Handbook of Research on Emerging Business Models and the New World Economic Order

Jose Manuel Saiz-Alvarez
Catholic University of Avila, Spain & Catholic University of Santiago de Guayaquil, Ecuador

A volume in the Advances in Business Strategy and Competitive Advantage (ABSCA) Book Series

Published in the United States of America by
IGI Global
Business Science Reference (an imprint of IGI Global)
701 E. Chocolate Avenue
Hershey PA, USA 17033
Tel: 717-533-8845
Fax: 717-533-8661
E-mail: cust@igi-global.com
Web site: http://www.igi-global.com

Copyright © 2022 by IGI Global. All rights reserved. No part of this publication may be reproduced, stored or distributed in any form or by any means, electronic or mechanical, including photocopying, without written permission from the publisher. Product or company names used in this set are for identification purposes only. Inclusion of the names of the products or companies does not indicate a claim of ownership by IGI Global of the trademark or registered trademark.
                              Library of Congress Cataloging-in-Publication Data

Names: Sáiz Álvarez, José Manuel, editor.
Title: Handbook of research on emerging business models and the new world economic order / Jose Manuel Saiz-Alvarez, editor.
Description: Hershey : Business Science Reference, 2021. | Includes bibliographical references and index. | Summary: "This book encouraged contributor to forecast future business changes and prospective models, structural or not, for guiding SMEs, multinationals, family firms, entrepreneurs, and NGOs in this pandemic time to survive, thus presenting strategies, economic policies, social, economic, and political trends that could affect organizations to increase their efficiency and labor productivity within he world's business and financial structures"-- Provided by publisher.
Identifiers: LCCN 2021013863 (print) | LCCN 2021013864 (ebook) | ISBN 9781799876892 (hardcover) | ISBN 9781799876908 (paperback) | ISBN 9781799876915 (ebook)
Subjects: LCSH: Business enterprises--Computer networks--Management. | Business networks. | Nonprofit organizations--Management. | Organizational change. | Social justice. | International cooperation. | COVID-19 Pandemic, 2020---Economic aspects.
Classification: LCC HD30.37 .E464 2021 (print) | LCC HD30.37 (ebook) | DDC 338.9--dc23
LC record available at https://lccn.loc.gov/2021013863
LC ebook record available at https://lccn.loc.gov/2021013864

This book is published in the IGI Global book series Advances in Business Strategy and Competitive Advantage (ABSCA) (ISSN: 2327-3429; eISSN: 2327-3437)

British Cataloguing in Publication Data
A Cataloguing in Publication record for this book is available from the British Library.

All work contributed to this book is new, previously-unpublished material. The views expressed in this book are those of the authors, but not necessarily of the publisher.

For electronic access to this publication, please contact: eresources@igi-global.com.

Advances in Business Strategy and Competitive Advantage (ABSCA) Book Series

Patricia Ordóñez de Pablos
Universidad de Oviedo, Spain

ISSN:2327-3429
EISSN:2327-3437

Mission

Business entities are constantly seeking new ways through which to gain advantage over their competitors and strengthen their position within the business environment. With competition at an all-time high due to technological advancements allowing for competition on a global scale, firms continue to seek new ways through which to improve and strengthen their business processes, procedures, and profitability.

The **Advances in Business Strategy and Competitive Advantage (ABSCA) Book Series** is a timely series responding to the high demand for state-of-the-art research on how business strategies are created, implemented and re-designed to meet the demands of globalized competitive markets. With a focus on local and global challenges, business opportunities and the needs of society, the **ABSCA** encourages scientific discourse on doing business and managing information technologies for the creation of sustainable competitive advantage.

Coverage

- Differentiation Strategy
- Strategy Performance Management
- Small and Medium Enterprises
- Adaptive Enterprise
- Strategic Management
- Customer-Orientation Strategy
- Value Creation
- Entrepreneurship & Innovation
- Strategic Alliances
- Competitive Strategy

IGI Global is currently accepting manuscripts for publication within this series. To submit a proposal for a volume in this series, please contact our Acquisition Editors at Acquisitions@igi-global.com or visit: http://www.igi-global.com/publish/.

The Advances in Business Strategy and Competitive Advantage (ABSCA) Book Series (ISSN 2327-3429) is published by IGI Global, 701 E. Chocolate Avenue, Hershey, PA 17033-1240, USA, www.igi-global.com. This series is composed of titles available for purchase individually; each title is edited to be contextually exclusive from any other title within the series. For pricing and ordering information please visit http://www.igi-global.com/book-series/advances-business-strategy-competitive-advantage/73672. Postmaster: Send all address changes to above address. © © 2022 IGI Global. All rights, including translation in other languages reserved by the publisher. No part of this series may be reproduced or used in any form or by any means – graphics, electronic, or mechanical, including photocopying, recording, taping, or information and retrieval systems – without written permission from the publisher, except for non commercial, educational use, including classroom teaching purposes. The views expressed in this series are those of the authors, but not necessarily of IGI Global.

Titles in this Series

For a list of additional titles in this series, please visit: www.igi-global.com/book-series

Leadership and Followership in an Organizational Change Context
Sajjad Nawaz Khan (Iqra University, Pakistan)
Business Science Reference • © 2022 • 361pp • H/C (ISBN: 9781799828075) • US $225.00

Emerging Ecosystem-Centric Business Models for Sustainable Value Creation
Xenia Ziouvelou (National Centre for Scientific Research "Demokritos", Greece & University of Southampton, UK) and Frank McGroarty (University of Southampton, UK)
Business Science Reference • © 2022 • 237pp • H/C (ISBN: 9781799848431) • US $195.00

Impact of Disruptive Technologies on the Sharing Economy
Ford Lumban Gaol (Bina Nusantara University, Jakarta, Indonesia) Natalia Filimonova (Vladimir State University, Russia) and Chandan Acharya (College of Staten Island, City University of New York, USA)
Business Science Reference • © 2021 • 269pp • H/C (ISBN: 9781799803614) • US $245.00

Global Corporate Social Responsibility Initiatives for Reluctant Businesses
Syed Abdul Rehman Khan (School of Management and Engineering, Xuzhou University of Technology, Xuzhou, China & Department of Business Administration, ILMA University, Karachi, Pakistan & Beijing Key Laboratory of Urban Spatial Engineering, Beijing, China) Zhang Yu (Chang'an University, China) Mirela Panait (Petroleum-Gas University of Ploiesti, Romania & Institute of National Economy, Bucharest, Romania) Laeeq Razzak Janjua (Poznan University of Economics and Business, Poland) and Adeel Shah (Institute of Business Management, Pakistan)
Business Science Reference • © 2021 • 280pp • H/C (ISBN: 9781799839880) • US $195.00

Impacts and Implications for the Sports Industry in the Post-COVID-19 Era
Armand Faganel (University of Primorska, Slovenia) Igor Rižnar (University of Primorska, Slovenia) and Arne Baruca (Texas A&M University San Antonio, USA)
Business Science Reference • © 2021 • 304pp • H/C (ISBN: 9781799867807) • US $215.00

Computational Thinking for Problem Solving and Managerial Mindset Training
Luisa Dall'Acqua (University of Bologna, Italy & LS TCO, Italy)
Business Science Reference • © 2021 • 293pp • H/C (ISBN: 9781799871262) • US $225.00

Bioentrepreneurship and Transferring Technology Into Product Development
Swati Agarwal (Banasthali University, India) Sonu Kumari (Banasthali University, India) and Suphiya Khan (Banasthali University, India)
Business Science Reference • © 2021 • 335pp • H/C (ISBN: 9781799874119) • US $245.00

701 East Chocolate Avenue, Hershey, PA 17033, USA
Tel: 717-533-8845 x100 • Fax: 717-533-8661
E-Mail: cust@igi-global.com • www.igi-global.com

Editorial Advisory Board

María Teresa Alcívar Avilés, *Catholic University of Santiago de Guayaquil, Ecuador*
Miguel Ángel Galindo-Martín, *University of Castile-La Mancha, Spain*
Jorge A. Gámez-Gutiérrez, *UNIMINUTO, Colombia & Fundación Universitaria del Area Andina, Colombia*
Mauricio Garita-Gutiérrez, *Francisco Marroquín University, Guatemala*
Sonia Esther González-Moreno, *Universidad Autónoma de Chihuahua, Mexico*
Delia Lizette Huezo-Ponce, *Tecnologico de Monterrey, Mexico*
Fernando Martínez Vallvey, *Pontifical University of Salamanca, Spain*
María Teresa Méndez-Picazo, *Complutense University of Madrid, Spain*
Edgar Muñiz Ávila, *Tecnologico de Monterrey, Mexico*
Sergio Luis Nañez Alonso, *Catholic University of Avila, Spain*
Lucía Rodríguez Aceves, *Tecnologico de Monterrey, Mexico*
Francisco Salinas Ramos, *Catholic University of Avila, Spain*

List of Reviewers

Neeta Baporikar, *Namibia University of Science and Technology, Namibia & University of Pune, India*
Danny Christian Barbery-Montoya, *Universidad Espíritu Santo, Ecuador*
Icek Kelly, *FIEC Research Institute (Swiss Branch), Switzerland*
Arturo Luque González, *Universidad Tecnica de Manabí, Ecuador & Universidad del Rosario, Ecuador*
Suja Ravindran Nair, *Educe Micro Research, Bengaluru, India*
Beatriz Olalla-Caballero, *Pontifical University of Salamanca, Spain*
Jesús Manuel Palma-Ruiz, *Universidad Autónoma de Chihuahua, Mexico*
Rafael Ignacio Pérez-Uribe, *Universidad Santo Tomás, Colombia*
Carlos Salcedo-Pérez, *Politecnico Grancolombiano, Colombia*
Bijoylaxmi Sarmah, *North-Eastern Regional Institute of Science and Technology, Nirjuli, India*
Jürgen Schdorfen, *FIEC Research Institute (Swiss Branch), Switzerland*
Eva Schöne, *FIEC Research Institute (German Branch), Germany*

List of Contributors

Alkorta, Aitor Bengoetxea / *Universidad del País Vasco, Spain & Euskal Herriko Unibertsitatea, Spain* 242
Baporikar, Neeta / *Namibia University of Science and Technology, Namibia & University of Pune, India* 287
Barbery-Montoya, Danny Christian / *Universidad Espíritu Santo, Ecuador* 183
Calderón Campos, Patricia / *Tecnológico Nacional de México. Secretaria Académica de Investigación e Innovación, Mexico* 1
Chang, Fa-Hsiang / *Wenzhou-Kean University, China* 163
Chen, Mingyi / *University of Edinburgh, UK* 214
Chen, Rongjuan / *Wenzhou-Kean University, China* 214
Coduras, Alicia / *Institut Opinòmetre, Spain & GEM Global, UK* 18
Coronel-Arellano, Dennisse A. / *Universitat de València, Spain* 183
Feng, Jiawei / *University of Warwick, UK* 214
Fernández-Villacañas Marín, Manuel Antonio / *San Pablo CEU University, Madrid, Spain* 99
Flores-Morales, Carmen Romelia / *Universidad Autónoma de Chihuahua, Mexico* 39
González, Arturo Luque / *Universidad Tecnica de Manabí, Ecuador & Universidad del Rosario, Ecuador* 242
Jiang, Sijia / *Wenzhou-Kean University, China* 326
Jiang, Zhongyue / *Independent Researcher, China* 343
Kamboj, Shampy / *National Institute of Technology, Hamirpur, India* 197
Kwok, Samuel / *Xi'an Jiaotong-Liverpool University, China* 343
Marjerison, Rob Kim / *Wenzhou-Kean University, China* 163, 214, 326, 365
Márquez, Enriqueta / *Universidad Anáhuac, Mexico* 304
Mata, Montserrat / *Deusto University, Spain* 267
Nair, Suja Ravindran / *Educe Micro Research, Bengaluru, India* 60
Olalla-Caballero, Beatriz / *Pontifical University of Salamanca, Spain* 267
Palma-Ruiz, Jesús Manuel / *Universidad Autónoma de Chihuahua, Mexico* 39
Pan, Jing / *University of Warwick, UK* 365
Pérez-Uribe, Rafael Ignacio / *Universidad Santo Tomas, Colombia* 80
Phookan, Neeraj Kumar / *North-Eastern Regional Institute of Science and Technology, Nirjuli, India* 197
Ramirez, Maria del Pilar / *EAN University, Colombia* 80
Roomi, Muhammad Azam / *Mohammed bin Salman College of Business and Entrepreneurship, Saudi Arabia* 18
Roy, Debasish / *Sikkim University, India* 125

Saiz-Alvarez, Jose Manuel / *Catholic University of Avila, Spain & Catholic University of Santiago de Guayaquil, Ecuador* 18
Salcedo, Jaime Leonidas Ordóñez / *Universidad del País Vasco, Spain & Euskal Herriko Unibertsitatea, Spain* 242
Salcedo-Perez, Carlos / *Politecnico Grancolombiano, Colombia* 80
Sánchez-Acosta, Luis Raúl / *Universidad Autónoma de Chihuahua, Mexico* 39
Sarmah, Bijoylaxmi / *North-Eastern Regional Institute of Science and Technology, Nirjuli, India* 197
Soria-Loor, Ariana / *Universidad Santa María, Ecuador* 183
Valles-Baca, Herik Germán / *Universidad Autónoma de Chihuahua, Mexico* 39
Vargas-Hernández, José G. / *Instituto Tecnológico Mario Molina Unidad Zapopan, Mexico* 1
Yu, Poshan / *Soochow University, China* 343
Zhou, Biqi / *School of Professional Studies, Columbia University, USA* 163

Table of Contents

Preface xx

Acknowledgment xxv

Section 1
Politics and Business

Chapter 1
Critical Analysis of the Evolving Process of Neoliberal Global Capitalism 1
    José G. Vargas-Hernández, Instituto Tecnológico Mario Molina Unidad Zapopan, Mexico
    Patricia Calderón Campos, Tecnológico Nacional de México. Secretaria Académica de
        Investigación e Innovación, Mexico

Chapter 2
How Have Governments and the Entrepreneurial Sector Reacted to the First COVID-19
Lockdown? 18
    Alicia Coduras, Institut Opinòmetre, Spain & GEM Global, UK
    Jose Manuel Saiz-Alvarez, Catholic University of Avila, Spain & Catholic University of
        Santiago de Guayaquil, Ecuador
    Muhammad Azam Roomi, Mohammed bin Salman College of Business and
        Entrepreneurship, Saudi Arabia

Chapter 3
Experiences, Perceptions, and Expectations of the Business Community in Mexico Amidst the
COVID-19 Crisis 39
    Jesús Manuel Palma-Ruiz, Universidad Autónoma de Chihuahua, Mexico
    Herik Germán Valles-Baca, Universidad Autónoma de Chihuahua, Mexico
    Carmen Romelia Flores-Morales, Universidad Autónoma de Chihuahua, Mexico
    Luis Raúl Sánchez-Acosta, Universidad Autónoma de Chihuahua, Mexico

Chapter 4
Impact of COVID-19 on Food Consumption and Marketing: A Behavioral Model Perspective 60
    Suja Ravindran Nair, Educe Micro Research, Bengaluru, India

Chapter 5
Organizational Components That Explain the Strategic Direction of SMEs for a New World Economic Order: The Case of Colombia 80
    Rafael Ignacio Pérez-Uribe, Universidad Santo Tomas, Colombia
    Carlos Salcedo-Perez, Politecnico Grancolombiano, Colombia
    Maria del Pilar Ramirez, EAN University, Colombia

Chapter 6
The New Concept of Disruptive Logistics: Global Sustainable Logistics 4.0 in a Future Post-New World Economic Order 99
    Manuel Antonio Fernández-Villacañas Marín, San Pablo CEU University, Madrid, Spain

Chapter 7
A Treatise on Isoattribute Curve Analysis, Consumer Induction Factor, and Country Brand Value: A Modern Proposal 125
    Debasish Roy, Sikkim University, India

Chapter 8
Chinese OEM Manufacturing Roadmap: SMEs – To Brand or Not to Brand 163
    Biqi Zhou, School of Professional Studies, Columbia University, USA
    Rob Kim Marjerison, Wenzhou-Kean University, China
    Fa-Hsiang Chang, Wenzhou-Kean University, China

Chapter 9
Omnichannel and Experience Approach as a Post-COVID-19 Economic Reactivation Mechanism 183
    Danny Christian Barbery-Montoya, Universidad Espíritu Santo, Ecuador
    Dennisse A. Coronel-Arellano, Universitat de València, Spain
    Ariana Soria-Loor, Universidad Santa María, Ecuador

Chapter 10
Determinants of RFID Adoption Intention in the Healthcare Industry for Patient Monitoring: A Special Reference to COVID-19 197
    Bijoylaxmi Sarmah, North-Eastern Regional Institute of Science and Technology, Nirjuli, India
    Shampy Kamboj, National Institute of Technology, Hamirpur, India
    Neeraj Kumar Phookan, North-Eastern Regional Institute of Science and Technology, Nirjuli, India

Chapter 11
Social Enterprise Awareness, Perception, and Purchase Influence in South East China: A Benchmark for Further Study 214
    Mingyi Chen, University of Edinburgh, UK
    Jiawei Feng, University of Warwick, UK
    Rob Kim Marjerison, Wenzhou-Kean University, China
    Rongjuan Chen, Wenzhou-Kean University, China

Chapter 12
The Social and Solidarity Economics, Public Policies, and Non-Monetary Economic Practices:
The Case of Associative Firms in Loja, Ecuador 242
    Arturo Luque González, Universidad Tecnica de Manabí, Ecuador & Universidad del
        Rosario, Ecuador
    Aitor Bengoetxea Alkorta, Universidad del País Vasco, Spain & Euskal Herriko
        Unibertsitatea, Spain
    Jaime Leonidas Ordóñez Salcedo, Universidad del País Vasco, Spain & Euskal Herriko
        Unibertsitatea, Spain

Chapter 13
Business Model Creation for Cost Saving in the New World Economic Order 267
    Beatriz Olalla-Caballero, Pontifical University of Salamanca, Spain
    Montserrat Mata, Deusto University, Spain

Section 2
Education

Chapter 14
Trends for Business Education Post COVID-19 287
    Neeta Baporikar, Namibia University of Science and Technology, Namibia & University of
        Pune, India

Chapter 15
Developments and Global Trends in the Education and Business Sectors in the Post-COVID-19
Period: The Mexican Case 304
    Enriqueta Márquez, Universidad Anáhuac, Mexico

Chapter 16
Initial Exploration of Cross-Generational Attitudes Towards Piracy of Chinese Online Literature .. 326
    Rob Kim Marjerison, Wenzhou-Kean University, China
    Sijia Jiang, Wenzhou-Kean University, China

Chapter 17
How COVID-19 Has Stimulated Innovation in the Chinese Education Sector 343
    Poshan Yu, Soochow University, China
    Samuel Kwok, Xi'an Jiaotong-Liverpool University, China
    Zhongyue Jiang, Independent Researcher, China

Chapter 18
Decision-Making Styles of the Next Generation of Chinese Business Leaders 365
    Rob Kim Marjerison, Wenzhou-Kean University, China
    Jing Pan, University of Warwick, UK

Compilation of References 387

About the Contributors 444

Index 451

Detailed Table of Contents

Preface xx

Acknowledgment xxv

Section 1
Politics and Business

Chapter 1
Critical Analysis of the Evolving Process of Neoliberal Global Capitalism 1
    José G. Vargas-Hernández, Instituto Tecnológico Mario Molina Unidad Zapopan, Mexico
    Patricia Calderón Campos, Tecnológico Nacional de México. Secretaria Académica de
        Investigación e Innovación, Mexico

This chapter aims to make a critical analysis of the evolving process of neoliberal capitalism globalization. It begins with the assumption that the neoliberal capitalism system is undergoing a mutation in the globalization processes as a dynamic element in continuous economic and financial crisis representing the development of the logic of capital based on the neoliberal ideology that promotes the free market. The evolving process of globalization is the history of international free trade framed by the classical liberal and neoliberal economic theory. The discussion focuses on a critical analysis of the paradigm of deglobalization as an alternative to the global capitalist regime that proposes local and regional economic protectionism solutions as an alternative to keep growing the national economies but still neglecting social justice and inequality inclusiveness and socio-ecological development.

Chapter 2
How Have Governments and the Entrepreneurial Sector Reacted to the First COVID-19
Lockdown?.. 18
    Alicia Coduras, Institut Opinòmetre, Spain & GEM Global, UK
    Jose Manuel Saiz-Alvarez, Catholic University of Avila, Spain & Catholic University of
        Santiago de Guayaquil, Ecuador
    Muhammad Azam Roomi, Mohammed bin Salman College of Business and
        Entrepreneurship, Saudi Arabia

At the end of 2019, the pandemic caused by COVID-19 and its different mutations is forcing the world to face a significant economic crisis that will change the business world. To cope with this socio-economic problem, a digitation process has been accelerated in the labor market, and a more vital public-private collaboration has been put into action to solve this situation. Despite these efforts, the world is facing a broader North-South gap, and a new business world has been created for the new generations to come. This chapter aims to analyze how the first lockdown caused by COVID-19 has influenced this changing process. The authors conclude that this lockdown has accelerated both the digitation process and the work-life balance. Also, more efforts are needed to fight the psychiatric problems associated with the lockdown.

Chapter 3
Experiences, Perceptions, and Expectations of the Business Community in Mexico Amidst the COVID-19 Crisis 39
    Jesús Manuel Palma-Ruiz, Universidad Autónoma de Chihuahua, Mexico
    Herik Germán Valles-Baca, Universidad Autónoma de Chihuahua, Mexico
    Carmen Romelia Flores-Morales, Universidad Autónoma de Chihuahua, Mexico
    Luis Raúl Sánchez-Acosta, Universidad Autónoma de Chihuahua, Mexico

The objective of this chapter is to provide a contextualized perspective about the effects of the COVID-19 health crisis for companies with economic activity and fixed installations in Mexico, mainly during the second to third phases of the contingency. For this purpose, data from the INEGI ECOVID-IE 2020 survey is analyzed, which used a sampling frame of 1,873,564 Mexican companies compared by size. Relevant information is provided about the reality of the Mexican business community to report the main sanitary measures implemented, the operational actions used, the sources and types of support received, the best support policies identified, and the income expectations for the following months. Faced with a negative scenario, targeted support strategies from governmental, chambers, and business organizations must be aligned to regain the confidence of the business community to support their continuity.

Chapter 4
Impact of COVID-19 on Food Consumption and Marketing: A Behavioral Model Perspective 60
    Suja Ravindran Nair, Educe Micro Research, Bengaluru, India

COVID-19 has greatly disrupted lives and affected buying behavior of individuals. Countries were forced to impose lockdowns, alongside the practices of wearing masks, social distancing and hygiene have become the 'new normal'. This situation forced consumers to re-work shopping habits, modify food patterns, develop healthy eating and online shopping behavior. With multiple waves of COVID-19 engulfing countries, pandemic effects are here to stay, suggesting food marketers explore the continuity of healthy food consumption with futuristic behavioral intention. For this purpose, this study uses a behavioral model perspective built upon the theory of planned behavior. A general review of the literature on food choice behavior is used. The literature review shows an integrated framework indicating linkages between the antecedents, consumers' behaviors, and behavior intentions/consequences from a sustainable behavioral model perspective.

Chapter 5
Organizational Components That Explain the Strategic Direction of SMEs for a New World Economic Order: The Case of Colombia 80
    Rafael Ignacio Pérez-Uribe, Universidad Santo Tomas, Colombia
    Carlos Salcedo-Perez, Politecnico Grancolombiano, Colombia
    Maria del Pilar Ramirez, EAN University, Colombia

This chapter aims to show some concepts related to the importance of planning and strategic direction as a fundamental tool for the sustainability of Colombian SMEs for a new world economic order and present the proportionality relationship between this concept of strategic management and the organizational components. Keys that explain it and facilitate its development, considering the modernization model for managing organizations (MMOM), were developed by a group of researchers from the EAN University in Bogotá-Colombia. It was found that market management, organizational culture, organizational structure, and knowledge and innovation management are the components that a high percentage explain the strategic direction of this type of company on which priority improvement and innovation activities should be developed in such a way ways that allow strategies to develop more smoothly to achieve business objectives of effectiveness, efficiency, profitability, and sustainable development.

Chapter 6
The New Concept of Disruptive Logistics: Global Sustainable Logistics 4.0 in a Future Post-New World Economic Order 99
Manuel Antonio Fernández-Villacañas Marín, San Pablo CEU University, Madrid, Spain

In an increasingly disruptive global environment, marked by the potential development of the Post-New World Economic Order, more innovative, effective, and efficient logistics solutions are demanded. It is necessary to offer radical improvements in logistics services through new models. It is considered necessary to define the new concept of disruptive logistics based on three fundamental pillars: globalization, digitization, and sustainability. This chapter aims to address the new concept, more effective and efficient, in a highly turbulent environment that has become disruptive, with unpredictable, substantial, and impactful changes. The most significant geoeconomics aspects that would condition a hypothetical Post-New World Economic Order are analyzed, the main factors of the global sustainable logistics are studied, and the development of the concepts of Logistics 4.0 and Supply Chain Management 4.0 is reviewed. Finally, as a result, the main aspects of the proposed new concept are analyzed.

Chapter 7
A Treatise on Isoattribute Curve Analysis, Consumer Induction Factor, and Country Brand Value: A Modern Proposal 125
Debasish Roy, Sikkim University, India

This research has endeavored to focus on three major issues that are yet to be explored as per the existing literature on marketing. The first issue focuses on the Isoattribute curve analysis, rooted in the theory of conjoint utility analysis. In other words, the first segment concentrates on the derivation of the Isoattribute curve model which helps to attain the consumer equilibrium condition in a two-commodity world (brand or non-brand products). The second segment of the chapter has transitioned from the microeconomic model to the macroeconomic perspective based on a 'single-country' approach, i.e., USA, based on a derivation of consumer induction factor (CIF). Finally, the third and final segment of the chapter extends its horizon at a larger scale by conducting a cross-country time-series study of 10 years (2009 – 2018) which redefines branding in an absolutely new dimension where the 'brand values' of seven sample countries are estimated by inculcating the socio-economic, political, and working environment factors as the major dimensions.

Chapter 8
Chinese OEM Manufacturing Roadmap: SMEs – To Brand or Not to Brand.................................. 163
    Biqi Zhou, School of Professional Studies, Columbia University, USA
    Rob Kim Marjerison, Wenzhou-Kean University, China
    Fa-Hsiang Chang, Wenzhou-Kean University, China

This study seeks to explore the strategic alternatives for the many small and medium-sized manufacturing firms in China that play an OEM role in the global value chain. Declining margins due to rising production costs and intense competition from emerging manufacturing industries in Southeast Asia necessitates the transformation of China's traditional manufacturing industry. The result is opportunities for the creation and manufacturing of domestic brands. A multiple-case study methodology is used with primary data collection through in-depth interviews, supported by secondary data on the subject firms. The findings reveal an awareness of the opportunities afforded by the trend towards the development of domestic brands as well as the vision, strategy, tactics, and forecasting related to a transition to brand creation. This chapter could be of interest to those with an interest in manufacturing transition, brand development, and providing direction to OEM SMEs in China that seek to develop a strategic roadmap during the imminent industrial evolution and transformation.

Chapter 9
Omnichannel and Experience Approach as a Post-COVID-19 Economic Reactivation Mechanism 183
    Danny Christian Barbery-Montoya, Universidad Espíritu Santo, Ecuador
    Dennisse A. Coronel-Arellano, Universitat de València, Spain
    Ariana Soria-Loor, Universidad Santa María, Ecuador

The aim of this chapter is to show how omnichannel tools must be applied through the process of creating experiences for the consumers. During the literature review, some authors make approaches to the key concepts connecting omnichannels and consumer experiences; therefore, they explain through the analysis of data the reality of the Ecuadorian environment and global trends. With this context, this chapter will present how, by using macro environment and accessibility, a unique experience may be created in the customer journey in omnichannel.

Chapter 10
Determinants of RFID Adoption Intention in the Healthcare Industry for Patient Monitoring: A Special Reference to COVID-19.. 197
    Bijoylaxmi Sarmah, North-Eastern Regional Institute of Science and Technology, Nirjuli, India
    Shampy Kamboj, National Institute of Technology, Hamirpur, India
    Neeraj Kumar Phookan, North-Eastern Regional Institute of Science and Technology, Nirjuli, India

Radio frequency identification (RFID) technology holds tremendous potential in improving the patient management system in hospitals attaining global importance in the healthcare industry due to the spread of the COVID-19 pandemic at present. RFID assists in wireless data storage and automatic retrieval, making systems efficient, improving patient safety, and decreasing costs. Although RFID is an emerging technology in the healthcare industry, its adoption is yet to gather momentum. This chapter will provide a background for healthcare practitioners and researchers about RFID technologies in the healthcare sector. Moreover, an integrated conceptual framework will be proposed consisting of factors that influence

RFID technology adoption intention in the healthcare industry. This study will be the first of its kind to identify and classify various factors of RFID adoption intention and provide a comprehensive model using an exploratory method laying the foundation for academicians and industry practitioners for the future scope of its research.

Chapter 11
Social Enterprise Awareness, Perception, and Purchase Influence in South East China: A Benchmark for Further Study 214
    Mingyi Chen, University of Edinburgh, UK
    Jiawei Feng, University of Warwick, UK
    Rob Kim Marjerison, Wenzhou-Kean University, China
    Rongjuan Chen, Wenzhou-Kean University, China

This study aims to explore awareness and interest in social enterprises in China and in doing so provide a benchmark for comparison with future research on the topic. There is a shortage of evidence in the previous literature with which to compare the present situation, but the regulatory emphasis and resources presently dedicated by the Chinese government to social enterprises makes research in this area relevant and makes it likely that the development of social enterprises would have an upward trend in awareness and interest. Primary data was collected from over 600 online surveys which measured awareness, purchase intention, and purchase motivation before and during the first year of the COVID-19 pandemic. The findings of this chapter may contribute to future research on the trends of social enterprise awareness and interest in China and may also be of interest to those with an interest in social entrepreneurship.

Chapter 12
The Social and Solidarity Economics, Public Policies, and Non-Monetary Economic Practices: The Case of Associative Firms in Loja, Ecuador 242
    Arturo Luque González, Universidad Tecnica de Manabí, Ecuador & Universidad del
        Rosario, Ecuador
    Aitor Bengoetxea Alkorta, Universidad del País Vasco, Spain & Euskal Herriko
        Unibertsitatea, Spain
    Jaime Leonidas Ordóñez Salcedo, Universidad del País Vasco, Spain & Euskal Herriko
        Unibertsitatea, Spain

The prevailing economic and social model contains great inequalities. Against this backdrop, the Republic of Ecuador, in its constitution of 2008, included recognizing ancestral practices at an economic and social level and granting special protection to "mother earth" or Pachamama based on the common element of solidarity between ecosystems and human beings. Despite this, continuous growth processes have blunted some of the tools and institutions created in Ecuador to redress poverty and rebalance existing economic and regulatory abuses. To analyze this situation, a series of group interviews were carried out in two communities of Loja (Ecuador) to analyze the scope and continuity of current ancestral practices and the effectiveness of processes established in the social economy. The analysis shows the lack of continuity of these practices and their associated benefits for people and communities with limited resources.

Chapter 13
Business Model Creation for Cost Saving in the New World Economic Order 267
    Beatriz Olalla-Caballero, Pontifical University of Salamanca, Spain
    Montserrat Mata, Deusto University, Spain

Globalization and economy features in this new world economic order due to SARS-CoV-2 pandemic crisis involve taking into account new ideas and proposals to keep the market share and to fight against competition. It is very important to consider and evaluate the business model of a company to drive all the objectives and the strategy towards the aimed position in the market to assure the market share in the future. Evaluation and analysis of a business model, together with new proposals regarding it may help a company to achieve all the objectives and to increase its competitiveness in the market.

Section 2
Education

Chapter 14
Trends for Business Education Post COVID-19 287
    Neeta Baporikar, Namibia University of Science and Technology, Namibia & University of
      Pune, India

COVID-19 has brought about tremendous changes in all occupations. Education in general and business education, in particular, is no exception. In the normal course, business education entailed students being on the campus as the courses are full-time residential with physical attendance to enable interaction and discussion. With COVID-19 lockdown and restrictions, the usual way of doing business is disrupted. Hence, by adopting systematic literature with grounded approach, the aim of this chapter is to understand the disruptions, faculty, and student difficulties and sketch out the future trends in business education post COVID-19.

Chapter 15
Developments and Global Trends in the Education and Business Sectors in the Post-COVID-19
Period: The Mexican Case 304
    Enriqueta Márquez, Universidad Anáhuac, Mexico

In this chapter, the author focuses on the reality of living through a pandemic that made people worldwide prioritize their matters of importance. Since the beginning of the pandemic, the educational sector was one of the most privileged ones thanks to the previous implementation of proper technologies and internet tools. The author will analyze the challenges faced by teachers, students, and parents, who had to adapt workplaces and focus their efforts to continuously innovate and capture the attention of students. On the business arena, the pandemic was a digital accelerator. Many businesses had to improve their digital platforms and different types of consumers emerged. The author will highlight the global consumer trends that emerged during the pandemic which will remain throughout the post-COVID-19 period and the challenges to capitalize on all the new trends that emerged to transform persons into better human beings and to contribute building a better world.

Chapter 16
Initial Exploration of Cross-Generational Attitudes Towards Piracy of Chinese Online Literature .. 326
    Rob Kim Marjerison, Wenzhou-Kean University, China
    Sijia Jiang, Wenzhou-Kean University, China

This chapter seeks to provide initial evidence and provide a baseline for further exploration of Chinese cross-generational audiences' attitude differences towards online literature and digital piracy. Globalization has complicated the many disparate cultural, generational, and national perspectives on intellectual property (IP) protection. IP and IP protection continue to grow in importance in global commerce and international relations. How attitudes towards IP and online content, in particular, evolve generationally is an area of relative under exploration. Data was gathered through an online survey and indicates a trend towards increased awareness and acceptance of IP value and protection. This study provides insight into cross-generational audiences in the important market of China. It may be helpful to those interested in commerce in the areas of online publishing or related industries to help make business decisions in targeting and marketing, to those interested in global commerce and international relations, or those who are researchers in the areas of IP and IP protection.

Chapter 17
How COVID-19 Has Stimulated Innovation in the Chinese Education Sector 343
    Poshan Yu, Soochow University, China
    Samuel Kwok, Xi'an Jiaotong-Liverpool University, China
    Zhongyue Jiang, Independent Researcher, China

This chapter aims to investigate the impacts of COVID-19 in China's education sector. It will capture the dynamics of the interlinked changing relationships between the availability and use of education technology (EdTech) and the demand for online learning among various stakeholders in the Chinese education market. In addition, this chapter examines whether and how these relationships enhance operational efficiency via transforming the current business models in the sector, in particular due to the COVID-19 pandemic. By analyzing the current practices of the sector, this chapter will critically discuss the challenges and opportunities for technology in education and how these changes in turn drive stakeholders (including students, educators, and regulators) to respond and engage with each other, and how these stakeholder engagements impact the sustainable development of delivery modes, such as digital education and remote learning by using EdTech strategies in the sector.

Chapter 18
Decision-Making Styles of the Next Generation of Chinese Business Leaders 365
    Rob Kim Marjerison, Wenzhou-Kean University, China
    Jing Pan, University of Warwick, UK

This study seeks to explore the relationships between decision-making styles, academic performance, and gender of educated Chinese millennials. As the millennial generation of college graduates in China comes of age, they will move into leadership roles in public and commercial organizations. They will have influence over considerable financial assets as well as economic and public policy which translates into global impact. There is a gap in the existing literature on the topic. This study utilized online self-report questionnaires to gather data, and the general decision-making style test to assess respondents' decision-making models culminating in correlation analysis and t-test. Based on the findings of related research, the authors hypothesized that there would be a difference in the decision-making styles based on gender and that there would be a significant difference in academic performance based on the decision-making styles. The findings may be of interest to a variety of those interested in decision-making styles, Chinese millennials, and future leaders of China.

Compilation of References 387

About the Contributors 444

Index 451

Preface

The global pandemic caused by COVID-19 is changing the world, both from a double geopolitical and social perspective, with the imposition of the 'new normal' defined by imposing lockdowns, alongside the practices of wearing masks, social distancing, and hygiene-based procedures. The sharp difference in vaccination terms between the richest and poorest countries on the planet increases the north-south gap, lengthening the pandemic's duration. As a consequence, with multiple waves of COVID-19 engulfing countries, pandemic effects are here to stay.

However, the effects of the COVID-19 pandemic are very intense and have a crucial structural change component as the impact occurs globally. Not only does it affect the health of individuals, but its geopolitical, economic, social, and even family effects are far-reaching to give rise to a New World Economic Order. Divided into two sections, the first devoted to politics, business, and economics, and the second to education, both focused on studying the new world economic order's traits for different sectors and countries.

Nearly forty authors from four continents (Africa, America, Asia, and Europe) and ten countries participate in this book to cope with this goal. Academicians and practitioners who are developing their ideas, theories, and professional skills in different universities and research centers of international prestige. This characteristic makes the book stand out for having a global vision, both from a North-South perspective, and above all, and what is more difficult to find in other books, with a South-South vision.

This book explores the need to advance into how the world is transforming and how some emerging business and educational models combined with social and geopolitical effects transform the business world into a New World Economic Order that will emerge during the post-COVID-19 era. Given this vision, the book's target audience, *Handbook of Research on Emerging Business Models and the New World Economic Order*, comprises scholar-practitioners, managers, policymakers, consultants, and undergraduate/graduate students. Still, it also appeals to anyone interested in these issues.

ORGANIZATION OF THE BOOK

The book is divided into two sections. The first section (Chapters 1–13) focuses on different aspects of the new world economic order from a triple-fold perspective, including political, economic, and business-related issues.

Chapter 1, entitled 'Critical Analysis of the Evolving Process of the Neoliberal Global Capitalism,' and written by Dr. José G. Vargas-Hernández, from the University Center for Economic and Managerial Sciences, University of Guadalajara (Mexico), aims to make a critical analysis of the evolving process

Preface

of neoliberal capitalism globalization. The author assumes that the neoliberal capitalist system promoting the free market is changing due to globalization and the pandemic. Consequently, in this chapter, the author focuses on the paradigm of deglobalization as an alternative to the global capitalist regime to propose protectionism-related local and regional economic measures to maintain nations' growth to keep in mind both social justice and socio-ecological development.

This two-fold perspective, including politics and economics, continues in Chapter 2 entitled 'How Have Governments and the Entrepreneurial Sector Reacted to the First COVID19 Lockdown?' written by Dr. Alicia Coduras, from Institut Opinòmetre, Spain and GEM Global, UK; Dr. José Manuel Saiz-Álvarez, from Catholic University of Santiago de Guayaquil, Ecuador and Mexican Academy of Sciences, and Dr. Muhammad Azam Roomi, from Mohammed bin Salman College of Business and Entrepreneurship, Saudi Arabia. At the end of 2019, the pandemic caused by COVID-19 and its different mutations is forcing the world to face a significant economic crisis that will change the business world., More vital public-private collaboration must be implemented to avoid a broader North-South gap to cope with this socio-economic problem, especially in the labor market. This chapter analyzes how the first lockdown caused by COVID-19 has influenced this changing process and concludes that this lockdown has accelerated both the digitation process and the work-life balance.

The following book chapters focus on the relationship between companies and the health and economic crisis generated by COVID-19. In this respect, Chapter 3 entitled 'Experiences, Perceptions, and Expectations of the Business Community in Mexico Amidst the COVID-19 Crisis', written by Dr. Jesús Manuel Palma-Ruiz, Prof. Herik Germán Valles-Baca, Dr. Carmen Romelia Flores-Morales, and Prof. Luis Raúl Sánchez-Acosta, all from Universidad Autónoma de Chihuahua, Mexico, aims to provide a contextualized perspective about the effects of the COVID-19 health crisis for Mexican firms, mainly during the second to third phases of the contingency. For this purpose, these authors analyze data from the INEGI ECOVID-IE 2020 survey, which uses a sampling frame of 1,873,564 Mexican companies compared by size, and conclude that public and private organizations must be aligned to regain the confidence of the business community to support their continuity.

This public-private alignment and cooperation are complemented in Chapter 4. entitled 'Impact of COVID-19 on Food Consumption and Marketing: A Behavioral Model Perspective', written by Dr. Suja Ravindran Nair, Educe Micro Research, Bengaluru, India, where the author affirms that consumers have re-worked shopping habits, modified food patterns, and developed healthy eating and online shopping because Covid19 has dramatically disrupted their lives and affected buying behavior of individuals. Dr. Nair assures that after multiple waves of COVID-19 engulfing countries, pandemic effects are here to stay, suggesting food marketers explore the continuity of healthy food consumption with futuristic behavioral intention. For this purpose, this chapter uses a behavioral model perspective; built upon the Theory of Planned Behavior to show an integrated framework indicating linkages between the antecedents, consumers' behaviors, and behavior intentions/consequences from a sustainable behavioral model perspective.

Also, SMEs' strategic policies have changed during the pandemic, as shown in Chapter 5 titled 'Organizational Components that Explain the Strategic Direction of SMEs for a New World Economic Order: The Case of Colombia', and written by Dr. Rafael Ignacio Pérez-Uribe, Universidad Santo Tomas, Colombia, Dr. Carlos Salcedo-Perez, Politecnico Grancolombiano, Colombia, and Dr. Maria del Pilar Ramirez, EAN University, Colombia. This chapter aims to show some concepts related to the importance of planning and strategic direction as fundamental tools for SMEs ' sustainability in a new world economic order. The authors explain SMEs' business policies for achieving effectiveness, efficiency, profitability, and sustainable development using an MMOM (modernization model for managing organizations) model combining organizational culture, knowledge, and innovation management.

Logistics play a crucial role in business as shown in Chapter 6, entitled 'The New Concept of Disruptive Logistics: Global Sustainable Logistics 4.0 in a Future Post-New World Economic Order', written by Dr. Manuel Antonio Fernández-Villacañas Marín, from Technical University of Madrid/Consulting M&M Planning and Project Management, Spain. Dr. Fernández-Villacañas affirms that in an increasingly disruptive global environment marked by the potential development of the post-New World Economic Order, more innovative, effective, and efficient logistics solutions are demanded. The author defines the new concept of Disruptive Logistics based on three fundamental pillars: globalization, digitization, and sustainability, to address logistics more effectively and efficiently in a highly turbulent, disruptive, and unpredictable business environment.

Another contribution to the business field is shown in Chapter 7 entitled 'A Treatise on Isoattribute Curve Analysis, Consumer Induction Factor, and Country Brand Value: A Modern Proposal,' written by Mr. Debasish Roy, Sikkim University, India, where the author introduces the Isoattribute curve analysis, rooted in the theory of Conjoint utility analysis, to attain the consumer's equilibrium condition in a two–commodity world (brand or non-brand products). Also, a new vision related to the Consumer Induction Factor (CIF) is shown. The author redefines branding in a new dimension where the 'brand values' of 7 sample countries are estimated.

Manufacturing is also analyzed in the book. Chapter 8 entitled 'Chinese OEM Manufacturing Roadmap: SMEs: To Brand or Not to Brand,' written by Ms. Biqi Zhou, Columbia University School of Professional Studies, United States, Prof. Rob Kim Marjerison, Wenzhou-Kean University, China, and Dr. Fa-Hsiang Chang, Wenzhou-Kean University, China, study this issue. Using a multiple-case study methodology with primary data collection through in-depth interviews, supported by secondary data on firms, the authors explore the strategic alternatives for the many SMEs manufacturing firms in China that play an OEM role in the global value chain. The authors focus on these firms, as they are the emerging manufacturing industries in Southeast Asia that need the transformation of China's traditional manufacturing industry to create and manufacture domestic brands.

Marketing has a crucial role for firms in the post-COVID-19 era. In this regard, Chapter 9 entitled 'Omnichannel and Experience Approach as a Post-Covid-19 Economic Reactivation Mechanism', and written by Dr. Danny Christian Barbery-Montoya, Universidad Espíritu Santo, Ecuador, Dennisse A. Coronel-Arellano, Universitat de València, Spain, and Ariana Soria-Loor, Universidad Santa María, Ecuador, aims to show how omnichannel tools must be applied through the process of creating experiences for the consumers in Ecuador. With this context, this chapter presents how a unique experience may be completed in the customer journey by following an omnichannel strategy using a macro environment and accessibility.

The healthcare industry is crucial to fight the pandemic. In this regard, Chapter 10 entitled 'Determinants of RFID Adoption Intention in Healthcare Industry for Patient Monitoring: A Special Reference to COVID-19', and written by Ms. Bijoylaxmi Sarmah, North-Eastern Regional Institute of Science & Technology, Nirjuli, Arunachal Pradesh, India, Dr. Shampy Kamboj, National Institute of Technology Hamirpur, India, and Mr. Neeraj Kumar Phookan, North Eastern Regional Institute of Science & Technology, India, describes how RFID (Radio Frequency Identification) technology improves the patient management system in hospitals by assisting in wireless data storage and automatic retrieval, making systems efficient, improving patient safety, and decreasing costs. This study is the first to identify and classify various factors of RFID adoption intention and provide a comprehensive model using an

Preface

experimental method laying the foundation for academicians and industry practitioners for the future scope of its research.

Continuing in Asia, Chapter 11 entitled 'Social Enterprise Awareness, Perception and Purchase Influence in South East China: A Benchmark for Further Study,' written by Mr. Mingyi Chen, Management, University of Edinburgh, UK, Ms. Jiawei Feng, Management, University of Warwick, UK, and Prof. Rob Kim Marjerison, Wenzhou-Kean University, China, explores the interest of the Chinese government to develop social enterprises in the country. To analyze the possibility of creating social entrepreneurship, the authors use primary data from over 600 online surveys to measure Awareness, Purchase Intention, and Purchase Motivation before and during the first year of the COVID-19 pandemic.

These ideas are complemented in Chapter 12, entitled 'The Social and Solidarity Economics, Public Policies, and Non-Monetary Economic Practices: The Case of Associative Firms in Loja, Ecuador', and written by Dr. Arturo Luque González, Universidad Tecnica de Manabí, Ecuador, & Universidad del Rosario, Colombia, Prof. Aitor Bengoetxea Alkorta, Universidad del País Vasco/Euskal Herriko Unibertsitatea UPV/EHU, Spain, and Prof. Jaime Leonidas Ordóñez Salcedo, Instituto Hegoa - Gezki, Universidad del País Vasco/Euskal Herriko Unibertsitatea UPV/EHU, Spain. From a Spanish-Ecuadorian perspective, these authors describe how the Republic of Ecuador, in its constitution of 2008, recognizes ancestral practices at an economic and social level to grant special protection to "mother earth" or Pachamama based on the common element of solidarity between ecosystems and human beings. The authors obtain data by conducting group interviews in Loja (Ecuador) communities to analyze the scope and continuity of current ancestral practices and the effectiveness of processes established in the social economy. They show the lack of continuity of these practices and their associated benefits for people and communities with limited resources.

From an entrepreneurial vision, business evaluation and cost savings are crucial to surviving in hostile business environments born in the post-COVID-19 era. In this respect, Chapter 13, entitled 'Business Model Creation for Cost Saving in the New World Economic Order,' and written by Dr. Beatriz Olalla-Caballero, Pontifical University of Salamanca, Spain, and Montserrat Mata, Deusto University, Spain, deals with these issues to assure the market share in the future and fight against competition.

The second section of this book (Chapters 14-18) deals with education-related issues and Covid19. In this regard, Chapter 14, entitled 'Trends for Business Education Post-COVID-19', written by Prof. Neeta Baporikar, Namibia University of Science and Technology, Namibia and University of Pune, India, affirms that Covid19 has brought about tremendous changes in business education in particular. In the ordinary course, business education entailed students being on the campus, and physical attendance enables interaction and discussion. With COVID-19 lockdown and restrictions, the usual way of doing business is disrupted. Hence, by adopting systematic literature and a grounded approach, this chapter aims to understand the disruptions, faculty, and student difficulties and sketch out the future trends in business education post-COVID-19.

This educational vision continues in Chapter 15, entitled 'Developments and Global Trends in the Education and Business Sectors in the Post-COVID-19 Period: The Mexican Case', written by Dr. Enriqueta Márquez, from Universidad Anáhuac, Mexico. The author affirms that the pandemic has made people worldwide prioritize their matters of importance and analyzes the challenges teachers, students, and parents faced, who had to adapt to workplaces and focus their efforts to innovate and capture students' attention continuously. Regarding firms, the pandemic was a digital accelerator, as different types of consumers emerged that will remain throughout the Post-COVID-19 period.

Preface

The last three chapters of this book are related to China. In this regard, Chapter 16, entitled 'Initial Exploration of Cross-Generational Attitudes Towards Piracy of Chinese Online Literature,' written by Prof. Rob Kim Marjerison, Wenzhou-Kean University, China, and Ms. Sijia Jiang, Wenzhou-Kean University, China, seeks to provide initial evidence and provide a baseline for further exploration of Chinese cross-generational audiences' attitude differences towards online literature and digital piracy. Globalization has complicated the cultural, generational, and national perspectives on intellectual property protection affecting global commerce and international relations. These authors indicate a trend towards increased awareness and acceptance of IP value and protection and provide insight into cross-generational audiences in the important market of China.

Education technology (EdTech) plays an emerging role in higher education institutions (HEIs). In this respect, Chapter 17, entitled 'How COVID-19 Has Stimulated Innovation in Chinese Education Sector', written by Mr. Poshan Yu, Soochow University, China; Dr. Samuel Kwok, International Business School Suzhou, Xi'an Jiaotong-Liverpool University, China, and Miss Zhongyue Jiang, Independent Researcher, China, investigates how COVID-19 has impacted in China's education sector. The authors capture the dynamics and operational efficiency of the interlinked changing relationships between the availability and use of EdTech and online learning demand among various stakeholders in the Chinese educational market. Besides, they study how these changes drive stakeholders towards digital education and remote learning by using EdTech strategies.

Finally, Chapter 18, entitled 'Decision-Making Styles of the Next Generation of Chinese Business Leaders', and written by Prof. Rob Kim Marjerison, Wenzhou-Kean University, China, and Ms. Jing Pan, University of Warwick, UK, seeks to explore the relationships between decision-making styles, academic performance, and gender of educated Chinese millennials, as future leaders in public and commercial organizations endowed with global impact. The authors gather data through online self-report questionnaires and the General Decision Making Style test to assess respondents' decision-making models culminating in correlation analysis and t-test. Based on the findings, the authors find a difference in the decision-making styles and academic performance based on gender. As the authors also state, these findings may be of interest to a variety of those interested in decision-making styles, Chinese millennials, and future leaders of China.

In short, this book includes a wide variety of approaches, problems, and discussions in some aspects related to business and economics in the post-COVID-19 era from double North-South and South-South perspectives. We expect the readers to find appealing ideas to implement into their organizations or to continue advancing in searching, conceiving, and starting new business-related and sociopolitical strategies to enhance richness and economic wealth in society.

José Manuel Saiz-Álvarez
Catholic University of Avila, Spain & Catholic University of Santiago de Guayaquil, Ecuador

Acknowledgment

To all 36 authors who participate in this book, and are working in universities and research centers located in Africa (Namibia), America (Colombia, Ecuador, Mexico, and the USA), Asia (China, India, and Saudi Arabia), and Europe (Spain and UK) for their excellent work and collaboration.

To all referees for their double-blind peer-review process and the EAB (Editorial Advisory Board) for their help and suggestions.

To the IGI Global Book Development Team, especially Gianna Walker, Assistant Development Editor–Book Development, for their support, patience, determination, and confidence.

To my family and friends for their encouragement while preparing this book.

Section 1
Politics and Business

Chapter 1
Critical Analysis of the Evolving Process of Neoliberal Global Capitalism

José G. Vargas-Hernández
https://orcid.org/0000-0003-0938-4197
Instituto Tecnológico Mario Molina Unidad Zapopan, Mexico

Patricia Calderón Campos
Tecnológico Nacional de México. Secretaria Académica de Investigación e Innovación, Mexico

ABSTRACT

This chapter aims to make a critical analysis of the evolving process of neoliberal capitalism globalization. It begins with the assumption that the neoliberal capitalism system is undergoing a mutation in the globalization processes as a dynamic element in continuous economic and financial crisis representing the development of the logic of capital based on the neoliberal ideology that promotes the free market. The evolving process of globalization is the history of international free trade framed by the classical liberal and neoliberal economic theory. The discussion focuses on a critical analysis of the paradigm of deglobalization as an alternative to the global capitalist regime that proposes local and regional economic protectionism solutions as an alternative to keep growing the national economies but still neglecting social justice and inequality inclusiveness and socio-ecological development.

INTRODUCTION

Neoliberal capitalism is undergoing a mutation, a shift towards deglobalization processes that require the resurgence of the nation-state. Capitalism is always in the process of creative destruction (Schumpeter, 1942), disruptive and in constant crisis, as in the use of digital and automation technologies that, while destroying some ways of working, create others, but also develop new losers and new winners. Globalization constitutes the most dynamic element in developing the neoliberal capitalist system characterized by recurring crises and instability of the system. However, Hardt and Negri (2002) and Browning and

DOI: 10.4018/978-1-7998-7689-2.ch001

Kilmister (2006) propose in Empire that capitalism has not delineated the processes of globalization but that socialism has also contributed to its characterization.

The economic integration processes have been implemented by an economic model that seeks the financialization of capital through free trade and capital agreements. That has specified international economic relations between countries. This form of economic globalization has been transcendent in the integration and cooperation of economic relations even though it is highly controversial.

Globalization has been described as a process of world economic integration through movements of goods and services, capital, technology, and labor, leading to economic decisions influenced by global conditions (Jenkins, 2004). The Committee for Development Policy defines economic globalization as the increasing interdependence between world economies at the growing integration scale of cross-border flow trade of goods, commodities and services, capital, and technologies.

The concept of globalization as a post-Westphalian phenomenon or as a process extends from movements, interconnectivity, and world economic exchanges to other fields such as social, political, cultural, etc., which Palomares (2006: 27), and more recently, Coppelli Ortiz (2018) consider that weaken the premise of the historical structure of the international Westphalian order and question the paradigms of international law that sustains that national states are entities that have control of their territory and their population, are self-sufficient and sovereign because they do not respond to superior austerities.

In this sense, these two conceptions are complementary, although diverse, to understand the dimensions of the observable phenomenon of globalization, as well as the measurable processes of globalization (García de la Cruz 2008: 72-74). The dimensions of economic globalization group classic productive factors, such as the international movement of goods and services, the free movement of capital, and the transit of people and labor.

Neoliberal global capitalism has been tightening its grip over almost the entire world, weakening regulatory mechanisms to the increasing mobility of capital and giving capitalism an unapologetic face, leading to global socio-economic problems, unprecedented inequality, and environmental degradation (Galent, & Soborski, 2020). As the third international division of labor processes, neoliberal global capitalism includes the specialized segmentation across the world to just produce a single commodity (Neilson, 2020). The factors that characterize globalization are the freedoms of trade, movement of people, and capital movements, which with the emergence of the health crisis have been seriously compromised.

Globalization represents the development of the logic of capital based on the neoliberal ideology that promotes the free market to transform the world into a global market, taking advantage of the trends of the free movement of people, goods, services and capital, the deregulation of international markets, low customs fees, free movement. Globalization is the integration into the markets of goods, services, capital, and people globally, which has come in waves.

The objective of this chapter is to make a critical analysis of the evolving process of neoliberal capitalism globalization. It begins with the assumption that the neoliberal capitalism system is undergoing a mutation in the globalization processes as a dynamic element in ongoing economic and financial crisis representing the development of the logic of capital based on the neoliberal ideology that promotes the free market.

EVOLVING GLOBALIZATION PROCESS

The pre-globalization process of European origin and with Asian manifestations until the 15th century moved to America. The Catholic Church, then the reforms, played a relevant role in globalizing the values of Greek, Roman, and Indo-European cultures. The first model of world economic integration was made with the agreements between Portugal, Spain, Great Britain, Holland, and France 500 years ago (Ferrer, 1998: 155).

In the 19th century, liberalism spread through international trade in the territorial markets of the great colonizing powers with the support of new industrial, transportation, and communication technologies. Globalization processes intensified at the end of the 19th century. The first stage or phase of globalization lasted from the 19th century until the outbreak of the First World War in 1914. During the periods 1850-1914 and 1950-2007, globalization has been the norm for most people, and therefore even periods of stagnant international economic and financial interaction are often seen as periods of deglobalization.

The manifestations of convergence processes between national states of the World Economy between 1870 and 1940, a product of the second industrial revolution, are considered as the first phase of globalization (Comín, 2011: 410) motivated by economic development, movement of goods, services and capital, labor, reduction of transport costs. This stage was interrupted by the First World War (ECLAC, 2002: 18; ECLAC, 2017).

The first wave occurred between 1870 and the Great Depression, with changes associated with the Industrial Revolution. What is considered the first period of economic globalization took place between 1870 and 1914, characterized by an increasing economic growth based on the exchange of goods and services, transfer of technology and factors of production, wages, and global prices converging among the national economies involved (Lascurain, 2017; Lascurain, & Villafuerte, 2016).

From the Beautiful Epoch that includes 1880-1914 and the glorious 20s that correspond to the first wave of globalization processes, interrupted with the bloody phase of the First World War, the Great Depression, the emergence of fascism leads to the Second World War. The first wave of globalization began at the end of the nineteenth century after pressure from prominent exporters of agricultural products that demanded a tariff increase on exports and the closure of the borders of some countries to migration.

The period between 1914 and 1980 was characterized by State intervention in capitalist and protectionist national economies with restrictions on international trade and capital exchanges (Bello, 2013). Before the First World War, the processes of globalization began a backward phase that ended with the Great Depression of 1930.

There is evidence that this great crisis was the product of pure individualism and sustained by the ideologies of liberalism and capitalism. However, nationalism and socialism create and develop governments with strong militarisms to expand their territories, leading to the First World War. Anti-globalization was a manifest sentiment in the population and one of the factors that caused the First World War, which, together with the economic problems caused by the Great Depression, motivated the implementation of protectionist and nationalist policies (Bordo, 2017). In this period of deglobalization, between 1929 and 1932, world trade contracted by one-third due to protectionist policies implemented by nations (Madse, 2001). During this period of economic globalization, capitalism developed until it fades later with World War II.

After the Second World War, between 1945 and 1973, after the Bretton Woods agreements of 1944, a new global liberal economic order was established to regulate trade and access to capital (Palomares,

2006: 217) through the creation of commercial and financial cooperation institutions, the International Monetary Fund (IMF), the World Bank (WB) and the General Agreement for Trade and Tariffs (GATT).

This new global economic order delimits the solution of international problems and the multilateral organization of the economy. With the Bretton Woods agreement, International Institutions emerge with the purpose of advancing the governance of capital and global trade, while some nations deepen the model of the Welfare State that seeks a balance between the development of capital and work. The Bretton Woods International Monetary Agreement lays down the rules for international trade and financial relations.

The latest period of economic globalization evolves from the early 1970s to the present times involving the spreading of capitalism based on an increasing reliance on markets though the world, shifting the national economies into a more open and export-oriented strategy based on cross-border production for foreign markets. The emergence and rise of contemporary global capitalism in the 1970s supported by neoliberal economic policies aimed at liberalizing and deregulating capital and financial markets have led to the contemporary process of financial globalization and increasing uneven development. Starting in 1991, the economic globalization promoted by the United States accelerated.

Economic globalization has increased the international movements of capital and investments, goods and services, and labor, facilitated by innovations in information and communication technologies (UNDP, 1999). Digital technologies are disruptive because using global digital platforms creates new networks through which the emerging activities in global markets of a new platform and surveillance capitalism are carried out as effects.

The rapid acceptance of this model of liberal globalization contributed to the capitalist economic redefinition with the disintegration of the Soviet Union from countries that were under its influence, added to the fall of the Berlin Wall and the economic growth of the countries of Southeast Asia (Fernández, 2010: 47). The defeat of real socialism and the fall of the Berlin Wall announced the proclamation of the end of history and the victory of the democratic system and the market economy. During the current period of intensified globalization with the fall of the Soviet bloc and the Berlin Wall, the free market's invisible hand tracked down the most efficient locations around the globe to locate its productive activities, with minimal intervention from nation-states.

Since the Bretton Woods agreements, the economic policies that govern relations in the international economic system are guided by the doctrine of free trade to eliminate protectionism and economic nationalism. For four decades, free trade achieved an increase in the volume of world trade and economic growth. The liberalism of Ruggie (1982) proposed the Bretton Woods type as the regime for global economic governance where the economic policies of the nation-state are made compatible and gave continuity to the regulatory system established by international institutions and agencies, such as the World Trade Organization.

1995 is considered the start date of globalization with the establishment of the World Trade Organization (WTO), the multilateral body regulating global trade transactions and exchanges between 164 member countries because of international negotiations. This vocation of the WTO is confirmed when, in 1996, in joint action with the World Bank and the International Monetary Fund, the other two Bretton Woods institutions declared to cooperate in designing and implementing a global economic policy. The institutional fragility of the WTO has not been able to advance the dispute settlement mechanism since the Doha Round. The multilateral system crumbles into a new generation of trade agreements that tend to undermine the global system's authority.

The world economy is more integrated until 2008 (Jiménez, 2009: 57) based on technological development that benefits the most advanced economies. During this period, emerging economies have positioned themselves in the global economy as relevant actors in determining international economic policies, as is the case of the BRICS countries and the Pacific Alliance.

Globalization has speedup the exchanges, interactions, and movements of human beings, goods, services, capital, knowledge, technologies, cultural practices, lifestyles, etc., all over the world and between different regions and populations. In 2019, China was one of the country's most open to international trade and was the world's largest exporter, which in 2018 represented 38.2% of GDP (World Bank).

The history of international free trade shows that globalization is transformed into its last phase dysfunctions with the contributions of the digital economy, the active participation of China, the erosion of democracy and values as the most significant challenges to combat inequality. An international model of unlimited production characterized global capitalism. Now, the current phase of global capitalism is characterized by an international model of limited production. The neoliberal global capitalism and technological change are the two factors shaping the current disorder by enabling the functioning and expansion of capital accumulation leading to severe turbulences in the capital and labor markets and introducing new patterns of social stratification (Galent, & Soborski, 2020)

The new phase of globalization shows characteristics that can be contextualized in an intensification of trade agreements and treaties that promote the privatization and liberalization of local economies, mainly in services. However, the pattern of relationship between political pro-capitalist violence and neoliberal restructuring for capital accumulation has increased in developing countries like Mexico and Colombia. According to Hristov (2020), neoliberal capitalism policies have enhanced the ability of capital to secure access to exploitable resources and labor employed by different modalities of structural state and non-state promotion of pro-capitalist violence.

THEORETICAL APPROACH

The global level of economic power is supported by capital. The economic globalization promoted by liberal policies pretended to create a borderless world only for capital without spatial and social responsibility attachments. In contrast, labor is subject to national boundaries and specific geographic spaces where people live in contexts of historical and cultural features with protection systems and collective solidarity.

The classical theory of economic integration and globalization supported by the principles of work division and specialization of national comparative advantage of each country motivated the international trade transactions giving access to the less developed countries to cheaper capital goods and technology. The theoretical foundations of globalization are found in David Ricardo's contributions to the comparative advantage of the nations. Ricardian ideas based on the location of productive activities in the places where it is produced more efficiently, a condition given by the factors of production such as costs and availability of raw materials and human capital.

The economic integration processes have been implemented by an economic model that seeks the financialization of capital through free trade, capital agreements, and specified international economic relations between countries. This form of economic globalization has been transcendent in the integration and cooperation of economic relations even though it is highly controversial.

The economic dimension of globalization contains trade, finance, cooperation, migration, and ideas (Goldin & Reinert, 2007: 38). On the other hand, Silva (2009) groups the components of globalization in international trade flows, foreign investment, financial capitals, movements of people, and knowledge and technology.

International trade liberalization and the global flow of foreign direct investment and capital mobility are current economic globalization elements that pose enormous challenges to the roles of international institutions and organizations and local governments and economies.

At the center of economic globalization processes are the FDI and capital flows, which may positively affect developing host countries that have advantages on location for the multinationals, despite the high risk of short-term mobility of capital. Large multinational corporations adopted the term to refer to the global markets for the consumption of goods and services and the exchange networks of financial services, capital movements, and speculative investments. Foreign direct investment (FDI) is the capital flow from a foreign company that acquires control over a local new or pre-existing business. This concept differs from portfolio investments because investors have no interest in having control over business operations.

The economic globalization process is determined by flows of trade liberalization, capital movements, and Foreign Direct Investment (FDI) through transnational and multinational enterprises (MNEs). Economic globalization has manifested through global capital flows. Commercial and financial free flows are promoted by large multinational and transnational companies, many of them with US capital. The FDI and portfolio investments have significantly increased in the last decades by integrating international finances based on liberalization of capital accounts and the ICT global advances.

The transfer of technology benefits the FDI and inputs of capital that promotes competition in local markets (Klein, 2015) besides contributing to the development of human capital and increasing the tax income (Sanna-Randaccio & Veugelers, 2003; Barrios *et al.*, 2003; Feldstein, 2000; Gilpin, 2001). Economic and financial global integration has been promoted by direct channels associated with increasing savings, reducing risks and transaction costs of capital, and developing local financial sectors (Feldstein, 2000). Indirect channels are related to economic policies and foreign investment flows to local markets (Prasad *et al..*, 2003).

Economic globalization is measured in the KOF index by exchanges of goods, services, and capital movements, restrictions on trade and capital with indicators, among others, the volume of exports and imports, foreign direct investment, and restrictions on investment in each country. According to the Golden Arches' theory, established in 1996 and later renamed as Dell's theory of conflict prevention, it affirms that prosperity makes people peaceful. So, it confirms that capitalist peace occurs among nations when there is at least one McDonald's in each country because nations integrated by logistics chains do not face wars.

The main features of economic globalization are the increase in commercial capital flows, recurring financial crises, the action of multinational companies, global competition, and the relocation of production (Requeijo, 2012: 346), as well as international movements of people, knowledge, and technology (Silva, 2009: 16). These situations have prompted more regulations in international financial markets in a world economy regulated by an institutional design framed by globalized Keynesian economics.

RESEARCH METHODOLOGY

This analysis employs exploratory and analytical instruments based on the literature review and the transference of findings to a specific implementation of cases. Postcolonial theory of capitalism is connected to the uneven development occurring on the periphery lacking paradigms of developed political analysis, constrained by the pre-neoliberal analysis and neoliberal global capitalism, which limit the discourse and practices (Neilson, 2020)

The objective of the exploratory analysis of information and qualitative data aimed to identify the different perspectives and theoretical models framed by the classical liberal and neoliberal economic theory, to delimit the critical analysis perspective of the neoliberal capitalism system considered the most appropriate to represent. This analysis is based on the study of the economic and financial crisis as the development of the logic of capitalism system based on the neoliberal ideology promoting the free market. In the critical analysis conducted, there is a particular emphasis to determine the evolving process of globalization as the history of international free trade, as well as the critical analysis of the periods of intense globalization processes leading to dysfunctionalities of the economic, financial, and sanitary crisis, and followed by periods of delocalization or deglobalization to transform the free market into a protected market.

THE ECONOMIC AND FINANCIAL CRISIS

Financial services are the most globalized sector of capital. Financial globalization promotes the deregulation of markets to increase speculation with financial derivatives, creating invisible accounting and tax havens. Financial globalization tends to concentrate the wealth of the owners of capital. The financial and economic stability and safety of developing countries are weak due to the enormous amount of floating international capital resulting from the rapid innovation, privatization, and expansion of financial instruments worldwide.

Countries maintained macroeconomic and financial stability by acquiring investments and technology, accumulation of capital (Irwin, 2005; Bhagwati, 2004). This massive amount of floating international capital leads to developing bubbles to cause economic and financial crises, weakening monetary sovereignty, and dysfunctional macroeconomic and monetary policies.

The free flow of speculative financial capital has created constant financial crises due to the instability and currency devaluation of the countries affected, as in Mexico in 1994, Southeast Asia in 1997, and Russia and Argentina in 2000. Crises from recent globalization emerged in Mexico, Russia, the Asian Southeast, and Argentina due to dysfunctional local financial market institutions to manage the capital flows in the international system. The experience shows the need to be cautious in opening the capital and maintaining discipline on regulations and supervision to confront the financial crises. The former financial turmoil of the 1990s in Mexico and East Asia, and the financial and economic crises of large capital management corporations, were caused due to the limitations that the international organizations have currently in managing the world economy.

After the 1980s and until the financial crisis of 2008-2009, economic integration reached a global scale while developing economies moved towards economic liberalization, free market, and democracy and dismantled trading barriers. While all these events were taking place, technology developments fueled the changes and improvements in information and communication technologies facilitating global supply chains and economic integration. Globalization processes were considered in the 80s and 90s of the last century as an opportunity to solve the problems of economic growth and social development, giving rise to countries and international organizations to discuss these issues. The release of tariff barriers and the reduction of customs duties, central to the concept of globalization based on the free market, reached its turning point in the crisis of 2008-2009.

The economic and financial crisis of 2007-2009 weakened the foundations of world capitalism. It exposed the inefficiency and inability of national and international financial systems, national states, and international financial institutions to manage financial risks. The financial crisis of 2008-2009 has pushed back capital investment flows. Since the economic and financial crisis of 2008-2009, world trade began to slow down the rate of its growth in terms of world GDP as the resurgence of nationalist market protectionism begins. An excellent example of this situation is the foreignization of banking and industry continues its ascendant trajectory in Mexico, responding to the profitability of the parent companies that results from a merger between the political elites and the financial oligarchy in a scheme of ambiguous neo-protectionism.

The profound economic-financial crisis of global capitalism of 2008-2009 surprised everyone, but the lack of a critical mass kept the existing system in check. Disenchantment over the lack of fulfillment of the promises of the economic globalization processes has affected the legitimacy of neoliberalism. It has generated high levels of discontent against political and economic elites for their inability to improve living standards and reduce economic inequality. The theory of globalization fails to fulfill the promises and promised benefits that have only benefited a few, the plutocracy that corresponds to 20% of the population and the holders of capital bonds.

The new events of the economic and financial crisis of 2008-2009, the advancement of information technologies and telecommunications, the digitization and robotization of the economy, the pressures of migratory movements of the population are just some of the events that have motivated a social discontent that generates a reaction panic and that promote populisms for a change in the world economic order. After this crisis, the advances of international trade flows are modified with an intensification of protectionist economic policies and the gradual abandonment of free trade policies.

The expansion of the coronavirus is facilitated by the intensity of social exchanges in a system of globalized capitalism of production, distribution, and consumption. The health crisis emerges in a global neoliberal capitalist economic system that was already destabilized and generated an impulse towards a post-capitalist system to continue the sacrifice of the southern countries. The health crisis emerges during a neoliberal capitalist economic system weakened and destabilized by a profound crisis of legitimacy and loss of control of the economic and political elites.

The adverse effects of the health crisis caused by the pandemic on trade, investment, capital, and people flows can deepen economic crises in countries that already have or drag countries on the brink into recessions. The economic and financial interdependence between the countries occurs more in the circuits of capital. Still, the current crisis shows that due to the excessive specialization in the production of goods and services, their costs have increased.

The current crisis of the economic model based on neoliberal capitalist globalization that has deteriorated economically and caused political conflicts between the great nations can give room for maneuver. So, countries not directly involved can accelerate their economic growth with a more endogenous orientation as a succession in previous crises of solidarity with the South. The immediate precedent of the current crisis of capitalism is the Second World War, which had significant effects on people's movements, commercial and financial exchanges. Solvency problems of individuals in their debts with the banking systems threaten to end, as has been the case on previous occasions, in public debt, which generates banking crises with more significant difficulties in accessing the capital markets and that require several years to achieve the recovery.

The health crisis of the pandemic, the financial crisis of 2008-2009, and cyberattacks are examples of the spread of risks that show the hidden face of the globalization processes of the global economic system that, although it has offered excellent benefits, has also implied significant risks. The dimensions of these risks are capitalized with substantial impacts for countries, organizations, and individuals, for which they require substantial changes such as the creation of new alternative sources of local supply of supplies regardless of the costs that replace the interruptions of global chains of supplies.

The first crisis of 2008-2009 and the second crisis of the financial capitalist globalization of the 21st century occurred with a difference of 12 years and have given greater emphasis to the social subjects and global protest movements that proclaim and fight for a transformation of the world. The health crisis has immediate and overwhelming economic and social effects leading to a general crisis of world democratic capitalism and creating opportunities for the emergence of a new world economic system based on new forms of capitalism that can be more aggressive and involve greater risks the survival of humanity.

Neoliberal-led global capitalism is currently going through a crisis due to the decreasing world trade and capital flows leading to growing protectionist tendencies and confronting nation-states in currency and trade wars and sanctions regimes. According to Komolog (2020), the expansive capitalist development subordinating the periphery to exploiting natural resources and cheap cost labor during the latest decades has intensified the contradictions of economic development with growing inequality, unemployment, financialization, etc.

TRANSITION OF THE GLOBAL NEOLIBERAL CAPITALISM

There is talk that global capitalism needs a profound neo-mercantile transformation. A transformation of neoliberal capitalist economic globalization processes depends on the reconfiguration of progressive groups that take advantage of the situation that results from the objective crisis of the system and the movement of subjective forces.

Globalization is an accelerated integration of markets and production from capital that seeks to increase the rate of profit. The processes of economic globalization have multidimensional impacts that involve the different economic actors and agents in a growing integration through the free exchange of factors, goods and services, capital, people, and technology (Barberá de la Torre, 2012) have expanded interdependence between nation-states. Nation-states are dependent on production and trade from global capitalism, so that local dysfunctions may lead to the systemic breakdown of the global economy and finance (Neilson, 2020). For more than 30 years, the continuous deepening of the processes of economic globalization based on the free flow of goods, capital, people, and technology brought, among other benefits, the economic growth of national economies and a reduction in the prices of consumer goods.

It is argued that globalization processes are beneficial for the economic growth and social development of nations and for all people who accept the status of global citizenship under the impersonal forces of the free market. At the same time, transnational corporations obtain the maximum benefits from an efficient combination of capital, land, labor, and technology resources.

The bourgeoning advance of global capitalism required governments to move towards structural adjustment policies and austerity measures that damaged the social policy to promote globalization further. The structural adjustment programs imposed by the International Monetary Fund in more than 70 developing countries during the eighties and nineties have been a failure because they have institutionalized the stagnation of economic growth with an increase in the levels of inequality and poverty. Numerous investigations have been carried out showing that the structural adjustment policies promoted by the Washington Consensus have been the main factor in the concentration of global income.

The economic globalization of neoliberal capitalism in the Washington Consensus proposal is inconsistent because it does not allow the free flow of labor. The Washington consensus is an ideological doctrine product of an intellectual consensus that underlies the promotion of economic globalization processes (Bergsten, 2000) with a strong component in the free flow of speculative capital.

The G20 leadership represents the most industrialized and developing economies accounting for around 80% of economic output and global trade, and is considered the political backbone of the global financial architecture that secures open markets, orderly capital flows, and a safety net for countries in difficulty. The G20 struggles to coordinate monetary and fiscal policies.

The processes of globalization delocalized production by enduring cheap labor, reduced sovereignty, and the ability of national governments to act, increased economic and social inequality, promoted capital migration and tax evasion. Less developed countries have not always received the infusions of foreign capital and technology. Moreover, governments' national sovereignty and their influence have been eroded by functions of international institutions and organizations, giving space to an increase of non-governmental organizations (Pyle 2001, 1999). These manifestations that defend and appeal to the principle of national sovereignty accentuate the processes of neoliberal globalization through the allegation that national interests are above global interests.

The processes of globalization have generated economic inequality in individuals and societies. Piketty and Goldhammer (2014) confirm the failure of capitalism with growing income and wealth inequality despite capitalism lifting billions out of extreme poverty.

However, outside of the technology companies that monopolize global markets, transnational companies compete with similar companies, and of the same category in other countries, as in companies that provide financial services with freedom of cross-border capital movements.

During the last period of neoliberal economic globalization, several countries have suffered a brutal assault on their economic and financial structures, losing their sovereignty. A similarity can be established between the First World War and the current health crisis as events that triggered changes and transformations in development models based on the intense globalization of economic processes. New alternatives emerge from the First World War. The responses to the current crisis of economic globalization processes must be alternatives that take advantage of the opportunities that arise from the exact relationship between synergy and the dialectic of the crisis.

The crisis of global neoliberal capitalism coupled with the failure of liberal democracy as systems to achieve people's equality has reinforced the space to create extreme-right movements favoring economic deglobalization processes that come to power because they are better positioned to take advantage of the discontent. Their programs in their paradigm come from the left, such as protectionism and State intervention in the economy, and the expansion of the Welfare State, which considers class social inclusion. Still, it is racial, cultural, and religiously exclusive.

The big problem is that the right has won the space to the left and has kidnapped and perverted for opportunistic gain for its authoritarian agenda. It is clearly demonstrated that a systemic crisis deepened by the health crisis has unleashed a subjective storm of resentment that is being exploited by the extreme right and left organized in populist movements. Social organizations and resistance to globalization processes are also in a crisis of indefiniteness because some expressions on the left have accepted the neoliberal ideology. Global neoliberalism supported by the most conservative national forces is protected with internal security and surveillance systems that feed repressive systems and endemic corruption that weaken the cross-border movements of counter-hegemonic globalization accused as an expression of international terrorism.

In a way, the far right is opportunistic and has hijacked popular discontent against the economic and political elites that promoted globalization. At the same time, the Social Democracy and Democrats and the left lack the legitimacy to take the responsibility of taking leadership outside of making a new commitment to neoliberalism. The strategies proposed by the left focus more on deglobalization, degrowth, food sovereignty, etc., without having a massive livelihood and involving them with the neoliberal system with a human face. Despite everything, the trend of deglobalization processes grows with a substitution of protectionist economies, giving rise to reversing policies focused on free trade.

The current phase of deglobalization is developing a new form of capital-centered global integration. This integration may be more brutal than in previous stages of economic globalization. Deglobalization proceeds along the route of regionalization based on regulations of mixed economies to strengthen national states with authority over private capital. Oriented deglobalization processes to economic regionalization are an alternative policy to opt for other scenarios defined by the postulates of the orthodox economy, that is, to the globalization model driven by the neoliberal capitalist economic model.

Another alternative scenario is what Jalife calls the "humanist neo-renaissance or socialism of the XXI century" that focuses exchanges on man and not on the market and where the transactional capitalist interests of the plutocracy become social interests with rights of equal conditions with the working class. Altermundism is not a real option for globalization because they lack a viable model to implement their projects to deglobalize the planet that they intend to be holistic, biospheric, and economical, but not financial.

For the deglobalization alternatives to deepen their changes, they must acquire the character of anti-capitalism. However, anti-globalization movements and religious fundamentalism in their most radical expression of terrorism show that capitalism is not assured of its hegemony. The growing problems of global insecurity and terrorism, of all kinds, negatively affect the control of the flows of goods, capital, and investments, etc. Investors and owners of capital privilege security and profitability that, in the presence of a scenario of deglobalization processes, currency evasion is made possible to refuge in the countries that offer greater security and profitability.

DEGLOBALIZATION PROCESSES OF CAPITALISM

Deglobalization processes show only one facet of the multiple crises of neoliberal capitalism that accuses the subordination of national economies and their limitations imposed by the globalizing interests of international organizations, multinationals, financial corporations, and global banks. What is relevant about these crises that affect the development of global capitalism is that if the lessons are learned to identify, manage, regulate, and control the inherent risks. Deglobalization is an inevitable process defined in a return of solid regulations to financial and capital movements that ensure that competition occurs between comparable social systems.

Deglobalization processes understand the different phases, deconstruction understood as resistance and confrontation to globalization expansion and the construction of alternatives to the capture of the world by capital (Bello, 2005). Deglobalization processes slide the world economy towards a decline in international flows of goods, services, capital, people, and technology. This setback represents challenges in return to the economic and financial control of the nation-states with protectionist policies and greater border control that are accompanied by new conflicts and social tensions, etc.

Several events have affected the deglobalization movement that drives the reversal of the world order and opposes advancing the values of globalizing capitalism, democracy, and the free market. In the wake of capital market crises that have occurred, the deglobalization processes are challenging rules and legitimacy and questioning the coordination of the capital market. Deglobalization aims to stop the trend of a system that tries to remove all political, social, and cultural obstacles that limit the expansive reproduction of capital. Even in some periods of increasing globalization processes, some developed countries against the crisis showed a tendency to "deglobalization," that is, isolationism.

The increasing flows of international capital and trade and the people movements have turned down into a deglobalization process with decreasing capital flows, trade, and people movements. Integration of trade, money, business, and governments of nation-states in the globalization processes has been followed by a hostile backlash driven by populist agendas and movements. The "Make America Great Again," the Brexit, the Continental European Populist, and the Brazilian Bolsonaro movements are examples of the critical deglobalization processes and the anti-globalization sentiment.

Recently, there have been some moves toward trade protection and its interrelationships with regulations of capital and investment flows, limitations of people´s movements. The US-China trade war has raised the risk of protectionism and distorted global capital and trade flows, pushing the global economy towards the deglobalization processes.

Companies tend to repatriate their capital and bring in processes of reshoring their displaced jobs to plants in other distant economies. The relocation of companies to the places of production and local consumption is supported by protectionist regulations, recovery of customs fees on imported goods and services, control of capital transfers, levies on financial transactions. Relocation is an effect of globalization that benefits prominent business people but has a perverse impact on the population. Citizens had been protesting these perverse effects of this relocation through free trade, movement of capital, the trade war and the health crisis are achieving it, the relocation of companies.

Following the US, other countries leverage trade and capital protectionism by tightening their export controls, expanding trade tariffs to relevant sectors, tightening technology transfers controls, and other measures in a race to the bottom. For example, China has adopted policies to face the provocations of the tech-trade war launched by the United States, to encourage the funding for Chinese tech firms and loosening financing regulations in a potential financial decoupling raising concerns over the tendency of globalization.

Countries reinforce their borders with protectionist measures of national economies that restrict capital flows less than goods, services, people, ideas, etc. Therefore, deglobalization processes occur in all sectors and constitute threats. One of the sectors that most deeply suffer its effects is higher education and research, which has severe consequences in training professionals with mentalities trapped by national borders without having international experiences.

The relocation of companies to the places of production and local consumption is supported by protectionist regulations, recovery of customs fees on imported goods and services, control of capital transfers, and levies on financial transactions.

Deglobalization processes affect a significant reduction in real GDP even in the most advanced countries. Still, those most affected by a breakdown in international trade are undoubtedly the economies of developing countries that lack natural resources and intellectual capital. However, for a small country, but well-governed and with close economic alliances with other countries, it creates advantages with globalization.

DISCUSSION

Neoliberalism and social democracy have exhausted their globalizing project. Progressivism offers several synergetic alternatives to deglobalization processes such as degrowth, ecosocialism, food sovereignty, neo-Marxist models and emancipatory feminisms, etc.

Modern capitalism has gone through a series of economic and financial crises, the most recent being the current deglobalization processes resulting from the economic and financial crisis of 2008 and 2009 that have deepened with the pandemic's health crisis. The primary beneficiaries of the processes of economic globalization have been the owners of capital and the plutocracy. In contrast, the most affected have been workers who remain in poverty, marginalization, and social inequality, in addition to the destruction of socio-ecosystems, biodiversity, and the environment. Social relations under capitalism are highly questionable.

Deglobalization, the slowing down of globalization or "slowbalization," has already been a precedent for several years in the traditional anti-globalization movements that denounce the advances of globalization processes as the promoters of savage capitalism. These anti-globalization movements are added the populist and nationalist claims that promote protectionist measures against the trend of free trade (Madsen, 2001). It is questioned whether these processes of slowing down globalization are temporary and reversible or represent the end of a cycle in the hostility of the world economy. The economic slowdown negatively affects trade and financial flows, investment, and capital movements, with the closure of the frontiers of the countries

Economic and financial globalization processes require rebalancing more the gains and benefits of cross-border investments by building capital infrastructure, labor, and environmental issues to prevent economic, social, and ecological crises. Therefore, deglobalization questions the process of world economic integration dominated by the logic of instrumental rationality of capital that erodes human values, human beings' decision-making capacity, and the needs of communities. The project of deglobalization processes is appropriated by the extreme right that previously promoted globalization with proposals of neoliberal capitalism. It now takes advantage of the opportunity of permanent unemployment and economic inequalities to claim the protection of workers' livelihoods and recovery of the industry.

The global economy needs a reorientation towards a new model based on digital technological advances capable of reorienting capitalism towards new forms and organizational structures that maintain the balance between all the factors of production. This new stage of post-capitalist globalization redirects productive activities to focus on local markets rather than exports. Local and national production systems must be oriented towards local or national consumption to meet their own needs. Exports cannot be sustained by extracting natural resources and raw materials, at the scales and scopes of global capitalist production, at the interventionist and colonialist investments because local socio-ecosystems, local production systems deteriorate, and in general, distort local economies.

A critical analysis of the paradigms of deglobalization as an alternative to the global capitalist regime proposes domestic solutions such as small-scale agriculture as an alternative to the socio-ecological and food crisis caused by capitalist corporate industrial agriculture and a key to avoid global warming. The reconfiguration phase of economic globalization processes is in line with food sovereignty as a right of peoples to have nutritious and culturally adequate food, so it cannot be subject to global standardization. For their progress, they need to be complemented with other alternatives with a broader scope, broader and deeper sovereign integration processes based on complementarity that break the logic of capital and the market.

For their advancement, they need to be complemented with other alternatives of broader scope, broader and deeper sovereign integration processes based on complementarity that break the logic of capital and the market. The alliances between the nation-states make it possible to advance in constructing an alternative model of globalization. The partnerships between nation-states allow progress in the construction of an alternative model of globalization.

The current deglobalization processes show an explicit subordination of emerging and less developed countries to powerful international financial interests, international organizations, and multinational companies. The construction of alternative integration processes requires national initiatives under a scheme different from the capitalist financial and transnational capital, not only at the economic and commercial level, which is supported by self-organization and self-management to satisfy social needs. These alternative processes of deglobalization have multiple economic, social, environmental, political, sociocultural, gender dimensions, etc. For the deglobalization alternatives to deepen their changes, they must acquire the character of anti-capitalism.

It is difficult for economic globalization to be reversed entirely after necessary adjustments that have slowed down progress to overcome the health crisis and the crisis of neoliberal financial capitalism. The construction of alternative integration processes requires national initiatives under a scheme different from the capitalist financial and transnational capital, not only at the economic and commercial level, which is supported by self-organization and self-management to satisfy social needs. These alternative processes of deglobalization have multiple economic, social, environmental, political, sociocultural, gender dimensions, etc.

The new phase of the processes of economic globalization must affirm the exchanges of goods, services, capital, people, and ideas in a free movement and transit that allows the development of the economies of communities, localities, and nations under the principles of subsidiarity, cooperation, respect for biodiversity and in entire exercise of democratic participation decisions. Deglobalization must recover an organized alternative path of the economy of secular stagnation characterized by low economic growth and high rates of prevailing unemployment that emerges from the crisis of capitalism. The health crisis of the pandemic aggravates that.

REFERENCES

Barberá de la Torre, R. (2012). Globalización. In J. Malfeito (Ed.), *Introducción a la economía mundial* (pp. 467–489). Delta Publicaciones.

Barrios, S., Görg, H., & Strobl, E. (2003). Foreign Direct Investment, Competition and Industrial Development in the Host Country. *European Economic Review, 49*(7), 1761–1784. doi:10.1016/j.euroecorev.2004.05.005

Bello, P. W. (2005). *Deglobalization: Ideas for a New World Economy*. Zed Books.

Bello, P. W. (2013). *Capitalism's Last Stand? Deglobalization in the Age of Austerity*. Zed Books. doi:10.5040/9781350218895

Bergsten, C. F. (2000). The Backlash against Globalization. *Tokyo 2000: The Annual Meeting of the Trilateral Commission*.

Bhagwati, J. (2004). *In Defence of Globalization*. Oxford University Press.

Bordo, M. (2017). *The Second Era of Globalization is Not Yet Over: An Historical Perspective.* NBER Working Papers.

Browning, G., & Kilmister, A. (2006). *Critical and Post-Critical Political Economy*. Palgrave Macmillan. doi:10.1057/9780230501522

Comín, F. (2011). *Historia económica mundial*. Alianza Editorial.

Comisión Económica para América Latina y El Caribe (CEPAL). (2002). *Globalización y desarrollo*. Santiago de Chile.

Comisión Económica para América Latina y El Caribe (CEPAL). (2017). *La inversión extranjera directa en América Latina y El Caribe*. Santiago de Chile.

Coppelli Ortiz, G. (2018). La globalización económica del siglo XXI. Entre la mundialización y la desglobalización. *Estudios Internacionales (Santiago)*, *50*(191), 57–80. doi:10.5354/0719-3769.2018.52048

Feldstein, M. (2000). *Aspects of Global Economic Integration: Outlook for the Future*. NBER Working Papers 7899.

Fernández, J. C. (2010). *Sistema de Derecho Económico Internacional*. Aranzadi.

Ferrer, A. (1998). América Latina y la globalización. *Revista CEPAL*, *10*, 155–168.

Galent, M., & Soborski, R. (2020). Introduction to the special issue: globalization thirty years on: promises, realities and morals for the future. *The International Journal of Interdisciplinary Global Studies*, *15*(4), 23–35. doi:10.18848/2324-755X/CGP/v15i04/0-0

García de la Cruz, J. M. (2008). La globalización económica. In *Sistema económico mundial* (pp. 53–74). Thomson Editores.

Gilpin, R. (2001). *Global Political Economy: Understanding the International Economic Order*. Princeton University Press. doi:10.1515/9781400831272

Goldin, I., & Reinert, K. (2007). *Globalización para el desarrollo*. The World Bank.

Hardt, M., & Negri, A. (2002). *Empire*. Harvard University Press.

Hristov, J. (2020). Pro-capitalist violence and globalization Lessons from Latin America. In The Routledge Handbook of Transformative Global Studies. Routledge.

Irwin, D. (2005). *Free Trade under Fire*. Princeton University Press.

Jenkins, R. (2004). Globalization, production, employment, and poverty: Debates and evidence. *Journal of International Development*, *16*(1), 1–12. doi:10.1002/jid.1059

Jiménez, J. C. (2009). Etapas del desarrollo de la economía mundial. In *Lecciones sobre Economía Mundial* (pp. 47–67). Aranzadi.

Klein, M. (2015). *Foreign Direct Investment and Intellectual Property Protection in Developing Countries*. Center for Applied Economics and Policy Research (CAEPR) Working Paper, 018.

Komolov, O. (2020). Deglobalization and the "Great Stagnation". *International Critical Thought, 10*(3), 424–439. doi:10.1080/21598282.2020.1846582

Lascurain, M. (2017). Challenges of economic globalization. *Revista de Relaciones Internacionales y de Estrategia de Seguridad, 12*(1), 23–50.

Lascurain, M., & Villafuerte, L. F. (2016). Primera globalización económica y las raíces de la inequidad social en México. *Ensayos de Economía, 26*(48), 67–90. doi:10.15446/ede.v26n48.59858

Madsen, J. (2001). Trade barriers and the collapse of world trade during the Great Depression. *Southern Economic Journal, 67*(4), 848–868. doi:10.2307/1061574

Neilson, D. (2020). Epistemic violence in the time of coronavirus: From the legacy of the western limits of Spivak's 'can the subaltern speak' to an alternative to the 'neoliberal model of development'. *Educational Philosophy and Theory, 53*(8), 760–765. doi:10.1080/00131857.2020.1750092

Palomares, G. (2006). *Relaciones internacionales en el siglo XXI*. Tecnos.

Piketty, T., & Goldhammer, A. (2014). *Capital in the twenty-first century*. The Belknap Press of Harvard University Press. doi:10.4159/9780674369542

Prasad, E., & ... . (2003). *Effects of Financial Globalization on Developing Countries: Some Empirical Evidence*. International Monetary Fund.

Pyle, J. L. (1999). Third World Women and Global Restructuring. In J. Chafetz (Ed.), *Handbook of the Sociology of Gender* (pp. 81–104). Kluwer.

Pyle, J. L. (2001). *International Encyclopedia of the Social & Behavioral Sciences*. Elsevier.

Requeijo, J. (2012). *Economía Mundial*. McGraw Hill.

Ruggie, J. (1982). International regimes, transactions, and change: Embedded Liberalism in the postwar economic order. *International Organization, 36*(2), 379–415. doi:10.1017/S0020818300018993

Sanna-Randaccio, M., & Veurgeles, R. (2003). Global Innovation strategies of MNE's: implications for host economies. In J. Cantwell & J. Molero (Eds.), *Multinational Enterprises, Innovative Strategies and Systems of Innovation, New Horizons in International Business*. Edward Elgar Publishing.

Silva, C. (2009). Globalización: Dimensiones y políticas públicas. *Hologramática, 10*, 3–25.

UNDP. (2009). *Human Development Report 2009: Overcoming Barriers–Human Mobility and Development*, NY.

ADDITIONAL READING

Piketty, T. (2020). *Capital and Ideology*. The Belknap Press of Harvard University Press. doi:10.4159/9780674245075

Saiz-Álvarez, J. M. (2020). 4-Helix Entrepreneurial Ecosystems, Poverty, and Violence. In R. Pérez-Uribe, C. Largacha-Martínez, & D. Ocampo-Guzmán (Eds.), *Handbook of Research on International Business and Models for Global Purpose-Driven Companies* (pp. 148–165). IGI Global.

Saiz-Álvarez, J. M., Huezo-Ponce, D. L., & Palma-Ruiz, J. M. (2020). Fostering Corporate Social Innovation through Sustainable Entrepreneurial Ecosystems in Developing Countries. In M. Ramírez-Pasillas, V. Ratten, & H. Lundberg (Eds.), *Social Innovation of New Ventures. Achieving Social Inclusion and Sustainability in Emerging Economies and Developing Countries*. Routledge. doi:10.4324/9781003034933-4

KEY TERMS AND DEFINITIONS

Capitalism: It is an economic and social system based on private ownership of the means of production, the importance of capital as a generator of wealth, and the allocation of resources through the market mechanism.

Deglobalization: Inverse phenomenon to that of globalization, one in which the economy (but also society, politics, or culture), after a stage of global interaction and interdependence, once again becomes more local or regional.

Economic Crisis: It is a period in an economic cycle in which an economy faces difficulties for a long time.

Economic Globalization: It consists of integrating the different countries of the world from the greater commercial exchange and investments.

Financial Crisis: It is a sudden disturbance that produces a considerable loss of value in institutions or assets

Neoliberalism: This is a political-economic theory that takes up the doctrine of classical liberalism and reconsiders it within the capitalist scheme. The priority is the price system, free entrepreneurship, free enterprise, and a solid and impartial State.

Chapter 2
How Have Governments and the Entrepreneurial Sector Reacted to the First COVID-19 Lockdown?

Alicia Coduras
https://orcid.org/0000-0003-3271-3673
Institut Opinòmetre, Spain & GEM Global, UK

Jose Manuel Saiz-Alvarez
https://orcid.org/0000-0001-6435-9600
Catholic University of Avila, Spain & Catholic University of Santiago de Guayaquil, Ecuador

Muhammad Azam Roomi
Mohammed bin Salman College of Business and Entrepreneurship, Saudi Arabia

ABSTRACT

At the end of 2019, the pandemic caused by COVID-19 and its different mutations is forcing the world to face a significant economic crisis that will change the business world. To cope with this socio-economic problem, a digitation process has been accelerated in the labor market, and a more vital public-private collaboration has been put into action to solve this situation. Despite these efforts, the world is facing a broader North-South gap, and a new business world has been created for the new generations to come. This chapter aims to analyze how the first lockdown caused by COVID-19 has influenced this changing process. The authors conclude that this lockdown has accelerated both the digitation process and the work-life balance. Also, more efforts are needed to fight the psychiatric problems associated with the lockdown.

DOI: 10.4018/978-1-7998-7689-2.ch002

How Have Governments and the Entrepreneurial Sector Reacted to the First COVID-19 Lockdown?

INTRODUCTION

At the end of 2019, the virus that will trigger the different mutations of COVID19, the global pandemic for years, began to spread from China to Europe, North America and Latin America, the rest of the Asian countries, Australia, Oceania, Middle East, and Africa. As a result, the sanitarian situation becomes global. Strict measures were adopted in most countries between February and July 2020, but the pandemic continues growing.

Among them was the unprecedented lockdown, in the form of quarantines, social and business restrictions, coercive governmental policies that affected personal life and professional life, and the economy of all countries to stop the virus. One aspect that has suddenly changed is human mobility, as it influences and modifies patterns of the virus (Chapin & Roy, 2021). Linked to human mobility, both tourism and the leisure industry have been affected by confinement and, where appropriate, less human mobility. As a result, new business models and market niches are emerging due to a substitution effect between foreign and domestic tourism in many countries, which has helped alleviate the decline in the tourism industry.

Although the tourism industry is one of the most affected, the impact of the virus continues to be strong in the rest of the economic sectors, both private and public. The arrival of Industry 4.0 is transforming companies, especially after the adoption of robotics, and hard skills and soft skills to impact sustainable development achieved after optimizing production and distribution networks and strengthening value chains (Walińska, & Dobroszek, 2021). The combination of remote working and the technological advances born from Industry 4.0 can contribute to surmounting this pandemic only if knowledge and techniques are internalized by human capital, and the public-private investment process contributes to increasing the use of socioeconomic wealth robots. In fact, service robots can work collaboratively with service employees (Van Doorn et al., 2017) to interact and co-create value with customers (Čaić, Mahr, & Oderkerken-Schröder, 2019). More importantly, the lower (or inexistent) interpersonal interaction can lower perceived viral transmission (Wan, Chan, & Luo, 2021).

Education has been altered due to COVID19. The global outbreak of COVID19 since January 2020 has forced the closure of schools and universities in over 180 countries to control the pandemic, affecting approximately 90% of students worldwide (Hsiao, 2021). As a result, the digitalization process has been accelerated in many higher education institutions (HEIs), especially in the developed countries.

There have been various types of impacts regarding entrepreneurial activity, mainly social, economic, and political. Ongoing nascent activities have been postponed or rejected for being adapted to the situation. Other companies have resisted with or without aid to others that have closed. Additionally, many entrepreneurs have identified opportunities associated or not with the pandemic and have set out to develop them.

In short, entrepreneurs have faced an unprecedented situation of different magnitude and characteristics depending on what happened in each country. To begin measuring and analyzing the impact of this new situation in the national entrepreneurial frameworks, the GEM observatory has carried out an initial experts' survey, the results of which are offered in this chapter. This chapter aims to present and analyze the results of this consultation, which allow the first approximation to the rapid changes that entrepreneurs face to adapt to the new scenario and help prevent the deterioration of the economy of their countries or its reconstruction in the cases most affected.

BACKGROUND

One of the keys that have fostered the searching for solutions in these pandemic times caused by COVID19 is how organizations have accelerated their digitalization processes. In this sense, Ahmad *et al.* (2021) show that senior management and technology infrastructure readiness positively impact digital transformation and organizational performance. Due to transformational digitalization, It has been possible to increase labor productivity in organizations, especially those in which the connection between the organization's stakeholders is made through high-speed networks endowed with the most advanced technology available. Therefore, a correct public-private collaboration must occur to succeed in this transformative process, which benefits society.

The arrival and spread of COVID19 have accelerated a digitization process already underway in the most developed countries on the planet. Confinement has favored remote work, which has had a positive impact on labor productivity and work-life balance. The fact is that the job changes produced by the virus will gradually become structural as time passes and professionals adapt to this new employment situation. As a result, technical skills have become more prominent, including STEM (Science, Technology, Engineering, and Mathematics). The acceleration of these STEM studies started in the European Union in 2000 to promote this kind of study throughout the continent, made Europe the first region globally in technological advances.

A substantial socioeconomic effect caused by the spread of COVID19 is transportation reduction or even collapse, with a lag not consistent over space or time. This fact is causing severe problems in transport companies, including air, land (rail and passenger transport by road), and maritime, which has led to numerous corporate bankruptcies all over the planet. This sudden decrease in mobility has caused locations near each other to share similar patterns due to COVID19 (Chapin & Roy, 2021).

Besides digitalization and transportation decrease, food and nutrition security have been altered significantly in the developing countries. In most low- and middle-income countries, micro, small, and medium-sized enterprises (MSMEs) play an essential role in food supply chains and thus in ensuring food and nutrition security. In this respect, Nordhagen *et al.* (2021) show that the youngest firms and those with the fewest employees (controlling for turnover) were less likely to be severely impacted. Also, over 80% of firms had taken actions to mitigate the pandemic's impact on their operations and/or staff, and about 44% were considering exploring new business areas, with some seeing opportunities for growth.

Another critical impact arises from the job market. In this sense, Guberina and Wnag (2021) posit that leadership and psychological well-being are most conducive to minimizing job insecurity, an integral part of enterprise sustainability. Also, entrepreneurial leadership leads to decreased job insecurity and improved psychological well-being. For these authors, fear of COVID19 leads to adverse psychological well-being and moderates the relationship between entrepreneurial leadership and job insecurity.

Regarding stock markets, Yong, Ziaei, and Szulczyk (2021) show that, despite slightly reduced, stock market returns are pretty persistent in the stock market, especially in European and Asian firms. Despite this, Pisedtasalasai (2021) suggests that gold generally provides a hedge for the stock market and industry indexes and works as a haven for stocks in some crises. However, bonds tend to offer a more negligible hedging effect.

Complementary to economic-related issues, it is crucial to fight COVID19 to dispose of highly socially admitted KAPs (knowledge, attitude, and practices) (Bhushan, & Rai, 2021), not only in the population but also in the organizations (public and private). In fighting COVID19, a good communication process is needed among all the agents affected, both from the economy and politics. If there is no such communication, or the economic resources are scarce, this impacts the population's mortality. Data that, in many countries, are fake for political or ideological reasons.

These KAPs are also observed in social networks through social media influencers and public participation. In this respect, Al Khasawneh, M. *et al.* (2021) argue that social media influencers can contribute to fighting COVID19 by giving governments and companies a chance to understand better the importance of social media influencers in contributing to the success of social media-based marketing campaigns, especially in millennials and centennials. When this importance is internalized by organizations (public and private), encouraging people's engagement in fulfilling health-based strategies will be enabled, and the COVID19's impact will be diminished (and ideally eliminated).

Regarding the psychological issues related to COVID19, Brown, Young, & Sacco (2021) affirms that humans have a suite of adaptations to satisfy belonging needs while avoiding diseased conspecifics. Competition between motivational systems may explain adherence and resistance to social distancing guidelines and how technologically mediated interactions further shape these decisions. Regions endowed with high-speed Internet thanks to the implementation of 5G and fiber optics encourage working remotely from home, with the consequent advantages in terms of comfort, more leisure time, transport cost savings, and the more efficient use of time. However, as negative aspects of confinement at home, the impact on the growing number of suicides in many countries, especially developed ones (Gratz, Mann, & Tull, 2021; Dubé *et al.*, 2021)), anxiety (Santabárbara et al., 2021), and the adverse effects on adults with autism (Oomen, Nijhof, & Wiersema, 2021).

Given these considerations, we aim to analyze the impact of the first lockdown from March to May 2020, with different intensities and effects on the countries studied. We will describe it in the next section.

METHODOLOGY

Analyzing the Impact of the First Lockdown from GEM

As the pandemic coincided with the start of data collection for the GEM 2020 cycle, its technical and scientific team reacted quickly and developed batteries of questions related to the situation in its information tools. Specifically, in the expert survey that GEM conducts annually, it inserted two blocks of questions. First, to capture the opinion of the experts about how the entrepreneurs' sector reacted to the confinement situation, and second, to press their opinion about the measures taken by national governments to help the industry.

The GEM observatory conducts the National Expert Survey (NES) annually in all participating countries to measure (subjectively) the average state of the main conditions determining the framework where entrepreneurs operate. These conditions are 1) financing for entrepreneurs, 2) government policies, 3) government programs for entrepreneurs, 4) entrepreneurial education and training, 5) R&D transfer, 6) commercial infrastructure, 7) internal market openness and dynamic, 8) physical infrastructure and services, and 9) social and cultural norms. A minimum of 36 GEM-selected experts (4 by condition) evaluate blocks of items on these nine conditions using 0-10 points Liker scales in each participating country. Later, these blocks are summarized in 12 principal components and their average results in the NECI composite index, representing the average state of the national entrepreneurial framework or context for entrepreneurial activity.

The NES survey is a flexible tool. Thus, at any moment, it can be extended by new blocks of items or constructs to measure new latent variables. In the year 2020, due to the pandemic, GEM included two constructs to measure and represent these variables related to the COVID19 lockdown:

Covid 1: Entrepreneurs' response to the COVID19 consequences
Covid 2: Government response to the COVID19 consequences

Table 1. Latent variables

Covid 1: Entrepreneurs' response to the COVID 19 consequences
A substantial number of new and growing firms are adopting new ways of doing business as a result of the COVID 19 pandemic
A substantial number of new and growing firms are promoting working from home as a result of the COVID 19 pandemic
A substantial number of new and growing firms are making adjustments to their current products and services to adapt to the COVID 19 pandemic
A substantial number of new and growing firms are identifying plenty of new opportunities because of the COVID 19 pandemic
Cooperation between and within new and growing firms and/or established firms has increased as a result of the COVID 19 pandemic
A substantial number of new and growing firms are collaborating on global social activities, challenges and proposals, as a result of the COVID 19 pandemic

Source: The Authors.

The items for the two constructs behind these latent variables are shown in Table 1.

In 2020, due to the exceptional situation faced by most countries, 42 countries had completed their experts' surveys. The information collected has no precedent and constitutes a valuable contribution to analyzing how entrepreneurs and governments reacted to the new scenario in different world regions.

RESULTS AND DISCUSSION

In 2020, 42 countries carried out the NES survey. Table 2 shows the list of countries, their world region, and the last income level provided by the Global Competitiveness Report n 2019.

As commented previously, two blocks of items designed as constructs to be summarized as principal components have been included this year in the NES questionnaire. The results of the principal components analysis are summarized in Table 3 and Table 4.

On the one hand, the results for the first principal component, representing entrepreneurs' response to the lockdown and first months of the sanitarian emergency, explain almost 61% of the original variance. The latent variable is reliable with a Cronbach's Alpha of 0.868, which ensures the internal coherence of the items' construct. Communalities indicate that the most robust evaluation of items in terms of agreement or coincidence among evaluators is when experts consider that a substantial number of new and growing firms are adjusting their products and services to adapt firms to the COVID19 pandemic (70.6% of its variance is used to build the principal component). This result is followed by considering that a substantial number of new and growing firms are identifying many opportunities due to the pandemic (67.2%) and so on. The less powerful statement contributing to the latent variable is that many

Table 2. GEM 2020: Countries that participated in the NES survey

COUNTRY	WORLD REGION	INCOME LEVEL
Angola	Sub-Saharan Africa	Low
Burkina Faso	Sub-Saharan Africa	Low
Egypt	Northern Africa and Western Asia	Low
Morocco	Northern Africa and Western Asia	Low
Kuwait	Northern Africa and Western Asia	High
Saudi Arabia	Northern Africa and Western Asia	High
Oman	Northern Africa and Western Asia	High
United Arab Emirates	Northern Africa and Western Asia	High
Qatar	Northern Africa and Western Asia	High
India	Central and Southern Asia	Low
Iran	Central and Southern Asia	Middle
Kazakhstan	Central and Southern Asia	Middle
Indonesia	Eastern and South-Eastern Asia	Low
South Korea	Eastern and South-Eastern Asia	High
Taiwan	Eastern and South-Eastern Asia	High
Brazil	Latin America and the Caribbean	Middle
Chile	Latin America and the Caribbean	High
Colombia	Latin America and the Caribbean	High
Guatemala	Latin America and the Caribbean	Middle
Mexico	Latin America and the Caribbean	Middle
Uruguay	Latin America and the Caribbean	High
Panama	Latin America and the Caribbean	High
Puerto Rico	Latin America and the Caribbean	High
Austria	Europe and Northern America	High
Croatia	Europe and Northern America	High
Cyprus	Europe and Northern America	High
Germany	Europe and Northern America	High
Greece	Europe and Northern America	High
Italy	Europe and Northern America	High
Luxembourg	Europe and Northern America	High
Netherlands	Europe and Northern America	High
Norway	Europe and Northern America	High
Poland	Europe and Northern America	High
Russia	Europe and Northern America	Middle
Slovak Republic	Europe and Northern America	High
Slovenia	Europe and Northern America	High
Spain	Europe and Northern America	High
Sweden	Europe and Northern America	High

Continued on the following page

Table 2. Continued

COUNTRY	WORLD REGION	INCOME LEVEL
Switzerland	Europe and Northern America	High
United Kingdom	Europe and Northern America	High
USA	Europe and Northern America	High

Source: The authors

new and growing firms are promoting working from home due to the COVID19 pandemic (54%). All the original variables or items show high and positive linear correlations with the principal components. This fact ratifies this set is representative of the construct. The principal component can be used as a variable to properly represent the proactiveness of response of the entrepreneurial sector facing the first lockdown and its consequences.

Table 3. Principal components analysis: Results about entrepreneurs' response

	Items	Communalities	Linear Correlation Coefficients with Principal component 1	% of variance explained
CV1	A substantial number of new and growing firms are adopting new ways of doing business as a result of the COVID19 pandemic	0.617	0.786	60.88%
CV2	A substantial number of new and growing firms are promoting working from home as a result of the COVID19 pandemic	0.540	0.735	Cronbach Alpha
CV3	A substantial number of new and growing firms are making adjustments to their current products and services to adapt to the COVID19 pandemic	0.706	0.840	0.868
CV4	A substantial number of new and growing firms are identifying plenty of new opportunities because of the COVID19 pandemic	0.672	0.820	N = 1450 valid cases
CV5	Cooperation between and within new and growing firms and/or established firms has increased as a result of the COVID19 pandemic	0.547	0.739	
CV6	A substantial number of new and growing firms are collaborating on global social activities, challenges, and proposals, as a result of the COVID19 pandemic	0.570	0.755	

Source: The authors

Regarding the previous results, it is interesting and important to note how experts appreciate the quick reaction of the entrepreneurial sector in terms of adaptation and adjustment of processes to detect opportunities and develop new ways of doing business, which is typical of entrepreneurs. On the other hand, the experts are more cautious in terms of their evaluations about the increase in cooperation between the large and consolidated companies with entrepreneurs, about the cooperation of entrepreneurs with global social activities, challenges and proposals resulting from the pandemic, and about a massive adoption of telework by entrepreneurial firms.

This diagnosis summarizes, at least partially, some trends that are developing in the exit and overcoming stage of the pandemic. Entrepreneurship intensifies its role as an engine of innovation and the detection of opportunities derived from the situation, seeking and rapidly adopting new ways of doing business where digital will be essential. Now, entrepreneurial companies require teamwork and a lot of interaction, which limits telework application to a certain degree, so its use will be rationalized. Likewise, early-stage companies, usually small, may participate in social projects and major global challenges but adjusted to their possibilities and capabilities, with a different impact than large companies.

On the other hand, the results for the second principal component, representing national governments' response to the lockdown and first months of the sanitarian emergency, explain almost 80% of the original variance. The latent variable is reliable with a Cronbach Alpha of 0.914, which ensures the internal coherence of the items' construct. Communalities indicate that the most robust evaluation of items in terms of experts' degree of agreement is the statement that proposes that the government has adopted effective measures to avoid massive loss of new and growing firms due to the COVID19 pandemic (88%). At the same time, there is less agreement or robustness about the statement that proposes that due to the COVID19 pandemic, the government has substantially increased the digital or online delivery of regulations for new and growing firms (63.8%). All the original variables show high and positive linear correlations with this second principal component ratifies that this set represents the construct. Also, the principal component can be used as a variable to adequately describe the governmental sector's proactiveness of response for the entrepreneurial sector facing the first lockdown and its consequences.

Table 4. Principal components analysis: Results about governments' response

	Items	Communalities	Linear Correlation Coefficients with Principal component 1	% of variance explained
CV7	The government has adopted effective measures for new and growing firms to adjust to the economic reality caused by the COVID19 pandemic	0.855	0.924	79.65%
CV8	The government has adopted effective measures to avoid massive loss of new and growing firms due to the COVID19 pandemic	0.880	0.938	Cronbach Alpha
CV9	The government has acted to protect workers and customers of new and growing firms from COVID19 during the pandemic	0.813	0.902	0.914
CV10	As a result of the COVID19 pandemic, the government has substantially increased the digital or online delivery of regulations for new and growing firms.	0.638	0.799	N = 1748 valid cases

Source: The authors

Therefore, in general, the experts have evaluated the performance of their respective governments in terms of the help provided to the entrepreneurial sector to avoid the loss of companies and jobs and protect workers, suppliers, and customers, in terms of facilitating new regulations to face these initial

Figure 1. Entrepreneurs' response to the COVID19 lockdown and consequences
(scale 0 = nothing proactive, 10 = fully proactive)
Source: The authors

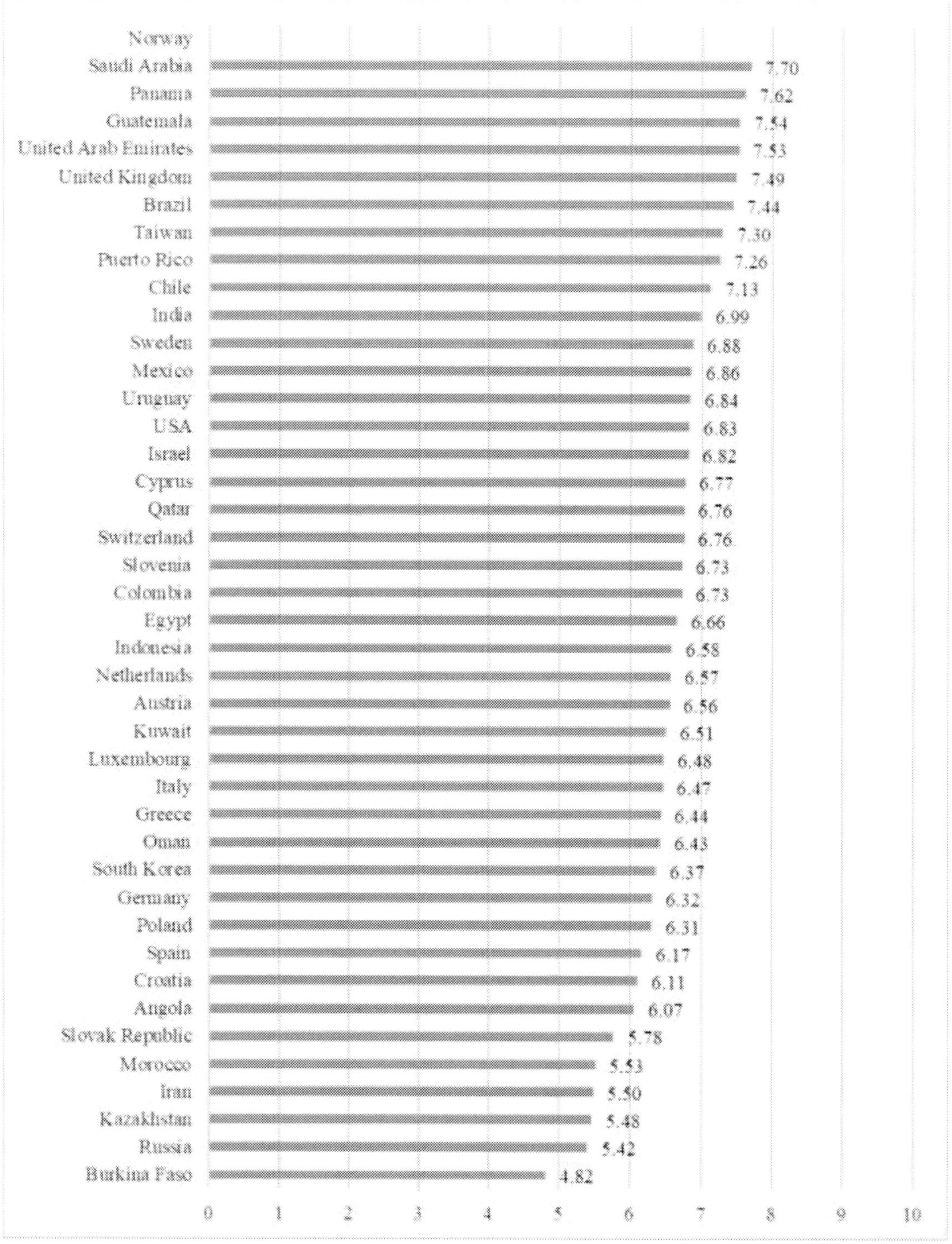

Norway	
Saudi Arabia	7.70
Panama	7.62
Guatemala	7.54
United Arab Emirates	7.53
United Kingdom	7.49
Brazil	7.44
Taiwan	7.30
Puerto Rico	7.26
Chile	7.13
India	6.99
Sweden	6.88
Mexico	6.86
Uruguay	6.84
USA	6.83
Israel	6.82
Cyprus	6.77
Qatar	6.76
Switzerland	6.76
Slovenia	6.73
Colombia	6.73
Egypt	6.66
Indonesia	6.58
Netherlands	6.57
Austria	6.56
Kuwait	6.51
Luxembourg	6.48
Italy	6.47
Greece	6.44
Oman	6.43
South Korea	6.37
Germany	6.32
Poland	6.31
Spain	6.17
Croatia	6.11
Angola	6.07
Slovak Republic	5.78
Morocco	5.53
Iran	5.50
Kazakhstan	5.48
Russia	5.42
Burkina Faso	4.82

stages electronically. As will be seen below, the results of the evaluation have been diverse depending on the countries.

Once shown that, with exciting nuances, these two variables obtained from the information provided by the experts adequately represent in statistical terms the concepts that it has been desired to measure, Figures 1 and 2 show, respectively, how GEM 2020 countries rank about them. The first rank suggests that nascent, new, and growing firms reacted proactively to the lockdown in general, with diverse intensity depending on the country. On a 10 points scale, all countries except Burkina Faso (although with almost 5 points) obtained experts' average scores above 5 points. The most prominent evaluations are given in Saudi Arabia, Panama, Guatemala, United Arab Emirates, United Kingdom, Brazil, Taiwan, Puerto Rico, and Chile. With average scores above 7 points, all these countries are those in which the experts perceive a greater degree of proactivity in the entrepreneurial sector.

The government response is perceived a non-satisfactory or insufficient by experts in 21 countries (50% of the sample). Regarding the countries where experts approve the governments' behavior, Saudi Arabia stands out in the first place with a high rating from experts that exceeds 8 points. It is closely followed by the United Arab Emirates and the Netherlands, where entrepreneurial activity enjoys excellent support and consideration.

Because of the previous rankings, we ask if the entrepreneurial response has depended, to some degree, on the governmental response. The linear correlation coefficient is positive but very low (0.31) between the two variables. A linear regression analysis shows no significant dependence between the reactions of both sectors to the lockdown when considering the whole sample of countries. Regarding this result, it must be regarded as that the experts from half of the countries deemed insufficient the government's response with some variability. Still, half of the countries considered it sufficient or higher. Both entrepreneurs and the government have reacted simultaneously and with different intensities depending on the country. So. the result suggests at least two types of behaviors or models within the general regression model, as shown in Figure 3.

1) A group of countries where the entrepreneurial sector reacted proactively almost independently from the insufficient governments' response (vertical ellipse)
2) A group of countries where governments and entrepreneurial sector reacted proactively at the same time coordinating their efforts to some degree (horizontal ellipse)

If we separate the two regression models, we obtain one regression in which the response of both sectors is weak but significantly related (Figure 4). And a second regression in which they are not related is that the entrepreneurial sector is perceived as proactive despite the government's insufficient response (Figure 5).

Figure 4. Countries = Egypt, Greece, Netherlands, Switzerland, Austria, UK, Poland, Germany, Chile, Indonesia, South Korea, India, Luxembourg, Cyprus, Croatia, Uruguay, Taiwan, KSA, Oman, UAE, and Qatar

Figure 5 Countries = USA, Russia, Spain, Italy, Sweden, Mexico, Brazil, Colombia, Iran, Morocco, Burkina Faso, Angola, Slovenia, Slovak Republic, Guatemala, Panama, Kazakhstan, Kuwait, Israel, and Puerto Rico

These results provide some lessons for policymakers. First, many governments are currently planning socioeconomic reconstruction, but these quick reactions could have been much more effective to save the economy if the sanitarian situation had been controlled. Although vaccines have indeed managed

Figure 2. National Governments' response to the COVID19 lockdown and its consequences for the entrepreneurial sector
(scale 0 = nothing proactive, 10 = fully proactive)
Source: The authors

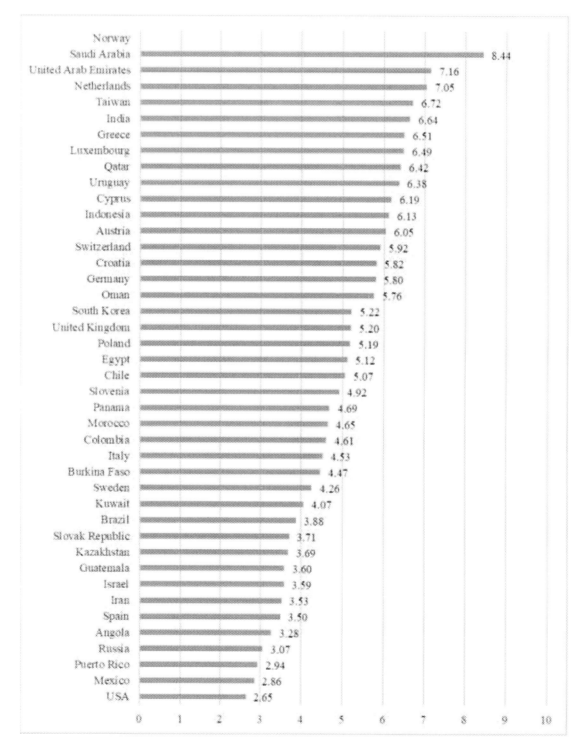

Figure 3. Linear regression between the entrepreneurial sector response and the government response to the first lockdown derived from the COVID19 pandemic
Source: The authors

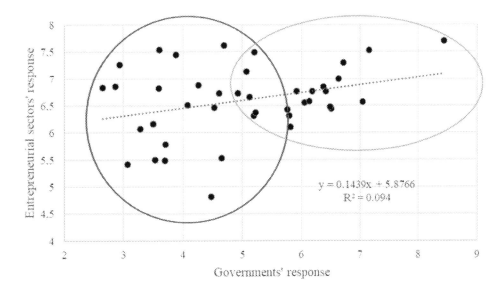

to slow down the spread of the virus, the truth is that their effectiveness is not 100% effective, and it is decreasing over time. As a result, governments have to race to prevent the spread of the virus before addressing economic recovery. Only a few countries globally (e.g., New Zealand and Australia, to a lesser extent) have successfully tackled the virus, so their economic growth is healthy.

Figure 4. Linear regression between the entrepreneurial sector response and the government response to the first lockdown derived from the COVID19 pandemic for the group of countries where both sectors reacted proactively at the same time
Source: The authors

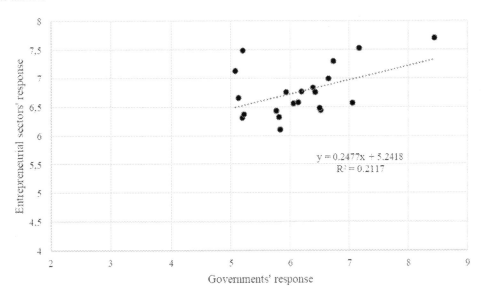

Figure 5. Linear regression between the entrepreneurial sector response and the governments' response to the first lockdown derived from the COVID19 pandemic for the group of countries where the entrepreneurial sector reacted proactively while the governments' response is perceived as insufficient
Source: The authors

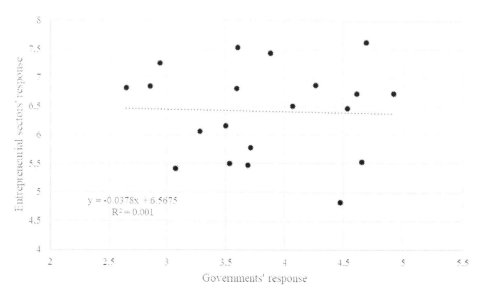

Second, to successfully fight against the virus, as shown in Figure 5, there must be a robust public-private collaboration, especially with the population and entrepreneurs, which must be willing to be vaccinated while avoiding social disruption (Kuznar, 2021). As Varma *et al.* (2021) show, people with a prior mental health diagnosis experienced more significant psychological distress expressed by poor sleep, lower levels of resilience, and even suicide behaviors (Dubé *et al.*, 2021; Efstathiou *et al.*, 2021) and psychosis (Alba *et al.*, 2021). Besides, these authors show that younger age and loneliness significantly mediated the links between stress and depression, and stress and anxiety. Hence, youngers were more vulnerable to stress, depression (Deng *et al.*, 2021), and anxiety symptoms, so they need more support.

Third, it is crucial to keep in mind that lockdowns will continue as the virus mutates and the effectiveness of vaccines decreases. This problem requires continuous investment processes in health research and policies for the economy's structural transformation to digitize it.

From the entrepreneurial perspective, GEM experts perceived that, on average, the proactive and quick reactions focused on adopting telework from home to continue their activities while making adjustments to their current products and services to adapt them to the COVID19 pandemic. In third place, firms began to adopt new ways of doing business. Depending on the country and somewhat less intensity, several firms could identify new opportunities because of the pandemic. Additionally, experts perceived a significant increment of cooperation between and within new and growing firms and/or established firms in some countries. This result is especially relevant in Saudi Arabia, India, Brazil, Guatemala, UAE, and Taiwan. Experts perceive a discrete but positive involvement of new and growing firms collaborating on global social activities challenges and proposals due to the pandemic. Countries where these activities are perceived as somewhat more intensive, are India, Uruguay, Brazil, UAE, Saudi Arabia, Taiwan, the UK, and Israel. In Table 5, it is possible to see the average scores for each country about the different actions evaluated by GEM experts for the entrepreneurial sector.

Table 5. Average scores for single items evaluated by experts by country to analyze the first reaction to lockdown within the entrepreneurial sector

	WAYS	HOME	P&S	OPP	COOP	GLOBAL
Average	**7.07**	**7.39**	**7.19**	**6.43**	**5.64**	**5.73**
Angola	6.56	6.59	6.57	6.35	5.21	5.18
Austria	6.70	7.65	6.86	6.27	5.91	5.40
Brazil	7.62	7.93	7.96	6.89	6.71	6.84
Burkina Faso	5.64	4.87	5.31	5.13	3.67	3.84
Chile	7.89	8.14	8.08	6.76	5.75	6.60
Colombia	7.02	7.40	7.26	6.60	6.33	5.98
Croatia	7.03	7.24	6.84	5.47	5.03	4.81
Cyprus	7.46	7.86	6.76	6.28	5.74	5.75
Egypt	7.26	7.00	7.23	6.51	5.95	5.70
Germany	6.86	8.15	7.01	5.97	5.24	4.86
Greece	6.78	7.83	6.94	6.17	5.39	5.42
Guatemala	8.19	8.14	8.03	7.34	6.75	6.06
India	7.04	6.75	7.07	7.05	6.85	7.12
Indonesia	6.80	7.06	6.80	6.77	6.26	6.12
Iran	6.08	5.97	5.84	5.51	5.08	4.46
Israel	6.76	8.31	7.68	6.76	5.96	6.63
Italy	6.68	7.47	6.66	6.46	5.14	5.97
Kazakhstan	5.89	6.37	6.69	4.81	4.67	3.97
Kuwait	7.43	7.19	7.35	6.24	5.06	5.41
Luxembourg	6.80	7.37	6.79	6.03	5.54	6.03
Mexico	7.38	7.15	7.46	7.15	5.87	6.06
Morocco	6.56	6.28	6.18	5.77	4.33	4.32
Netherlands	7.14	8.22	7.23	6.15	5.26	5.94
Oman	6.21	6.79	7.03	6.06	5.63	5.55
Panama	8.06	8.25	8.44	7.92	6.17	6.31
Poland	7.03	7.84	7.11	6.39	4.10	5.10
Puerto Rico	7.97	7.83	7.89	7.03	6.43	6.24
Qatar	7.46	7.18	7.55	6.36	6.13	5.78
Russia	6.39	6.54	6.89	4.89	4.48	4.12
Saudi Arabia	8.16	8.02	8.24	7.45	7.24	6.83
Slovak R.	6.39	7.06	6.14	5.29	4.72	4.73
Slovenia	7.29	7.92	7.08	6.83	5.19	5.77
South Korea	7.04	6.77	7.13	6.49	5.20	5.54
Spain	6.39	6.72	6.50	6.06	5.49	5.75
Sweden	6.76	7.55	7.72	6.78	5.92	5.86
Switzerland	7.03	7.69	7.03	6.50	6.39	5.92

Continued on following page

Table 5. Continued

	WAYS	HOME	P&S	OPP	COOP	GLOBAL
Average	**7.07**	**7.39**	**7.19**	**6.43**	**5.64**	**5.73**
Taiwan	7.14	7.20	7.75	7.98	6.57	6.82
UAE	8.11	8.19	7.94	7.65	6.67	6.94
UK	7.95	8.54	8.31	6.74	6.09	6.48
Uruguay	7.28	7.72	7.60	6.14	5.66	6.88
USA	7.65	8.29	7.89	6.43	5.28	5.70

Legend: WAYS (A substantial number of new and growing firms are adopting new ways of doing business as a result of the COVID19 pandemic), HOME (A significant number of new and growing firms are promoting working from home as a result of the COVID19 pandemic), P&S (A substantial number of new and growing firms are making adjustments to their current products and services to adapt to the COVID19 pandemic), OPP (A sizeable number of new and growing firms are identifying plenty of new opportunities because of the COVID19 pandemic), COOP (Cooperation between and within new and growing firms and/or established firms has increased as a result of the COVID19 pandemic), GLOBAL (A substantial number of new and growing firms are collaborating on global social activities. challenges and proposals. as a result of the COVID19 pandemic), UK (United Kingdom), UAE (United Arab Emirates), USA (United States of America).

Source: The authors

By taking the sample of countries globally, the most appreciated by the government, on average, has been its action to protect workers, consumers, and suppliers and facilitate new regulations to adapt companies to the situation digitally. In turn, on average, it has been perceived as insufficient the behavior about adopting effective measures for new and growing firms to adjust to the economic reality caused by the COVID19 pandemic and to avoid massive loss of new and growing firms due to the COVID19 pandemic. However, in several countries, these measures have been considered adequate. Experts believe their governments have adopted effective measures for new and growing firms to adjust to the economic reality caused by the COVID19 pandemic in Saudi Arabia, Taiwan, the Netherlands, UAE, India, and other countries to avoid massive loss of new and growing firms. Table 6 shows the average evaluation of the four statements proposed to experts about the government response during the first lockdown.

As shown in Table 6, the highest average scores arise when governments have acted to protect workers and customers of new and growing firms from COVID19 during the pandemic (5.30 on average), having Saudi Arabia (8.26) the highest score. Strong results are also achieved when the government has substantially increased the digital or online delivery of regulations for new and growing firms (5.29 on average), also reaching Saudi Arabia (8.95) with the highest score. This situation has been shown in developed countries as they are equipped with the economic and financial means to fight COVID19, digitize to avoid displacement, and vaccinate the population.

Table 6. Average scores for single items evaluated by experts by country to analyze the first reaction to lockdown within the government sector

	The government has adopted effective measures for new and growing firms to adjust to the economic reality caused by the COVID19 pandemic	The government has adopted effective measures to avoid massive loss of new and growing firms due to the COVID19 pandemic	The government has acted to protect workers and customers of new and growing firms from COVID19 during the pandemic	As a result of the COVID19 pandemic, the government has substantially increased the digital or online delivery of regulations for new and growing firms.
Average	**4.80**	**4.65**	**5.30**	**5.29**
Angola	3.29	2.78	3.69	3.00
Austria	6.00	5.89	6.79	5.21
Brazil	3.56	3.24	4.00	4.45
Burkina Faso	4.72	4.79	4.44	3.85
Chile	4.95	4.54	5.24	5.73
Colombia	4.65	4.40	5.09	4.73
Croatia	5.47	5.50	6.13	5.80
Cyprus	5.78	5.97	6.59	6.23
Egypt	4.97	4.80	4.85	5.61
Germany	5.96	5.58	6.87	5.05
Greece	6.24	5.97	6.62	7.32
Guatemala	3.03	2.92	4.56	4.00
India	6.58	6.65	6.56	6.79
Indonesia	6.14	6.08	6.06	6.25
Iran	3.49	3.14	3.16	4.46
Israel	3.31	3.06	3.19	4.69
Italy	4.14	3.86	4.92	4.95
Kazakhstan	3.23	3.09	3.94	4.66
Kuwait	3.56	3.46	4.41	5.14
Luxembourg	6.06	6.00	7.06	6.12
Mexico	2.90	1.98	3.08	3.66
Morocco	4.47	4.51	5.04	4.89
Netherlands	6.71	7.18	7.64	6.88
Oman	5.59	5.41	6.00	6.09
Panama	4.31	3.72	4.69	6.28
Poland	4.81	5.38	5.38	4.65
Puerto Rico	2.44	2.17	3.34	3.58
Qatar	6.13	5.74	6.69	7.02
Russia	2.78	2.86	2.95	3.33
Saudi Arabia	8.07	8.05	8.26	8.95
The Slovak Rep.	2.89	2.94	5.00	3.69
Slovenia	4.53	4.34	5.94	4.52

Continued on following page

Table 6. Continued

	The government has adopted effective measures for new and growing firms to adjust to the economic reality caused by the COVID19 pandemic	The government has adopted effective measures to avoid massive loss of new and growing firms due to the COVID19 pandemic	The government has acted to protect workers and customers of new and growing firms from COVID19 during the pandemic	As a result of the COVID19 pandemic, the government has substantially increased the digital or online delivery of regulations for new and growing firms.
Average	4.80	4.65	5.30	5.29
South Korea	5.11	4.97	5.20	5.81
Spain	2.83	2.75	3.14	5.56
Sweden	4.14	4.33	5.03	4.08
Switzerland	6.11	5.67	6.50	5.36
Taiwan	7.02	6.71	6.95	5.67
UK	5.05	4.64	5.82	5.45
UAE	6.66	6.67	6.91	8.13
Uruguay	6.28	6.22	7.00	6.11
USA	2.79	2.51	2.66	2.96

Legend: UK (United Kingdom), UAE (United Arab Emirates), USA (United States of America)
Source: The authors.

CONCLUSIONS AND RECOMMENDATIONS

It is essential to fight against COVID19 by implementing public-private collaboration policies focused on health research and vaccination of the population until herd immunity is reached. There is a significant difference in this immunization process between the vaccination speed of nations whose health systems are the most advanced and equipped on the planet and those countries where health systems are underdeveloped or non-existent. For this reason, the achievement of fruitful cooperation among aid policies carried out by supranational and national organizations, close with the efforts of public and private (religious and civil) NGOs, is essential to attain success in the fight against the virus.

One of the collateral damages of the virus, primarily due to the economic crisis generated by the confinement, is the psychiatric problems associated with the virus, including suicide. According to the World Health Organization, suicide is the second leading cause of death for young people between 15 and 29, only behind traffic accidents. As Dubé et al. (2021) show, strong protections from governments (e.g., implementing best practices in suicide prevention) are urgently needed to reduce suicidal behaviors and prevent psychosis during the COVID19 pandemic.

The digitization process that began at the beginning of the 21st century and accelerated with the pandemic leads to structural changes that will be irreversible in many labor markets. Changes that will affect both labor productivity and the work-life balance will be improved for many professionals. The countries that take the most advantage of new technologies, vaccinate their population, and implement policies based on digitization will be the ones that first overcome this double health and economic crisis.

It is foreseeable that lockdowns will continue as the virus mutates and the effectiveness of vaccines decreases after these mutations. These mutations require continuous investment processes in health research and policies for the economy's structural transformation to digitize it. But we think that the research carried out to combat the virus will finally bear fruit and lead to new treatments that will be more effective than the current ones, which will help heal better in less time.

The virus has had a substantial impact on the labor market worldwide. Many partial changes, initially thought of as a temporal remedy, only will become structural, in many cases, after the digitization process and R&D investments carried out in the organization. As a result, for many professionals, purchasing habits and transportation processes will change and vary to achieve a work-life balance that benefits society. New labor-related professional relationships have emerged and will transform societies and economies worldwide.

Unfortunately, the struggle against COVID19 will be long, and it is foreseeable a lost decade of economic growth for a good part of the countries, predominantly located in developing countries. This fact will tend to widen the North-South gap, but also the South-South breach. The collaboration of multilateral development organizations (International Monetary Fund, the World Bank, and regional development banks) is needed to reduce this gap. Multilateral organizations are forced to collaborate, directly or indirectly, with the new development and growth instruments launched by China, among which the AIIB (Asian Infrastructure Investment Bank) stands out. As a result, a bipolar world is emerging again with the rise of China on the world economic scene, mainly concerning international trade. An accelerated process based on the *heping jueqi* (peaceful rise) strategy favoring China during this pandemic.

REFERENCES

Ahmad, A., Alshurideh, M. T., Al Kurdi, B. H., & Salloum, S. A. (2021). Factors Impacts Organization Digital Transformation and Organization Decision Making During Covid19 Pandemic. *Studies in Systems. Decision and Control, 334*, 95–106.

Al Khasawneh, M., Abuhashesh, M., Ahmad, A., Masa'deh, R., & Alshurideh, M. T. (2021). Customers' Online Engagement with Social Media Influencers' Content Related to COVID 19. *Studies in Systems. Decision and Control, 334*, 385–404.

Alba, L., Coll, C., Sáez, S., Alonso, L., Pérez, H., Palma, S., Vallés, V., & Ortiz, S. (2021). New-onset psychosis: A case report of brief psychosis related to COVID-19 infection. *Psychiatry Research, 301*, 113975. doi:10.1016/j.psychres.2021.113975 PMID:33990069

Bhushan, V., & Rai, S. (2021). Knowledge, attitude, and practices regarding COVID19 outbreak among the personnel providing emergency services in India. *International Journal of Academic Medicine, 7*(2), 107–112. doi:10.4103/IJAM.IJAM_2_21

Brown, M., Young, S. G., & Sacco, D. F. (2021). Competing motives in a pandemic: Interplays between fundamental social motives and technology use in predicting (Non)Compliance with social distancing guidelines. *Computers in Human Behavior, 123*, 106892. doi:10.1016/j.chb.2021.106892

Čaić, M., Mahr, D., & Oderkerken-Schröder, G. (2019). Value of social robots in services: Social cognition perspective. *Journal of Services Marketing, 29*(2), 178–205.

Chapin, C., & Roy, S. S. (2021). A Spatial Web Application to Explore the Interactions between Human Mobility. Government Policies. and COVID19 Cases. *Journal of Geovisualization and Spatial Analysis*, *5*(1), 12. doi:10.100741651-021-00081-y

Deng, J., Zhou, F., Hou, W., Silver, Z., Wong, C. Y., Chang, O., Drakos, A., Zuo, Q. K., & Huang, E. (2021). The prevalence of depressive symptoms, anxiety symptoms and sleep disturbance in higher education students during the COVID-19 pandemic: A systematic review and meta-analysis. *Psychiatry Research*, *301*, 113863. doi:10.1016/j.psychres.2021.113863 PMID:33984824

Dubé, J. P., Smith, M. M., Sherry, S. B., Hewitt, P. L., & Stewart, S. H. (2021). Suicide behaviors during the COVID-19 pandemic: A meta-analysis of 54 studies. *Psychiatry Research*, *301*, 113998. doi:10.1016/j.psychres.2021.113998 PMID:34022657

Efstathiou, V., Michopoulos, I., Yotsidi, V., Smyrnis, N., Zompola, C., Papadopoulou, A., Pomini, V., Papadopoulou, M., Tsigkaropoulou, E., Tsivgoulis, G., Douzenis, A., & Gournellis, R. (2021). Does suicidal ideation increase during the second COVID-19 lockdown? *Psychiatry Research*, *301*, 113990. doi:10.1016/j.psychres.2021.113990 PMID:34020218

Gratz, K. L., Mann, A. J. D., & Tull, M. T. (2021). Suicidal ideation among university students during the COVID19 pandemic: Identifying at-risk subgroups. *Psychiatry Research*, *302*, 114034. doi:10.1016/j.psychres.2021.114034 PMID:34098158

Hsiao, Y.-C. (2021). (in press). Impacts of course type and student gender on distance learning performance: A case study in Taiwan. *Education and Information Technologies*. Advance online publication. doi:10.100710639-021-10538-8 PMID:33867809

Kuznar, L. A. (2021). A tale of two pandemics: Evolutionary psychology, urbanism, and the biology of disease spread deepen sociopolitical divides in the U.S. *Humanities and Social Sciences Communications*, *8*(1), 42. doi:10.105741599-021-00719-8

Nordhagen, S., Igbeka, U., Rowlands, H., Heneghan, E., & Tench, J. (2021). COVID19 and small enterprises in the food supply chain: Early impacts and implications for longer-term food system resilience in low- and middle-income countries. *World Development, 141,* 105405.

Oomen, D., Nijhof, A. D., & Wiersema, J. R. (2021). The psychological impact of the COVID19 pandemic on adults with autism: A survey study across three countries. *Molecular Autism*, *12*(1), 21. doi:10.118613229-021-00424-y PMID:33658046

Pisedtasalasai, A. (2021). Hedging stocks in crises and market downturns with gold and bonds: Industry analysis. *Asian Economic and Financial Review*, *11*(1), 1–16. doi:10.18488/journal.aefr.2021.111.1.16

Santabárbara, J., Lasheras, I., Lipnicki, D. M., Bueno-Notivol, J., Pérez-Moreno, M., López-Antón, R., De la Cámara, C., Lobo, A., & Gracia-García, P. (2021). Prevalence of anxiety in the COVID-19 pandemic: An updated meta-analysis of community-based studies. *Progress in Neuro-Psychopharmacology & Biological Psychiatry*, *109*, 110207. doi:10.1016/j.pnpbp.2020.110207 PMID:33338558

Van Doorn, J., Mende, M., Noble, S. M., Hulland, J., Ostrom, A. L., Grewal, D., & Petersen, J. A. (2017). Domo arigato Mr. Roboto: Emergence of automated social presence in organizational frontlines and customers' service experiences. *Journal of Service Research*, *20*(1), 43–58. doi:10.1177/1094670516679272

Varma, P., Junge, M., Meaklim, H., & Jackson, M. L. (2021). Younger people are more vulnerable to stress, anxiety, and depression during COVID-19 pandemic: A global cross-sectional survey. *Progress in Neuro-Psychopharmacology & Biological Psychiatry*, *109*, 110236. doi:10.1016/j.pnpbp.2020.110236 PMID:33373680

Walińska, E., & Dobroszek, J. (2021). The functional controller for sustainable and value chain management: Fashion or need? A sample of job advertisements in the COVID19 period. [Switzerland]. *Sustainability*, *13*(13), 7139. doi:10.3390u13137139

Wan, L. C., Chan, E. K., & Luo, X. (2021). ROBOTS COME to RESCUE: How to reduce perceived risk of infectious disease in Covid19-stricken consumers? *Annals of Tourism Research*, *88*, 103069. doi:10.1016/j.annals.2020.103069 PMID:33071394

Yong, J. N. C., Ziaei, S. M., & Szulczyk, K. R. (2021). The impact of COVID19 pandemic on stock market return volatility: Evidence from Malaysia and Singapore. *Asian Economic and Financial Review*, *11*(3), 191–204. doi:10.18488/journal.aefr.2021.113.191.204

ADDITIONAL READING

Baporikar, N. (Ed.). (2021). *Handbook of Research on Strategies and Interventions to Mitigate COVID-19 Impact on SMEs*. IGI Global., doi:10.4018/978-1-7998-7436-2

Ceesay, E. K. (2021). Assessing the Impact of the COVID-19 Crisis on the Socio-Economic Situation in Africa. *International Journal of Business Strategy and Automation*, *2*(2), 41–53. doi:10.4018/IJBSA.20210401.oa4

McCall, M. K., Skutsch, M. M., & Honey-Roses, J. (2021). Surveillance in the COVID-19 Normal: Tracking, Tracing, and Snooping – Trade-Offs in Safety and Autonomy in the E-City. *International Journal of E-Planning Research*, *10*(2), 27–44. doi:10.4018/IJEPR.20210401.oa3

Perez-Uribe, R., Ocampo-Guzman, D., Moreno-Monsalve, N. A., & Fajardo-Moreno, W. S. (Eds.). (2021). *Handbook of Research on Management Techniques and Sustainability Strategies for Handling Disruptive Situations in Corporate Settings*. IGI Global., doi:10.4018/978-1-7998-8185-8

Scassa, T. (2021). COVID-19 Contact Tracing: From Local to Global and Back Again. *International Journal of E-Planning Research*, *10*(2), 45–58. doi:10.4018/IJEPR.20210401.oa4

Wildenauer, A. A., & Basl, J. (2021). An Exploration of COVID-19 and Its Consideration as a Black Swan for the Construction Industry in Switzerland. *International Journal of Digital Innovation in the Built Environment*, *10*(1), 62–82. doi:10.4018/IJDIBE.20210101.oa1

KEY TERMS AND DEFINITIONS

Cronbach's Alpha: It is a statistical measure of internal consistency focused on measuring how closely related a set of items are as a group.

Early-Stage Companies: They are firms located in their early stages of business operations.

GEM: Acronym of global entrepreneurship monitor, it is the most comprehensive organization devoted to studying entrepreneurship in the world.

NES Questionnaire: The acronym of National Expert Survey consists of three blocks of questions in which experts provide open-ended responses.

North-South Gap: It is the difference in growth, wealth, and employment between the first and the third worlds.

Principal Components Method: This technique is used to describe a data set in terms of new uncorrelated variables ('components') ordered by the amount of original variance they represent.

South-South Gap: It is the difference in growth, wealth, and employment between the third and fourth world countries.

Chapter 3
Experiences, Perceptions, and Expectations of the Business Community in Mexico Amidst the COVID-19 Crisis

Jesús Manuel Palma-Ruiz
https://orcid.org/0000-0002-1039-6243
Universidad Autónoma de Chihuahua, Mexico

Herik Germán Valles-Baca
Universidad Autónoma de Chihuahua, Mexico

Carmen Romelia Flores-Morales
Universidad Autónoma de Chihuahua, Mexico

Luis Raúl Sánchez-Acosta
Universidad Autónoma de Chihuahua, Mexico

ABSTRACT

The objective of this chapter is to provide a contextualized perspective about the effects of the COVID-19 health crisis for companies with economic activity and fixed installations in Mexico, mainly during the second to third phases of the contingency. For this purpose, data from the INEGI ECOVID-IE 2020 survey is analyzed, which used a sampling frame of 1,873,564 Mexican companies compared by size. Relevant information is provided about the reality of the Mexican business community to report the main sanitary measures implemented, the operational actions used, the sources and types of support received, the best support policies identified, and the income expectations for the following months. Faced with a negative scenario, targeted support strategies from governmental, chambers, and business organizations must be aligned to regain the confidence of the business community to support their continuity.

DOI: 10.4018/978-1-7998-7689-2.ch003

INTRODUCTION

The COVID-19 pandemic has underlined both the relevance and opportunity to approach several strategic management topics, entrepreneurship, and supply chain management in a synchronized way to better understand organizational success, particularly during such times of emergency (Ketchen & Craighead, 2020). As a result, academic research has gradually been building valuable insights and practical lessons from a qualitative and quantitative standpoint about how to steer through crises.

Faced with the limitations and unfavorable conditions derived from COVID-19, companies have had to implement (and often improvise or comply) operational actions to face the pandemic (Caligiuri et al., 2020; Palma-Ruiz, Castillo-Apraiz, et al., 2020). Thus, administrators have been pressured by such adversity to conceive and apply strategic decisions in the short term about their ways of operating, organizing, directing, and communicating with their staff, reducing expenses, prioritizing activities and tasks, defining new ways of attention and service to its customers and suppliers, learn and implement new technological tools, innovate in its operations and business model, among several others (García-Muñoz Aparicio et al., 2020; Katare et al., 2021). In this way, companies have been pressured to respond to the urgent demands in the environment, prioritize, direct their resources and adapt their operations, aiming for more outstanding performance in the short term (Luger et al., 2018; Marín-Idárraga et al., 2016).

The adverse environment caused by COVID-19 has brought companies to test their strategic capacity to act quickly, having to respond to pressing needs and new changing conditions in the environment. Such an adverse scenario represents a valuable opportunity to revisit the strategy and its orientation in organizations in different contexts. Primarily, more than 98% of formal and informal business structures in different countries represent micro and small and medium-sized enterprises (SMEs) (Lemes & Machado, 2007). Therefore, the deterioration of such a business structure will certainly negatively affect economic development and recovery (Obi et al., 2018).

Although studies examining the effects of previous crises on SMEs have been documented (Eggers, 2020), the relevance to address the topic during the present pandemic remains open (Saiz-Álvarez, 2022). Thus, an opportunity arises due to the current context disrupted by COVID-19 to document the perceptions and expectations of the Mexican business community by addressing the following research questions: What were the main health measures and operational actions implemented in the organizations in response to COVID-19? What sources and sorts of support were received to deal with COVID-19? What should be the best support policies for companies to face recovery? And what are the income expectations for the following months? While answering these questions, this chapter contributes to the limited studies with a qualitative organizational approach on COVID-19 in Mexico. Likewise, as a response to the call for recent studies by considering other relevant aspects of strategic management, such as transformation and organizational behavior, as well as a business strategy from a contingency approach in different contexts, which can have an impact on business recovery from this health crisis (Aslam et al., 2020; Gil Robles, 2020; Palma-Ruiz, Castillo-Apraiz, et al., 2020).

The experiences and learnings documented in the various settings across the globe provide valuable insights into the overall situation of the region´s productive sector and regain confidence in the face of potential recovery scenarios (OCDE, 2020b). In this way, for this chapter, we will concentrate on the economic impact of COVID-19 in Mexico, analyzed from the private sector companies´ perspective, mainly during phases 2 and 3 of this health crisis in Mexico (Santana Juárez et al., 2020); concentrating on the adjustment measures and operational actions implemented by businesses retrieved during April

2020, and as noted before, outlining the support instruments available for companies in such difficult time, and the income expectations for the upcoming months.

This chapter is organized into six sections, with this introduction included. Section two addresses the background information to contextualize the relevance of this study. Section three revisits distinct aspects of strategic management from a contingency approach to highlight the relevance of adapting and responding appropriately to new adverse demands of the environment and facing adversities. Section four describes the study´s methodology. The results and the discussion of the leading indicators are shown in section five. Finally, section six addresses the conclusions and recommendations.

BACKGROUND

On March 11th, 2020, as the number of infected people and deaths increased exponentially; the World Health Organization declared a pandemic crisis due to the COVID-19 virus (WHO, 2020). For this reason, countries declared themselves in a state of emergency, suspending economic and social activities, also imposing a whole series of health measures and regulations, such as confinement and social distancing. Companies in various sectors were forced to limit their economic activities, carrying out technical shutdowns and temporary closures as measures to contain the spread of the virus (OCDE, 2020a). Furthermore, the governments across regions responded rapidly by planning and executing several support instruments and policies on the macroeconomic and labor fronts that greatly conditioned the economic advances for the following months in each country (ECLAC & ILO, 2020).

Through the Health Ministry and the General Direction of Epidemiology, Mexico determined three phases of contingency for the COVID-19 pandemic. The first case of COVID-19 in the country was detected on February 27th, 2020. As a result, the government decided to carry out preventive measures against COVID-19 as of March 16th, 2020, known as the first phase of contingency. The second phase included containment measures starting on March 23rd and beginning on March 30th. The government declared the suspension of non-essential activities in various economic sectors, prolonging it until May 30th, 2020. By April 30th, there were already 19,224 confirmed cases in the country and 1,859 deaths (Suárez et al., 2020). During the third phase of contingency, starting in July 2020, Mexico was already one of the most affected countries, with 299,759 confirmed cases and 35,006 deaths (Ibarra-Nava et al., 2020). As of July 2021, Mexico has confirmed more than 2.5 million cases and 234,192 deaths, resulting in one of the most affected countries worldwide (Dong et al., 2020).

The economic slowdown derived by the suspension of all those activities considered non-essential, as well as the limited reopening of the same, has been carried out slowly and gradually during the second and third phases of contingency for the pandemic to maintain social distancing and avoid an increase in the rate of infections. As a result, this health crisis has contracted the economy (Santana Juárez et al., 2020), causing a deep and generalized fall in the nation´s imports and exports, halting many aspects of social life and economic development, endangering all types of business operations (Esquivel, 2020).

The Organization for Economic Cooperation and Development (OECD) made an urgent call in the face of COVID-19 to take decisive and collective action on five main fronts, the first referring to support the working class, and the second to support micro, and small and medium-sized enterprises (SMEs). Micro and SMEs make up the bulk of the business structure worldwide with a relevant contribution to generating wealth and employment. The relevance of micro and SMEs has recently been reinforced by the International Labor Organization (ILO) to maintain wages jobs during the stage of the COVID-19 pandemic (ECLAC & ILO, 2020; ILO, 2021).

The OECD estimated that for every month of confinement due to COVID-19, it could represent a loss of up to 2.0 points in annual GDP (OCDE, 2020a). The Economic Commission for Latin America and the Caribbean (ECLAC) forecasted a drop of 8.4% in GDP for Mexico during 2020, being one of the countries with the most remarkable effects in Latin America (ECLAC, 2020). Official data confirmed a historic drop of 8.5% in GDP for 2020 (INEGI, 2021). The economic activity collapsed during the second trimester of 2020, even exceeding the worst expectations and confirming the severe effects of the confinement (ECLAC, 2020). In fact, Mexico registered a massive -18.6% GDP fall during such a trimester, facing an extremely complex and uncertain scenario for the upcoming months. Enterprises have been forced to implement technical shutdowns or temporary closures following government regulations (OCDE, 2020a). Indeed, this has caused a historical negative economic impact with effects in the short and long term, even driving various economic sectors at risk (Fana et al., 2020).

In most countries in the Latin America and the Caribbean (LAC) region, almost all the companies experienced at least one type of effect caused by COVID-19, such as a decrease in income, a decline in demand for their products or a shortage of inputs and outputs. Moreover, the region's most significant percentage of absent workers was documented during April 2020 (ILO, 2021).

In Mexico, 59.6% of the companies reported that they had suspended operations or closed temporarily, negatively impacting employment and wages. As a result, 21.9% of employees were temporarily absent from their jobs during April 2020 (compared to 1.7% in March 2020). More specifically, the percentage of employees present at work for less than 15 hours per week increased from 6.2% in March 2020 to 13.9% in April 2020, while the rate of people working between 15 and 34 hours increased from 16.9% to 23.8% in the same period. Meanwhile, underemployment (measured by the number of working hours) increased from 8.5% to 25.5% from the first to second quarter in 2020 (ECLAC & ILO, 2020).

STRATEGY AND ENTREPRENEURSHIP TOPICS DURING COVID-19

Organizational strategy is likely one of the topics that generate the most interest in business management (Palma-Ruiz, Barros-Contreras, et al., 2020). Earlier literature discussed the relevance of administrative tasks or management processes to shift a company's strategic direction (Prahalad & Bettis, 1986). The exemplification of these processes helps denote the mobilization and use of resources and knowledge, such as "the choice of key individuals, processes of planning, budgeting, control, compensation, career management, and organizational structure" (p. 490). Additionally, these administrative processes are necessary but a challenging task to accomplish goals and make the right decisions in the business, particularly during difficult times such as crises.

The strategic management literature emphasizes the importance of strategy development, which involves developing and maintaining a competitive advantage for wealth creation (Hitt et al., 2001). Sharma and Chrisman (1999, p. 17) defined strategy as to how organizations align their critical resources with the environment they develop, including its core competencies, resources, and procedures. Nowadays, due to the COVID-19 pandemic, business survival and endurance are the immediate top priorities for organizations, while wealth and growth are deferred to the long term (Lesser & Reeves, 2020).

Strategic management relates to the ability of firms to respond to uncertain environments through internal strategic and structural adaptation (Gavetti, 2005; McMullen & Shepherd, 2006). These processes emphasize action-based mechanisms for organizational adaptation and are often referred to as routines or task-oriented actions (Dosi et al., 2000; Winter, 2003). Hence, organizations draw on existing practices developed in prior environments and initiate steps to execute specific tasks. Moreover, managers import routines they know from previous professional experience (Helfat & Peteraf, 2003). Authors have highlighted the significance of considering contextual factors and circumstances in the immediate environment of the entrepreneur, which influences the behavior of critical economic agents (Kalantaridis, 2006). However, a real challenge exists when facing the unknown such as the current health crisis. Strategic management requires focusing on the internal and external environment (Kuratko & Audretsch, 2009) to encompass factors of opportunity and innovation as a continuous search for new resources and ways that support business decisions. In this way, scholars sustain that strategic management provides an ideal context to develop entrepreneurial activities (Hitt et al., 2001), in addition to being an indispensable requirement for growth and performance in dynamic environments characterized by adversity (Weismeier-Sammer, 2011).

Environmental factors can be hostile and not only affect business growth or development but also hinder and put its continuity at risk (Barros et al., 2017). In our days, indeed, all types of organizations have faced the need to make a series of difficult decisions while facing the abrupt crisis caused by the COVID-19 pandemic. Small and medium-sized enterprises have been particularly vulnerable to the negative impact of this health crisis due to the change of consumer habits resulting from social distancing and fear of contagion, decrease in purchasing power, and more cautious spending due to the shift in priorities, etc. The reality is that such effects to counter the virus spread have had destructive implications for many organizations, particularly micro and SMEs.

Therefore, companies must develop a strategic position or orientation (Rauch et al., 2009). A strategic direction then refers to the principles that direct and influence the company's activities and generate the behaviors designed to ensure its viability and performance (Hakala, 2011, p. 199). Likewise, it has also been defined as the strategic actions implemented by the company to create the appropriate behaviors for superior business performance in a sustained way (Arzubiaga et al., 2020; Deutscher et al., 2016). Other authors recently refer to the development of strategic agility (Clauss et al., 2020; Shams et al., 2020) to adapt and respond quickly to opportunities and threats in the environment (Mao et al., 2015, p. 316).

For example, supply chain agility denotes the effectiveness of firms, and their supply chains respond to customers´ needs when changes in supply and demand (Swafford et al., 2006). The significance of supply chain agility has been pivotal during COVID-19 (Arora et al., 2020; Belhadi et al., 2021; Kuo et al., 2021). The constant occurrence of inventory depletion and sluggish restocks amid COVID-19 has revealed the opportunities for businesses to develop such agility dimension, setting the path for entrepreneurial venues (Short et al., 2010).

Many businesses pre-COVID-19 base their operations on a single distribution channel; however, those that have been able to shift channels during the pandemic had an advantage over others that could not respond. However, the resource orchestration theory points out about implementing a multiple channel approach, adding complexity to the firm's resources management, and creating new opportunities to realize value from those resources (Sirmon et al., 2007). Additionally, derived from the preventive measures during the pandemic, stay-at-home orders demanded micro, SMEs, and large companies to truly address online distribution channels and assess the advantages of social media. As a result, many businesses have reexamined their business models and explored further possibilities to team up with third-party firms (Duprey, 2020). Moreover, organizations have shifted to a more entrepreneurial strategic orientation, which has been of great benefit versus those that have remained stagnant with previous business models (Breier et al., 2021).

METHODOLOGY

The foremost governmental institution in Mexico that integrates statistic-economical and geographical information regarding the national business network is the National Institute of Statistics and Geography (INEGI for its acronym in Spanish); this material is relevant for different purposes, including the academic part of scientific research.

In an effort to know on time the economic impact caused by COVID-19 in Mexican companies during April 2020, the INEGI carried out a particular survey by telephone to the national level called ECOVID-IE 2020. The general objective of this study was to generate qualitative indicators about the effects of the contingency derived from COVID-19 with a representative stratified sample of the economic units of the country (INEGI, 2020). Therefore, the units of analysis were micro-enterprises, small and medium-sized enterprises (SMEs), and large companies with economic activity and fixed installations in Mexico in the industrial, commercial, and service sectors. As part of the methodological and conceptual framework, INEGI considers the economic units located in the Mexican territory considering the 32 federal entities, with its corresponding towns and rural/urban zones.

The sampling frame was made up of 1,873,564 companies by their different strata considering employed personnel (micro, SMEs, and large enterprises). For a confidence level of 95% and a relative error of 10%, a probabilistic and stratified sample size of 4,920 companies was obtained. The period for retrieving responses was from May 7th to June 12th, 2020. Table 1 below describes the distribution of the companies in the sample.

Table 1. Description of the sampling frame and sample size

Company size by employed personnel	Total	Sample
Micro (1 to 10)	1,728,410	1,735
SMEs (11 to 100)	128,261	1,360
Large (101 or more)	16,893	1,825
Total	1,873,564	4,920

Source: INEGI (2020). Survey on the Economic Impact Generated by COVID-19 in Companies (ECOVID-IE) 2020.

Regarding the implemented questionnaire, it was divided into eight main topics of interest, including sanitary measures implemented, operational actions implemented, days of technical shutdowns or temporary closure, effects due to the contingency, sources of support received and causes for not receiving them, types of support received, necessary policies to support companies, and income expectations in the next six months. The following section provides a descriptive analysis of the main results of this survey.

INFORMATION ANALYSIS AND DISCUSSION

First, the results on the sanitary measures implemented by the companies during April 2020 are presented. Figure 1 shows the total number of companies that implemented sanitary measures.

Figure 1. Sanitary measures implemented
Source: Own elaboration with data from INEGI (2020). Survey on the Economic Impact Generated by COVID-19 in Companies (ECOVID-IE) 2020.

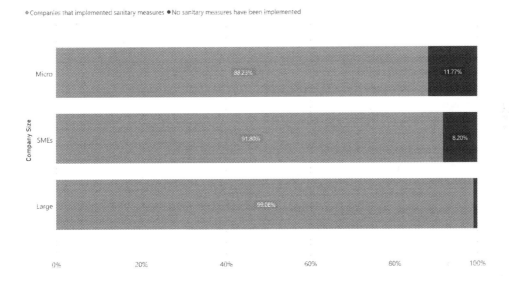

Figure 2. Types of sanitary measures implemented
Source: Own elaboration with data from INEGI (2020). Survey on the Economic Impact Generated by COVID-19 in Companies (ECOVID-IE) 2020.

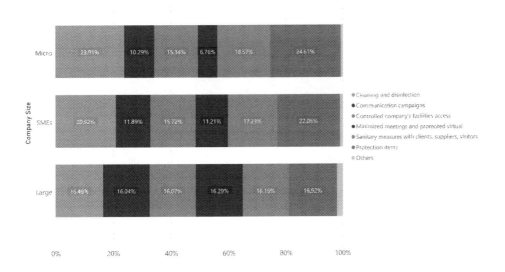

Only 11.4% of all companies did not implement sanitary measures during April 2020, representing 214,129 companies, most of which were micro-enterprises (203,455) and SMEs (10,520). While, of the large companies, only 155 did not implement any measure.

On the other hand, Figure 2 describes the types of sanitary measures implemented and the percentage of companies according to size.

Interestingly, the highest sanitary measure implemented in all companies was to provide personal protection items to their employees (24.3%), followed by cleaning and disinfection of facilities (23.5%). The lower types of implementation identified were that of minimizing face-to-face meetings and promoting communication through virtual means (7.3%), as well as other unidentified ones (0.8%) for all companies. However, within large companies, this type of sanitary measure represents 16.3%, while in micro-enterprises, it is only 6.8%, and among SMEs was 11.2%. The foregoing is understandable since, in general, micro and small companies include among the owners their relatives and staff who work receiving only tips, volunteers, among others. This data becomes more relevant during the pandemic as it shows the extraordinary efforts made by micro-enterprises and SMEs to preserve their operations and jobs, thus reinforcing the call of the OECD regarding the role of micro and SMEs as mentioned before in section 2.

Regarding the operational actions implemented against COVID-19, Figure 3 describes the types of actions by enterprise size.

Figure 3. Types of operational actions implemented by enterprise size
Source: Own elaboration with data from INEGI (2020). Survey on the Economic Impact Generated by COVID-19 in Companies (ECOVID-IE) 2020.

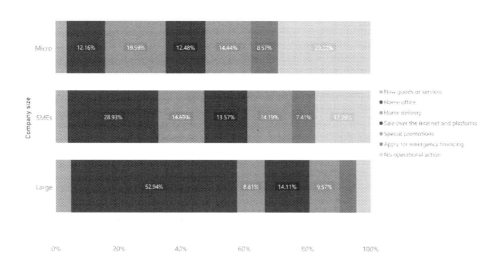

In order to complement the information concerning the health measures implemented, Figure 3 shows that the primary type of action for SMEs and large companies was the home office with 28.9% and 52.9%, respectively. This data is of distinctive relevance for strategic organizational management due to the challenges involved in implementing in the short term new forms and procedures for information and communications technology (ICT) management, such as work and communication tools, managing and sharing information, work documents, and other resources through networks and systems (García-Muñoz Aparicio et al., 2020), and considering the issues of stress and productivity of working at home (Madero Gómez et al., 2020).

Another essential issue shows that 29.2% of micro-enterprises and 17.4% of SMEs did not implement any operational action. These indicators are important since it suggests a deeper study of organizations that, when facing adversity and uncertainty in the environment, simply cannot respond and could end up extinct due to their indifference or lack of capacity to respond to the current demands of the domain. Similarly, other topics to further expansion suggest the management of information sources to document decision-making, managerial capacities, and attitudes to respond agilely with a planned strategy, or if faced with a real threat of health damage constitutes a determinant for termination of operations (especially when it comes to family businesses, see Serrano-Bedia et al., 2019).

Although several scenarios or reasons could be inferred to discern these indicators, among them the lack of resources to face COVID-19, a central issue refers to the lack of a strategic vision to act on the opportunities and adversities in the environment. As previously mentioned, micro-enterprises and SMEs generally lack a professional structure for their operations, and, in a majority of their cases, members of the same family participate, directed by the decisions of the founder or owner of the company or business. Faced with such a complex scenario, there are opportunities to address organizational leadership in family-owned versus non-family-owned firms, the professionalization of business operations, including issues of digital literacy, technology implementation, product or service innovation, to name a few (Saiz-Álvarez et al., 2019).

On the other hand, a percentage of micro-enterprises and SMEs did engage in operational actions, such as home order deliveries (19.6% and 14.7%, respectively), special promotions, such as discounts and rebates, deferred payments, buy 1 get 2, among others (14.4% and 14.2%, respectively), and sale of goods and services online or social media platforms (12.5% and 13.6%, respectively). These indicators also demonstrate the importance of delving into issues of strategic orientation by acting on opportunities in the environment and focusing their resources appropriately on certain types of operational actions that could both be implemented and that would be profitable in the short term given the current demand or needs, thus ensuring the viability and continuity of operations. However, it should also be noted that the least operational action implemented was the offer of new goods or services to attend to the health emergency with 3.4% of all companies. Although it is true that, due to the scope of this survey, business experiences were addressed during April 2020, it would not ignore the possibility that innovation attempts and results could be shown in the coming months.

The percentages of implementation of technical shutdowns or temporary closures derived from COVID-19 are contained in Figure 4. It is noticeable that 40.4% of all enterprises did not implement technical shutdowns or temporary closures during April 2020. It should also be noted that the distribution was relatively balanced between micro, SMEs, and large enterprises with 39.7%, 48.5%, and 55.9%, respectively.

The number of calendar days that the enterprises did implement a technical shutdown or temporary closure is shown in Figure 5. The majority implemented more than 21 calendar days (46.7%), being 68.1% among large enterprises, 54.0% for SMEs, and 46.1% for micro-enterprises. Considering these indicators, it is interesting to distinguish the type of activities carried out by said companies and the type of actions previously addressed in Figure 3.

Figure 4. Implementation of technical shutdown or temporary closure due to COVID-19
Source: Own elaboration with data from INEGI (2020). Survey on the Economic Impact Generated by COVID-19 in Companies (ECOVID-IE) 2020.

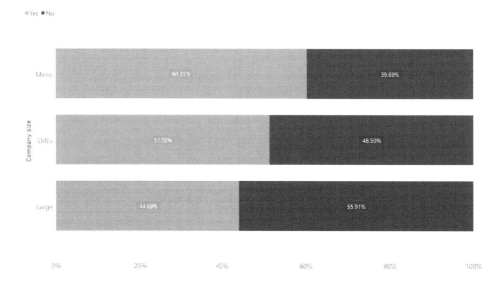

Figure 5. Calendar days of the technical shutdown or temporary closure due to COVID-19
Source: Own elaboration with data from INEGI (2020). Survey on the Economic Impact Generated by COVID-19 in Companies (ECOVID-IE) 2020.

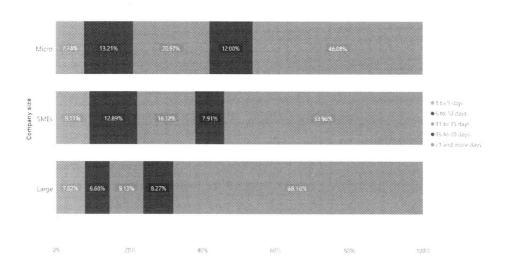

The main types of effects on companies derived from COVID-19 are described in Figure 6. As is to be expected, the effects due to decreased income represent the major impact among all companies

Figure 6. Types of effects on companies due to COVID-19
Source: Own elaboration with data from INEGI (2020). Survey on the Economic Impact Generated by COVID-19 in Companies (ECOVID-IE) 2020.

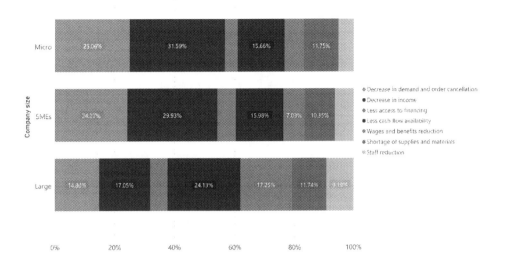

(30.5%), followed by a decrease in the demand and order cancellation (24.3%), lower availability of cash flow (15.3%), and a shortage of supplies, raw materials, finished goods or materials acquired for resale (11.3%). This same order of affectations is maintained among the micro-enterprises and SMEs. In contrast, in large companies, the main affectation referred to the lower cash flow and the reduction of the total amount of the salaries and/or personnel benefits with 24.1% and 17.25%, respectively.

An interesting topic to study refers to the reception of support and the sources of such support available during the pandemic, as well as the leading causes for not receiving them. This information is summarized in Figures 7 and 8 below.

As shown in Figure 7 and Table 2, only 7.6% of the micro-enterprises, 10.3% of the SMEs, and 11.46% of the large enterprises received some support to face the health crisis, and the primary source was coming from governmental instances. These indicators highlight the lack of an emerging support plan and leadership of the Mexican government to counteract the effects of the pandemic, at least in the short term, which has also been pointed out by other authors (Ibarra-Nava et al., 2020). This fact raises additional research questions to expand on institutional conditions that can affect organizational performance. In addition, to topics of strategic management from a contingency perspective within governmental institutions. Table 2 below describes in greater detail the distribution of support received by type of source.

Figure 8 indicates the main reasons why companies did not receive support against COVID-19. The leading cause for all the firms corresponded to the lack of knowledge on support (37.4%), followed by the complexity of requesting the support (18.2%), and the non-receipt of the support despite having asked for it (17.5%). It is worth mentioning that for large companies, 26.1% indicated that it was not necessary to request support, and 21.6% affirmed that the requirements asked were not met.

To complement the information above, Figure 9 describes the main types of support received, and Figure 10 lists the most necessary policies to deal with COVID-19.

Figure 7. Reception of support due to COVID-19
Source: Own elaboration with data from INEGI (2020). Survey on the Economic Impact Generated by COVID-19 in Companies (ECOVID-IE) 2020.

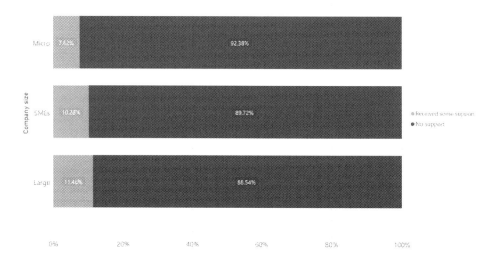

Figure 8. Causes for not receiving support due to COVID-19
Source: Own elaboration with data from INEGI (2020). Survey on the Economic Impact Generated by COVID-19 in Companies (ECOVID-IE) 2020.

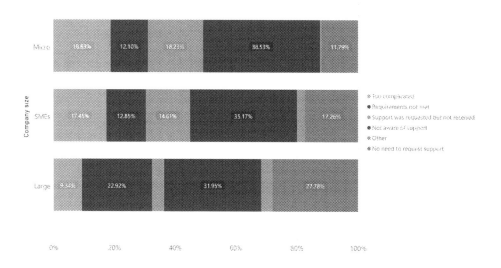

While micro-enterprises and SMEs received support in cash transfers, large companies received tax exemptions or reductions, tax deferrals, and payroll subsidies.

Figure 9. Types of support received due to COVID-19
Source: Own elaboration with data from INEGI (2020). Survey on the Economic Impact Generated by COVID-19 in Companies (ECOVID-IE) 2020.

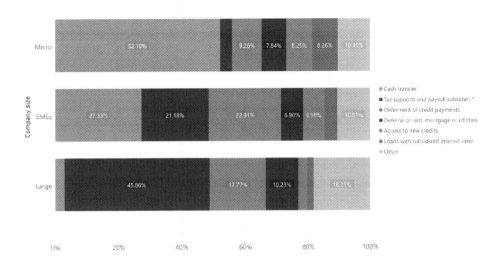

In line with the previous information, Figure 10 indicates that for micro-enterprises, the most necessary policies correspond to the deferral of rent, mortgage, or charges for public services, closely followed by cash transfers and access to new credit. On the other hand, SMEs and large companies indicate that tax deferral and tax exemptions or reductions represent the most necessary policies. These findings are

Figure 10. Most necessary policies to face COVID-19
Source: Own elaboration with data from INEGI (2020). Survey on the Economic Impact Generated by COVID-19 in Companies (ECOVID-IE) 2020.

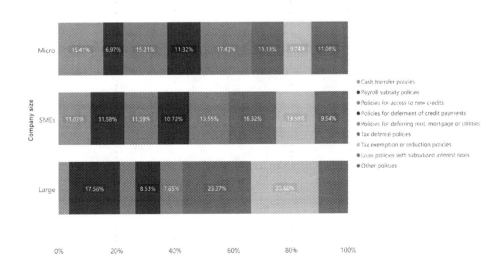

Table 2. Sources of support amid COVID-19

Company size	Total	Total number of companies that received some type of support	Government (Federal, State or Municipal / Mayor´s Office)	Chambers and business organizations	Other	Had not received any type of support
Micro	1,728,410	131,654	120,307	3,198	8,149	1,596,756
SMEs	128,261	13,191	8,849	1,791	2,999	115,070
Large	16,893	1,937	1,195	349	545	14,956
Total	1,873,564	146,782	130,352	5,338	11,693	1,726,782

Source: INEGI (2020). Survey on the Economic Impact Generated by COVID-19 in Companies (ECOVID-IE) 2020.

similar to studies in different contexts, such as Russia, where the most demanded measures to support SMEs tax payment deferral regarding all taxes (Razumovskaia et al., 2020). Thus, the information on these indicators is critical as it could lay the basis for developing support policies targeting companies' various sectors and sizes. Therefore, the importance of deepening its analysis and triggering profiles of companies that could benefit the most from the economic recovery plans for the following months and probably years.

To finish with this analysis of qualitative indicators, Figure 11 recovers the income expectations of the companies during the next six months.

Figure 11. Expectations of income for the next six months
Source: Own elaboration with data from INEGI (2020). Survey on the Economic Impact Generated by COVID-19 in Companies (ECOVID-IE) 2020.

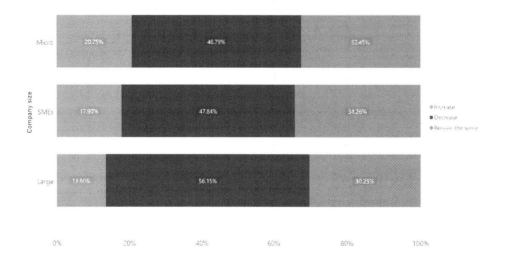

Out of the total number of firms, 46.8% of micro-enterprises indicated that their income expectations would decrease in the next six months, and 47.8% of SMEs and 56.15% of large enterprises. Although these indicators refer to a specific period in time, a negative outlook looms with a long-term impact.

CONCLUSION

Derived from the need to identify the economic impact of COVID-19 in different productive sectors in Latin America, this study provides relevant information about the reality of Mexican business. As a result, the authors have identified the main health measures implemented, the operational strategies or actions implemented, the sources and types of support received, the best support policies for companies, and income expectations for the coming months. The approach to a descriptive study with qualitative indicators allowed the authors to identify a series of issues related to strategic management in organizations facing adversity situations as a call for future studies to deepen their analysis and better understand the effects of the pandemic in various axes.

On the other hand, the indicators presented in this study show the importance of deepening the analysis of companies according to the characteristics of size by employed personnel to design a justified support strategy to reactivate those companies in a situation of emergency. Although the third and fourth quarters of 2020 suppose negative expectations and records for Mexico, governments must propose strategies aligned to the reality that entrepreneurs are experiencing in the face of the pandemic. Thus, for micro-enterprises, the most necessary policy corresponds to deferral of rent, mortgage, or charges for public services, closely followed by cash transfers and access to new credits. For SMEs and large companies, tax deferrals and tax exemptions or reductions represent the most necessary policies that the Mexican business community has indicated as decisive factors towards economic recovery. Policies that will also condition the expected restrictions or limitations in the strategy of the economic reopening plan towards the stage known as the "new normal," such as those that have been clearly defined in other areas (Torres-Toukoumidis et al., 2021).

The implementation of well-defined support policies could not only benefit companies in terms of exemption from payments or extensions and access to new credits. Still, it could also provide the necessary resource to implement more profitable strategic actions and even encourage product innovation and services adapted to the latest market demands. In this study, it has been identified that only 7.8% of Mexican companies received some support against COVID-19. Future studies should delve into whether, in the face of this lack of support, the implementation of strategic actions in companies and innovation could be conditioned and measure the organizational performance of those who did receive it.

The importance of regaining business confidence will be critical to face the following months and possibly years. To a large extent, this trust will be supported by adequate and focused institutional support programs and the right strategic decisions by the business community. All this requires being attentive to the conditions in the environment, focusing resources more effectively, and implementing operational actions to maintain viability and competitiveness in the market. The experience of the COVID-19 crisis has once again demonstrated that valuable knowledge of organizational strategy could inform and support the practice of strategic management. There are many reasons for this, as noted in this study. However, the "big questions" cannot be answered unless knowledge is shared and multidisciplinary research is deepened.

REFERENCES

Arora, R., Arora, P. K., Kumar, H., & Pant, M. (2020). Additive Manufacturing Enabled Supply Chain in Combating COVID-19. *Journal of Industrial Integration and Management*, *05*(04), 495–505. doi:10.1142/S2424862220500244

Arzubiaga, U., Castillo-Apraiz, J., & Palma-Ruiz, J. M. (2020). Organisational learning as a mediator in the host-home country similarity–international firm performance link: The role of exploration and exploitation. *European Business Review*, *33*(3), 409–426. doi:10.1108/EBR-09-2019-0238

Aslam, F., Mohti, W., & Ferreira, P. (2020). Evidence of Intraday Multifractality in European Stock Markets during the recent Coronavirus (COVID-19) Outbreak. *International Journal of Financial Studies*, *8*(2), 31. doi:10.3390/ijfs8020031

Barros, I., Palma-Ruiz, J. M., Cantarero-Prieto, D., & González-Moreno, S. E. (2017). Las empresas familiares en el desarrollo regional: un llamado al reenfoque de la investigación en México. In Los Retos del Cambio Económico Actual: Revisión y Aplicaciones para el Caso Mexicano (pp. 128–152). Ediciones de Laurel / Universidad Autónoma de Chihuahua.

Belhadi, A., Kamble, S., Jabbour, C. J. C., Gunasekaran, A., Ndubisi, N. O., & Venkatesh, M. (2021). Manufacturing and service supply chain resilience to the COVID-19 outbreak: Lessons learned from the automobile and airline industries. *Technological Forecasting and Social Change*, *163*, 120447. doi:10.1016/j.techfore.2020.120447 PMID:33518818

Breier, M., Kallmuenzer, A., Clauss, T., Gast, J., Kraus, S., & Tiberius, V. (2021). The role of business model innovation in the hospitality industry during the COVID-19 crisis. *International Journal of Hospitality Management*, *92*, 102723. doi:10.1016/j.ijhm.2020.102723

Caligiuri, P., De Cieri, H., Minbaeva, D., Verbeke, A., & Zimmermann, A. (2020). International HRM insights for navigating the COVID-19 pandemic: Implications for future research and practice. *Journal of International Business Studies*, *51*(5), 697–713. doi:10.105741267-020-00335-9 PMID:32836500

CEPAL. (2020). *Estudio Económico de América Latina y el Caribe 2020: Principales condicionantes de las políticas fiscal y monetaria en la era pospandemia de COVID-19* (LC/PUB.20). Comisión Económica para América Latina y el Caribe (CEPAL).

Clauss, T., Kraus, S., Kallinger, F. L., Bican, P. M., Brem, A., & Kailer, N. (2020). Organizational ambidexterity and competitive advantage: The role of strategic agility in the exploration-exploitation paradox. *Journal of Innovation & KNOWLEDGE*. doi:10.1016/j.jik.2020.07.003

Deutscher, F., Zapkau, F. B., Schwens, C., Baum, M., & Kabst, R. (2016). Strategic orientations and performance: A configurational perspective. *Journal of Business Research*, *69*(2), 849–861. doi:10.1016/j.jbusres.2015.07.005

Dong, E., Du, H., & Gardner, L. (2020). An interactive web-based dashboard to track COVID-19 in real time. *The Lancet. Infectious Diseases*, *20*(5), 533–534. doi:10.1016/S1473-3099(20)30120-1 PMID:32087114

Dosi, G., Nelson, R. R., & Winter, S. G. (2000). *The nature and dynamics of organizational capabilities* (G. Dosi, R. R. Nelson, & S. G. Winter, Eds.). Oxford University Press.

Duprey, R. (2020). *Uber eats gains Grubhub lags during Coronavirus pandemic*. Motley Fool. https://www.fool.com/ investing/2020/04/09/ uber-eats- gains- grubhub- lags- during- coronavirus- pa.aspx

ECLAC & ILO. (2020). Employment trends in an unprecedented crisis: policy challenges. In *Employment Situation in Latin America and the Caribbean* (Issue 23 (LC/TS.2020/128)). United Nations. https://repositorio.cepal.org/bitstream/handle/11362/46309/4/S2000600_en.pdf

Eggers, F. (2020). Masters of disasters? Challenges and opportunities for SMEs in times of crisis. *Journal of Business Research*, *116*, 199–208. doi:10.1016/j.jbusres.2020.05.025 PMID:32501306

Esquivel, G. (2020). The Economic Impacts of the Pandemic in Mexico. *Economía UNAM*, *17*(51). Advance online publication. doi:10.22201/fe.24488143e.2020.51.543

Fana, M., Tolan, S., Torrejón Pérez, S., Urzi Brancati, M. C., & Fernández-Macías, E. (2020). The COVID confinement measures and EU labour markets. In *JCR Technical Reports*. Publications Office of the European Union. doi:10.2760/079230

García-Muñoz Aparicio, C., Pérez Sánchez, B., & Navarrete Torres, M. del C. (2020). Las Empresas ante el COVID-19. *Revista de Investigación En Gestion Industrial, Ambiental, Seguridad y Salud En El Trabajo- GISST, 2*(2), 85–143. doi:10.34893/gisst.v2i2.83

Gavetti, G. (2005). Cognition and Hierarchy: Rethinking the Microfoundations of Capabilities' Development. *Organization Science*, *16*(6), 599–617. doi:10.1287/orsc.1050.0140

Gil Robles, M. A. (2020). Organizational Transformation During COVID-19. *IEEE Engineering Management Review*, *48*(3), 31–36. doi:10.1109/EMR.2020.3014280

Hakala, H. (2011). Strategic Orientations in Management Literature: Three Approaches to Understanding the Interaction between Market, Technology, Entrepreneurial and Learning Orientations. *International Journal of Management Reviews*, *13*(2), 199–217. doi:10.1111/j.1468-2370.2010.00292.x

Helfat, C. E., & Peteraf, M. A. (2003). The dynamic resource-based view: Capability lifecycles. *Strategic Management Journal*, *24*(10), 997–1010. doi:10.1002mj.332

Hitt, M. A., Ireland, R. D., Camp, S. M., & Sexton, D. L. (2001). Strategic entrepreneurship: Entrepreneurial strategies for wealth creation. *Strategic Management Journal*, *22*(6–7), 479–491. doi:10.1002mj.196

Ibarra-Nava, I., Cardenas-de la Garza, J. A., Ruiz-Lozano, R. E., & Salazar-Montalvo, R. G. (2020). Mexico and the COVID-19 Response. *Disaster Medicine and Public Health Preparedness*, *1–2*(4), e17–e18. Advance online publication. doi:10.1017/dmp.2020.260 PMID:32713412

ILO. (2021). *COVID-19 and the World of Work*. https://www.ilo.org/ global/topics/ coronavirus/ lang- -en/index.htm

INEGI. (2020). *Encuesta sobre el Impacto Económico Generado por COVID-19 en las Empresas 2020 (ECOVID-IE): Síntesis metodológica*. Instituto Nacional de Estadística y Geografía.

INEGI. (2021). *Gross Domestic Product per Economic Activity*. https://www.inegi.org.mx/temas/pib/

Kalantaridis, C. (2006). A study into the localization of rural businesses in five European countries. *European Planning Studies*, *14*(1), 61–78. doi:10.1080/09654310500339133

Katare, B., Marshall, M. I., & Valdivia, C. B. (2021). Bend or break? Small business survival and strategies during the COVID-19 shock. *International Journal of Disaster Risk Reduction*, *61*, 102332. doi:10.1016/j.ijdrr.2021.102332

Ketchen, D. J. Jr, & Craighead, C. W. (2020). Research at the Intersection of Entrepreneurship, Supply Chain Management, and Strategic Management: Opportunities Highlighted by COVID-19. *Journal of Management*, *46*(8), 1330–1341. doi:10.1177/0149206320945028

Kuo, S., Ou, H.-T., & Wang, C. J. (2021). Managing medication supply chains: Lessons learned from Taiwan during the COVID-19 pandemic and preparedness planning for the future. *Journal of the American Pharmacists Association*, *61*(1), e12–e15. doi:10.1016/j.japh.2020.08.029 PMID:32919923

Kuratko, D. F., & Audretsch, D. B. (2009). Strategic Entrepreneurship: Exploring Different Perspectives of an Emerging Concept. *Entrepreneurship Theory and Practice*, *33*(1), 1–17. doi:10.1111/j.1540-6520.2008.00278.x

Lemes, A., & Machado, T. (2007). *SMEs and Their Space in the Latin American Economy*. https://www.eumed.net/ eve/resum/ 07-enero/alb.htm

Lesser, R., & Reeves, M. (2020). *5 Priorities for Leaders in the New Reality of COVID-19*. World Economic Forum. https://www.weforum.org/ agenda/2020/05/ 5-things- leaders- succeed- new-reality- coronavirus/

Luger, J., Raisch, S., & Schimmer, M. (2018). Dynamic balancing of exploration and exploitation: The contingent benefits of ambidexterity. *Organization Science*, *29*(3), 449–470. doi:10.1287/orsc.2017.1189

Madero Gómez, S., Ortiz Mendoza, O. E., Ramírez, J., & Olivas-Luján, M. R. (2020). Stress and myths related to the COVID-19 pandemic's effects on remote work. *Management Research: Journal of the Iberoamerican Academy of Management*. doi:10.1108/MRJIAM-06-2020-1065

Mao, H., Liu, S., & Zhang, J. (2015). How the effects of IT and knowledge capability on organizational agility are contingent on environmental uncertainty and information intensity. *Information Development*, *31*(4), 358–382. doi:10.1177/0266666913518059

Marín-Idárraga, D. A., Hurtado González, J. M., & Cabello Medina, C. (2016). The Antecedents of Exploitation-Exploration and Their Relationship with Innovation: A Study of Managers' Cognitive Maps. *Creativity and Innovation Management*, *25*(1), 18–37. doi:10.1111/caim.12139

McMullen, J. S., & Shepherd, D. A. (2006). Entrepreneurial Action and The Role of Uncertainty in The Theory of The Entrepreneur. *Academy of Management Review*, *31*(1), 132–152. doi:10.5465/amr.2006.19379628

Obi, J., Ibidunni, A. S., Tolulope, A., Olokundun, M. A., Amaihian, A. B., Borishade, T. T., & Fred, P. (2018). Contribution of small and medium enterprises to economic development: Evidence from a transiting economy. *Data in Brief*, *18*, 835–839. doi:10.1016/j.dib.2018.03.126 PMID:29900247

OCDE. (2020a). *Covid-19 en América Latina y el Caribe: Panorama de las respuestas de los gobiernos a la crisis.* https://www.oecd.org/ coronavirus/ policy-responses/ covid-19- en-america- latina-y- el-caribe- panorama- de-las-respuestas- de-los-gobiernos -a-la-crisis- 7d9f7a2b/

OCDE. (2020b). *Generar confianza ante una recuperación incierta.* https://www.oecd.org/ perspectivas- economicas

Palma-Ruiz, J. M., Barros-Contreras, I., & Gnan, L. (Eds.). (2020). Handbook of Research on the Strategic Management of Family Businesses. IGI Global. doi:10.4018/978-1-7998-2269-1

Palma-Ruiz, J. M., Castillo-Apraiz, J., & Gómez-Martínez, R. (2020). Socially Responsible Investing as a Competitive Strategy for Trading Companies in Times of Upheaval Amid COVID-19: Evidence from Spain. *International Journal of Financial Studies*, 8(3), 41. doi:10.3390/ijfs8030041

Prahalad, C. K., & Bettis, R. A. (1986). The dominant logic: A new linkage between diversity and performance. *Strategic Management Journal*, 7(6), 485–501. doi:10.1002mj.4250070602

Rauch, A., Wiklund, J., Lumpkin, G. T., & Frese, M. (2009). Entrepreneurial Orientation and Business Performance: An Assessment of Past Research and Suggestions for the Future. *Entrepreneurship Theory and Practice*, 33(3), 761–787. doi:10.1111/j.1540-6520.2009.00308.x

Razumovskaia, E., Yuzvovich, L., Kniazeva, E., Klimenko, M., & Shelyakin, V. (2020). The Effectiveness of Russian Government Policy to Support SMEs in the COVID-19 Pandemic. *Journal of Open Innovation*, 6(4), 160. doi:10.3390/joitmc6040160

Saiz-Álvarez, J. M. (2022). *Emerging Business Models and the New World Economic Order* (1st ed.). IGI Global. https://www.igi-global.com/ submission/ book-project-chapters/ ?projectid= 1032c361- 0b19- 48a4-8f0d-6ae9b2dc9dce

Saiz-Álvarez, J. M., Leitao, J., & Palma-Ruiz, J. M. (Eds.). (2019). Entrepreneurship and Family Business Vitality: Surviving and Flourishing in the Long Term. Springer International Publishing AG. doi:10.1007/978-3-030-15526-1

Santana Juárez, M. V., Santana Castañeda, G., Sánchez Carillo, C., Sánchez Carrillo, R., & Ortega Alcántara, R. (2020). COVID-19 en México: Asociación espacial de cara a la fase tres. *Hygeia; Revista Brasileira de Geografia Médica e da Saúde*, 36–48. doi:10.14393/Hygeia0054317

Serrano-Bedia, A. M., Palma-Ruiz, J. M., & Flores-Rivera, C. (2019). Innovation and Family Firms: Past and Future Research Perspectives. In Handbook of Research on Entrepreneurial Leadership and Competitive Strategy in Family Business (pp. 371–398). IGI Global. doi:10.4018/978-1-5225-8012-6.ch018

Shams, R., Vrontis, D., Belyaeva, Z., Ferraris, A., & Czinkota, M. R. (2020). Strategic agility in international business: A conceptual framework for "agile" multinationals. *Journal of International Management*, 100737. doi:10.1016/j.intman.2020.100737

Sharma, P., & Chrisman, J. J. (1999). Toward a Reconciliation of the Definitional Issues in the Field of Corporate Entrepreneurship. *Entrepreneurship Theory and Practice*, 23(3), 11–28. doi:10.1177/104225879902300302

Short, J. C., Ketchen, D. J. Jr, Shook, C. L., & Ireland, R. D. (2010). The Concept of "Opportunity" in Entrepreneurship Research: Past Accomplishments and Future Challenges. *Journal of Management*, *36*(1), 40–65. doi:10.1177/0149206309342746

Sirmon, D. G., Hitt, M. A., & Ireland, R. D. (2007). Managing firm resources in dynamic environments to create value: Looking inside the black box. *Academy of Management Review*, *32*(1), 273–292. doi:10.5465/amr.2007.23466005

Suárez, V., Suarez Quezada, M., Oros Ruiz, S., & Ronquillo De Jesús, E. (2020). Epidemiología de COVID-19 en México: Del 27 de febrero al 30 de abril de 2020. *Revista Clínica Española*, *220*(8), 463–471. doi:10.1016/j.rceng.2020.05.008

Swafford, P. M., Ghosh, S., & Murthy, N. (2006). The antecedents of supply chain agility of a firm: Scale development and model testing. *Journal of Operations Management*, *24*(2), 170–188. doi:10.1016/j.jom.2005.05.002

Torres-Toukoumidis, A., González-Moreno, S. E., Pesántez-Avilés, F., Cárdenas-Tapia, J., & Valles-Baca, H. G. (2021). Políticas públicas educativas durante la pandemia: Estudio comparativo México y Ecuador. *Education Policy Analysis Archives*, *29*, 88. doi:10.14507/epaa.29.6362

Weismeier-Sammer, D. (2011). Entrepreneurial behavior in family firms: A replication study. *Journal of Family Business Strategy*, *2*(3), 128–138. doi:10.1016/j.jfbs.2011.07.003

WHO. (2020). *WHO Timeline - COVID-19*. Newsroom. https://www.who.int/news-room/detail/27-04-2020-who-timeline---covid-19

Winter, S. G. (2003). Understanding dynamic capabilities. *Strategic Management Journal*, *24*(10), 991–995. doi:10.1002mj.318

ADDITIONAL READING

Aristizábal Tamayo, J. M., Tarapuez, E., & Vasquez, J. C. (2020). Application of a Fuzzy System to the Analysis of Entrepreneurial Intention in Brazil, Mexico, and Colombia. In J.M. Saiz-Álvarez, & J. Gámez-Gutiérrez (Ed.), Senior Entrepreneurship and Aging in Modern Business (pp. 237-258). IGI Global. http://doi:10.4018/978-1-7998-2019-2.ch013

Palma-Ruiz, J. M., Saiz-Álvarez, J., & Herrero-Crespo, Á. (Eds.). (2020). *Handbook of Research on Smart Territories and Entrepreneurial Ecosystems for Social Innovation and Sustainable Growth*. IGI Global. doi:10.4018/978-1-7998-2097-0

Saiz-Alvarez, J. M. (2020). Entrepreneurial Knowledge-Based Strategies for Organizational Development: A Case of Tecnológico de Monterrey Mexico. In Disruptive Technology: Concepts, Methodologies, Tools, and Applications (pp. 513-530). IGI Global. doi:10.4018/978-1-5225-9273-0.ch025

Saiz-Alvarez, J. M. (2021). Innovation-Based Lateral Thinking and Intrapreneurship Strategies for Handling Corporate Chaordism. In R. Perez-Uribe, D. Ocampo-Guzman, N. Moreno-Monsalve, & W. Fajardo-Moreno (Eds.), Handbook of Research on Management Techniques and Sustainability Strategies for Handling Disruptive Situations in Corporate Settings (pp. 89-107). IGI Global. http://doi:10.4018/978-1-7998-8185-8.ch005

Saiz-Alvarez, J. M., Castillo-Nazareno, U. H., Matute de León, J. S., & Alcívar-Avilés, M. T. (2021). Post-COVID Indigenous Women Entrepreneurship: A Case of the Kichwa-Puruha in Ecuador. In N. Baporikar (Ed.), *Handbook of Research on Strategies and Interventions to Mitigate COVID-19 Impact on SMEs* (pp. 430–456). IGI Global. doi:10.4018/978-1-7998-7436-2.ch021

Tomas, C. M., Pinto-López, I. N., & Amsler, A. (2021). Scenario Planning as a Tool to Manage Crises in Chaotic and Uncertain Environments: The Case of the COVID-19 Pandemic. In R. Perez-Uribe, D. Ocampo-Guzman, N. Moreno-Monsalve, & W. Fajardo-Moreno (Ed.), Handbook of Research on Management Techniques and Sustainability Strategies for Handling Disruptive Situations in Corporate Settings (pp. 184-205). IGI Global. doi:10.4018/978-1-7998-8185-8.ch009

Vargas-Hernández, J. G., & Cervantes-Guzman, J. N. (2020). La Barranca del Rio Santiago as Tourist and Eco Touristic Attraction for the Brand Guadalajara, Focused on a National Tourism. *International Journal of Tourism and Hospitality Management in the Digital Age, 4*(1), 10–28. doi:10.4018/IJTHMDA.2020010102

KEY TERMS AND DEFINITIONS

Agility: It is a way to adapt and respond quickly to opportunities and threats in the environment.

Contingency Perspective: The contingency approach suggests that an organization's most suitable management style depends on the context or environment.

ECLAC: It refers to the Spanish acronym for CEPAL and stands for the Economic Commission for Latin America and the Caribbean as one of the five regional commissions of the United Nations across the globe with headquarters in Chile.

INEGI: Refers to the Spanish acronym for the National Institute of Statistics and Geography in Mexico.

Information and Communications Technology: (ICT): It refers to information technology (IT) that integrates communications and computers, including software, and information manipulation, such as storage, retrieval, and access.

State of Emergency: The government under extreme circumstances executes a series of policies to regulate all types of activities for the safety and protection of its society.

Strategy: How organizations align their critical resources with the environment they develop, including the organization´s core competencies, use of resources, and techniques.

Technical Shutdown: It is defined as a total stoppage of a plant´s production for a determined period.

Chapter 4
Impact of COVID-19 on Food Consumption and Marketing:
A Behavioral Model Perspective

Suja Ravindran Nair
https://orcid.org/0000-0002-9803-0552
Educe Micro Research, Bengaluru, India

ABSTRACT

COVID-19 has greatly disrupted lives and affected buying behavior of individuals. Countries were forced to impose lockdowns, alongside the practices of wearing masks, social distancing and hygiene have become the 'new normal'. This situation forced consumers to re-work shopping habits, modify food patterns, develop healthy eating and online shopping behavior. With multiple waves of COVID-19 engulfing countries, pandemic effects are here to stay, suggesting food marketers explore the continuity of healthy food consumption with futuristic behavioral intention. For this purpose, this study uses a behavioral model perspective built upon the theory of planned behavior. A general review of the literature on food choice behavior is used. The literature review shows an integrated framework indicating linkages between the antecedents, consumers' behaviors, and behavior intentions/consequences from a sustainable behavioral model perspective.

INTRODUCTION

Consumption of food is a basic human need, and as a part of the social system is greatly influenced by many factors including sociocultural, economic, marketing, amongst others. Steenkamp (1993) had stated that given the complexity and diversity of the factors influencing individual food choice and consumption is a call for researchers to draw insights on food behavior from the wide range of science and social science disciplines that include food science, nutrition, medicine, psychology, physiology, psychophysics, sociology, economics, marketing, and anthropology. In line to this, researchers have found there are various factors influencing food consumption. For instance, Mak *et al.* (2012) identified cultural/religious influences, socio-demographics, food-related personality traits, exposure effect/past

DOI: 10.4018/978-1-7998-7689-2.ch004

experience, and motivational factors that affect tourist food consumption. Deshpande *et al.* (2009) found that perception of current dietary, quality, perceived importance of eating a healthy diet, self-efficacy or individual perception of being able to perform the advocated behavior and other environmental variables are likely to influence healthy food consumption. Meanwhile, during times of crisis (like-economic recession) factors such as product features and natural contents, economic issues, identity and sensory appeal, mood, weight control and health, and convenience influence consumers' food purchasing behavior, noted Theodoridou *et al.* (2017). Recent researchers (Liu *et al.*, 2020) found feelings of disgust, knowledge, phobia, and social demographic factors such as age, household size, household income and region are the main factors that influence specific food (e.g., insect) purchases and consumption. Thus, as the above studies indicate there are various factors (sociocultural, personal, psychological, and so on) which influence the purchase and consumption of food.

Meanwhile, during specific situational crisis like the unprecedented Covid-19 pandemic, people were compelled to fundamentally change not only their way of living but also their consumption behavior of goods and services. In fact, studies suggest that many people across the globe have started looking at products and product-brands through a new lens. Indeed, Covid-19 has greatly affected the consumption behavior of people, more so post the lockdowns that were imposed and, alongside the need to practice the guidelines suggested by the World Health Organization (WHO) of social distancing, wearing masks and maintaining hygiene, which have become the 'new normal' (Sheth, 2020), disrupting many of the existing customers' purchase and shopping behavior. For example, when the lockdowns were imposed across nations consumers were forced to rework their shopping habits, they became more cost conscious, developed a preference towards local products, started to engage in healthy eating habits, and, so on. More interestingly was visible the dramatic shift towards e-commerce and online shopping (Asti *et al.*, 2021; Badenhop & Frasquet, 2021; UNCAD, 2020). Furthermore, with the Covid-19 pandemic spread; the way consumers shop for their groceries has also changed. In that, to limit contact, people have modified their buying pattern (and behavior), preferring to opt for online purchase of groceries through orders placed via the internet, smart phones, delivery apps, etc. Consequently, this also required them to make less number of shopping trips to a grocery store. Thus, unlike pre Covid-19 times, now people have started living differently, purchasing differently, and in many ways, even thinking differently. Of course, partly this can also be attributed to their line of thinking and reasoning which drastically changed when lockdowns were imposed across nations. Needless to mention that the changed circumstances have compelled people to realize the importance of consuming healthy and nutritious food, and alongside, the need to purchase sustainable brands which offer them 'valued choices'. In fact, a visible change in consumer behavior was that instead of engaging in 'impulsive' and/or 'on the go shopping and eating', people started doing 'more' cooking at home, and carefully plan their weekly shopping trips with the focus being on 'the core values' rather than on the 'weekly special offers' (FoodMatters, 2020).

Incidentally, to gain an understanding on the Covid-19 pandemic effect which brought about widespread changes in the way consumers buy food, their concern regarding food safety, and what they eat, during April 2020 the International Food Information Council (IFIC) conducted a Covid-19 IFIC consumer research survey through holding interviews with 1000 individuals. The key takeaways from this study were identified as: (1) people are doing less in-person shopping and cooking more, with the spotlight being on online grocery shopping, (2) there is scope for improvement with regards recommended health habits and grocery shopping, (3) at grocery stores, employees need to take more actions regarding the food safety, (4) food shoppers were most concerned about the health of the other shoppers and grocery store employees, along with the fear of running out of staple foods, (5) although consumers purchased more packaged foods, they were concerned about the 'healthfulness' of these products, (6) there have been changes in consumers' eating habits, and lastly, (7) most people were confident regarding the safety of the food supply and in the ability of the food producers to meet their needs (Food Insight, 2020).

The visible changes in consumers' behavior due to the Covid-19 pandemic crisis were also observed by other research scholars. For instance, the impact of Covid-19 on consumer food habits was found to inversely vary based on personal attitudes, individual and household experiences, and characteristics (Borsellino *et al.*, 2020), changes are visible in the food consumption patterns of individuals before and during the Covid-19 pandemic, noted Eftimov *et al.* (2020). Interestingly, Danley (2020) reiterates this by referring to the International Food Information Council's (IFIC) 2020 Food and Health Survey, which indicated that 85% of Americans have made changes in the food they eat or in the way they prepare food because of the coronavirus (Covid-19) pandemic. Additionally, this study found the biggest change was seen among 60% of consumers who stated that they were cooking at home more, one-in-three who said they were snacking more, and a quarter who had said that they were thinking about food more than usual, and about 20% who had reported that they were eating healthier than usual, more than usual, and more pre-made meals from their own pantry or freezer too (Danley, 2020).

Thus far, studies have indicated the impact of post Covid-19 pandemic, and its effect on changing the food consumption behavioral process of people across the world. While, this pandemic made consumers learn to improvise and develop new consumption behavioral habits, scholars argue that even if consumers go back to their earlier habits, it is likely to be in line to the current 'new normal' ways when shopping and purchasing products and services (Mehta *et al.*, 2020; Sheth, 2020). Also, the changing demographics, government policies that discourage or encourage consumption (compulsory to wearing masks, etc.) and technology advances (e.g., digital technology like mobile, cloud computing, etc.) are likely to be major contextual forces in the development of new habits and consumption behavior in the future, opined Sheth (2020). Furthermore, Mehta *et al.* (2020) suggest that the next normal could be explored through adopting a spiritual approach in understanding consumer behavior; along with keeping in mind the drivers of economies of consumption, saving and health.

Research scholars argue that consumer behavior varies significantly from place to place depending on the cultures, geographies, location, etc. Usage of AI-augmented chatbots can help in creating valued customer experiences (Sidaoui *et al.*, 2020), and now with the pandemic spread, consumption behavior has become more complex especially with consumer migration to virtual world and exposure to newer influences. Hence, it is likely that consumers will adopt new habits and patterns of behavior for a longer time, in response to the multiple waves of the pandemic (Puttaiah *et al.*, 2020). Meanwhile, a recent study (Radojeviíc *et al.*, 2021) observed that health consciousness and healthy lifestyle can influence food consumption behavior. Furthermore, given that a significant proportion of consumers are moving towards buying healthier and more sustainable food, Borsellino *et al.* (2020) suggested this be treated as an opportunity by manufacturers and retailers to explore re-engineering of the agro-food market towards transition and adoption of more sustainable supply and production patterns.

While Covid-19 has initiated a conscious, healthier food consumption behavior among people, given the unprecedented situation of multiple waves of the pandemic that seem to be affecting people across countries is a call upon marketers to analyze the changed food consumption pattern of their market and work out suitable food marketing strategies to cater to the modified consumer behavior, opined Sheth (2020). Meanwhile, changes in the market dynamics due to the Covid-19 pandemic that led to a forced/modified consumption behavior needs to be explored from a post Covid-19 scenario, which may throw up possibilities of new consumer segments exhibiting new behaviors in the future, argued Mehta *et al.*

(2020). This is suggestive of a research gap that needs to examine the modified consumption behavior in the light of the 'new normal', and its likelihood to continue in the future. Extending this to food behavior would raise the research question on identifying which variables (antecedents) led to changed food behaviors and how to channelize the behavior intentions to create impact from a long term perspective? Information in this context would be useful to work out marketing strategies that create awareness, for bettering communications, and for the promotion of food products, which would help in building up effectiveness in the long run.

Prior research scholars have used different theories like the theory of reasoned action (e.g. Petrovici *et al.* (2004), and Randall and Sanjur's (1981) food preference model (as cited in Mak *et al.*, 2012) to determine variables/factors influencing consumers' food choice behavior. Going by these studies, we propose to examine antecedents that influenced food consumption during the Covid-19 pandemic and consumers' intention to continue to engage in such behavior, and also determine whether these could be extended to create a positive impact in the long-term consumption pattern. Accordingly, this study has attempted to build upon the Theory of Planned Behavior (TPB)(Ajzen, 1991; 2020) and proposes a framework suggesting marketers to evaluate peoples' food consumption behavior by looking into antecedents that lead to the purchase and consumption of healthier food products, and also to examine whether intention to engage in such behaviors could be explored from a sustainable, customer centric perspective. This line of contention is duly supported by prior studies which used the theory of Reasoned Action/TPB to analyze different aspects of marketing (Shin *et al.*, 2020; Yakasai & Jusoh, 2015). So, also are researchers who noted consumer's emotions (Jin *et al.*, 2020), as well as attitudes are intention-driven and affect their purchase intention (Woo & Kim, 2019), and emotional values affect consumer trust, and motivates purchase intention (Watanabe *et al.*, 2020), and others who claim that action and motivational factors (categorized into symbolic, obligatory, contrast, extension, and pleasure) affect food consumption (Mak *et al.*, 2012).

Thus, the main aims of this study are: (1) To provide a general review of the literature on food choice behavior that adds to the existing knowledge of how food consumption behavior is currently determined; as well as to address knowledge gap from a post Covid-19 effectiveness perspective, and (2) To apply the TPB by synthesizing the literature review themes into proposing an integrated framework; indicating the linkages between the antecedents, consumers' behaviors and the consequences or behavior intentions.

The chapter is structured as follows: in the following section, under literature review a brief on food consumption behavior and its antecedents are discussed. In the section which follows this, effectiveness on food consumption behavior through application of the TPB is first examined, and then the conceptual framework suggesting extending the TPB to influence the behavioral intention in the context of healthier food consumption behavior is proposed. Thereafter in the last section, the study's conclusion is drawn, the implications for both theory and practice are presented, and finally limitations that lead to avenues for future research are discussed.

LITERATURE REVIEW

Food Consumption Behavior

Food as a basic human need is a vital source of nutrition and energy. Food consumption plays an important role in the development of a healthy lifestyle as well as in the creation of hedonic experiences. Analyzing of food consumption behavior, involves a lot of complexity and diversity as it tends to vary depending upon the social and cultural influences that exist in regions across the world. Given the involvement of these influences in food choice and consumption decisions, Steenkamp (1993) had suggested the need to draw insights from a wide range of science and social science disciplines, such as food science, nutrition, medicine, psychology, physiology, psychophysics, sociology, economics, marketing, and anthropology. In fact, prior studies on food consumption behavior have also supported this. For instance, cultural, socio-economic, demographic, consumer attitudes, consumption habits, amongst others influence wine consumption and consumers' preferences (Gunay & Baker, 2011), socio-cultural and psychological factors (e.g., cultural/religious influences, socio-demographic factors, food-related personality traits, exposure effect/past experience, and motivational factors) can impact tourist food consumption (Mak *et al.*, 2012), the interplay of diverse fields on the consumer behavior can affect consumers' choice of food (Nair & Maram, 2014), food consumption behavior get influenced by a variety of factors including individual (cooking skills, taste of food, knowledge, etc.), societal (social norms and peer pressure), university related (campus culture and frequency of examination), and environmental factors (cooking resources, food prices, etc.) (Kabir *et al.*, 2018), social value plays a key role in influencing consumer attitudes and intention to purchase green food products (Woo & Kim, 2019), in-store attributes and consumer demographics influence food and grocery shopping behavior (Nair, 2018b; Nair & Shams, 2020). Apart from the above factors, researchers noted certain key external influences related to the food itself (food-attributes and food values) could affect consumers' food decisions (Martinez-Ruiz & Gómez-Cantó, 2016).

Consuming food is important for all human beings, and, given that there are various factors which affect consumers' food purchase behavior/decisions, an understanding of the consumption pattern of one's target market would help organizations to work out suitable food marketing strategies. Moreover, in the aftermath of the Covid-19 pandemic spread, the imposition of lockdowns and the social distancing practices that are in vogue currently, has resulted in disruption of existing food purchase habits and the related shopping behavior (Borsellino *et al.*, 2020; FoodMatters, 2020; Sheth, 2020; UNCAD, 2020). Indeed, the Covid-19 pandemic has driven consumers to opt for healthier and more sustainable food patterns (Murphy *et al.*, 2021; Borsellino *et al.*, 2020).Another visible impact of the Covid-19 pandemic spread is that e-grocery shopping has increased (Asti *et al.*, 2021), with customers shopping for food products at e-grocers operating multichannel supermarkets (Badenhop & Frasquet, 2021). Interestingly, while the Covid-19 pandemic forced customers to opt for online shopping, research by GlobalData revealed that around 68% of shoppers in the U.S. stated they would be using curbside pickup at stores more in the future, and about 60% stated they would collect more of their online purchases from inside stores (Repko & Thomas, 2020). This implies that in the future, customers are likely to look for phygital shopping experiences. Hence, the post COVID-19 scenario will need retailers to blend these two channels and provide new customer centric experiences. Additionally, Sheth (2020) noted that while prevailing marketing strategies focused on research areas such as social media, emerging markets, and societal marketing, the new promising frontiers of research is definitely going to be on 'customer centricity'. So, if one were to delve on this perspective in the post Covid-19 pandemic situation, it implies the need of research to examine the influence of 'customer centric' factors that impacted people, modified their food consumption behavior and their likely or proposed behavior in the future.

Antecedents to Food Consumption Behavior

Given the importance of food consumption and its outcomes, literature review indicated prior research scholars who focused on understanding consumers' behavior and attitudes and/or perceptions towards consuming food products (Deshpande *et al.*, 2009; Mak *et al.*, 2012; Nair & Maram, 2014; Nair and Shams 2020, etc.) In fact, some scholars attempted to understand the antecedents that influence food behavior, and how these have impacted consumers' responses towards food consumption behavior. For instance, consumer attitudes towards the food (Khalek, 2014; Nystranda & Olsen, 2020; Torri *et al.*, 2020) as well as their personality traits and knowledge can affect their food-choice decisions and behavior (Ardebili & Rickertsen, 2020). Meanwhile, the Covid-19 pandemic spread has brought about changes in peoples' attitudes with a growing awareness on the need to consume healthy food and alongside consumers are displaying willingness to change their food habits too (Borsellino *et al.*, 2020; Danley, 2020; Demarest, 2020). Additionally, researchers like White *et al.* (2020) found cognitive processes (e.g., attention, language, memory, learning, and metacognition) could affect human perceptions and their responses to food. Hence, the following research proposition:

RP1: *Psychological factors affect consumers' responsiveness in food consumption behavior*

Since a long time, research scholars have referred to the role of attitudes and beliefs in human behavior (Fishbein & Ajzen 1975), and that attitudinal factors and external conditions acting in combination can influence human behavior (Guagnano *et al.*, 1995). According to Fishbein and Ajzen (1975), attitudes are determined by individual's salient beliefs, and his behavioral intention depends upon prior formation of the attitude and the subjective probability (or norms) of the particular beliefs. For instance, interaction of experiential attitude and norms have a positive association with green travel intention, whereas, interaction of instrumental attitude and norms have a negative association with green travel intention (Ru *et al.*, 2018). Similarly, prior studies related to food consumption behavior found beliefs and attitudes affected behavioral intentions. For instance, Aikman *et al.* (2006) suggested the need to understand how attitudes can influence food choice decisions and behavior, Minbashrazgah *et al.* (2017) found consumer's level of trust, food beliefs and perceived environmental responsibility had a positive impact on green purchase intention. This implies that - more positively a person regards a certain behavior or action and, this behavior is perceived as being important for human beings or the society (e.g. environment friendly), the more likely he/she is to form intentions to engage in such behaviors. Furthermore, a recent study also found that attitude, subjective norms, and perceived behavioral control can be helpful in the prediction of purchase intention (Lim & An, 2021). Hence, the following research proposition:

RP2: *Consumer's beliefs and attitudes can influence intentions affecting consumption behavior.*

Typically, the culture and the society in which people live, the kind of contact these individuals have with one another and the social groups they interact with, etc., influence their food choices. Indeed, since long, researchers have been referring to the influence of socio-cultural factors such as culture, family, peers, amongst others on the food behavior. Musaiger (1993) had found that socio-cultural factors including beliefs, religion, food preferences, education, gender discrimination, and women employment impacted food consumption patterns in Arab countries. Verstraeten *et al.* (2014) noted inter-related factors such as the individual's personal, culture-specific key factors (perceived food safety, lack of self-control, financial autonomy, habit's strength) and changes in socio-cultural environment (socio-economic status and setting) can influence food eating behaviors. Woo and Kim (2019) observed social value was a key variable that influenced consumers' attitudes and intention to purchase green food products. And, Povey *et al*. (2000) found perceived social support moderated the relationship between perceived behavioral control and intention, as well as the relationship between attitude and intention for healthy food consumption. Hence, the following research proposition:

RP3: *Socio-cultural variables can affect decisions concerning healthy food behavior intention.*

The TPB can be used to examine the motivation of people's intention and behavior, as well as to explain the determinants and antecedents of purchase intentions (Ajzen & Manstead, 2007; Fishbein & Ajzen, 1975). In fact, going by the assumption that intentions and behavioral processes of change are a part of the larger goal construct, Bandura (2004) had asserted that goals include the motivation (e.g., intention) to enact the goal and the strategies used to engage in the behavior. In today's globalized world, there is a need to gain a broader understanding on consumers' motivation and the characteristics of their decision-making process so that it facilitates effective customer engagement, observed Suki (2017). Consumer emotions' (Jin *et al*., 2020), as well as emotional values affect consumer trust, and motivates purchase intention (Watanabe *et al*., 2020). Consumer motivations encompassing both environmental and hedonic dimensions can trigger green purchase intentions noted, Choi and Johnson (2019). Hence, the following research proposition:

RP4: *Emotions, Motivations affect peoples' intentions as well as the subsequent behaviors.*

Prior research studies have also referred to the influence of demographics on behavioral intentions and food consumption behaviors. Demographics such as education have a positive influence on consumer's attitude towards buying of organic food (Paul & Rana, 2012). While, age (Nair & Shams, 2020) as well as gender, education and annual household income affect the purchase of food and groceries (Nair, 2018b). Determinants and intentions to engage in collaborative consumption can vary based on certain demographics like education, income, etc., observed Lindblom and Lindblom (2018). Gender wise differences were found even though consumers' attitude, subjective norm, and perceived behavioral control significantly influenced their product purchase intention (Beldad & Hegner, 2018). Subjective norms significantly moderated the relationship between attitudes and buying intention and between perceived behavior control and buying intention (Al-Swidi *et al*., 2014). Hence, the following research proposition:

RP5: *Demographics can affect the impact of subjective norm on purchase intentions.*

THEORY OF PLANNED BEHAVIOR AND FOOD CONSUMPTION

The TPB is one of the most widely employed social-cognitive theories to understand the relationship between intentions and behavior. According to this theory, 'attitude,' is defined as "the degree to which a person has a favorable or an unfavorable evaluation of the behavior in question" (Ajzen, 1991, p. 188) and can encompass an individual's behavioral intentions (which may be either positive or negative), after assessing these to be affective (for example, pleasant or unpleasant) and instrumental (for example, easy or difficult) (Baker & White, 2010).This theory also refers to one's behavioral intention e.g. a person's willingness or the amount of effort he/she is willing to exert to attain a goal (Ajzen, 1991), and is said to be a very prominent predictor of one's behavior too. Using of the TPB in food consumption is illustrated in Figure 1. In this context, other researchers have also supported this theory. For example, Kim and Han (2010) asserted that intention is related to one's relative strength of purpose in order to perform certain behavior, while, Verma and Chandra (2018) claim attitude positively affect young consumers' intention to visit green hotels.

Figure 1. Using the Theory of Planned Behavior in food consumption

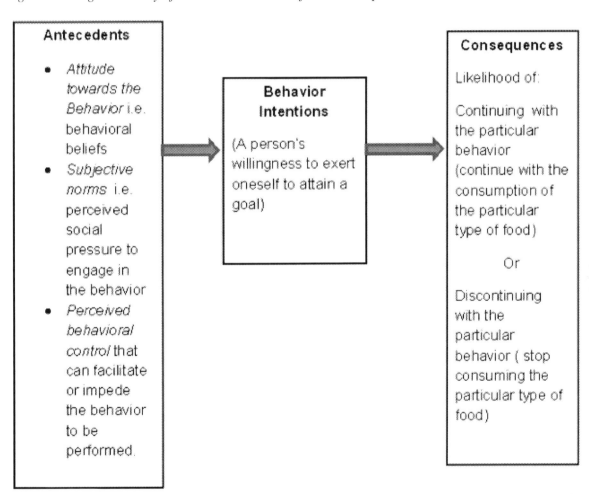

(Source: Adapted from: Ajzen, I. 2020, The theory of planned behavior: Frequently asked questions Human Behavior and Emerging Technologies)

Given that studies have reported about consumers having acquired new habits and shopping behavior due to the Covid-19 pandemic (Sheth, 2020) which has also affected their food consumption behavior

(Food Insight, 2020; FoodMatters, 2020), the current study intends to build upon the TPB in the context of food behavior and examine it with a futuristic behavioral intention perspective. Also, variables such as personality traits, demographic characteristics, life values etc., could be considered as background factors that indirectly influence intentions and behavior, stated Ajzen (2020).Giving due consideration to this, and building up on the TPB we have proposed a framework suggesting that food behavior acquired during the Covid-19 pandemic, triggered by the *Antecedents* (attitudes or beliefs and evaluation of the attributes and outcomes, along with the value in consuming the chosen food), *Subjective Norms* (beliefs about whether others are in agreement or disagreement to continue with the food consumption, along with the degree of motivation involved in complying with the broad views), and *Perceived Behavioral Control* (continue with the food choices later on in the future due to knowledge, awareness, health consciousness, etc.) is likely to have an impact on the purchase intentions and food choice behavior of people in the future too. Also, going by previous studies that found attributes and demographics influence food consumption behavior (Mak *et al.*, 2012; Nair & Shams, 2020), we have incorporated these factors into our proposed framework, suggesting these variables could also influence consumers' food purchase intentions. A further consequence suggests using effective communications and promotional programs that help to convert food purchase intentions to actual purchases, and that satisfaction of these could lead to customer loyalty in the long run.

Accordingly, is illustrated the proposed framework (Figure 2), which extends on TPB and recognizes certain antecedents, subjective norms and perceived behavioral control factors that affect food consumption behavior. We argue that the healthy food choice behavior displayed during the Covid-19 pandemic are shaped on the basis of certain antecedents, subjective norms, perceived behavior controls, food/store-attributes and socio-demographics that create certain consequences, visible in their behavioral intentions in food consumption, and eventually purchase satisfaction could lead to customer loyalty in the future.

Previous studies have indeed referred to a link between peoples' attitudes and their subsequent food behaviors. For instance, Aikman *et al.* (2006) argued the need to develop a better understanding of consumer attitudes (e.g., likes and dislikes), which influence people's behavior and their food choice decisions. Khalek (2014) found young consumers' positive attitude towards halal food influenced its consumption. Woo and Kim (2019) noted that while, conditional values (discounts, promotional incentives, etc.) create positive consumers' attitude, social values influence the purchase intentions of green foods. And, Nystrand and Olsen (2020) found that utilitarian eating values are strongly and positively associated to individuals' attitude towards the consumption of functional foods, whereas, hedonic eating values are less strongly and negatively related to consumer attitude. Thus, it can be inferred that consumers' attitudes, beliefs and values act as antecedents to influence their food consumption behavior.

Many researchers have referred to the influence of social acceptance, and the related motivating factors that affect food consumption intentions and behavior. Higgs and Thomas (2016) argued on social norms that influence eating behavior. Mak *et al.* (2012) in fact, identified five major socio-cultural and psychological factors, namely, cultural/religious influences, socio-demographic factors, food-related personality traits, exposure effect/past experience, and motivational factors (categorized into: symbolic, obligatory, contrast, extension, and pleasure) which influence tourist food consumption. González *et al.* (2019) noted culture, motivational factors and food-related personality traits significantly predict travelers' propensity to consume local foods. Interestingly, Shin *et al.* (2018) observed attitude, subjective norms, etc. can positively impact consumers' intention to visit restaurants offering organic menu, and also that this affected their intentions to purchase state-branded food products (Shin *et al.*, 2020). Thus,

Impact of COVID-19 on Food Consumption and Marketing

Figure 2. Proposed framework: Extending Theory of Planned Behavior to futuristic food behavioral intentions

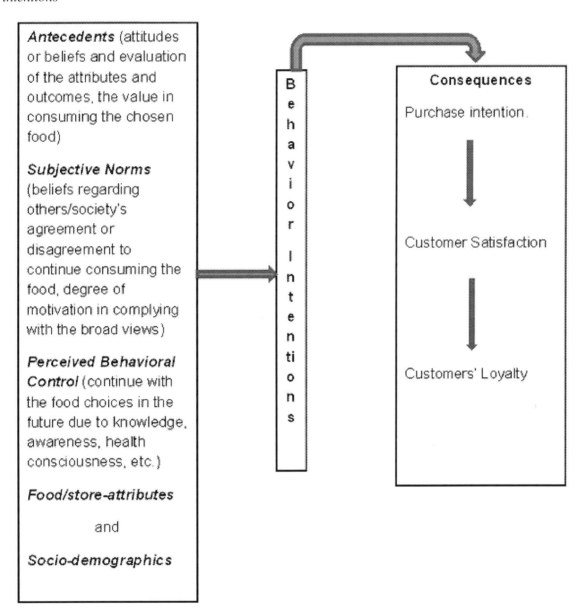

going by prior studies; social and motivational factors can be considered as antecedents that affect food consumption behaviors.

Meanwhile, recent studies found consumers' perceived behavioral control affect their food behavior intentions. Pacho (2020) observed knowledge about organic food and health consciousness can indirectly affect the relationship between attitude, subjective norms, and intention to buy it. While, Aliaga-Ortega *et al*. (2019) claim nutritional warning (NW) labels on processed foods influence consumer attitudes and affect their perceived behavioral control visible in their behavior e.g., either to choose or to eliminate processed food consumption. Thus, it can be stated that consumers' behavioral control affects their food choice behavior.

Additionally, in food consumption research, socio-demographics are recognized as factors that explain the variations in food consumption behavior (González et al., 2019; Mak et al., 2012; Nair, 2018b; Nair & Shams, 2020). For instance, gender wise differences are observed in the impact of subjective norms on purchase intentions (Beldad & Hegner, 2018), socio-economic characteristics of consumers' influences organic food purchase decisions (Radojevi´c, et al., 2021). Changing demographics (age and family/ household size) are contextual forces (due to Covid-19) that may result in the development of new habits and/or giving up old consumption habits claims Sheth (2020).

So, the discussion thus far, and as indicated in the proposed framework (Figure 2) consumer attitude, belief and values, social and motivational factors, perceived behavioral control, and socio-demographic characteristics are seen as antecedents that impact food consumption behavioral intentions. Consumer satisfaction is regarded as a fundamental determinant of the long-term success of any business, and researchers have investigated the impact of consumer satisfaction based on post consumption evaluations such as behavioral and attitudinal loyalty (e.g., Cooil, et al., 2007). Hence, in the proposed framework we argue that marketers must strive to convert the behavior intentions into actual food purchases, and then work towards consumer satisfaction that earns customer loyalty in the long run.

CONCLUSION, IMPLICATIONS, LIMITATIONS AND FUTURE RESEARCH

While food is a basic human need; food consumption behavior is greatly influenced by the interplay of a wide range of science and social science disciplines including food science, psychology, physiology, sociology, marketing, amongst many others. So, gaining an understanding on the factors affecting food behavior will enable food marketers to learn about their market's consumption pattern which helps to work out suitable marketing strategies. Additionally, the current Covid-19 pandemic has brought about changes in the food consumption behavior, and initiated a conscious, healthier food consumption behavior among the people at large. Meanwhile, recent scholars argue that the modified consumption behavior due to Covid-19 throw up possibilities of new consumer segments exhibiting such behaviors in the future (Mehta, et al., 2020; Puttaiah et al., 2020), and that this behavior is accepted as the 'new normal' which is likely to continue; albeit modified by new regulations and procedures in the way consumers shop and buy products and services (Sheth, 2020).

In the light of this situational requirement, to gain an understanding on the antecedents that triggered the modified food consumption, and on how to cater to this changed food pattern in a sustainable manner, the current study suggested a behavioral model perspective that is built upon the TPB. This is in line to prior studies which indicated there were certain antecedents that led to the purchase and consumption of healthier food products during the Covid-19 pandemic spread (e.g., Radojevi´c, et al., 2021; Sheth, 2020). Moreover, with the multiple waves of the pandemic continuing to affect countries across the world, its impact on food consumption behavior, in turn, is very likely to be felt for a longer period; probably even in post Covid-19 scenario. For instance, a Deloitte consumer tracker survey revealed that while 40% of consumers want to buy groceries online, only 29% would like to buy them in-store (Ramanathan, 2020). This implies, food marketers will need to invest on creating hybrid physical and digital (or phygital) store experiences, with the focus being on providing more personalized or customer centric buying experience. A further indication is that food marketers and retailers would need to work out marketing strategies keeping these in minds, as well as from a sustainable, long term perspective.

Applicability of the extension of TPB in food consumption behavior is visible in studies that found food quality attributes elicit customer satisfaction and enhances return visits (Namkung & Jang, 2007), as well as on purchase importance influence on customer satisfaction formation process and their loyalty intentions (Tam, 2011). Furthermore, given that prior studies on food purchase behavior have brought out the link between satisfaction and patronage intentions (Nair, 2018a), the impact of Covid-19 pandemic with consumers' shifting towards purchase of healthier and more sustainable food in the new world of phygital reality needs to be strategically explored. Moreover, amidst phygital reality and the contemporary competitive scenario, food marketers would need to focus on customer centricity, e.g., by keeping customers in the forefront, the entire marketing team should work at creating fundamental beliefs about customer service, customer relationship management, and customer lifetime value. Such moves would foster positive valued customer experiences that can lead to satisfaction and loyalty in the long run. Alongside, food marketers will be required to work for transiting towards more sustainable supply and production patterns, as opined by Borsellino *et al.* (2020), is suggested.

The study provides implications for both theory and practice, which are discussed in detail below:

Implications of the Study

An implication of the study is building upon the TPB to examine the impact of the antecedents on food consumption behavior during the Covid-19 pandemic spread, as well as proposing its scope from a long-term perspective. In fact, going by prior studies that extended the application of the TPB in food consumption (Lim & An, 2021), and other researchers who investigated the role of social norms, personal norms (Higgs & Thomas, 2016; Pacho, 2020), and perceived behavioral control on food consumption (Aliaga-Ortega *et al.*, 2019), we feel that consumers food behavior in the post Covid-19 situation are shaped based on these antecedents, thus, creating respectively certain consequences (e.g., behavioral intentions) that needs to be explored. In that, the Covid-19 pandemic's impact on food-purchasing behavior has indicated a consumer shift towards buying more healthier and sustainable food (Murphy, *et al.*, 2021), which should be strategically exploited by food marketers not only to satisfy this demand but also in transiting towards a more sustainable supply and production pattern (Borsellino *et al.*, 2020). Trip Tripathy (Kaufman Rossin's CEO, Board & Shareholder Business Advisory Services) stated "recent data shows more consumers are shopping and buying online while brick and mortar continues to be an important part of the customer journey for many brands. Thus, omnichannel is here to stay" (DeAngelis, 2021). In this context, a related challenge for marketers will be in figuring out the suitable customer delivery model for catering to such changing behavioral patterns times.

While, Covid-19 has led to dramatic societal shifts affecting changes in consumers' food practices (Eftimov *et al.*, 2020), this has also initiated healthier food consumption behavior (Danley, 2020; Food-Matters, 2020; Food Insights, 2020; Murphy, *et al.*, 2021), but with the occurrences of multiple waves of the pandemic this 'new normal' is here to stay for a longer time too (Puttaiah *et al.*, 2020; Sheth, 2020). Also, now, with consumer acceptance of shopping online as well as at physical stores, they are expecting phygital personalized/customer centric experiences, which need to be explored by the marketers. Furthermore, these situational requirements imply that to gain profitably, food marketers would need to examine how to adopt phygital practices that lead to food consumption satisfaction at all the outlets, and, also can be sustained for a longer time in the future. Thus, future researchers could focus on exploring how food marketers can develop customer centric models (Sheth, 2020), and through engaging with customers in proactive, predictive, and personalized ways provide valued customer centricity experiences which will further help them to create long-term, profitable customer relationships and improve future viability (Komulainen & Saraniemi, 2019).

Another practical implication of the study is that given the influence of consumer demographics and lifestyles of food purchase behavior (e.g., Nair, 2018a; 2018b) food marketers and retailers would need to identify the specific socio-demographics, physiological, psychological, etc. factors (e.g., antecedents) affecting their market's food consumption pattern and work out suitable communications and promotional programs. Furthermore, they should involve and encourage repetitive purchases by consumers through adopting positive habit formation techniques (White *et al.*, 2019), as well as by using trusted, reputable sources of information (or media) to dispel fears/perceived stress on limited access to food as the pandemic spreads (Je˙zewska-Zychowicz *et al.*, 2020). Thus, in short, the management should aim at involving and sharing value filled information on their food product and service offerings; prompting consumers who have shifted towards healthy food patterns during the Covid-19 pandemic to continue with the same for a longer period of time.

Another implication for the management is that consumers who have now learnt to order food online may also opt for combining this with offline shopping once things get back to normal. So as to help them in this new behavioral journey, the management must make strategic investments in technological inputs usage to create lasting post-purchase customer experiences, prompting customers to remain connected to their food brands in the future too. This may call for marketers to provide phygital experience, e.g., they would need to adopt a multichannel approach and use marketing automation strategies and digital technologies such as artificial intelligence, chatbot and augmented reality (Sidaoui *et al.*, 2020), for this purpose.

Limitations and Recommendations for Future Research

While secondary data (review of previous literature) has helped in providing insights on the different aspects of food consumption behavior during the covid-19, it is not exhaustive. Empirical studies providing deeper insights regarding the influence of the antecedents (prevalent during pre Covid-19 times) and its effect on the conscious, healthy food consumption behavior in the post Covid-19 times, needs to be explored. Such studies throwing up insights on the specific aspects and/or factors that encourage consumers to continue or discontinue their food consuming patterns in the future, could be examined by future researchers.

When things get back to normal in the future and people start traveling to other places, a challenge for the hospitality industry will be to develop innovative ways through adoption of newer technologies which would facilitate work, travel and food consumption in a more convenient manner. Given that work from home has gained popularity during the Covid-19 pandemic spread; how newer technologies can aid in providing convenience at combining work, travel and food consumption is an area which needs be explored.

REFERENCES

Aikman, S. N., Min, K. E., & Graham, D. (2006). Food attitudes, eating behavior, and the information underlying food attitudes. *Appetite*, *47*(1), 111–114. doi:10.1016/j.appet.2006.02.004 PMID:16621134

Ajzen, I. (1991). The theory of planned behavior. *Organizational Behavior and Human Decision Processes*, *50*(2), 179–211. doi:10.1016/0749-5978(91)90020-T

Ajzen, I. (2020). The theory of planned behavior: Frequently asked questions. *Human Behavior and Emerging Technologies*, *2*(4), 314–324. doi:10.1002/hbe2.195

Ajzen, I., & Manstead, A. S. (2007). Changing health-related behaviors: An approach based on the theory of planned behavior. In M. Hewstone, J. B. F. de Wit, K. van den Bos, H. Schut, & M. Stroebe (Eds.), *The Scope of Social Psychology: Theory and Applications* (pp. 43–63). Psychology Press.

Al-Swidi, A., Mohammed Rafiul Huque, S., Haroon Hafeez, M., & Noor Mohd Shariff, M. (2014). The role of subjective norms in theory of planned behavior in the context of organic food consumption. *British Food Journal*, *116*(10), 1561–1580. doi:10.1108/BFJ-05-2013-0105

Aliaga-Ortega, L., Adasme-Berríos, C., Méndez, C., Soto, C., & Schnettler, B. (2019). Processed food choice based on the theory of planned behavior in the context of nutritional warning labels. *British Food Journal*, *121*(12), 3266–3280. doi:10.1108/BFJ-10-2018-0695

Ardebili, A. T., & Rickertsen, K. (2020). Personality traits, knowledge, and consumer acceptance of genetically modified plant and animal products. *Food Quality and Preference*, *80*, 103825. doi:10.1016/j.foodqual.2019.103825

Asti, W. P., Handayani, P. W., & Azzahro, F. (2021). Influence of Trust, Perceived Value, and Attitude on Customers' Repurchase Intention for E-Grocery. *Journal of Food Products Marketing*, *27*(3), 157–171. doi:10.1080/10454446.2021.1922325

Badenhop, A., & Frasquet, M. (2021). Online Grocery Shopping at Multichannel Supermarkets: The Impact of Retailer Brand Equity. *Journal of Food Products Marketing*, *27*(2), 89–104. doi:10.1080/10454446.2021.1894296

Baker, R. K., & White, K. M. (2010). Predicting adolescents' use of social networking sites from an extended theory of planned behaviour perspective. *Computers in Human Behavior*, *26*(6), 1591–1597. doi:10.1016/j.chb.2010.06.006

Bandura, A. (2004). Health promotion by social cognitive means. *Health Education & Behavior*, *31*(2), 143–164. doi:10.1177/1090198104263660 PMID:15090118

Beldad, A., & Hegner, S. (2018). Determinants of Fair-Trade Product Purchase Intention of Dutch Consumers According to the Extended Theory of Planned Behaviour, The Moderating Role of Gender. *Journal of Consumer Policy*, *41*(3), 191–210. doi:10.100710603-018-9384-1

Borsellino, V., Kaliji, S. A., & Schimment, E. (2020). COVID-19 Drives Consumer Behaviour and Agro-Food Markets towards Healthier and More Sustainable Patterns. *Sustainability*, *12*(20), 8366. doi:10.3390u12208366

Choi, D., & Johnson, K. K. P. (2019). Influences of environmental and hedonic motivations on intention to purchase green products: An extension of the theory of planned behavior. *Sustainable Production and Consumption*, *18*, 145–155. doi:10.1016/j.spc.2019.02.001

Cooil, B., Keiningham, T. L., Aksoy, L., & Hsu, M. (2007). A Longitudinal Analysis of Customer Satisfaction and Share of Wallet: Investigating the Moderating Effect of Customer Characteristics. *Journal of Marketing*, *71*(1), 67–83. doi:10.1509/jmkg.71.1.067

Danley, S. (2020 December 6). Eight in ten consumers changed their eating habits due to COVID-19. *Food Business News*. Available at: https://www.foodbusinessnews.net/articles/16226-eight-in-ten-consumers-changed-their-eating-habits-due-to-covid-19

DeAngelis, S. (2021 May 24). *The Changing Face of Retail*. Available at: https://enterrasolutions.com/blog/the-changing-face-of-retail/

Demarest, A. A. (2020 June 10). New Survey Reveals Covid-19's Impact on American Food Habits. *Forbes*. Available at: https://www.forbes.com/sites/abigailabesamis/2020/06/10/new-survey-reveals-covid-19s-impact-on-american-food-habits/?sh=18697fdf6a77

Deshpande, S., Basil, M. D., & Basil, D. Z. (2009). Factors Influencing Healthy Eating Habits among College Students: An Application of the Health Belief Model. *Health Marketing Quarterly*, *26*(2), 145–164. doi:10.1080/07359680802619834 PMID:19408181

Eftimov, T., Popovski, G., Petković, M., Seljak, B. K., & Dragi Kocev, D. (2020). COVID-19 pandemic changes the food consumption patterns. *Trends in Food Science & Technology*, *104*, 268–272. doi:10.1016/j.tifs.2020.08.017 PMID:32905099

Fishbein, M., & Ajzen, I. (1975). *Belief, Attitude, Intention, and Behavior: An Introduction to Theory and Research*. Addison-Wesley.

Food Insight. (2020 April 14). Consumer Survey: COVID-19's Impact on Food Purchasing, Eating Behaviors and Perceptions of Food Safety. *Food Insight*. Available at: https://foodinsight.org/consumer-survey-covid-19s-impact-on-food-purchasing/

FoodMatters. (2020 June 4). COVID-19 is changing consumer behaviour. *FoodMatters*. Available at: https://www.foodmatters.co.uk/industry-insight/covid-19-is-changing-consumer-behaviour/

González, A. F., Curtis, C., Washburn, I. J., & Shirsat, A. R. (2019). Factors in tourists' food decision processes: A US-based case study. *Journal of Tourism Analysis: Revista de Análisis Turístico*, *27*(1), 2–19. doi:10.1108/JTA-01-2019-0002

Guagnano, G. A., Stern, P. C., & Dietz, T. (1995). Influences on Attitude-Behavior Relationships: A Natural Experiment with Curbside Recycling. *Environment and Behavior*, *27*(5), 699–718. doi:10.1177/0013916595275005

Gunay, G. N., & Baker, M. J. (2011). The factors influencing consumers' behaviour on wine consumption in the Turkish wine market. *EuroMed Journal of Business*, *6*(3), 324–334. doi:10.1108/14502191111170150

Higgs, S., & Thomas, J. (2016). Social influences on eating. *Current Opinion in Behavioral Sciences*, *9*, 1–6. doi:10.1016/j.cobeha.2015.10.005

Jeżewska-Zychowicz, M., Plichta, M., & Królak, M. (2020). Consumers' Fears Regarding Food Availability and Purchasing Behaviors during the COVID-19 Pandemic: The Importance of Trust and Perceived Stress. *Nutrients*, *12*(9), 2852. doi:10.3390/nu12092852 PMID:32957585

Jin, H., Lin, Z., & McLeay, F. (2020). Negative emotions, positive actions: Food safety and consumer intentions to purchase ethical food in China. *Food Quality and Preference*, *85*, 103981. doi:10.1016/j.foodqual.2020.103981

Kabir, A., Miah, S., & Islam, A. (2018). Factors influencing eating behavior and dietary intake among resident students in a public university in Bangladesh: A qualitative study. *PLoS One*, *13*(6), e0198801. Advance online publication. doi:10.1371/journal.pone.0198801 PMID:29920535

Khalek, A. A. (2014). Young consumers' attitude towards halal food outlets and JAKIM's halal certification in Malaysia. *Procedia: Social and Behavioral Sciences*, *121*, 26–34. doi:10.1016/j.sbspro.2014.01.1105

Kim, Y., & Han, H. (2010). Intention to pay conventional-hotel prices at a green hotel – a modification of the theory of planned behavior. *Journal of Sustainable Tourism*, *18*(8), 1014–1037. doi:10.1080/09669582.2010.490300

Komulainen, H., & Saraniemi, S. (2019). Customer centricity in mobile banking: A customer experience perspective. *International Journal of Bank Marketing*, *37*(5), 1082–1102. doi:10.1108/IJBM-11-2017-0245

Lim, H.-R., & An, S. (2021). Intention to purchase wellbeing food among Korean consumers: An application of the Theory of Planned Behavior. *Food Quality and Preference*, *88*, 104101. doi:10.1016/j.foodqual.2020.104101 PMID:33071469

Lindblom, A., & Lindblom, T. (2018). Applying the Extended Theory of Planned Behavior to Predict Collaborative Consumption Intentions. In A. Smedlund, A. Lindblom, & L. Mitronen (Eds.), *Collaborative Value Co-creation in the Platform Economy. Translational Systems Sciences, 11*. Springer. doi:10.1007/978-981-10-8956-5_9

Liu, A.-J., Li, J., & Gómez, M. I. (2020). Factors Influencing Consumption of Edible Insects for Chinese Consumers. *Insects*, *11*(1), 10. doi:10.3390/insects11010010 PMID:31861955

Mak, A. H. N., Lumbers, M., Eves, A., & Chang, R. C. Y. (2012). Factors influencing tourist food consumption. *International Journal of Hospitality Management*, *31*(3), 928–936. doi:10.1016/j.ijhm.2011.10.012

Martínez-Ruiz, M. P., & Gómez-Cantó, C. M. (2016). Key External Influences Affecting Consumers' Decisions Regarding Food. *Frontiers in Psychology*, *7*. Advance online publication. doi:10.3389/fpsyg.2016.01618 PMID:27803686

Mehta, S., Saxena, T., & Purohit, N. (2020). The New Consumer Behaviour Paradigm amid COVID-19: Permanent or Transient? *Journal of Health Management*, *22*(2), 291–301. doi:10.1177/0972063420940834

Minbashrazgah, M. M., Maleki, F., & Torabi, M. (2017). Green chicken purchase behavior: The moderating role of price transparency. *Management of Environmental Quality*, *28*(6), 902–916. doi:10.1108/MEQ-12-2016-0093

Murphy, B., Benson, T., McCloat, A., Mooney, E., Elliott, C., Dean, M., & Lavelle, F. (2021). Changes in Consumers' Food Practices during the COVID-19 Lockdown, Implications for Diet Quality and the Food System: A Cross-Continental Comparison. *Nutrients*, *13*(1), 20. doi:10.3390/nu13010020 PMID:33374619

Musaiger, A. O. (1993). Socio-Cultural and Economic Factors Affecting Food Consumption Patterns in the Arab Countries. *Journal of the Royal Society of Health*, *113*(2), 68–74. doi:10.1177/146642409311300205 PMID:8478894

Nair, S. R. (2018a). Analyzing the relationship between store attributes, satisfaction, patronage-intention and lifestyle in food and grocery store choice behavior. *International Journal of Retail & Distribution Management*, *46*(1), 70–89. doi:10.1108/IJRDM-06-2016-0102

Nair, S. R. (2018b). Consumption dynamics and demographics effect on food and grocery shopping behaviour. *IIMS Journal of Management Science*, *9*(2), 137–154. doi:10.5958/0976-173X.2018.00013.1

Nair, S. R., & Maram, H. K. (2014). Consumer Behavior in Choice of Food and Branding. *The Future of Entrepreneurship, 7th Annual Conference of the EuroMed Academy of Business*.

Nair, S.R., & Shams, R.S.M. (2020). Impact of store-attributes on food and grocery shopping behavior: insights from an emerging market context. *EuroMed Journal of Business,* *16*(3), 324-343. doi.10.1108/EMJB-10-2019-0128 doi:10.1108/EMJB-10-2019-0128

Namkung, Y., & Jang, S. (2007). Does Food Quality Really Matter in Restaurants? Its Impact on Customer Satisfaction and Behavioral Intentions. *Journal of Hospitality & Tourism Research (Washington, D.C.)*, *31*(3), 387–409. doi:10.1177/1096348007299924

Nystrand, B. T., & Olsen, S. O. (2020). Consumers' attitudes and intentions toward consuming functional foods in Norway. *Food Quality and Preference*, *80*, 103827. doi:10.1016/j.foodqual.2019.103827

Pacho, F. (2020). What influences consumers to purchase organic food in developing countries? *British Food Journal*, *122*(12), 3695–3709. doi:10.1108/BFJ-01-2020-0075

Paul, J., & Rana, J. (2012). Consumer behavior and purchase intention for organic food. *Journal of Consumer Marketing*, *29*(6), 412–422. doi:10.1108/07363761211259223

Petrovici, D. A., Ritson, C., & Ness, M. (2004). The Theory of Reasoned Action and Food Choice. *Journal of International Food & Agribusiness Marketing*, *16*(1), 59–87. doi:10.1300/J047v16n01_05

Povey, R., Conner, M., Sparks, P., Rhiannon, J., & Shepherd, R. (2000). The theory of planned behaviour and healthy eating: Examining additive and moderating effects of social influence variables. *Psychology & Health*, *14*(6), 991–1006. doi:10.1080/08870440008407363 PMID:22175258

Puttaiah, M. H., Raverkar, A. K., & Avramakis, E. (2020 December 10). *All change: how COVID-19 is transforming consumer behaviour*. Available at: https://www.swissre.com/institute/research/topics-and-risk-dialogues/health-and-longevity/covid-19-and-consumer-behaviour.html

Radojevi'c, V., Tomaš Simin, M., Glavaš Trbi'c, D., & Mili'c, D. (2021). A Profile of Organic Food Consumers—Serbia Case-Study. *Sustainability*, *13*(1), 131. doi:10.3390u13010131

Ramanathan, A. (2020 September 30). Elevating consumer experience in a phygital world. *Retail News*. Available at: https://retail.economictimes.indiatimes.com/news/industry/elevating-consumer-experience-in-a-phygital-world/78406271

Repko, M., & Thomas, L. (2020 September 29). 6 ways the coronavirus pandemic has forever altered the retail landscape. *CNBC*. Available at: https://www.cnbc.com/2020/09/29/how-coronavirus-pandemic-forever-altered-retail.html

Ru, X., Wang, S., Chen, Q., & Yan, S. (2018). Exploring the interaction effects of norms and attitudes on green travel intention: An empirical study in eastern China. *Journal of Cleaner Production, 197*(Part 1), 1317–1327. doi:10.1016/j.jclepro.2018.06.293

Sheth, J. (2020). Impact of Covid-19 on consumer behavior: Will the old habits return or die? *Journal of Business Research, 117*, 280–283. doi:10.1016/j.jbusres.2020.05.059 PMID:32536735

Shin, Y. H., Im, J., Jung, S. E., & Severt, K. (2018). The theory of planned behavior and the norm activation model approach to consumer behavior regarding organic menus. *International Journal of Hospitality Management, 69*, 21–29. doi:10.1016/j.ijhm.2017.10.011

Shin, Y. H., Jung, S. E., Im, J., & Severt, K. (2020). Applying an extended theory of planned behavior to examine state-branded food product purchase behavior: The moderating effect of gender. *Journal of Foodservice Business Research, 23*(4), 358–375. doi:10.1080/15378020.2020.1770043

Sidaoui, K., Jaakkola, M., & Burton, J. (2020). AI feel you: Customer experience assessment via chatbot interviews. *Journal of Service Management, 31*(4), 745–766. doi:10.1108/JOSM-11-2019-0341

Steenkamp, J.-B. E. M. (1993). Food Consumption Behavior. In E-European Advances in Consumer Research, 1. Provo, UT: Association for Consumer Research.

Suki, N. M. (Ed.). (2017). *The Handbook of Research on Leveraging Consumer Psychology for Effective Customer Engagement*. IGI Global. doi:10.4018/978-1-5225-0746-8

Tam, J. L. M. (2011). The moderating effects of purchase importance in customer satisfaction process: An empirical investigation. *Journal of Consumer Behaviour, 10*(4), 205–215. doi:10.1002/cb.330

Theodoridou, G., Tsakiridou, E., Kalogeras, N., & Mattas, K. (2017). Food Consumption Patterns in Times of Economic Recession. *International Journal of Food and Beverage Manufacturing and Business Models, 2*(1), 56–69. doi:10.4018/IJFBMBM.2017010105

Torri, L., Tuccillo, F., Bonelli, S., Piraino, S., & Leoned, A. (2020). The attitudes of Italian consumers towards jellyfish as novel food. *Food Quality and Preference, 79*, 103782. doi:10.1016/j.foodqual.2019.103782

UNCAD. (2020 October). *COVID-19 and E-commerce, Findings from a survey of online consumers in 9 countries*. Available at https://unctad.org/system/files/official-document/dtlstictinf2020d1_en.pdf

Verma, V. K., & Chandra, B. (2018). An application of theory of planned behavior to predict young Indian consumers' green hotel visit intention. *Journal of Cleaner Production, 172*, 1152–1162. doi:10.1016/j.jclepro.2017.10.047

Verstraeten, R., Van Royen, K., Ochoa-Avilés, A., Penafiel, D., Holdsworth, M., Donoso, S., Maes, L., & Kolsteren, P. (2014). A Conceptual Framework for Healthy Eating Behavior in Ecuadorian Adolescents: A Qualitative Study. *PLoS One*, *9*(1), e87183. doi:10.1371/journal.pone.0087183 PMID:24489865

Watanabe, E. A. M., Alfinito, S., Curvelo, I. C. G., & Hamza, K. M. (2020). Perceived value, trust and purchase intention of organic food: A study with Brazilian consumers. *British Food Journal*, *122*(4), 1070–1184. doi:10.1108/BFJ-05-2019-0363

White, K., Habib, R., David, J., & Hardisty, D. J. (2019). How to SHIFT Consumer Behaviors to be More Sustainable: A Literature Review and Guiding Framework. *Journal of Marketing*, *83*(3), 22–49. doi:10.1177/0022242919825649

White, T. L., Thomas-Danguin, T., Olofsson, J. K., Zucco, G. M., & Prescott, J. (2020). Thought for food: Cognitive influences on chemosensory perceptions and preferences. *Food Quality and Preference*, *79*, 103776. doi:10.1016/j.foodqual.2019.103776

Woo, E., & Kim, Y. G. (2019). Consumer attitudes and buying behavior for green food products: From the aspect of green perceived value (GPV). *British Food Journal*, *121*(2), 320–332. doi:10.1108/BFJ-01-2018-0027

Yakasai, A. B. M., & Jusoh, W. J. W. (2015). Testing the Theory of Planned Behavior in Determining Intention to Use Digital Coupon among University Students. *Procedia Economics and Finance*, *31*, 186–193. doi:10.1016/S2212-5671(15)01145-4

ADDITIONAL READING

Ballina, F. J., Valdes, L., & Del Valle, E. (2019). The Phygital experience in the smart tourism destination. *International Journal of Tourism Cities*, *5*(4), 656–671. doi:10.1108/IJTC-11-2018-0088

Becker, L. (2018). Methodological proposals for the study of consumer experience. *Qualitative Market Research*, *21*(4), 465–490. doi:10.1108/QMR-01-2017-0036

Chaney, D., Lunardo, R., & Mencarelli, R. (2018). Consumption experience: Past, present and future. *Qualitative Market Research*, *21*(4), 402–420. doi:10.1108/QMR-04-2018-0042

Hall, M. C., Prayag, G., Fieger, P., & Dyason, D. (2021). Beyond panic buying: Consumption displacement and COVID-19. *Journal of Service Management*, *32*(1), 113–128. doi:10.1108/JOSM-05-2020-0151

Panzone, L. A., Larcom, S., & She, P.-W. (2021). Estimating the impact of the first COVID-19 lockdown on UK food retailers and the restaurant sector. *Global Food Security*, *28*, 100495. doi:10.1016/j.gfs.2021.100495

KEY TERMS AND DEFINITIONS

Antecedents to Food Behavior: The antecedents to food behavior refer to preceding or preexisting phenomenon, events, variables, factors etc. that affect the food consumption behavior of people.

Behavioral Intentions: Behavioral intentions refer to the perceived likelihood or subjective probability of an individual to engage in a given behavior.

Customer Centricity: This refers to keeping 'the customer' as the focal point for all decisions concerning the delivery of the products, services, and experiences so as to create valued customer experiences, satisfaction, patronage intentions and loyalty in the long run.

Customer Satisfaction: Customer satisfaction is a quality of measurement that determines how happy customers are with a company's products, services, and capabilities.

Extension of Theory of Planned Behavior (TPB): Building upon the TPB which suggests that an individual's intention to perform a given behavior is a function of his or her attitude toward performing the behavior, their beliefs regarding what others think they should do, and their perception of the difficulty or ease in performing that behavior.

Food Consumption Behavior: Food consumption behavior is with reference to peoples' food shopping and consumption patterns which provide key insightful information to food retailers and manufacturers, who can then adapt their food products to suit the changing environment.

Healthy Food Consumption: A balanced intake of food choices that helps one to experience feelings of calmness, high energy levels and alertness.

Impact of COVID-19 on Food Habits and Behavior: This refers to how the COVID-19 pandemic has affected the day-to-day lives and especially the food intake behavior of people across the globe.

Phygital Experience: A marketing strategy that combines both online (digital) and offline (physical) store environments, makes use of technology to create a digital experience that is user-friendly and seamless for the customer.

Societal Shifts and Changes: These are social norms or social movements due to external factors such as environmental shifts or technological innovations, etc. that bring about disruptive shift in the social status quo and behavior.

Sustainable Consumption: Consumer behavior displaying sustained food products choices and patterns of consumption for a longer period of time.

Chapter 5
Organizational Components That Explain the Strategic Direction of SMEs for a New World Economic Order:
The Case of Colombia

Rafael Ignacio Pérez-Uribe
https://orcid.org/0000-0001-9924-6657
Universidad Santo Tomas, Colombia

Carlos Salcedo-Perez
Politecnico Grancolombiano, Colombia

Maria del Pilar Ramirez
https://orcid.org/0000-0002-9462-0897
EAN University, Colombia

ABSTRACT

This chapter aims to show some concepts related to the importance of planning and strategic direction as a fundamental tool for the sustainability of Colombian SMEs for a new world economic order and present the proportionality relationship between this concept of strategic management and the organizational components. Keys that explain it and facilitate its development, considering the modernization model for managing organizations (MMOM), were developed by a group of researchers from the EAN University in Bogotá-Colombia. It was found that market management, organizational culture, organizational structure, and knowledge and innovation management are the components that a high percentage explain the strategic direction of this type of company on which priority improvement and innovation activities should be developed in such a way ways that allow strategies to develop more smoothly to achieve business objectives of effectiveness, efficiency, profitability, and sustainable development.

DOI: 10.4018/978-1-7998-7689-2.ch005

INTRODUCTION

The Colombian economy relies on MSMEs (Micro, small and medium enterprises), as they represent at least 90% of all firms, generate 73% of employment, and represent 53% of the gross production on manufacturing, trade, and services (Ramírez-Garzón, Pérez-Uribe, & Espinoza-Mosqueda, 2020). Their importance has made them the main objective for several industries, and there is an interest to strengthen them due to their role as job creators and their contribution to non-traditional exports (Rodríguez, 2005).

Regardless of their importance, there is still a lot to know about them, especially of microenterprises. There is no consensus yet about the number of microenterprises in Colombia. For this chapter, the authors use the definition of Law 905 issued in 2004, which considers as a micro, small, and medium enterprise any economic activity performed by a person or organization belonging to the entrepreneurial, agricultural, manufacturing, trade, or services sector, either rural or urban (Congress of the Republic of Colombia, 2004).

Since the 70s, strategic planning has been a guide to fulfill organizational goals. At the same time, top managers accepted strategic planning, but mid-managers and employees had lower acceptance levels, considering it another way of filling forms (Castro, 2010; Perez-Uribe, 2018; Ansoff & McDonell, 1990). Since the 80s, strategic management arises as a continuous process to achieve long-term goals stated by enterprises, in which managers and employees participate based on executing strategic plans (Perez-Uribe, 2018).

This research aims to clarify some aspects and definitions of strategic management for a new world economic order, oriented towards the construction, implementation, and feedback of strategic direction in firms. Then, we propose the main topics related to its importance for SMEs (Small and Medium enterprises). Finally, we establish the proportional relationships that may exist in firms by connecting their strategic direction and long-term sustainability for a new world economic order. We will analyze this relationship with the use of the organizational components of the MMOM (Model of Modernization for Organizational Management) (López, Ocampo-Guzmán, & Pérez–Uribe, 2013) applied in 316 Colombian SMEs.

THEORETICAL FRAMEWORK

Hill and Jones (1996), Vidal (2004), Fuentelsaz, Polo and Maicas (2003), Dixit and Nalebuff (1991), Manso (1991), Fernández (2001), Perez-Uribe, Ocampo-Guzmán, Salcedo-Perez, Piñeiro-Cortes, and Ramírez-Salazar (2020), and others, state the importance of implementing strategy as an essential tool of direction in a changing environment. As a result, strategic planning, as a primary methodology of strategic management, is done in the short, mid, and long terms, usually in five stages (Pérez-Uribe, 2018):

1. *Description of the current strategy*. It identifies what the organization has done during the last taxing term regarding vision, mission, purpose, principles, values, objectives, process, and organizational structure to identify and document them in the organization.
2. *Strategic assessment*, with the implementation of internal (strengths and weaknesses) and external (opportunities and threats) analyses.
3. *Strategic conclusions*. They come from the two previous stages by proposing strategic options linked to the objectives set in the organization. These two concepts are prioritized using adequate

tools to define mid-term (2-3 years) goals and corporate or organizational strategies, depending on the focus used.
4. *Strategic direction.* Based on the previous stage, it is proposed by stating the vision, principles, and values (long-term) to align them to goals and strategies (mid-term) of each process to structure the fifth stage.
5. *Less than one-year action plans.* They are composed of activities, responsibilities, budget, due dates, and management indicators to measure periodical advances.

Authors such as Arnaud, Mills, Legrand, and Maton (2016), Certo (2001), Rodríguez (2005), Mintzberg, Quinn, and Ghoshal (2006), CETDIR (2007), and Pérez- Uribe (2018) have highlighted the importance of strategic planning from its position as an administrative function and as an activity that affects all other functions and the organization as a whole.

Valencia-Maldonado and Erazo (2016) state that strategic planning aims to enable a consistent development of organizations and coordinate actions of different areas by using unified criteria to solve conflicts of interest, providing clarity to all organizational departments about the objectives and methods to achieve them. This fact is crucial since it unifies the goals of all areas with those of top management.

The direction that is managed strategically is the focus allowing top management to establish a clear path and to promote those activities necessary. Hence, all the organization moves in the same direction (Camacho, 2002). This methodology provides managers different elements to prepare them to face changes in the environment and all complex situations that managers must deal with (Dabic, González-Loureiro & Furrer, 2014).

Strategic direction or management's primary objective for a new world economic order is to support the manager in the continuous search for methods by developing a set of tools and conceptual maps that allow finding systemic relations that exist between the manager's decisions and organizational performance (Saloner, Shepard, & Podolny, 2005).

The activity of strategic direction is related to setting objectives and goals for the organization and keeping its relations with the environment to achieve its objectives, its coherence with the organizational capabilities, and its awareness of the environment's demands (Ansoff, 1997).

After defining different authors, it is necessary to consider that SMEs must use the strategic direction to remain in business for a new world economic order (Perez-Uribe, Triviño, & Ramírez, 2015). Therefore, the most accurate definition comes from Thompson and Strickland (2004), who define it as the administrative process of creating a strategic vision, set objectives, formulate, introduce, and execute a strategy, and then through time, adjust vision, objectives, procedure, or its execution if necessary.

Strategic direction is essential for the entrepreneurial development of Colombian SMEs for a new world economic order, being a key factor for their sustainability and growth (Pérez-Uribe, Ocampo-Guzmán, Ospina-Bermeo, Cifuentes-Valenzuela, & Cubillos-Leal, 2016). The instrument for SMEs' strategic management is different from that of big enterprises because of technological resources required, language used, and the structure and culture under which it operates (Botero, 2011). All enterprises must buy, transform, sell, and supply products. Therefore, regardless of the differences in size that influence amounts invested, organizational cultures, and other operating differences, there is the possibility to set a general tool for strategic direction (Pérez-Uribe *et al.*, 2016) where corporate social responsibility is of core importance (Saiz-Alvarez, 2018a).

To achieve its potential development, a firm must have a strategy to guide its path and values that identify the company and the mission and vision as part of an adequate and planned direction. This fact will take to the integration of different areas or the organization around a planning system that breaks cultural paradigms, allowing to visualize the way clearly and orderly in which organizational objectives are being achieved, forecasting itself in the future. Thus, according to Perez-Uribe (2018), both mission and vision are directional parameters that clarify the entrepreneurial goals for a new world economic order.

As mentioned in the abstract, this research is based on applying the MMOM in a group of Colombian SMEs. This Model was created by the G3Pymes Research Group of the EAN University. It proposes an improvement path to have better planning and strategies for SMEs to be sustainable by evaluating comprehensively and systematically the state of the firm. This goal is achieved by prioritizing projects or modernization of management and proposing descriptors, activities, and elements needed for establishing the paths to optimize the critical features of the firm (Lopez *et al.*, 2012).

Between 2004-2019 the Model was applied to 316 Colombian SMEs from different industries. The instrument evaluates 16 organizational components to identify managerial modernization and innovation, valued and classified in four different levels, from 1 (basic) to 4 (most advanced) levels. An enterprise reaches level 4 when implementing the best practices, therefore being considered a world-class SME (Arias, Hernández & Pérez-Uribe, 2018) (Figure 1).

Figure 1. Brief of the Model for Organizational Modernization
Source: Adapted from Ramírez-Garzón, et al. (2020, p. 28).

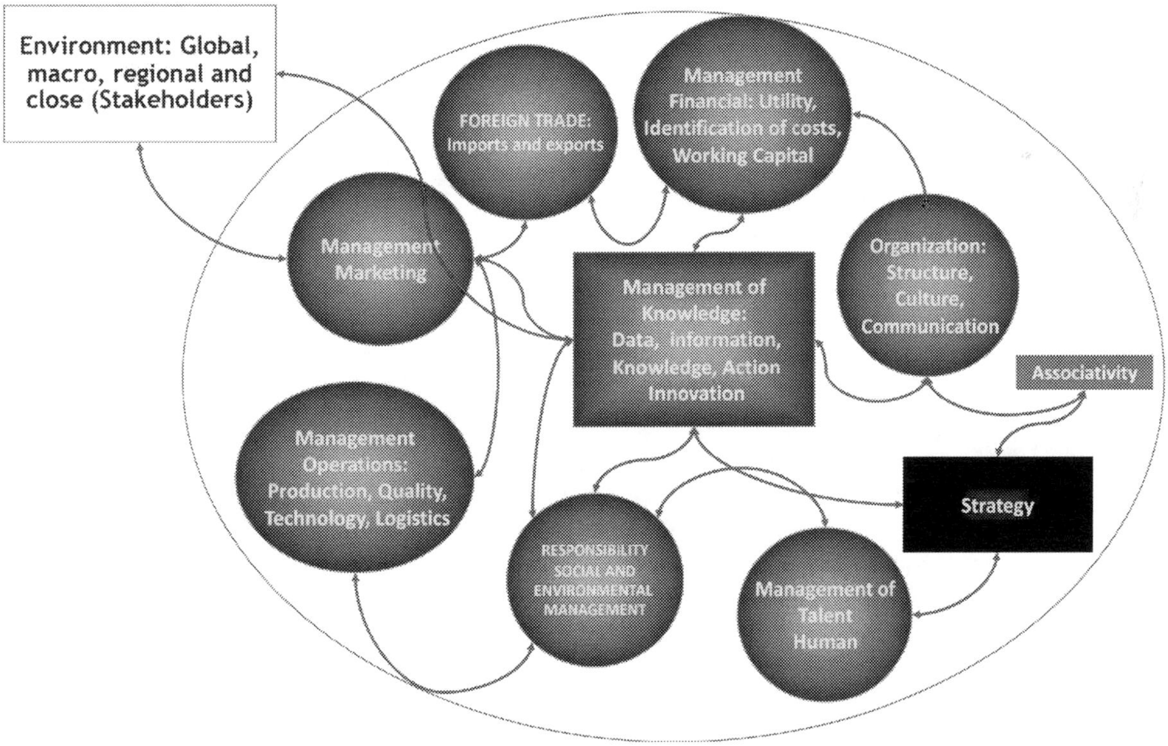

The Model contains graphs for each component and a summary that shows the results of all 16 components. The information obtained with this assessment proposes a path for organizational improvement and innovation to describe the current enterprise's situation, find problems, potentials, and make recommendations to execute plans, evaluate and innovate managerial practices that make sustainable firms (Arias *et al.*, 2018).

RESEARCH PROBLEM AND HYPOTHESIS

Based on the implementation of the Model as of December 2019, imports, we find two scores defined by levels 1 and 2. Level 1 (survival level, the component with the lowest score) is determined when SMEs do not have foreign suppliers. All other components are at level 2 (Figure 2), indicating that the organizational components of management of the SMEs analyzed are at an internal development level.

Figure 2. Stages or levels in the MMOM
Source: Adapted from Ramírez-Garzón, et al. (2020, p. 28).

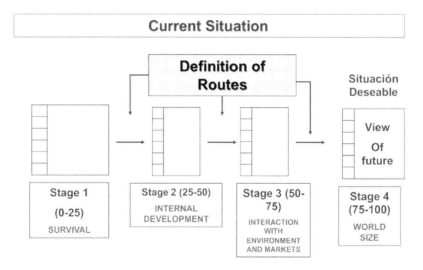

The strategic direction plays a crucial role in developing this type of firm where challenges are to find differences regarding management, criteria, and components to explain entrepreneurial behavior. This result indicates the best strategies according to their characteristics, considering the impact of obstacles when interacting with other firms that employ the best managerial practices. This fact is central to developing Colombian SMEs for a new world economic order (Gálvez, Cuéllar, Restrepo, Bernal, & Cortés, 2014). Therefore, the research hypothesis is:

H1. The strategic direction is essential for the development and sustainability of Colombian SMEs for a new world economic order, which depends on causal organizational components.

METHODOLOGY

Based on the concepts and the application of the MMOM (Applicative 1, version 9E) until 2019, the authors used a statistical analysis model based on multivariate linear regression. In this model, qualitative and quantitative discrete variables were used to describe the influence of organizational components on strategic planning, and therefore, on SMEs' success in the long term.

Thus, 15 variables were chosen. According to the study concept shown in this document, strategic direction, strategic planning, management, and strategic direction are considered proxies. As planning is part of management and the strategic direction is a result of strategic planning (dependent variable), the remaining 14 are independent variables. These independent variables are human resources management, operation management, marketing management, organizational culture, organizational structure, knowledge and innovation management, associativity, logistic management, social and environmental responsibility, international business (imports and exports), technology, communication and information, environmental economic surveillance and analysis, and financial management.

Ten hypothesis tests were conducted, assigning specific weights to each variable to determine which of them have a more decisive influence on strategic direction as deciding factor for SMEs' long-term development. This article shows the results of the tenth test, which results in an equation with the variables that allow a smoother development of strategic direction (Table 1).

Table 1 Analysis of Hypothesis Testing

ANALYSIS	DESCRIPTION
Dependent variable: Strategic direction. Independent variables: marketing management; organizational culture; organizational structure; knowledge and innovation management.	Since the P-value in the ANOVA table is less than 0.05, there is a statistically significant relationship between the variables with a confidence level of 95.0%. The R-Square statistic indicates that the adjusted model explains 76.5122% of the variability in STRATEGIC DIRECTION. The adjusted R-Squared statistic, which is more appropriate for comparing models with a different number of independent variables, is 76.2111%. The standard error of the estimate shows that the standard deviation of the residuals is 9,77749. The mean absolute error (MAE) of 7.39187 is the average value of the waste. The Durbin-Watson (DW) statistic examines the residuals to determine any significant correlation based on the order in which they are presented in the data file. Since the P-value is less than 0.05, there is an indication of a possible serial correlation with a confidence level of 95.0%. Graph the residuals versus the row number to see if any patterns can be detected. To determine if the model can be simplified, note that the highest P-value of the independent variables is 0.0088, which corresponds to KNOWLEDGE AND INNOVATION MANAGEMENT. Since the P-value is less than 0.05, that term is statistically significant with a confidence level of 95.0%. As a result, it probably would not want to eliminate any variable from the model.

Source: The authors using Statgraphics Centurión XVI

FINDINGS

Statgraphics recommended removing ten components from the model given the weights, confidence intervals, and statistical parameters. The components extracted were associativity technology, communication, and information; human resources management; exports; financial management; imports; environmental economic surveillance and analysis; social and environmental responsibility; logistic management and operation management. The resulting equation is as follows:

Strategic Direction = -4,00917 + 0,213812*Market Management + 0,14467*Organizational Culture + 0,537331*Organizational Structure + 0,105254*Knowledge and Innovation Management

Tables 2 and 3 and Figure 2 show results of the multiple regression model that describes the relationship between strategic direction and four independent variables, for which:

R-Squared = 76.5122%
R-Squared (adjusted for degrees of freedom) = 76.2111%
Standard Error of the Estimated = 9.77749
Median Absolute Error = 7.39187
Durbin-Watson = 1.79161 (P=0.0317)
Autocorrelation of residuals with delay 1 = 0.103455

These results show that 76% of strategic direction in the 316 SMEs analyzed is explained by marketing management, organizational structure, organizational culture, and innovation and knowledge management. Therefore, the hypothesis is confirmed. This finding is essential for academic, scientific, and business environments since it proves the necessity of conducting activities in those four components to have more agile strategies.

Table 2. Multiple Regression Analysis (Dependent variable: Strategic planning)

Parameter	Estimation	Standard Error	Statistical t	P Value
CONSTANT	-4,00917	1,63568	-2,45107	0,0148
Market.Man	0,213812	0,0430803	4,9631	0,0000
Organ. Cult.	0,14467	0,0430714	3,35885	0,0009
Organ.struc.	0,537331	0,0396799	13,5416	0,0000
Kimanagement	0,105254	0,0399512	2,63457	0,0088

Source: The authors using Statgraphics Centurión XVI

Table 3. Variance Analysis

Source	Sum of Squares	Gl	Median Square	F Value	P Value
Model	97162,3	4	24290,6	254,09	0,0000
Residual	29827,0	312	95,5994		
Total (Corr.)	126989,	316			

Source: The authors using Statgraphics Centurión XVI

Numbers for each variable correspond to its weight in the equation. Weights refer to the relevance of each variable in the strategic management of SMEs. Therefore, the most relevant variable is organizational structure (0,537331), followed by marketing management (0,213812), organizational culture (0,14467), innovation and knowledge management (0,105254).

CONCLUSIONS

Conclusions are presented for each of the variables of the equation. SMEs managers must concentrate on them to have an effective strategic direction for a new world economic order:

Organizational Structure

It is the first variable to consider as it is of the highest importance. In organizational design, the structure formally specifies the behavior of individuals in the organization. It aims to perform actions to reach objectives, implicitly leading to establishing tasks and interactions necessary among all parties accurately and successfully (Arévalo, Perez-Uribe, & Ocampo-Guzmán, 2015). Besides, it creates ways and spheres of communication among members and formal methods to behave and control (Denison & Mishra, 1995; Pertuz, 2013). It can be considered a tool to put together coordination, division of labor, and technical and social systems of an organization (Olabuénaga, *1995;* Marín-Idárraga, 2012). If a person working in an organization decides to leave, the organization must be capable of finding a person to replace him/her. This fact enables the organization to face risks and strengthen itself as a unique and essential party to have good management and function throughout the organization (Cruz, 2016).

Marketing Management

It is the second component in order of importance to strategic direction for a new world economic order. According to Kotler (1999), it is based on two foundational perspectives:

1. **Marketing Management.** Learning, projecting, doing, and confirming the elaboration, recognition, promotion, and distribution of a particular idea, good or service, obtain a mutual benefit between the organization that supplies and the individual who obtains benefits. Marketing is a human activity aimed at satisfying needs and wants by exchange processes. Considering a more open perspective in which the firm is continuously exchanging, Marketing has a new focus in which organizations reach their goals whenever they direct their efforts towards satisfying customer needs. Such focus links to customers and the market economy, which assumes that what is produced, the way to create and the way to distribute are linked to the customers' preferences that influence individual decisions in a free market (Leonidou & Leonidou, 2011), and

2. **Strategic Management.** It is based on a continuous study and analysis of customers' needs as an initial step to direct the enterprise's management towards obtaining benefits. A strategic focus means, first, studying the enterprise's current situation and the evolution of its markets; and second, identifying products, needs, and segments that could be attractive, to evaluate the degree of attractiveness of the product, market, and segment (Ambrose, Anaza, & Rutherord, 2017).

Organizational Culture

It is the third component that explains the strategic direction for a new world economic order. Allaire and Firsirotu (1984) found multiple theories regarding organizational culture. These authors classified them as functionalist, structural-functionalist, ecological, historical, structuralism, mutualistic, symbolic, and cognitive. This broad theoretical categorization can be synthesized into two general types of studies on organizational culture. The first group deals with identifying variables that define corporate culture and their relationship with organizational results. The second group comprises cross-cultural studies to associate characteristics of cultures from different countries or regions with organizational cultures.

In the first case, different models about characteristics shaping organizational culture have been developed. One of the first was produced by Harrison (1972). He created a typology oriented to power, role, task, and people, describing the foundational traits of an organization's culture. Among the main aspects of organizational culture are involvement, consistency, adaptability, and mission (Denison & Mishra, 1995; Denison & Neale, 1996; Smerek & Denison, 2007, mentioned by Reyes-Martínez, Barboza-Carrasco, & Vicuña-Tapia, 2017).

Besides, like Denison and colleagues, Cameron and Quinn (1999) and Perez-Uribe (2012) developed a theoretical framework for assessing and changing organizational culture and work environment. Such authors proposed five types of organizational culture: hierarchy, clan, adhocracy, commitment, and market.

Among cross-cultural studies, the work developed by Hofstede (1980), cited by Oyserman, Coon, and Kemmelmeier (2002), is recognized as fundamental. This work was the first to identify traits that allow comparing organizational cultures between different countries. Its essential variables have been used in several cross-cultural studies about organizational behavior. Such variables, initially, were individualism, power distance, masculinity, and uncertainty avoidance; later, orientation to the future was included. According to Oyserman *et al. (2002),* the Hofstede Model organized cultural differences into general patterns, allowing comparative research, being the base for subsequent studies about cross-cultural research.

Innovation and Knowledge Management

It is the fourth component that explains strategic direction. It covers the whole organization, and from a focus proposed by Dess and Lumpkin (2003), Johnson and Scholes (1997), and Perez-Uribe and colleagues (2020), there are three core factors related to the process of strategic planning: strategic analysis (analysis), strategic formulation (election, decision), and strategic implementation (action). These planning processes are composed of different types of knowledge: physical, chemical, logic, social, which have been incorporated into products and processes of the firm by qualified, experienced people who work for the organization of third parties (universities, labs, consulting firms, etc.)

Knowledge, innovation, and technology are the most critical strengths when competing for a market segment, given the social impact generated (Saiz-Alvarez, 2018b). The manager must recognize the environment in which the enterprise competes, plans strategies, and develops plans and projects. This fact implies the formal knowledge of clients to know their current and future needs, their behavior as consumers, and the capabilities and weaknesses of competitors, suppliers, and associates who could provide support if needed (López *et al., 2012*). In this relation, technology is a crucial factor for development. Current developments were almost unimaginable a decade ago, and their usefulness increases exponentially. This fact is related to ICTs, which allow enterprises to accumulate large amounts of information (Ramírez-Salazar, 2016). Sometimes, this situation is perceived as an increase of data for decision-making that may cause an excess load. That is why technology becomes adequate support for modern organizations in which strategic direction is used to reach objectives (Calderon-Hernandez, 2017). Thus, it is necessary to consider the strategic value and usefulness for the promotion that ICTs can play for organizational sustainability (Perez-Uribe, 2018). The previous authors mention that the main direct contribution of ICT for organizations is the increase of connectivity and information flows with other business players linked to the firm. These relations facilitate reaching effectiveness, efficiency, profitability, and improving quality of life and environmental management.

CONTRIBUTIONS TO MANAGERIAL THEORY

Organizational Structure

This variable is the first to be considered with the highest importance. Every organizational structure has dimensions that put together its essential characteristics: complexity, formalism, and centralization, as follows,

1. *Complexity* explains how organizational activities separate from each other, which can be of three types horizontal, vertical, and transversal. *Horizontal*: whenever there is a large number of diverse activities, more specialized labor is required, which makes relations difficult since communication becomes too technical and complex, with diversified terminologies, which leads to having multiple commands. *Vertical* refers to the hierarchy of the organization. The higher the number of levels, the higher the complexity. In addition, *spatial or transversal* differences increase the geographic dispersion among people in the organization (Denison & Neale, 1996; Calixto, Plazas & Balaguera, 2013).
2. *Formalism* refers to the degree of standardization in the organization defined by the degree of freedom that an individual must make decisions that directly or indirectly affect the organization. Depending on the individual's position, the organization will bestow on him/her a higher/lower level of formalization. Thus, the lower the level of formalism, the higher the specialization and training the worker must have (Al-Qatawneh, 2014), and
3. *Centralization* refers to the concentration of power to make decisions in an organization. There is high centralization when top management makes decisions alone. Other levels only obey. When centralization is low, people who can make decisions must be highly prepared (Madueny, Oluremi, Fadeyi, & Akintunde, 2015).

Activities related to organizational structure that could facilitate the development of strategies for a new world economic order, are, according to López *et al.* (2013) and Pérez–Uribe (2007):

1) Structure adjusted to strategy:
    a. The structure must adjust to guarantee the success of strategies implemented and clear for all involved.
    b. The organization and functions manual must be periodically used, evaluated, and communicated to improve processes.
2) Decisions must be made based on strategic planning:
    a. Decisions are made after consulting and with the participation of those directly involved.
    b. Decisions are adjusted to strategic direction; indicators and results are evidence of this.
3) Standardization *vs.* Strategic planning:
    a. There is a certification for standardization and normalization. Both characteristics are part of a worker's daily habits.
    b. Handbooks or other standardization tools provide added value to strategic planning, evidenced by indicators.
4) Adaptation of the organizational structure:

a. The organization chart, handbooks, and other tools for organizational structure are permanently updated.
   b. Strategic direction sets the path for updating the structure, handbooks, or other systems.
5) Working in teams and by projects:
   a. Workers work and form teams naturally. Indicators and results evidence this fact.
   b. The way of doing things enables permanently working by projects.
6) Records:
   a. They are complete and updated to learn and make decisions in real-time.
   b. Changes in the structure are based on strategic direction.
7) Information systems related to the organizational structure:
   a. Information systems provide relevant data to trace and evaluate changes in the organizational structure. Such data is used for decision-making.
   b. Information is helpful for indicators to measure the relation between structure and strategic direction.
   c. The information system is systemic, integrated, and facilitates change-oriented decisions.

Marketing Management

As the second component in order of importance to strategic direction for a new world economic order, the marketing management activities that could be performed to facilitate the development of strategies are (López *et al.*, 2013; Botero, 2011; Pérez-Uribe *et al.*, 2009):

1) Orientation of the organization towards the market:
   a. The organization considers first the needs and wants of social actors, clients, users, or consumers. The most important is to exceed their expectations and needs.
   b. The enterprise's positioning and brands result from a researched and planned management controlled by the owner and its team.
2) Marketing planning and control:
   a. It has written marketing plans, forecast for at least four years.
   b. Marketing plans are traced, taking the corresponding corrective actions.
3) Market research: Market researchers applied to the needs of the enterprise are performed.
4) The behavior of the social actor, client, user, consumer, and clients' segmentation.
   a. The buying behavior of customers and other social actors is known in detail.
   b. The enterprise knows the buying and consumption behavior of consumers and works based on them.
   c. The firm knows the lifecycle of social actors and consumers and plans marketing action to retain them. Results are traced.
5) Product strategy:
   a. Marketing research is performed, their results are used to develop new processes and products.
   b. Levels of products are known. There is a strategy to keep and attract satisfied customers. Differentiated products are offered to the market.
   c. The lifecycle is known in detail. The product is differentiated, forecasting its future in the market, and satisfying the social actors and clients.
6) Price strategy:

    a. There is a cost system that is constantly updated, calculated by an expert.
    b. The price strategy responds to the needs of the enterprise and the market.
    c. The organization is ready to respond to price changes from competitors or similar organizations quickly.
7) Distribution strategy and structure:
    a. The distribution strategy is well defined according to opportunities in the market. Constant controls are performed to guarantee results.
    b. Distribution is performed, having complete information, control, and evaluation of market penetration, product turnover, availability, and sales volume of each distribution channel.
8) Sales strategies:
    a. The sales force is constantly planned, managed, motivated, controlled, and promoted to get the best results for it, the enterprise, and the market.
    b. The sales budget is calculated based on a planned sales and marketing research process, working with the sales force, forecasting scenarios, and control mechanisms.
    c. Sales strategies and tactics are based on the type of products and the market's needs, clients, buyers, and users. New technologies support tactics.
9) Communication strategy:
    a. There is a funded advertisement plan, which is controlled and whose results are known.
    b. There is a promotion plan based on market research, which is controlled and evaluated.
    c. The enterprise plans its participation in events such as fairs, trade missions, showrooms, etc. The enterprise is aware of the effectiveness and favorable results of such participation.
    d. The enterprise performs promotion activities to channels and consumers and evaluates their results.
    e. Public relations are adequately planned, and workers are trained to participate. Results are evaluated considering benefits for the enterprise.
    f. There is a funded plan for direct marketing activities plan. Results are evaluated considering benefits for the enterprise.
    g. There is permanent planning of promotional and personal merchandising, whose effects are known and controlled.
10) Service to social actors, clients, users, and consumers:
    a. The enterprise has a clear customer service philosophy; it plans and controls customer loyalty and trains and empowers its workers to offer the best customer service.
    b. Clients consider that the customer services offered by the firm are excellent.

Organizational Culture

It is the third component that explains the strategic direction for a new world economic order. According to Pérez-Uribe (2011 & 2012), Lozano, Pérez-Uribe, and Ocampo-Guzmán (2015), actions regarding organizational culture that could facilitate the development of strategies are:

1) To promote leadership:
    a. Management responsibilities (board of directors or board of family members) in the enterprise are clearly defined, documented, and known by those interested and are perfectly fulfilled.

b. The role and participation of management as a leader to create, promote and keep a culture of harmony at work is evident throughout the enterprise. There are indicators to demonstrate this.
   c. The activities to promote leadership skills at all levels are explicit throughout the enterprise.
   d. The assessment and improvements of organizational culture work smoothly. There are indicators to demonstrate this fact.
2) To encourage participation and commitment:
   a. The activities to improve the authority and autonomy skills of workers work excellently. There are indicators to demonstrate this.
   b. The strategies to form teams to facilitate reaching organizational objectives work skillfully.
   c. Formal and explicit commitments to provide a quick and satisfactory response to workers' initiative work excellently.
3) To promote development and recognition:
   a. The application of worker's development expertly plans works.
   b. Programs prepare workers for their retirement work in an excellent manner.
   c. The organization references and compares its practices of development and recognition to others applied at national and international levels. This fact works expertly, and the information obtained is used for decision-making.
   d. Recognition to individuals and teams that contribute to reaching organizational objectives is explicit and visible throughout the firm.
4) To create a dynamic environment for all workers:
   a. Methods to analyze and provide a concrete response to alienation, anguish and stress generated by the climate work excellently.
   b. Actions developed to promote human dignity and respect work skillfully.

Innovation and Knowledge management

It is the fourth component that explains strategic direction. According to Ramírez-Salazar (2016), Ramírez-Salazar, Perez-Uribe, and Salcedo-Perez (2018) and Pérez-Uribe and Ramírez-Salazar (2018), actions regarding innovation and knowledge that could facilitate the development of strategies are:

1) For innovation players,
   a. The organization acquires external talent and combines it with internal talent.
   b. The firm has the knowledge required to develop sustainable innovation activities.
   c. The enterprise disposes of skilled and experienced workers to develop innovation activities.
   d. The organization makes possible that worker's ideas become projects and products.
2) To develop a culture of sustainable innovation,
   a. The firm integrates internal and external processes to innovate operations in economic, social, and environmental dimensions.
   b. The organization integrates its workers into open innovation networks.
   c. The company recognizes innovations. Besides, it provides stimulus for it.
   d. The enterprise is recognized as a leader in sustainable innovation in its industry.
   e. The organization supports its innovation activities in the interaction and contribution of all stakeholders with equity and justice.

      f. The company makes it possible for all its workers to contribute to sustainable innovation processes.
3) To develop infrastructure for innovation,
      a. The firm has established a management system of innovation activities, with indicators for processes and results in economic, social, and environmental aspects.
      b. The organization has implemented an innovative program based on values, looking for a balance of economic, social, and environmental aspects.
      c. The corporation allocates funds to be used specifically and exclusively in innovation activities.
      d. The enterprise has mechanisms, instruments, and regulations to protect the results obtained with innovation activities and has established policies and strategies to protect its innovations.
4) For the use of different types of innovation,
      a. The firm has an innovative program that includes product development focused on comprehensive sustainability.
      b. The corporation has a program of systemic innovation of its productive processes aimed at improving productivity, competitiveness, and sustainability.
      c. The organization keeps looking for new markets and ways to commercialize its products, using fair practices.
      d. The enterprise develops capacities to adapt its organizational structures and management systems to social, economic, and environmental circumstances.
      e. The company keeps looking for new ways of comprehensive sustainable development for its stakeholders.
5) To manage innovation capabilities,
      a. The firm can create innovation in its products, production processes, ways to reach markets, management systems, and business models.
      b. The organization anticipates opportunities and threats in the environment.
      c. The enterprise develops systematic solutions to take advantage of opportunities and threats previously anticipated.
      d. The company has developed capabilities to replicate innovation processes systematically.
6) Regarding technological matters,
      a. The firm must fully use technology to have friendly relations with the environment and the community.
      b. The organization needs to establish a technological action plan according to the strategy that guarantees its sustainability.
      c. The corporation must foresee technological changes and take anticipated actions to become sustainable.
      d. The company must use knowledge to adapt the technology to its social, environmental, and economic needs.
7) Regarding knowledge management,
      a. The company acquires knowledge from collaborators from the industry and the environment.
      b. The firm acquires, in an easy way, the necessary knowledge to solve problems.
      c. The corporation shares knowledge with its stakeholders.
      d. The organization uses its knowledge to solve problems.

From the MMOM perspective, if its application continues, the same analysis could be carried out with a larger sample of companies to observe if this affects the results obtained in the present study. Likewise, other variables could be taken as dependent on testing their correlation with the rest of the variables as independent and carry out their respective analyzes.

REFERENCES

Al-Qatawneh, M. I. (2014). The Impact of Organizational Structure on Organizational Commitment: A Comparison between Public and Private Sector Firms in Jordan. *European Journal of Business and Management*, 6(12), 23–32.

Allaire, Y., & Firsirotu, M. (1984). Theories of organizational culture. *Organization Studies*, 5(3), 193–226. doi:10.1177/017084068400500301

Ambrose, S. C., Anaza, N. A., & Rutherord, B. N. (2017). The role of prior sales experience of buyers and duration in buyer-seller relationships. *The Marketing Management Journal*, 27(1), 16–30.

Ansoff, I. H. (1997). *La dirección estratégica en la práctica empresarial* (2nd ed.). Pearson.

Ansoff, I. H., & Mcdonell, E. (1990). *Implanting Strategic Management* (2nd ed.). Prentice-Hall.

Arévalo Pardo, N. J., Perez-Uribe, R., & Ocampo-Guzmán, D. (2015). *MIIGO (Modelo de intervención e innovación de la gestión organizacional): Intervención e innovación de la estructura organizacional*. Universidad EAN.

Arias, A. D., Hernández, A., & Pérez-Uribe, R. I. (2018). Model of Modernization for Organizational Management Component Evaluation. In R. Perez-Uribe, C. Salcedo-Perez, & D. David Ocampo-Guzman (Eds.), *Handbook of Research on Intrapreneurship and Organizational Sustainability in SMEs* (pp. 217–249). IGI Global. doi:10.4018/978-1-5225-3543-0.ch011

Arnaud, N., Mills, C. E., Legrand, C., & Maton, E. (2016). Materializing Strategy in Mundane Tools: ¿the Key to Coupling Global Strategy and Local Strategy Practice? *British Journal of Management*, 27(1), 38–57. doi:10.1111/1467-8551.12144

Botero, A. J. L. (2011). *Modelo de direccionamiento estratégico para PYMES*. Universidad EAN.

Calderón-Hernández, G. (2017). *La generación de conocimiento en estrategia organizacional en Colombia*. Universidad Sergio Arboleda and Ascolfa.

Camacho, M. (2002). Direccionamiento estratégico: Análisis de una herramienta poderosa. *Revista VíaSalud*, 21, 6–12.

Castro, A. A. (2010). *Direccionamiento estratégico y crecimiento empresarial: algunas reflexiones en torno a su relación*. Universidad del Norte.

Certo, S. (2001). *Administración moderna: diversidad, calidad, ética y el entorno global* (8th ed.). Pearson Education.

CETDIR. (2007). Dirección estratégica integrada. *Ingeniería Industrial*, 28(1), 14–23.

Cruz, R. W. L. (2016). *La estructura organizacional y el análisis de la capacidad institucional: un referente en la Universidad de los Llanos*. Universidad Nacional de Colombia.

Dabic, M., González-Loureiro, M., & Furrer, O. (2014). Research on the strategy of multinational enterprises: Key approaches and new avenues. *BRQ Business Research Quarterly, 17*(2), 129–148. doi:10.1016/j.brq.2013.09.001

de la Republica de Colombia, C. (2004). *Ley 905 de 2004*. Retrieved from http://web.presidencia.gov.co/leyes/2004/agosto/Ley%20No.%20905.pdf

Denison, D., & Neale, W.S. (1996). *Denison organizational culture survey: facilitator guide*. Aviat.

Denison, R., & Mishra, A. (1995). Toward a theory of organizational culture and effectiveness. *Organization Science, 6*(2), 204–223. doi:10.1287/orsc.6.2.204

Dess, G. G., & Lumpkin, G. T. (2003). *Dirección estratégica: Creando ventajas competitivas*. McGraw-Hill Interamericana.

Dixit, A. K., & Nalebuff, B. J. (1991). *Pensar estratégicamente: un arma decisiva en los negocios, la política y la vida diaria*. Antoni Bosch.

Fernández G.R. (2001). *Manual para el desarrollo y crecimiento empresarial*. 3R Editores.

Fuentelsaz, L., Polo, Y., & Maicas, J. P. (2003). Economía digital y estrategia empresarial: Un análisis desde la dirección estratégica. *Revista de Empresa, 5*, 57–63.

Gálvez, A. E. J., Cuéllar, L. K., Restrepo, R. C., Berna, C. A., & Cortés, J. A. (2014). *Análisis estratégico para el desarrollo de las MiPymes en Colombia*. Programa Editorial Universidad del Valle. doi:10.25100/peu.35

Harrison, R. (1972). Understanding your organization's charter. *Harvard Business Review*, (May-June), 119–128.

Hill, W. L., & Jones, G. R. (1996). *Administración estratégica: un enfoque integrado* (3rd ed.). McGrawHill.

Jarillo, C. (1992). *Dirección Estratégica*. McGraw-Hill.

Johnson, G., & Scholes, K. (1997). *Dirección Estratégica: Análisis de la estrategia de las organizaciones*. Prentice Hall.

Leonidou, C. N., & Leonidou, L. C. (2011). Research into environmental marketing/management: A bibliographic analysis. *European Journal of Marketing, 45*(1-2), 68–103. doi:10.1108/03090561111095603

López, I. I. A., Ocampo, G. D., & Pérez–Uribe, R. (2013). *Model of Modernization for organizational Management (MMOM)*. Ediciones EAN., doi:10.13140/2.1.3437.4727

Lozano, L. J., Perez-Uribe, R., & Ocampo-Guzmán, D. (2015). *MIIGO (Modelo de intervención e innovación de la gestión organizacional): Intervención e innovación de la cultura organizacional*. Universidad EAN.

Madueny, S., Oluremi, A., Fadeyi, O., & Akintunde, M. (2015). Impact of organization structure on organization performance. *International Conference on African Development Issues (CU-ICADI)*. Retrieved from https://www.researchgate.net/publication/291336611

Manso, C. F. J. (1991). *Curso de dirección estratégica comercial*. ESIC Editorial.

Marín-Idárraga, D. A. (2012). Estructura organizacional y sus parámetros de diseño: Análisis descriptivo en pymes industriales de Bogotá. *Estudios Gerenciales*, *28*(123), 43–63. doi:10.1016/S0123-5923(12)70204-8

Mintzberg, H., Quinn, J. B., & Ghoshal, S. (1999). *El proceso estratégico*. Prentice Hall.

Olabuenga, R. J. I. (1995). *Sociología de las organizaciones*. Universidad de Deusto.

Oyserman, D., Coon, H. M., & Kemmelmeier, M. (2002). Rethinking Individualism and Collectivism: Evaluation of Theoretical Assumptions and Meta-Analyses. *Psychological Bulletin*, *128*(1), 3–72. doi:10.1037/0033-2909.128.1.3 PMID:11843547

Pérez–Uribe, R. (2007). Estructura y Cultura organizacional en la PYME Colombiana: Análisis en empresas Bogotanas. *Cuadernos Americanos*, *38*, 73–85.

Pérez–Uribe, R. (2011). *Compromiso de la alta gerencia como eje en el desarrollo de una cultura organizacional de excelencia y su efecto en el desempeño de la firma: Un estudio en medianas empresas del sector de maquinaria y equipo en la ciudad de Bogotá*. Editorial Académica Española.

Pérez–Uribe, R. (2012). *El ambiente laboral y su incidencia en el desempeño de las organizaciones: estudio de las mejores empresas para trabajar en Colombia* (PhD Dissertation). Universidad Antonio de Nebrija.

Pérez–Uribe, R. (2018). *Gerencia Estratégica Corporativa*. Ediciones Ecoe.

Pérez-Uribe, R., Ocampo-Guzmán, D., Ospina-Bermeo, J., Cifuentes-Valenzuela, J., & Cubillos-Leal, C. A. (2016). *MIIGO - Modelo de Intervención e Innovación para el direccionamiento estratégico*. Ediciones EAN. doi:10.21158/9789587564143

Perez-Uribe, R., Ocampo-Guzmán, D., Salcedo-Perez, C., Piñeiro-Cortes, L., & Ramírez-Salazar, M. P. (2020). Preface. In R. Perez-Uribe, D. Ocampo-Guzmán, C. Salcedo-Perez, L. Piñeiro-Cortes, & M. P. Ramírez-Salazar (Eds.), *Handbook of Research on Increasing the Competitiveness of SMEs*. IGI Global. doi:10.4018/978-1-5225-9425-3

Pérez-Uribe, R., & Ramírez-Salazar, M. P. (2018). Organizational Components that Explain the Management of Innovation and Knowledge in Colombian SMEs. In R. Perez-Uribe, C. Salcedo-Perez, & D. David Ocampo-Guzman (Eds.), *Handbook of Research on Intrapreneurship and Organizational Sustainability in SMEs* (pp. 1–27). doi:10.4018/978-1-5225-3543-0.ch001

Pertuz, R. A. (2013). Estudio de los tipos de estructura organizacional de los institutos universitarios venezolanos. *Revista Electrónica de Investigación Educativa*, *15*(3), 53–67.

Ramírez-Garzón, M. T., Perez-Uribe, R., & Espinoza-Mosqueda, R. (2020). Organizational components that explain profitability as a key factor of competitiveness. Colombian SMEs Case. In R. Perez-Uribe, D. Ocampo-Guzmán, C. Salcedo-Perez, L. Piñeiro-Cortes, & M. P. Ramírez-Salazar (Eds.), *Handbook of Research on Increasing the Competitiveness of SMEs* (pp. 26–53). IGI Global. doi:10.4018/978-1-5225-9425-3.ch002

Ramírez-Salazar, M. P. (2016). *Modelo de Innovación Abierta Colaborativa para la Banca de Fomento, Caso Bancóldex* (PhD Dissertation). Universidad Antonio de Nebrija & Universidad EAN. DOI: doi:10.13140/RG.2.2.12496.92166

Ramírez-Salazar, M. P., Perez-Uribe, R., & Salcedo-Perez, C. (2018). A Triple Helix Model Based on Open Collaborative Innovation in Colombia: A Proposal for Higher Education Institutions. In N. Suja & J. M. Saiz-Alvarez (Eds.), *Handbook of Research on Ethics, Entrepreneurship, and Governance in Higher Education* (pp. 238–261). IGI Global. doi:10.4018/978-1-5225-5837-8.ch011

Reyes-Martínez, L., Barboza-Carrasco, M., & Vicuña-Tapia, H. (2017). Diagnóstico Cultura Organizacional de la Empresa Grupo Fadomo Reproser, S.A. de C.V. *Revista de Desarrollo Económico.*, *4*(12), 67–78.

Rodríguez, V. J. (2005). *Cómo aplicar la administración estratégica a la pequeña y mediana empresa* (5th ed.). Thompson.

Saiz-Álvarez, J. M. (2018a). An Entrepreneurship-based Model to Foster Organizational Wellbeing. In P. Ochoa, M. T. Lepeley, & P. Essens (Eds.), *Wellbeing for Sustainability in the Global Workplace* (pp. 159–178). Routledge. doi:10.4324/9780429470523-8

Saiz-Álvarez, J. M. (2018b). Managing Social Innovation through CSR 2.0 and the Quadruple Helix. A Socially Inclusive Business Strategy for the Industry 4.0. In A. Guerra (Ed.), *Organizational Transformation and Managing Innovation in the Fourth Industrial Revolution* (pp. 228–244). IGI Global.

Saloner, G., Shepard, A., & Podolny, J. (2005). *Administración estratégica*. LimusaWiley.

Thompson, A., & Strickland, A. J. (2004). *Administración estratégica: textos y casos* (13th ed.). McGraw-Hill.

Valencia-Maldonado, G., & Erazo, M. A. (2016). El reto de la planificación estratégica en las Pymes. *Revista Publicando*, *3*(8), 335–344.

Vidal, A. E. (2004). *Diagnóstico organizacional: evaluación sistémica del desempeño empresarial en la era digital*. Ecoe.

KEY TERMS AND DEFINITIONS

ANOVA: Acronym of analysis of variance is a collection of statistical models and their associated procedures. The variance is partitioned into specific components due to different explanatory variables. It is used intensively in the analysis and design of experiments to evaluate the effect of treatments on the variability of the response variable.

CETDIR: From Spanish, *Centro de Estudios de Técnicas de Dirección*. It is an official Cuban organism dedicated to the business development and training of executives of the Cuban business system and its governing bodies. It relies on research and consulting to promote more effective management dynamics in organizations.

MMOM: The model of modernization for organizational management comprises 16 organizational components that allow diagnosing the level of management of SMEs considering four levels of development on a 0-100% scale defined by survival (level 1), internal development (level 2), interaction with environments and markets (level 3), and world-class with best business practices (level 4).

MSMEs: Acronym of micro, small, and medium-sized companies. Depending on each country, they are classified by the number of workers, sales, and total assets. In Colombia, they are classified according to the manufacturing, commercial, and service sectors by the level of sales according to the taxing unit defined annually by the National Tax and Customs Department (In Spanish: DIAN, *Departamento de Impuestos y Aduana Nacional*). Sometimes, it is also used by the number of workers: Micro company (up to 9 workers), small company (between 10 and 50 workers), medium company (between 51 and 200 workers), and large company (greater than 200 workers).

Organizational Components: They are the factors or elements that make up any business organization in the light of the MMOM to achieve its objectives of effectiveness, efficiency, profitability, and sustainability.

P-Value: In null hypothesis significance testing, the *p*-value is the probability of obtaining test results at least as extreme as the results observed, assuming that the null hypothesis is correct. A very small *p*-value means that such an extreme observed outcome would be very unlikely under the null hypothesis. Reporting *p*-values of statistical tests is common practice in academic publications of many quantitative fields. Since the precise meaning of *p*-value is hard to grasp, misuse is widespread and has been an essential topic in metascience.

Statgraphics Centurión XVI: It is designed for anyone who wishes to do serious data analysis without investing weeks learning how to use a statistical package. It contains over 180 statistical procedures, covering everything from summary statistics to graphical representation of data. Yet users do not need to be a statistician to use the program. Everything is completely menu-driven, and there are tools such as StatWizard and StatAdvisor to help the user use the program most effectively.

Strategic Direction: It is the "flight log" or the route that must be developed in the short, medium, and long term of an organization that generally contains a vision (long term), a mission (short term), objectives, and strategies in the medium term, an action plan (short term, less than a year) and a battery of indicators.

Chapter 6
The New Concept of Disruptive Logistics:
Global Sustainable Logistics 4.0 in a Future Post–New World Economic Order

Manuel Antonio Fernández-Villacañas Marín
https://orcid.org/0000-0001-7397-6395
San Pablo CEU University, Madrid, Spain

ABSTRACT

In an increasingly disruptive global environment, marked by the potential development of the Post-New World Economic Order, more innovative, effective, and efficient logistics solutions are demanded. It is necessary to offer radical improvements in logistics services through new models. It is considered necessary to define the new concept of disruptive logistics based on three fundamental pillars: globalization, digitization, and sustainability. This chapter aims to address the new concept, more effective and efficient, in a highly turbulent environment that has become disruptive, with unpredictable, substantial, and impactful changes. The most significant geoeconomics aspects that would condition a hypothetical Post-New World Economic Order are analyzed, the main factors of the global sustainable logistics are studied, and the development of the concepts of Logistics 4.0 and Supply Chain Management 4.0 is reviewed. Finally, as a result, the main aspects of the proposed new concept are analyzed.

INTRODUCTION

The COVID-19 pandemic has generated a global crisis that has completely disrupted the social, economic, and political spheres, showing the high vulnerability of most countries to this type of threat, as evidenced by their inability to respond effectively to these new crises generated by growing environmental uncertainty (Haarhaus & Liening, 2020). This crisis has altered traditional socio-economic systems, and the hypothesis that it will lead to restructuring towards a new world order, post-coronavirus, is beginning to gain strength. Furthermore, this increased risk associated with infectious diseases, resulting from

DOI: 10.4018/978-1-7998-7689-2.ch006

a global change that is rapidly altering human relationships and the environment, could trigger other crises related to the imbalance of the environment, whose scope could be very harmful (McMichael et al., 2020). Phenomena such as the use and abuse of resource consumption generating significant imbalances in ecosystems, extensive migratory processes involving large population movements, population aging, the tendency to concentrate the population of many countries in large urban centers, or climate change and consequent increase in temperatures, seem to be driving forces for the contagion and spread of these diseases.

However, in the face of the potential spread of these diseases, governments' response and crisis management capacities in many Western countries have proven improvised, late, ineffective, and insufficient. And these threatening triggers are also present in other equally devastating environmental phenomena, such as the water crisis, failures in action in favor of the climate, natural disasters, combating extreme weather, man-made environmental disasters, loss of biodiversity, or other increasingly present social phenomena, such as cyber-attacks, political corruption, failures in global governance, economic war, social instability, etc. It seems that humanity will be doomed over the next few years to have to live with a succession of severe crises that will give rise to an almost permanent emergency (World Economic Forum, 2020). It seems clear that this extraordinary situation is a new opportunity to promote an in-depth process review of the global socio-economic system and its structural transformation to explore a new economic order entirely focused on the principles of sustainability and sustainable economic development.

Indeed, we are witnessing an unprecedented modification since the New World Economic Order that emerged after World War II. The global pandemic of COVID 19 has been the primary catalyst. The United States and the Soviet Union then rose as the triumphant nations, with an ideological struggle to impose and expand the benefits of their respective economic-political systems, which lasted until the disintegration of the Soviet Union in 1991. The Bretton Woods Accords gave rise to the Monetary and Financial Conference of 1944, in which the first world economic institutions emerged (among them, the World Bank and the International Monetary Fund), and the creation years later, in 1948, of the General Agreement on Tariffs Customs and Trade (GATT). Starting in the eighties of the previous century, a new economic model emerged under the political auspices of Reagan and Thatcher, which has been called neoliberalism, as a response to the economic crises generated in nations by excessive public interventionism. The integration of national economies was also sought to promote international commercial and financial integration in incipient and unstoppable globalization. To consolidate this process, the World Trade Organization (WTO) was created in 1995, establishing a multilateral trading system. However, starting with the terrorist attacks against the Twin Towers in New York in 2001, which showed a tremendous real weakness of the society that until then had been a world leader, the hegemony of the United States began to be questioned, and very particularly at the end of that decade with the irruption of the international financial crisis. These significant changes have made many of these institutions obsolete, increasingly pressured by the surge of emerging countries with a great capacity for growth and influence. These institutions are forced to undertake a profound transformation not to disappear. China's new and increasingly prominent leadership with the United States, and a more and more weakened EU, have been facilitated by the global evolution of the COVID-19 pandemic. A context defined like a Third World War, but without violent conflicts or weapons of destruction, where economic intelligence and strategic management are the keys to victory. In addition, a new ideological struggle has been generated to impose and expand the benefits of their respective economic-political systems between the United States and China in their struggle for world leadership (Arbeláez-Campillo & Villasmil, 2020).

The New Concept of Disruptive Logistics

The impetus that the GATT and the WTO gave to world trade and the phenomenon of globalization since the end of the 20th century is well known. This momentum led to the transformation of logistics into an essential function. Logistics has become a critical element of business strategy in an increasingly complex, dynamic, and uncertain global environment. It is the primary source of competitive advantage, in whose evolution the polysemic and polyhedral concept of what is known as New Logistics (Fernández-Villacañas, 2020). It is worth highlighting two factors that add to globalization: logistics sustainability and its digital transformation.

Beyond the implementation of practices defined by environmental respect and the expanded concept of sustainability to include social and economic dimensions, such as responsibility, ethics of social behavior, sustainable economy, or new needs demanded by consumers, all of which is promoting very significant changes in the distribution of value-added and global economic surplus. Although there have been clearly positive effects on the environment because of the current pandemic, it is necessary to emphasize that environmental problems have not disappeared. The climate crisis is part of our life and represents an emergency that is still present. Thus, the importance of the circular economy, as an overcoming of the traditional linear economy models of use and disposal, should be promoted and developed through operational models that allow transforming waste as a resource capable of generating a new economic benefit. Without a doubt, the Post-New World Economic Order that might be established should be entirely focused on sustainability.

On the other hand, the digital transformation effort of the public and private sector is being translated into a new innovative scenario of value generation, the result of the connection and optimization of all production, management, logistics, and commercial processes (Borda, 2016). This new scenario is technologically defined by the physical and digital world's hybridization, where all the value chain elements are interconnected (factories, machines, tools, warehouses, administration systems, vehicles, products, among others). They work automatically, making logistics smart and creating global value networks focused on the customer (Navarro & Sabalza, 2016). Thus, logistics models need to have innovative, more effective, and efficient solutions capable of generating radical changes for the improvement and rapid adaptation of the logistics services offered to this new disruptive environment. In addition to the use of digital technologies, this requires integrating traditional lean & agile approaches into solutions and the use of logistics intelligence, strategic anticipation, and prospective planning strategies, which allow avoiding surprises and improvised logistics responses, deviant and insufficient. In this way, a global, competitive, changing, and interdependent business logistics environment becomes hybrid and hyperconnected. All this will allow us to achieve immediate responses in decision-making through intelligent systems and processes, without variability, without errors, based on information captured in real-time.

In a highly disruptive environment, endowed with unforeseen, substantial, and impactful changes, restructuring the Post-New World Economic Order will also affect leadership. It will be necessary to promote a new concept of disruptive logistics supported on three fundamental pillars: globalization, digitization, and sustainability. Therefore, it is needed to design this new concept that incorporates the development of its permanent digital transformation processes within the paradigm of Global Sustainable Logistics.

This chapter aims to study the most significant aspects of this new concept of disruptive logistics, identifying the key elements to advance towards its implementation in strategic terms within the framework of the Post-New World Economic Order established after the pandemic. After the introductory section, the chapter is divided into four more sections. In the first place, the most significant strategic and geoeconomics aspects that will condition the Post-New World Economic Order are analyzed. Subsequently, the main determinants of the Global Sustainable Logistics paradigm are studied. Third, the most significant conceptual aspects of Logistics 4.0 and Supply Chain 4.0 are examined, such as the evolution of the new logistics, the conceptual basis of disruptive logistics. Finally, as a result, the main aspects of the new concept are developed.

RESEARCH METHODOLOGY

The research has been developed using a qualitative documentary research methodology, applying a descriptive and explanatory method on the research problem, generating new orientations, approaches, and trends to properly guide the new proposed conceptual definition and the solution it represents.

The literature review has been used to include concepts and prior approaches essential to the investigated problem. The study has been carried out with sufficient detail, seeking its original aspects to guarantee objectivity and avoiding incurring interpretive biases. An attempt has been made to perceive the reality of the problem and integrate it coherently, guided by the author's research and professional experience in logistics.

TOWARDS A POST-NEW WORLD ECONOMIC ORDER

The world order can be defined as a systemic space determined by the union of political, strategic, economic, diplomatic, and military interests, among others, where nations converge with marginal or very marked influential patterns, and where regional conflicts, alliances, power blocs (e.g., European Union), and multilateral organizations (e.g., United Nations) are solved. Its theoretical purpose is to manage differences and support common objectives that allow the well-being of the people to be achieved (Arbeláez-Campillo et al., 2019). However, it seems that the strongest states have always imposed a general law to force their will on the rest to ensure survival and achievement of their national goals.

Despite the asymmetric power relations developed in the bipolar world of the Cold War dominated by the United States and the USSR, that would end with the Soviet collapse in the last decade of the 20th century and the proclamation of liberal democracy, the market economy, and respect for human rights. In the face of major conflicts or international catastrophes, it has always been possible to reach agreements with good cooperation and exchange between the least aligned countries. Indeed, the prevailing world order for many decades has been the consequence of the world reorganization after the Second World War, when the victorious big economic powers, the United States, and the USSR, determined their areas of geopolitical influence and the contours of the New World Economic Order.

All of this has also been a consequence of the consolidation of the project to update economic systems. It should be noted that during the second half of the 20th century, the global community has experienced an intense process of economic growth, doubling the standard of a living average of humanity since the end of the Second World War (Kasper, 2015). This new global economic order is ideologically based on two antagonistic approaches: capitalism and socialism. These approaches, despite conflicting, coincided in their perspective of promoting economic development from the modernization of the economy and society through better production systems and industrialization processes shaped by scientific and technological advances.

However, during the first two decades of the 21st century, the ideological contradictions of the current international order and the shared drive for economic development have worsened, as a consequence of the fact that their political-economic models are totally incapable of providing solutions to the significant problems that arise against the humanity: climate change, natural disasters, loss of biodiversity, terrorism, drug trafficking, organized crime, food crises, infectious disease epidemics, cyberattacks, political corruption, human rights violations, the extreme polarization of wealth, public and private waste, unemployment, gender violence, etc. And all of this is especially shocking in the poorest countries. The advantages of modernity have been selectively oriented for the exclusive benefit of privileged groups, leaving large populations relegated to extreme poverty (Morales et al., 2019).

This situation has progressively degraded the institutions and political discourses that have served as cement to the globalizing order, socially deteriorating the legitimacy of the representatives. However, until the COVID-19 pandemic spread in 2020, there were few public statements about the decline of the prevailing world order. From then on, the most impactful social media began to disseminate opinions about the meaning of the ravages of the pandemic as a turning point in the world economic order, given its profound and dramatic consequences driving a global economic recession, growing political tensions, and even a major armed conflict, exceeding the capacities of many of nation-states (Lissardy, 2020; Barría, 2020).

The clearest example of these revision proposals is the World Economic Forum (WEF)'s "COVID-19: The Great Reset" initiative to transform the global economic model after the pandemic. This initiative offers to rebuild the world economy and international relations sustainably after the damage caused by COVID-19. The plan was presented at the WEF headquarters in Davos (Switzerland) in May 2020, and new meetings are planned to deepen its initiative and align it with the UN 2030 Agenda. "The Great Reset" proposes restarting capitalism to put nature at the heart of the new economic system and establish a new social contract that extols the dignity of every human being. The WEF proposes promoting fiscal stimuli to relaunch the economy and use new parameters to measure the economic capacity of countries since GDP, used as the primary indicator, does not consider the division of wealth or the quality of life of people. In addition, companies are asked to modernize their ethical and environmental standards, reducing carbon emissions, and investing in renewable energy and innovation. Beyond these measures, the plan presents some ambiguity in the specific economic policy proposals. The supporters of "The Great Reset" consider that if the appropriate measures are not taken, the world will become less and less sustainable and egalitarian, which is why they request the participation of all global actors from the public and private spheres (Schwab & Malleret, 2020). However, this plan does not seem to have generated much interest in international public opinion, at less in this time.

In any case, from ending 2020 and the first months of 2021, a discourse of support for the current model has been imposed in the face of these proposals for major reforms, proposing only the changes and reforms necessary to alleviate the crisis and gradually return to the lost normality. The current world economic order will probably continue its course. However, the contradictions of the prominent dominant paradigms will surely deepen until, in another future conjuncture of great crisis, the conditions are sufficient and necessary to achieve the proposal of a Post-New World Economic Order. In this sense, this new order must address essential aspects to guarantee global sustainability. On the one hand, it would be necessary to deconcentrate the accumulation of world wealth in a polarized and extreme way like the one that exists today, making excessive use of non-renewable natural resources in an excessive desire for profit. On the other hand, production systems must subordinate the search for economic growth to the planet's sustainability, using clean technologies and exceeding the energy use of fossil fuels (Parra, 2020).

Today's world is divided into three significant areas of influence formed around three great superpowers: the United States, China, and the European Union, which try to shape the world according to their economic interests. Using their significant influence, these areas and the nations involved compete against each other.

Figure 1. Strategic triangle: Great power rivalry in the 21ˢᵗ century
Source: Koziej (2020)(GIS)

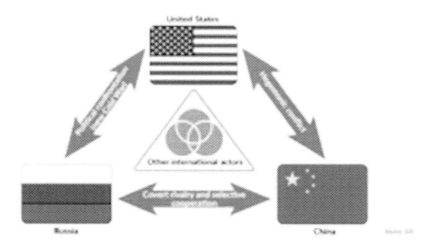

However, during the last decade, there has been a progressive international weakness of the European Union, among other factors, for not having a strict foreign, defense, and security policy, a lukewarm immigration policy, the Brexit crisis, and, above all, the failure of its management in the face of the problem of the COVID-19 pandemic. As a result, the increasingly prominent role played by Russia in the international arena has finally prevailed, in a relationship of political confrontation with the United States based on its great military capacity and global influence, and a covert rivalry but of selective cooperation with China. Figure 1 shows the strategic triangle of the current great rivalry for power, mainly in military terms, between the United States, China, and Russia (Koziej, 2020).

In any case, many analysts already consider that the current world can no longer be considered unipolar or multipolar, but nonpolar. This fact means that the world is dominated by multiple actors who possess and exercise various types of power. Many are not nation-states that have diluted their power in favor of a large global structure made up of various regional and international institutions, global corporations, civil society organizations, militias, and non-governmental organizations (Haass, 2008). Therefore, the current geopolitical scheme is sustained by a community of actors that is very diverse and plural than the one that existed at the end of the 20th century, which makes this scheme more complex and unstable, and hinders the real possibility of achieving efficient governance at the global level.

Everything indicates that the hegemonic position of the United States will continue to weaken, and other powers that are currently emerging, especially in Asia, will consolidate as poles of power with the force to challenge the hitherto hegemonic power. A new consolidated order can take various forms of governance. Still, it is evident that the forces shaping it are based on the rise of new powers in Asia, the consequent power and wealth shifts from the West to the East, and the central nation in the geopolitical transformation underway is China (Peel, 2009).

An excellent example of this is the trade war that the USA and China have been waging in recent years, where the WTO exercises an increasingly irrelevant position (Colombatto, 2020) and has not been able to impose its regulatory capacity and act as a conciliator of the conflict. But the process by which China has surpassed the USA as a world trading partner has been evolutionary and progressive. During 2000-2018, trade has increased by almost 150% in terms of its weight over world GDP, representing 59% in 2018. During these nearly two decades, international trade has progressively transformed in the composition and volume of the merchandise traded and the nations in which the rest of the world relies on its commercial relations.

Through this period, international trade has significantly transformed, not only in volume and composition but also in the countries in which the rest of the world relies upon its most important trade relations, surpassing China to the USA in the global leadership as a business partner.

Based on the Direction of Trade Statistics Database of the International Monetary Fund, the Lowy Institute based in Australia analyzed the evolution of the bilateral trade flows of different countries globally to determine the most important trading partner between the USA or China, evaluating year by year, from 1980 to 2018 (Ghosh, 2020). Figure 2 shows the initial and final situation, from the US dominance to the Chinese dominance. Before 2000, the USA was at the forefront of world trade, achieving the American power 80% more commercial activity than China. In 2018, this figure had been reduced to only 30%, with the Chinese giant becoming the leader in 128 of the 190 countries analyzed and achieving a totally dominant position in Africa and Asia and a very significant one in Latin America.

China's entry into the World Trade Organization in 2001 is seen as a turning point in its international trade relations. A rapid change in its commercial economic policy began to occur from that year, especially between 2005 and 2010. Over time, China's dominance has grown dramatically, assuming leadership and unseating, as we said, the United States.

But the matter must consider other dimensions. The USA and China compete in many ways to impose their global hegemony, including in the commercial sphere, but it is also true that both nations need to promote lines of cooperation, even in commercial matters, which obviously must be of mutual benefit. It was necessary to reach a stable trade agreement that would guarantee that both superpowers would benefit, a deal that we do not know if it has already been definitively attained.

Since the beginning of 2018, both parties have faced each other through an increasingly tense relationship, raising mutual tariffs on bilateral imports of many industrial and consumer goods (see Figure 3), until reaching a stabilized relationship in February 2020, with tariffs of approximately 20% by both parties.

While there appeared to have been a truce in the trade war in early 2020, having had a strong negative impact on global growth, the COVID-19 pandemic seems to have tipped the balance in China's favor, allowing its sphere of influence has increased rapidly.

It is a struggle that is not exclusively commercial but is based on the rivalry for world leadership and global hegemony. However, as a synthesis of this section, there is a multiplicity and diversity of actors on the worldwide scene. Significant changes are taking place in terms of their ability to influence. Whatever new world order may be generated, not only will it not be free from conflict and tension, but it can be a very conducive means of creating them. We believe that, as J. Sachs has argued, the Post-New World Economic Order of the 21st century will undoubtedly be based on the promise of shared prosperity that does not currently exist but will very possibly carry the risk of global conflict (Sachs, 2008).

Figure 2. The USA vs. China: A trade war to achieve global hegemony
Source: Ghosh (2020)(Lowy Institute)

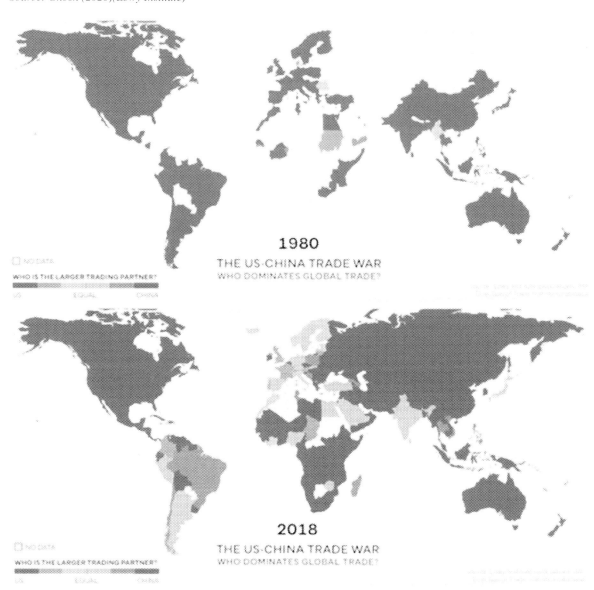

The New Concept of Disruptive Logistics

Figure 3. The USA vs. China: Trade-Weighted average tariffs (%)
Source: Ghosh (2020)(Lowy Institute), from Peterson Institute for International Economics, FT

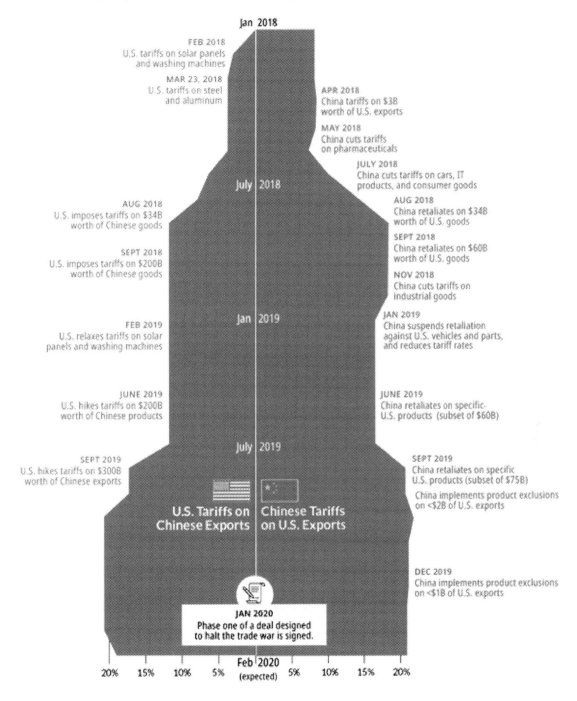

GLOBAL SUSTAINABLE LOGISTICS

Logistics has become a fundamental area to compete successfully in the global business environment within the framework of an increasingly turbulent digital environment. The development of logistics models has been spectacular in recent decades, exponentially increasing the effectiveness and efficiency of logistics services. With it, the value provided to customers is increasingly concerned with corporate social responsibility and global sustainability.

In conceptual terms, the global sustainability of the supply chain and, in general, of logistics management implies a strategy of combining the organization's environmental, economic, and social objectives. This strategy must be transparent within the framework of the coordination system of business processes within the company, which tries to optimize the economic results of each company and long-term supply chains (Carter & Rogers, 2008). This approach to sustainable global logistics is detailed in Figure 4, which shows its main aspects of strategy, risk management, corporate culture, and transparency.

Figure 4. Concept and Implications of Global Sustainable Logistics
Source: Fernández-Villacañas (2019)(adapted from Carter & Rogers, 2008)

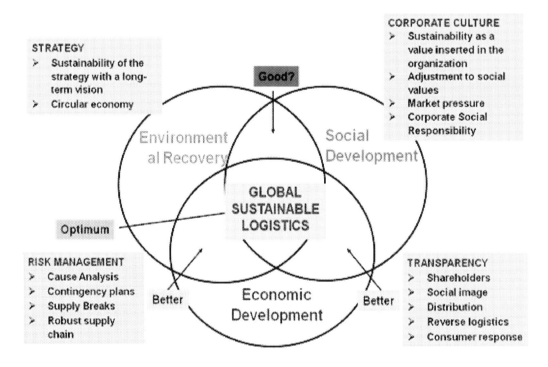

In 2015, the UN 2030 Agenda established the Sustainable Development Goals, calling countries of the international community and all significant social actors to a more intense effort in the social, economic, and ecological spheres, above all, to fight poverty, reduce human inequalities, and combat environmental damage. Although the achievements have been modest since the promulgation of the 2030 Agenda, sustainability has become a crucial aspect of business management (Rosati & Diniz, 2019) but insufficient to achieve global sustainability in such a degraded world (Caiado et al., 2018).

The New Concept of Disruptive Logistics

It is still indispensable to continue promoting more sustainable business and logistics management in all international community countries, implicitly integrating a critical assessment of all its activities concerning social, economic, and environmental aspects (Yun et al., 2019).

The growing economic importance derived from the Post-New World Economic Order trends, which we have analyzed, has derived the geoeconomics weight towards Asia-Pacific and African countries. Also, it is necessary to extend and emphasize the search for less polluting energy transport solutions and more sustainable solutions. Multinational logistics companies that offer their transportation services globally are the most interested in sustainability, as they value it as an essential source of competitive advantage (Bask et al., 2018). Likewise, sustainability has become a crucial factor in the competitiveness of industrial manufacturing companies, which is generating changes in the distribution of global added value (Le et al., 2013).

As proof of the growing importance assigned to logistics sustainability for global competitiveness is found on the sensitivity of the stock prices' value to the awarding of awards for logistics sustainability more than to other types of business awards, indirectly valuing investors the importance of sustainability concerning business performance (Eroglu et al., 2016). On the other hand, a synergistic relationship has been found between innovation in logistics sustainability and the implementation of logistics chains (Cherrafi et al., 2018). Likewise, it has been found that the success of implementing sustainable practices in logistics chains depends, among other factors, on the proper use of technological resources for transformation, information processing, and management and transportation operations (Watanabe et al., 2018).

After analyzing the concept of Global Sustainable Logistics, we can highlight the following aspects as fundamental bases for its development (Fernández-Villacañas, 2019):

- Cultural change to reconcile economic growth with responsible consumption.
- A long-term vision of the politicians responsible for its implementation, with the determination of a competitive and efficient national and regional framework that facilitates an adequate allocation and use of resources, favoring the effective development of macro-logistics infrastructures on which it relies, the competitiveness and productivity of companies.
- The progressive social diffusion of environmental respect for a natural basis of sustainable progress.
- The development of a social policy considers citizens both "means" and "ends" to achieve non-demagogic socio-economic progress.
- The need to promote a permanent structured collaboration between public and private sectors.

Finally, it is necessary to briefly analyze the concept of sustainable investment, an approach that is part of the philosophy of ethical investment. Today it is vital that companies comply with a series of sustainable parameters when investing. Since the late 1990s, progress in applying the concept of sustainable investing has been continuous, with the decision to launch the Dow Jones Sustainability Index, the first global index to introduce sustainability criteria.

For an investment to be considered socially responsible and within the framework of sustainability, it must meet environmental, social, and governance (ESG) criteria. It is critical for companies always to act based on them since they achieve greater profitability and commitment to society. The ESG criteria cover the following aspects (Halbritter & Dorfleitner, 2015):

- Environmental criterion (E) allows making decisions based on how the activities of the companies affect the environment.
- Social criterion (S), according to which the impact that the activities carried out by companies have on the community must be considered, in terms of diversity, human rights, or health care, among others.
- Governance criterion (G) emphasizes the impact that shareholders and management have, analyzing the repercussions of government decisions on stakeholders in matters such as the boards of directors' structure, shareholders' rights, and transparency.

NEW LOGISTICS, LOGISTICS 4.0, AND SUPPLY CHAIN 4.0

New Logistics and Digital Transformation

As we discussed earlier, the phenomenon of globalization within the framework of the New World Economic Order has driven for several decades a profound transformation of global business structures and promoted a new strategic mindset in business management based on the performance of international markets. As a result, the logistics function has undergone in parallel a continuous process of development and exponential transformation, becoming the fundamental support to satisfy the increasingly demanding needs of customers at a global level and one of the primary sources of competitive advantage for transnational companies. As a functional area with a minimal scope, logistics has developed and evolved in all industrial sectors, giving rise to the so-called new logistics capable of responding to the needs born from an increasingly complex, hostile, dynamic environment and global and uncertain. This evolved concept of new logistics was based on the conceptual transition from a "push" strategic supply perspective to a "push" demand perspective, developing new logistics models that are more sustainable, efficient, agile, intelligent, adaptable, resilient, and scalable.

The response to the new determinants of the global environment has also caused changes in companies' relationships with their suppliers and customers. Both groups are increasingly heterogeneous and are moving from one focused on reducing supply, storage, distribution, and waste costs to one focused on consumers. As a result, firms are more flexible and adaptive, systematically improving and integrating service levels and managing supply chains from the beginning to the end of the string. Beyond the linear supply chain in which the consumer is at the end, a complex network of socio-economic actors focused on the consumer is identified. The consumer in this network plays the role of the evaluator of all these actors involved, opting in their consumption by those they consider that best adapt to their changing needs (Fernández-Villacañas, 2018). Figure 5 summarizes the main aspects of traditional logistics and its evolution towards the new logistics.

On the other hand, we define digital transformation as the set of systemic processes, understood integrally and necessary for applying digital technologies, which implies the strategic, organizational, and cultural reinvention of the entity applied. It uses data, information, and intelligence to improve its performance and the necessary capacity to adapt quickly to the disruptive changes that are generated in the environment (Fernández-Villacañas, 2018). The result is a new technological scenario that is inducing a shortening of management cycles. Environmental changes are continuous and increase rapidly, at a rate that will undoubtedly continue to accelerate exponentially. This technological revolution is causing profound changes in the industry and society, economic prospects, work planning models, and how man-machine interactions should be oriented (Barreto, 2017).

Figure 5. The Traditional Logistics vs. the New Logistics
Source: Fernández-Villacañas (2018)

THE TRADITIONAL LOGISTICS	THE NEW LOGISTICS
Competition for price	Competition for service
Transportation of large lots, rare	Transport of smaller and more frequent lots
Supply type push, driven by the offer	Supply type pull, driven by demand
Existence of large inventories	Inventory zero (just in time)
Focus on business by contracts	Focus on the integration of processes, with the use of ICTs for coordination and control
Distribution networks organized at multiple levels with reduced areas of influence	Global networks of logistics platforms and integrated distribution centers
Producers and marketers with their own organization, including transportation	Outsourcing to logistics operators (3PL and above), focus of the entrepreneur on activities of greater added value
Provision and sales focused on the country itself	Globalization of suppliers and customers
Low environmental awareness	Greater environmental awareness, circular economy and reverse logistics

The engine that drives change and causes this continuous acceleration is the digital revolution, motivated by the global expansion of the internet and the solid exponential evolution of information and communication technologies. Thus, today we are totally immersed in the deployment process of digital technologies that are profoundly modifying society in general and the business world (Evtodieva et al., 2017). Although at the time, the development of information technologies represented a very significant advance in the mechanization and automation of processes and an immense qualitative leap with the subsequent connection of equipment between them, the development of digital technologies has exponentially multiplied the connectivity of all public and private actors, including people.

The analysis of the evolution of disruptive technologies concerning their adoption and habitual application by citizens, the productive-distributive sector, public administration, and educational systems are shown in Figure 6. The practically reactive attitude that characterizes most countries' public and educational sectors generates an increasingly wide gap about the exponential evolution of technologies. This attitude becomes more proactive in people and the productive-distributive sector, whose adoption is more significant but insufficient. The growing gap in the adoption of digital technologies between the public administration and the productive-distributive sector is worrying since it generates a potential future conflict between the public and private sectors, with a delay and desynchronization that will tend to grow due to exponential technology evolution.

Figure 6. Disruptive technologies evolution and social changes
Source: Author

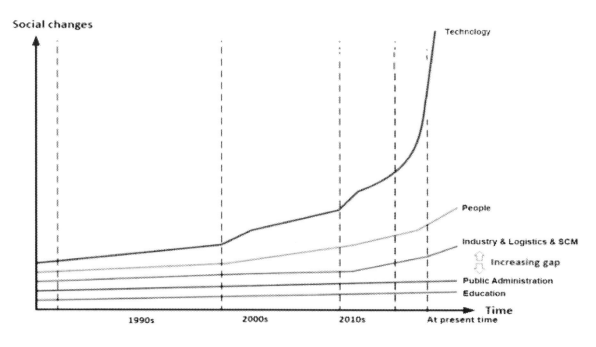

Figure 7. Digital Age evolution: Industry age, Logistics age, and SCM age
Source: Frazzon et al. (2019)

	INDUSTRY AGE	LOGISTICS AGE	SCM AGE
2020 / 2010	**Industry 4.0** Strong products individualization under production conditions with great flexibility (current...)	**Logistics 4.0** Intelligent Transportation Systems (ITS), Real Time Locating Systems (RTLS) (current...)	**SCM 4.0** Total network integration (current)
2000 / 1990 / 1980	Industry 3.0 Micro-processors. First programmable logic controller (PLC). Use of electronics and Information Technology (1969 to 2000s)	Logistics 3.0 System of Logistics Management (from the 1980s)	SCM 3.0 Integration between two channels (beginning of the 1980s)
1970 / 1960 / 1880 / 1870	Industry 2.0 Mass production using electrical energy (1870 to 1969)	Logistics 2.0 Automation of handling system (from the 1960s)	There is no SCM concept in this period
1860 / 1850 / 1800 / 1790 / 1780	Industry 1.0 Mechanical weaving loom, water, steam power (1784 to 1870)	Logistics 1.0 Mechanization of transport (late 19th century and early 20th century)	

The New Concept of Disruptive Logistics

In any case, beyond these relative problems of adoption and technological evolution, the result of the technical application to the productive-distributive field will allow immediate responses in decision-making based on information captured in real-time, through systems and smart processes, without variability or errors, with total traceability in the process chains and total sustainability. Following Frazzon et al. (2019), to summarize the impact of industrial-technological evolution on inventory and physical distribution area, Figure 7 draws a parallel between the phases of Industry evolution (Thoben et al., 2017), Logistics (Wang, 2016), and Supply Chain Management (SCM). In this comparative digital age evolution, it is possible to highlight some relevant aspects (Frazzon et al., 2019):

- Logistics 2.0 begins almost a century after Industry 2.0.
- Phase 3.0 has started almost simultaneously for all areas: Industry 3.0 in 1969, Logistics 3.0 in 1980, and SCM 3.0 in 1985.
- There is an absence of the SCM 1.0 and SCM 2.0 phases due to the characteristics and techniques of SCM 3.0, which is the first phase of SCM and is more related to industry 3.0 and logistics 3.0.
- SCM 4.0 is still a theoretical phase, not fully applied, whose practical application has not yet been consolidated to achieve full integration of supply networks.

Logistics 4.0

Industry 4.0 represents an essential evolution of the traditional approach to product optimization. During the last decades, the design and location of the plants responded to the search for economies of scale based on the volume of manufacturing and the economies derived from offshoring based on the lower costs of the productive factors of the location areas. However, Industry 4.0 proposes an intelligent relocation process derived from other elements of specialization and synergies. As a result, it creates different and immense interconnected networks of production and storage units, with an intelligent operation, which will achieve those raw materials, intermediate components, semi-finished products, and final product, will have the necessary mobility. They will be perfectly synchronized in their guaranteed flows, participating in global supply networks and an intra-industry trade system. The result of all this is a new form of the digital economy, known as hyper-connected and intelligent manufacturing (Evtodieva et al., 2019).

As an induced development of Industry 4.0 from which it comes, the concept of Logistics 4.0 arises which, based on the advanced approach of the new logistics, has gained significant importance in the business sector, both in entities that operate in local markets and, above all, those who distribute their products in global markets (Tang & Veelenturf, 2019). Clearly, the development of Industry 4.0 could not have been driven without addressing such a fundamental element of the industrial sector as logistics (Winkelhaus & Grosse, 2019).

Following Szymańska et al. (2017), we define Logistics 4.0 from a double approach, as a set of firm and mutually related processes among independent members using large amounts of data, and as a group of autonomous systems and self-organized within other systems to create logistics systems integrating separate subsystems made up of digital tools and technologies to support logistics' processes.

The main objective of Logistics 4.0 is to solve the logistical and management difficulties derived from reducing the life cycles of the products in global markets and, in general, the shortening of the management cycles. The implications on the continuous variation of demand that makes its calculation very complex make it necessary for more excellent connectivity and integration of global supply chains, fully linking their final and initial links. Likewise, it is required to have a great capacity to aggregate large masses of data to estimate demand in real-time, rigorously and automatically, and to be equipped with the capabilities of artificial intelligence and expert systems. These expert systems support specific decision-making processes in uncertain and increasingly complex environments (Fernández-Villacañas, 2018).

On the other hand, Logistics 4.0 implies the intelligent connection and optimization of all the processes and elements of the distribution and supply networks to improving logistics functionalities such as, among others, individual manufacturing fully adapted to each client with personalized offers, global customer geolocation, and optimization of global routes, a greater capacity to manage orders and physical shipments of products; flexibility, and automation of payments; complete international traceability of shipments; simultaneous multimodal omnichannel, international routes' optimization, and reduction of intermediate stocks and storage space (Strandhagen et al., 2019).

The main objective of Logistics 4.0 is to link the physical and the virtual in a symbiotic way to make the industry, logistics, and markets intelligent, to implement an innovative and collaborative model, in which the productive means are connected, the supply chains integrated, and the customer service channels are digital. This new hyper-connected and intelligent logistics will also facilitate the location with greater precision to customers, both current and potential, and the knowledge in detail of their purchasing behavior. Doing this will develop an effective treatment and interpretation of the data collected concerning all processes. They are key concepts that support the development of Logistics 4.0 integration, holistic vision, coherence, collaboration, innovation, and flexibility. The implementation of Logistics 4.0 will require the design and establishment of a new logistics strategy and the structure of a brand new organization. Change management towards a new digital culture is necessary to design and implement new methodologies and processes within the scalable framework of the progressive incorporation of new digital technologies (Fernández-Villacañas, 2020).

The future development of Logistics 4.0 has founded the Physical Internet logistics model (Montreuil et al., 2010), which has been valued as an essential conceptual reference in the US and the EU to guide the goal of the 2050 global logistics system. Physical internet would be a global logistics system that integrates physical and digital media and total operational interconnectivity. This integration would be achieved through the encapsulation, interfaces, and the design of the necessary systemic protocols supported by digital technologies. The system would be responsible for moving and storing physical objects around the planet effectively, efficiently, and sustainably in economic, social, and environmental terms. The main objective pursued by this logistics approach is the elimination of the voluminous inefficiencies currently present in the logistics and waste management networks of international transport, emulating, as a matrix idea, what the internet has developed concerning information flows on a global level.

It will be necessary to create an open market for transporting goods to implement this initiative globally and to offer a unique business consortium throughout the planet, equipped with shared, open, and adjustable distribution chains. As a result, products are transported in intelligent, modular, and standardized containers, which would allow comprehensive monitoring and control of each unit. For this, it will be necessary to achieve a maximum level of global collaboration, redefining the competitive space, eliminating the logistical processes of competition between companies, and concentrating the activity of the competition only in the points of sale, physical or digital, in which the consumers will determine the market shares (Montreuil, 2011).

Supply Chain Management 4.0

Following Frazzon et al. (2019), we define SCM 4.0 as the approach to integrating and synchronizing the entire value chain extended through the participating companies, using digital technologies to build an interconnected, intelligent, and transparent system with multidirectional communication in real-time. As a result, it allows managing the flows and the automation itself, creating an autonomous network focused on the client, adaptable, intelligent, agile, and dynamic. End-to-end integration is undoubtedly the core of SCM 4.0 through digital technologies, such as the Internet of Things, Internet of Service, and other technical elements, allowing a network to be integrated, synchronized, remarkably dynamic, and flexible in its applications. It is an innovation from the factory to the consumer (Figure 8).

Figure 8. Supply Chain 4.0 delivers innovation from factory to customer
Source: Alicke et al. (2017)(McKinsey & Company)

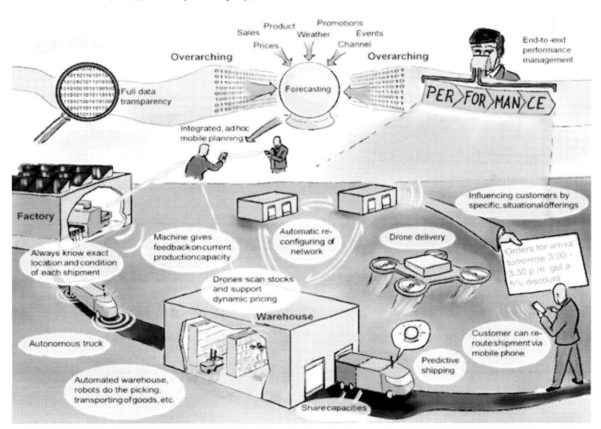

The SCM function has focused on the analytical planning processes of supply, operations, and demand and sales, based on its complete integration of suppliers to customers (Castro, 2019). The strong trend towards individualization and personalization of products progressively increases the number of references, with a permanent increase in customer expectations regarding service, order, and delivery management and intense competition between the different supply chains. The result is needed to redesign the chain for which digitization will be the fundamental tool to improve effectiveness and efficiency. We obtain the SCM 4.0 that offers the following functional advantages (Alicke et al., 2017):

- Faster, significantly reducing delivery time and advancing shipments through predictive demand analysis, even before the customer places their order.
- Greater flexibility, dynamic replanning through a continuous process in real-time, and the reorganization of the chain, supply changes generated by changes in demand or supply, in changing requirements or restrictions.
- More individualization in demand management, micro-segmentation techniques, mass customization, more sophisticated scheduling, and deliveries in the "last mile."
- Higher precision through logistical and economic performance-related key indicators automatically inform the establishment of goals at more realistic levels. Also, automatic identification by the expert system of risks and exceptions without human participation allows modifying aspects of the SCM to eliminate or reduce risks.
- Cost reduction, through the automation and robotization of physical handling tasks in the logistics processes of reception, storage, collection, packaging, and shipping, as well as with the use of autonomous trucks. The use of Artificial Intelligence and Machine Learning supports optimizing the use of storage and transport media.

RESULT: THE NEW CONCEPT OF DISRUPTIVE LOGISTICS

The previous sections have analyzed the substantial evolution of logistics in recent decades to become an essential element of business strategy in an increasingly global, dynamic, complex, technological, and uncertain environment. Likewise, the circumstances that could generate the emergence of the Post-New World Economic Order, fuelled by the global crisis of the COVID-19 pandemic, are a degraded globalizing system, with a social tendency towards political delegitimization, and great existing difficulties for the sustainability of the planet. In any case, it seems undeniable that the changes and reforms necessary to alleviate the crisis will be implemented in the short term, and little by little, they will return to the lost normality. The significant changes of a new order will not occur now. However, the evidence shows that the turbulent environment has become disruptive.

It seems necessary that from the development of Logistics 4.0 and Supply Chain Management 4.0, with the help of digital technologies, logistics will continue to evolve rapidly to face disruptive environments. Changes are unforeseen, substantial, and impactful. Companies and global consumer markets demand innovative, more effective, and efficient logistics solutions, generating radical improvements in the logistics services developed.

Disruptive Logistics arises to advance and create the necessary business models that will make the previous ones obsolete, integrating and emphasizing the latest disruptive technological solutions, the traditional lean & agile logistics models. On the one hand, Lean Logistics corresponds to the long-term efficiency of the organization, and to obtain the correct results, in the right place, at the right time, in the right amount, minimizing costs, being flexible and open to change (Hinterhuber, 1994). On the other hand, Agile Logistics corresponds to the effectiveness of specific operations in short-term approaches. The rapid reaction to change and frequent deviations from plans make agility essential (Christopher, 2000).

The New Concept of Disruptive Logistics

Given that the "lean" and "agile" approaches are opposite and complementary, logistics strategies must combine Lean Logistics and Agile Logistics to respond to the different needs derived from the disruptive environment, low costs (lean), and speed of delivery and response (agile), both of great value to achieve effective and efficient logistics performance in disruptive environments (Aronsson et al., 2011; Vázquez-Bustelo & Avella, 2006).

The new concept of Disruptive Logistics must be fully integrated into the analyzed paradigm of Sustainable Global Logistics 4.0. The sustainability of the supply chain and logistics management, in general, implies the establishment of a strategy that integrates the sustainability objectives within the business process coordination system and in a transparent way. Figure 9 combines Logistics 4.0, SCM 4.0, and Lean & Agile Logistics to cope with disruptive environments. Also, the development and implementation of a global logistics solution, similar to the Physical Internet, comply with the ecological, social, and economic restrictions that limit optimal logistics solutions and will condition operations and activities.

Figure 9. Disruptive Logistics concept
Source: Author

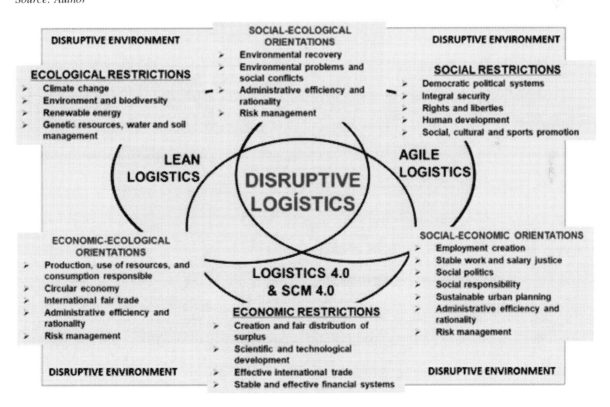

As Figure 9 shows, a series of socio-economic, economic-ecological, and socio-ecological guidelines will guide the planning, definition, and implementation of the systems transformation processes. The new Disruptive Logistics has an excellent capacity for innovation and added social influence to modify people's behavior, eliminate harmful products, and generate changes in consumption habits typical of the traditional linear market economy to promote a renewed circular digital economy.

SOLUTIONS AND RECOMMENDATIONS

Global logistics management develops in a highly disruptive environment, in which changes are increasingly substantial, unforeseen, and impactful. Today, innovative, more effective, and efficient logistics solutions are demanded within a global sustainability framework, capable of generating radical improvements through the integration of traditional lean & agile logistics models and disruptive technologies.

Regardless of when a restructuring of the Post-New World Economic Order would be imposed, it is necessary to promote a new concept of Disruptive Logistics that has been defined and that is based on three fundamental pillars: globalization, digitization, and sustainability. This new idea incorporates the potential of the digital transformation processes of logistics systems within the paradigm of Global Sustainable Logistics.

FUTURE RESEARCH DIRECTIONS

The study carried out on the concept of Disruptive Logistics within Global Sustainable Logistics 4.0 shows interesting lines derived from the research concerning a possible implementation of the Post-New World Economic Order. Within these multidisciplinary lines of research, it would be necessary to develop a new logistics concept related to the application of different disruptive technologies with environmental, social, and economic restrictions. Also, socio-economic, economic-ecological, and socio-ecological guidelines should guide planning, defining, and implementing this transformation process. On the other hand, it is necessary to broaden the analysis of applied Disruptive Logistics, studying its impact on logistics activities in real cases. These studies could be related to the reforms, changes, and policies that nations will foreseeably propose, both in the public and private spheres, to alleviate the economic and social crisis induced by the COVID-19 pandemic.

CONCLUSION

A conceptual review has been carried out of the aspects that condition the definition of a new concept of Disruptive Logistics that can respond to the logistics management needs deriving from a hypothetical restructuring of the current New World Economic Order and a real and moving disruptive environment. As the most significant conclusions obtained from the research, we can highlight the following:

First, the New World Economic Order that the United States and the USSR imposed as victorious powers after World War II has progressively degraded over the past two decades. Both institutions and political discourses were the basis of the globalizing order that has deteriorated close with the legitimacy of the representatives and the political system itself. Devastating environment, such as water crisis, inaction in favor of the climate, natural disasters, the fight against extreme weather events, man-made environmental disasters, loss of biodiversity, pandemics, added to other social phenomena, such as cyberattacks, corruption, failures in global governance, economic war, and social instability have revealed the significant weaknesses of the current world order. It seems that this extraordinary situation, catalyzed by the consequences of the COVID-19 pandemic, represents a window of opportunity to promote an in-depth review process of the global socio-economic system.

Second, although the decline of the prevailing order is evident, the current world economic order will probably continue its course. However, the contradictions of the great dominant paradigms will surely deepen until, in another future conjuncture of great crisis, the conditions are sufficient and necessary to achieve the proposed Post-New World Economic Order.

Third, system degradation has transformed a turbulent environment into a disruptive and destructive event, so it is essential to urgently integrate logistics systems into the sustainable global logistics paradigm we have been analyzing. After this, humankind will fully assume the three-fold environmental, social, and economic sustainability-related commitments.

Fourth, the Logistics 4.0 and SCM 4.0 development has evolved logistics to face disruptive environments, where changes are unforeseen, substantial, and impactful. Firms and global consumer markets demand innovative, more effective, and efficient logistics solutions, generating radical improvements in the logistics services developed. The exponential technological development creates a growing gap concerning its application by people, companies, public administration, and educational systems.

Finally, because of all these ideas, the enriched concept of Disruptive Logistics has been proposed, which arises for the advancement and creation of new business models, together with new digital technology solutions and traditional Lean & Agile approaches. It will be necessary to develop and implement a global logistics solution, similar to the Physical Internet, to fulfill ecological, social, and economic restrictions limiting optimal logistics solutions and its capacity for innovation and social influence. As a result, it modifies people's behavior, eliminates harmful products, and generates changes in consumer habits to promote a renewed circular digital economy.

REFERENCES

Alicke, K.; Rexhausen, D., & Seyfert, A. (2017). *Supply Chain 4.0 in consumer goods.* McKinsey & Company.

Arbeláez-Campillo, D. F., Dudareva, A., & Marianna, M. J. (2019). Las pandemias como factor perturbador del orden geopolítico en el mundo globalizado. *Cuestiones Políticas, 36*(63), 134–150.

Arbeláez-Campillo, D. F., & Villasmil, J. J. (2020). Escenarios prospectivos de un nuevo orden internacional que se vislumbra luego de la pandemia COVID-19. *Telos. Revista de Estudios Interdisciplinarios en Ciencias Sociales, 22*(3), 494–508. doi:10.36390/telos223.02

Aronsson, H., Abrahamsson, M., & Spens, K. (2011). Developing lean and agile health care supply chains. *Supply Chain Management, 16*(3), 176–183. doi:10.1108/13598541111127164

Barreto, L., Amaral, A., & Pereria, T. (2017) Industry 4.0 implications in logistics: an overview. *Proceedings of the Manufacturing Engineering Society International Conference MESIC 2017.* 10.1016/j.promfg.2017.09.045

Barría, C. (2020, March 30) Coronavirus: "Estamos frente a una crisis generalizada del capitalismo democrático mundial y del no democrático, como el de China". *BBC News / Mundo.* https://www.bbc.com/mundo/noticias-52055657

Bask, A., Rajahonka, M., Laari, S., Solakivi, T., Töyli, J., & Ojala, L. (2018). Environmental sustainability in shipper-LSP relationships. *Journal of Cleaner Production, 172*, 2986–2998. doi:10.1016/j.jclepro.2017.11.112

Borda, J. (2016). *La Fábrica del Futuro: Humana, inteligente, tecnológica y digital*. Sisteplant.

Caiado, R. G., Filho, W. L., Quelhas, O. L. G., de Mattos, D. L., & Avila, L. V. (2018). A literature-based review on potentials and constraints in the implementation of the sustainable development goals. *Journal of Cleaner Production, 198*, 1276–1288. doi:10.1016/j.jclepro.2018.07.102

Carter, C. R., & Rogers, D. S. (2008). A framework of sustainable chain management: Moving toward new theory. *International Journal of Physical Distribution & Logistics Management, 38*(5), 360–387. doi:10.1108/09600030810882816

Castro, J. (2019, June 11). *Qué es la cadena de suministro Supply Chain 4.0 y qué puede hacer por tu negocio*. Blog Corponet. https://blog.corponet.com.mx/que-es-la-cadena-de-suministro-o-supply-chain-4-0-y-que-puede-hacer-por-tu-negocio

Cherrafi, A., Garza-Reyes, J. A., Kumar, V., Mishra, N., Ghobadian, A., & El-Fezazi, S. (2018). Lean, green practices and process innovation: A model for green supply chain performance. *International Journal of Production Economics, 206*, 79–92. doi:10.1016/j.ijpe.2018.09.031

Christopher, M. (2000). The Agile Supply Chain Competing in Volatile Markets. *Industrial Marketing Management, 29*(1), 37–44. doi:10.1016/S0019-8501(99)00110-8

Colombatto, E. (2020, Nov 27). *Opinion: The WTO drifts toward irrelevance*. Geopolitical Intelligence Services GIS. https://www.gisreportsonline.com/opinion-the-wto-drifts-toward-irrelevance,economy,3373.html

Eroglu, C., Kurt, A. C., & Elwakil, O. S. (2016). Stock Market Reaction to Quality, Safety, and Sustainability Awards in Logistics. *Journal of Business Logistics, 37*(4), 329–345. doi:10.1111/jbl.12145

Evtodieva, T. E., Chernova, D. V., Ivanova, N. V., & Kisteneva, N. S. (2019). Logistics 4.0. In S. Ashmarina & M. Vochozka (Eds.), *Sustainable Growth and Development of Economic Systems* (pp. 207–219). Springer. doi:10.1007/978-3-030-11754-2_16

Evtodieva, T. E., Chernova, D. V., Voitkevich, N. I., Khramtsova, E. R., & Gorgodze, T. E. (2017). Transformation of logistics organizations forms under the conditions of a modern economy. In E. G. Popkova (Ed.), *Russia and the European Union* (pp. 177–182). Springer. doi:10.1007/978-3-319-55257-6_24

Fernández-Villacañas, M.A. (2018) Las plataformas logísticas 4.0 y la mejora del comercio global: Creando ventaja competitiva logística y desarrollo sostenible. *VI Simposio Internacional Online de Logística y Competitividad, High Logistics Simposios*.

Fernández-Villacañas, M. A. (2019) Desarrollo e Implementación de Plataformas Logísticas de Carga 4.0. *Proceedings of Primer Congreso Internacional de Tecnología e Innovación en Logística 4.0*.

Fernández-Villacañas, M. A. (2020). The New Concept of Logistics Platforms 4.0: Creating Competitiveness Within the Paradigm of Global Sustainable Logistics. In U. Akkucuk (Ed.), *Handbook of Research on Sustainable Supply Chain Management for the Global Economy* (pp. 36–62). IGI Global. doi:10.4018/978-1-7998-4601-7.ch003

Frazzon, E., Rodriguez, C. M., Pereira, M., Pires, M., & Uhlmann, I. (2019). Towards Supply Chain Management 4.0. *Brazilian Journal of Operations & Production Management, 16*(2), 180–191. doi:10.14488/BJOPM.2019.v16.n2.a2

Ghosh, I. (2020). *How China Overtook the U.S. as the World's Major Trading Partner.* Visual Capitalist. https://www.visualcapitalist.com/china-u-s-worlds-trading-partner/

Haarhaus, T., & Liening, A. (2020). Building dynamic capabilities to cope with environmental uncertainty: The role of strategic foresight. *Technological Forecasting and Social Change, 155*(3), 120033. doi:10.1016/j.techfore.2020.120033

Haass, R. N. (2008). The age of non-polarity: What will follow U. S. dominance? *Foreign Affairs, 87*(3), 44–56.

Halbritter, G., & Dorfleitner, G. (2015). The wages of social responsibility - where are they? A critical review of ESG investing. *Review of Financial Economics, 26*, 25–35. doi:10.1016/j.rfe.2015.03.004

Hinterhuber, H. H. (1994). The European way to lean management. *The International Executive, 36*(3), 275–290. doi:10.1002/tie.5060360303

Kasper, W. (2015). *Libertad Económica y Desarrollo*. Universidad Francisco Marroquin.

Koziej, S. (2020, May 5). *The U.S. and China: The rivalry escalates irrelevance.* Geopolitical Intelligence Services GIS. https://www.gisreportsonline.com/the-us-and-china-the-rivalry-escalates,defense,3155,report.html

Le, F., Olivier, B., & Mognol, J. H. (2013). Sustainable manufacturing: Evaluation and modeling of environmental impacts in additive manufacturing. *International Journal of Advanced Manufacturing Technology, 69*(9-12), 1927–1939. doi:10.100700170-013-5151-2

Lissardy, G. (2020). *Coronavirus: los 2 grandes escenarios mundiales que plantean algunos expertos para después de la pandemia*. BBC News/Mundo. https://www.bbc.com/mundo/noticias-internacional-52526090

McMichael, A. J. (2020). *Climate change and human health. Risks and responses*. World Health Organization.

Montreuil, B. (2011). Toward a Physical Internet: Meeting the global logistics sustainability grand challenge. *Logistics Research, 3*(2-3), 1–29. doi:10.100712159-011-0045-x

Montreuil, B., Meller, R. D., & Ballot, E. (2010). Towards a Physical Internet: the impact on logistics facilities and material handling systems design and innovation. In K. Gue (Ed.), *Progress in Material Handling Research* (pp. 1–23). Material Handling Industry of America.

Morales, Y. R., Villasmil, J. J., & Martínez, R. D. (2019). Democracia a la palestra: ¿Gobierno del pueblo o degeneración del poder? *Revista de Ciencias Sociales*, *25*, 236–252.

Navarro, M. & Sabalza, X. (2016) Reflexiones sobre la Industria 4.0 desde el caso vasco. *Ekonomiaz. Revista vasca de Economía, 89*, 142-173.

Parra, R. (2020). Una perspectiva del mundo que se nos avecina. *Revista de la Universidad del Zulia*, *11*(29), 3–5. doi:10.46925/rdluz.29.01

Peel, Q. (2009, May 4) El primer paso de un nuevo orden geopolítico. *Cronista, Impresa General*. https://www.cronista.com/impresa-general/el-primer-paso-de-un-nuevo-orden-geopolitico-20090504-0035.html

Rosati, F., & Diniz, L. G. (2019). Addressing the Sustainable Development Goals in sustainability reports: The relationship with institutional factors. *Journal of Cleaner Production*, *215*, 1312–1326. doi:10.1016/j.jclepro.2018.12.107

Sachs, J. (2008). *Common Wealth: Economics for a Crowded Planet*. Penguin Group.

Schwab, K., & Malleret, T. (2020). *COVID-19: The Great Reset.* World Economic Forum, Forum Publishing.

Strandhagen, J. O., Vallandingham, L. R., Fragapane, G., Strandhagen, J. W., Stangeland, A. B. H., & Sharma, N. (2019). Logistics 4.0 and emerging sustainable business models. *Advanced Manufacturing*, *5*(4), 23–32.

Szymańska, O., Adamczak, M., & Cyplik, P. (2017). Logistics 4.0 - a new paradigm or set of known solutions? *Research in Logistics and Production*, *7*(4), 299–310. doi:10.21008/j.2083-4950.2017.7.4.2

Tang, C. S., & Veelenturf, L. P. (2019). The Strategic Role of Logistics in the Industry 4.0 Era. *Transportation Research Part E, Logistics and Transportation Review*, *129*, 1–11. doi:10.1016/j.tre.2019.06.004

Thoben, K. D., Wiesner, S., & Wuestet, T. (2017). "Industrie 4.0" and Smart Manufacturing – A Review of Research Issues and Application Examples. *International Journal of Automotive Technology*, *11*, 4–19.

Vazquez-Bustelo, D., & Avella, L. (2006). Agile manufacturing: Industrial case studies in Spain. *Technovation*, *26*(10), 1147–1161. doi:10.1016/j.technovation.2005.11.006

Wang, K. S. (2016) Logistics 4.0 Solution: New Challenges and Opportunities. *6th International Workshop of Advanced Manufacturing and Automation*. 10.2991/iwama-16.2016.13

Watanabe, E. H., Da Silva, R. M., Blos, M. F., Junqueira, F., Filho, D. J., & Miyagi, P. E. (2018). Framework to evaluate the performance and sustainability of a dispersed productive system. *Journal of the Brazilian Society of Mechanical Sciences and Engineering*, *40*(6), 277–286. doi:10.100740430-018-1032-9

Winkelhaus, S., & Grosse, E. (2019). Logistics 4.0: A systematic review towards a new logistics system. *International Journal of Production Research*, *1*, 18–43.

World Economic Forum. (2020) *The Global Risks Report 2020*. Author.

Yun, G., Yalcin, M. G., Hales, D. N., & Kwon, H. Y. (2019). Interactions in sustainable supply chain management: A framework review. *International Journal of Logistics Management*, *30*(1), 140–173. doi:10.1108/IJLM-05-2017-0112

ADDITIONAL READING

Abd Hamid, M. S., Isa, S., & Boon Cheong, C. (2021). A Study of Quality Tools and Techniques for Smart Manufacturing in Industry 4.0 in Malaysia: The Case of Northern Corridor Economic Region. In Research Anthology on Cross-Industry Challenges of Industry 4.0 (pp. 792-816). IGI Global. http://doi:10.4018/978-1-7998-8548-1.ch040

Aslan, E. (2021). How Supply Chain Management Will Change in the Industry 4.0 Era? In Research Anthology on Cross-Industry Challenges of Industry 4.0 (pp. 1015-1035). IGI Global. http://doi:10.4018/978-1-7998-8548-1.ch051

Baporikar, N. (2020). Logistics Effectiveness Through Systems Thinking. *International Journal of System Dynamics Applications*, *9*(2), 64–79. doi:10.4018/IJSDA.2020040104

Munsamy, M., Telukdarie, A., & Dhamija, P. (2021). Logistics 4.0 Energy Modelling. In Research Anthology on Cross-Industry Challenges of Industry 4.0 (pp. 436-460). IGI Global. http://doi:10.4018/978-1-7998-8548-1.ch023

Saiz-Alvarez, J. (2018). *Business Strategies and Advanced Techniques for Entrepreneurship 4.0*. IGI Global. doi:10.4018/978-1-5225-4978-9

Saiz-Álvarez, J., & Olalla-Caballero, B. (Eds.). (2021). *Quality Management for Competitive Advantage in Global Markets*. IGI Global. doi:10.4018/978-1-7998-5036-6

Uslu, B. Ç., & Fırat, S. Ü. (2021). A Comprehensive Study on Internet of Things Based on Key Artificial Intelligence Technologies and Industry 4.0. In Research Anthology on Cross-Industry Challenges of Industry 4.0 (pp. 171-191). IGI Global. http://doi:10.4018/978-1-7998-8548-1.ch010

KEY TERMS AND DEFINITIONS

Digital Economy: An economic system that primarily employs digital technology, especially electronic transactions made using the internet.

Disruptive Environment: It is considered one in which the changes are unforeseen, substantial, and impactful, or in which the appearance of a new technology or work method directly influences the entities.

Disruptive Technology: It is an innovation that significantly alters how consumers, industries, or businesses operate. A disruptive technology sweeps away the systems or habits it replaces because it has attributes that are recognizably very superior.

ESG Criteria: Environmental, social, and governance (ESG) criteria are standards for a company's operations. Environmental criteria consider how a company performs as a steward of nature. Social criteria examine how it manages relationships with employees, suppliers, customers, and the communities where it operates. Governance deals with a company's leadership, executive pay, audits, internal controls, and shareholder rights.

Global Logistics: It is technically the process of managing goods through an international supply chain, from its production to other parts of the world through intermodal transport system, transport via ocean, air, rail, and truck. The effectiveness of global logistics is measured using international logistics performance indexes.

Logistics 4.0: It is a strategic technological direction that integrates different types of technologies to increase both the efficiency and effectiveness of the supply chain, shifting the focus of the organizations to value chains, maximizing the value delivered to the consumers as well as the customers, by raising the levels of competitiveness, transparency, and decentralization among the different parties through digitalization.

New Logistics: This evolved concept of logistics is based on the conceptual transition from a push strategic supply perspective to a push demand perspective, developing logistics models that are more sustainable, efficient, agile, intelligent, adaptable, resilient, and scalable. The response to the new determinants of the global environment has also caused logistics changes in companies' relationships with their suppliers and customers. Both groups are increasingly heterogeneous. They initially focused on reducing supply costs, storage, distribution, and waste. Now, they concentrate on consumers to be more flexible and adaptive, improve service levels systematically, and manage supply chains in an integrated manner.

New World Economic Order: This is the name given to the world economic order that prevailed for many decades because of the world reorganization produced after the Second World War, with particular geopolitical and geoeconomics areas of influence two victorious great powers, the USA and the USSR. Despite the bipolar world of the cold war dominated by these superpowers, it was always possible to reach agreements with good cooperation and exchange between the least aligned countries.

Post-New World Economic Order: A set of proposals for the reform of the New World Economic Order that supports political-economic models that are considered obsolete, given that they are totally incapable of providing solutions to the significant problems that arose against humanity: climate change, natural disasters, loss of biodiversity, terrorism, drug trafficking, organized crime, food crises, infectious disease epidemics, cyber-attacks, political corruption, human rights violations, the extreme polarization of wealth, and private waste, unemployment, gender violence, etc.

Supply Chain Management 4.0: Logistics approach that integrates and synchronizes the entire value chain extended through the participating companies, using digital technologies to build an interconnected, intelligent, and transparent system, with multidirectional communication in real-time that allows managing the flows and the automation itself, creating an autonomous network focused on the client, adaptable, intelligent, agile, and dynamic.

Sustainable Logistics: It is a logistics strategy that combining the environmental, economic, and social objectives of the organization transparently, within the framework of the coordination system of business processes within the company, which tries to optimize the economic results of each company and long-term supply chains. The result wanted is to produce and distribute goods in a sustainable way, taking into account environmental, economic, and social factors.

Chapter 7
A Treatise on Isoattribute Curve Analysis, Consumer Induction Factor, and Country Brand Value:
A Modern Proposal

Debasish Roy
https://orcid.org/0000-0002-0706-9743
Sikkim University, India

ABSTRACT

This research has endeavored to focus on three major issues that are yet to be explored as per the existing literature on marketing. The first issue focuses on the Isoattribute curve analysis, rooted in the theory of conjoint utility analysis. In other words, the first segment concentrates on the derivation of the Isoattribute curve model which helps to attain the consumer equilibrium condition in a two-commodity world (brand or non-brand products). The second segment of the chapter has transitioned from the microeconomic model to the macroeconomic perspective based on a 'single-country' approach, i.e., USA, based on a derivation of consumer induction factor (CIF). Finally, the third and final segment of the chapter extends its horizon at a larger scale by conducting a cross-country time-series study of 10 years (2009 – 2018) which redefines branding in an absolutely new dimension where the 'brand values' of seven sample countries are estimated by inculcating the socio-economic, political, and working environment factors as the major dimensions.

INTRODUCTION

This research work is my sole contribution to the existing literature of applied marketing, which is totally original and seminal in nature in the sense that it has contributed to introducing three new concepts of *Isoattribute curve* and *Isopartworth line*, *Consumer Induction Factor (CIF)*, and *Country Brand Value*

DOI: 10.4018/978-1-7998-7689-2.ch007

(CBV) that would definitely help to advance the evolving domain of marketing analytics holistically as they have originated from the foundations of Conjoint utility analysis, Consumer behavior, and Brand analytics respectively.

The *first* segment of this article begins with the concept of *Conjoint utility analysis*. Conjoint utilities measure customer preference levels depending on the *attribute* levels of the commodities (brands) consumed and the *partworths* (relative weights) of the goods (brands) consumed. To quote Toubia (2018): "The premise of Conjoint Analysis is to decompose a product or service into attributes (e.g., number of minutes included, number of GB of data, charge for additional minutes, base price, etc.) that each has different levels (e.g., 500 minutes, 1,000 minutes, unlimited). The output of a Conjoint Analysis study is an estimation of how much each consumer in a sample values each level of each attribute. Such preferences are called partworths because they capture how much each part of the product is worth to the consumer".

Conceptualization of the Isoattribute Curve and Isopartworth Line

By using the premise of the conjoint utility analysis, the foundations of the *Isoattribute* curve and the *Isopartworth* line could be structured from a *microeconomic* perspective. An *isoattribute* curve may be defined as a *locus* of points, each representing a combination of quantities consumed for two commodities under the non – brand category or two products under the same brand category which will yield a fixed level of aggregate attribute at a given time. By maintaining parity with the property of indifference curve, it may be stated that a *higher* isoattribute curve represents a *higher* attribute level for a consumer, *ceteris paribus*.

An *isopartworth* line may be defined as the *locus* of points, each representing a combination of different partworths of two commodities under non – brand category or two products under the *same* brand category within a *fixed* budget of a consumer for a given time.

The *traditional tangency solution may attain the consumer's equilibrium condition*, i.e., by the point of tangency between the isoattribute curve and the isopartworth line where the Marginal Rate of Change (MRC) in the partworth (W) of each good must be equal to its Marginal Rate of Change (MRC) in the attribute level.

The *convexity* condition of the isoattribute curve refers to the *diminishing* rate of Marginal Rate of Technical Change (MRTC) between the attribute levels and partworths of two goods consumed. These concepts are discussed in detail under the "Methodology" section and the "Theoretical framework of Isoattribute curve analysis" subsection.

Derivation of Consumer Induction Factor (CIF): A Single Country Approach

In order to derive the Consumer Induction Factor (CIF) for the US economy, three major variables are taken into account, and they are as follows:

- Household final consumption expenditure per capita (in constant 2010 US$) growth rate or simply Consumption Per Capita Growth Rate (CPCGR)(World Bank);
- The Global Innovation Index (GII)® (A joint collaboration of Cornell University, INSEAD Business School, and World Intellectual Property Organization (WIPO)); and
- The American Customer Satisfaction Index (ACSI)®.

These three factors (variables) are chosen very carefully, with specific objectives pertinent to the formulation of CIF. The first variable, i.e., CPCGR, is to be considered the determining factor to interpret the changes in the *purchasing power* of the consumers (population) of a given economy. An increase in CPCGR is treated as a positive economic indicator of an economy regarding the growth perspective. The second variable, GII, emphasizes the importance of *innovation* which *positively* influences the consumption pattern of the population in general. The estimation of missing observations for GII of USA for the years 2008 - 2010 are as follows (Table 1).

Table 1. Estimation of missing observations for the Global Innovation Index (GII) for USA

Year	GII	x	GII*x	x*x
2011	56.67	-4	-226.28	16
2012	57.70	-3	-173.10	9
2013	60.31	-2	-120.62	4
2014	60.09	-1	-60.09	1
2015	60.10	0	0	0
2016	61.40	1	61.40	1
2017	61.40	2	122.80	4
2018	60.13	3	180.39	9
2019	61.73	4	246.92	16
	539.43	0	31.42	60

X = (Year − 2015) GII = 59.94 + 0.524x
GII for the year 2008 = 56.272 | GII for the year 2009 = 53.795 | GII for the year 2010 = 57.320

To quote Lam (2006, p.124): "Innovation can be understood as a process of learning and knowledge creation through which new problems are defined, and new knowledge is developed to solve them." There are four major characteristics of factors that affect both the first and repeat purchases of a new product/service by customers: adopter characteristics, innovation characteristics, firm characteristics, and environmental characteristics. The adopter characteristics directly affect the purchase of a new product and include adopter class, risk disposition, geodemographics, economic value need, and word of mouth behavior. The innovation characteristics include relative advantage, relative cost price, perceived usefulness, ease of use, and network externality. The firm characteristics comprise firm size, firm marketing efforts, and firm reputation. The environment characteristics that drive new product trials and repeat purchases include infrastructure, availability, demand for related products, and market conditions (Shankar, 2009). The *sixth* and present generation of innovation model (Marinova and Phillimore, 2003; pp. 45–51), termed as *Innovation Milieux,* states that "innovation stems from a creative combination of generic know-how and specific competencies" and "territorial organization is an essential component of the process of techno-economic creation" (Bramanti and Ratti, 1997; p. 5). Hence, technological innovation plays a significant role in diversifying the range of products/services in the market and boosting the consumption demand and GDP of an economy.

Finally, customer satisfaction is considered to be one of the most significant indicators of market perceptions. Its principal use is twofold, as mentioned below:

a) The collection, analysis, and dissemination of data send a message to send a statement about the importance of tending to customers and ensuring that they have a positive experience with the company's goods and services;
b) Although sales or market share can indicate how well a firm is performing *currently*, satisfaction is perhaps the best indicator of how likely the customers would opt for *repeat purchase* in the *future* (Bendle *et al.*, 2016; p. 49).

Thus, ACSI would be the automatic choice to gauge the country's overall customer satisfaction across all industry segments in the US economy.

The CIF is enumerated as the *geometric mean* of the Consumption per capita Relative (CPCR), Global Innovation Index Relative (GIIR), and The American Customer Satisfaction Index Relative (ACSIR) respectively for the period 2009 – 2018 (CIF = 100 for Base Year = 2008) [Discussed in detail under "Methodology" section and "Theoretical framework of Consumer Induction Factor (CIF)" subsection].

Derivation of Country Brand Value (CBV): A Cross-Country Empirical Study

Although there is no universally accepted definition of "Brand," the American Marketing Association's (AMA) 1960's definition of a brand is well-accepted by the academics (especially from North America) as 'a name, term, design, symbol or any other feature that identifies one seller's good or service as distinct from those of other sellers'(www.ama.org/resources/Pages/Dictionary.aspx?dLetter=B, accessed Sept 24, 2020).

The AMA's Dictionary of Marketing Terms has amended the definition of 'Brand and Branding' as below:

A brand is a customer experience represented by a collection of images and ideas; often, it refers to a symbol such as a name, logo, slogan, and design scheme. Brand recognition and other reactions are created by the accumulation of experiences with the specific product or service, both directly relating to its use, and through the influence of advertising, design, and media commentary (www.ama.org/resources/Pages/Dictionary.aspx?dLetter=B, accessed Sept 24, 2020).

De Chernatony and McDonald (2003) produced a more comprehensive definition of *successful branding* as: "an identifiable product, service, person or place, augmented in such a way that a buyer or user perceives relevant and unique added values which match their needs more closely. Furthermore, its success results from being able to sustain these added values in the face of competition". Clearly, the concept of successful branding of an entity should be *multidimensional* in nature. Although the branding of the countries around the world had been attempted by the introduction of an index named *Anholt Ipsos Nation Brands Index® (NBI)* (A joint collaboration between Simon Anholt and Ipsos) and it had gained substantial popularity among its target audience over time, however, it failed to focus on the multidimensional aspects related to the core objective of *branding* – especially, when it comes to the point of branding countries across the globe that are uniquely diversified in terms of multiethnic, socio-economic, political-legal, cultural and linguistic backgrounds.

The NBI was formulated using six dimensions: *Exports, Governance, Culture and Heritage, People, Tourism,* and *Investment and Immigration* (https://www.ipsos.com/sites/default/files/20-03-60_anholt-ipsos_place-branding.pdf, accessed Sept 24, 2020). This Index, though it seems to be quite comprehensive in nature, fails to address the major glaring issues that the countries are facing in the current global scenario, such as economic recession, inequality in income distribution, level of human development, quality of life, and social well-being, levels of unemployment and vulnerable employment, social cohesion, and democratic environment. In order to address those issues, the concept of Country Brand Value (CBV) has been introduced by applying the technique of Present Value (PV) criterion. There are eight variables required to estimate the CBV of a country, and they are as follows:

a) Gross Domestic Product (Annual) Growth Rate (GDPGR): It is required as an indicator of a country's economic performance;

b) Unemployment Rate (Annual) (UNEMR): It is required to evaluate the impact of economic growth on the labor market of an economy;

c) Vulnerable Employment Rate (Annual) (VEMR): It plays an essential role in determining the portion of the labor force of an economy that is vulnerable to demand and supply *shocks* of the system;

d) Secured Employment Rate (Annual) (SEMPR): The annual SEMPR is calculated as the *difference* between 100 and the *sum* of UNEMR and VEMR;

e) Human Development Index (HDI): The annual HDI estimates are required to analyze a country's progression/retrogression in terms of the scale of human development;

f) Job Quality Index (JQI): The JQI (annual) is itself a broad-based index computed as the *geometric mean* of 6 important variables termed as Earning Quality Relative (EQR), Job Market Security Rate Relative (JMSRR), Quality of Working Environment Rate Relative (QWERR), Mean Personal Income Relative (MPIR), Life Satisfaction Index Relative (LSIR), and Dependent Employees Ratio Relative (DERR) respectively (Base Year: 2007) which provides us a comprehensive overview of the 'job quality' for the employees of a country;

g) Gini Coefficient (GC): The annual estimates of Gini Coefficient (GC) have been included in the formulation of CBV because it helps to give us a clear idea about the extent of unequal distribution of income and wealth among the targeted recipient population of an economy;

h) Fragile States Index (FSI): The FSI is itself a highly comprehensive weighted average based on four broad dimensions of cohesion, economic, political, and social indicators. The higher score on the scale for a country contemplates greater vulnerability in terms of *failing* to handle the socio-political issues; and

i) Fragile States Index Rate (FSIR): The FSIR is a simple ratio of the FSI score of a country divided by the maximum possible score of 120 [Discussed in detail under "Methodology" section and "Theoretical framework of Country Brand Value (CBV)" subsection].

Data Descriptions

The Metadata for the chosen variables to estimate Consumer Induction Factor (CIF) and Country Brand Value (CBV) respectively are given below:

Consumer Induction Factor (CIF)

Household final consumption expenditure per capita, or simply "(private consumption per capita), is calculated using private consumption in constant 2010 prices and World Bank population estimates. Household final consumption expenditure is the market value of all goods and services, including durable products (such as cars, washing machines, and home computers) purchased by households. It excludes purchases of dwellings but includes imputed rent for owner-occupied dwellings. It also includes payments and fees to governments to obtain permits and licenses. Here, household consumption expenditure includes the expenditures of nonprofit institutions serving households, even when reported separately by the country. Data are in constant 2010 US dollars" (World Bank).

The Global Innovation Index (GII)® is a collaborative effort among Cornell University (USA), INSEAD Business School (France), and World Intellectual Property Organization (WIPO). "The Global Innovation Index (GII) is an evolving project that builds on its previous editions while incorporating newly available data and that is inspired by the latest research on the measurement of innovation. The GII relies on two sub-indices—the Innovation Input Sub-Index and the Innovation Output Sub-Index—each built around pillars. Three measures are calculated:

1. Innovation Input Sub-Index: Five input pillars capture elements of the national economy that enable innovative activities.
2. Innovation Output Sub-Index: Innovation outputs are the result of innovative activities within the economy. Although the Output Sub-Index includes only two pillars, it has the same weight in calculating the overall GII scores as the Input Sub-Index.

The overall GII score is the average of the Input and Output Sub-Indices (Score: 0–100) (https://www.globalinnovationindex.org/about-gii#framework)

The American Customer Satisfaction Index (ACSI)® is the only national cross-industry measure of customer satisfaction in the United States. This strategic economic indicator is based on customer evaluations of the quality of goods and services purchased in the United States and produced by domestic and foreign firms with substantial US market shares. The ACSI measures the quality of economic output as a complement to traditional economic output measures. The ACSI was started in the United States in 1994 by researchers at the University of Michigan, in conjunction with the American Society for Quality in Milwaukee, Wisconsin, and CFI Group in Ann Arbor, Michigan. The national ACSI score continues to be updated quarterly on a rolling basis, factoring in data from 10 economic sectors and 46 industries" (Score: 0–100) (https://www.theacsi.org/about-acsi/history)

Country Brand Value (CBV)

GDP Growth Rate (Annual) (GDPGR):

"Annual percentage growth rate of GDP at market prices based on constant local currency. Aggregates are based on constant 2010 US dollars. GDP is the sum of gross value added by all resident producers in the economy plus any product taxes and minus any subsidies not included in the value of the products. It is calculated without making deductions for depreciation of fabricated assets or depletion and degradation of natural resources" (World Bank).

- Unemployment Rate (Annual) (UNEMR): It "refers to the share of the labor force that is without work but available for and seeking employment" (World Bank).
- Vulnerable Employment Rate (Annual) (VEMR): It "is contributing family workers and own-account workers as a percentage of total employment" (World Bank).
- Secured Employment Rate (Annual) (SEMPR): It is calculated as the difference between 100 and the sum of the Unemployment rate and Vulnerable employment rate. The labor force pertaining to secured employment could be treated as resilient to demand and/or supply shocks of the labor market.
- Human Development Index (HDI): It "is a summary measure of average achievement in key dimensions of human development: a long and healthy life, being knowledgeable and have a decent standard of living. The HDI is the geometric mean of normalized indices for each of the three dimensions.

The health dimension is assessed by life expectancy at birth. The education dimension is measured through schooling years for adults aged 25 years and more and expected years of schooling for school-age children entering age. The standard of living dimension is measured by gross national income per capita. The HDI uses the logarithm of income to reflect the diminishing importance of income with increasing GNI. The scores for the three HDI dimension indices are then aggregated into a composite index using geometric mean" [United Nations Development Programme (UNDP)]

- Job Quality Index (JQI): It "is estimated as a Geometric Mean of six Quantity Relatives of Earnings Quality (EQ), Job Market Security Rate (JMSR) which is calculated as the difference between 1 and Job Market Insecurity Rate (JMIR) (expressed as a percentage), Quality of Working Environment Rate (QWER) which is estimated as the difference between 1 and Job Strain (JSTR) (expressed as a percentage), Mean Personal Income (MPI), Life Satisfaction Index (LSI), and Dependent Employees Ratio (DER) (expressed as a percentage) [Base Year = 2007]. The Quantity Relatives are termed as Earnings Quality Relative (EQR), Job Market Security Rate Relative (JMSRR), Quality of Working Environment Rate Relative (QWERR), Mean Personal Income Relative (MPIR), Life Satisfaction Index Relative (LSIR), and Dependent Employees Ratio Relative (DERR), respectively.

Formally,

$JQI = (EQR \times JMSRR \times QWERR \times MPIR \times LSIR \times DERR)^{1/6}$ (Roy, 2019)

The datasets of all the indicators (variables) are available at Better Life Index – Edition 2017 (Organization for Economic Co-operation and Development, OECD) http://stats.oecd.org/OecdStat_Metadata/ShowMetadata.ashx?Dataset=BLI&Coords=&Lang=en.

The Gini Coefficient (GC) "measures the extent to which the distribution of income (or, in some cases, consumption expenditure) among individuals or households within an economy deviates from a perfectly equal distribution. A Lorenz curve plots the cumulative percentages of total income received against the cumulative number of recipients, starting with the poorest individual or household. The Gini index measures the area between the Lorenz curve and a hypothetical line of absolute equality, expressed as a percentage of the maximum area under the line. Thus, a Gini index of 0 represents perfect equality, while an index of 100 implies perfect inequality" (World Bank);

The Fragile States Index (FSI)® "produced by The Fund for Peace (FFP), is a critical tool in highlighting not only the normal pressures that all states experience but also in identifying when those pressures are outweighing the states' capacity to manage those pressures. By highlighting pertinent vulnerabilities which contribute to the risk of state fragility, the Index — and the social science framework and the data analysis tools upon which it is built — makes political risk assessment and early warning of conflict accessible to policy-makers and the public at large". The FSI consists of 12 dimensions divided into four major *indicators* having three dimensions per group, namely; Cohesion indicator with dimensions Security Apparatus, Fractionalized Elites, and Group Grievance; Economic indicator with dimensions Economic Decline, Uneven Economic Development, and Human Flight and Brain Drain; Political indicator with dimensions State Legitimacy, Public Services, and Human Rights and Rule of Law; and Social and Cross-cutting indicators with dimensions Demographic Pressures, Refugees and Internally Displaced Persons (IDP), and External Interventions respectively. Each dimension's score ranges from 0 to 10 ('0' being the 'Best,' and '10' the 'Worst'), totaling a *maximum* possible score of 120 (https://fragilestatesindex.org/).

The Fragile States Index Rate (FSIR) is the ratio of a country's FSI score to 120.

LITERATURE REVIEW

By maintaining the structure of this article, this section has also been divided into three sections emphasizing conjoint utility analysis, consumer behavior, and branding, which are closely related to the three core topics of Isoattribute curve analysis, CIF, and CBV analysis, respectively.

Conjoint Utility Analysis

Conjoint utility analysis is one of the oldest and commonly used tools in the field of marketing analytics. Its origin dates back to the early 1970s' (Green and Rao, 1971) and has its foundation in Mathematical Psychology (Luce and Tukey, 1964). The conjoint utility analysis is a study of quantifying customer preferences. One of the essential properties of conjoint utility analysis is that the number of attribute levels may estimate the number of partworths in a sample. The number of partworths is estimated as the number of levels (L) *minus* 1. However, each attribute at each profile has to be at the same level. It is possible to describe the level of each profile of an attribute by using L–1 variables, given the number of levels as L (Toubia, 2018). The conjoint utility function may be expressed as below (Toubia, 2018):

$$u_{ij} = \alpha_i + \sum_k \beta_{ik} x_{jk} + \varepsilon_{ij} \tag{1}$$

where u_{ij} = Utility of i-th consumer for j-th profile,
α_i = Intercept of the regression line for consumer i,
β_{ik} = Coefficient that determines the partworths of consumer i for attribute k. If there are L levels in attribute k, this coefficient vector has a single row and L–1 columns,
x_{jk} = Vector that captures the level of profile j on attribute k. If there are L levels in attribute k, this coefficient vector has a single row and L–1 columns,

ε_{ij} = Error terms.

The additive nature of the utility function above implies that it is 'compensatory' in nature. In other words, there always remains a chance to *compensate* the lower value of an attribute by increasing the value of another attribute. However, there always remains the scope of non-compensatory research in the conjoint utility analysis. The non-compensatory rules are of *five* types (Toubia, 2018):

a) Conjunctive: This rule allows consumers to 'pass' a profile if it meets a list of criteria, e.g., a car with a certain body type and below a price level;
b) Disjunctive: This rule allows consumers to 'pass' a profile if it meets any *one* of the lists of criteria, e.g., a car with a certain body type *or* below a price level;
c) Disjunction of conjunctions: This rule allows consumers to 'pass' a profile if it meets *at least* one conjunctive rule from the set conjunctive rules (Hauser *et al.*, 2010);
d) Lexicographic: This rule is applied when profiles are ranked based on criteria that are sequentially listed, e.g., cars are ranked based on price followed by their designs; and
e) Elimination by aspect: This rule is applied when profiles are eliminated from the choice set by considering various criteria in a sequential manner (Tversky, 1972).

There are several formats of conjoint utility analysis. The most traditional format is "Ratings-based Conjoint Analysis." It requires the respondents to rate several profiles (usually between 12 to 20). These profiles are assumed to be rated independently from each other by the consumer. This method has its major limitation in the sense that it does not reflect the real-world situations where consumers have their alternative choices. A popular format of conjoint utility analysis that is more technically sound is "Choice-Based Conjoint Analysis (CBC)." This format has the option to *choose* among alternatives accompanied by the option of "no choice" also. This format is much closer to real-world scenario since a consumer always opts for 'better' alternatives than the existing products/services available in the market, and in case no such alternative is found, he/she may opt for "no choice" (Louviere *et al.*, 2000).

The major disadvantage of this format is that it is both time-consuming and expensive. Apart from predicting market shares and optimizing product lines, conjoint analysis is also used to infer the "Willingness to pay (WTP)" for any product/service. For example, if the partworth for a price level p_1 is β_{p1} and at the price level p_0 of another partworth is β_{p0}, then if $p_0 < p_1$; the condition $\beta_{p_0} > \beta_{p_1}$ holds for the consumer as she prefers the lower price. Hence it may be stated that for a reduction in the price of $1, the consumer's change in utility level will be $(\beta_{p_0} - \beta_{p_1})/(p_1 - p_0)$. Assuming that the utility level is linear in nature, in case of change in partworths from β_{l1} to β_{l0} with attribute levels l_1 and l_0 respectively, the WTP for the consumer may be estimated as $(\beta_{l_1} - \beta_{l_0})(p_1 - p_0)/(\beta_{p_0} - \beta_{p_1})$ - which may be used as a standard equation to estimate the WTP of a consumer for partworths of two different attribute levels.

Finally, it must be essential to treat conjoint utility analysis as a market research tool that can only *approximate* real-world scenarios. Innovation and the introduction of new technologies would definitely help advance its methodical applications in the future to quantify consumer preferences better.

Consumer Behavior

The foundations of consumer behavior models are stated below (Lilien, Kotler, and Sridhar Moorthy, 1992; pp. 19-135):

a) <u>Behavioral learning</u>: This theory states that a consumer's experience determines her future behavior of purchasing;
b) <u>Personality research</u>: The attribution theory of reconciliation of a consumer's purchasing behavior with the behaviors of others and existing social normative beliefs dictate her future consumption behavior;
c) <u>Information processing</u>: It studies both the idiosyncratic structure of an individual consumer's decision-making processes along with her behavioral changes about pre-conceived norms and standards; and
d) <u>Attitude models</u>: This paradigm deals with studying a consumer's intention and her resulting attitude towards existing social norms and beliefs.

There are five stages that a consumer supposedly goes through before purchasing a product/service: need arousal, information search, evaluation, purchase, and post-purchase feelings (Lilien, Kotler, and Sridhar Moorthy, 1992; pp. 19 - 135). These stages are briefly described below:

I) <u>Need Approach</u>: The epoch of purchasing process is need arousal. A need can be activated through internal or external stimuli. The internal stimuli are often *physical needs,* and external stimuli consist of audio-visual triggers such as advertisements, announcements, sales promotions, etc.
II) <u>Information Search</u>: Depending on the intensity of stored need, the consumer is faced with two states. The first state is known as *heightened attention,* where the individual becomes extremely alert regarding the information about need and its instant gratification. The second state is called *active information search,* where the consumer, under the conditions of more intense need, searches for relevant information pertinent to his / her complete satisfaction and gratification.
III) <u>Evaluation</u>: The evaluation stage has two components. The first component is called *perception*, which refers to the consumer's perceptive belief(s), guiding him/her to influence the buying decision. The second component is termed preferences driven by the buyer's perceptions.
IV) <u>Purchase</u>: The purchasing stage involves the consumer's perception of the brand, expected utility from the brand, and uncertainty that affects purchase probability.
V) <u>Post-purchase feelings</u>: The post-purchase feelings of a customer are twofold: first, if he/she is satisfied with the quality of the product/service, then he/she will purchase it again, and second, the consumer is likely to communicate his / her feelings about the product to other potential customers who are seeking information.

Modern theories of consumer behavior are based upon a *behavioral perspective*. The behavioral perspective model treats behavior at the *molar* level compared to individual responses (Foxall, 2010). The central perspective of the behavioral perspective model is the consumer *situation* which directly influences the shaping and maintenance of consumer behavior (Foxall, 2007). The dependent variable in the consumer behavior analysis is response rate (Fagerstrøm and Sigurdsson, 2016). When a response is strengthened or weakened by the presence/absence of stimuli that follow a consumer's response is called *operant behavior* (Catania, 2013).

The *key* independent variables incorporated in the behavioral perspective model related to the consequences of consumer behavior are *reinforcement (utilitarian or informational)* and *punishment (utilitarian or informational)*, where reinforcement is the tangible functional and economic benefits derived from the purchase of products/services, ownership, and consumption (utilitarian), social appreciation or appreciation (informational); and punishment, as a process, encompasses those factors which have yielded *negative* reinforcements to the consumers like the cost of consuming, relinquishment of funds, etc. (utilitarian), and aversive consequences of consumer behavior guided by social network (informational). The different types of stimuli are a) *physical* (e.g., point-of-purchase promotion, store brand, etc.), b) *social* (e.g., salesperson, other consumers in the store, etc.), c) *temporal* (related to specific occasions), and d) *regulatory* (rules and regulations related to contingencies) (Foxall, 2005).

The Behavioral Perspective Model (BPM) is essentially an extension of "three-term contingency" based on operant behaviorism. Formally, it may be expressed as below:

$$S^D \to R \to S^r$$

where S^D: An element in the environment; R: Response; and S^r: Another element (external) in the background facilitates reinforcement (Foxall, 2016) (Figure 1).

Figure 1. Summative behavioral perspective model (BPM)
Source: Foxall, 2016

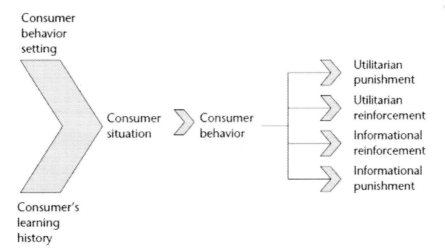

Finally, when principles and techniques developed in fundamental behavior analysis get transferred from the animal laboratories (as a part of the behavioral study) to analyzing consumer choice patterns in real open settings (Sigurdsson and Foxall, 2016), the concept of *matching analysis* emerges. The *matching law* was discovered by Herrnstein (1961, 1970), and now it has been researched worldwide (Baum, 2002; Logue, 2002). The matching law is a *molar law* which states that *relative response rate* (behavior) matches its *relative reinforcement* on concurrent interval schedules of equilibrium (Davison and McCarthy, 1988; Herrnstein, 1997). For two response possibilities, the *strict matching law* may be expressed as:

$$B_a / (B_a + B_b) = R_a / (R_a + R_b) \qquad (2)$$

where B stands for specific choice for actions 'a' and 'b' respectively, and R stands for a response for actions 'a' and 'b' respectively.

The concept of melioration succeeds the matching law. Melioration predicts that the customer will always prefer a higher reinforcement value each time commensurate with his/her behavior (Sigurdsson and Foxall, 2016). It is applicable for short-run consumer behavior analysis and not the long run (as per rational choice analysis). The process of melioration may be expressed by an equation below:

$$\frac{d[C_a / (C_a + C_b)]}{dt} = f_x (V_a - V_b) \qquad (3)$$

where C_a and C_b are money spent on actions a and b in time t, and V_a and V_b are values of reinforcement (action a) and punishment (action b) in time t.

The function f_x is differentiable and monotonically increasing with $f_x(0)=0$ (Vaughan, 1985) and $C_a+C_b=1$. At equilibrium, $V_a=V_b$ and the payoff for the consumer in the situation i may be defined as:

$$V_i = g[(R_i - P_i) / t_i] \qquad (4)$$

where V_i = Payoff for the consumer in situation i.
R_i = Reinforcement for the consumer in situation i.
P_i = Reinforcement for the consumer in situation i.
t_i = Time taken in situation i.

The matching law and melioration are the future trendsetters in consumer behavior analysis which are still in development in light of the experimental interventions in real market environments such as retailing (Curry *et al.*, 2010).

Brand and Branding

The term 'brand' is usually referred to a branded product (e.g., Pepsi, Coca-Cola, etc.), service (e.g., T-mobile, UPS, etc.), company (e.g., Wal-Mart, Amazon, Microsoft, etc.), person (politician, celebrity, painter, scientist, etc.), team (soccer, basketball, rugby, etc.), organization (e.g., UNICEF, etc.) or place (e.g., a city brand) (Park *et al.*, 2008).

The brand-customer relationships vary on the *degree* of strength dimension – ranging from weaker forms like simple liking and purchasing to more robust states of "involving customers' desire to stay in brand relationships" like repeat purchase, resisting negative brand information, etc. (Figure 2).

The successful branding of a product or service requires *branding attachment*. The branding attachment is purely a combination of psychological and behavioral actions. To quote Park *et al.* (2008): "In

Figure 2. Consumers' behavioral hierarchy
Source: Park et al., 2008

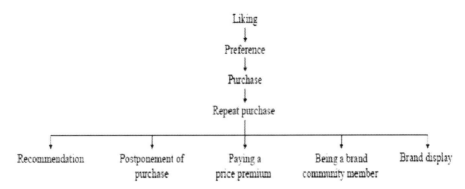

this context, we define attachment as the *strength of the cognitive and affective link between a consumer and a brand*. It denotes a psychological state of mind in which a strong cognitive and affective bond connects a brand to an individual in such a way that the brand is an extension of the self". The hierarchy of brand attachment may be summarized below (Figure 3):

Figure 3. A schematic representation of the determinants and effects of brand attachment
Source: Park et al., 2008

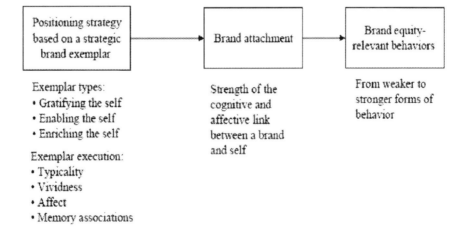

Fournier (1998) identified 15 types of consumer-brand relationships: love, commitment, passion, the feeling of attachment, etc., at the 'core of all strong brand relationships.' After brand attachment, *Brand identity* is an important concept that serves as the basis for brand strategy or corporate strategy. Esch (2008) has pointed out *three* fundamental criteria for a brand identity from identity research as follows:

1. Self–image: Self–image refers to the subjective perception of brand identity, and it reflects the vision of the corporate managers and employees who promote this brand.
2. Identity–reflecting attributes: These attributes comprise continuous and visible features through which the brand identity becomes visible to others.

3. <u>Brand image</u>: Brand image is a derived output defined by a *picture* that target groups perceive by contacting the brand. Continual cognitive processes form the external image.

Brand identity should be considered the cornerstone of brand strategy and vital to brand management (Kapferer, 2004). Brand positioning is the basis of brand identity (Esch, 2007). Proper positioning of a brand helps to emphasize the distinctive characteristics of brand identity that differentiates the brand from other brands and makes it attractive to the stakeholders (Esch, 2008).

The relationship between brand identity, brand positioning, and brand image may be illustrated as below (Figure 4):

Figure 4. Relationship between brand identity, brand positioning, and brand image
Source: Esch et al., 2005

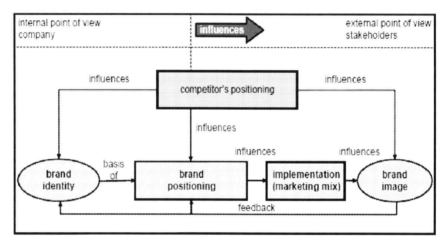

In the case of conceptualizing brand identity, the following aspects should be taken into account (Esch, 2007):

a) Brand identity is *more* than the summation of separate criteria. In the case of a brand identity, 'the sum of parts does not equal the whole.' In other words, while judging a brand, one should not judge it by its one or a few attributes; however, the brand should be judged holistically with correlations between single attributes.
b) For the development of strong brand associations, emotions and modality-based impressions play an important role.
c) Collection of all brand identity attributes must ensure that all-important and continuous attributes of the brand have been considered.
d) The brand identity tools should reflect brand identity so that all its contents are easily applicable.
e) The product range of a brand determines its brand identity. The degree of heterogeneity is directly proportional to the level of complexities for brand identity.
f) It is crucial to analyze the relationship between brand identity and brand strategy. The brand strategy must be different between "a house of brands" and "a branded house" (Aaker and Joachimsthaler,

A Treatise on Isoattribute Curve Analysis, Consumer Induction Factor, and Country Brand Value

2000). For 'a house of brands', each brand must have distinguishing attributes that should not overlap.

In brand equity research, three qualities, namely, favorability, top–of–mind salience, and uniqueness, are considered significant factors influencing brand strength in the marketplace (Keller, 1993). However, Fournier et al. (2008) termed a more innovative approach as *brand meaning resonance* has been able to create a landmark in the study of brand equity. To quote Fournier *et al.* (2008): "Resonance refers to the reverberation of a brand's meanings within the contexts of the organization, the broader culture, and the person's life." They have defined three levels of resonances: The *personal resonance* level reflects the degree of correlation between the brand's architecture of claimed meanings and the meanings a consumer seeks to find from his/her life; *cultural resonance* level refers to the degree by which claimed brand meanings reflect, reinforce, and shape meanings from the collective social space connect to the consumers in terms of interpretation and exchange of brand's experience; and *organizational resonance* level refers to the degree of correlation between the brand's claimed implications, operational business structure, values and goals, and behaviors of its employees and delivering the 'goods' by the brand (Figure 5).

Figure 5. A meaning-based model of brand equity
Source: Fournier et al., 2008

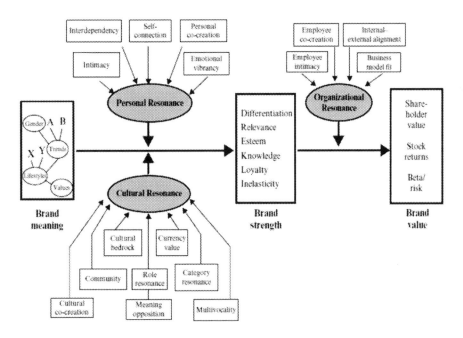

Apart from the scholarly works mentioned above, there had been a significant amount of research work in the field of brand equity and its allied subjects. Smith *et al.* (2007), in their research spanning six years (1999–2004) with a sample size of 198 observations (brands), have shown that advertising expenditure has the "least significant relationship with the brand equity based on current and previous year data." However, advertising and gross profit showed increased statistical significance based on the previous year's data following a lagged linear model. The regression analysis revealed that the three variables taken together would help increase the level of statistical significance.

Leone *et al*. (2006) have emphasized that "The power of the brand lies in the minds of consumers" (p. 126). On the other hand, Customer Lifetime Value (CLV) is a financial measure that has immediate application as a metric for assessing customer prospecting, as an objective to be managed, and as a method for valuing the firm (Blattberg, Kim, and Neslin 2008; Gupta, Lehmann, and Stuart 2004; Gupta and Lehmann, 2005).

Leone *et al*. (2006), Peppers and Rogers (2004, p. 31), and Rust *et al*. (2000, p. 55) have chosen Brand Equity as the logical precursor of CLV. By winning the consumers' hearts and minds, it is easier for the marketing managers to retain and sustain the customer base. Keller and Lehmann (2006) have identified the link between Brand Equity and CLV as a *key* area for future research. Ailawadi, Lehmann, and Neslin (2003) and Srinivasan, Park, and Chang (2005) have shown how marketing actions are associated with Brand Equity. Aaker and Jacobson (1994, 2001) found a positive relationship between brand quality, attitude, and stock prices. The relationship between brand quality and the stock price has also been established by Kerin and Sethuraman (1998), Mizik and Jacobson (2008), and Madden, Fehle, and Fourier (2006). There are two primary methods for calculating CLV (Dwyer 1989; Berger and Nasr 1998; Blattberg *et al*. 2008, 2009):

(I) The *simple retention model assumes* that a customer is acquired, retained with a certain probability every year, and ceases to be a customer after a specific time. This model does not consider the 'return factor' of a customer and treats the customer as a 'perishable' commodity.

(II) On the other hand, the *Markov migration model* considers the factor of the *temporary* defection of a customer and accepts the customer's return after temporary defection as the process of reacquisition.

The simple retention model is mainly driven by profit (contribution margin) and retention rates, whereas the Markov migration model is guided by profit, retention rate, and reacquisition rates. Stahl *et al*. (2012), in their empirical study based on a unique database of 39 automobile brands in the US for ten years (1999 – 2008) about the relationship between Brand Equity and the components of CLV like customer acquisition, retention and profitability envisaged the following important results:

- Brand Equity has a predictable and meaningful impact on all the significant components of CLV like customer acquisition, retention, and profitability;
- The relationship is effective even after controlling all other major marketing activities;
- In particular, brand differentiation increases customer profitability but decreases customer retention and acquisition.

To sum up, conjoint utility, consumer behavior analysis, and brand management are intertwined, which may be studied either separately or collectively to conduct research works in the dynamic and ever-changing world of marketing analytics.

METHODOLOGY

The Theoretical Framework of Isoattribute Curve Analysis

Let the number of consumers in a finite space be i (i = 1, 2, 3, ..., n), and the possible attribute levels of available consumer goods be A_j and the partworths associated with the attribute levels be W_j (j = 1, 2, 3, ..., m). Hence the *aggregate conjoint utility* function (U_C^i) may be expressed as:

$$U_C^i = \sum_{i=1}^{n} \sum_{j=1}^{m} A_j W_j \tag{5}$$

Now let the demand function for j-th commodity be:

$$q_j = q_j(A_j, W_j) \text{ with } \partial q_j / \partial A_j, \ \partial q_j / \partial W_j > 0 \tag{6}$$

Thus, the *aggregate demand* function may be expressed as:

$$Q_j^i = \sum_{i=1}^{n} \sum_{j=1}^{m} q_j(A_j, W_j) \tag{7}$$

Hence, the *aggregate budget* equation for the consumers would be:

$$m_j^i = \sum_{i=1}^{n} \sum_{j=1}^{m} p_j \times q_j(A_j, W_j) \tag{8}$$

where m_j^i = Expenditure on commodity j by consumer i; and p_j = Price of commodity j.

Now, society's problem is maximizing its aggregate conjoint utility subject to the aggregate budget constraint (Henderson and Quandt, 1980). Hence, the required Lagrangian equation would be:

$$Ł = \sum_{i=1}^{n} \sum_{j=1}^{m} A_j W_j + \lambda [m_j^{\bar{i}} - \sum_{i=1}^{n} \sum_{j=1}^{m} p_j \times q_j(A_j, W_j)](\lambda \geq 0) \tag{9}$$

The required first-order conditions are:

$$\partial Ł / \partial A_j = \sum_{i=1}^{n} \sum_{j=1}^{m} W_j - \lambda p_j \sum_{i=1}^{n} \sum_{j=1}^{m} \partial q_j / \partial A_j = 0 \tag{10}$$

$$\partial Ł / \partial W_j = \sum_{i=1}^{n}\sum_{j=1}^{m} A_j - \lambda p_j \sum_{i=1}^{n}\sum_{j=1}^{m} \partial q_j / \partial W_j = 0 \qquad (11)$$

$$\partial Ł / \partial \lambda = m_j^{\bar{i}} - \sum_{i=1}^{n}\sum_{j=1}^{m} p_j \times q_j(A_j, W_j) = 0 \qquad (12)$$

From equations (10) and (11), we have:

$$\sum_{i=1}^{n}\sum_{j=1}^{m}(\partial q_j / \partial A_j) / \sum_{i=1}^{n}\sum_{j=1}^{m}(\partial q_j / \partial W_j) = \sum_{i=1}^{n}\sum_{j=1}^{m} W_j / \sum_{i=1}^{n}\sum_{j=1}^{m} A_j \qquad (13)$$

$$\rightarrow \sum_{i=1}^{n}\sum_{j=1}^{m} \partial W_j / \partial A_j = \sum_{i=1}^{n}\sum_{j=1}^{m} W_j / \sum_{i=1}^{n}\sum_{j=1}^{m} A_j \qquad (14)$$

$$\rightarrow \sum_{i=1}^{n}\sum_{j=1}^{m} \partial W_j / W_j = \sum_{i=1}^{n}\sum_{j=1}^{m} \partial A_j / A_j \qquad (15)$$

Marginal rate of change in the aggregate partworth for commodity j for the society = Marginal rate of change in the total attribute level of commodity j for the society. Equation (15) represents the *society's consumers' equilibrium condition*.

Equation of the Isoattribute Curve

In a two–commodity (*branded or non – branded products*) world, the equation of the Isoattribute curve may be expressed as:

$$A = f(W_1 q_1, W_2 q_2) = A^o \text{ (fixed)} \qquad (16)$$

where A = Attribute level
W_1 = Partworth of good 1
q_1 = Quantity of good 1
W_2 = Partworth of good 2
q_2 = Quantity of good 2

Equation of the Isopartworth Line

$$M \geq W_1 p_1 q_1 + W_2 p_2 q_2 \qquad (17)$$

where M = Income of the consumer

p_1 = Price per unit of good 1
p_2 = Price per unit of good 2

At the point of tangency (T) between the isoattribute curve I_1 and the isopartwoth line MM_1, the Marginal Rate of Change (MRC) in the partworth (W) of each good must be equal to its Marginal Rate of Change (MRC) in the attribute level (Figure 6).

Figure 6. Consumer's equilibrium for brand/non-brand consumption

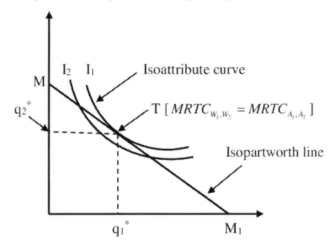

Formally,

$$MRC_W^1 = MRC_A^1 \text{ and } MRC_W^2 = MRC_A^2 \tag{18}$$

where MRC_W^1 = Marginal Rate of Change in the partworth of Good 1
MRC_A^1 = Marginal Rate of Change in the attribute level of Good 1,
MRC_W^2 = Marginal Rate of Change in the partworth of Good 2, and
MRC_A^2 = Marginal Rate of Change in the attribute level of Good 2.

The second-order condition for consumer's utility maximization requires the *bordered Hessian determinant (Đ)* to be positive (Henderson and Quandt, 1980).
In other words,

$$Đ = \begin{vmatrix} q_{AA} & q_{AW} & -W \\ q_{WA} & q_{WW} & -A \\ -W & -A & 0 \end{vmatrix} > 0 \quad (19)$$

where

$$q_{AA} = \frac{\partial^2 q}{\partial A^2}, \; q_{AW} = \frac{\partial^2 q}{\partial A \partial W}, \; q_{WA} = \frac{\partial^2 q}{\partial W \partial A}, \; \text{and} \; q_{WW} = \frac{\partial^2 q}{\partial W^2} \quad (20)$$

It should be noted that the *attribute* levels of commodities should be measurable *quantitatively*. For example, by using Brand Finance's Brand Strength Index (BSI)® (Scale: 0 – 100) as a *proxy variable* for the attribute levels of branded products, the *equilibrium* levels of attributes and partworths could be estimated for branded commodities.

The Theoretical Framework of Consumer Induction Factor (CIF)

By keeping in mind, the premise of Consumer Induction Factor (CIF), it may be estimated as the *Geometric Mean (GM)* of the Consumption per capita Relative (CPCR), Global Innovation Index Relative (GIIR), and The American Customer Satisfaction Index Relative (ACSIR) respectively for the period 2009 – 2018 (CIF = 100 for Base Year = 2008). The missing observations for the variable GII had been estimated using the Least Squares method.
Formally,

$$CIP = (CPCR \times GIIR \times ASCIR)^{1/3} \quad (21)$$

The estimated results for the CIF are econometrically tested by the Ordinary Least Squares (OLS) method at a 5 percent level of significance or better to provide a holistic picture about the respective distribution of weights of the relevant dimensions included for the study (Table 2).

The Theoretical Framework of Country Brand Value (CBV)

The Country Brand Values (CBV) for 7 sample European countries were estimated using the Customer Lifetime Value (CLV) criterion. The CLV equation may be expressed as below (Bendle *et al.*, 2016):

$$CLV = (C \times RR) / (1 + DR - RR) \quad (22)$$

where C = Contribution, RR = Retention Rate, and DR = Discount Rate.

Identical to the concept of CLV, CBV is also a *discounted* estimate by taking into account all six variables, namely, Gross Domestic Product (Annual) Growth Rate (GDPGR), Secured Employment Rate (Annual) (SEMPR), Human Development Index (HDI), Job Quality Index (JQI), Gini Coefficient (GC), and Fragile States Index Rate (FSIR) respectively. The missing observations of GC for Germany (Table 3) and the UK (Table 4) are estimated by the Least Squares method (Das, 2000).

Table 2. Estimation of the Consumption Induction Factor (CIF) for USA (2009-2018)

Year	CPC	GII	ACSI	CPCGR	GIIR	ACSIR	CIF
2008	33337.9	56.27	75.7				
2009	32632.4	53.79	75.9	97.883	95.599	100.264	97.897
2010	32929.1	57.32	75.3	98.773	101.862	99.471	100.027
2011	33310.3	56.57	75.8	99.917	100.530	100.132	100.193
2012	33566.0	57.70	76.3	100.684	102.538	100.793	101.335
2013	33821.0	60.31	77.9	101.449	107.176	102.906	103.816
2014	34569.7	60.09	76.8	103.695	106.785	101.453	103.955
2015	35583.1	60.10	74.8	106.735	106.803	98.811	104.047
2016	36295.8	61.40	78.3	108.873	109.113	103.435	107.108
2017	37008.3	61.40	78.1	111.010	109.113	103.170	107.712
2018	37921.7	60.13	77.4	113.750	106.856	102.246	107.514

Base year: 2008 = 100

Table 3. Missing observations for the Gini coefficient (Germany)

Year	GC	x	GC*x	x*x
1991	29.2	-14	-408.8	196
1994	29.2	-11	-321.2	121
1995	28.9	-10	-289.0	100
1998	28.3	-7	-198.1	49
2000	28.8	-5	-144.0	25
2001	30.3	-4	-121.2	16
2002	29.9	-3	-89.7	9
2003	30.0	-2	-60.0	4
2004	30.4	-1	-30.4	1
2005	32.1	0	0	0
2006	31.3	1	31.3	1
2007	31.3	2	62.6	4
2008	31.1	3	93.3	9
2009	30.5	4	122.0	16
2010	30.2	5	151.0	25
2011	30.5	6	183.0	36
2013	31.1	8	248.8	64
2015	31.7	10	317.0	100
2016	31.9	11	350.9	121
	576.7	**-7**	**-102.5**	**897**

x = (Year − 2005) GC = 30.4 + 0.124x
GC for the year 2012 = 31.3 | GC for the year 2014 = 31.5 | GC for the year 2017 = 32

Table 4. Missing observations for the Gini coefficient (UK)

Year	GC	x	GC*x	x*x
1969	33.7	-36	-1213.2	1296
1974	30.0	-31	-930.0	961
1979	28.4	-26	-738.4	676
1986	31.9	-19	-606.1	361
1991	35.9	-14	-502.6	196
1994	36.1	-11	-397.1	121
1995	36.3	-10	-363.0	100
1999	37.0	-6	-222.0	36
2004	36.0	-1	-36.0	1
2005	34.3	0	0	0
2006	34.6	1	34.6	1
2007	35.7	2	71.4	4
2008	34.1	3	102.3	9
2009	34.3	4	137.2	16
2010	34.4	5	172.0	25
2011	33.2	6	199.2	36
2012	32.3	7	226.1	49
2013	33.2	8	265.6	64
2014	34.0	9	306.0	81
2015	33.2	10	332.0	100
2016	34.8	11	382.8	121
	713.4	**-88**	**-2779.2**	**4254**

x = (Year = 2005) GC = 34.2 + 0.054x
GC for the year 2017 = 35

Formally, for the *first* year, the CBV of a nation may be expressed as:

$$CBV_1 = (GDPGR_1 \times SEMPR_1 \times HDI_1 \times JQI_1) / [(1+GC_1) \times (1+FSIR_1)] \qquad (23)$$

The CBV for the *second* year could be estimated as:

$$CBV_2 = (GDPGR_2 \times SEMPR_2 \times HDI_2 \times JQI_2) / [(1+GC_2)^2 \times (1+FSIR_1)^2] \qquad (24)$$

Proceeding likewise, the CBV for year n is expressed as:

$$CBV_n = (GDPGR_n \times SEMPR_n \times HDI_n \times JQI_n) / [(1+GC_n)^n \times (1+FSIR_n)^n] \qquad (25)$$

where $CBV_1, CBV_2, \ldots, CBV_n$ = CBVs' for year 1, 2, …, n;

$GDPGR_1, GDPGR_2, ..., GDPGR_n$ = GDPGRs' for year 1, 2, ..., n;<

$SEMPR_1, SEMPR_2, ..., SEMPR_n$ = SEMPRs' for year 1, 2, ..., n;

$HDI_1, HDI_2, ..., HDI_n$ = HDIs' for year 1, 2, ..., n;

$GC_1, GC_2, ..., GC_n$ = GCs' for year 1, 2, ..., n; and

$FSIR_1, FSIR_2, ..., FSIR_n$ = FSIRs' for year 1, 2, ..., n.

There is one *primary* reason for choosing GC and FSIR as the *discount factors* – an increase in values for both of them would invariably *diminish* the value of CBV of a nation. Hence both GC and FSIR are basically *negative* contributing factors for a country, whereas the remaining four variables act as *positive* contributing factors.

The CBVs' for 7 sample countries are estimated by using equation (25), and the derived results are econometrically tested by the Ordinary Least Squares (OLS) method at a 5 percent level of significance or better.

RESULTS AND FINDINGS

Mathematical Illustration of Isoattribute Curve Analysis

In order to illustrate the concept in a real-world scenario, an example of a multi-product brand is considered. Let there be two products, Sneaker and T-shirts, under the brand name of Nike®. According to Brand Finance's® annual report (2017) on the world's most valuable brands, Nike's Brand Strength Index (BSI) was 92.1 (out of a scale of 100).

Hence, in order to derive the equilibrium demand functions for Sneaker and T-shirts for the consumer, it has to be *assumed* that the Brand Strength Index (BSI) might be used as the *proxy variable* for a total attribute (A).

Now let the consumer's attribute function be: $A = (W_1 q_1 \times W_2 q_2)^{1/2} = A^o = 92.1$

The required Lagrangian for the optimization problem may be expressed as:

$$Z = W_1 p_1 q_1 + W_2 p_2 q_2 + \mu[92.1 - (W_1 q_1 \times W_2 q_2)^{1/2}](\mu \geq 0) \tag{26}$$

(p_1 and p_2 are priced per unit corresponding to quantities of q_1 and q_2, respectively)

The necessary first-order conditions are:

$$\partial Z / \partial q_1 = W_1 p_1 - \mu (W_1 W_2)^{1/2} q_2^{1/2} q_1^{-1/2} = 0 \qquad (27)$$

$$\partial Z / \partial q_2 = W_2 p_2 - \mu (W_1 W_2)^{1/2} q_1^{1/2} q_2^{-1/2} = 0 \qquad (28)$$

$$\partial Z / \partial \mu = 92.1 - (W_1 q_1 \times W_2 q_2)^{1/2} = 0 \qquad (29)$$

From equations (27) and (28), the following result may be derived as:

$$q_2 / q_1 = W_1 p_1 / W_2 p_2 \rightarrow q_2 = (W_1 p_1 / W_2 p_2) \times q_1 \qquad (30)$$

By substituting the value of q_2 in equation (29) and simplifying, we have:

$$W_1 (p_1 / p_2)^{1/2} q_1 = 92.1 \qquad (31)$$

$\rightarrow q_1^*$ = Equilibrium demand function for sneaker = $92.1 (p_2 / p_1)^{1/2} / W_1$

Now let $W_1 = 0.6$, $W_2 = (1-0.6) = 0.4$, p_1 = Price of Sneaker = \$60 per pair, p_2 = Price of T – Shirt = \$15 per unit. By plugging the values in the demand functions for Sneaker and T – Shirt, the following results may be derived as:

$\rightarrow q_1^* = $ = Equilibrium demand for sneaker = $92.1 (p_2 / p_1)^{1/2} / W_1$ pairs, and

q_1^* Equilibrium demand for T – shirt = $(W_1 p_1 / W_2 p_2) \times q_1 = (36 / 6) \times 77 = 462$ units.

The above hypothetical example would help justify the concept of isoattribute curve in the context of the two–commodity (branded) world scenario and how equilibrium quantities/partworths of two commodities (brand or non – brand) could be derived if values of one of the variables are known. Calculated for the years 2008-2017, the estimation of the Country Brand Values (CBV) for Belgium (Table 5), Finland (Table 6), Germany (Table 7), Norway (Table 8), Greece (Table 9), Czech Republic (Table 10), and the UK (Table 11) are shown.

Table 5. Estimation of the Country Brand Value (CBV) for Belgium

Year	GDPGR	UNEMR	VEMR	SEMPR	HDI	JQI	GC	FSI	FSIR	CBV
2008	0.44692	6.976	10.022	83.002	0.899	100.852	28.4	29.0	0.24167	0.2103
2009	-2.0207	7.908	10.325	81.767	0.899	101.020	28.6	33.5	0.27917	-0.554
2010	2.86429	8.292	9.891	81.817	0.903	99.5543	28.4	32.0	0.26667	0.4896
2011	1.6945	7.14	10.169	82.691	0.904	100.865	28.1	34.1	0.28417	0.1744
2012	0.73923	7.542	10.251	82.207	0.905	101.261	27.5	33.5	0.27917	0.0482
2013	0.45923	8.425	10.78	80.795	0.908	101.347	27.7	30.9	0.25750	0.0199
2014	1.57852	8.523	10.504	80.973	0.910	101.927	28.1	32.0	0.26667	0.0400
2015	2.03279	8.482	10.882	80.636	0.913	102.609	27.7	30.5	0.25417	0.0354
2016	1.4783	7.83	10.683	81.487	0.915	102.133	27.6	29.0	0.24167	0.0179
2017	1.90386	7.086	10.203	82.711	0.917	100.838	27.4	30.8	0.25667	0.0131

Table 6. Estimation of the Country Brand Value (CBV) for Finland

Year	GDPGR	UNEMR	VEMR	SEMPR	HDI	JQI	GC	FSI	FSIR	CBV
2008	0.78402	6.369	9.019	84.612	0.904	100.390	27.8	18.4	0.2	0.54330
2009	-8.0746	8.249	9.547	82.204	0.899	100.941	27.5	19.2	0.2	-4.9858
2010	3.18591	8.394	9.227	82.379	0.903	101.555	27.7	19.3	0.2	1.80791
2011	2.54753	7.781	9.276	82.943	0.907	101.736	27.6	19.7	0.2	1.35095
2012	-1.3974	7.689	9.554	82.757	0.908	102.101	27.1	20.0	0.2	-0.6986
2013	-0.902	8.193	9.442	82.385	0.916	102.530	27.2	18.0	0.2	-0.3811
2014	-0.3649	8.663	9.769	81.568	0.918	102.158	26.8	18.7	0.2	-0.4160
2015	0.54356	9.376	9.986	80.638	0.919	102.056	27.1	17.7	0.1	0.18147
2016	2.71052	8.818	9.985	81.197	0.922	102.428	27.1	18.8	0.2	0.88982
2017	3.10038	8.640	9.246	82.114	0.924	104.220	27.4	18.7	0.2	0.92622

Table 7. Estimation of the Country Brand Value (CBV) for Germany

Year	GDPGR	UNEMR	VEMR	SEMPR	HDI	JQI	GC	FSI	FSIR	CBV
2008	0.96227	7.524	6.889	85.587	0.916	101.168	31.1	37.3	0.31083	0.7631
2009	-5.6972	7.742	6.758	85.500	0.916	102.687	30.5	36.2	0.30167	-4.558
2010	4.17897	6.966	6.713	86.321	0.920	103.914	30.2	35.4	0.2950	3.3933
2011	3.92413	5.824	6.893	87.283	0.925	103.941	30.5	33.9	0.2825	3.0717
2012	0.41955	5.379	6.817	87.804	0.927	105.721	31.3	31.7	0.2641	0.2987
2013	0.42824	5.231	6.475	88.294	0.927	114.576	31.1	29.7	0.2475	0.2981
2014	2.22569	4.981	6.320	88.699	0.930	117.386	31.5	30.6	0.2550	1.5542
2015	1.73975	4.624	6.130	89.246	0.933	116.632	31.7	28.1	0.23417	1.0048
2016	2.23000	4.122	5.990	89.888	0.936	116.946	31.9	28.6	0.23833	1.2433
2017	2.46503	3.746	5.839	90.415	0.938	116.183	32.0	28.1	0.23417	1.2399

Table 8. Estimation of the Country Brand Value (CBV) for Norway

Year	GDPGR	UNEMR	VEMR	SEMPR	HDI	JQI	GC	FSI	FSIR	CBV
2008	0.47638	2.550	5.714	91.736	0.938	101.038	27.0	16.8	0.140	0.37178
2009	-1.7270	3.103	5.862	91.035	0.938	102.024	26.2	18.3	0.1525	-1.2548
2010	0.70183	3.521	5.554	90.925	0.942	102.919	25.7	18.7	0.1558	0.4810
2011	0.98147	3.215	5.180	91.605	0.943	104.237	25.3	20.4	0.170	0.67184
2012	2.70307	3.123	5.164	91.713	0.942	105.575	25.7	23.9	0.1991	1.94816
2013	1.03407	3.423	5.139	91.438	0.946	106.520	26.4	24.5	0.1791	0.62801
2014	1.96954	3.484	5.303	91.213	0.945	108.396	26.8	23.0	0.1916	1.19157
2015	1.96713	4.296	5.309	90.395	0.948	106.570	27.5	20.9	0.1741	0.92934
2016	1.07156	4.679	5.148	90.173	0.951	108.741	28.5	21.2	0.1766	0.45229
2017	2.32326	4.162	4.739	91.099	0.953	109.562	27.0	20.5	0.1708	0.98012

Table 9. Estimation of the Country Brand Value (CBV) for Greece

Year	GDPGR	UNEMR	VEMR	SEMPR	HDI	JQI	GC	FSI	FSIR	CBV
2008	-0.3352	7.760	26.672	65.568	0.857	104.167	33.6	45.4	0.3783	-0.2024
2009	-4.3007	9.616	26.999	63.385	0.859	108.866	33.6	46.1	0.3841	-2.7364
2010	-5.479	12.713	27.752	59.535	0.857	110.480	34.1	45.9	0.3825	-3.3842
2011	-9.1325	17.865	28.546	53.589	0.853	110.132	34.8	47.4	0.3950	-5.2731
2012	-7.3005	24.439	29.587	45.974	0.856	110.239	36.3	50.4	0.4200	-3.8872
2013	-3.2414	27.466	30.335	42.199	0.858	110.479	36.1	50.6	0.4216	-1.6844
2014	0.73978	26.491	29.640	43.869	0.866	111.134	35.8	52.1	0.4341	0.45764
2015	-0.4378	24.897	28.077	47.026	0.868	113.239	36.0	52.6	0.4383	-0.3168
2016	-0.191	23.539	26.693	49.768	0.866	114.848	35.0	55.9	0.4658	-0.1983
2017	1.5051	21.488	26.758	51.754	0.871	119.588	34.4	57.5	0.4791	2.11541

Table 10. Estimation of the Country Brand Value (CBV) for the Czech Republic

Year	GDPGR	UNEMR	VEMR	SEMPR	HDI	JQI	GC	FSI	FSIR	CBV
2008	2.68228	4.392	12.550	83.058	0.854	99.4287	26.3	42.1	0.35083	2.0232
2009	-4.8026	6.662	13.046	80.292	0.857	98.6582	26.2	42.6	0.35500	-3.758
2010	2.27342	7.279	14.080	78.641	0.862	98.7937	26.6	41.5	0.34583	1.8291
2011	1.77783	6.711	14.438	78.851	0.865	98.6589	26.4	42.4	0.35333	1.5721
2012	-0.7998	6.978	15.028	77.994	0.865	98.1868	26.1	39.5	0.32917	-0.689
2013	-0.4837	6.953	14.500	78.547	0.874	96.5230	26.5	39.9	0.33250	-0.437
2014	2.71512	6.108	14.536	79.356	0.879	97.3405	25.9	39.4	0.32833	2.6830
2015	5.30924	5.046	13.815	81.139	0.882	97.2601	25.9	37.4	0.31167	5.1291
2016	2.45054	6.951	14.020	82.029	0.885	95.6426	25.4	40.8	0.34000	3.0909
2017	4.3526	2.890	13.984	83.126	0.888	96.1091	24.9	40.1	0.33417	5.9722

Table 11. Estimation of the Country Brand Value (CBV) for the UK

Year	GDPGR	UNEMR	VEMR	SEMPR	HDI	JQI	GC	FSI	FSIR	CBV
2008	-0.2812	5.615	10.529	83.856	0.896	99.3741	34.1	32.9	0.27417	-0.122
2009	-4.2478	7.537	10.816	81.647	0.899	100.044	34.3	33.6	0.28000	-2.833
2010	1.94952	7.787	11.344	80.869	0.905	99.340	34.4	33.9	0.28250	1.2315
2011	1.54015	8.037	11.663	80.300	0.899	99.2319	33.2	34.1	0.28417	0.9531
2012	1.47892	7.885	12.099	80.016	0.897	99.3428	32.3	35.3	0.29417	0.9445
2013	2.13949	7.525	12.123	80.352	0.914	99.1507	33.2	35.2	0.27667	1.2077
2014	2.60748	6.110	12.694	81.196	0.918	99.7551	34.0	34.3	0.28583	1.4524
2015	2.35552	5.301	12.542	82.157	0.916	100.347	33.2	33.4	0.27833	1.2801
2016	1.91816	4.813	13.008	82.179	0.918	99.1376	34.8	32.4	0.27000	0.8389
2017	1.89208	4.335	12.978	82.687	0.919	99.8823	35.0	33.2	0.27667	0.8215

Consumer Induction Factor (CIF)

The regression result for CIF of the US economy (2009–2018) may be expressed as follows:

$$CIF = 0.33CPCGR + 0.33GIIR + 0.34ACSIR \tag{32}$$

Equation (18) gives us a fair idea that for the US economy, the CIF shares equal weightage for Consumption Per Capita Growth Relative (CPCGR), Global Innovation Index Relative (GIIR), and American Customer Satisfaction Index Relative (ACSIR), respectively.

In other words, per capita consumption expenditure, level of innovation, and the degree (level) of customer satisfaction are equally important in determining the degree of consumer induction or consumer attraction towards the market. The regression results of CIF on CPCGR, GIIR, and ACSIR, respectively, were derived using the Ordinary Least Squares (OLS) method. The results were found to be statistically significant at a 5 percent level of significance or better. They successfully passed Granger and Newbold's (1974) *Thumb rule test of Econometric Regression* using the software GRETL v.1.9.4 (Table 12, Annex).

Country Brand Value (CBV)

The regression results of CBV on GDP Growth Rate (GDPGR), Secured Employment Rate (SEMPR), Human Development Index (HDI), Job Quality Index (JQI), Gini Coefficient (GC), and Fragile States Index Rate (FSIR), respectively for 7 sample countries are summarized as follows:

Box 1.

Country	Regression equation	Reference
Belgium	$CBV = 44 + 0.21GDPGR - 34HDI - 0.21GC - 5FSIR$	Table 13, Annex
Finland	$CBV = 121 + 0.67GDPGR + 0.18SEMPR - 104HDI + 0.2JQI - 1.91GC - 56FSIR$	Table 14, Annex
Germany	$CBV = 48.55 + 0.83GDPGR$	Table 15, Annex
Norway	$CBV = 0.65GDPGR$	Table 16, Annex
Greece	$CBV = 0.74GDPGR$	Table 17, Annex
Czech Republic	$CBV = 0.8GDPGR - 0.91GC + 12FISR$	Table 18, Annex
UK	$CBV = 13.5 + 0.67GDPGR - 18HDI$	Table 19, Annex

Regression results of Country Brand Value (CBV) on GDP Growth Rate (GDPGR), Secured Employment Rate (SEMPR), Human Development Index (HDI), Job Quality Index (JQI), Gini Coefficient (GC), and Fragile States Index Rate (FSIR) respectively for 7 sample countries (2009 – 2018) are as follows,

- GDP Growth Rate (GDPGR) plays the *most* significant role in influencing the Country Brand Value (CBV) of the sample countries. It is the *common* variable that is statistically significant at 1 percent level or better for all the 7 sample countries;
- Apart from GDPGR, the three variables Human Development Index (HDI), Gini Coefficient (GC), and Fragile States Index Rate (FSIR) play essential roles in determining the Country Brand Value

(CBV). They are *common* variables that are statistically significant at 5 percent level or better for 3 out of 7 sample countries;

- Barring one country, i.e., Finland; the variables Secured Employment Rate (SEMPR) and Job Quality Index (JQI) do not play any significant (statistically) role in inferring CBV;
- In the case of 3 out of 7 sample countries (Germany, Norway, and Greece), GDPGR is the *only* statistically significant variable to regress CBV;
- Finland is the *only* nation for which all the six dependent variables are statistically significant at 5 percent level or better;
- Quite interestingly, *contrary* to the fundamental hypothesis related to the *positive* effect of the Human Development Index (HDI) on CBV, three countries (Belgium, Finland, and the UK) displayed a robust *negative correlation* between CBV and HDI. This phenomenon somehow proves that the positive effect of HDI on CBV could be achieved for the *developing* countries with low values of HDIs'. However, for the *developed* countries with already existing high levels of HDI, the effect is reversed; and
- As per the hypothesis related to the *Gini Coefficient (GC) negative effect* on CBV, the regression results corroborated the fundamental logic behind the hypothesis as 3 sample countries (Belgium, Finland, and the Czech Republic) displayed a negative correlation between CBV and HDI. In the other negative contributing factor Fragile States Index Rate (FSIR), surprisingly, Czech Republic was the only country that showed a *positive* relationship between CBV and FSIR. The valid explanation behind this aberration probably may be attributed to the higher arithmetic mean of FSIR for the Czech Republic compared to two other countries, i.e., Belgium and Finland, respectively.

The econometrical results were derived using the Ordinary Least Squares (OLS) method, and the results were statistically significant at a 5 percent level of significance or better. They successfully passed Granger and Newbold's (1974) *Thumb rule test of Econometric Regression* using the software GRETL v.1.9.4.

Limitations

a) The primary issue surrounding this research work is related to the fact that the CBV analysis is restricted among a 'privileged' few developed countries, and it does not take into account the developing nations or the major Asian economies that are driving the global growth trend;

b) Apart from the USA, the study regarding Consumer Induction Factor (CIF) analysis could be extended to other nations as well provided those countries formulate comprehensive Customer Satisfaction Indices of their own, and

c) In the case of Isoattribute curve analysis, it would be interesting to find out how the model works in terms of choosing an *appropriate* index for non-branded commodities like food and beverage items, Fast Moving Consumer Goods (FMCG), etc. as the proxy variable for aggregate attribute level (A) in a two – commodity world.

CONCLUSION

This book chapter has comprehensively analyzed three perspectives of marketing analytics ranging from microeconomic to macroeconomic aspects. The research yielded interesting results and findings, especially in formulating the Consumer Induction Factor (CIF) for USA and Country Brand Values (CBV) for seven sample countries. The USA, per capita consumption growth rate, Global Innovation Index (GII), and American Customer Satisfaction Index (ACSI) played an equal role in determining consumer behavior.

However, the GDP growth rate proved to be the commonest and most significant factor in determining the CBV for the sample countries. The Gini coefficient proved to be a determining factor for some sample countries.

In the rapidly changing global scenario characterized by an economic recession, rising trends of neoliberalism, unequal distribution of income and wealth among the populations, and pandemic scourge due to COVID–19 virus. These fresh concepts definitely have the potential to change the face of marketing analytics constructively and open new vistas of research from a much larger perspective across the world.

DATA AVAILABILITY STATEMENT

Data available at:

    https://www.theacsi.org/news-and-resources/customer-satisfaction-reports/report-archive
    https://www.ama.org/resources/Pages/Dictionary.aspx?dLetter=B
    https://www.ipsos.com/sites/default/files/20-03-60_anholt-ipsos_place-branding.pdf
    https://brandfinance.com/knowledge-centre/reports/
    https://brandfinance.com/images/upload/global_500_2017_locked_website.pdf
    https://www.globalinnovationindex.org/analysis-indicator
    http://stats.oecd.org/OecdStat_Metadata/ShowMetadata.ashx?Dataset=BLI&Coords=&Lang=en.
    https://data.worldbank.org/indicator?tab=all
    https://data.worldbank.org/indicator/NE.CON.PRVT.KD
    https://www.undp.org/content/undp/en/home/search.html?q=HDI
    https://fragilestatesindex.org/data/

ABBREVIATIONS

CIF: Consumer Induction Factor
CBV: Country Brand Value
MRC: Marginal Rate of Change (Attributes/Partworths)
MRTC: Marginal Rate of Technical Change (Between attributes and partworths)
CPCGR: Consumption Per Capita Growth Rate
CPCR: Consumption per capita Relative
GII: Global Innovation Index
GIIR: Global Innovation Index Relative
ACSI: American Customer Satisfaction Index
ACSIR: American Customer Satisfaction Index Relative

GDPGR: Gross Domestic Product (Annual) Growth Rate
VEMR: Vulnerable Employment Rate (Annual)
SEMPR: Secured Employment Rate (Annual)
HDI: Human Development Index
JQI: Job Quality Index
GC: Gini Coefficient
FSI: Fragile States Index
FSIR: Fragile States Index Rate

CONFLICTS OF INTERESTS STATEMENT

The author has NO interests with/or involvement in any organization or entity with any financial interest (such as honoraria; educational grants; participation in speakers' bureaus; membership, employment, consultancies, stock ownership, or other equity interest; and expert testimony or patent-licensing arrangements), or non-financial interest (such as personal or professional relationships, affiliations, knowledge or beliefs) in the subject matter or materials discussed in this manuscript.

REFERENCES

Aaker, D. A. (1991). *Managing Brand Equity: Capitalizing on the Value of a Brand Name*. Free Press.

Aaker, D. A. (1996). *Building Strong Brands*. Free Press.

Aaker, D. A. (2004). *Brand Portfolio Strategy*. Free Press.

Aaker, D. A., & Jacobson, R. (1994). The Financial Information Content of Perceived Quality. *JMR, Journal of Marketing Research*, *31*(2), 191–201. doi:10.1177/002224379403100204

Aaker, D. A., & Jacobson, R. (2001). The Value Relevance of Brand Attitude in High – Technology Markets. *JMR, Journal of Marketing Research*, *38*(4), 485–493. doi:10.1509/jmkr.38.4.485.18905

Aaker, D. A., & Joachimsthaler, E. (2000). *Brand Leadership*. The Free Press.

Ailawadi, K. L., Lehmann, D. R., & Neslin, S. A. (2003). Revenue Premium as an Outcome Measure of Brand Equity. *Journal of Marketing*, *67*(4), 1–17. doi:10.1509/jmkg.67.4.1.18688

Baum, W. M. (2002, May). The Harvard pigeon lab under Herrnstein. *Journal of the Experimental Analysis of Behavior*, *77*(3), 347–355. doi:10.1901/jeab.2002.77-347 PMID:12083686

Bendle, N. T., Farris, P. W., Pfeifer, P. E., & Reibstein, D. J. (2016). *Marketing Metrics: The Manager's Guide to Measuring Marketing Performance* (3rd ed.). Pearson Education, Inc.

Berger, P. D., & Nasr, N. I. (1998). Customer Lifetime Value: Marketing Models and Applications. *Journal of Interactive Marketing*, *12*(1), 17–30. doi:10.1002/(SICI)1520-6653(199824)12:1<17::AID-DIR3>3.0.CO;2-K

Blattberg, R. C., Byung-Do, K., & Neslin, S. A. (2008). Database Marketing: Analyzing and Managing Customers. New York, NY: Springer-Verlag. doi:10.1007/978-0-387-72579-6

Blattberg, R. C., Malthouse, E. C., & Neslin, S. A. (2009, May). Customer Lifetime Value: Empirical Generalizations and Some Conceptual Questions. *Journal of Interactive Marketing*, *23*(2), 157–168. doi:10.1016/j.intmar.2009.02.005

Bramanti, A., & Ratti, R. (1997). The multi-faceted dimensions of local development. In R. Ratti, A. Bramanti, & R. Gordon (Eds.), *The Dynamics of Innovative Regions: The GREMI Approach* (pp. 3–44). Ashgate.

Catania, A. C. (2013). Learning (5th ed.). Cornwall on Hudson, NY: Sloan Publishing.

Curry, B., Foxall, G. R., & Sigurdsson, V. (2010, May). On the tautology of the matching law in consumer behavior analysis. *Behavioural Processes*, *84*(1), 390–399. doi:10.1016/j.beproc.2010.02.009 PMID:20178838

Das, B. C., & Mukherjee, B. N. (2000). *Integral Calculus* (50th ed.). U. N. Dhur & Sons Private Limited.

Davison, M., & McCarthy, D. (1988). *The matching law: A research review*. Lawrence Erlbaum Associates, Inc.

de Chernatony, L., & McDonald, M. H. B. (2003). *Creating Powerful Brands in Consumer, Service and Industrial Markets* (3rd ed.). Elsevier / Butterworth – Heinemann.

Dwyer, F. R. (1989). Customer Lifetime Valuation to Support Marketing Decision Making. *Journal of Direct Marketing*, *3*(4), 8–15. doi:10.1002/dir.4000030404

Esch, F. R. (2007). *Strategie und Technik der Markenführung* (4th ed.). Vahlen.

Esch, F. R. (2008). Brand identity: the guiding star for successful brands. In B. H. Schmitt & D. L. Rogers (Eds.), *Handbook on Brand and Experience Management* (pp. 58–73). Edward Elgar Publishing. doi:10.4337/9781848446151.00010

Esch, F. R., Langner, T., & Rempel, J. E. (2005). Ansätze zur Erfassung und Entwicklung der Markenidentität. In F. R. Esch (Ed.), *Moderne Markenführung, Grundlagen – Innovative Ansätze – Praktische Umsetzungen* (4th ed., pp. 103–129). Springer Gabler Verlag., doi:10.1007/978-3-8349-4541-9_4

Fagerstrøm, A., & Sigurdsson, V. (2016). Experimental analyses of consumer choices. In G. R. Foxall (Ed.), *The Routledge Companion to Consumer Behavior Analysis* (pp. 25–39). Routledge.

Fournier, S. (1998, March). Consumers and Their Brands: Developing Relationship Theory in Consumer Research. *The Journal of Consumer Research*, *24*(4), 343–373. doi:10.1086/209515

Fournier, S., Solomon, M. R., & Englis, B. G. (2008). When brands resonate. In B. H. Schmitt & D. L. Rogers (Eds.), *Handbook on Brand and Experience Management* (pp. 35–57). Edward Elgar Publishing. doi:10.4337/9781848446151.00009

Foxall, G. R. (2005). *Understanding Consumer Choice*. Palgrave Macmillan. doi:10.1057/9780230510029

Foxall, G. R. (2007). *Explaining Consumer Choice*. Palgrave Macmillan. doi:10.1057/9780230599796

Foxall, G. R. (2010). *Interpreting Consumer Choice: The Behavioral Perspective Model*. Routledge.

Foxall, G. R. (2016). Consumer behavior analysis comes of an age. In G. R. Foxall (Ed.), *The Routledge Companion to Consumer Behavior Analysis* (pp. 3–21). Routledge.

Granger, C. W. J., & Newbold, P. (1974). Spurious regressions in econometrics. *Journal of Econometrics*, *2*(2), 111–120. doi:10.1016/0304-4076(74)90034-7

Green, P. E., & Rao, V. R. (1971, August). Conjoint measurement for quantifying judgmental data. *JMR, Journal of Marketing Research*, *8*(3), 355–363. doi:10.2307/3149575

Gujarati, D. N. (2003). *Basic Econometrics* (4th ed.). McGraw – Hill, Inc.

Gupta, S., & Lehmann, D. R. (2005). *Managing Customers as Investments*. Wharton Business School Publishing.

Gupta, S., Lehmann, D. R., & Stuart, J. A. (2004). Valuing Customers. *JMR, Journal of Marketing Research*, *41*(1), 7–18. doi:10.1509/jmkr.41.1.7.25084

Henderson, J. M., & Quandt, R. E. (1980). Microeconomic Theory: A Mathematical Approach (3rd ed.). McGraw-Hill Book Company.

Herrnstein, R. J. (1961, July). Relative and absolute strength of response as a function of frequency of reinforcement. *Journal of the Experimental Analysis of Behavior*, *4*(3), 267–272. doi:10.1901/jeab.1961.4-267 PMID:13713775

Herrnstein, R. J. (1970, March). On the law of effect. *Journal of the Experimental Analysis of Behavior*, *13*(2), 243–266. doi:10.1901/jeab.1970.13-243 PMID:16811440

Herrnstein, R. J. (1997). The matching law: Papers in psychology and economics. In H. Rachlin & D. Laibson (Eds.). Russel Sage Foundation.

Kapferer, J. N. (2004). *The New Strategic Brand Management: Creating and Sustaining Brand Equity Long Term* (3rd ed.). Kogan Page.

Keller, K. L. (1993). Conceptualizing, Measuring, Managing Customer-Based Brand Equity. *Journal of Marketing*, *57*(1), 1–22. doi:10.1177/002224299305700101

Keller, K. L., & Lehmann, D. R. (2006). Brands and Branding: Research Findings and Future Priorities. *Marketing Science*, *25*(6), 740–759. doi:10.1287/mksc.1050.0153

Kerin, R. A., & Sethuraman, R. (1998). Exploring the Brand Value – Shareholder Value Nexus for Customer Goods Companies. *Journal of the Academy of Marketing Science*, *26*(14), 260–273. doi:10.1177/0092070398264001

Lam, A. (2006). Organizational innovation. In J. Fagerberg, D. C. Mowery, & R. R. Nelson (Eds.), *The Oxford Handbook of Innovation* (pp. 115–147). Oxford University Press.

Leone, R. P., Rao, V. R., Keller, K. L., Luo, A. M., McAlister, L., & Srivastava, R. (2006). Linking Brand Equity to Customer Equity. *Journal of Service Research*, *9*(2), 125–138. doi:10.1177/1094670506293563

Lilien, G. L., Kotler, P., & Sridhar Moorthy, K. (1992). *Marketing Models*. Englewood Cliffs, NJ: Prentice-Hall, Inc.

Logue, A. W. (2002, May). The living legacy of the Harvard Pigeon Lab: Quantitative analysis in the wide world. *Journal of the Experimental Analysis of Behavior*, 77(3), 357–366. doi:10.1901/jeab.2002.77-357 PMID:12083687

Louviere, J. J., Hensher, D. A., & Swait, J. D. (2000). *Stated Choice Methods: Analysis and Applications*. Cambridge University Press. doi:10.1017/CBO9780511753831

Luce, R. D., & Tukey, J. W. (1964, January). Simultaneous conjoint measurement: A new type of fundamental measurement. *Journal of Mathematical Psychology*, 1(1), 1–27. doi:10.1016/0022-2496(64)90015-X

Madden, T. J., Fehle, F., & Fournier, S. (2006). Brands Matter: An Empirical Demonstration of the Creation of Shareholder Value Through Branding. *Journal of the Academy of Marketing Science*, 34(2), 224–235. doi:10.1177/0092070305283356

Marinova, D., & Phillimore, J. (2003). Models of Innovation. In L. V. Shavinina (Ed.), *The International Handbook on Innovation* (pp. 44–53). Elsevier Science Ltd. doi:10.1016/B978-008044198-6/50005-X

Mizik, N., & Jacobson, R. (2008). The Financial Value Impact of Perceptual Brand Attributes. *JMR, Journal of Marketing Research*, 45(1), 15–32. doi:10.1509/jmkr.45.1.15

Park, C. W., MacInnis, D. J., & Priester, J. (2008). Brand attachment and a strategic brand exemplar. In B. H. Schmitt & D. L. Rogers (Eds.), *Handbook on Brand and Experience Management* (pp. 3–17). Edward Elgar Publishing. doi:10.4337/9781848446151.00007

Peppers, D., & Rogers, M. (2004). *Managing Customer Relationships*. John Wiley & Sons.

Roy, D. (2019). Managerial grid in macroeconomic perspective: An empirical study (2008–2017). *Journal of Transnational Management*, 24(3), 165–184. doi:10.1080/15475778.2019.1632636

Rust, R. T., Lemon, K. N., & Zeithaml, V. A. (2004). Return on Marketing: Using Customer Equity to Focus Marketing Strategy. *Journal of Marketing*, 68(1), 109–127. doi:10.1509/jmkg.68.1.109.24030

Shankar, V. (2009). The Evolution of Markets: Innovation Adoption, Diffusion, Market Growth, New Product Entry, and Competitor Responses. In S. Shane (Ed.), *The Handbook of Technology and Innovation Management* (pp. 57–112). John Wiley & Sons Ltd.

Sigurdsson, V., & Foxall, G. R. (2016). Experimental analyses of choice and matching: from the animal laboratory to the marketplace. In G. R. Foxall (Ed.), *The Routledge Companion to Consumer Behavior Analysis* (pp. 78–95). Routledge.

Srinivasan, V., Park, C. S., & Chang, D. R. (2005). An Approach to the Measurement Analysis and Prediction of Brand Equity and Its Sources. *Management Science*, 51(9), 1433–1448. doi:10.1287/mnsc.1050.0405

Stahl, F., Heitmann, M., Lehmann, D. R., & Neslin, S. A. (2012). The Impact of Brand Equity on Customer Acquisition, Retention, and Profit Margin. *Journal of Marketing*, 76(4), 44–63. doi:10.1509/jm.10.0522

Toubia, O. (2018). Conjoint Analysis. In N. Mizik & D. M. Hanssens (Eds.), *Handbook of Marketing Analytics* (pp. 52–75). Edward Elgar Publishing. doi:10.4337/9781784716752.00011

Tversky, A. (1972). Elimination by aspects: A theory of choice. *Psychological Review, 79*(4), 281-299. https://psycnet.apa.org/doi/10.1037/h0032955

KEY TERMS AND DEFINITIONS

American Customer Satisfaction Index (ACSI)®: It is the only national cross-industry measure of customer satisfaction in the United States, scaling between 0 and 100.

Consumer Induction Factor (CIF): It may be defined as an index that influences the consumers' behavioral purchasing pattern based on three factors (variables).

Country Brand Value (CBV): It refers to the *discounted* method of estimating a country's 'brand' value using the present value (PV) analysis technique by using six factors (variables).

Fragile States Index (FSI)®: It is a critical tool to highlight the normal socio-economic and political pressures experienced by the states and identify the impacts of those pressures on states' capacities based on 12 dimensions.

Global Innovation Index (GII)®: It is a composite index that emphasizes the importance of innovation in positively influencing the consumption pattern of the population in general.

Isoattribute Curve: It may be defined as a locus of the combination of quantities consumed for two commodities (brand/non-brand) which will yield the same level of attribute for the consumer.

Isopartworth Line: It may be defined as a locus of points, each representing a combination of different partworths of two commodities (brand/non–brand) consumed within a fixed budget of the consumer.

Job Quality Index (JQI): It is itself a broad-based index computed as the *geometric mean* of 6 important variables, which provides us a comprehensive overview of the 'job quality' for the employees of a country.

APPENDIX

Table 12. Regression results for Consumer Induction Factor (CIF) (2009 – 2018)

	Coefficient	Std. Error	t-ratio	p-value	
const	−0.0189550	0.334944	−0.05659	0.9567	
CPCGR	0.326602	0.00151563	215.5	<0.0001	***
GIIR	0.334710	0.00160526	208.5	<0.0001	***
ACSIR	0.338694	0.00359576	94.19	<0.0001	***
Mean dependent var	103.3603		SD dependent var	3.437588	
Sum squared resid	0.001737		SE of regression	0.017014	
R-squared	0.999984		Adjusted R-squared	0.999976	
F(3, 6)	266410.0		P-value(F)	9.25e-16	
Log-likelihood	29.10220		Akaike criterion	−50.20440	
Schwarz criterion	−48.99406		Hannan-Quinn	−51.53214	
rho	−0.205816		Durbin-Watson	2.200449	

(USA)
Model 1: OLS, using observations 2009-2018 (T = 10)
Dependent variable: CIF
HAC standard errors, bandwidth 1 (Bartlett kernel)

Table 13. Regression results of Country Brand Value (CBV) (2008 – 2017)

	Coefficient	Std. Error	t-ratio	p-value		
const	43.6442	3.87592		11.26	0.0015	***
GDPGR	0.207359	0.00921865	22.49	0.0002	***	
SEMPR	−0.0167082	0.0180312	−0.9266	0.4225		
HDI	−34.2488	2.67671	−12.80	0.0010	***	
JQI	−0.0409877	0.0202338	−2.026	0.1359		
GC	−0.214431	0.0306863	−6.988	0.0060	***	
FSIR	−4.73376	0.533374	−8.875	0.0030	***	
Mean dependent var	0.049478		SD dependent var	0.258971		
Sum squared resid	0.011412		SE of regression	0.061676		
R-squared	0.981094		Adjusted R-squared	0.943281		
F(6, 3)	639.3315		P-value(F)	0.000095		
Log-likelihood	19.68908		Akaike criterion	−25.37816		
Schwarz criterion	−23.26007		Hannan-Quinn	−27.70171		
rho	−0.301931		Durbin-Watson	2.571933		

(Belgium)
Model 1: OLS, using observations 2008-2017 (T = 10)
Dependent variable: CBV
HAC standard errors, bandwidth 1 (Bartlett kernel)

Table 14. Regression results of Country Brand Value (CBV) (2008 – 2017)

	Coefficient	Std. Error	t-ratio	p-value	
const	120.738	11.3758	10.61	0.0018	***
GDPGR	0.670672	0.00835708	80.25	<0.0001	***
SEMPR	0.183019	0.0231776	7.896	0.0042	***
HDI	−104.301	11.9102	−8.757	0.0031	***
JQI	0.196502	0.0510721	3.848	0.0310	**
GC	−1.90889	0.128509	−14.85	0.0007	***
FSIR	−55.6630	8.49539	−6.552	0.0072	***
Mean dependent var	−0.051188		SD dependent var	1.901997	
Sum squared resid	0.050712		SE of regression	0.130015	
R-squared	0.998442		Adjusted R-squared	0.995327	
F(6, 3)	23148.39		P-value(F)	4.39e-07	
Log-likelihood	12.23153		Akaike criterion	−10.46306	
Schwarz criterion	−8.344962		Hannan-Quinn	−12.78660	
rho	−0.378296		Durbin-Watson	2.644704	

(Finland)
Model 1: OLS, using observations 2008-2017 (T = 10)
Dependent variable: CBV
HAC standard errors, bandwidth 1 (Bartlett kernel)

Table 15. Regression results of Country Brand Value (CBV) (2008 – 2017)

	Coefficient	Std. Error	t-ratio	p-value	
const	48.5545	10.9270	4.444	0.0212	**
GDPGR	0.826067	0.00687499	120.2	<0.0001	***
SEMPR	−0.246301	0.262946	−0.9367	0.4180	
HDI	−22.4493	34.9124	−0.6430	0.5660	
JQI	−0.00510489	0.0151754	−0.3364	0.7587	
GC	−0.0636013	0.0643125	−0.9889	0.3956	
FSIR	−14.2167	6.77961	−2.097	0.1269	
Mean dependent var	0.830897		SD dependent var	2.162685	
Sum squared resid	0.052549		S.E. of regression	0.132350	
R-squared	0.998752		Adjusted R-squared	0.996255	
F(6, 3)	19233.17		P-value(F)	5.80e-07	
Log-likelihood	12.05355		Akaike criterion	−10.10710	
Schwarz criterion	−7.989006		Hannan-Quinn	−12.43065	
rho	−0.102588		Durbin-Watson	2.086898	

(Germany)
Model 1: OLS, using observations 2008-2017 (T = 10)
Dependent variable: CBV
HAC standard errors, bandwidth 1 (Bartlett kernel)

Table 16. Regression results of Country Brand Value (CBV) (2008 – 2017)

	Coefficient	Std. Error	t-ratio	p-value	
const	−4.18920	15.8002	−0.2651	0.8081	
GDPGR	0.651834	0.0565496	11.53	0.0014	***
SEMPR	0.110859	0.0936691	1.184	0.3218	
HDI	0.660014	12.8093	0.05153	0.9621	
JQI	−0.0898530	0.0364351	−2.466	0.0904	*
GC	0.0380011	0.0575488	0.6603	0.5562	
FSIR	10.6818	4.02675	2.653	0.0768	*
Mean dependent var	0.639930		SD dependent var	0.812322	
Sum squared resid	0.070768		SE of regression	0.153589	
R-squared	0.988084		Adjusted R-squared	0.964251	
F(6, 3)	1327.552		P-value(F)	0.000032	
Log-likelihood	10.56525		Akaike criterion	−7.130499	
Schwarz criterion	−5.012403		Hannan-Quinn	−9.454045	
rho	−0.668237		Durbin-Watson	3.122685	

(Norway)
Model 1: OLS, using observations 2008-2017 (T = 10)
Dependent variable: CBV
HAC standard errors, bandwidth 1 (Bartlett kernel)

Table 17. Regression results of Country Brand Value (CBV) (2008 – 2017)

	Coefficient	Std. Error	t-ratio	p-value	
const	82.2684	28.2062	2.917	0.0617	*
GDPGR	0.741095	0.0994135	7.455	0.0050	***
SEMPR	0.0500021	0.0398454	1.255	0.2984	
HDI	−137.728	55.0419	−2.502	0.0875	*
JQI	0.184526	0.140273	1.315	0.2799	
GC	0.375262	0.338871	1.107	0.3489	
FSIR	1.49774	14.5980	0.1026	0.9248	
Mean dependent var	−1.510961		SD dependent var	2.278599	
Sum squared resid	0.699434		S.E. of regression	0.482851	
R-squared	0.985032		Adjusted R-squared	0.955096	
F(6, 3)	3617.594		P-value(F)	7.11e-06	
Log-likelihood	−0.889040		Akaike criterion	15.77808	
Schwarz criterion	17.89618		Hannan-Quinn	13.45453	
rho	−0.392595		Durbin-Watson	2.327682	

(Greece)
Model 1: OLS, using observations 2008-2017 (T = 10)
Dependent variable: CBV
HAC standard errors, bandwidth 1 (Bartlett kernel)

Table 18. Regression results of Country Brand Value (CBV) (2008 – 2017)

	Coefficient	Std. Error	t-ratio	p-value	
const	−59.9042	42.3278	−1.415	0.2519	
GDPGR	0.796289	0.0323178	24.64	0.0001	***
SEMPR	0.0419669	0.0329593	1.273	0.2926	
HDI	57.9372	25.1541	2.303	0.1047	
JQI	0.267745	0.212600	1.259	0.2970	
GC	−0.914239	0.252398	−3.622	0.0362	**
FSIR	12.4667	3.54324	3.518	0.0390	**
Mean dependent var	1.741412		SD dependent var	2.850108	
Sum squared resid	0.408616		SE of regression	0.369060	
R-squared	0.994411		Adjusted R-squared	0.983232	
F(6, 3)	2686.483		P-value(F)	0.000011	
Log-likelihood	1.798439		Akaike criterion	10.40312	
Schwarz criterion	12.52122		Hannan-Quinn	8.079576	
rho	−0.659688		Durbin-Watson	2.627056	

(Czech Republic)
Model 1: OLS, using observations 2008-2017 (T = 10)
Dependent variable: CBV
HAC standard errors, bandwidth 1 (Bartlett kernel)

Table 19. Regression results of Country Brand Value (CBV) (2008 – 2017)

	Coefficient	Std. Error	t-ratio	p-value	
const	13.4962	3.16050	4.270	0.0236	**
GDPGR	0.668796	0.0133087	50.25	<0.0001	***
SEMPR	−0.0116769	0.0263001	−0.4440	0.6871	
HDI	−18.4841	4.82959	−3.827	0.0314	**
JQI	0.0482045	0.0608670	0.7920	0.4862	
GC	−0.00463105	0.0325805	−0.1421	0.8960	
FSIR	−2.08094	5.25628	−0.3959	0.7187	
Mean dependent var	0.577364		SD dependent var	1.274253	
Sum squared resid	0.030346		SE of regression	0.100575	
R-squared	0.997923		Adjusted R-squared	0.993770	
F(6, 3)	45015.03		P-value(F)	1.62e-07	
Log-likelihood	14.79895		Akaike criterion	−15.59790	
Schwarz criterion	−13.47981		Hannan-Quinn	−17.92145	
rho	0.196663		Durbin-Watson	1.446963	

(UK)
Model 1: OLS, using observations 2008-2017 (T = 10)
Dependent variable: CBV
HAC standard errors, bandwidth 1 (Bartlett kernel)

Chapter 8
Chinese OEM Manufacturing Roadmap:
SMEs – To Brand or Not to Brand

Biqi Zhou
School of Professional Studies, Columbia University, USA

Rob Kim Marjerison
https://orcid.org/0000-0003-1181-8695
Wenzhou-Kean University, China

Fa-Hsiang Chang
Wenzhou-Kean University, China

ABSTRACT

This study seeks to explore the strategic alternatives for the many small and medium-sized manufacturing firms in China that play an OEM role in the global value chain. Declining margins due to rising production costs and intense competition from emerging manufacturing industries in Southeast Asia necessitates the transformation of China's traditional manufacturing industry. The result is opportunities for the creation and manufacturing of domestic brands. A multiple-case study methodology is used with primary data collection through in-depth interviews, supported by secondary data on the subject firms. The findings reveal an awareness of the opportunities afforded by the trend towards the development of domestic brands as well as the vision, strategy, tactics, and forecasting related to a transition to brand creation. This chapter could be of interest to those with an interest in manufacturing transition, brand development, and providing direction to OEM SMEs in China that seek to develop a strategic roadmap during the imminent industrial evolution and transformation.

DOI: 10.4018/978-1-7998-7689-2.ch008

INTRODUCTION

Small and medium-sized enterprises (SME) in the manufacturing sector in China mainly play an original equipment manufacturing (OEM) and original design manufacturing (ODM) role in the global value chain. Over time, as other nations have increased their manufacturing capability, Chinese SMEs have been faced with rising production costs and the competitive intensification from emerging manufacturing industries, especially in Southeast Asian countries. The profit margin of Chinese OEM manufacturers has been reduced, making it necessary to transform and upgrade OEM manufacturers in China.

When considering the OEM manufacturers' strategies, two strategies are mainly suggested and practiced by OEM manufacturers. The first one is strengthening ODM/OEM by improving production efficiency and management efficiency. The process and machine drive improvement in production efficiency. OEM manufacturers apply a Lean System to enhance productivity. Industry 4.0 provides another opportunity for the manufacturing industry. OEM manufacturers also tend to develop smart factories by introducing automatic equipment. The improvement in management, most accessible but limited, is driven by organization structure and employee retention. However, the cost of adopting mechanization and electrification is burdensome for small and middle-sized manufactures.

The second is to cultivate a self-owned brand created from independent research and development. Increasingly OEM firms transform themselves from a full-package manufacturer into an original brand-name manufacturer and retailer (Tokatli, 2013a). OEM manufacturers establish the self-owned brand to gain the latest market information, interact with customers, and cultivate their retailer capability. Chinese manufacturers have started to establish original domestic brands that target 1.4 billion Chinese customers. Unlike international prestige brands, the brand image of the original domestic brand negatively impacts the customer's purchase intention. Chinese customers' acceptance of this original brand is critical to brand success. However, the stronger consumption power, the superior quality of China-made goods, the recognition of China's brands, the strengthening of patriotism, and more factors are jointly changing the attitude of Chinese consumers towards original Chinese brands. Therefore, understanding the Chinese customer could guide the manufacturer on what to do and how to do it.

This chapter aims to investigate the strategy development of upgrading and transformation of Chinese consumer apparel manufacturers through the multi-case study method. Five companies from consumer apparel manufactures have been selected to gain insights from their innovation performance and their own brand development efforts. These five companies are at two different stages of their upgrading process. Similarly, the brands of companies are also at different stages of their progression. The diverse backgrounds of these brands are helpful to investigate their development paths and understand the factors that help OEM companies create their own brands.

LITERATURE REVIEW - BACKGROUND

The inexorable growth of China's economy after a series of economic reforms post-1978 has been the primary driver of the booming manufacturing sector (Tokatli, 2013a). The rising cost squeezed the margin of OEM manufacturers, in particular, small and medium-sized manufacturers. OEM manufacturers in China are looking for upgrading opportunities available to manufacturers. The challenges and cost of transformation and upgrades add to the pressure for OEM factories to adapt to survive. The transformation and upgrade are taxing in the update process; either OEM upgraded to ODM or OBM. Manufacturers that operate in global networks upgrade in production. Still, they face discouragement and obstacles when upgrading into higher value-added activities, such as design, brand-name manufacturing, marketing, and retailing (Tokatli & Kizilgün, 2004a).

Original Equipment Manufacturer (OEM)

OEM maintains its comparative competitiveness on the low cost of production through economies of scale. OEM manufacturers usually do not participate in marketing. OEM manufacturers' advantages come from lower manufacturing costs and flexibility in mass customization (Feng & Chern, 2008). As for the international brand companies, it is an economical way to outsource production, as OEM allows the purchasing company to obtain needed components or products without owning and operating a factory. In other words, the purchasing companies are price sensitive and money orientated. Only OEM factories that have the advantage in price and cost could survive. The key to the success of Chinese companies in the new round of international market competition is to change from a passive position to a favorable position (Zhongqun, 2011). No single best strategy is suitable for all OEM firms (B.-W. Lin, 2004).

Given that SMEs can rarely achieve such a transition, we have elaborated on this dynamic process through case studies. These SMEs have created their own path, not to follow the forerunners. These paths are neither new nor original but are spliced together from different strategies according to their own situation (Lee et al., 2015). Particularly in the clothing industry, global buyers have come to play an increasingly important role in the global value chain (Tokatli & Kizilgün, 2004a).

Growing Global Competitors in Emerging Economics

Data shows that China's labor costs are no longer the lowest, and emerging low-cost producers such as Vietnam, Cambodia, and Laos are squeezing their market share (L. Li, 2018). At the same time, China is not the most powerful player in the high-tech sector. Developed countries (U.S., Germany, and Japan) effectively use technologies such as digital technology to lead the creation of new industrial environments, produce new products, and improve their mature brands (L. Li, 2018). Six Asian countries, Indonesia, Malaysia, Philippines, Singapore, Thailand, and Vietnam, have become investment destinations due to their abundant natural and human resources and a rich market for goods and services (Jayadi & Aziz, 2017). As a fast-growing and fast-developing ASEAN economy, Vietnam has tremendous market potential for EU companies and plays a vital role in political relations with the EU. After more than 20 years of export, the footwear industry has become one of Vietnam's major export sectors. In addition to providing many employment opportunities, the Vietnamese footwear industry has brought more foreign currency to the national economy, met the needs of the nationals, and established the relationship between national with international footwear manufacturing (Hoang & Pham, 2016). The EU was one of Vietnam's largest overseas markets, buying nearly 19% of the country's global exports in 2015. In 2015, Vietnam's exports to the EU exceeded 27 billion euros. The EU is still the third-largest trade partner for Vietnam after China and the United States. In 2015, the EU ranked first among Vietnam's major foreign direct investment countries. Vietnam has the opportunity to increase its competitiveness and reduce its dependence on imports from China. It can also help Vietnam create a more liberal business and investment environment (Hoang & Pham, 2016).

Lean Production System (LPS)

Manufacturers seek to use the available resources most efficiently to create value and eliminate waste and deficits to improve productivity. Companies are looking for an opportunity to eliminate waste and improve their competitiveness (C. Li, 2011). The concept of LPS in the book named "The Machine That Changed the World" has attracted a growing number of companies. The Automotive industry has implemented LPS over many years, as Toyota initially created it. LPS is one of the tools that, along with information systems, is used to improve productivity. The goal of LPS is to eliminate waste from the production cycle and add customer value. OEM Manufacturers have also begun to accept lean thinking. Presently, their motivation is to develop a faster, higher quality, and lower cost lean model (C. Li, 2011). Lean assurance will bring huge benefits in reducing waste and increasing communication and integration between organizations and supply chains (Scherrer-Rathje et al., 2009).

Original Brand Manufacturer (OBM)

The manufactory sector in China has a strong capability in production; most of them manufacture products as full-package producers for international brands. "Doing things better" and "making better things" represent upgrading within production and revolve around the dimensions of quality, flexibility, and productivity. Still, they do not bring design-related benefits to the manufacturer because the value added to garments by designers and the related skills resides with the buyer firms (Tokatli & Kizilgün, 2004a). The limiting margins in manufacturing, low price bargaining power, low cost skilled and semi-skilled labor, information asymmetry, to name a few, all drive firms to transform and upgrade. Then, many firms transform themselves from a full-package manufacturer into original brand-name manufacturer and retailer (Tokatli & Kizilgün, 2004a). Their products are sold in direct owned and operated flagship stores (Tokatli & Kizilgün, 2004a). The transition from OEM to ODM and OBM reflects the expansion of the range of activities of manufacturers in the vertical value chain and the inevitable result of business upgrades and enhanced international competitiveness (Zhongqun, 2011). The original brand created by the manufacturer faces tremendous challenges from the market. In most places, according to Humphrey and Schmitz (2002), it is difficult for manufacturers to break out of the "lock-in" and emerge as brand-name manufacturers, global marketers, or retailers (Tokatli & Kizilgün, 2004a). At the same time, it is difficult for manufacturers to move to higher value-add stages and achieve this functional upgrading, such as design, branding, and retailing, because such a transformation requires the use of intangible and intermediates assets and requires differently skilled labor (Gereffi & Frederick, 2010).

Manufacturing Transformation and Upgrade

Both Kaplinsky (2000) and Porter (1990) believe that upgrading is the best response to the competitive pressure to remain competitive under intense pressure. Activities that make better products make them more efficient or enter more skills are called upgrading (B. Chen et al., 2018). Similarly, "Upgrading is an unending and complicated process that requires a consideration of the variety of ways in which firms can balance or replace manufacturing with higher value-added activities" (Tokatli, 2013b). Although upgrading is a universal phenomenon in every industry, it plays a significant role in the consumer apparel and footwear industry. They can choose to become a dedicated OEM service provider or choose to sell their own branded products (B.-W. Lin, 2004)

As global competition intensifies, contract manufacturers' disadvantages, such as poor pricing power, are unable to achieve higher profit margins and are growing. The external environment becomes one of significant concern. The wave of controversy about corporate transformation to upgrade technology or build private label manufacturing (OBM), which involves producing and selling products under its own brand, has become a key topic (Yan, 2012). The process of manufacturing upgrades can be described as progression along a value creation chain from OEM, ODM, OBM. Functional upgrades in manufacturing can be further divided into CMT (Cut, Manufacturing, Trim), OEM (Original Equipment Manufacturer), ODM (Original Design Manufacturer), and OBM (Original Brand Manufacturer) (S. Lin et al., 2019). It has been observed that upgrading mostly follows a common trajectory (Kaplinsky, 2000). It has been found that as economies develop, there is a trend for companies to gradually move from OEA to OEM to ODM to OBM (Y. Chen et al., 2020). Achieving a strategic transformation from OEM to upstream ODM and downstream OBM can result in a country move from large-scale manufacturing to strong manufacturing (Zhongqun, 2011).

The foremost necessity for upgrading is for the firm to have a strategic intent to move up the value chain. Financial investments are another utmost important capability of upgrading the firm (Peng & Chen, 2011). Besides eight economic conditions, eight different marketing capabilities influence manufacturing upgrade performance. In particular, product development, marketing communication, and channel management capabilities are crucial for manufacturing upgrades (Eng & Spickett-Jones, 2009a). Therefore, design and branding are capabilities that, once acquired, can push companies up the chain.

Table 1. Different stages of functional upgrading

Firm Role	Other Names	Functions/Characteristics
Sub-contractor	Assembler Cut-Make-Trim (CMT) Producer Jobber Second or Lower Tier Supplier	Export-Platform Manufacturer Component Supplier
OEM	Commercial (Sub) Contractor Full Package Supplier Contractor Turn-key Supplier	Process and Production Specialization
ODM	Supplier- Subcontractor	Independent supplier with complete control over the development, design, and fabrication of its product design. Process and production specialization
OBM	Independent Exporter	OBM designs, markets, and even sometimes retail own brands. Actual production often becomes less important—product and Marketing Specialization.

Source: Authors.

Attention must be paid to the firm's strategy and national policies to address workers' rising wages, material, and energy costs, and pressure from competition from other low-cost producers in Asia (Zhu & Pickles, 2014). Large and mature firms are blessed with both tangible and intangible assets compared to smaller firms, making them more likely to be the most competitive players and a contender in transformation and upgrading (Y. Chen et al., 2020). Large and mature companies tend to prioritize upgrades and establish a trend in their industry (Zhu & He, 2018). The political, institutional, and economic environment has played a key role in the escalation process, suggesting that it is not enough to focus solely on the dynamics of corporate upgrading. Previous studies have found that the government also emerged as a catalyst for upgrading efforts (Zhu & He, 2018). The supporting role of the government could facilitate the upgrading process.

Additionally, Zhu & He (2018a) also found that smaller firms are more reliant on government support than large and mature firms. Previous studies have identified that production upgrading is a demand necessitated by the global nature of buyers (Ghadge et al., 2017). Global buyers have been found to have a considerable influence on their suppliers' sales and the type of upgrading strategies open to them (Ghadge et al., 2017; Tokatli & Kizilgün, 2004b).

RESEARCH QUESTION AND HYPOTHESES

Previous studies have identified a typical trajectory of manufacturing firm upgrading, and companies are gradually moving up from OEM to ODM to OBM (Eng & Spickett-Jones, 2009b).

Research Question (RQ): What strategies could OEM manufacturers of consumer apparel and footwear in China develop?

There are only two major strategies that OEM firms would develop. Based on the existing body of knowledge reported above, the following hypotheses are derived.

H1: OEM firms in the consumer appeal and footwear industry should maintain OEM/ODM business but improve efficiency.
　1a – Promote a Lean Production System to reduce waste and cost.
　1b – Introduce automated processes in crucial stages and adapt to Intelligent Manufacturing.

H2: OEM firms in the consumer appeal and footwear industries should invest in creating and promoting their own brands and transform them into OBM.
　2a – Cultivate a Chinese brand that targets Chinese customers.
　2b – Cultivate an international brand that targets global customers.

This chapter followed the qualitative research method to study five cases of Chinese apparel and footwear industry companies to investigate the factors affecting their strategy development and resource investment in a time of national upgrading. Each company accepted an on-site visit and in-depth interview. The interviews were recorded and took live notes. The qualitative data were collected, and the results were presented in tabular form.

METHODOLOGY

Multiple-Case Study (Qualitative Method)

A descriptive, multiple-case research design will be used to understand a phenomenon, and data will be collected through multiple sources (Yin, 2017). A multiple-case study methodology was conducted to satisfy the goal of qualitative research design, which was to investigate OEM manufactories' upgrading strategies and recent innovative performance on the automation level, promotion, and brand cultivation. Five companies from the apparel and footwear industry are investigated, consisting of two footwear manufacturers, two clothing manufacturers, and one dye manufacturing company. These five firms represent a range of company types based on the nature of the organization. Five manufacturers were interviewed by the same questions. The practitioners were interviewed face-to-face within their natural working environment (Rempel et al., 2013a). In-depth interviews with senior management (c-suite or project leader) were conducted during a series of field visits. Additionally, a semi-structured interviewing technique was employed to ensure that the investigations were guided by our research questions while keeping the flexibility to react to unforeseen informants' responses and to explore unexpected phenomena (Rempel et al., 2013a).

The interview questions were derived from methodology previously used by Rempel et al. (2013b) and consisted of three parts:

- General information about the firm's industry setting, its competitive position, and the most significant challenge they are facing.
- The firm's strategies and innovative performance on functional and operational upgrading in the lean production system and automation level.
- Detailed information about the application of automation equipment, its incentives, and the expectations of the equipment performance was collected.
- OBM cultivation progression, what motivates and enables them to become OBM suppliers, and how to enter into a market with their brand.

Description of Case Companies

Case Company A

Company A was founded in 1979. After 40 years of development, it has gradually established a brand-based clothing industry, is involved in real estate development, financial investment, diversified and professional development, and has more than 50,000 employees. Company A is a large multinational group company. Company A has 772 self-operated stores nationwide, with 2,632 commercial outlets. The suit product has maintained first place in the market for 12 consecutive years.

Case Company B

Company B is a knitwear company specializing in producing men's and women's sportswear, casual wear, pajamas, and children's clothing. Company B is located adjacent to an international city and port with the convenience and advantages of ocean transport and direct access to foreign markets. Since its establishment in 1995, it has been the gateway to foreign markets. In 2002, Company B invested in the establishment of a knit dyeing and weaving company.

Case Company C

Company C was established in 1993. It is a footwear enterprise specialized in research and development, production, sales, and services. It is a footwear enterprise that has the largest volume and value for export within a local province. The products are sold in more than twenty countries and regions in Europe and America. For five consecutive years, its footwear exports ranked first in the entire province of Zhejiang in SE China.

Table 2. Description of case companies

	Company A	Company B	Company C	Company D	Company E
Industry	Apparel	Apparel	Footwear	Footwear	Dying
Year of incorporation	1997	1995	1993	1997	2007
Position in the industry	Large and Mature; Tier 1	SME	Large and Mature; Tier 1	SME	SME
Export Destination/Domestic	Domestic Trade/ Export Globally	Export to USA, EU	Extensively export to one German client	Set stores in Russia, small retailers in Russia	Domestic Trade
Subordinary	1 HQ, 4 SB in China, 1 SB in Romania	1 HQ	1 HQ, 3 SB in China	1 HQ, 1 SB in North Korea	1 HQ
Sales (billion USD 2018)	2100	40	171	---	13
Employees (2019)	202 (HQ)	800	6000	300	250
# of own brands	5+	---	1 (since 2017)	---	1 (since 2017)
Business Strategy	OEM ODM OBM	OEM	OEM ODM OBM	OEM	OEM ODM OBM
Category	Apparel, Leather production, Apparel Design Technology, Apparel Sales Retail, Wholesale	Knitting garment manufacturing, Self-employed and agents of import and export business	A modern footwear company integrating R&D, production, sales, and service	Leather shoe processing, manufacturing, operation of the export business of the company's own products	Manufacture, processing, dyeing, and finishing of needle textiles and garments
Attitude to Invest	Positive	Partly positive	Positive	Partly positive	Not positive
Major Suppliers	Integrated Supply in China	Close to its supplier	Close to its supplier. Partly integrated supplier	Close to its supplier	Close to its supplier
R&D	0.48% of sales. 1.84% of employees	---	6000 new types	100 new types	6% of sales
# of outputs (units)	960,000	4,000,000	25,000,000	2,600,000	6,300 t

Legend: HQ (Headquarter), SB (Subordinary)
Source: Authors

Case Company D

Company D was founded in 1997. It develops, produces, and sells men's and women's domestic and foreign shoes. The company has over 1,000 employees, including ten senior managers, more than 100 college graduates, and many international first-class production lines, with an annual output of 2 million pairs of leather shoes. An average of 2-3 new varieties is developed every day to meet the needs of domestic and foreign merchants. Company D commits to establish a modern management system and fully introduce the CIS system.

Case Company E

Company E was established in 2007 with developed equipment. Company E commits to the "quality-oriented, commitment is gold, development and innovation, mutual benefit and win-win" business value. It is specialized in all types of knitted fabric dyeing and finishing, new fabrics, functional fabric research and development, production, and sales. Products can be produced for branded clothing enterprises. Products have been praised as "the fashion pioneer of new and functional fabrics."

ANALYSIS / RESULTS

The responses to the in-depth interviews with the five companies were presented in tabular form. The interview focused on the company's transformation and upgrading and deepening the company's operational strategy in the development of lean manufacturing systems and automated smart factories. On the other hand, the interviews investigated the development of OBM strategy, factors stimulating the company's adoption of OBM, and the expectation towards the brand development. Detailed data and actual case information were collected during the interview.

1. What is/are a competitive advantage(s) of your company?

Table 3. Competitiveness of companies

Company A   The first smart men suit production line in China. Affluent cash flow: Invest in the introduction of new production lines and products. Achieve lean production, high production efficiency. Penetrate the market with multi-brands. Integrated the upper and lower supply chain to ensure a stable supply and innovation ability.
Company B   Production base industry chain, supporting industrial chain is complete. The customer order is large and stable—a good relationship with customers. Good quality management, high unit price.
Company C   Production base industry chain, supporting industrial chain is complete. The customer order is large and stable— a good relationship with customers. Good quality management, high unit price.
Company D   Start to streamline staff cutting as costs rise. Directly connect with clients by the sales team in China and overseas. Purchasing link personally control. Partly integrated supply chain to reduce costs. Customers in multiple regions, no off-season in one year, ten months of production throughout the year.
Company E   Emphasis on R&D since 2001. Differentiation strategy, target clients' order that demand relatively high-tech, does not compare with price advantage. Introduce a large number of professional specialists from universities and vocational colleges. The upstream dyeing and finishing business has bottlenecks and began integrating the downstream value-added fabric industry, avoiding pure price competition.

Source: Authors.

All five companies have mature supply chains to support them. The small businesses are located close to local suppliers. The large enterprises are more advanced in their transition to lean production and have higher efficiency, but they are also constantly improving production and management efficiency. Large companies are more capable of developing, investing, and acquiring influence upstream and downstream of their supply chains and setting up production bases in many places. The R&D capability of large enterprises is generally more robust than in small firms, but small corporations also regard innovation and technology development as their core competitiveness. The output of large enterprises is larger than that of small firms, resulting in an economy of scale effect. Large companies are more willing to invest capital in new equipment and technology, and the degree of automation is significantly higher than that of small businesses.

All five companies mentioned the current shift, emphasizing that they are beginning to pay more attention to product quality than quantity. Large companies are more willing to invest capital in new equipment and technology, and the level of automation is significantly higher than that of small Businesses. The speed and support of a large enterprise layout brand rollout are greater than that of a small business. In addition to individual small businesses that want long-term development, small businesses often stabilize production, so there is a lesser need for brand development.

2. What is the most significant challenge you are presently facing?

Table 4. Significant challenges of companies

Company A
Labor costs are rising, but the manufacturing industry relies on skilled workers. Simplify and reduce reliance on skilled workers. For example, automatically draw simple designs, such as typesetting (the 3D scan to the body dimension, the database has a model that can automatically design the layout). The design's information automation can replace the experienced and data-oriented master, thus reducing labor requirements and training time. Set up factories in other Chinese regions with lower labor costs.
Company B
The rise in labor costs. A large number of orders flow to Southeast Asia. The price advantage no longer exists.
Company C
The government does not support the footwear industry and the upstream and downstream industries that manufacture footwear, such as the hardware and printing and dyeing industries. Many closed small firms are suppliers of the company, and the firm has lost the advantage of a developed and convenient supply chain. The profit is reduced, the labor cost of the order is rising, and the skilled workers are returning to the inland cities. European customers have expressed the hope that firms can move to Southeast Asia.
Company D
Labor cost and the cost of raw materials.
Company E
The long-term development of enterprises has become the most significant challenge. External national policies are the biggest challenge, as 60% of the core business is dyeing and finishing, and it is the first to be defined as a highly polluting industry. Therefore, policy suppression has become an obstacle that enterprises cannot change and greatly hinder. The biggest internal challenge is a drop in profits. Order prices are not high, but costs are rising. Since 2016, the price of gas has incremented by 20%, and the price of fuel has increased by 10%. In the fabric sector, the biggest challenge is the lack of talent for development. The biggest challenge for brands is capital, training brand teams, and marketing.

Source: Authors.

According to the five interviews, labor, export tax, and government policy are the most significant challenges.

Labor issue: Regardless of size, large and mature companies, or SMEs, all suffer from the rising labor cost. The clothing, footwear, and dying industries are labor-intense industries, so all five companies heavily rely on cheap labor and skilled labor. First, many middle-aged and skilled front-line workers have returned to their homes in central China cities which severely hampers the sustainable development of the manufacturing firms(Tombe & Zhu, 2019). Second, young people are reluctant to be blue-collar workers. Due to the shortage of young skilled and semi-skilled workforce, companies need to invest heavily in training new and young laborers who have not received professional vocational training in schools (Tombe & Zhu, 2019; Yi et al., 2018).

Export Tax: European and American buyers must pay a 15%-19% tax on Chinese footwear (and other manufactured products) but only a 13% tax on footwear made in Vietnam (Cali, 2018; Itakura, 2020). The difference in export tax cannot be mitigated through increasing efficiency by Chinese manufacturing companies. Therefore, there is a trend for many Chinese companies to buy or contract with companies overseas in Viet Nam and other lower-cost countries and then export them to Europe and the United States to reduce tariff pressure (Bown, 2019; Itakura, 2020).

Government Policy: Another inevitable challenge is the changing of policies that impact the industry in China. As the government enacts policies to reduce environmental impact, some industries such as the footwear, clothing, and dying industries which are relatively high in pollution, are highly affected. Thus, the policies would not positively promote the development of these industries, and improved efficiency is necessary to offset the costs associated with pollution reduction in manufacturing.

3. How to reduce cost and improve efficiency?

Table 5. Strategies for reducing cost and improve efficiency

Company A The company has completed the lean production transformation, so the number of people in each process is reasonable. From the perspective of intelligent manufacturing workshops, reducing costs is to reduce labor in the transportation sector. Improve quality and product stability to reduce the cost of waste and deficits. After using the smart hanging system, the ten pieces of flow were changed into a single piece flow, reducing the costs of error and rework.
Company B Cutting is a key process in making garments. Cutting is the most challenging part of manual control and the most work-related injury. In the cutting process, two automatic cutting machines worth 1 million were introduced, each of which can replace eight workers and significantly improve quality and production safety.
Company C We are using lean production. The IE department records the time of each process and calculates the wages of workers. The accuracy of the color is improved. The downtime is reduced, and the raw material guarantee is shipped to the factory before production.
Company D Reducing personnel: a production line has been reduced from 85 people seven years ago to 60 or 45 now. Cut people down by half. In the key cutting process, introducing a computer laser machine can make the slicing faster and more accurate. Use a hot press to reduce the use of raw materials. In addition, improving production efficiency is also a cost-saving one. It can save workers time by using a faster sewing machine to achieve automatic line change.
Company E Since the main business is now printing and dyeing, energy consumption is the primary source of cost. Adjust the finishing process to reduce energy consumption. Improve 2% successful pass rate and reduce the defective rate, saving 6% of the cost. Process improvement, streamlining off labor cost.

Source: Authors.

All companies mentioned reducing the rate of defective products, rework, and the cost of deficits. The primary cost of most companies is labor cost. The first solution for the labor issue is to adjust the process and reduce the number of employees. The second solution is to replace the labor in key processes with automation, machines, and robotics. The third solution is to consider logistics for maximum efficiency and economic value, and companies may transfer part of production lines to cities where the cost of labor is lower. Additionally, companies mentioned that improvement of management efficiency, motivation of employees, and saving of energy cost also contribute to cost reduction and efficiency improvement.

4. How is the extent of intelligent manufacturing operated in the company, and what automated equipment is applied to the production line?

Table 6. Intelligent manufacturing application level

Company A 　　a) Save time and replace the workforce in transportation, packaging, and inventory management. 　　b) The ability to increase flexible production enables high-volume production and single-piece mixing production. 　　c) Sales data and production time data appear in the dashboard visualization, so sales and production could have a more timely and accurate response, reducing unnecessary inventory and responding faster to the market. 　　d) Large-scale production of production planning and raw material inventory is more accurate when selling small quantities. It is clearer how long it can be completed. 　　e) Energy consumption is -10%, production is 10%, and the number of people on the overall production line is not much reduced because lean production has been determined to work. 　　f) The machine processes data in the cut stage, designing a fixed graphic, cutting work.
Company B In logistics, the automation equipment is applied in the transmission during the whole operation—the automation machine is used in the cutting process. With the automation machine, product quality is more unstable, and avoid human injury. The investment in equipment is expected to return in two years.
Company C 3D design, computer needles, and production lines have introduced a higher automation level of the machine. Because of the large number of orders, economies of scale are more likely to afford the cost of new equipment. It reduces a process into more than 30 simple processes, thereby reducing the reliance on workers' technical capabilities and better measuring the time and processes' costs.
Company D Partly automatic cutting. The equipment for the computer needle car was purchased. Still, due to the high cost of making the original template, the order of the small amount of change could not bear the template production's cost. Hence, the computer automatic sewing machine equipment was temporarily not used. The company intends to introduce the ERP system to calculate the compensation of workers' companies more accurately and reduce management costs.
Company E Key equipment's improvement at the production line level of automated equipment. The main dyeing tanks (leading production equipment) and laboratories are equipped for R&D.

Source: Authors.

Larger and more mature companies have progressed farther in the overall value chain from customer information collection, logistics, warehousing, procurement of raw materials, scheduling of production, production, quality management, inspection, and packaging and delivery. Companies begin their intelligent manufacturing upgrading with the automation of customer information collection, logistics, and packaging. They were followed by warehousing, raw material procurement, and scheduling of production. Eventually, production and quality management would be possible to achieve full automation. However, in terms of the application of intelligent manufacturing at the enterprise level, larger and more mature companies significantly differ from SMEs. SMEs still operate outdated machines and do not take advantage of using a management information system. This significant difference is caused by funding, capability, and company goals.

Funding: Big corporations have more cash flow to invest on a percentage basis. Also, the volume and value of each large order that larger corporations fill are higher and more efficient than SMEs. Thus, it is more likely to have a scale effect so that the ROI on upgrade investment is more rapid. In other words, the larger and more mature companies are abler to afford upgrades and are more financially capable of introducing and investing in more automation on the production line. Greater access to funding fuels the larger and more mature companies to promote speedy intelligent manufacturing upgrading. Investment in automation is a substantial investment; thus, SMEs are much slower in the process of transformation to more advanced, efficient, and intelligent manufacturing.

Capability: Big companies, like Company A and Company C, have well-developed lean production systems in a relatively advanced state. In other words, the amount of labor in one production line and the producing processes in place are already at a reasonably efficient state. There is not much space for larger companies to adjust. To break through this bottleneck, larger and more mature companies tend to find other methods for sustainable development, such as upgrading to intelligent manufacturing. By contrast, SMEs could achieve considerable benefits by adopting lean production systems in both production and management to improve their performance immediately.

Company goals: Each company has its unique goals. Large-scale manufacturing firms aim to integrate the value chain; thus, they invest in design, logistics, warehousing, and information systems. On the contrary, SMEs are more likely to aim to stabilize production, optimize performance, and reduce costs based on current production, so their automation equipment is more likely to be concentrated on the production line. Companies that want to exit the market or are uncertain about the external business environment are typically cautious about making substantial investments in new automation equipment.

5. What is the main purpose of investing in automation machines and intelligent manufacturing?

Table 7. Purpose of adopting intelligent manufacturing

Company A This intelligent pilot production line is mainly designed to increase the flexibility and flexibility of flexible production. For future brand development and customized services to improve the production capacity, improve to whatever style of products, you can mix and match government subsidies. From the company's overall strategy and production, the layout of the higher value of the industry is 6+1, design, raw materials, warehousing, transportation, and sales. From the production line, the machine can simply repeat the process that needs to stabilize the production capacity, such as pressing the arc. The effect is that product quality is more stable and uniform.
Company B First, the most effective automation is the improvement of crucial processes. In the crucial process-cutting, the automatic cutting machine can reduce the number of human workers and stabilize the quality, mainly solving the toughest problems of labor injury. Production capacity increased by 20%, profit margin increased by 10%. Second, the automation of the hanging system is on the transport transmission, and the whole process is faster. Third, the government subsidizes the degree of automation. The overall automation degree of the firm is 30%
Company C First, to achieve technological breakthroughs in crucial processes. Second, to relieve the dependence on skilled workers, reduce the requirements for recruiting workers, and make it easier to recruit more labor.
Company D First, the key process changes on the production line, saving more use of raw materials. Second, the use of information management systems to more precisely control the time and production costs and reduce management efficiency.
Company E Improve quality, error rate, and cost reduction.

Source: Authors.

6. What are the latest trends, and what are your three to five-year strategies?

Table 8. Three to five year plan

Company A In the long-term strategy, the integrated industrial chain has reached a rapid response market, transforming and upgrading into a dominant brand. Intelligentization and temporarily replace actions that require stability. If there are changes, soft materials, materials that change, and intelligent mechanization are not easy to achieve. The simplest thing is transportation logistics, customer information database, design innovation.
Company B We hope that information technology and automation equipment become more mature. Much existing equipment is imported, and it is too expensive for the company. It is expected that domestically produced equipment can be developed in several years. Our company has plans to withdraw from the market and lease the factory to exit the market.
Company C We expect that the local government could position the footwear industry as a sunrise industry. Enterprises drive a large number of local employment, pay a high amount of tax, and there is not much pollution to the environment. Therefore, we hope to get support from the government, especially the support of the land. Because of the demolition and reconstruction of the city, the land price has risen, and the company has no way to get cheap land for use as an employee dormitory.
Company D Comply with the rising cost trend, streamline the number of employees and raw materials' use. When the development of new types of automation equipment is more mature, more suitable for adapting to the situation of enterprises, our company will invest.
Company E Entrepreneurs suggested that the position of traditional manufacturing enterprises can be high-tech, green, and fashionable. This industry can drive employment and taxation. If the policy is unstable, the uncertainty of land requirements for environmental protection will cause enterprises to have concerns about future development. They are in a wait-and-see state, whether they need to introduce the latest equipment and limit the automation development of the industry.

Source: Authors.

Social entrepreneurs suggest that the position of traditional manufacturing enterprises can be transitioned to high-tech, green, and sustainable fashion (Gudiel et al., 2021). Consumer appeal can translate into high sales volume, and in the footwear industry, sales volume can drive employment and tax revenue. Additionally, the external environment is unstable, with continuous change such as the uncertainty of land requirements, export/import tariffs, and environmental protection requirements. These will cause enterprises to be concerned about further investment in a rapidly changing and unpredictable business climate. SMEs are more likely to be in a wait-and-see state, and they are cautious about whether they need to introduce the latest equipment to expand the use of automation development in the industry.

7. Does your company adopt an OEM strategy and develop its own brand?

Companies pursuing long-term growth have begun to explore their own brands, and companies that want to continue maintaining the status quo have not tried to create their own brands. For companies that have never developed a brand, the strategy used is less radical, and the investment is relatively conservative when making the first brand. Manufacturing companies can use their production lines to develop their products and manage their inventory, but their sales and marketing capabilities are insufficient. Brand-owned manufacturing companies have chosen a multi-brand strategy to create different brands for different age groups, consumption levels, and gender customers. As the number of brands increases, the flexibility of the production process and the responsiveness to the market will increase significantly.

Table 9. Brands owned by case companies

Company A   Multiple brands, more than five brands, for all ages, genders, price segments, and materials, also represent the sales of foreign brands. Starting with a men's suit shirt, the products are excellent, and the price is good. In recent years, Youngor's strategy is to enrich the brand into the market, targeting all ages, high-end mid-end low-end brands are covered, cotton and hemp products are available, domestic and foreign products. Mainly target Chinese customers.
Company B   No
Company C   One Brand. PU women's shoes fashion luxury positioning, online and offline sales, the average prices is 200-500. Brands have higher pricing power and are able to directly get market trends and feedback to provide accurate information for development targets.
Company D   No
Company E   One Brand. Bedclothes and baby clothes that use plant dyeing are mainly environmentally friendly and have no chemically harmful additions. Combined with its own production advantages, it will develop to the final product end and extend to the downstream industrial chain.

Source: Authors.

8. What kind of resources are invested? What are your expectations for the brand?

Table 10. Efforts on OBM strategy

Company A   The brand of men's shirts began 20 years ago, and the market share of men's suits still ranks first in China. The company has invested heavily in the R&D department to innovating high-quality products. Brand operations require rapid response and collaboration across all parts of the value chain. The company's star brand is a high-end customized brand dedicated to improving the quality of the user experience, using 3D scanning and database, customizing clothes that are more in line with the customer's size, and increasing customer loyalty and customer value.
Company B   No
Company C   The brand is registered in Shanghai to create a more international brand image. The former Ogilvy design team designed the brand packaging design and promotion team, and the German design team developed the UI. The design plan costs 1 million yuan. The brand's products are relatively high-end, and in order to ensure product quality, the company introduced two production designs from Italy. In 2017, a brand was officially launched. Currently, shopping malls in two cities in China have invested in offline stores, and there are currently five offline stores. The company expects to cultivate brand talents and cultivate teams to accumulate experience. Improve the company's retail and sales capabilities and reduce the risk of only one customer. It is expected that the brand will break even in three years.
Company D   No
Company E   Since 2017, the company has started to form a brand team from the outside to hire experienced brand development managers, designers, and salespeople to create a team of four. This year, the company mainly engaged in product development and inventory management, coordinated by the R&D department and the fabric department of the factory headquarters. Participate in the exhibition layout booth in different Canton Fair exhibitions. In 2018, the first physical store in the shopping mall was opened. The total investment and inventory for two years is 5 million.

Source: Authors.

When profit margins in production are being squeezed, companies are actively looking for new opportunities. The primary purpose of developing a brand is to move to a higher value-added niche in the value chain, namely, design and sales. Company A expects that brand development could grow its profit margins and result in profit growth. Company C is preparing in advance for the future turbulent market environment against the risk of uncertain clients and orders shortly. Company E expects to continue developing during the transformation and upgrading and plans for the resource allocation of the enterprise.

CONCLUSION

This study found that in five sample case companies, 60% of the OEM companies consider product quality and R&D capabilities as their main advantages, and 40% of OEM companies consider low product prices as their main advantages. 80% of OEM companies seek long-term development; 60% of OEM companies are cautious about continuing to invest heavily. Large enterprises adopt state-of-the-art equipment earlier than small enterprises. The more firmly a company pursues long-term development, the more capital it invests.

The fundamental purpose of developing their brand is that OEM firms are eager to transform the focus to make higher value-added products at increased profit margins. Thereby, OEM firms start to integrate upstream and downstream in the supply chain. The upstream production processes low-profit margins as a result of price pressure as a result of government policies. Thus, firms realize that if they commit resources to pursue sustainable business growth, they must move up to the high value-added part of the supply chain. OEM manufacturers are in the position where they must seek higher autonomy in price setting.

The main challenge of implementing the OBM strategy is the lack of a sales team or expertise within the organization who knows how to penetrate the market through the effective positioning of the brand. Manufacturing companies are conservative in brand investment. In the process of developing brands, manufacturing companies generally believe that the most severe difficulty is in sales. Brand visual design, how brand value is passed on to consumers, and what consumers want to or will buy are areas that make these companies that are good at managing production feel unfamiliar. The professional marketing staff who hire young people outside will also adopt the method of cautious use of the budget because of the high cost of training the team.

We found that manufacturing companies have unique advantages to transfer to OBM compared to a company that possesses design capability only. Manufacturing companies have production lines, product design departments, and warehousing, which provide a vital advantage in the early stage of product production-proofing. In the early stage of development, a small batch of tests and proofing is required. The relative cost is high because the number is small, and the outsourcing company is unwilling to do it. Therefore, compared with brand design companies, manufacturing companies have faster product iterations, more stable product production, and more reliable product quality.

Regarding the question of whether a company should be cultivating its own brand or not, different companies should have different strategies, and companies can adopt a combination of different strategic approaches. This study found some common trajectory and consensus among the strategies of these five case companies. Therefore, OEM firms can refer to these five different development stages and different companies and get some suggestions in the transformation and upgrading stage.

This study found that established and mature OEM companies have different strategies than SME firms. In many cases, large OEM firms have reached the highest production efficiency in production and performed lean production outstandingly. There is no way to reduce costs significantly. When the production cost is not significantly reduced, the company's strategy shifts to vertical integration, upstream and downstream on the supply chain, rather than production improvements. That means that OEM firms are more likely to be ready to develop a brand design and develop smart logistics.

Furthermore, brand development also facilitates the upgrading of production in turn. The lot size of the brand production order is different from that of the OEM production order. Brand orders are small but frequently change and also require a shorter delivery time. In contrast, the OEM lot-size order is larger, but the frequency is lower. Because the company's production needs to meet changing market demands, the update rate of production determines the rapid production speed and intense collaboration of the entire supply chain. Therefore, the firm's production lines need to be more flexible and agile so that the whole process of the new design, ordering, production, packaging, and store logistics can be completed quickly. As for more extensive and more mature OEM companies, the primary purpose of introducing smart devices is not to reduce production costs but to improve the production line's flexible production and rapid response capabilities.

In small and medium-sized OEM enterprises, the processes are not the same capability for access to capital and management expertise as larger firms. The investment in new equipment or brand development will have a relatively larger negative impact on SMEs, which increases the financial burden on these SMEs. OEM SMEs have meager bargaining power, with global buyers able to control and drive the product prices low, so OEM/ODM SMEs have to reduce their costs. Some OEM/ODM's main cost is labor cost, while others are the cost of energy. Therefore, OEM/ODM SMEs will usually reduce their primary source of production costs. Enterprises whose main expense is the cost of labor will adopt layoffs, replace people with machines at the crucial stages, and transfer some production lines to cities with lower costs. If the main production expense is energy, SME firms will optimize the production efficiency transition process.

LIMITATIONS AND FUTURE RESEARCH

Although the multiple cash study methodology supports the validity of findings for research that includes five cases, due to the diversity of firm size and industry, a replicative study of a more significant number of firms would be valuable. Further studies could include more firms and also consider different industries beyond consumer apparel and footwear. The finding could be strengthened through additional and more specific questions and interviews with multiple individuals at each firm.

REFERENCES

Bown, C. P. (2019). The 2018 US-China trade conflict after forty years of special protection. *China Economic Journal*, *12*(2), 109–136. doi:10.1080/17538963.2019.1608047

Cali, M. (2018). The impact of the US-China trade war on East Asia. *VoxEU. Org, 16*.

Chen, B., Wan, J., Shu, L., Li, P., Mukherjee, M., & Yin, B. (2018). Smart Factory of Industry 4.0: Key Technologies, Application Case, and Challenges. *IEEE Access: Practical Innovations, Open Solutions*, 6, 6505–6519. doi:10.1109/ACCESS.2017.2783682

Chen, Y., Han, Z., Cao, K., Zheng, X., & Xu, X. (2020). Manufacturing upgrading in industry 4.0 era. *Systems Research and Behavioral Science*, 37(4), 766–771. doi:10.1002res.2717

Eng, T.-Y., & Spickett-Jones, J. G. (2009a). An investigation of marketing capabilities and upgrading performance of manufacturers in mainland China and Hong Kong. *Journal of World Business*, 44(4), 463–475. doi:10.1016/j.jwb.2009.01.002

Eng, T.-Y., & Spickett-Jones, J. G. (2009b). An investigation of marketing capabilities and upgrading performance of manufacturers in mainland China and Hong Kong. *Journal of World Business*, 44(4), 463–475. doi:10.1016/j.jwb.2009.01.002

Feng, C.-M., & Chern, C.-H. (2008). Key Factors Used by Manufacturers to Analyze Supply-Chain Operational Models: An Empirical Study among Notebook Computer Firms. *International Journal of Management; Poole*, 25(4), 740-755,779.

Gereffi, G., & Frederick, S. S. (2010). *The Global Apparel Value Chain, Trade and the Crisis: Challenges and Opportunities for Developing Countries*. doi:10.1596/1813-9450-5281

Ghadge, A., Dani, S., Ojha, R., & Caldwell, N. (2017). Using risk sharing contracts for supply chain risk mitigation: A buyer-supplier power and dependence perspective. *Computers & Industrial Engineering*, 103, 262–270. doi:10.1016/j.cie.2016.11.034

Gudiel, K. C., Marjerison, R. K., & Zhao, Y. (2021). Scope for Sustainability in the Fashion Industry Supply Chain: Technology and Its Impact. In Entrepreneurial Innovation for Securing Long-Term Growth in a Short-Term Economy (pp. 71–89). IGI Global.

Hoang, L. T. P., & Pham, H. T. T. (2016). An Analysis of Vietnamese Footwear Manufacturers' Participation in the Global Value Chain Where They Are and Where They Should Proceed? *VNU Journal of Science: Economics and Business*, 32(5E). https://js.vnu.edu.vn/EAB/article/view/4063

Humphrey, J., & Schmitz, H. (2002). How does insertion in global value chains affect upgrading in industrial clusters? *Regional Studies*, 36(9), 1017–1027. doi:10.1080/0034340022000022198

Itakura, K. (2020). Evaluating the impact of the US–China trade war. *Asian Economic Policy Review*, 15(1), 77–93. doi:10.1111/aepr.12286

Jayadi, A., & Aziz, H. A. (2017). Comparative advantage analysis and products mapping of Indonesia, Malaysia, Philippines, Singapore, Thailand and Vietnam export products. *Journal of Development Economics*, 2(1), 12–27.

Kaplinsky, R. (2000). Globalization and unequalisation: What can be learned from value chain analysis? *The Journal of Development Studies*, 37(2), 117–146. doi:10.1080/713600071

Lee, K., Song, J., & Kwak, J. (2015). An Exploratory Study on the Transition from OEM to OBM: Case Studies of SMEs in Korea. *Industry and Innovation*. https://www.tandfonline.com/doi/pdf/10.1080/13662716.2015.1064257?needAccess=true

Li, C. (2011). *A customized lean model for a Chinese aerospace OEM (Original Equipment Manufacturer)*. https://dspace.lib.cranfield.ac.uk/handle/1826/5716

Li, L. (2018). China's manufacturing locus in 2025: With a comparison of "Made-in-China 2025" and "Industry 4.0.". *Technological Forecasting and Social Change, 135*, 66–74. doi:10.1016/j.techfore.2017.05.028

Lin, B.-W. (2004). Original equipment manufacturers (OEM) manufacturing strategy for network innovation agility: The case of Taiwanese manufacturing networks. *International Journal of Production Research, 42*(5), 943–957. doi:10.1080/00207540310001622449

Lin, S., Cai, S., Sun, J., Wang, S., & Zhao, D. (2019). Influencing mechanism and achievement of manufacturing transformation and upgrading. *Journal of Manufacturing Technology Management, 30*(1), 213–232. doi:10.1108/JMTM-05-2018-0126

Nguyen, N. T. T. (n.d.). *The reform of Vietnamese Economic institutions under the impact of Free Trade Agreements A case study of the EU and Vietnam Free Trade Agreement*. Academic Press.

Peng, M. W., & Chen, H. (2011). Strategic Responses to Domestic and Foreign Institutional Pressures. *International Studies of Management & Organization, 41*(2), 88–105. doi:10.2753/IMO0020-8825410204

Porter, M. E. (1990). The competitive advantage of nations. *Competitive Intelligence Review, 1*(1), 14–14. doi:10.1002/cir.3880010112

Rempel, P., Mader, P., & Kuschke, T. (2013). An empirical study on project-specific traceability strategies. *2013 21st IEEE International Requirements Engineering Conference (RE)*, 195–204. 10.1109/RE.2013.6636719

Scherrer-Rathje, M., Boyle, T. A., & Deflorin, P. (2009). Lean, take two! Reflections from the second attempt at lean implementation. *Business Horizons, 52*(1), 79–88. doi:10.1016/j.bushor.2008.08.004

Tokatli, N. (2013). Toward a better understanding of the apparel industry. *Journal of Economic Geography, 13*(6), 993–1101. doi:10.1093/jeg/lbs043

Tokatli, N., & Kizilgün, Ö. (2004). Upgrading in the Global Clothing Industry: Mavi Jeans and the Transformation of a Turkish Firm from Full-Package to Brand-Name Manufacturing and Retailing. *Economic Geography, 80*(3), 221–240. doi:10.1111/j.1944-8287.2004.tb00233.x

Tombe, T., & Zhu, X. (2019). Trade, migration, and productivity: A quantitative analysis of china. *The American Economic Review, 109*(5), 1843–1872. doi:10.1257/aer.20150811

Yan, H.-D. (2012). Entrepreneurship, Competitive Strategies, and Transforming Firms from OEM to OBM in Taiwan. *Journal of Asia-Pacific Business, 13*(1), 16–36. doi:10.1080/10599231.2012.629877

Yi, H., Li, G., Li, L., Loyalka, P., Zhang, L., Xu, J., Kardanova, E., Shi, H., & Chu, J. (2018). Assessing the quality of upper-secondary vocational education and training: Evidence from China. *Comparative Education Review, 62*(2), 199–230. doi:10.1086/696920

Zhongqun, S. (2011). *Road of Strategic Transformation for Chinese OEM Enterprises: Issues and Countermeasures*. Academic Press.

Zhu, S., & He, C. (2018). Upgrading in China's apparel industry: International trade, local clusters and institutional contexts. *Post-Communist Economies*, *30*(2), 193–215. doi:10.1080/14631377.2017.1362099

Zhu, S., & Pickles, J. (2014). Bring In, Go Up, Go West, Go Out: Upgrading, Regionalization and Delocalisation in China's Apparel Production Networks. *Journal of Contemporary Asia*, *44*(1), 36–63. doi:10.1080/00472336.2013.801166

KEY TERMS AND DEFINITIONS

ASEAN (Association of Southeast Asian Nations): An economic union comprising ten member states in Southeast Asia, the largest of which include: Singapore, Malaysia, Indonesia, Philippines, and Thailand.

EU (European Union): A political and economic union of 27 member states located primarily in Europe and have a shared currency and single internal market and system of laws.

LPS (Lean Production System): Also known as lean production, just-in-time manufacturing and just-in-time production (JIT) is a production method derived from Toyota's operating model and aims primarily at reducing times within the production system as response times from suppliers and to customers.

ODM (Original Design Manufacturer): A contract manufacturer that uses its own designs and intellectual property (IP). An ODM product can either be the result of the supplier's own product development efforts – or a replica of another product already on the market and can be branded with the buyer's logo.

OEM (Original Equipment Manufacturer): An Original Equipment Manufacturer or OEM is a company that manufactures and sells products or parts of a product that their buyer, another company, sells to its own customers while putting the products under its own branding. OEMs commonly operate in the auto and computer industries.

SME (Small and Medium-Sized Enterprises): The sizing or categorization of a company as an SME can be based on a number of characteristics. The traits include annual sales, number of employees, the number of assets owned by the company, market capitalization, or any combination of these features. Generally, they are independent firms with less than 50 employees and not more than 250 employees. However, the maximum number of employees is different from one country to the next.

Chapter 9
Omnichannel and Experience Approach as a Post-COVID-19 Economic Reactivation Mechanism

Danny Christian Barbery-Montoya
https://orcid.org/0000-0002-6005-4997
Universidad Espíritu Santo, Ecuador

Dennisse A. Coronel-Arellano
Universitat de València, Spain

Ariana Soria-Loor
Universidad Santa María, Ecuador

ABSTRACT

The aim of this chapter is to show how omnichannel tools must be applied through the process of creating experiences for the consumers. During the literature review, some authors make approaches to the key concepts connecting omnichannels and consumer experiences; therefore, they explain through the analysis of data the reality of the Ecuadorian environment and global trends. With this context, this chapter will present how, by using macro environment and accessibility, a unique experience may be created in the customer journey in omnichannel.

INTRODUCTION

According to the World Health Organization (OMS, 2020), COVID19 is an infectious disease that had its outbreak in Wuhan (China) and has become a worldwide pandemic caused by the new coronavirus. According to Shiller, Nobel prize of Economics in 2013, a pandemic is more dangerous than an earthquake. This fact happens because the first one generates a greater feeling of anxiety and concern. As a

DOI: 10.4018/978-1-7998-7689-2.ch009

result of these, a "second pandemic" may appear as a financial and economic crisis that would alter the market around the world (BBC, 2020), causing a severe impact in many industries as tourism (Madrid & Diaz-Rebolledo, 2020).

Regarding this situation, some mechanisms are being recommended to the organizations to fight the crisis, as an example: plans for operational continuity, crisis management, financing and liquidity, labor management, among other aspects (PWC-Chile, 2020); however, many companies have shown how fragile they are in the matter of productivity in the value chain and must focus in a new business model strategy, in rearrange the manufacturing process and to strengthen the safety protocols for the employees and clients (Comisión Económica para América Latina y El Caribe, 2020). In this final topic, a Euromonitor report shows how consumer behavior changed in 2020 because of the pandemic, creating an anxious consumer, someone preoccupied with health and safety, who has turned his home into his office (Angus, 2020); he has tried to find connections with the outside world through social media and online communications; and also new entertainments in streaming platforms: movies, music, videogames (Ortega-Vivanco, 2020); now the whole experience process has changed, and it plays an essential part in industries as retailing (Tyrväinen, Karjaluoto, & Saarijärvi, 2020).

Facing this situation, the omnichannel is an alternative to homogenize the buying process through offline and online channel, provoking the customer to experiment with the brand and becoming companies' main interest (Lorenzo-Romero et al., 2020), creating emotions that take them to recommend the brand and resulting in loyalty (Arconada Muñoz, 2016). Nevertheless, it may also have a negative result, as the risk being perceived by the customer sharing his information (Quach, Barari, Vit Moudry, & Quach, 2020) or it may engage in additional logistic costs (Guerrero-Lorente et al., 2020).

With everything said before, one can question: How omnichannels help economic reactivation? Or, being specific: how are facilities driven to consumers by the omnichannels and the economy is reactivated?

Based on the literature review, the next chapter aims to show how omnichannel and the approach to improve the consumer experience may be applied to reactivate the economy revealing and classifying valuable tools to lead companies to digital transformation.

To achieve the objective, three parts will be addressed in this chapter: a) Literature review explaining the concept of omnichannels and consumer´s purchasing experiences through this strategy; b) A review on Covid19 impact on the Ecuadorian consumer´s behavior; and c) Suggestions, recommendations and possible solutions based on the topics previously described.

BACKGROUND

Omnichannel

By the end of the 90s, the internet has exponential growth. This situation causes many changes in society, such as how people communicate with each other and how high the influence of traditional transactions while buying and selling goods and services (Universidad Autónoma de México, 2018). For Universitat Oberta de Catalunya (2018), the action of buying and selling goods and services performed by websites or mobile applications (apps) between two individuals is known as E-Commerce. This fact has many crucial matters when individuals desire to purchase something, bringing up an effective omnichannel environment. The term omnichannel refers to the presence of multichannels where the consumer may find the good he/she is looking for, providing comfort and easing the decision-making process while shopping. This fact may happen, so it could exist a market development in front of the competitors, being a challenger in a market that is not mature in an omnichannel, and finally to achieve cost reduction in infrastructure and/or transactions (Jo, Kim, & Choi, 2018). About this opening, the services gotten by the omnichannels provide a high experiential level that relates with a wide range of the channel and the interactions generated by clients and suppliers.

On the contrary to the multichannel o cross-channel services, the omnichannel service involves a small segment and all the channels available for consumers. The omnichannel grows with the digital era, which doesn't happen with multichannels or single channels because technology has changed profoundly how retailers and consumers interact (Sun et al., 2020). Picot-Coupey et al. (2016) define omnichannel administration as a strategy to manage channels as merged contact points that allow consumers to live an experience inside the brand ecosystem.

Omnichannel Retailing

In a conventional system, clients purchase products at offline stores or e-commerce sites, while retailers do their channel marketing management separately (Sun et al., 2020). However, the concept of omnichannel retailing is oriented to be for clients where and when they want to, turning the consumer journey into a much complex and complete one by the presence of many contact points (Lynch & Barnes, 2020). For retailers, bringing a solid and standard shopping experience through offline and online channels has been very complex. This fact happens because the process requires compensations among quality of the responses, product mix, and consumer convenience (Lynch & Barnes, 2020). Nowadays, it's hard to compare a physical store with an online one as the last one may offer a broader catalog than the physical one (Reyneke & Barnardo, 2019).

Omnichannel must have some specific characteristics that, according to Lynch and Barnes (2020), are defined as dimensions which are: a) A perfect customer experience (fuzzy and integrated); b) be customer-centered with a simple vision; c) to create an experience and a brand commitment; d) the use of different channels simultaneously; e) the consistency of independent channels; f) Holistic and integrated, and g) the consumer journey. These dimensions lead us to an emphatic vision of the consumer himself, who sees a company's value offer, integrated, personalized, and adapted to his comfort, coming closer to the conceptualization of Grönroos (1994), who determines a marketing approach focus on the market and not to an extreme oversimplification of a 4Ps based mix.

The companies are moving forward to an integrated channel strategy, but the results are better for the online channel than for the offline one. This fact can be seen in integrating both the website and social media by linking consumers from one to another, interconnecting them by profiles, posts, or the purchase option in social media.

Incorporating the physical store in the online channel is much more developed, even more through the tools helping consumers find stores near them. This effect is more powerful when the stores give information about the products available, pick-up options, or even if they have return policies about online purchases. By using these strategies, companies adapt their services to meet consumers' needs. The integration has been improving these last years when we found more and more companies' allowing to return in physical stores some of the online purchases (López-Hernández & López, 2019). To be specific, in a multichannel retailer, channels are not integrated and also are managed separately, while in an omnichannel retailer, there is a considerable number of channels that are highly connected and integrated (Rodríguez-Torrico et al., 2020)

Nowadays, three forces are working together to promote retailers: 1) The spread of channels where their products could be upgraded, physical or virtual. 2) Consumer segments are defined by their channel preferences: offline, online, the mix; 3) The retailer's choice to manage the channels to offer a synergic experience to the consumer.

Valentini, Neslin, and Montaguti (2020) reference this in three phases: First of all, consumers' background based on their motivations, opportunities, and abilities (MOA); then, those segments open to omnichannel agreements, those who can access procurement channels (websites, banners, ads, apps, e-mail, social, special-deal websites, stores, mail, newspaper) and use channels (PC, mobile, stores, call center, catalog); and finally, the consequences where we find consumption, the change or loyalty to a brand/retailer. The retailers should consider the consumer's emotions to understand the attitudes they will develop. They also should build spaces that feel environments, designs, and social aspects as crucial elements to create positive feelings. In the same way, a follow-up to the consumers' journey among the channels should be done to identify those omniconsumers and how they travel (Rodríguez-Torrico et al., 2020). As already said, omnichannel contributes to obtaining loyalty from clients. With positive emotions during the experience, these act as conduct between omnichannel strategy and client's commitment (Mainardes et al., 2020).

The New Consumer: From Multichannels to Omnichannels

The digital era is tearing apart shopping routines motivating consumers to trust their mobile gadgets more and more every time and to use them to search and compare products and services (Sun et al., 2020). These days, consumers have become more intelligent. They have switched their traditional decision-making process by being careful with the trending situations, using discussion as a path to social acceptance, researching and comparing by utilizing both online and offline methods to conclude if making a purchase is the best choice (Mehta et al., 2020). The consumer is an omnichannel consumer, an evolution from the one in multichannel, someone whose behavior has changed from using few channels in parallel to someone who plays with all the contact points simultaneously.

They are turning personal attributes, and sales strategies in retailers have changed some of the consumer´s behavioral patterns, from purchasing one or more channels to the interest in using omnichannel services. Digitalization has also impacted these behavioral patterns, the retail environment, and the follow-up with the consumer. The consumer may feel satisfied with omnichannel when he believes there is an ability to give service and expectations regarding the channel performance (Sun et al., 2020). Now, the consumer makes decisions about online shopping by convenience and sales. Financial wellness affects the frequency and the average spending in online shopping but not in the desired benefits (Mehta et al., 2020).

It has to be considered that the consumer has evolved, and the way he tries to reach the companies have done it too. The digital channel has become a well know way to make contact, and according to Jo *et al.* (2018), there are the following types of online consumers:

Multichannel consumers: This type of consumer uses more than one channel when they have to purchase. The fact that the potential client prefers to have the option to visit a store physically becomes a challenge for the company as some of them won´t be able to fulfill this requirement.

Categorizing consumers: These are the ones who are actively looking for the lowest price in the market.

Webrooming consumers: These consumers are the ones who prefer to find their product by surfing websites but also decide to do the purchasing process in a physical store.

Showrooming consumers: They enjoy having a wholly physical experience. Both searching and purchasing are done in a store.

Logistics as an Inflection Point in Omnichannel Strategy

The way to do marketing is relatively new when meeting how changing media consumption habits are. This phenomenon pushes companies to find innovative ways to communicate with consumers. They have discovered that the key may be more interested in the customer experiences than in the products themselves (Baños González & de Aguilera Moyano, 2017). Retailing models (RBM) are still making efforts to develop omnichannels (OC); however, these changes respond to how omnichannels create and capture value. This fact suggests that integration of all the contact points must exist to assure an experience that the consumer could assess as perfect. With that established, processes must be created and carefully administrated by placing the consumer as the center of the strategy (Davis-Sramek et al., 2020).

Still, there is a big division between the supply chain and how retailers are organized inside their stores. Years before, stores used to be considered a perfect way to create experiences for the consumers. Nowadays, everything is integrated and participates in the supply chain (Davis-Sramek et al., 2020). The omnichannel strategy has forced retailers to reinvent supply chain management. Inside this decision, there is a new concept emerging: SFSTS (ship-from-store-to-store). By adopting SFSTS, the store becomes a distribution center (DC) prepared to supply other stores near it and end this way any trouble regarding inventory control or management and increasing product availability for consumers (Li, 2020).

SFTS is the main reason why in retailers' omnichannel websites, consumers may find many delivery options for their purchases and many others to handle returns. The chance to have all these options allows consumers to select what comes better for their needs considering time, place, transportation fee, etc. (Guerrero-Lorente et al., 2020). Online orders are prepared for shipping in any of the following: a) Distribution centers to combine tasks as the supply for other stores; b) Logistic Centers where inventory is stored specially for online orders, and c) Stores to allow both physical and online shopping and have just the limited resources to prepare online orders deliveries. (Guerrero-Lorente et al., 2020). Here is how the ability to have a synergy through channels is shown; for example, the inventory may be managed online to make a physical sale on online sale that could be picked up at a store (Lorenzo-Romero et al., 2020).

There is also a typical delivery system. It can be divided into two channels: Traditional existing channels such as post offices and New channels, taking into consideration convenience stores and home deliveries (Guerrero-Lorente et al., 2020). Companies want to achieve with any of these systems to have the consumer as a center and allow him to contact the brands whenever and wherever he would like to. The primary purpose is to make the consumer feel the brand and not the channel, and ultimately the consumer has perceived these efforts (Lorenzo-Romero et al., 2020). Nevertheless, with many channels available, the perceived risk is widely decreased whether it is financial, performance (how the product may work), physical (is the product broken?), social, or psychological (Hoffman & Bateson, 2008).

Creating Purchase Experience

Slow Retail Model is known for its capability to discover, explore, execute, create a community, learn, buy and share. These dimensions are conceptualized in future experiential store models, and they suggest four designed spaces: storytelling, fluid, digital zones, and community centers (Alexander & Blazquez Cano, 2020).

Storytelling: Space where the brand can be personified in 3D and show its identity

Fluid: Spaces speed, interchange, and interaction are the "beta mode." These spaces allow consumers to experiment, try new technologies and immersive experiences

Digital zones: Micro spaces inside physical stores were using technology, and the consumers have new experiences.

Community center: This space is programmed to lead communities, socialize, and live. Usually, these spaces are centered on human interaction.

As it was said before, creating a stimulus for consumers generates motivations. The concept of stimulus-organisms- response S-O-R under the omnichannel definition includes topics as digital atmosphere or webmospherics. Regarding online sales, the stimulus is defined by adding visible and hearable signs for online consumers (e-consumer or e-shopper). In the same matter, other variables as "how big is the picture" or "number of products available to sight" are different wars to understand and measure stimulus. In the same way, physical stores have their dimensions to care about: temperature, smells, textures, and others that stimulate the senses. (Paz & Delgado, 2020)

Covid19 and its implications in consumer behavior

In May 2020, a new era in commercial departments began, affecting how companies perform their daily activities. With the Covid19 pandemic, people were forced to stay inside their homes to take care of themselves and their health and activities as getting supplies could not stop. As a result of this situation, the digital channel had a significant increase in sales indicators around the world. Still, Ecuador´s reality has made its people untrust online channels, and taking that option during a pandemic felt forced. This statement is demonstrated by a study done by the Universidad Espìritu Santo (UEES) and *Cámara Ecuatoriana de Comercio Electrónico* in 2020, where even though perceived risk has been decreasing, people fear when doing online transactions, as they think their personal and financial information could be stolen or products may never arrive. On the other hand, it also can be said that prices are the primary motivation that people find if they must use this channel. Some others were also mentioned as payment methods and quality guarantees offered post-sales. This example takes us to the conclusion that every market should keep innovating in its processes to maintain the best possible experience each time a consumer is making a purchase (Davis-Sramek et al., 2020). At the same time, we could adopt two theories analyzed by Mart (Mart, 2020): 1) The Life cycle of the retailer, defined concerning the life´s cycle of the products and its four phases: innovation, accelerated development, maturity, and fall. 2) The environment theory is based on the belief that the market itself will generate different ways to do business and assures that success will result from continuous adaptation.

With Covid19 on the map, the frequency of online purchases increased drastically. In figure 1, it can be seen that the number of people who were keen on using digital channels once a month increased from 19% to 40%. This growth is explained by the family's concern for health and wellness during April 2020 (Angus & Westbrook, 2020). The tendency of online shopping in Ecuador will keep going up; however, this does not mean that people will only seek this experience.

The same study performed by the UEES (2020) demonstrates a clear intention to try online shopping, but still, people will shop traditionally in physical stores. This fact means the population is not fractioned but with the desire to have this omnichannel opportunity, as shown in figure 2.

Just as it was said before, there are four main reasons why people wouldn't shop online: a) fear of being scammed; b) fear that personal and financial information would be stolen; c) People prefer to see

Figure 1. Frequency of online shopping during Pandemic
Source: Universidad Espíritu Santo (2020)

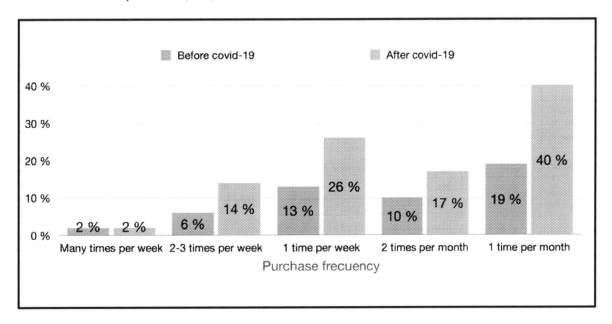

Figure 2. The intention of online shopping
Source: Universidad Espíritu Santo (2020)

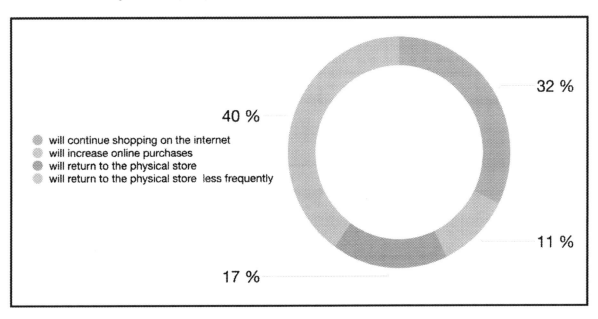

and touch what they are going to buy; and d) Untrusting of payment methods. These arguments could be better understood using financial risk and psychological context, as was stated by Bateson and Hoffman (2008). However, it should be taken into consideration the other side of the moon: Motivations. With these criteria, having a guaranteed delivery and payment, best quality, and the chance to split payments are arguments mentioned as the three principal motivations por people to consider online shopping an actual benefit. At this point, motivation is a deal-breaker.

On the other hand, the consumer is searching for information before making decisions about a purchase. This information-seeking makes them look for what prosumers have to say about the matter, visits to websites, social media, and even blogs or forums. The channel hopping is happening 25% of the time when going from online to physical stores (31% almost every time and 4% every time), which guarantees a blended behavior. This channel hopping does not indicate that the sale is made because some technological factors, such as apps or websites, are not working correctly (48%), causing dropouts. As delivery times (30%), some others are having these adverse effects also decreasing effectivity ratio in sales for companies.

When analyzing both the Ecuadorian consumer and the tendencies presented in some reports of Angus (2020) and Westbrook and Angus (2021), some behavioral changes merging physical and virtual actions are explained. The *phygital* reality referred to by these reports tells us about how people feel the experience while shopping at home on websites and the virtual experiences in the physical stores. These second generate a sense of safety and health through shoppers leaving their homes. The tendency studied un Euromonitor 2021 indicates that people from 15 to 29 are the group that has engaged more in digital transactions or augmented reality. This phenomenon happens for some reasons: smartphone dependency, some country´s restrictions making people stay at home asking people to avoid contact, the obsession with health and wellness, new work environments, and resiliency. Having identified these factors, they turn into opportunities for companies to act fast and adapt to new consumption habits that are now affecting the economy.

SOLUTIONS AND RECOMMENDATIONS

Access to Omnichannels

Covid19 pandemic has created a new challenge for organizations pushing them to adapt faster in a competitive and technological market while behaviors on consumers are also changing as people learn how to live in new normal.

As Lynch and Barnes (2020) referred to, having the consumer as a center gives companies a hint on what the strategy should be: as simple as making the experience transparent and unique where the consumer co-creates value with them. Companies have already achieved some levels where consumers feel one with brands and feel very involved. Some authors as Bateson and Hoffman (2008) and Lovelock and Wirtz (2009) defined this no-separation between consumers and companies even though they did not refer to *phygital* reality like the one we live in nowadays.

By this matter, we may understand omnichannel as a fully integrated experience as Picot-Coupey et al. (2016) defines it. It is presented as static and portable in every dimension. If a company offers a physical experience, then sanitary safety should be considered because of the pandemic; while in online security, one must consider access infallibility, the payment method's security, and the logistic quality based on effectiveness and efficiency (figure 3). This is how it is expected that the consumer adapts to this reality.

Figure 3. Physical and Virtual Spaces in Omnichannels

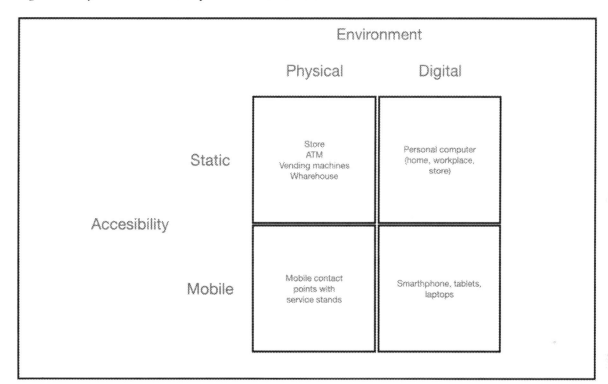

In omnichannel matters, logistics should bring to consumers the feeling that getting the products will be easy through the contact points that suit their convenience and, of course, help the company get efficient with delivery expenses. Creating Distribution centers, logistic centers, and stores has become investments for Guerrero-Lorente et al. (2020). However, they constitute physical growth for them as they would be occupying spaces in the land. The investments shortly would become a chance to have franchises contributing to brand awareness.

The Customer Journey in Omnichannels

Even though there are some tools to determine the customer journey, omnichannels have been getting more complex by having the inflection points in Pandemic times: a) Sanitary safety seeked by consumers and b) new workspaces invading personal life. Following the context, the first actions to be taken to reactivate consumption and, therefore, the economy itself generate a path where spending money is not retained. A simple model is proposed to define moments in consumers' lives: before, during, and after purchasing.

Before making the purchase, it makes us look closely right to where the consumer is doing research and defining what they need. The physical environment takes in all the information gathered around the traditional channels of communication (radio, tv, newspapers, magazines), word-of-mouth from acquaintances, communication tools in the store, flyers, POP, product packaging, or any other tangible element that contributes to the evaluation. On the other hand, the virtual environment takes the eWOM happening in social media or any other website.

In a hybrid environment, a smartphone merges the channel by introducing an online experience in a store, such as QRs.

During the purchase: Factors must be established to let consumers *identify the brand*. In this matter, when talking about physical spaces, the brand could use any element that can be perceived by the consumer´s senses to communicate with him and make him notice. The digital environments contemplate using easy names for their websites, exclusive apps, and so on. Beyond the brand, some *security mechanisms* should be considered, while in the physical world, brands take care of the consumer´s health. In the virtual world, brands should take care of their information and privacy. It´s recommended that they implement responses to guarantee that the consumer is safe, such as return policy, giving the money back when necessary.

Finally, *promotions, discounts, and prices should be established to fulfill both worlds' needs to keep the consumer coming back and forth fro*m the channels.

After purchase: This is where emotions are born in the consumer's heart. When the world is going through difficult times, make someone feel safe and calm causes a deep connection and creates value. In the digital channel, emotion is created when the purchasing is regular because it can be understood that the consumer has had a riskless experience saving time. In the physical world, the guarantee of a safe space with sanitary protocols is the best way to assure loyalty.

Figure 4. Vital elements for omnichannels in Customer Journey

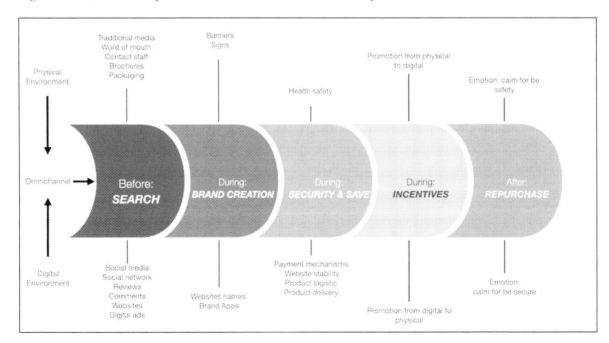

The steps and elements described in Figure 4 show how omnichannels contribute to creating "relatively" new experiences for consumers, one that must make develop positive emotions that guarantee the buyback of the products and turning into trust as a result to contrasts and improve the consumption system lost by the pandemic times. Homes had restricted their purchases because of the lack of confidence in digital channels. However, with omnichannels actions, companies could show themselves as transparent and accessible to keep the contact with these new consumers that now is looking for new experiences where security has two meanings: health and information.

CONCLUSION AND FUTURE RESEARCH DIRECTIONS

One of the main exciting subjects is which is the change that the pandemic brought. Before Covid19 came as a reality, people in Ecuador had the digital experience as an additional alternative to reach products or even get closer to the companies. The core interest in using digital channels was focused on the pre-purchase phase. This information-seeking seldom turned into a genuine purchase because of the trusting issues addressed before in this chapter. This fear about security was pausing the development of the digital experience, but it helped the consumers get online information and then pursuing their purchases through physical channels.

Covid19 turned the alternative into a must. Online purchasing became a need based on the urge to keep healthy, helping consumers overcome fear in the channel and finally come through with the whole transaction. With this sudden phenomenon, companies had to move faster to an omnichannel strategy. The digital transformation driven by the organizations has been abrupt and full of incidentals; however, it wills to achieve adaptability in the environment, proximity to the customers, and the possibility to move forward in their competitive development.

Discuss Omnichannels are big bets generated by the Covid19 pandemic. Many authors have put some effort into studying all decisions companies are making and the actions taken to defeat the economic fall the pandemic has caused. The literature review and this theoretical proposal pretend to be a start point for future studies in marketing, logistics, and administration. It is recommended that the investigation continues regarding the elements that contribute to unique experiences for new consumers and so the purchasing process. The authors of this study don't pretend to reach that hyper-simplification mentioned by Gröonross applied to omnichannels. Still, we hope this could guide where to start for companies and those entrepreneurs born post-pandemic looking forward to achieving sustainability.

Omnichannels must be the starting point for new business models where the companies must provide static and mobile accesses by considering how both physical and digital worlds merge. Firms must classify contact points based on how convenient they are for consumers and how environments could help them achieve the best experience. Consumers have an active role in the value chain as they have good experiences while making a purchase.

The key points that should be studied from the consumer's journey are investigation, brand creation, the seek for physical (health), financial, transactional, and logistic safety, promotions, and finally, how to generate positive emotions based on calm and tranquility. However, it is probably that with the technological evolution, some behavioral changes will accelerate and not only be studied but anticipated by companies.

REFERENCES

Alexander, B., & Blazquez Cano, M. (2020). Store of the future: Towards a (re)invention and (re)imagination of physical store space in an omnichannel context. *Journal of Retailing and Consumer Services, 55*(August), 101913. doi:10.1016/j.jretconser.2019.101913

Angus, A. (2020). *How Is COVID19 Affecting The Top 10 Global Consumer Trends 2020?* Euromonitor International.

Arconada Muñoz, D. (2016). La Experiencia de Cliente y la Omnicanalidad. *Contact Center,* (83), 18–21.

Baños González, M., & de Aguilera Moyano, J. (2017). Las comunicaciones en el nuevo paradigma de marketing. Experiencias, relevancia, engagement y personalización. Presentación. *Revista ICONO14 Revista Científica de Comunicación y Tecnologías Emergentes, 15*(2), 1–15. doi:10.7195/ri14.v15i2.1098

BBC. (2020). *Mundo-Noticias: BBC News*. Obtenido de BBC: https://www.bbc.com/mundo/noticias-52748371

Comisión Económica para América Latina y El Caribe. (2020). *Repositorio: CEPAL*. Obtained from CEPAL:https://repositorio.cepal.org/bitstream/handle/11362/45734/S2000438_es.pdf?sequence=4&isAllowed=y

Davis-Sramek, B., Ishfaq, R., Gibson, B. J., & Defee, C. (2020). Examining retail business model transformation: A longitudinal study of the transition to omnichannel order fulfillment. *International Journal of Physical Distribution & Logistics Management, 50*(5), 557–576. doi:10.1108/IJPDLM-02-2019-0055

Grönroos, C. (1994). *Marketing y gestión de servicios*. Ediciones Díaz de Santos S.A.

Guerrero-Lorente, J., Gabor, A. F., & Ponce-Cueto, E. (2020). Omnichannel logistics network design with integrated customer preference for deliveries and returns. *Computers & Industrial Engineering, 144*(March), 106433. doi:10.1016/j.cie.2020.106433

Hoffman, K. D., & Bateson, J. E. G. (2008). Services Marketing. In Acta Theologica (4e ed.). doi:10.4314/actat.v27i2.52312

Jo, W., Kim, J., & Choi, J. (2018). *Who are the multichannel shoppers, and how can retailers use them? Evidence from the French apparel industry*. Emerald Insight.

Li, R. (2020). Reinvent Retail Supply Chain: Ship-from-Store-to-Store. *Production and Operations Management, 29*(8), 1825–1836. doi:10.1111/poms.13195

López-Hernández, A. M., & López, M. (2019). Estudio omnicanal de las empresas minorista del sector cosmético en España. *Red Marka - Revista de Marketing Aplicado, 23*(2), 19–41.

Lorenzo-Romero, C., Andrés-Martínez, M. E., & Mondéjar-Jiménez, J. A. (2020). Omnichannel in the fashion industry: A qualitative analysis from a supply-side perspective. *Heliyon, 6*(6), e04198. Advance online publication. doi:10.1016/j.heliyon.2020.e04198 PMID:32577571

Lynch, S., & Barnes, L. (2020). Omnichannel fashion retailing: Examining the customer decision-making journey. *Journal of Fashion Marketing and Management, 24*(3), 471–493. doi:10.1108/JFMM-09-2019-0192

Madrid, F., & Diaz-Rebolledo, J. (2020). *México: Red de Universidades Anáhuac*. Obtained from Red de Universidades Anáhuac: https://www.anahuac.mx/mexico/cicotur/sites/default/files/2020-03/Doc06_Coronavirus_Turismo_CICOTUR.pdf

Mainardes, E. W., Rosa, C. A. de M., & Nossa, S. N. (2020). Omnichannel strategy and customer loyalty in banking. *International Journal of Bank Marketing, 38*(4), 799–822. doi:10.1108/IJBM-07-2019-0272

Mart, C. J. (2020). Walmart China. *Evolución de los formatos comerciales hasta la omnicanalidad, 3*, 110–120.

Martínez, A., Romero, L., & Jimenez, M. (2017). La ominicanalidad como medio de homogeneización de la experiencia de compra. In XXIX Congreso de Marketing Aemark 2017 (pp. 1597-1599). Sevilla: ESIC.

Mehta, R., Singh, H., Banerjee, A., Bozhuk, S., & Kozlova, N. (2020). Comparative analysis of the consequences of purchasing models transformation within the global digitalization of the economy. *IOP Conference Series. Materials Science and Engineering, 940*(1), 012071. Advance online publication. doi:10.1088/1757-899X/940/1/012071

OMS. (2020). *Orientaciones para el Público: OMS*. Obtained from Organización Mundial de la Salud: https://www.who.int/es/emergencies/diseases/novel-coronavirus-2019/advice-for-public/q-a-coronaviruses

Ortega-Vivanco, M. (2020). Efectos del Covid19 en el comportamiento del consumidor: Caso Ecuador. *RETOS. Revista de Ciencias de la Administración y Economía, 10*(20), 233–247.

Paz, M. D. R., & Delgado, F. J. (2020). Consumer Experience and Omnichannel Behavior in Various Sales Atmospheres. *Frontiers in Psychology, 11*(August), 1–11. doi:10.3389/fpsyg.2020.01972 PMID:32849155

PWC-Chile. (2020). *Nuestros Servicios: PWC*. Obtained from PWC: https://www.pwc.com/cl/es/Nuestros-Servicios/COVID19-como-puede-responder-tu-empresa-ante-la-crisis.html

Quach, S., Barari, M., Vit Moudry, D., & Quach, K. (2020). Service integration in omnichannel retailing and its impact on customer experience. *Journal of Retailing and Consumer Services*, 102267. doi:10.1016/j.jretconser.2020.102267

Rodríguez-Torrico, P., San-Martín, S., & San José Cabezudo, R. (2020). The role of omnichannel tendency in digital information processing. *Online Information Review, 44*(7), 1347–1367. doi:10.1108/OIR-08-2019-0272

Sun, Y., Yang, C., Shen, X. L., & Wang, N. (2020). When digitalized customers meet digitalized services: A digitalized social cognitive perspective of omnichannel service usage. *International Journal of Information Management, 54*(July), 102200. doi:10.1016/j.ijinfomgt.2020.102200

Tyrväinen, O., Karjaluoto, H., & Saarijärvi, H. (2020). Personalization and hedonic motivation in creating customer experiences and loyalty in omnichannel retail. *Journal of Retailing and Consumer Services, 57*.

Universidad Autónoma de México. (2018). El Comercio Electrónico y principios económico-comerciales. *Biblioteca Juridica Virtual del Instituto de Investigaciones Jurídicas de la UNAM, 1*.

Universidad de Catalunya. (2018). La logística como fuente de valor añadido al eCommerce. *Oikonomics*, 28-30.

Valentini, S., Neslin, S. A., & Montaguti, E. (2020). Identifying omnichannel deal-prone segments, their antecedents, and their consequences. *Journal of Retailing*, 96(3), 310–327. doi:10.1016/j.jretai.2020.01.003

KEY TERMS AND DEFINITIONS

Consumer Centrality or Consumer-Centered Strategy: Integral activities that companies engage in create experiences for their clients.

Customer Journey: The concept addresses the consumer´s purchasing process and the different contact points. This process drives through the need identification to how the consumer behaves post-purchase.

Hybrid Environments: It refers to an atmosphere where the consumer may have both physical and technological experiences. These technologies may be based on social media, collaborative tools, compilations, or video sharing.

Inseparability Is the Service: The concept of service marketing in which it is defined that there is joint participation between the client and the company for the creation and provision of the service. If the client does not participate in the provision, the service is not generated.

Multichannel: Multiple touchpoints that work independently to provide an isolated consumer experience. The consumer can access the company's contact channels in parallel but not intermixed.

Phygital: Referring to the inseparability of physical and digital environments. It is achieved with an interaction at the points of contact with mobile applications and portable devices such as smartphones.

S.O.R. (Stimulus, Organism, Reply): Psychologic concept applied to Marketing of services to the point that creating environments generates an organic reaction in human beings. This reaction translates into positive or negative answers about consumption.

Service Inseparability: Marketing of services' concept. It defines joint participation between the client and the company to create and give service. If the client is not involved in delivering the service, then the service is not generated.

Word-of-Mouth: Term used to refer to what people say about a product based on their experience with it. In the digital world, it is known as eWOM (electronic word of mouth).

Chapter 10
Determinants of RFID Adoption Intention in the Healthcare Industry for Patient Monitoring:
A Special Reference to COVID-19

Bijoylaxmi Sarmah
North-Eastern Regional Institute of Science and Technology, Nirjuli, India

Shampy Kamboj
National Institute of Technology, Hamirpur, India

Neeraj Kumar Phookan
https://orcid.org/0000-0003-2676-8731
North-Eastern Regional Institute of Science and Technology, Nirjuli, India

ABSTRACT

Radio frequency identification (RFID) technology holds tremendous potential in improving the patient management system in hospitals attaining global importance in the healthcare industry due to the spread of the COVID-19 pandemic at present. RFID assists in wireless data storage and automatic retrieval, making systems efficient, improving patient safety, and decreasing costs. Although RFID is an emerging technology in the healthcare industry, its adoption is yet to gather momentum. This chapter will provide a background for healthcare practitioners and researchers about RFID technologies in the healthcare sector. Moreover, an integrated conceptual framework will be proposed consisting of factors that influence RFID technology adoption intention in the healthcare industry. This study will be the first of its kind to identify and classify various factors of RFID adoption intention and provide a comprehensive model using an exploratory method laying the foundation for academicians and industry practitioners for the future scope of its research.

DOI: 10.4018/978-1-7998-7689-2.ch010

INTRODUCTION

Radio Frequency Identification (RFID) Technology is attaining global importance in the healthcare industry due to the spread of SARS and nCOVID-19 pandemics. It has seen increasing adoption rates in various sectors, including the health care industry. In hospitals deploying RFID application devices, the existing hospital information system is integrated with the RFID application network for developing a platform to synthesize data collected via RFID and other sources. According to the World Health Organization's (WHO) guidelines, the hospitals have to follow proper hand hygiene, barrier precautions, personal protective equipment (PPE), safe injection practices, etc. RFID technology assists in patient monitoring and managing patient hygiene through tags used at hand hygiene dispensers (Burbano, et al., 2009) in hospitals.

The application of RFID technology for patient monitoring and management system is crucial for good quality in health care services. It helps store wireless data and automatic retrieval, which further helps identify, track, and store data and the barcode system. RFID application also improves patient safety, minimizes patients' waiting time, and decreasing costs (Maroo, 2016). In India, Apollo Hospital Chennai, one of the most extensive healthcare facilities, implemented RFID in various areas such as patient waiting for time reduction, patient location tracking, care for patients, etc. Apollo could offer lots of patient assistance by implementing RFID in hospitals, such as selecting the proper departments and tracking their file's progress that reduce delays and bottlenecks through unique ID numbers assigned to each patient (Maroo, 2016).

However, RFID adoption is still in its infancy (Tzeng et al., 2008). A few empirical studies have been conducted to assess RFID technology's potential in healthcare (Fosso Wamba, Anand, & Carter, 2013; Yazici, 2014; Reyes, Li, & Visich, 2016). Fosso Wamba et al. (2016) use empirical analysis to explore the role of technological, organizational, environmental, and managerial characteristics of small and mid-sized enterprises (SMEs) in their intention to adopt RFID technology. Despite RFID technology's promise in the literature, healthcare organizations are still in the early stages of using this RFID technology (Carr et al., 2010; Yao, Chu, & Li, 2012). Moreover, it has been viewed that there is a lack of studies discussing the antecedents, mediators, and moderators of RFID adoption intention in healthcare services.

Keeping in mind these research gaps, this chapter aims to highlight the role of RFID technologies in the healthcare sector. It discusses the antecedents, mediating, and moderating factors affecting RFID enabled application adoption intention with a proposed conceptual framework. The remaining part of this chapter is structured as follows: first, the literature review on RFID adoption intention has been discussed, followed by a proposed conceptual framework, research methodology, discussion, the theoretical and practical implications of this study, and lastly, the conclusion and future research directions are being presented.

LITERATURE REVIEW

RFID is a wire-less auto-identification and data capture (AIDC) technology that includes optical recognition, barcoding, biometrics, touch or contact memory technology, and card technology (Burbano et al., 2009). RFID tools and technologies use radio-frequency to find tagged items via wireless transmission, which can be automatically tracked. RFID tags assist in individual item identification. RFID technologies are embedded in the packaging of products (Burbano et al., 2009).

Determinants of RFID Adoption Intention in the Healthcare Industry for Patient Monitoring

For the patient-care process, RFID technologies help collect biological data information, blood tracking, monitoring signs, and patient environments (Reyes, Li, & Visich, 2012). Previous literature discussed RFID adoption in the context of various purposes. Sharma et al. (2007) integrated the models proposed by Iacovou, Benbasat, and Dexter (1995) and Teo et al. (2003) and adapted them to explore the context of RFID adoption. Bensel et al. (2008) and Pigni and Ugazio (2009) discussed RFID adoption for potential benefits and business performance. Krasnova et al. (2008) and Tewari and Gupta (2020) used case studies to discuss RFID adoption intentions. Madlberger (2009) studied the antecedents of RFID adoption intention by firms and other aspects such as perceived internal and inter-organizational benefits, expected future cost of RFID, firm size.

During the Severe Acute Respiratory Syndrome (SARS) epidemic in Taiwan, hospitals benefited by adopting RFID technologies for patient care and analyzing the workload of medical staff (Tzeng et al., 2008). RFID-based solutions help in tracking patients and improving patient care. In Italy, pharmacies provided customers passive 13.56 MHz RFID cards to create health diaries and track prescription purchases. Hassinen and Marttila-Kontio (2008) highlighted the RFID bracelets and wireless sensors for automating documentation processes, and Chowdhury and Khosla (2007) studied the use of wrist bands for patient identification purposes.

Earlier studies discussed the benefit of RFID in a multitude of areas, such as reducing labor costs through improved real-time visibility (De Marco et al., 2012), lead time variability within the supply chain (Chang, Klabjan, & Vossen, 2010), and facilitating the promotion or cross-selling of new products more effectively and efficiently (Wong et al., 2012). Moreover, improved customer satisfaction Bhattacharya et al., 2010), customer loyalty (Lee, Fiedler, & Smith, 2008), inventory management (De Marco et al., 2012; Reaidy, Gunasekaran, & Spalanzani, 2015), patient care, security, and safety (Reyes, Li, & Visich, 2012). Yazici (2014) explored how RFID Technology can help meet hospital real-time asset and information management requirements. A systematic review was done to study RFID applications and issues in the health care industry (Fosso Wamba, Anand, & Carter, 2013). Fosso Wamba et al. (2015) also identified and rated the critical technological, security and privacy, and financing issues related to RFID-enabled health care transformation projects. Reyes, Li, & Visich (2016) researched the antecedents and outcomes of RFID technology in the health care sector by surveying 88 health care organizations.

RFID helps mitigate drug counterfeiting, simplifies the clinical trial process, improves patient identification accuracy, eases inventory management, streamlines patient tracking, improves communications between caregivers and patients, and eradicates the risk of administering the wrong medications. RFID also plays a vital role during surgical procedures as it helps surgeons and operation theatre staff track all required devices in a matter of seconds. RFID offers many advantages over existing technologies such as bar codes, which are 'read-only.' At the same time, RFID tags are 'read-write.' This means bar codes must be individually read. In contrast, groups of RFID tags are read simultaneously (Verdict Medical Devices, 2017). A few limitations of RFID technologies such as its cost, cannot withstand extreme temperatures, the requirement of Internet, and electricity requirements. Moreover, the lifespan of RFID tags depends on replaceable batteries.

CONCEPTUAL FRAMEWORK DEVELOPMENT

Antecedents

Psychological Characteristics

New technology adoption in an organization is driven by the user's need, conceptualized by terms like need-pull and technology push (Zmud, 1984). The literature on total quality control (Blauw & During, 1990) and benchmarking adoption (Forker & Mendez, 2001) also suggests that adopting new practices increases to mitigate the firm's existing problems. In turn, these problems can create a perception of a performance gap that establishes the relevance of need-pull.

Holmqvist and Stefansson (2006) argued that RFID implementation could reduce handling costs, facilitate identifying items within the operational premises, and improve process design. Other advantages include real-time tracking and faster replenishment of items (Spekman & Sweeny, 2006), thus reducing stockout chances. Keeping in line, healthcare organizations face a myriad of operational issues viz. critical patient safety, the pressure to reduce operational costs, prevent counterfeit drugs, reducing time for nurses and hospital management to source and locate medical equipment, assessing the utilization rate of the equipment, reducing errors in laboratory tests, inventory losses due to unnecessary waste and theft (Yazici, 2014). Operationally complicated issues such as blood management and distribution can be benefitted by utilizing temperature-sensitive RFID tags using real-time tracking data thus, ensuring that only blood stored in optimal temperatures can be distributed to the patient (Wicks, Visich, & Li, 2006). These issues can be categorized under three heads- control and management of assets, monitoring people, integration of people, and assets that can be addressed by RFID application (Mogre, Gadh, & Chattopadhyay, 2009).

Technological Characteristics

Rogers identified five key technological factors- 'relative advantage,' 'compatibility,' 'complexity,' 'observability,' and 'trialability' that play a prominent role while adopting or rejecting IT innovation (Rogers, 1995). Relative advantage is the degree to which an innovation can be beneficial to the organization. Compatibility is the degree to which an innovation can be implemented within the existing business processes and systems. Complexity is the degree to which an innovation is complicated to use. Observability is the degree to which results are visible after implementing the innovation. Trialability is the degree to which an innovation allows experimentation to be possible. But, relative advantage, compatibility, and complexity were found to have a significant and consistent relationship with innovation adoption (Tornatzky, & Klein, 1982).

In RFID adoption intention, a relative advantage is the most cited facilitator (Sharma, & Citurs, 2005) and predictor (Premkumar, & Roberts, 1999). In healthcare systems, RFID application increases efficiency in the healthcare delivery process, thereby saving time and reducing data entry errors (Bunduchi, Weisshaar, & Smart, 2011), facilitating the identification, keeping track and trace of the patient (Fisher, & Monahan, 2008); reduce patient care errors such as a mismatch in medication distribution, medication dosage and allergies caused from the drug (Thuemmler, Buchanan, & Kumar, 2007; Tu, Zhou, & Piramuthu, 2009); facilitate monitoring, tracking and tracing of blood during management and distribution from the blood bank to healthcare unit (Najera, Lopez, & Roman, 2011). Furthermore, integrating

RFID also has an indirect positive benefit on inventory handling viz, reducing stockouts, reducing time in sourcing misplaced items, and losing items due to theft (Yazici, 2014).

Brown and Russel (2007) and Wang et al. (2010) have suggested high compatibility as an essential predictor of RFID adoption intention. Combining RFID technology along with current operational practices such as barcode-based data collection can bring a magnitude of improvement within the organization (Niederman et al., 2007). Although resisting this change may act as a grave issue for its implementation (Ngai et al., 2007).

On the contrary, complexity negatively affects adoption intention (Premkumar & Roberts, 1999). Many organizations' RFID implementation is still in the nascent stage, thus creating a lower level of confidence among people (Ngai et al., 2007) that may lead to the assumption that bar code is sufficient (Yazici, 2014). Technological obstacles due to false reads arising from the presence of electromagnetic interference, security obstacles such as availability of secured data storage and communication channels between RFID readers and tags, and delay due to slow cultural change of nurses and employees in the healthcare facility make RFID implementation complex (Yazici, 2014).

Organizational Characteristics

Organizational characteristics is a widely studied antecedent in technology adoption intention literature. In this regard, firm size has been extensively studied (Masters et al., 1992) as a key finding that plays a vital role in technology adoption intentions. The advantage of having more resources in finance, slack, and technical expertise makes it easier for larger firms to adopt new technological practices (Rogers, 1995). On the other hand, small firms take up new technology under different circumstances (Jun, & Cal, 2003), such as when coming under pressure from their bigger trading partners (Iacovou, Benbasat, & Dexter, 1995). Several case studies argue that even smaller firms apply RFID if the business processes are closed-loop in nature or gain a competitive advantage (Madlberger, 2009). In healthcare systems, RFID implementation can yield a significant improvement in efficiency by reducing unwanted medical errors, enabling a higher level of patient care and safety, and maintaining regulatory compliance (Yazici, 2014). Thus, RFID can yield a competitive advantage over others.

Environmental Characteristics

Competitive pressure, competitive environment, the firm's geographic location, and standards and regulations are the key environmental factors studied in IT adoption (Fosso Wamba et al., 2016). Competitive pressure as a factor of IT adoption intention is suggested in multiple studies (Sharma, Dominic, & Benn, 2008; Wang, Wang, & Yang, 2010) and as one of the best (Jeyaraj, Rottman, & Lacity, 2006). Adopting IT, innovations in situations of market uncertainty facilitates organizations to be more agile in responding to competitive threats (Sambamurthy, Bharadwaj, & Grover, 2003) and creates an edge in a competitive environment (Chau, & Tam, 1997). The healthcare industry faces uncertainty in changing government regulations, privacy issues of patients, moving to electronic record keeping, and volatile relationships between doctors, hospitals, and insurers. This provides an opportunity for RFID implementation to improve overall efficiency, thus, attaining a strong position in the uncertain environment (Cao et al., 2012). Coronado, Acosta, and Fernández (2008) argue that the firm's geographical location and the availability of technological opportunities create a positive attitude towards adoption intention.

Applied Information Systems

Previous studies have found technical readiness to be an antecedent of technology adoption (Madlberger, 2009) referred to as the available resources- financial and technological in the firm; people and physical assets; and different understanding of technology (Iacovou, Benbasat, & Dexter, 1995; Zhu, Mukhopadhyay, & Kurata, 2012). Current IT innovations require sophisticated technology levels, and, for attaining benefits, RFID requires the same. Therefore, for successful implementation, the prerequisites will be advanced levels of information system capabilities.

Expected Future Costs of RFID

Frequent inhibitors of RFID are the high cost involved hindering firms from taking a back seat (Saran, 2005). Driedonks et al. (2005) considered a negative relationship between perceived costs and the intention to adopt RFID. A tag ranges between 4 cents to as high as $50, and tag readers can cost from $1000 to $3000 (Yazici, 2014). As such, it is imperative to consider expected future costs and not concentrate on present costs during RFID implementation (Madlberger, 2009).

Mediators

Perceived Benefits of RFID

Perceived benefits of RFID are two-pronged: perceived internal benefits and perceived inter-organizational benefits. In the context of perceived internal benefits, implementing RFID technology improves automation efficiency, productivity improvements, and labor costs. Li and Benton (2006) observed that decisions for technology adoption and cost and quality performance of the hospital have a significant relationship. Measures related to cost focus on reducing patient costs, handling inventory to reduce stockouts, higher capacity utilization, and labor productivity. Furthermore, RFID adoption reduces errors in the data entry process, reducing overall steps in the healthcare delivery process, and increasing overall efficiency (Yazici, 2014). Therefore, maintaining a favorable relationship between cost and perceived internal benefit will positively affect RFID adoption intention (Madlberger, 2009).

Moderators

Industry Sector

The industry sector and the firm's country can influence the strength of the relationship that the antecedents have on RFID adoption intention. The country's structure- infrastructure, legal policies, the education system will play a significant role in influencing the decisions taken in IT adoption investment (Coe, Helpman, & Hoffmaister, 1997). Previous literature has also found a connection between a firm's willingness to adopt IT innovation based on its industry sector (Harland et al., 2007; Oliveira & Martins, 2010).

Managerial Characteristics

Adopting IT innovation in an organization depends on the quality of Managerial functionaries' (Marcati, Guido, & Peluso, 2008). The age factor of Managerial functionaries plays an important role in adopting and using IT-based technologies to improve organizations. According to former studies, with the advancement of age, the ability to handle/process complex information slows down. As such, they do not show interest in adopting new technology because they must acclimatize with the changing working environment for which they have to re-learn things to perform their activities (Venkatesh, Sykes, & Venkatraman, 2014). On the other hand, adopting new technology is a valuable addition to young managers' working environments for their recent education and learning capabilities (Kitchell, 1997).

Consequences

RFID Technology Adoption Intention

The 21st-century health care system's critical goal is the adoption of IT and its effective use in the healthcare sector (Menachemi, & Brooks, 2006). Technology adoption intention at the firm level is prominently studied under two models viz. Diffusion of innovation (DOI) (Rogers, 1995) and technology, organization, and environment (TOE) framework (Tornatzky, Fleischer, & Chakrabarti, 1990). At the firm level, the DOI theory reflects how innovation spreads within a social system. The rate has a significant relationship with individual-level characteristics (e.g., manager-leader), structural features of the organization, and external organizational characteristics (Rogers, 1995). Technological context, organizational context, and environmental context are the three aspects determined by the TOE framework. These aspects influence how an enterprise adopts and implements technological innovation (Oliveira, & Martins, 2011).

Multiple studies show that RFID implementation has led to benefits in automation, improvements in productivity, patient and labor cost reduction, efficient inventory handling, thus, reducing stockouts and losses, patient safety, reducing data entry and laboratory tests errors, reduced loss due to theft and critical operations like blood management and distribution (Yazici, 2014). The perceived performance gap can be addressed only indirectly through the mediation of perceived benefits, resulting in RFID adoption intention. This is dependent on the levels of satisfaction that the firm has on the current operational processes and systems. Schon (1967) and Zmud (1984) studied that factors like need-pull and technology-push facilitate technology adoption intention. But when considering need pull factors, Rai and Patnayakuni (1996) found it indirectly related to technology adoption. Technological adoption intention has been studied extensively. It is stated that to pace with the more significant trading partners, the smaller firms tend to adopt innovation (Iacovou, Benbasat, & Dexter, 1995), thereby having the advantage of experiencing various technological opportunities (Jun, & Cal, 2003). Menachemi and Brooks (2006) propounded that implementing IT in the healthcare system is the paramount goal of the century. The health care system will be experiencing fewer errors (Yacizi, 2014) and would have transparency and efficiency with the RFID adoption (Reaidy, Gunasekaran, & Spalanzani, 2015; Madlberger, 2009), leading to potential safety savings (Sherer, 2010).

METHODOLOGY

RFID technologies play an important role in the efforts against COVID-19 and possibly add to solutions faster than we would otherwise attain in various fields and applications. As the outburst of the epidemic, there has been a rise in the study and use of RFID technologies in many areas. In addition, the advents of machines powered by RFID technologies have already robustly influenced the healthcare industry, and the effects of its adoption in hospitals have been a highly debated issue. This chapter addresses how the various factors (psychological factors, organizational factors, human factors, technological factors, external factors, institutional factors, and supply chain readiness factors) affect hospitals' RFID technologies adoption intention. For the same purpose, a conceptual framework is proposed in Figure 1 that represents the antecedents, mediating, and moderating factors affecting RFID-enabled application adoption intention.

Figure 1. Conceptual Framework of RFID Adoption
Source: Authors

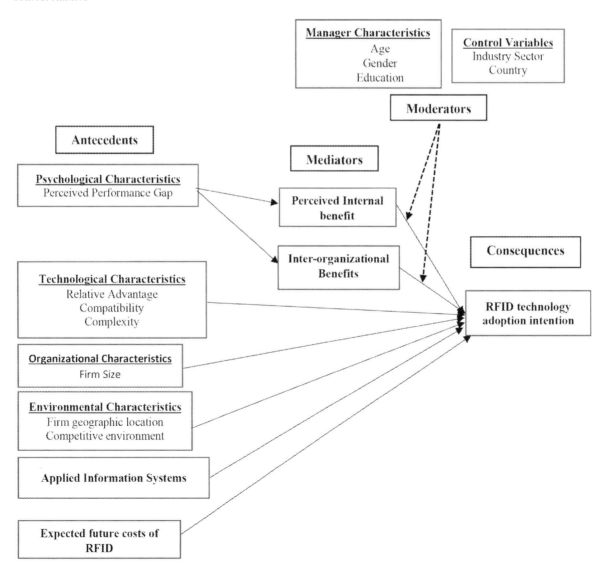

DISCUSSION

Previous works revealed a call for further research from the practitioner viewpoint, which has been inspired via actual life applications to accept what implements RFID in the healthcare industry (Ferrer, Dew, & Apte, 2010; Zhu, Mukhopadhyay, & Kurata, 2012). Several scholars focused on the significance of client approval and executed the TAM model for proper use or acceptance of RFID and its comparable techniques (Fisher & Monahan, 2008; Hossain & Prybutok, 2008). Indeed, Sykes, Venkatesh, and Rai (2011) argued about their intended societal network viewpoint, which is derived from peer approval, the contribution of staff in affecting how the scheme is arranged and organized, improved their knowledge of technical know-how and its use. The present chapter corroborates with the earlier work in user approval and discloses relevant findings for adopting RFID techniques, specifically in the Healthcare industry. The chapter describes that RFID may be planned and implemented by considering the specific requirements of hospitals. This chapter addresses the impact of various factors (psychological, technological, organizational, and environmental) affecting hospitals' RFID technologies adoption intention. A conceptual framework is proposed representing the antecedents, mediating, and moderating factors affecting RFID-enabled application adoption intention.

A few previous studies depict that the directors who operate the hospitals understand and agree about the real-time locating, recording, and tracking of relevant patient health-related data before actual adoption. Thus, identifying and examining patients throughout their health healing was established as the most important real-time data requisites, along with hospital staff workflow constraints.

This fact supports a few works suggesting RFID uses at bed face, emergency wards, tracking the surgical patients, watching severe patients, and contacting health check-up staff (Fosso Wamba, Anand, & Carter, 2013; Yao, Chu, & Li, 2012). Thus, regarding asset-related requisites, requirements for tracking objects such as pumps, biologicals, and implants, which are usually used for patients, are pursued via archiving and recovering charts of patients. Similarly, tracing of the equipment that is not working and proper safeguarding are also essential requisites. Therefore, RFID adoption benefits facilitate decreasing response time, increasing safety, ease of tracking the assets and patients to enhance efficiency, and added to patient satisfaction via answering in good health to patient appeals and grievances.

Regarding psychological characteristics, RFID intensive people tracking is much about to answer in enhanced reply to patient requirements, increased patient relief, and superior contact among patients and health check-up staff in hospitals. It is also consistent with earlier work by Reyes, Li, and Visich (2016) and Bunduchi, Weisshaar, and Smart (2011) that described the advantages of RFID tools on patient security, concern, and ultimate satisfaction. Reyes, Li, and Visich (2016) argued that RFID tools' upcoming implementers were deemed to increase patient care with superior assistance. Further, this works also defined that the health care group not employed RFID during their study but believed it was put into action shortly. Consequently, if healthcare organizations' key objective is to enhance patient satisfaction, spending in RFID tools for real-time person recognition, watching patient healing and thus is more beneficial.

Further, as a part of technological, organizational, and environmental characteristics, the following are observed in the literature. There should be an association shortly outlay in patient data systems and RFID effectiveness, and further patient liking reveals the significance of IT infrastructure before RFID adoption. It is in line with Van der Togt, Bakker, and Jaspers (2011) that suggested RFID infrastructure device, which consists of information systems and RFID hardware tools. In addition, it also shores up results of the study of Kim and Garrison (2010) that managerial willingness facilitated monetary resources and technical understanding are entirely connected with the RFID assessment stage, which sequentially is connected with RFID adoption. Moreover, Adhiarna et al. (2013) pointed out that it is critical that the organization's IT structure, software, and hardware completely adapt during the initial steps of RFID execution. The spending on information systems, which will be afterward incorporated with RFID hardware and software, contributes more to user approval and identification of the technology-related benefits.

Additionally, it is established in the literature that the perceived competence, efficiency, and system enhancement advantages of RFID tools significantly link with asset and person-related real-time data requisites. It is based on the fact that improved competence, efficiency may be achieved via meeting real-time people and asset tracing/placing/watching requirements. It is also consistent with a few studies cited previously (Bunduchi, Weisshaar, & Smart, 2011; Reyes, Li, & Visich, 2016) and described how the enhancement in competence, efficiency, patient security, workflow, preparation, and management might be achieved via RFID enabled tracking tools. These tools are time spent locating mobile phone-based medical tools, time spent stocking tools, identifying where the equipment requires intermittent continuation and robotically/mechanically watching patients' crucial symptoms and emergencies. Every staff person's workflow requires gathering information about workflow and inefficiencies, tracking staff movements, checking the patients and visitors to know if somebody was getting in touch with patients with infectious diseases, and reducing the message gap among doctors, nurses, and other medical personnel staff. A few mediators and moderators of RFID technology adoption intention are also presented in this chapter. Among the mediators, the most affecting are perceived Internal benefit, Inter-organizational benefits, applied information systems in logistics, and expected future RFID costs. These all partially or fully contributed to mediate between the different factors identified (psychological, technological, organizational, and environmental) and RFID technology adoption intention. Further, manager characteristics in terms of their age, gender, and education may moderate RFID technology adoption intention.

IMPLICATIONS OF THE STUDY

Theoretical Implications

This study will help to address a few research gaps. Literature reveals a scant number of researches regarding RFID application in healthcare services; this study will be contributed to close the gap. Again, this study develops a conceptual framework development that can further be tested. Further, the present study stresses applying technology (RFID) to solve the problems faced by society by following the Government and World Health Organization's guidelines and SOPs during the COVID-19 situation.

Practical Implications

The adoption of RFID technologies is used for service delivery, operational efficiency, improved operational capability, and useful intelligence data. Healthcare efficiency depends on operational and informational improvement that leads to "lean health care management."

This chapter guides healthcare service managers to understand the importance and use of RFID technologies for patients' caring and tracking. Again, RFID's increased significance during the pandemic COVID-19 can guide managers to implement it in other hospitals. Managers from other service sectors can also use the study to learn the issue of RFID adoption intention.

It has been viewed that more awareness campaign about the use of RFID among healthcare workers is needed. The hospitals can also consider different training programs for different users to improve RFID acceptance among healthcare workers. The training program may be organized for more innovative users with a higher inclination towards technology adoption.

CONCLUSION

The present chapter is focused on the determinants of adoption intention in the context of RFID application in the healthcare industry. This study highlights the antecedents, mediators, and moderators of RFID adoption intention, contributing to the emerging literature on RFID adoption intention. Although there is increased focus on RFID technology adoption in the health care industry, its intention to use for minimizing service employee-patient contact, service delivery, and service recovery happen to be crucial in the context of a pandemic- SARS and nCOVID-19, which is stressed as future research scope by the researchers. Thus, this study focuses on health care sectors' RFID adoption intentions and contributes to the existing research by identifying the determinants that significantly impact RFID adoption intention in healthcare services during the COVID-19 pandemic. This study is exploratory, and future research may empirically test the inter-relationship among the factors in the proposed conceptual framework in any empirical context.

REFERENCES

Adhiarna, N., Hwang, Y. M., Park, M. J., & Rho, J. (2013). An integrated framework for RFID adoption and diffusion with a stage-scale-scope cubicle model: A case of Indonesia. *International Journal of Information Management*, *33*(2), 378–389. doi:10.1016/j.ijinfomgt.2012.10.001

Bensel, P., Gunther, O., Tribowski, C., & Vogeler, S. (2008). Cost-benefit sharing in cross-company RFID applications: a case study approach, ICIS 2008 Proceedings, 129.

Bhattacharya, M., Chu, C. H., Hayya, J., & Mullen, T. (2010). An exploratory study of RFID adoption in the retail sector. *Operations Management Research*, *3*(1-2), 80–89. doi:10.100712063-010-0029-z

Blauw, J. N., & During, W. E. (1990). Adoption of an organizational innovation: Total quality control in industrial firms. *International Journal of Production Research*, *28*(10), 1831–1846. doi:10.1080/00207549008942837

Brown, I., & Russell, J. (2007). Radio frequency identification technology: An exploratory study on adoption in the South African retail sector. *International Journal of Information Management*, *27*(4), 50–265. doi:10.1016/j.ijinfomgt.2007.02.007

Bunduchi, R., Weisshaar, C., & Smart, A. U. (2011). Mapping the benefits and costs associated with process innovation: The case of RFID adoption. *Technovation*, *31*(9), 505–521. doi:10.1016/j.technovation.2011.04.001

Burbano, A., Saka, B., Rardin, R., & Rossetti, M. (2009). Technology assessment for an inventory management process in a hospital unit. In *Proceedings of the 2009 industrial engineering research conference* (pp. 791–796). Academic Press.

Cao, Q., Baker, J., Wetherbe, J., & Gu, V. (2012). Organizational adoption of innovation: Identifying factors that influence RFID adoption in the healthcare industry. *Proceedings of the European Conference on Information Systems*, 94.

Carr, A. S., Zhang, M., Klopping, I., & Min, H. (2010). RFID technology: Implications for healthcare organizations. *American Journal of Business*, 25(2), 25–40. doi:10.1108/19355181201000008

Chang, S., Klabjan, D., & Vossen, T. (2010). Optimal radio frequency identification deployment in a supply chain network. *International Journal of Production Economics*, 125(1), 71–83. doi:10.1016/j.ijpe.2010.01.004

Chau, P. Y., & Tam, K. Y. (1997). Factors affecting the adoption of open systems: An exploratory study. *Management Information Systems Quarterly*, 21(1), 1–24. doi:10.2307/249740

Chowdhury, B., & Khosla, R. (2007). RFID-based hospital real-time patient management system. In *6th IEEE/ACIS international conference on computer and information science (ICIS 2007)* (pp. 363-368). IEEE. 10.1109/ICIS.2007.159

Coe, D. T., Helpman, E., & Hoffmaister, A. W. (1997). International R&D spillovers and institutions. *European Economic Review*, 53(7), 723–741. doi:10.1016/j.euroecorev.2009.02.005

Coronado, D., Acosta, M., & Fernández, A. (2008). Attitudes to innovation in peripheral economic regions. *Research Policy*, 37(6-7), 1009–1021. doi:10.1016/j.respol.2008.03.009

De Marco, A., Cagliano, A. C., Nervo, M. L., & Rafele, C. (2012). Using System Dynamics to assess the impact of RFID technology on retail operations. *International Journal of Production Economics*, 135(1), 333–344. doi:10.1016/j.ijpe.2011.08.009

Driedonks, C., Gregor, S., Wassenaar, A., & Wassenaar, A. (2005). Economic and social analysis of the adoption of B2B electronic marketplaces: A case study in the Australian beef industry. *International Journal of Electronic Commerce*, 9(3), 49–72. doi:10.1080/10864415.2005.11044337

Ferrer, G., Dew, N., & Apte, U. (2010). When is RFID right for your service? *International Journal of Production Economics*, 124(2), 414–425. doi:10.1016/j.ijpe.2009.12.004

Fisher, J. A., & Monahan, T. (2008). Tracking the social dimensions of RFID systems in hospitals. *International Journal of Medical Informatics*, 77(3), 176–183. doi:10.1016/j.ijmedinf.2007.04.010 PMID:17544841

Forker, L. B., & Mendez, D. (2001). An analytical method for benchmarking best peer suppliers. *International Journal of Operations & Production Management*, 21(1–2), 195–209. doi:10.1108/01443570110358530

Fosso Wamba, S., Anand, A., & Carter, L. (2013). A Literature Review of RFID enabled Healthcare Applications and Issues. *International Journal of Information Management*, 33(5), 875–891. doi:10.1016/j.ijinfomgt.2013.07.005

Fosso Wamba, S., Gunasekaran, A., Bhattacharya, M., & Dubey, R. (2016). Determinants of RFID adoption intention by SMEs: An empirical investigation. *Production Planning and Control*, *27*(12), 979–990. doi:10.1080/09537287.2016.1167981

Fosso Wamba, S., & Ngai, E. W. (2015). Importance of Issues Related to RFID enabled Healthcare Transformation Projects: Results from a Delphi Study. *Production Planning and Control*, *26*(1), 19–33. doi:10.1080/09537287.2013.840015

Harland, C. M., Caldwell, N. D., Powell, P., & Zheng, J. (2007). Barriers to supply chain information integration: SMEs adrift of eLands. *Journal of Operations Management*, *25*(6), 1234–1254. doi:10.1016/j.jom.2007.01.004

Hassinen, M., & Marttila-Kontio, M. (2008). EMS coordination in large scale emergencies using automated patient monitoring. In *2008 Second International Conference on Pervasive Computing Technologies for Healthcare* (pp. 86-87). IEEE. 10.1109/PCTHEALTH.2008.4571035

Holmqvist, M., & Stefansson, G. (2006). 'Smart goods' and mobile RFID a case with innovation from Volvo. *Journal of Business Logistics*, *27*(2), 251–272. doi:10.1002/j.2158-1592.2006.tb00225.x

Hossain, M. M., & Prybutok, V. R. (2008). Consumer acceptance of RFID technology: An exploratory study. *IEEE Transactions on Engineering Management*, *55*(2), 316–328. doi:10.1109/TEM.2008.919728

Iacovou, C. L., Benbasat, I., & Dexter, A. S. (1995). Electronic data interchange and small organizations: Adoption and impact of technology. *Management Information Systems Quarterly*, *19*(4), 465–485. doi:10.2307/249629

Jeyaraj, A., Rottman, J. W., & Lacity, M. C. (2006). A review of the predictors, linkages, and biases in IT innovation adoption research. *Journal of Information Technology*, *21*(1), 1–23. doi:10.1057/palgrave.jit.2000056

Jun, M., & Cal, S. (2003). Key Obstacles to EDI Success: From the US Small Manufacturing Companies' Perspective. *Industrial Management & Data Systems*, *103*(3), 192–203. doi:10.1108/02635570310465670

Kim, S., & Garrison, G. (2010). Understanding users' behaviors regarding supply chain technology: Determinants impacting the adoption and implementation of RFID technology in South Korea. *International Journal of Information Management*, *30*(5), 388–398. doi:10.1016/j.ijinfomgt.2010.02.008

Kitchell, S. (1997). CEO characteristics and technological innovativeness: A Canadian perspective. *Canadian Journal of Administrative Sciences/Revue Canadienne des Sciences de l'Administration*, *14*(2), 111–121, Doi:10.1111/j.1936-4490.1997.tb00123

Krasnova, H., Weser, L., & Ivantysynova, L. (2008). Drivers of RFID adoption in the automotive industry. AMCIS 2008 Proceedings, 287.

Lee, L. S., Fiedler, K. D., & Smith, J. S. (2008). Radio frequency identification (RFID) implementation in the service sector: A customer-facing diffusion model. *International Journal of Production Economics*, *112*(2), 587–600. doi:10.1016/j.ijpe.2007.05.008

Li, L., & Benton, W. C. (2006). Hospital technology and nurse staffing management decisions. *Journal of Operations Management*, *24*(5), 676–691. doi:10.1016/j.jom.2005.06.001

Madlberger, M. (2009). A model of antecedents of RFID adoption intention in the supply chain. In *Proceedings of the 42nd Hawaii International Conference on System Sciences*-2009 (pp. 1-10). IEEE.

Marcati, A., Guido, G., & Peluso, A. M. (2008). The role of SME entrepreneurs' innovativeness and personality in the adoption of innovations. *Research Policy*, *37*(9), 1579–1590. doi:10.1016/j.respol.2008.06.004

Maroo, P. (2016). Need for Deployment of RFID Technology in Indian Hospitals. In *Proceedings - International Conference on Industrial Engineering and Operations Management* (pp. 3427-3431). Academic Press.

Masters, J. M., Allenby, G. M., LaLonde, B. J., & Maltz, A. (1992). On the adoption of DRP. *Journal of Business Logistics*, *13*(1), 47. doi:10.1108/09574099410805117

Menachemi, N., & Brooks, R. G. (2006). EHR and other IT adoption among physicians: Results of a large-scale state wide analysis. *Journal of Healthcare Information Management*, *20*(3), 79–87. PMID:16903665

Mogre, R., Gadh, R., & Chattopadhyay, A. (2009). Using survey data to design a RFID centric service system for hospitals. *Service Science*, *1*(3), 189–206. doi:10.1287erv.1.3.189

Najera, P., Lopez, J., & Roman, R. (2011). Real-time location and inpatient care systems based on passive RFID. *Journal of Network and Computer Applications*, *34*(3), 980–989. doi:10.1016/j.jnca.2010.04.011 PMID:34170999

Ngai, E. W. T., Cheng, T. C. E., Lai, K. H., Chai, P. Y. F., Choi, Y. S., & Sin, R. K. Y. (2007). Development of an RFID-based traceability system: Experiences and lessons learned from an aircraft engineering company. *Production and Operations Management*, *16*(5), 554–568. doi:10.1111/j.1937-5956.2007.tb00280.x

Niederman, F., Mathieu, R. G., Morley, R., & Kwon, I.-W. (2007). Examining RFID applications in supply chain management. *Communications of the ACM*, *50*(7), 92–101. doi:10.1145/1272516.1272520

Oliveira, T., & Martins, M. F. (2010). Firms' patterns of e-business adoption: Evidence for the European Union-27. *Electronic Journal of Information Systems Evaluation*, *13*(1), 47–56.

Oliveira, T., & Martins, M. F. (2011). Literature review of information technology adoption models at firm level. *Electronic Journal of Information Systems Evaluation*, *14*(1), 110–121.

Pigni, F., & Ugazio, E. (2009). Measuring RFID benefits in supply chains. *AMCIS 2009 Proceedings*, 635.

Premkumar, G., & Roberts, M. (1999). Adoption of new information technologies in rural small businesses. *Omega*, *27*(4), 467–484. doi:10.1016/S0305-0483(98)00071-1

Rai, A., & Patnayakuni, R. (1996). A structural model for CASE adoption behavior. *Journal of Management Information Systems*, *13*(2), 205–234. doi:10.1080/07421222.1996.11518129

Reaidy, P. J., Gunasekaran, A., & Spalanzani, A. (2015). Bottom-up approach based on Internet of Things for order fulfillment in a collaborative warehousing environment. *International Journal of Production Economics*, *159*, 29–40. doi:10.1016/j.ijpe.2014.02.017

Reyes, P. M., Li, S., & Visich, J. K. (2012). Accessing Antecedents and Outcomes of RFID Implementation in Health Care. *International Journal of Production Economics*, *136*(1), 137–150. doi:10.1016/j.ijpe.2011.09.024

Reyes, P. M., Li, S., & Visich, J. K. (2016). Determinants of RFID adoption stage and perceived benefits. *European Journal of Operational Research*, *254*(3), 801–812. doi:10.1016/j.ejor.2016.03.051

Rogers, E. M. (1995). *Diffusion of Innovations* (4th ed.). Free Press. doi:10.2307/30036530 10.1146/annurev.soc.28.110601.141051

Sambamurthy, V., Bharadwaj, A., & Grover, V. (2003). Shaping Agility Through Digital Options: Reconceptualizing the Role of Information Technology in Contemporary Firms. *Management Information Systems Quarterly*, *27*(2), 237–263. doi:10.2307/30036530

Saran, C. (2005). Costs Set to Rise as RFID and Barcodes Battle. *Computer Weekly*, 2-8. doi:10.1108/01443571011029994

Schon, D. (1967). *Technology and social change*. Delacorte. doi:10.1016/j.techfore.2020.120054

Sharma, A., & Citurs, A. (2005). Radio frequency identification (RFID) adoption drivers: A radical innovation adoption perspective. AMCIS 2005 Proceedings, 211.

Sharma, A., Citurs, A., & Konsynski, B. (2007). Strategic and institutional perspectives in the adoption and early integration of radio frequency identification (RFID). In *2007 40th Annual Hawaii International Conference on System Sciences (HICSS'07)*. IEEE.

Sharma, A., Dominic, T., & Benn, K. (2008). Strategic and institutional perspectives in the evaluation, adoption and early integration of radio frequency identification (RFID): an empirical investigation of current and potential adopters. In *Proceedings of the 41st Annual Hawaii International Conference on System Sciences (HICSS 2008)* (pp. 407-407). IEEE. 10.1109/HICSS.2008.412

Sherer, S. (2010). Information systems and healthcare: An institutional theory perspective on physician adoption of electronic health records. *Communications of the Association for Information Systems*, *27*(7), 127–140. doi:10.17705/1CAIS.02607

Spekman, R. E., & Sweeney, P. J. II. (2006). RFID: From concept to implementation. *International Journal of Physical Distribution & Logistics Management*, *36*(10), 736–754. doi:10.1108/09600030610714571

Sykes, T. A., Venkatesh, V., & Rai, A. (2011). Explaining physicians' use of EMR systems and performance in the shakedown phase. *Journal of the American Medical Informatics Association: JAMIA*, *18*(2), 125–130. doi:10.1136/jamia.2010.009316 PMID:21292704

Teo, H. H., Wei, K. K., & Benbasat, I. (2003). Predicting intention to adopt interorganizational linkages: An institutional perspective. *Management Information Systems Quarterly*, *27*(1), 19–49. doi:10.2307/30036518

Tewari, A., & Gupta, B. B. (2020). An Analysis of Provable Security Frameworks for RFID Security. In *Handbook of Computer Networks and Cyber Security* (pp. 635–651). Springer., doi:10.1007/978-3-030-22277-2_25

Thuemmler, C., Buchanan, W., & Kumar, V. (2007). Setting safety standards by designing a low-budget and compatible patient identification system based on passive RFID technology. *International Journal of Healthcare Technology and Management*, 8(5), 571–583. doi:10.1504/IJHTM.2007.013524

Tornatzky, L. G., Fleischer, M., & Chakrabarti, A. K. (1990). *The processes of technological innovation*. Lexington Books. doi:10.1007/BF02371446

Tornatzky, L. G., & Klein, K. J. (1982). Innovation characteristics and innovation adoption-implementation: A meta-analysis of findings. *IEEE Transactions on Engineering Management*, 29(1), 28–45. doi:10.1109/TEM.1982.6447463

Tu, Y. J., Zhou, W., & Piramuthu, S. (2009). Identifying RFID-embedded objects in pervasive healthcare applications. *Decision Support Systems*, 46(2), 586–593. doi:10.1016/j.dss.2008.10.001

Tzeng, C. T., Chiang, Y. C., Chiang, C. M., & Lai, C. M. (2008). Combination of radio frequency identification (RFID) and field verification tests of interior decorating materials. *Automation in Construction*, 18(1), 16–23. doi:10.1016/j.autcon.2008.04.003

Van der Togt, R., Bakker, P. J., & Jaspers, M. W. (2011). A framework for performance and data quality assessment of Radio Frequency Identification (RFID) systems in health care settings. *Journal of Biomedical Informatics*, 44(2), 372–383. doi:10.1016/j.jbi.2010.12.004 PMID:21168526

Venkatesh, V., Sykes, T. A., & Venkatraman, S. (2014). Understanding e-Government portal use in rural India: Role of demographic and personality characteristics. *Information Systems Journal*, 24(3), 249–269. doi:10.1111/isj.12008

Verdict Medical Devices. (2017). *Radio-frequency identification technology in healthcare*. https://www.medicaldevice-network.com/comment/commentradio-frequency-identification-technology-in-healthcare-5848545/

Wang, Y. M., Wang, Y. S., & Yang, Y. F. (2010). Understanding the determinants of RFID adoption in the manufacturing industry. *Technological Forecasting and Social Change*, 77(5), 803–815. doi:10.1016/j.techfore.2010.03.006

Wicks, A. M., Visich, J. K., & Li, S. (2006). Radio frequency identification applications in healthcare. *International Journal of Healthcare Technology and Management*, 7(6), 522–540. doi:10.1504/IJHTM.2006.010414

Wong, W. K., Leung, S. Y. S., Guo, Z. X., Zeng, X. H., & Mok, P. Y. (2012). Intelligent product cross-selling system with radio frequency identification technology for retailing. *International Journal of Production Economics*, 135(1), 308–319. doi:10.1016/j.ijpe.2011.08.005

Yao, W., Chu, C. H., & Li, Z. (2012). The adoption and implementation of RFID technologies in healthcare: A literature review. *Journal of Medical Systems*, 36(6), 3507–3525. doi:10.100710916-011-9789-8 PMID:22009254

Yazici, H. J. (2014). An Exploratory Analysis of Hospital Perspectives on Real Time Information Requirements and Perceived Benefits of RFID Technology for Future Adoption. *International Journal of Information Management*, 34(5), 603–621. doi:10.1016/j.ijinfomgt.2014.04.010

Zhu, X., Mukhopadhyay, S. K., & Kurata, H. (2012). A review of RFID technology and its managerial applications in different industries. *Journal of Engineering and Technology Management*, *29*(1), 152–167. doi:10.1016/j.jengtecman.2011.09.011

Zmud, R. W. (1984). An examination of push-pull theory applied to process innovation in knowledge work. *Management Science*, *30*(6), 727–738. doi:10.1287/mnsc.30.6.727

ADDITIONAL READING

Ganapathi, P., & Abu-Shanab, E. A. (2019). Utilizing Radio Frequency Identification in Libraries: The Case of Qatar. *International Journal of Public Administration in the Digital Age*, *6*(4), 14–29. doi:10.4018/IJPADA.2019100102

Mouattah, A., & Hachemi, K. (2021). Estimation of Medication Dispensing Errors (MDEs) as Tracked by Passive RFID-Based Solution. *International Journal of Healthcare Information Systems and Informatics*, *16*(3), 89–104. doi:10.4018/IJHISI.20210701.oa6

Prodanoff, Z., White-Williams, C., & Chi, H. (2021). Regulations and Standards Aware Framework for Recording of mHealth App Vulnerabilities. *International Journal of E-Health and Medical Communications*, *12*(3), 1–16. doi:10.4018/IJEHMC.20210501.oa1

Smith, A. D. (2021). Green Supply Chains and Enabling RFID Technology. In M. Khosrow-Pour D.B.A. (Eds.), Encyclopedia of Organizational Knowledge, Administration, and Technology (pp. 2403-2420). IGI Global. http://doi:10.4018/978-1-7998-3473-1.ch166

Smith-Ditizio, A. A., & Smith, A. D. (2018). Radio Frequency Identification Technologies and Issues in Healthcare. In M. Khosrow-Pour, D.B.A. (Ed.), Encyclopedia of Information Science and Technology, Fourth Edition (pp. 5918-5929). IGI Global. http://doi:10.4018/978-1-5225-2255-3.ch515

KEY TERMS AND DEFINITIONS

Benchmarking: Mainly applied in business, it is a process of measuring key metrics and practices and comparing them.

DOI: The acronym of Diffusion of Innovation consists of spreading the innovation inside and outside the organization.

RFID Technology: Acronym of Radio Frequency Identification is defined by a technology applied to patients that helps store wireless data and automatic retrieval, which helps identify, track, and store data and the barcode system.

SOP: The acronym of Standard Operating Procedures defines how to behave in specific emergencies and situations.

TOE Framework: It is formed by the combination of technology, organization, and environment.

Total Quality Control: It consists of integrating efforts toward improving performance at every level.

Chapter 11
Social Enterprise Awareness, Perception, and Purchase Influence in South East China:
A Benchmark for Further Study

Mingyi Chen
University of Edinburgh, UK

Jiawei Feng
University of Warwick, UK

Rob Kim Marjerison
https://orcid.org/0000-0003-1181-8695
Wenzhou-Kean University, China

Rongjuan Chen
Wenzhou-Kean University, China

ABSTRACT

This study aims to explore awareness and interest in social enterprises in China and in doing so provide a benchmark for comparison with future research on the topic. There is a shortage of evidence in the previous literature with which to compare the present situation, but the regulatory emphasis and resources presently dedicated by the Chinese government to social enterprises makes research in this area relevant and makes it likely that the development of social enterprises would have an upward trend in awareness and interest. Primary data was collected from over 600 online surveys which measured awareness, purchase intention, and purchase motivation before and during the first year of the COVID-19 pandemic. The findings of this chapter may contribute to future research on the trends of social enterprise awareness and interest in China and may also be of interest to those with an interest in social entrepreneurship.

DOI: 10.4018/978-1-7998-7689-2.ch011

INTRODUCTION

The concept of social enterprise (SE) is becoming more well-known globally with the relevance and attention to the concept increased dramatically in the wake of the global pandemic of 2020 (Bacq & Lumpkin, 2020). The role that SE can play both economically and as a driver of social well-being is substantial is not overlooked by the government of China, which has increasingly shown willingness to encourage social entrepreneurship and SEs (Yu, 2013, 2016; Zhao, 2020). In the 1990s, the concept of SE was still novel in China (Lee, 2009). With the development of the nonprofit sector, which was encouraged by the Chinese government in recent years, those traditional nonprofit organizations (NPOs) are changing themselves to newer and more dynamic forms, which adopt commercial or market mechanisms to resolve social problems (Evers, 2005; Tian et al., 2018). The market sector has become stronger, and importantly, there are some new forms of organizations named social enterprises (SEs) appearing (Young, 2001). According to the Organization for Economic Co-operation and Development (OECD), SE can be defined as "an organization that operates outside the purely private business and state sectors," and integrated with the explanation of "a kind of business-like activity with a social purpose (Young, 2001). Thus, SEs' core values are located in the middle of "social value creation" and "economic value creation" (Alter, 2006), which means SEs aim to provide social value to the welfare or public by using the earned profit which is from the for-profit sector of the organization (Wang et al., 2015)

This paper aims to research the awareness of SEs activity. Due to the social structure of China, SEs, and other social sector organizations historically receive little attention (Howell, 2007; Ma, 2005; Wang et al., 2015). However, awareness has increased in recent years with the increased cognition of the close relationship between firms' operations and the impact on society, including such factors as pollution management and benefits to disadvantaged people (Muttakin & Khan, 2014). Many countries have highlighted SEs as business strategies to overcome the problems related to the environment and balance the development and protection of natural resources (Türkel et al., 2016; White et al., 2017).

During the COVID-19 pandemic in 2020, many SEs, including pharmaceutical and transportation companies, played a significant role in their regions to help society. This chapter seeks to explore public awareness of those activities and determine whether people would change their cognition to SEs as a result of the COVID-19 pandemic.

LITERATURE REVIEW

SEs in China

The emergence of SEs in China has transpired for several reasons. First, the unequal development between urban and rural China has spawned a series of social problems that cannot be easily resolved. As a result of these and other issues, SEs have emerged to respond to social needs (Ma, 2005). Second, support and encouragement from the government are conducive to SE formation. Since 1978, the Chinese government has increased the availability of economic subsidies provided to public sectors, which has also contributed to the emergence of SEs (Ma, 2005). Third, because of the development and affluence of Chinese society, consumers have more options in their purchasing activity. Many of them prefer to purchase from nonprofit SEs, which is not limited to selecting private or public SEs. These purchasing behaviors are not all aimed at saving money but instead can be seen as seeking products or services from organizations aligned with their personal values. As merchants, SEs aim to achieve philanthropic goals, satisfying their desires to help society (Lee, 2009).

Finally, international achievements by SEs have contributed to cultivating the spirit of social entrepreneurship in China. Zhao (2016) reported that Lv Zhao had participated in the Skoll World Forum held at Oxford University in 2006 and then led the work of training others in the development and operation of Chinese nonprofit institutions. The Skoll Centre for Social Entrepreneurship, which aims to promote the advancement of social entrepreneurship worldwide, cooperates with the International Forum on Social Entrepreneurship held at Zhejiang University. Lee (2009) proposed the building of potential relationships between Chinese and European social entrepreneurship development initiatives.

Tian et al. (2018) proposed that SEs emerged in China in the 1990s because of the ideology of the New Public Management (NPM). Zhou (2016) suggested that the Chinese government's move towards market-oriented mechanisms (e.g., authoritative procurement, philanthropic ventures, contract tendering) in public sectors to diversify the services and increase the efficiencies of the transitions of activities in the services sector. Thus, SEs emerge in China as a result of five nonprofit sector trends: marketization of NPM, the growing awareness of corporate social responsibility, the appearance of privatizing the public social welfare institutions, the emergence of public interest venture capital, tri-partnerships, and global cooperation (Tian et al., 2018).

The Cognition Degree of SEs in China

According to Defournay and Nyssens (2006), SEs do not have a clearly defined and well-accepted definition; however, the standard cognition of SEs is that their primary goal is to benefit society. The definition of SE has changed in China, according to Chinese people's understanding. In the past, Chinese governmental sectors and the public were not familiar with SEs, but knew the concept of nonprofit institutions which aimed to do philanthropy. Therefore, people tend to understand the SEs' practical purpose, benefit others, but overlook its organizational form in which financial sustainability is sought (Zhao & Wry, 2016). However, with the recent changes in the perceptions of Chinese society, people's acceptance and understanding of SEs have increased.

In China, SEs can be considered institutions that work outside the general two sectors: the private and state sectors. Young (2001) finds that it takes a series of operations to reach the social or philanthropic purpose. SEs are organizations with a social or philanthropic mission: the attainment of which will benefit the public. Among other goals, SEs aim to provide social help for vulnerable groups such as low-income groups, disabled people, children, women, homeless people (Pache & Santos, 2012; Zhao & Wry, 2016).

H1: *Cognition degree has a significant impact on public awareness of SE.*

Lee (2009) reported that SEs are nonprofit institutions that offer goods or services as part of a business model to reach their goals of benefiting society. SEs have two primary purposes: to serve the community or the environment and maximize profit (Muñoz & Tinsely, 2008). The customers' purchasing intentions are positively related to SEs' primary purposes. To satisfy the compatibility goals with their ethical and moral values, customers prefer to choose SEs that serve society or the environment.

H2: *Purchasing intention has a significant impact on public awareness of SE.*

SEs' two purposes are not in conflict but are fulfilled concurrently. By distributing profits to shareholders, SEs receive the opportunity of reinvestment and achieve sustainable development instead of waiting for a subsidy from the government (Kim & Lim, 2017). SEs in China tend to be more sustainable than traditional Chinese philanthropic institutions because Chinese SEs have reinvestments to support sustainable development (Wang et al., 2015).

Classification of SEs in China

The classification of Chinese SEs has different categories and standards. According to Lee (2009), the current Chinese regime identifies the SE into four constitutional parts: non-governmental and nonprofit organizations, cooperative institutions, social welfare corporations, and community service departments. Non-governmental and nonprofit organizations include social organizations, foundations, and civil non-enterprises organizations. Social organizations and civil non-enterprise organizations are voluntary organizations that work on not-for-profit social activities. At the same time, foundations are identified as not-for-profit civil organizations that utilize donated assets to be engaged in philanthropy (Lee, 2009). Cooperative organizations are not-for-profit organizations that have small scales, such as worker cooperatives. Social welfare corporations refer to SEs, including those aiming to provide job choices for the disabled to satisfy their life demands (Yu, 2020). It is one of the most popular forms of SE in China. Lee (2009) claims that the government supports community service activities at various levels in China. They offer social services to the public (e.g., elderly care services, construction of infrastructure for basic sanitation, and other related facilities).

Based on the level of integration within social activities and commercial events, Alter (2006) proposed that SEs are classified into three parts: externality, integration, and embeddedness. Embedded SE refers to SEs with similar meanings of social programs and business activities by achieving financial and social profits simultaneously. Leung et al. (2019) attribute integrated SEs as SEs whose social programs overlap with business activities. Assets, spending, and attributes often are shared in the overlap part. For external SEs, business activities are excluded from social programs. They are comparatively dependent but supportive. Business activities offer to fund the holding of social programs (Alter, 2006).

Importance of SEs in China

There is no consensus around the definition of SEs currently because researchers are still finding the appropriate location for them in the market and trying to get more awareness from the public; however, in Carroll's well-known theory (1991), SEs commit to seeing the public as their stakeholders and think about bringing more benefits when they operate the company (Frederick, 2006; Griffin, 2008). The importance of the social benefits can be shown by the benefits they bring to society.

Economic Sector Benefits

According to Bui (2010), in research-based in Vietnam, which is also categorized as a developing country, SEs' activities helped the public become sensitive to social issues. The results showed that two-thirds of the participants have increased purchasing intention towards products that look or are indicated to be "green" or "clean" (Suki, 2016). When consumers act on their purchasing decisions, social benefits will be one of the factors that influence them. This means that SEs' products will be more popular and presumable will achieve greater commercial success (Pop et al., 2020). Most customers confirmed their intention to buy products from SEs because of the information communicated by SEs on the internet or other public places (Bui, 2010). SEs can use such methods as social media to increase their brand's popularity and perceived value to increase economic development, which will distribute to society (Munerah et al., 2021). The pattern in research findings shows that SEs help society increases the degree of ethical morality and make more people aware of the significance of SEs (Bui, 2010).

Environmental Benefits

Minimizing environmental damage is one of the core objectives of SEs, and sustainability in the environmental aspects requires maintaining the natural balance, which includes conserving the diversity of species, preserving the natural resources needed for support of the biological systems, and human society to ensure that nature can self-renew (Kim & Lim, 2017). SEs are devoted to producing and trading sustainable products such as green organic vegetables, green livestock and poultry, and innovative biodegradable handicrafts (Yu, 2020). Although those kinds of products may not be manufactured on a large scale, the primary purpose of producing them is twofold: firstly, as experiments to gain expertise in biodegradable and green manufacturing techniques, and secondly, to expand the scale with which such products can be produced and marketed to increase the popularity of those products among the public in the future (Yu, 2016). Thus, SEs' activities can help society divert the resource base and release the pressure on intensive limited resources. There is a broader recognition that most economic activities are closely related to environmental impact, which means SEs will operate their businesses while paying attention to those concepts of environmentally friendly operations such as clean production (Jackson, 1993), eco-efficiency, and innovation in the design of manufacturing processes or services in order to minimize the use of resources and the subsequent pollution (Vickers, 2010).

Social Sector Benefits

The third perspective of benefit brought by SEs is the social sector. It mostly includes the governance issues like institutional values, board identity, the method and criteria for recruiting board members, board function, and arrangement of profit distribution (Yu, 2020, 2013).

Institutional Value

For the SEs which were taken into the analysis proceeding, none of them consider values of demographic participation and stakeholder engagement as their organizational mission. Instead, they looked highly at the institutional values which prioritize performance enhancement, especially for the business-focused SEs. Those SEs generate revenue through business trading activities in the market, maintaining companies' financial sustainability. Still, their performance-orientated value has been expressed clearly by providing some social benefits services, such as using the profits gained from business trading activities, for example, to help children with dyslexia and reading disabilities (Yu, 2013). When considering the institutional value, it is essential to consider what type of value the organization's goals include and how it should be distributed to the stakeholders (Wieland et al., 2016). The kind of governance applied for SEs shows that the profit distribution is significantly different from the profit-driven business model (Buchanan et al., 2018). SEs comply with ethically based self-restrictions on profit distribution by investors. Also, some SEs' founders support giving up benefits and distributing most of the revenue to employees or some other combination of stakeholders, generally to alleviate the gap of wealth (Yu, 2013).

Public Awareness of SEs in China

The Occurrence of Public Awareness of SEs in China

According to Tian et al. (2018), the concept of SEs has been occurring in China since the 1990s due to the implementation of market-oriented mechanisms by the Chinese authority. However, during that time, the public awareness of this newly introduced concept is weak. Later, during the first decade of the 2000s, the words "SE" incorporated the Chinese public policy and official discourse, which attracted public awareness of SE (Man & Terence, 2011).

Well-publicized conferences issued professional periodicals, and important events increased public awareness of SEs in China. Due to various conferences and official symposiums, the public awareness of SE occurred in 2004 in China. In 2006, the International Conference on Social Innovation held in the Chinese capital Beijing received active affirmation from the Chinese authorities. The ideas of developing SEs to solve social issues (e.g., poverty, unemployment) then become a hot topic for many officials and even the public (Man & Terence, 2011). In the same year, David Bornstein's book *How to Change the World* (Bornstein, 2007) was published in China to inspire many Chinese SEs to offer social help by establishing SEs (Yu, 2020). The year 2008, identified as "The Year of Civil Society," is the special year that increases the Chinese public awareness of SEs. In 2008, the 5.12 Wenchuan Earthquake in China indirectly attracted the public's attention to SEs, such as the Red Cross Society of China (Yu, 2020).

The Development of Public Awareness of SEs in China

Both non-governmental organizations and Chinese authorities make efforts to develop Chinese public awareness of SEs. Non-governmental organizations in China attempted to offer certifications to SEs to help them receive support from the public. Because of the absence of legal certifications and regulatory approval, earlier Chinese SEs were not widely recognized by the people in China (Yu, 2020). To solve this problem, the first unofficial SE Certification was launched by five well-known organizations in China at the annual China Charity Fair, which helps the application of SEs in China. Xia (2019) argued the SE certification inspires social entrepreneurs and increases the numbers of Chinese SEs. Also, this certification develops public awareness of SEs by having SE-certified symbols on their goods and marketing collaterals(L. Yu, 2020). With the development of the economic market and the popularization of corporate social responsibility, more and more Chinese corporations tend to have philanthropic activities to benefit others. Also, more and more individuals in China work in philanthropy and invest in Chinese SE (Chan et al., 2013). Therefore, public awareness of SEs in China increases based on the effort of non-governmental organizations or individuals.

Chinese authorities issued a series of regulatory guidelines to develop Chinese SEs and strengthen the public recognition of SEs in China. In 2017, Chinese authorities launched 'Beijing Social Enterprise Initiatives' to accelerate the development of SEs in China (Tian et al., 2018). Yu (2020) points out that the Beijing municipal administration issued a SE Certification program to provide official certifications for SEs in 2018. According to Meyer (2018), this program revealed that Chinese SEs are recognized from the institutional and governmental levels. The official recognition of Chinese SEs promotes public awareness of SEs in China.

The Deficiencies of Public Awareness of SEs in China

Due to the lack of a widely recognized standard, the classification of SEs is not precise, which led to incorrect public awareness of SEs in China (Tian et al., 2018). The current categories of SEs in China cannot capture part of the characteristics of SEs. Also, under the current Chinese system, the law does not recognize SEs as a unique legal entity but treats them as organizations with the purpose of doing philanthropy (Lee, 2009). In China, owners of SEs can register SEs as business companies, Civil Non-Enterprise Units, social welfare institutions, farmers' cooperatives, and individual educational organizations (Yu, 2013). However, these complex classifications can reduce public awareness of SEs in China (Defourny & Nyssens, 2006).

Costanzo et al. (2014) argued that SEs are motivated to achieve financial and philanthropic goals, implying that SEs will face more considerations. For most entrepreneurs, it is not an optimal investment because SEs sacrifice part of the economic benefits. As a result, few entrepreneurs in China will invest in SEs. Due to this reason, and compared with traditional business corporations, the scale of SEs in China is small; thus, the public has fewer opportunities to get in touch with SE, implying low public awareness of SE (Davies et al., 2019).

Public Interest in SEs in China

Chinese Customers' Purchasing Behavior

Concerns for environmental and health issues have become one of the top topics for various societal stakeholders since the early 1770s (Grunert, n.d.). Almost all the populations around the world are worrying about the hazardous impacts of environmental deterioration, which has a big impact on their enjoyment of life (Alsmadi, 2007; Dagnoli, 1991; Skrentny, 1993; Yang et al., 2019). Chinese citizens, especially those who reside in urban areas, have realized the importance of ecological well-being (Chan, 2001). According to the survey taken by Ye (Shieh et al., 2018; Wang et al., 2017), over 75% of the Chinese customers expressed their strong intention to purchase social or environment-protective products from SEs, and over 90% of enterprises showed their willingness to be SEs to sell green products (Sun et al., 2020). The survey results indicate that the development of SEs in China is exceptionally potential (Chan & Lau, 2002; Zhu & Sarkis, 2016).

The food industry is one of the most obvious fields which showed Chinese customers' purchasing intention on the products from SEs (Peng et al., 2015). Food safety problems, including adulteration, fraud, and misleading advertising, have frequently been reported during the last five years, and those problems have become a deep concern for the public. With the food safety regulations and administrative intervention, actions have been taken by the Chinese government, the awareness of the food-safety problem, and the interest in buying eco-friendly food has widened up (Leggett, 2020; Qi & Ploeger, 2019).

Interest in Social Factors

Social factors can be defined as elements that are beneficial to society, such as enterprises' responsibility for the environment, sustainable development, or public health. Those factors can be used as the foundation for the increased interest in SEs. Since China's economic reforms and opening up after 1978, the problem of balancing economic development and protecting the environment has become a big challenge (Fumero et al., 2018). Although the Chinese government put forward some regulations on alleviating pollution and increasing the use of non-fossil fuel-based energy, the country is still struggling to achieve the ambitious goal of decreasing energy consumption and pollution emissions (Jennings et al., 2011). However, with the trend of using eco-friendly energy and promoting a green lifestyle, Chinese people paid more attention to those issues and were interested in learning about the reasons that cause the pollution and other social factors (Li et al., 2019). Some studies have also shown that the awareness of social and environmental problems would inspire the public to change their lifestyles and increase their interest in eco-friendly products produced by SEs (Brounen et al., 2014; Gadenne et al., 2011; Von Borgstede et al., 2013).

Cognition of Emerging Purpose

With billions of under-privileged people, a growing number of entrepreneurs want to create innovative business models to create social value to help them (Chandra et al., 2021; Dees, 2007). The results of those efforts can transform the poor and underprivileged into producers, create job opportunities and family income for them, provide safe drinking water and food supplies, and provide opportunities for access to education and health care services (Sodhi & Tang, 2011). That can be seen as one of the main drivers of the emergence of SEs (Hockerts, 2017; Tiwari et al., 2017). Another emerging purpose of SEs is that SEs may be considered to connect with micro-entrepreneurs to fill gaps in the supply chain (Sodhi & Tang, 2011). How SEs are viewed as a success factor in business is of interest because a comprehensive supply chain's importance extends well beyond its immediate transactions (Marshall et al., 2015; Sodhi & Tang, 2011).

Another factor in the growing awareness of SE is the importance of gaining access to financial backing through the banking and credit system (Sullivan Mort et al., 2003). Based on the core premise of transforming the poor into producers, some new banking and lending models have emerged, including the Grameen Bank in Bangladesh, based on the belief that the poor are reliable and trustworthy because they are willing to work hard to change their lives (Faizah & Husaeni, 2019; Hossain, 1988). Thus, those kinds of banks became SEs to make loans for the small entrepreneurs and promote those businesses, starting up SEs. With the increased awareness and interest in SEs and green lifestyles, entrepreneurs are more likely to start up SEs to create social value and make better living standards for the whole society (Sodhi & Tang, 2011). The creation of social benefits can also be used to increase the entrepreneurs' reputation and drive revenues that may ultimately be used to create profit and add social value (Alter, 2006).

SEs' Behavior during the COVID-19 Epidemic in China

The SE is identified as "an initiative of social outcomes established by farseeing social entrepreneurs" by Yunus, a Nobel Laureate (Chen and Kelly, 2015). SEs receive high social recognition because of their social values, and SEs, which aim to serve communities, the environment, and societies, are essential catalysts for surmounting social challenges (Boolkin, 2017). For example, SEs were advanced in providing specialized support, including integrating citizen's information, transferring assistance resources, and maintaining cohesive communication within communities during the COVID-19 pandemic in China (Shen et al., 2020).

Shenzhen LianDi Accessibility Co., Ltd, is a certified B Corporation in China engaged in testing, consulting, and training. "The vision of this company is to help everyone work and live in an accessible information environment" (Certified B Corporations, 2016). It offers systematic accessibility solutions for citizens and provided adequate visual information for visually impaired persons through the internet during the COVID-19 epidemic in China. *First Respond*, the first Chinese SE that received a B Corps certification, provides online courses for first aid training and related media, such as a course on the proper use of masks during the COVID-19 pandemic. *BottleDream*, a SE that disseminates information regarding the importance and opportunities related to social innovation to young people, organized an online team to assist 5 million Wuhan citizens who were outside Wuhan (Shen, 2020). Chinese SEs are doing their best to assist China in overcoming the risks of COVID-19 and in order regions of the world (Saiz-Alvarez et al., 2020).

These and other SEs in China attempted to make contributions in their fields during the COVID-19 Pandemic outbreak. Their assistance was reported to be of value to Chinese society during the 100-day lock-down period in Spring 2020 and the ensuing months of economic recovery.

H3: *The impact of cognitive social benefits on SE awareness is more substantial during the COVID-19 pandemic.*
H4: *There is a positive relationship between purchasing behavior and interest in SE.*
H5: *There is a stronger positive relationship between the social factor and interest in SE during the COVID-19 pandemic.*
H6: *There is a stronger positive relationship between emerging purpose and interest in SE during the COVID-19 pandemic.*

CONCEPTUAL FRAMEWORK

Figure 1. The conceptual model

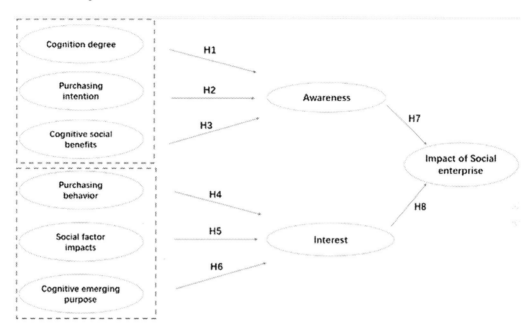

ANALYSIS/RESULTS

Data was gathered through an online survey and analyzed below using a combination of statistical methods. The primary data was collected from 608 anonymous online surveys where respondents self-selected to participate. The data was gathered via the popular online social media platform WeChat. The respondents were self-selecting and were assured of anonymity. The instrument used was adapted from prior related research and used; cognition degree, purchasing intention, cognitive social benefits to measure awareness and purchasing behaviors, social factor impacts, and emerging cognitive purpose to measure the public interest in SEs. The respondents were 61% female and 38% male. The largest age group represented was the 20-30 group which comprised 74% of the sample. The 20 age group comprised 16% of the sample, and the 31-40 group, 3%. The 41-50 age group was 6% of the total. The educational level of the respondents was overwhelmingly college-educated with 85%, with 2% at postgraduate level, 6% with the junior college or technical school education, and 5% with high school education.

The Impact of Cognition Degree on Awareness of SEs

The survey results present the mean score of cognition (Mean = 4.02) and standard deviation (SD = 1.77) and indicate that cognition degree can significantly impact awareness of SEs (adjusted R^2 = .55, $p < .001$). Since results have been collected for the condition of before COVID-19 only, H1 is partially supported.

Figure 2 shows the distribution of subjects' responses of cognition degree. Figure 3 demonstrates the relationship between cognition degree and awareness of SEs.

Figure 2. Cognition degree on a scale of 1-7

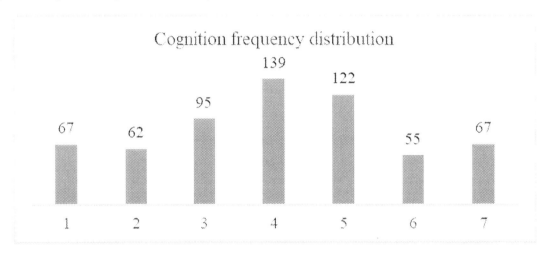

Figure 3. The relationship between cognition degree and awareness of SEs

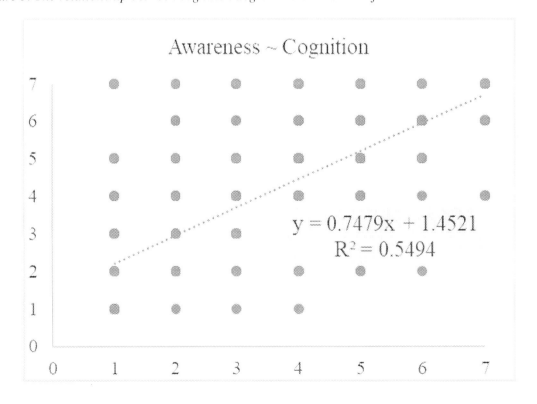

The Impact of Purchasing Intention on Awareness of SEs

The survey results capture the significant difference between the self-rated scores of purchasing intention before (Mean = 4.92, SD = 1.48) and during (Mean = 5.21, SD = 1.40) COVID-19 (t = -3.58, p < .001). Figure 4 shows the mean comparison of purchasing intention.

Figure 4. Purchasing intention during COVID-19 is significantly higher than before

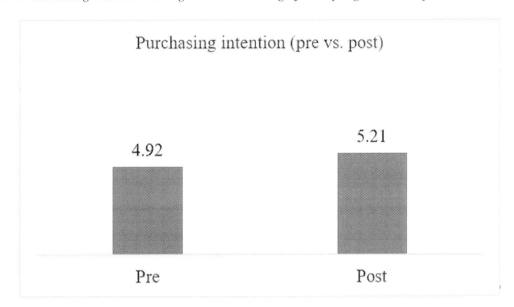

Assuming there is a difference between people's awareness of SEs concerning purchasing intention at different stages, two separate regression models have been developed to demonstrate the relationship before and during COVID-19. Both analyses have found the significant impact of purchasing intention on awareness of SEs (before COVID-19: adjusted R^2 = .18, p < .001; during COVID-19: adjusted R^2 = .29, p < .001), as shown in Figure 5 and Figure 6. Thus, H2 is fully supported.

The Impact of Cognitive Social Benefits on Awareness of SEs

The survey results reveal that cognitive social benefits during COVID-19 (Mean = 5.26, SD = 1.24) is significantly lower than before (Mean = 5.57, SD = 1.21; t = 4.30, p < .001). Figure 7 shows the mean comparison of purchasing intention.

Assuming there is a difference between people's awareness of SEs in relation to cognitive social benefits at different stages, two separate regression models have been developed to demonstrate the relationship before and during COVID-19. The impact of cognitive social benefits on awareness of SEs is found to be much stronger during COVID-19 (adjusted R^2 = .37, p < .001) as compared to before (adjusted R^2 = .04, p < .001), as shown in Figure 8 and Figure 9. Thus, H3 is partially supported in the condition of during COVID-19 only.

Figure 5. The relationship between purchasing intention and awareness of SEs (before COVID-19)

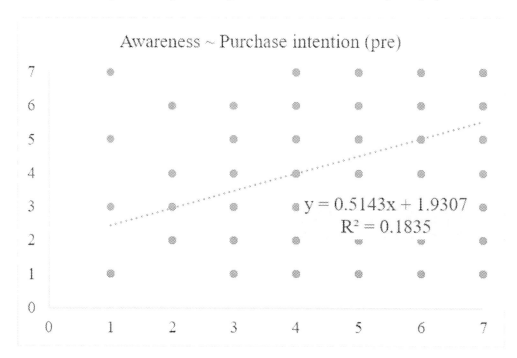

Figure 6. The relationship between purchasing intention and awareness of SEs (during COVID-19)

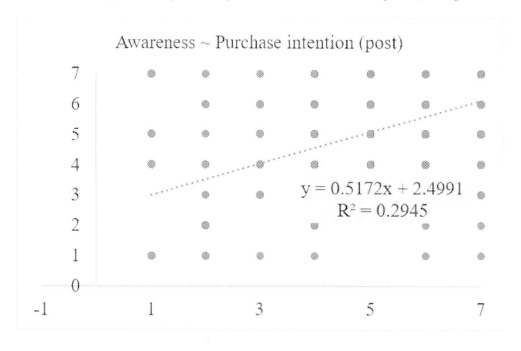

Figure 7. Cognitive social benefits during COVID-19 is significantly lower than before

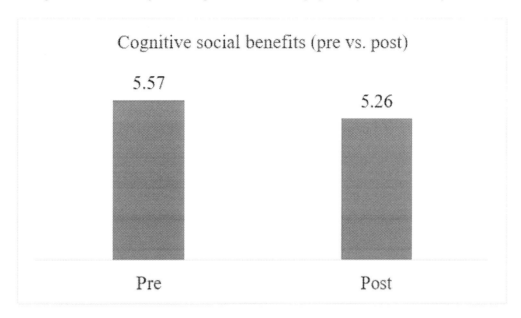

Figure 8. The relationship between cognitive social benefits and awareness of SEs (before COVID-19)

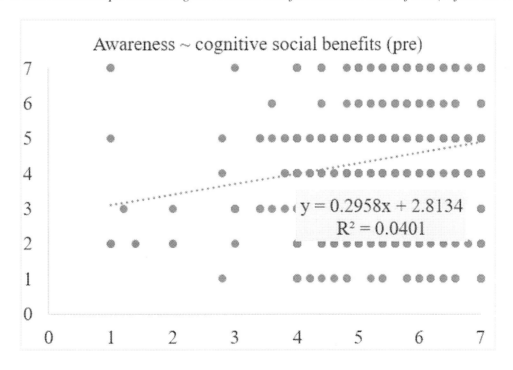

Figure 9. The relationship between cognitive social benefits and awareness of SEs (during COVID-19)

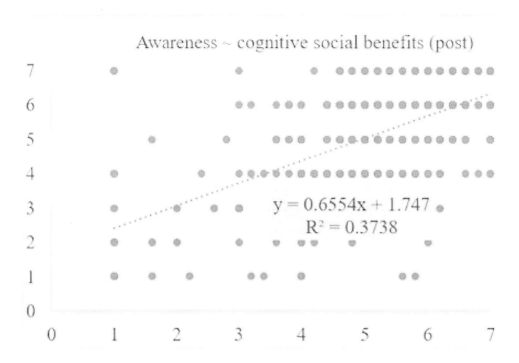

The Prediction of Awareness of SEs Based on Cognition Degree, Purchasing Intention, and Cognitive Social Benefits

The results reported in previous sections, focusing on the impacts of proposed factors on awareness of SEs, indicate that awareness of SEs can be predicted by cognition degree, purchasing intention, and cognitive social benefits, given some of their impacts found to be significant before and during COVID-19. Figure 10 illustrates the predictive model of awareness of SEs, using cognition degree and purchasing intention as two effective predictors before COVID-19. Figure 11 depicts the relationships between purchasing intention, cognitive social benefits, and awareness of SEs. Please note that only the impacts that have been measured and tested to be significant are presented below.

Taken together, the patterns regarding how awareness of SEs is impacted by these factors, including cognition degree, purchasing intention, and cognitive social benefits, vary across the two time periods, before and during COVID-19.

The Impact of Purchasing Behavior on Interest in SEs

The survey results present the mean score of cognition (Mean = 3.82) and standard deviation (SD = 1.79) and indicate that purchasing behavior can significantly impact interest in SEs (adjusted R^2 = .55, $p < .001$). Since results have been collected for the condition of before COVID-19 only, H4 is partially supported.

Figure 12 shows the distribution of subjects' responses to purchasing behavior. Figure 13 demonstrates the relationship between purchasing behavior and interest in SEs.

Figure 10. Cognition degree and purchasing intention can determine awareness of SEs before COVID-19

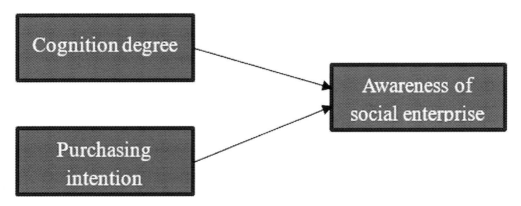

Figure 11. Purchasing intention and cognitive social benefits can determine awareness of SEs during COVID-19

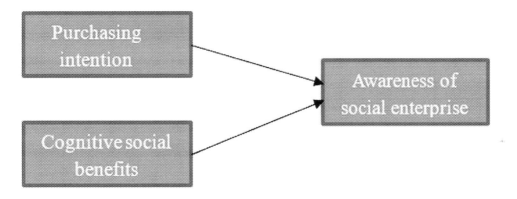

Figure 12. Purchasing behavior on a scale of 1-7

Figure 13. The relationship between purchasing behavior and interest in SEs

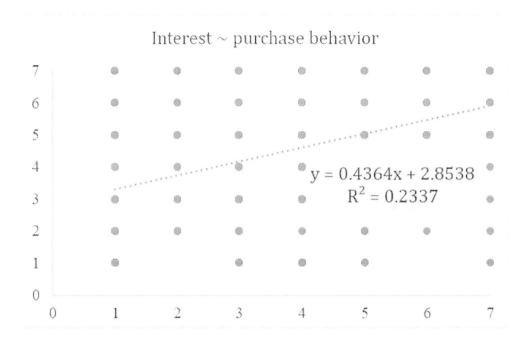

The Impact of the Social Factor on Interest in SEs

The survey results show that social factor during COVID-19 (Mean = 5.30, SD = 1.31) is significantly higher than before (Mean = 4.75, SD = 1.36; $t = -7.14, p < .001$). Figure 14 shows the mean comparison of social factor.

Assuming there is a difference between people's interest in SEs in relation to social factors at different stages, two separate regression models have been developed to demonstrate the relationship before and during COVID-19. The impact of social factor on interest in SEs is found to be relatively strong during COVID-19 (adjusted $R^2 = .27, p < .001$) as compared to before (adjusted $R^2 = .11, p < .001$), as shown in Figure 15 and Figure 16. Thus, H5 is partially supported, in the condition of during COVID-19 only.

The Impact of the Emerging Cognitive Purpose on Interest in SEs

The survey results present the mean score of the emerging cognitive purpose (Mean = 5.26) and standard deviation (SD = 1.05). As we assume there should be no significant difference in the emerging cognitive purpose before and during COVID-19, we measured this variable in a general sense in the survey. But, based on the two separate regression models developed to test the relationship between the emerging cognitive purpose and interest in SEs, before and during COVID-19 respectively, this factor is more likely to have an impact during COVID-19 (before COVID-19: adjusted $R^2 = .08, p < .001$; during COVID-19: adjusted $R^2 = .16, p < .001$). Thus, H6 is partially supported.

Figure 17 shows the distribution of subjects' responses to emerging cognitive purposes. Figure 18 demonstrates the relationship between the cognitive emerging purpose and interest in SEs.

Figure 14. Social factor during COVID-19 is significantly higher than before

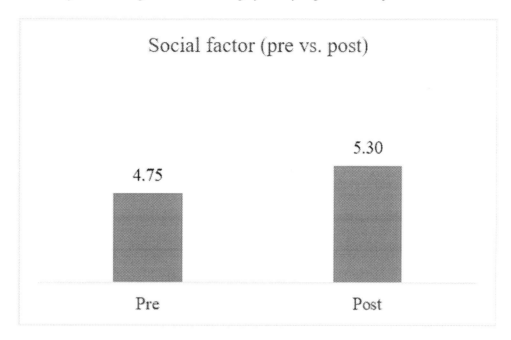

Figure 15. The relationship between the social factor and interest in SEs (before COVID-19)

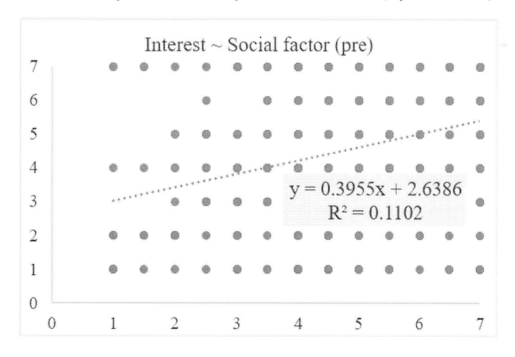

Figure 16. The relationship between the social factor and interest in SEs (during COVID-19)

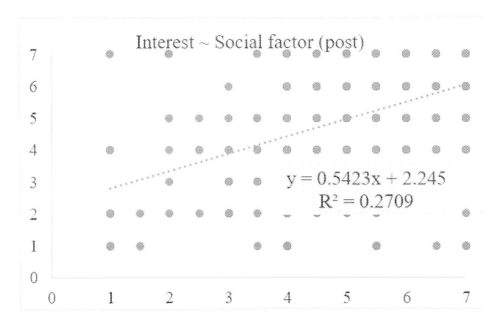

Figure 17. The emerging cognitive purpose on a scale of 1-7

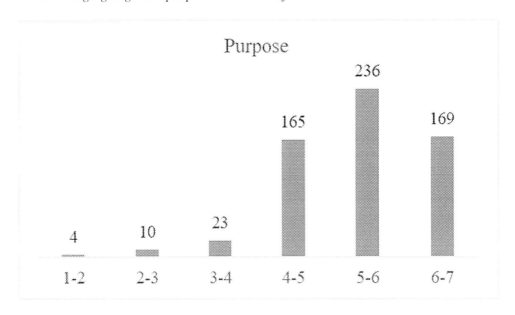

Figure 18. The relationship between cognitive emerging purpose and interest in SEs (before and during COVID-19)

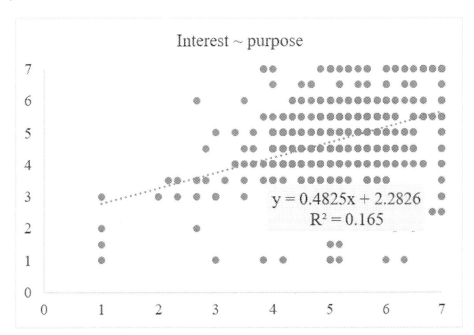

The Prediction of Interest in SEs based on Purchasing Behavior, Social Factor, and Emerging Cognitive Purpose

The results reported in previous sections, focusing on the impacts of the proposed factors on interest in SEs, indicate that interest in SEs can be predicted by purchasing behavior, social factor, and emerging cognitive purpose, given some of their impacts found to be significant before and during COVID-19. Figure 19 illustrates the predictive model of interest in SEs, using purchasing behavior, social factor, and emerging cognitive purpose as three effective predictors before COVID-19. Figure 20 depicts the relationships between purchasing intention, cognitive social benefits, and awareness of SEs. Please note that only the impacts that have been measured and tested to be significant are presented below.

Taken together, the patterns regarding how interest in SEs is impacted by these factors, including purchasing behavior, social factor, and the emerging cognitive purpose, vary across the two time periods, before and during COVID-19.

CONCLUSION AND IMPLICATIONS

The results of this research suggest that awareness of SEs and interest in SEs are impacted by the factors proposed in a theoretical model (see Figure 1) through different patterns. First, before COVID-19, awareness of SEs is more likely to be impacted by cognition and purchasing intention; however, cognitive social benefits have no impact. On the other side, during COVID-19, awareness of SEs is more likely to be impacted by purchasing intention and cognitive social benefits. The reason why cognition degree

Figure 19. Purchasing behavior, social factor, and the emerging cognitive purpose can determine interest in SEs before COVID-19

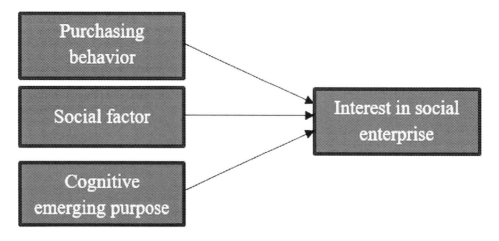

Figure 20. Social factor and the emerging cognitive purpose can determine interest in SEs during COVID-19

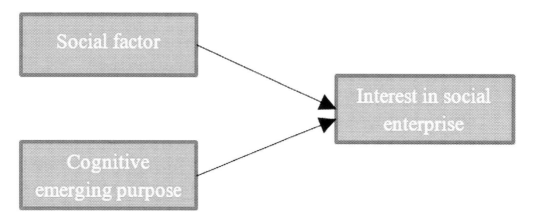

does not appear in the predictive model of awareness of SEs during COVID-19 is because this variable has not been addressed in our survey. Yet, why cognitive social benefits would not impact awareness of SEs during COVID-19 may need some further explanation. Overall, awareness of SEs has significantly increased during COVID-19 compared to before (before vs. during: 4.46 vs. 5.20, $p < .001$), which can be impacted by the proposed factors differently. Additionally, these factors can successfully predict awareness of SEs, which is considered one of the most significant findings of this research.

Second, before COVID-19, interest in SEs is significantly impacted by the three factors proposed, purchasing behavior, social factor, and emerging cognitive purpose. By contrast, because the impact of purchasing behavior has not been captured in the survey, the impact of this factor on interest in SEs is unknown. Besides purchasing behavior, the other two factors, social factor, and emerging cognitive purpose are found to have significant impacts on interest in SEs. Similar to awareness of SEs, interest in SEs has significantly increased during COVID-19 than before (before vs. during: 4.52 vs. 5.12, p

< .001), which can be impacted by the proposed factors differently. Overall, all these factors, except purchasing behavior not tested in this work, can successfully predict interest in SEs, which is the other significant finding of this study.

Third, as a side finding of this work awareness of SEs and interest in SEs are not two exclusive variables. In particular, the correlation between these two outcome variables is strong in both periods, before and during COVID-19 (before: $r = .43, p < .001$; during: $r = .75, p < .001$). The results suggest that in future research, we can propose a more comprehensive model addressing the impacts of all proposed factors, such as cognition degree and purchasing intention, on the perceptions of SEs, including awareness, interest, and perhaps, other additional concepts related to people's understanding of SEs. To test this comprehensive model, regarding the attitudes toward SEs and people's related knowledge and perceptions, more advanced analytical methods can be applied, and more detailed empirical results can be produced.

LIMITATIONS AND FUTURE RESEARCH

The sample size of this study is fairly strong. Still, the lack of diversity in the geographical location of the respondents could be a weakness due to variations in the implementation strategies for SEs in differing regions of China. A future study could explore the relationship between relative affluence and SEs awareness between different provinces of China. This study relies heavily on the perceptions of the respondents. While primary first-hand data is often valuable and useful, a future study using a longitudinal methodology for data collection would be useful to validate the results of this research.

REFERENCES

Alsmadi, S. (2007). Green marketing and the concern over the environment: Measuring environmental consciousness of Jordanian consumers. *Journal of Promotion Management*, *13*(3–4), 339–361. doi:10.1080/10496490802306905

Alter, S. K. (2006). SE models and their mission and money relationships. *Social Entrepreneurship: New Models of Sustainable Social Change*.

Bacq, S., & Lumpkin, G. (2020). Social Entrepreneurship and COVID-19. *Journal of Management Studies*.

Boolkin, J. (2017). *Good reads: Best books for social entrepreneurs and changemakers*. Academic Press.

Bornstein, D. (2007). *How to change the world: Social entrepreneurs and the power of new ideas*. Oxford University Press.

Brounen, D., Kok, N., & Quigley, J. (2014). Energy literacy and capitalization. *Energy Economics*, *38*(7), 42–50.

Buchanan, B., Cao, C. X., & Chen, C. (2018). Corporate social responsibility, firm value, and influential institutional ownership. *Journal of Corporate Finance*, *52*, 73–95. doi:10.1016/j.jcorpfin.2018.07.004

Bui, T. L. H. (2010). The Vietnamese consumer perception on corporate social responsibility. *Journal of International Business Research*, *9*(1), 75–87.

Carroll, A. B. (1991). The pyramid of corporate social responsibility: Toward the moral management of organizational stakeholders. *Business Horizons*, *34*(4), 39–48. doi:10.1016/0007-6813(91)90005-G

Chan, K.-M., Yuen, Y., & Wong, H. (2013). *Realities of social service purchasing in China: A political transaction cost perspective*. Academic Press.

Chan, R. Y., & Lau, L. B. (2002). Explaining green purchasing behavior: A cross-cultural study on American and Chinese consumers. *Journal of International Consumer Marketing*, *14*(2–3), 9–40. doi:10.1300/J046v14n02_02

Chan, R. Y. K. (2001). Determinants of Chinese consumers' green purchase behavior. *Psychology and Marketing*, *18*(4), 389–413. doi:10.1002/mar.1013

Chandra, Y., Lee, E. K. M., & Tjiptono, F. (2021). Public versus private interest in social entrepreneurship: Can one serve two masters? *Journal of Cleaner Production*, *280*, 124499. doi:10.1016/j.jclepro.2020.124499

Chen, X., & Kelly, T. F. (2015). B-Corps—A Growing Form of SE: Tracing Their Progress and Assessing Their Performance. *Journal of Leadership & Organizational Studies*, *22*(1), 102–114. doi:10.1177/1548051814532529

Costanzo, L. A., Vurro, C., Foster, D., Servato, F., & Perrini, F. (2014). Dual-Mission Management in Social Entrepreneurship: Qualitative Evidence from Social Firms in the United Kingdom. *Journal of Small Business Management*, *52*(4), 655–677. doi:10.1111/jsbm.12128

Dagnoli, J. (1991). Consciously green. *Advertising Age*, *62*(38), 14–14.

Davies, I. A., Haugh, H., & Chambers, L. (2019). Barriers to SE Growth. *Journal of Small Business Management*, *57*(4), 1616–1636. doi:10.1111/jsbm.12429

Dees, J. G. (2007). Taking social entrepreneurship seriously. *Society*, *44*(3), 24–31. doi:10.1007/BF02819936

Defourny, J., & Nyssens, M. (2006). Defining SE. *SE: At the Crossroads of Market. Public Policies and Civil Society*, *7*, 3–27.

Evers, A. (2005). Mixed Welfare Systems and Hybrid Organizations: Changes in the Governance and Provision of Social Services. *International Journal of Public Administration*, *28*(9–10), 737–748. doi:10.1081/PAD-200067318

Faizah, S. I., & Husaeni, U. A. (2019). Economic Empowerment for Poor Women Using Grameen Bank Model in Indonesia. *KnE Social Sciences*, 880–913.

Frederick, W. C. (2006). *Corporation, be good!: The story of corporate social responsibility*. Dog Ear Publishing.

Fumero, A., Marrero, R. J., Voltes, D., & Penate, W. (2018). Personal and social factors involved in internet addiction among adolescents: A meta-analysis. *Computers in Human Behavior*, *86*, 387–400. doi:10.1016/j.chb.2018.05.005

Gadenne, D., Sharma, B., Kerr, D., & Smith, T. (2011). The influence of consumers' environmental beliefs and attitudes on energy-saving behaviours. *Energy Policy*, *39*(12), 7684–7694. doi:10.1016/j.enpol.2011.09.002

Griffin, A. (2008). *New strategies for reputation management: Gaining control of issues, crises & corporate social responsibility*. Kogan Page Publishers.

Grunert, S. C. (n.d.). *Everybody seems concerned about the environment: But is this concern reflected in (Danish) consumers' food choice?* Academic Press.

Hockerts, K. (2017). Determinants of social entrepreneurial intentions. *Entrepreneurship Theory and Practice*, *41*(1), 105–130. doi:10.1111/etap.12171

Hossain, M. (1988). *Credit for alleviation of rural poverty: The Grameen Bank in Bangladesh* (Vol. 65). Intl Food Policy Res Inst.

Howell, J. (2007). Civil Society In China: Chipping away at the edges. *Development*, *50*(3), 17–23. doi:10.1057/palgrave.development.1100416

Jackson, T. (1993). *Clean Production Strategies Developing Preventive Environmental Management in the Industrial Economy*. CRC Press.

Jennings, M., Munuera, L., & Tong, D. (2011). *An Assessment of China's 2020 Carbon Intensity Target*. Grantham Institute for Climate Change Report GR1.

Kim, D., & Lim, U. (2017). SE as a Catalyst for Sustainable Local and Regional Development. *Sustainability*, *9*(8), 1427. doi:10.3390u9081427

Lee, R. (2009). The Emergence of SEs in China. *The Quest for Space and Legitimacy.*, *2*, 21.

Leggett, A. (2020). Bringing green food to the Chinese table: How civil society actors are changing consumer culture in China. *Journal of Consumer Culture*, *20*(1), 83–101. doi:10.1177/1469540517729009

Leung, Z. C., Ho, A. P., Tjia, L. Y., Tam, R. K., Chan, K., & Lai, M. K. (2019). Social Impacts of Work Integration SE in Hong Kong–Workfare and Beyond. *Journal of Social Entrepreneurship*, *10*(2), 159–176. doi:10.1080/19420676.2018.1541007

Li, J., Zhang, D., & Su, B. (2019). The Impact of Social Awareness and Lifestyles on Household Carbon Emissions in China. *Ecological Economics*, *160*, 145–155. doi:10.1016/j.ecolecon.2019.02.020

Ma, Q. (2005). *Non-governmental organizations in contemporary China: Paving the way to civil society?* Routledge. doi:10.4324/9780203029367

Man, C. K., & Terence, Y. Y. K. (2011). An overview of SE development in China and Hong Kong. *Journal of Ritsumeikan Social Sciences*, *5*, 165–178.

Marshall, D., McCarthy, L., McGrath, P., & Claudy, M. (2015). Going above and beyond: How sustainability culture and entrepreneurial orientation drive social sustainability supply chain practice adoption. *Supply Chain Management*, *20*(4), 434–454. doi:10.1108/SCM-08-2014-0267

Meyer, K. E., Ding, Y., Li, J., & Zhang, H. (2018). Overcoming distrust: How state-owned enterprises adapt their foreign entries to institutional pressures abroad. In *State-Owned Multinationals* (pp. 211–251). Springer. doi:10.1007/978-3-319-51715-5_9

Munerah, S., Koay, K. Y., & Thambiah, S. (2021). Factors influencing non-green consumers' purchase intention: A partial least squares structural equation modelling (PLS-SEM) approach. *Journal of Cleaner Production*, *280*, 124192. doi:10.1016/j.jclepro.2020.124192

Muttakin, M. B., & Khan, A. (2014). Determinants of corporate social disclosure: Empirical evidence from Bangladesh. *Advances in Accounting*, *30*(1), 168–175. doi:10.1016/j.adiac.2014.03.005

Pache, A.-C., & Santos, F. (2012). Inside the Hybrid Organization: Selective Coupling as a Response to Competing Institutional Logics. *Academy of Management Journal*, *56*(4), 972–1001. doi:10.5465/amj.2011.0405

Peng, Y., Li, J., Xia, H., Qi, S., & Li, J. (2015). The effects of food safety issues released by we media on consumers' awareness and purchasing behavior: A case study in China. *Food Policy*, *51*, 44–52. doi:10.1016/j.foodpol.2014.12.010

Pop, R.-A., Săplăcan, Z., & Alt, M.-A. (2020). Social Media Goes Green—The Impact of Social Media on Green Cosmetics Purchase Motivation and Intention. *Information (Basel)*, *11*(9), 447. doi:10.3390/info11090447

Qi, X., & Ploeger, A. (2019). Explaining consumers' intentions towards purchasing green food in Qingdao, China: The amendment and extension of the theory of planned behavior. *Appetite*, *133*, 414–422. doi:10.1016/j.appet.2018.12.004 PMID:30537527

Saiz-Alvarez, J. M., Vega-Muñoz, A., Acevedo-Duque, A., & Castillo, D. (2020). B Corps: A Socioeconomic Approach for the COVID-19 Post-crisis. *Frontiers in Psychology*, *11*, 1867. doi:10.3389/fpsyg.2020.01867 PMID:32849095

Shen, H., Fu, M., Pan, H., Yu, Z., & Chen, Y. (2020). The impact of the COVID-19 pandemic on firm performance. *Emerging Markets Finance & Trade*, *56*(10), 2213–2230. doi:10.1080/1540496X.2020.1785863

Shieh, M.-D., Chen, C.-N., & Lin, M.-C. (2018). Discussion of Correlations between Green Advertising Design and Purchase Intention based on Consumers' Environmental Attitude. *Ekoloji*, *27*(106), 1153–1159.

Skrentny, J. D. (1993). Concern for the environment: A cross-national perspective. *International Journal of Public Opinion Research*, *5*(4), 335–352. doi:10.1093/ijpor/5.4.335

Sodhi, M. S., & Tang, C. S. (2011). SEs as supply-chain enablers for the poor. *Socio-Economic Planning Sciences*, *45*(4), 146–153. doi:10.1016/j.seps.2011.04.001

Suki, N. M. (2016). Green product purchase intention: Impact of green brands, attitude, and knowledge. *British Food Journal*.

Sullivan Mort, G., Weerawardena, J., & Carnegie, K. (2003). Social entrepreneurship: Towards conceptualisation. *International Journal of Nonprofit and Voluntary Sector Marketing, 8*(1), 76–88. doi:10.1002/nvsm.202

Sun, Y., Luo, B., Wang, S., & Fang, W. (2020). What you see is meaningful: Does green advertising change the intentions of consumers to purchase eco-labeled products? *Business Strategy and the Environment.*

Tian, R., Chui, C. H.-K., & Hu, X. (2018). Emergent models and strategies of SEs in China. *Asia Pacific Journal of Social Work and Development, 28*(2), 111–127. doi:10.1080/02185385.2018.1453372

Tiwari, P., Bhat, A. K., & Tikoria, J. (2017). An empirical analysis of the factors affecting social entrepreneurial intentions. *Journal of Global Entrepreneurship Research, 7*(1), 1–25. doi:10.118640497-017-0067-1

Türkel, S., Uzunoğlu, E., Kaplan, M. D., & Vural, B. A. (2016). A Strategic Approach to CSR Communication: Examining the Impact of Brand Familiarity on Consumer Responses. *Corporate Social Responsibility and Environmental Management, 23*(4), 228–242. doi:10.1002/csr.1373

Vickers, I. (2010). *SE and the environment: A review of the literature.* Third Sector Research Centre Working Paper, 22.

Von Borgstede, C., Andersson, M., & Johnsson, F. (2013). Public attitudes to climate change and carbon mitigation—Implications for energy-associated behaviours. *Energy Policy, 57,* 182–193. doi:10.1016/j.enpol.2013.01.051

Wang, H., Alon, I., & Kimble, C. (2015). Dialogue in the dark: Shedding light on the development of SEs in China. *Global Business and Organizational Excellence, 34*(4), 60–69. doi:10.1002/joe.21615

Wang, J., Bao, J., Wang, C., & Wu, L. (2017). The impact of different emotional appeals on the purchase intention for green products: The moderating effects of green involvement and Confucian cultures. *Sustainable Cities and Society, 34,* 32–42. doi:10.1016/j.scs.2017.06.001

White, C. L., Nielsen, A. E., & Valentini, C. (2017). CSR research in the apparel industry: A quantitative and qualitative review of existing literature. *Corporate Social Responsibility and Environmental Management, 24*(5), 382–394. doi:10.1002/csr.1413

Wieland, H., Koskela-Huotari, K., & Vargo, S. L. (2016). Extending actor participation in value creation: An institutional view. *Journal of Strategic Marketing, 24*(3–4), 210–226. doi:10.1080/0965254X.2015.1095225

Xia, D., Zhang, M., Yu, Q., & Tu, Y. (2019). Developing a framework to identify barriers of Green technology adoption for enterprises. *Resources, Conservation and Recycling, 143,* 99–110. doi:10.1016/j.resconrec.2018.12.022

Yang, X., Dong, X., Jiang, Q., & Liu, G. (2019). Factors influencing public concern about environmental protection: An analysis from China. *Discrete Dynamics in Nature and Society, 2019,* 2019. doi:10.1155/2019/5983160

Young, D. R. (2001). Organizational Identity in Nonprofit Organizations: Strategic and Structural Implications. *Nonprofit Management & Leadership, 12*(2), 139–157. doi:10.1002/nml.12202

Yu, L. (2020). The emergence of social entrepreneurs in China. *Journal of the International Council for Small Business*, *1*(1), 32–35. doi:10.1080/26437015.2020.1714359

Yu, X. (2013). *The governance of SEs in China*. SE Journal.

Yu, X. (2016). Social Entrepreneurship in China's Nonprofit Sector. The Case of Innovative Participation of Civil Society in Post-disaster Reconstruction. *China Perspectives, 2016*(3), 53–61. doi:10.4000/chinaperspectives.7051

Zhao, E. Y., & Wry, T. (2016). Not All Inequality Is Equal: Deconstructing the Societal Logic of Patriarchy to Understand Microfinance Lending to Women. *Academy of Management Journal*, *59*(6), 1994–2020. doi:10.5465/amj.2015.0476

Zhao, M. (2020, September 13). *The SE Emerges in China (SSIR)*. https://ssir.org/articles/entry/the_social_enterprise_emerges_in_china

Zhu, Q., & Sarkis, J. (2016). Green marketing and consumerism as social change in China: Analyzing the literature. *International Journal of Production Economics*, *181*, 289–302. doi:10.1016/j.ijpe.2016.06.006

ADDITIONAL READING

Cotte, A., Muñoz, A. G., & Correa, G. (Eds.). (2016). *Development, Growth, Environment, and Social Equity*. Nova.

Gamez-Gutierrez, J., & Saiz-Alvarez, J. M. (2021). *Entrepreneurial Innovation for Securing Long-Term Growth in a Short Term Economy*. IGI Global. doi:10.4018/978-1-7998-3568-4

Marjerison, R. K., Lin, Y., & Chen, R. (2021). *Analysis of Entrepreneurial Mindset as Predictor of Startup Desire in South-East China: Considering Social Cause Interest. Journal of International Business and Entrepreneurship Development*. doi:10.1504/JIBED.2021.10034397

Marjerison, R. K., & Songcheng, G. (2020). Social Media Influencers' Effect on Chinese Gen Z Consumers: Management and Use of Video Content Platforms. *Journal of Media Management and Entrepreneurship*, *2*(2), 1–18. doi:10.4018/JMME.2020070101

Palma-Ruiz, J. M., Saiz-Alvarez, J. M., & Herrero-Crespo, A. (2020). *Handbook of Research on Smart Territories and Entrepreneurial Ecosystems for Social Innovation and Sustainable Growth*. IGI Global. doi:10.4018/978-1-7998-2097-0

Saiz-Alvarez, J. M. (2018). *Business Strategies and Advanced Techniques for Entrepreneurship 4.0*. IGI Global. doi:10.4018/978-1-5225-4978-9

Saiz-Alvarez, J. M. (Ed.). (2019). *Handbook of Research on Digital Marketing Innovations in Social Entrepreneurship and Solidarity Economics*. IGI Global. doi:10.4018/978-1-5225-8939-6

KEY TERMS AND DEFINITIONS

B Corporations: They are hybrid companies defined as for-profit and are socially responsible beyond corporate social responsibility, as they make profits but not at the expense of stakeholders.

Beijing Social Enterprise Initiatives: Public funded program launched to accelerate the development of social enterprises in China.

Embedded Social Enterprise: It refers to social enterprises with similar meanings of social programs and business activities to achieve financial and social profits simultaneously.

Foundations: Not-for-profit civil organizations that use donated assets to be engaged in philanthropy.

New Public Management: A type of public management is defined by incorporating market-oriented mechanisms (e.g., authoritative procurement, philanthropic ventures, contract tendering) in public sectors to increase efficiency in the services sector.

Social Enterprise: It is a sort of organization defined by being operated outside the purely private business and state sectors.

Social Welfare Corporations: They are social enterprises focused on providing job choices for the disabled to satisfy their life demands.

Year of Civil Society: Officially set in 2008, it was the special year to increase the Chinese public awareness of social enterprises.

Chapter 12
The Social and Solidarity Economics, Public Policies, and Non-Monetary Economic Practices:
The Case of Associative Firms in Loja, Ecuador

Arturo Luque González
https://orcid.org/0000-0002-7447-7560
Universidad Tecnica de Manabí, Ecuador & Universidad del Rosario, Ecuador

Aitor Bengoetxea Alkorta
Universidad del País Vasco, Spain & Euskal Herriko Unibertsitatea, Spain

Jaime Leonidas Ordóñez Salcedo
Universidad del País Vasco, Spain & Euskal Herriko Unibertsitatea, Spain

ABSTRACT

The prevailing economic and social model contains great inequalities. Against this backdrop, the Republic of Ecuador, in its constitution of 2008, included recognizing ancestral practices at an economic and social level and granting special protection to "mother earth" or Pachamama based on the common element of solidarity between ecosystems and human beings. Despite this, continuous growth processes have blunted some of the tools and institutions created in Ecuador to redress poverty and rebalance existing economic and regulatory abuses. To analyze this situation, a series of group interviews were carried out in two communities of Loja (Ecuador) to analyze the scope and continuity of current ancestral practices and the effectiveness of processes established in the social economy. The analysis shows the lack of continuity of these practices and their associated benefits for people and communities with limited resources.

DOI: 10.4018/978-1-7998-7689-2.ch012

The Social and Solidarity Economics, Public Policies, and Non-Monetary Economic Practices

INTRODUCTION

Economic and social inequality points towards alarming prospects for the majority of the globalized world. More wealth is concentrated in the hands of 1% of the global population than in the remaining 99%. Even more starkly, 62 individuals have amassed fortunes equivalent to the combined resources of 3.6 billion people, demonstrating the current lack of fairness in the redistribution of wealth and the need to introduce and develop an economic and social system within everyone's reach (Oxfam, 2016). Economic models guided by private interests enable the accumulation of power and influence, obeying the common denominator of continuous growth (Passet, 2013; Piketty, 2014; Mason, 2016). There is a vested interest in maintaining methods for accumulating wealth by one part of the population-based on the dispossession of the rest of the globalized world (Harvey, 2007). Processes of labor exploitation, extractivism, pollution, and a sham collaborative economy are becoming the norm. The markets are gaining power, and endemic corruption is the rule rather than the exception (Luque, 2018, 2019). This pattern is repeated in Ecuador, where national poverty stands at 23.2% and extreme poverty at 8.4%. The poverty percentage reaches 40% in the rural sector, while extreme poverty stands at 17.7% above specific estimates (INEC, 2019).

As a result of this, today's reality drives significant swathes of the population towards living standards far removed from models of anthropocentrism and consumerism. Certain corporations impose choices, trends, and tastes by their overwhelming offer of new products and services in the guise of modernity and necessity (Luque, 2017). They are driven to obtain the highest possible returns by promoting disproportionate processes of individualism and consumerism in the face of existing inequalities (Acosta, 2017). The Earth's limits are broken by techniques such as extractivism of natural resources (and its consequences) and the associated continually rising pollution. Regulations favor transnational developments. According to Banerjee (2019), reducing taxes for companies to boost investments is a myth. By doing so, we are merely giving incentives to the rich who already have excessive cash reserves. Once again, we see that lowering taxes—for corporations—creates extra wealth for those who least need it. By the same process, millions of people are squeezed out of an economic and social system geared towards production. The enjoyment of leisure, holidays, and the family is unattainable for many globalized populations who lack the resources and time (Sassen, 2015). Business is protected over and above human rights, fostering competition to land the next order between factories, even within the same group. Governments desperate for investment create legislation favorable to transnational corporations (TNCs), compromising human rights and the general interest (Hernández Zubizarreta and Ramino, 2016; Oliván, 2019; Luque and Herrero García, 2019).

Given this constant assault of the consume-dispose-consume mindset, the resulting social problems have led to solidarity initiatives such as cooperatives, mutual societies, associations, and all kinds of ancestral practices. In these, precedence is given to the redistribution of wealth, and collective values replace ownership by the few over the many. This fact stands in stark contrast to the traditional business paradigm in which wage differences between workers and CEOs can be of several orders of magnitude and decision making is concentrated in the hands of only a few.

Socially-based economic models arise spontaneously from the current needs or act as an escape valve for a production system that, by act or omission, forces some to look for alternatives. According to the Encyclical, *Laudato Si: on care for our common home,* by Pope Francis and Beroglio (2015, p.73), "Christian tradition has never recognized the right to private property as absolute or inviolable, and has stressed the social purpose of all forms of private property," hence the need to explore new social, political and legal horizons shifting from morality towards social regulations as a backdrop focused on eliminating vital imbalances.

Today, alternatives that are complementary to the private system are being created (Velecela, 2017). According to the International Cooperative Alliance (2019), cooperative members represent at least 12% of the global population and employ 280 million people worldwide and notably contribute to generating steady employment (CICOPA, 2014). The cooperative system is financially highly resistant and has a strong capacity for adapting to continually shifting social transformations and needs. These aspects arose from the First Industrial Revolution to provide male and female workers with fairer and more decent work and protect them by establishing adequate welfare and social security systems (International Labour Organisation, 2019).

In Latin America, the processes of the Social and Solidarity Economy (SSE) of recent decades have acted as an essential element in building developmental models (Pianovi, 2012; Luque and Casado, 2020). SSE processes have served as a vehicle between extreme poverty and an effective way out of the equality trap. They are based on social identity, including different organizational formats under alternative economic processes and social contextualization (da Ros, 2007). In Ecuador, the experiences of the solidarity economy are connected to a deep-lying history of ancient practices, many of which are dependent on the traditional indigenous economy (Jiménez, 2016; Luque, Ortega and Carretero, 2019). These origins have marked the way solidarity economy enterprises function in communities. They are expressed in many practices, such as *cambio de manos* and *minga,* that, while often overlooked, are essential for the proper functioning of the local economy (Donoso, 2014; Yépez, 2015).

From 2008 onwards, under the new constitutional framework of the Republic of Ecuador, and until 2017, an alternative model of development was promoted focused on human beings and nature. Article 283 of the constitution states that the economic system is socially orientated and mutually supportive. It seeks a comprise between public, private, mixed-economy, and social and solidarity forms of economy. The SSE consists of the cooperative, associative, and community sectors (Constitution of the Republic of Ecuador CRE, 2008). This fact enables the enactment of regulations and the creation of institutional bodies to regulate, control, foster, and promote the sector. However, it has been a model in constant conflict since 2017. Public policies have chosen a new amalgam of contradictory terminology such as the "market social economy" when defining the economic model, juxtaposing the pejorative and the ameliorative in the same concept.

With this objective in view and following the central thesis of this research, an analysis was made of 1) the public policies implemented in Ecuador and their compatibility with SSE institutions, specifically with those that base their activity on non-monetary economic transactions (in many cases of a marked indigenous origin); and 2) the traditional exchange methods based on non-monetary economic transactions generated between those making up the Asociación de Productores Agropecuarios Micro Cuenca Mataderos [Association of Agricultural Micro-Producers of the Mataderos Basin], located in Loja's Macará Canton and the Asociación de Servicios de Alimentación, Limpieza y Mensajería Inkan Samana (ASOINKAN) [Association of Grocery, Cleaning and Delivery Services, "Inkan Samana"] from Loja's Saraguro Canton. An analysis was made of their sustainability and viability per se and the relationships established by the fulfillment of SSE policies within the framework of their entrepreneurial activity. Lastly, a detailed examination was made of the challenges faced by ancestral practices regarding their survival over time and the sustainability of their management while complying with constitutional precepts.

Constitutional Framework and Institutionalization of the Social and Solidarity Economy in Ecuador

Because of the extreme levels of poverty and the erosion of principles and values (as opposed to focusing solely on development), it is necessary to examine the new public policies that have emerged from Ecuador's "Good Living" initiative (Buen Vivir), which seeks to "rebuild harmony and balance, and later create policies to protect the harmony and balance of life" (Huanacuni, 2010, p.58). Logically, over time, different forms of economic organization have emerged in Ecuador's economy. Despite the scarce employment and social opportunities, these have survived amid a dominant economic system by adopting the SSE model. These endeavors seek to generate their subsistence-level work based on cultural legacies, the intrinsic organization of each community, or the dissemination of alternative social realities existing in rural and urban sectors. These include cooperatives, associations, and irrigation communities, among others (Sánchez, 2016).

The political instability in Ecuador from 1996 to 2006 saw seven presidents come and go. A profound financial crisis underlies this reality. The political uncertainty and economic recession of the last years of the 20th century brought on a mass exodus towards Europe and specifically towards Spain (Jokisch, 2001). During this period, more than half of the private banks folded. On January 9, 2000, under the presidency of Jamil Mahuad, the US dollar's adoption was decreed (25,000 Sucres were equivalent to 1 dollar), with the subsequent exchange of all deposits. This aspect entailed a loss in the value of deposits held by citizens (Oleas, 2016). The scenario triggered the loss of confidence in private banking and the state by many citizens. The economic crisis prompted a move by many savers from the banking sector towards savings and credit cooperatives. The extent of the repercussions in favor of the cooperative financial industry was that, during 1998 and 2006, fixed-term deposits rose by a yearly average of 58.48% (Miño, 2013). After this turbulent decade, Ecuador turned to a government that would offer the impetus of a more democratic economy and a society where the human being was above material interests. For the first time in Latin America, the year 2008 saw the approval of a constitution based on the ancestral vision of the Andean peoples. In general, Ecuador's new constitution obliged the state and society to move toward *Sumak Kawsay*[1], with a permanent commitment to caring for nature (Sánchez, 2012). The constitution, in article 283, declares that the economic system is socially oriented and mutually supportive, thereby surpassing the concepts of market economy and market social economy expressed in the constitutions of 1978 and 1998 (Naranjo, 2016).

In Act number 055 of May 30, 2008, of the Montecristi Assembly, the construction of a social and solidarity economic system was shown to imply moving from an economy focused on the market and the accumulation of capital to one that prioritizes, above all, human life. This system would have to:

Guarantee economic sovereignty, gradual replacement of the extractivist model, recognition of human beings and their labor as the only real source of value, enable the strengthening of more supportive forms of exchange and promote consumer models that compromise neither our present time nor the material foundations of future generations (Assembly, 2008, p.8).

Nonetheless, despite the consecration of the SSE in the 2008 constitution, and despite the importance of articles 283, 309, and 311, the institutional structure of SSE processes has failed to be strengthened (Oleas, 2016).

The Organic Law of the Social and Solidarity Economy (OLSSE), in article 5, establishes that the act of economic solidarity is carried out between organizations and their members to which the law refers, within the exercise of their activities corresponding to their corporate purpose. These do not constitute commercial or civil acts but supporting acts and are subject to the same legislation. On the other hand, article 139 establishes that *acts of solidarity carried out by members of the organizations referred to in the law, as part of the performance of their corporate activities, are not considered taxable; however, acts and other operations carried out with third parties are subject to the common tax system*. Article 145 provides that *regulations be issued separately for both the individuals and organizations making up the Social and Solidarity Economy, as well as the Social and Solidarity Financial Sector, and refer to the protection, promotion, incentives, operation, and monitoring of all relevant economic activities, in keeping with the regulations issued by other state institutions to protect the rights of users and consumers.* (Organic Law on the Social and Solidarity Economy, OLSSE, 2008).

Despite that which is stipulated in the OLSSE, in fulfilling its attributions and functions, the Ministry of Employment (ME) regulates the implementation of the Labour Law (LL) to all companies, including SSE associations to which it has issued sanctions for failure to comply concerning the non-recording of contracts of associations with their workers (article 28 of the OLSSE stipulates that members be also workers, a circumstance that does not lead to a relationship of dependence). Furthermore, as part of compliance with the LL, 15% of the overall profits must be shared among the workers, except when they are contracted by third parties (i.e., they are not members). The legal dilemma occurs when the workers are also members of the organizations. By including them in the distribution of profits, compliance with the ME would contradict their articles of association and, therefore, the OLSSE. This latter indicates that enterprises' equity comprises 1) the original capital investment and 2) the total profits of the previous period. In other words, organizations are sanctioned by the ME if they fail to include members in the register of 15% of the profits while being admonished by the Superintendency of the Social and Solidarity Economy (SSSE) if they proceed with dividend distribution.

On the other hand, the OLSSE does not oblige organizations to enter employment contracts with their worker-members; instead, it currently invokes Internal Revenue Service resolution NAC-DGERC-GC16-00000343[2], creating the Simplified SSE System, which establishes the following benefits: *As is the case of organizations in the general scheme, they will issue purchase bonds to sustain acts of economic solidarity, even if the members to whom these bonds are issued have a tax number, being able to consolidate the transactions with every member of the organization annually.* This fact means that an employment contract does not need to be signed between the organization and the worker.

Some of the public institutions that contract SSE goods and services (mainly their financial managers) oblige managers of SSE organizations to provide proof of having complied with their Ecuadorian Social Security Institute (ESSI) (especially their financial managers) obligations before paying the amounts due under the contracts established. It should be noted that this requirement opens up the possibility that, on crossing the ESSI databases with those of the ME and following the obligations of the Employment Code, many members of the organizations who pay voluntary insurance and are also part of the Rural Social Security Scheme could incur difficulties in meeting these obligations. It is fundamental that the relevant authorities establish a common criterion when interpreting the legal regulations found in the constitution and the various organic laws, codes, and all other rules governing the actions of SSE organizations. This fact would avoid tensions and disagreement when SSE organizations endeavor to fulfill any obligation or restriction.

Article 288 of the CRE states: "*[...] Priority shall be given to domestic products and services, in particular, those originating in the Social and Solidarity Economy, and in micro, small and medium-sized production units*". In 2018, public procurement contracts worth 301.4 million dollars involved SSE actors. Among the prominent contract awards were cleaning and maintenance services of buildings (71.20 million dollars), garment manufacturing services (54.3 million), food preparation and supply services for other companies and other institutions (40.6 million), other cleaning and maintenance services (27.0 million), lightweight and mixed freight transport services (15.1 million), window cleaning services in houses and other buildings (8.3 million), services of painting building interiors and similar services (8.0 million), carpentry (7.5 million), meter readings (7.4 million) and passenger transport services on routes with predetermined timetables (6.8 million dollars). In the same year, public procurement awards to the ten biggest national suppliers (which do not belong to the SSE sector) amount to 705.5 million dollars (SERCOP, 2019). In this analysis, there is no evidence of activity involving organizations in the rural sectors; it is clear, then, that the SSE sector constitutes a marginal production and commercialization niche. However, the SSE sector competes with consolidated market economy companies to supply goods and services to the state.

In public policy development, these envisage the introduction and development of programs in production, food, construction, manufacturing, tourism, services, and the social and solidarity financial sector. This translates as the Ecuadorian state's decision to promote and strengthen the SSE employing 1) promoting the transition from ways of organizing the social economy to ways of organizing the SSE, whether these be cooperative, associative, or communitarian; 2) articulating ways of organizing the SSE to strengthen and boost processes that produce, distribute, circulate, finance and consume goods and services; 3) consolidating SSE actors in social, economic and political subjects that promote processes of endogenous development articulated within the National Plan for Good Living (later renamed *Toda una Vida* [Lifelong]); and 4) consolidating SSE processes as triggers for the construction of the new alternative system of development and of the social and solidarity economy system, prioritizing work over the capital as the dominant axis of society (Ministry of Economic and Social Inclusion, 2013). There are also different measures for promoting the SSE, such as 1) the law on fostering production; 2) the law controlling market power; 3) the different resolutions of the SSSE and Institute of Social and Solidarity Economy (ISSE); 4) the BanEcuador finance project; and 5) the devolved organs of decentralized regional governments (DAGs).

National Development Plan (NDP)

Article 280 of the Constitution of the Republic of Ecuador (2008) indicates that the NDP is the instrument to which public policies, programs, and projects shall adhere. It determines the assigning of public resources, clearly mandating compliance for the whole public sector. From its first edition in 2007 through to the Lifelong Plan, published in 2017, the NDP promotes the objective of establishing, consolidating, and supporting the social and solidarity economic system (Senplades, 2019). The achievement of this objective is currently in a phase of political deceleration. According to Villalba (2019):

Ecuador is not at the stage of sustaining a consolidated solidarity system concerning the Good Living and Lifelong national plans. However, one of the 12 objectives for 2009-2013 and 2013-2017 was establishing the social and solidarity system. If you read the project in detail, you will see that problems already existed, i.e., that there were no specifically consistent goals and policies. The title of the objective was appropriate, but later the specific and political goals intended to achieve the object were unrealistic and at times somewhat incoherent, or in the majority of cases, non-existent. In other words, it was more a question of fostering the SSE than of transforming the system towards a social and solidarity economic system; that's why the country is now at the stage of establishing that system. Of course, some things have been started, and they must be consolidated. Things that were shored up must be sustained, but, in general, the country is still in the process of building the system, and what has already been established, or has achieved some degree of consolidation, must be re-assessed.

Organic Law on the Social and Solidarity Economy (OLSSE)

The year 2011 saw the passing of the OLSSE, the law that Coraggio states "is possibly the most developed specific legal instrument of SSE institutionalization in the region" (2014, p.16). In article 2, the law states that, according to the constitution, all forms of an organization making up the SSE and the social and solidarity finance sector (SSFS) are governed by this law, as well as by the institutions commissioned by the state to proceed with SSE governance, regulation, monitoring, strengthening, promotion, and accompaniment. The purpose of the law, according to article 3, is to recognize, foster, and strengthen the SSE and the SSFS in their functioning and connection with the other sectors of the economy and the state (OLSSE, 2011). According to Andino (2013, p.15), this regulatory framework "is principally a mechanism to identify, govern and monitor the sector, as well as to reform the institutions that govern the sector, rather than a legal instrument to foster development, promotion, and incentives." In an endeavor to bring about changes in the OLSSE, on January 23, 2017, the National Assembly of Ecuador presented the executive with the Bill Amending the Organic Law on the SSE. This text was rejected by the president at that time, arguing that:

We must point out that, despite the regulatory framework proposed in different spheres, it neither comprises all of the organizations involved with sufficient scope and extension, nor do we see that the typical particularities of the undertakings and activities of the individuals within the social and solidarity economy are included with sufficient accuracy. In this respect, a national debate must be launched. This reflection must necessarily consider those who have traditionally belonged to the sector (Bill of the Organic Law on Social and Solidarity Economy, 2017, p.2).

State Bodies Intervening in the SSE

In Ecuador, the Organic Law on Social and Solidarity Economy and on the Social and Solidarity Financial Sector created a number of institutions responsible for fostering, promoting and controlling the SSE, each with different functions, as follows: 1) the SSE Inter-institutional Committee, which defines the forms of organisation and coordinates public policies on development and control; 2) The Advisory Board, made up of the DAGs and SSE organisations by means of inclusive participatory processes; 3) the Social and Solidarity Financial Sector Control Board (this has an executive function and is made up of members of the Coordination for Social Development, for Economic Policy, and a delegate of the president of the republic); 4) the Superintendency of the Social and Solidarity Economy (SSSE), which has supervisory and monitoring functions; 5) the National Institute of the Social and Solidarity Economy (ISSE), which coordinates programmes related to the legislation on the SSE; and 6) the National Corporation of Social and Solidarity Finances, a body which provides financial services (Lanas, 2014).

The Social and Solidarity Economics, Public Policies, and Non-Monetary Economic Practices

Ecuador's constitutional mandate on SSE programs remains in effect, despite the lack of institutions favorable to the establishment and development of the SSE. The OLSSE (2011), in article 142, establishes the Inter-institutional Committee (IC) as the governing body of the SSE and the SSFS. This body pertains to various ministries of state whose relationship with SSE processes is defined by the presidency. At the governance level, an effort has been made to connect the coordinating authorities of the IC's economic, productive, and social aspects to carry out joint work. Still, their participation has been limited (Sánchez, 2016). On the other hand, article 46 of the same law determines that the SSSE will control the SSE and the SSFS. Table 1, Active Organisations, describes the active composition of the elements making up the SSE sector.

Table 1. Active organizations

Active Organizations	2019	Percentage
Associations	11,915	77.38
Non-financial Cooperatives	2,730	17.73
Federations	4	0.03
Community Organisations	49	0.32
Networks	1	0.01
Integration Networks	29	0.19
Unions	51	0.33
Financial Sector Cooperatives	618	4.01
CONAFIPS	1	0.01
TOTAL	15,398	100

Source: Compiled by the authors based on data from the SSSE 2019a, the 2019 official register of the non-financial sector, and the 2018 Financial Report.

According to the interview with the former Superintendent of the SSE:

In recent years, there has been a very significant increase in new associations. Many of these have participated in government procurement, enabling many people to obtain employment, means of production, economic activity, and, through these, improvements in their living conditions (Jácome, 2019).

One of the bodies created is the National Institute of the Social and Solidarity Economy (ISSE). By way of example, the institute received investments of 7,094,389 dollars in 2014; 10,680,206 in 2015; 4,496,140 for 2016; in 2017, the investment fell to 101,163 and for 2018, the figure was 533,014 (ISSE, 2019). According to the interview with the former director of the ISSE:

The Institute has limited financial resources for executing the truly great needs of the sector. The public policy for the SSE is to recover its leading position through a public body such as the ISSE, but also through the SSFS and, above all, through the representation of this sector through SSE chambers, associations, and cooperatives; it is these who must recapture the importance of the sector in a country where the constitution states that there is a social and solidarity economic system (Zurita, 2019).

Table 2, Legislation, gives a chronological summary of the regulations created to foster the SSE in the last ten years.

Table 2. Legislation

Regulation	Year	Article	Remarks
National Development Plan for the "Citizen Revolution"*	2007	11	Establishes a supportive and sustainable economic system.
Constitution of the Republic	2008	283	Declares a social and solidarity economic system at the national level.
Organic Law on the Food Sovereignty Regime	2009	14	Fosters agro-ecological and organic production utilizing training, credit, and commercialization.
Regulation of the Special Small-Scale Mining Regime	2009	44	Allows the National Mining Corporation to enter into contracts with SSE organizations or establish associations with persons carrying out individual mining activities.
Organic Code on Territorial Organisation, Autonomy, and Decentralisation	2010	4	Plans for participatory development to transform and boost the Social and Solidarity Economy.
Organic Law and Regulation on the Social and Solidarity Economy	2011	2; 4; 8	Determines who is protected by this legislation; sets out the principles of the organizations; determines who makes up the SSE.
Organic Law for the Regulation and Control of Market Power	2011	29	Supports and promotes the production of the Social and Solidarity Economy.
Organic Code of Production, Commerce, and Investments	2013	4	Democratizes access to production factors with an emphasis on the SSE and promotes social responsibility in microenterprises.
National Development Plan for Good Living	2013	8	Sustainably consolidates the social and solidarity system.
Mining Law	2014	137	Contemplates SSE associations to promote mining development in small-scale mines, emphasizing the principle of social responsibility.
Organic Law for the Public Service of Electric Energy	2015	10	Regulates the electricity sector in the business field that must also act through SSE companies and associations.
Regulation on the Suppression of Outsourcing and Labour Immediacy	2015	2; 4	Regulates the sale of complementary services (surveillance, security, groceries, delivery, and cleaning) from associations to the public sector.
Organic Law on Rural Land and Ancestral Territories	2016	22; 85	Regulates the right to land for the association sector.
The regulation implementing the Fishing and Fisheries Development Law	2016	1.3	Regulates how fishing associations are defined themselves as being part of the artisan ship-owning group.
Organic Law on the Government Procurement System	2016	25	Gives preference to SSE actors for the procurement of goods, works, and services.
The regulation implementing the Organic Law on the Government Procurement System	2016	16	Mandates SERCOP (the government procurement service) to establish criteria of preference for the SSE in government procurement (Resolutions 25 and 99) – Inclusive Fairs and Inclusive Dynamic Catalogue.
National Plan for the Development of Good Living	2017	4	Consolidates sustainability of the social and solidarity economic system and strengthens dollarization.

Source: Compiled by the authors based on Luque, Ordóñez, and Ruales (2017); *includes development plans that are not regulations.

The legislation drawn up over the last decade in Ecuador endeavors to achieve viability in the productive activities carried out by associations. Article 15 of the Organic Law on the Food Sovereignty Regime (OLFSR) states that the government must foster the agro-industrial production of small and medium-sized producers in rural areas, organized into associations (LORSA, 2009). This law is strengthened by directly relating to one of the goals of the decentralized regional authorities (DAGs) indicated in article 133 of the OLSSE. This states that these bodies are legitimately allowed to include the execution of programs and projects to foster the strengthening of these producers in their annual planning and budget. The laws for achieving the territorial promotion of the SSE are even more explicit, establishing that the goals of the DAGs within their territories should include "planned participatory development to transform the reality of and boost the SSE, to eradicate poverty, equitably distributing resources and wealth, and achieving Good Living" (COOTAD, 2010, p.8).

At a constitutional, legislative and institutional level, Ecuador has taken essential steps to strengthen the SSE. However, the actions generated by these authorities have limited scope in comparison with the free-market policies implemented from 2017 to 2019. The policies that drive the solidarity economy are framed along the lines of a market economy based on obtaining maximum profits, which raises the issue of a new hypothesis concerning the exciting possibilities of the solidarity economy in the current context within these combined interests (Jiménez, 2016).

THE CASE OF ECUADOR: HIGHLAND INDIGENOUS PEOPLES AND THEIR SOLIDARITY ECONOMY PRACTICES

Ecuador's economic history during the colonial period was marked by the labor exploitation forced on the Native Americans from the Inter-Andean region by *hacienda* landowners[3]. Despite this oppression, the indigenous inhabitants were able to generate initiatives and express some of the behaviors typical of their forebears (although there is sometimes a tendency to forget their active role in inter-ethnic trade, their perception of objects and processes of exchange, the way they articulated these relations, the cooperation between families and the distribution of tasks, etc., (Lanas, 2010). During the colonial and republican periods, the period of the haciendas distanced the indigenous people from their agricultural roots. However, in 1940, how the Native Americans of Otavalo continued to practice reciprocity through different exchange relations remained evident (Korovkin, 2002). Indigenous communities have different ways of relating at the economic level: by reciprocity and not using money as a payment method (Donoso, 2014). These roots of cooperation and solidarity date back to the time of the Incas. Before the Spanish invasion and conquest, forms of voluntary collaboration were already in place among the agricultural collectives when carrying out community and family work. These expressions continue to exist in the rural sectors and are known as *minga, cambio de manos*, and *trabajo mancomunado* among others (da Ros and Flores, 2006).

Minga or *Minka*

Minga is a Quechua word that translates as the equivalent of "a meeting between people invited for some kind of work" and served as the basis of subsistence and coexistence of the *ayllus*[4] (Guevara, 1957, p.22). It is an ancestral practice that has remained firmly in place over time (Obando, 2015) and constitutes the highest expression of indigenous reciprocity and forms the basis of Andean social organization; it strengthens the community's interests based on solidarity redistribution. Minga remains very widely practiced within the family and community sphere and is reflected at times of agricultural activity in building houses and in pre-construction activities (de la Torre and Sandoval, 2004).

Ranti-ranti (Lend-a-Hand)

This is a form of exchange involving the transfer of values, products, and work. Suppose someone shares some of their harvest with a person. In that case, the person receiving that harvest acquires the obligation to act reciprocally and deliver some of their crops to the other in return. This fact means that giving and taking are a never-ending cycle (de la Torre and Sandoval, 2004). The exchange is similar to the *minga*, with the difference that all of the community do not carry it out, but within the family or domestic unit. (Guamán, 2007).

Chucchir (Gleaning)

This is a practice carried out after harvesting, whereby poor people with no land can go to the fields to pick the farmed products (barley, wheat) left behind by the farming machinery (gleaning). The landowners who allow this *chucchir, in turn,* increase their social capital, which they can use in the future. In other words, this practice is considered a transaction of moral credit to be repaid later (Ferraro, 2004).

P'aina

This is a kind of labor that can be carried out by an individual in a short time, such as sweeping, washing plates, making clothes, looking after a vegetable garden, among others; these actions allow the individual to receive food, agricultural products, or clothes in return (de la Torre and Sandoval, 2004).

Barter

This is also a historical practice found in ancient economies. It is a small or large-scale transaction and is present in different types of societies (Humphrey and Hugh-Jones, 1998). Barter is a form of non-monetary exchange. All opportunities to buy and sell must be appropriately balanced; in other words, each bilateral exchange must be proportionate. The value of the article sold by each party equals the value of the purchase (Anderlini and Sabourian, 1998).

Uyanza

Here, those buying new clothes for the major indigenous celebrations must give their used clothes (uyanza) to the community's most impoverished people or those helping with the celebration preparations (de la Torre and Sandoval, 2004).

Uniguilla

This fact is the reciprocal exchange of farm products between different ecological regions based on an ongoing moral commitment between the parties involved. It is expected that the products will be received and reciprocated quickly (Ferraro, 2004).

Prestamanos (Lend-a-Hand)

It is a system whereby an individual asks others to hand in a task to benefit the person asking for help. The others lend their time and effort to completing tasks such as preparing land for sowing, harvesting, building houses, and helping to prepare celebrations, etc. During the day of the labor, the host provides food and drink for all those who have come to help them as a form of exchange for their work. During harvest time, the host will give part of the harvest to the people who have helped them. The person to have asked for help must be prepared to return the favor when asked. (Ferraro, 2004). The quality and quantity of payment are established depending on who benefits from the work. If the person were to refuse to fulfill their responsibilities, they would be qualified as a debtor, meaning that they would be in debt to those who helped them (Fonseca, 1974, p.88).

Changing from a capitalist system to a model focused on community and a sustainable format is a challenge with significant obstacles. Business logic and physical money have entered the lives of indigenous communities, but the forms of economic relationships existing between them refuse to disappear (Acosta, 2013). Given this reality, Andino (2014, p. 121) states that:

Without losing their emancipating character, the viability of these solidarity endeavors is one of the aspects to which we must pay most outstanding attention in our effort to position the Sumak Kawsay paradigm [....]. It is, therefore, a priority to strengthen their viability, which, at least for now, is geared towards achieving minimum sustainability within a capitalist system while deepening their emancipatory character through an increasingly more complete application of the principles of Sumak Kawsay.

METHODOLOGY

The methodology established for this work is far from typical. This fact is because the processes to be examined have no regulations within the conventional economic system. In addition, despite being understood, not all of the necessary information is available for their normalized analysis generates difficulties when attempting to access that information reliably, suitable for reproduction. Hence the complexity of the undertaking and the need to incorporate different research methods to obtain direct, indirect, and informal knowledge. The idea is not to compare the two case studies but to analyze them through processes of implicit contextualized ethnography. Both cases have their own identity and, despite the particular connotations of each collective, the results may be valid for reproduction in other communities. An analytic-synthetic qualitative methodology was chosen based on breaking down the problem to analyze each part separately (history, regulations, group interviews). To make this a valid path for achieving the objectives indicated, the following steps were employed:

1. An extensive and exhaustive analysis was made of academic information to define the object of study (Rodríguez and Valldeoriola, 2007). An investigation was made of similar research by universities in Ecuador, such as the Simon Bolivar Andean University, the Central University of Ecuador, the Latin American Faculty of Social Sciences, the University of Cuenca, etc. Searches were also carried out for works index-linked in high-impact databases (Wos, Scopus, and JCR) using Boolean search strings such as, for example, "Native American justice," "indigenous culture," "alternative economies," "non-monetary economies," "alternative exchanges," "indigenous inequality," "poverty," "Good Living," "Montecristi Constitution," "SSE Ecuador," "public policies," "economic sustainability," etc.
2. A descriptive analysis was made of the existing legislation to discover its evolution and scope, showing a clear development of SSE processes between 2007 and 2017 and 2017 to 2019.
3. Participatory action-research initiatives were developed since the study was approached from an intentional and proactive perspective (Colmenares, 2012). While this phase of the process focused mainly on individuals, this was not exclusively the case, and interpretation of the interviews was, instead, the core element.
4. The qualitative data were collected through interviews with focus groups. This is a scientific tool of recognized use and scope (Rabiee, 2004). The focus group was organized to learn about ancestral practices. It offered considerable advantages over other methods. It enabled the recording of information through feedback on the process between participants that might be missed if another methodology were used (e.g., personal interview, questionnaire, etc.).
5. Furthermore, the focus adopted was easily accessible for researchers and participants (Krueger and Casey, 2014). Indeed, a great deal of theoretical and philosophical literature supports this approach (Draper, 2004). In this case, a group of people was selected who shared similar social characteristics and were comfortable interacting with the interviewer and with one another (Richardson and Rabiee, 2001). The groups consisted of 8 people, aged between 38 and 53 years, from Saraguro and mixed-race groups within the Saraguro and Macará cantons. The interviews were carried out from April 15 to 17, 2019. The participants were invited to recall ancestral practices from their youth through to the present day, thereby making it possible to reach a deeper level of analysis (Morgan, 1997) through interpretation of the information obtained (Fade, 2004) (as shown below).
6. A theoretical study was made of the social phenomena before immediately proceeding with their substantive interpretation based on the taxonomy of incoherencies in the existing legislation, the public policies implemented, and the subsequent synthesis of the participants' opinions.

Case Study Analysis

The Andean community economy enriches and provides content and strength to the solidarity economy. Its logic and approach to the family, which must be maintained throughout the community, makes it necessary to contemplate the collective as a whole even when no blood relationship exists. For example, all suffer if one of the members is ill or falls into poverty and if one of the parties no longer supports the community economy. The current culture of waste and the pillaging and destruction of nature brought about by humans requires an urgent sense of community coexistence to guarantee the lives of individuals and life on the planet (Andrade, Cáceres, and Vásquez, 2014). In this context, the productive initiatives of Ecuador's SSE organizations are guided by principles focused on placing the collective before the

The Social and Solidarity Economics, Public Policies, and Non-Monetary Economic Practices

individual interest and the precedence of work over the capital, based on relations of solidarity, cooperation, and reciprocity[5] (OLSSE, 2011).

1)"Asociación de Servicios de Alimentación, Limpieza y Mensajería Inkan Samana" (ASOINKAN) located in the Saraguro Parish, Saraguro Canton, in the Province of Loja, established on November 19, 2013 (SPSE, 2019b). The association has 25 members (4 men and 21 women) and, according to its corporate purpose, is dedicated to the sale of cleaning and courier services, for which the state is its potential client; 92% of its members are Saraguro Native Americans, and 8% are of mixed race.

According to the Association members, in 1991 and 1992, the government helped by creating crèches in almost all of the communities in the canton. Thanks to these spaces, women could leave their children to work the land in the hills and look after livestock. Some of the women who are now part of the organization worked in these crèches, looking after children for up to twenty years. But in 2012, the state changed the way these centers were run, leaving many women out of work; this situation prompted several of the former workers to create groups and look for work in institutions such as the Ministry of Economic and Social Inclusion (MESI), the ISSE and the SSSE, going on to shape what is now the ASOINKAN. Thanks to this initiative, the members have participated in government procurement processes, becoming suppliers of outsourced food services for the Good Living Centres for Child Development (CDIBV), now called Centres for Child Development, promoted by the former president of Ecuador, Rafael Correa Delgado, who also implemented a state project enabling the acquisition of equipment to increase the productive capacity of the undertaking.

Traditionally, the association members live in communities such as San Jorge, Ilincho, and Kuiskinchir. According to their testimonials, these lands were bought by their parents, grandparents, and great-grandparents with the proceeds obtained from working and tilling the land:

The majority of our forebears saved the money they earned from their work and would put it away to buy land. Money was considered sacred, something that had to be kept, and today in our houses, we still use the saying, "silver to buy land." They earned that money with their livestock, crops, and harvests. My grandparents had quite a lot of land, resulting from those savings and their effort (Medina, 2019a)[6].

The land they bought was used for sowing crops, and that was the basis of the *mingas*:

When people saw that we were getting ready to work, they would come along to help, unsolicited, bringing hoes and oxen; we young people would prepare cucayo (lunch) and take it to them, also doing our bit to help; we had set days for going to these mingas. The mingas were not only communal: families and neighbors would also help one another when sowing, harvesting, clearing scrub and building adobe houses. Sometimes up to 80 of us would gather to work in a minga so that a home would be built in no time; some would flatten the mud, others would cut and place the reeds, and we women would prepare the food (Medina, 2019b).

To prepare celebrations, there were *priostes*[7] and *muñidores*[8], and the guests would bring gifts in the shape of bags of rice, yucca, potatoes, and cabbage, among others, to help the person organizing the celebration. Even though the *priostes* and *muñidores* still exist today, the *pinshir* (help) offered when preparing celebrations is rare, and there is no longer widespread community participation. The same applies to an even lesser extent when referring to clearing scrub, sowing, harvesting, and building houses. Those interviewed consider that help in these aspects has also decreased:

Today you have to pay for everything. For example, before, we would take our oxen to help at the mingas, and in exchange, the landowner would give you a rice dish with a roast guinea pig, cheese, bread, corn beer, and a bottle of alcohol. That was for the person who brought their oxen. Nowadays, if they have to get their oxen, the price is 70 dollars. And if you want them to plow the land, you also have to provide food for the animal owners. Before we shared things, today the oxen have to be rented and cost much more than renting a machine; a machine costs 20 dollars, so I prefer to use a device than oxen. Today you have to pay for everything; if you want to clear scrub, you can't count on people coming to the minga anymore; instead, you have to find someone you can pay to do the job, and the same applies to the harvests (Medina, 2019c).

The Association considers that products obtained from the vegetable gardens and used to make up their diet were largely grain-based. They depended very little on shops. That's why they remember how their parents and grandparents would barter; people from the warmer areas of the canton would bring yucca to exchange for pulses and grains, while others would travel from Saraguro to exchange fresh cheese for sugarcane *panela*. According to their testimonials, such practices are disappearing over time.

Regarding the non-monetary practices carried out by ASOINKAN for the sustainability of its business activity, nobody is paid for the cleaning work according to the members who participated in the focus group. They, as the owners, wash the dishes, dust, and sweep and do not hire employees to do these activities. Between them, they carry out what they call "a daily *minga*," enabling them to sell their services to the state. They buy materials and prepare and distribute food to children's centers, thereby guaranteeing work for all. But an essential practice is *Makitakushun* (lend-a-hand), in which all contribute by carrying out different daily activities in the business. One of the youngest participants believes that the traditional methods of exchange carried out by her forebears are disappearing. According to another of the participants in the study, "*I believe we no longer practice traditional methods of exchange, today money is more important.*" (Cango, 2019).

2) Asociación de Productores Agropecuarios Micro Cuenca Mataderos. This association is located in the Mataderos district of Larama Parish, Macara Canton, in Loja Province. It was established on August 23, 2013 (SPSE, 2019b). It has 23 members (3 women and 20 men) dedicated to farming and fishing according to its corporate purpose. All members of the Association are of mixed race.

The participants in the focus group consider that, 20 years ago, the support for the rural sector was poor, referring to the fostering of their productive initiatives. Such backing came from the president of the government at that time as a result of his political initiative and from institutions such as the Mancomunidad Bosque Seco in the Macará Canton of Larama Parish and the ISSE. These were institutional actions that enabled the Association to start its cheese business. They say that to obtain that backing:

We realized that a legally established organization could launch projects and find openings in different public institutions. This fact encouraged us to create the Association and obtain the necessary backing to build a cheese-making factory. In exchange, we provided the workforce, which is why we love what we do; perhaps if they'd given us everything on a plate, we would not appreciate it today (Valle, 2019a).

The members of the organization, their parents and grandparents, have lived for decades in these territories, but they did not always own these lands:

The Social and Solidarity Economics, Public Policies, and Non-Monetary Economic Practices

These lands belonged to a hacienda bordered the Sozoranga Canton; the owner was a Spanish man called Gustavo Samaniego. He would arrive on horseback, elegantly dressed; his lips were so red they looked as if they were bleeding. This man became the owner by buying the land at ridiculous prices, and once he had purchased the hacienda, he allowed us to live there, paying for the right to stay with our labor. My father worked for around 35 weeks a year at the hacienda, as did all farming families. Control of the weeks to be paid by the owner was recorded on a tarja (a piece of cane), as it was for everyone else. With the agrarian reform, the owners had to sell the land, and he sold 60 hectares to my father, not considering that he had worked that land for him for 40 years (Valle, 2019b).

Those who lived in the Mataderos district would organize *mingas* to do the sowing and would only use hoes; the hosts would provide the food and prepare the *guanchana* (liquor), and the guests would have to do the same when it was their turn to be the hosts.

My father would say to a few folks, "Come to a minga with me, my friend," and they would prepare pork or goat meat and condensed milk. They would be given quite a lot to take home; they would also get coffee, lunch, and supper, and they were given a decent dish of large tamales and marzipan and other foodstuffs to take home. The work wasn't paid, and people were grateful. The mingas were only organized at sowing and harvest time (Valle, 2019c).

The celebrations were hugely exciting occasions and would last for a week, with many people's participation. To build houses, each owner would do the work themselves with their family members, and professionals were rarely hired. According to the information gathered in the sector, the *mingas* have practically disappeared. But they still practice *el vuelto* (return of favors). Today, the celebrations last for a day and build houses; family participation is generally the norm. Furthermore, the way income is obtained has changed; whereas it used to be that, when there were no harvests, there was no money, today, thanks to the milk obtained from their livestock, income is weekly for those who are also involved in that activity.

When there were no harvests, there was no money to be had. That explains the bartering carried out by the parents of some members of the organization. According to their testimonials, they would exchange fresh cheese for agricultural products like yucca, banana, oranges, or plantains in the warmer areas. According to the same testimonials, bartering is rare in the community; given that, today, the rural sector also depends on the market.

Regarding the non-monetary economic practices carried out by the association to sustain their business, they say that the *minga* was the best way to build their cheese factory, substituting money for labor. But they also say that their business activity is maintained by a traditional form of exchange known in the sector as *cambio de manos* or *el vuelto*, practiced by the women who make the cheese at the factory:

At work, we operate based on the cambio de manos system. Our business is made up of three women who produce the cheese; if a sudden situation means that one of us cannot come to work, she speaks to one or both of the others, asking us to lend a hand because she cannot go to make the cheese, saying that she'll return the favor one day or whenever we want. It all works because it is reciprocal (Valle, 2019d).

DISCUSSION

The Constitution of the Republic of Ecuador (2008) states that the national economy is a social and solidarity system, despite the incoherencies existing concerning its implementation and development. Villalba (2019) examines the lack of precision in the National Development Plans and points out the difficulties of shifting from a traditional economic system to a social and solidarity economic system. Today, Ecuador is in the process of establishing and consolidating the processes of sustainability of this "new system." It is essential to point out that the OLSSE is more of a management tool or means of encouragement (including incentives) that will gradually enable this new economy to position itself (Andino, 2013). It is, therefore, the state that must take up the analysis of the project to reform this law, proposed in 2017, to achieve more refined and less theoretical elements based on the reality of the organizations making up the SSE.

The government has implemented myriad institutions and an array of legislation that recognizes SSE processes. However, in Jácome's view (2019):

The state has acknowledged these actors in the constitution and some laws but has not given them recognition, despite knowing that they exist and appreciating the way they live, their principles, the way they function, and their identities. In practical terms, the state does recognize them by expressing in this constitutional mandate or the OLSSE policies, programs, and projects in favor of these organizations, which is where the process of recognition comes into play. Not recognizing them implies only looking at them from the point of view of production; the SSE sector must not therefore only be approached from the economic aspect, it must be considered integrally, redirecting the economic element towards the social, cultural, and political spheres, and that is what is not currently happening.

Therefore, it is necessary to rethink the balance and harmony of public policies and prevent the organizational destructuring of the sectors making up the SSE instead of only focusing on strengthening economic aspects as the core element of well-being.

The two businesses in the case study correspond to specific government policies introduced by the Ecuadorian state to foster the solidarity economy from 2008. On the one hand, ASOINKAN operates successfully in government procurement and the co-financing projects promoted by the ISSE. At the same time, the Micro Cuenca Mataderos Association also successfully develops its activity based on the SSE programs and projects promoted by the Mancomunidad Bosque Seco association to build and strengthen organizations protected by the OLSSE. According to the SSSE (2019) and the official register of non-financial sector businesses, Loja province has 382 active organizations. But in the last five years, only one organization in the province has received co-financing from the ISSE to strengthen the organizational aspect of the association and boost the productive capacity of the business, thereby highlighting the meager budget assigned by the state to promote the business activity of SSE organizations. According to Zurita (2019), the financial arm of the ISSE is too limited to respond to the widespread needs of the sector. Furthermore, its territorial impact is likely to be affected by the national cutbacks launched by the government this year.

In both case studies, the organization members believe that traditional practices of exchange are disappearing. Dependence on the market inexorably pushes them to put a price on the services they would once have lent one another reciprocally, complementary actions focused on the sustainability of their lives and, therefore, of the community. The introduction of work in exchange for wages and micro-farming are behind the rapid disappearance of the *minga* as a communal system of work among the Saraguro Native Americans (Patiño, 2012). Non-monetary economic practices such as the *makitakushun* (lend-a-hand) or el *vuelto*, *minga,* and barter are giving way, over time, to the pressures of the trading system in the era of immediacy. Thus, the logic of capitalism spreads to "all social relations until making it the basis of our lives" (Laval and Dardot, 2017, p.11).

CONCLUSION

Ten years into the constitutional mandate recognizing the economy of Ecuador as being a social and solidarity system, it is evident that the policies implemented during the period have concentrated on development (focused on supervision and control) rather than on implementing real changes to achieve transformation of the system (productive infrastructure) in its territories. The state must examine the processes established for shifting from a mercantilist system to a new economic system combining all of the social and economic realities implicitly developed by the *Sumak Kawsay* principles. In the post-Montecristi Constitution era, it can be said that the work carried out in this decade has done nothing to build the solid pillars needed to ensure the consolidation and future sustainability of this political project as an appropriate instrument of change for the population of Ecuador as a whole, while also meeting its most pressing necessities. These needs arise from the established processes of persistent inequality, in turn, nourished by a de facto change in SSE policies between 2017 and 2019. Consistent changes in the consolidation of the market economy (despite the constitution indicating the contrary) support free trade agreements with made-to-measure arbitration tribunals and an evident dependence on external credit agreements that, once signed, are very difficult to reverse.

The state has sacrificed social and solidarity economic processes to social policy. They are considered an accessory and, to a certain extent, dispensable. Indirectly, Ecuador relates SSE processes to philanthropic methods in which the poor are helped according to capitalist principles rather than by economic policy as stipulated in the constitution. The current regulatory approach to the solidarity economy processes is paradoxical. These processes do not fall under the Ministry of Economic and Finances umbrella but are assigned, de facto, to the Ministry of Economic and Social Inclusion. These actions are also part of processes recognizing the SSE sector as a vehicular economic system and not, as is today, as being subordinate to big business.

Organizations in the solidarity economy manage to make headway amid a dominant economic system rather than a social and solidarity system, with scarce opportunities in the face of today's developmental and effective growth policies. In these conditions, solidarity practices are consigned to memory and are not evident in practice. Thus, the state must return to the path of disseminating SSE processes to all areas of government as an instrument for achieving real social change and local transformations, rather than following the economic mirages of advanced countries in which knowledge and resources that they have no intention of sharing are concentrated. Today, Ecuador must find its own path, and this will never be simply to follow the same course as other countries with disruptive economies focused on capital accumulation. On the contrary, it will always have, within arm's reach, the dignity of its ancestral non-monetary practices as a vital tool for covering the needs of many communities and social realities, such as migrants from rural areas to the city. Here, many find themselves moving from one misery to another, searching for a solution in an unfortunately designed economy only to benefit the few.

REFERENCES

Acosta, A. (2013). *El Buen Vivir. In Sumak kawsay una oportunidad para imaginar otro mundo*. Icaria.

Acosta, A. (2017). Los buenos convivires: Filosofías sin filósofos, Prácticas sin teorías. *Estudios Críticos del Desarrollo V*, 7(12), 153–192. doi:10.35533/ecd.0712.aa

Anderlini, L., & Sabourian, H. (1998). Algunas notas sobre la economía del trueque, dinero y crédito. In *Trueque, intercambio y valor: Aproximaciones Antropológicas*. Abya - Yala.

Andino, V. (2013). *Políticas Públicas para la Economía Popular y Solidaria Caso de Estudio de Ecuador*. RELIESS.

Andino, V. (2014). Continuidades y rupturas entre los enfoques de economía solidaria y desarrollo local. In Y. Jubeto, L. Guridi, & V. Fernández (Eds.), *Diálogos sobre Economía Popular y Solidaria en Ecuador* (p. 121). UPV-Hegoa.

Andrade, C., Cáceres, M., & Vásquez, A. (2014). Cosmovisión andina, Sumak Ally Kawsay y economía comunitaria. In Y. Jubeto, L. Guridi, & V. Fernández (Eds.), *Diálogos sobre Economía Popular y Solidaria en Ecuador* (pp. 174–178). UPV-Hegoa.

Assembly, C. (2008). *Acta 055, Sumario 30 of May 2008*. Quito, Ecuador: Gobierno de Ecuador. Retrieved from https://montecristivive.com/wp-content/uploads/2014/05/acta-055-30-05-2008.pdf

Báez, R., Ospina, P., & Ramón, G. (2004). *Desarrollo Local con énfasis en la gestión de los recursos naturales: Una breve Historial del espacio ecuatoriano*. Camaren.

Banerjee, A. (2019). *Portafolio: El mito de bajar los impuestos a las empresas para subir la inversión*. Retrieved from https://www.portafolio.co/internacional/el-falso-mito-de-bajar-los-impuestos-para-impulsar-la-inversion-534814

Bill of the Organic Law on Social and Solidarity Economy. (2017). Quito, Ecuador: Gobierno de Ecuador. Retrieved from http://2013-2017.observatoriolegislativo.ec/media/archivos_leyes/Objeci%C3%B3n_Total_ Presidente_de_la_Rep%C3%BAblica_Tr._275224.pdf

Cango, C. (2019). *La Economía Popular y Solidaria en Ecuador: Políticas públicas y prácticas económicas no monetarias y sostenibles en los emprendimientos asociativos* (J. Ordoñez, Interviewer). Academic Press.

Cicopa. (2014). *Cooperativas y empleo: un informe mundial*. Bruselas: CICOPA & Grupo Desjardins. Retrieved from http://www.cicopa.coop/cicopa_old/IMG/pdf/ cooperativas_y_empleo_cicopa_es__web_1_pagina.pdf

Código Orgánico de Organización Territorial. (2010). *Autonomía y Descentralización*. Lexis.

Colmenares, E. A. M. (2012). Investigación-acción participativa: Una metodología integradora del conocimiento y la acción. Voces y Silencios. *Revista Latinoamericana de Educación*, 3(1), 102–115.

Constitution of the Republic of Ecuador CRE. (2008). Government of Ecuador.

Coraggio, J. (2014). *La presencia de la Economía Popular y Solidaria y su institucionalización en América Latina, 16*. Ginebra. Retrieved from https://www.coraggioeconomia.org/ jlc/archivos%20 para%20descargar/A%20Ponencia%20ES%20estados%20generales%20junio%202011.pdf

Daros, G. (2007). Economía Solidaria: Aspectos teóricos y experiencias. *Unircoop, 5*(1), 9–19.

Daros, G., & Flores, R. (2006). Realidad y perspectivas de la Economía Popular en Ecuador. In J. Pérez & M. Rodrigán (Eds.), *La Economía Popular en Iberoamérica*. Fundibes.

De La Torre, L., & Sandoval, C. (2004). *La Reciprocidad en el Mundo Andino*. Abya Yala.

Donoso, E. (2014). *Lecciones de las prácticas económicas de las comunidades indígenas Andino-Amazonicas para ser aplicadas en las PYMES*. Retrieved from http://repositorio.flacsoandes.edu.ec:8080/handle/10469/7518

Draper, A. (2004). The principles and application of qualitative research. *The Proceedings of the Nutrition Society, 63*(4), 641–646. doi:10.1079/PNS2004397 PMID:15831137

Fade, S. (2004). Using interpretative phenomenological analysis for public health nutrition and dietetic research: A practical guide. *The Proceedings of the Nutrition Society, 63*(4), 647–653. doi:10.1079/PNS2004398 PMID:15831138

Ferraro, E. (2004). *Reciprocidad, don y deuda Formas de relaciones de intercambios en los Andes de Ecuador: la comunidad de Pesillo*. Abya - Yala.

Fonseca, C. (1974). Modalidades de la Minka. In Reciprocidad e intercambio en los Andes peruanos (p. 88). Lima, Peru: Industrial.

Francisco, P., & Bergoglio, J. (2015). *Carta Encíclica Laudato Si: sobre el cuidado de la casa común. Vaticano*. Retrieved from http://w2.vatican.va/content/dam/ francesco/pdf/encyclicals/documents/papa-francesco_20150524_enciclica-laudato-si_sp.pdf

Guamán, J. (2017). *La perspectiva indígena de la equidad, la reciprocidad y la solidaridad como aporte a la construcción de un Nuevo Orden Económico Internacional*. Retrieved from https://es.scribd.com/document/130539491/La-perspectiva-indigena-de-la-equidad-la-reciprocidad-y-la-solidaridad

Guevara, D. (1957). *Las Mingas en el Ecuador: orígenes, tránsito, supervivencia*. Universitaria.

Harvey, D. (2007). *Breve historia del neoliberalismo*. Akal.

Hernández Zubizarreta, J., & Ramiro, P. (2016). *Contra la Lex Mercatoria*. Icaria.

Huanacuni, F. (2010). *Vivir Bien / Buen Vivir: Filosofía, políticas, estrategias y experiencias regionales*. Instituto Internacional de Integración. Retrieved from https://www.escr-net.org/sites/default/files/Libro%20Buen%20Vivir%20y%20Vivir%20Bien_0.pdf

Humpbrey, C., & Hugb Jones, S. (1998). *Trueque intercambio y valor: Aproximaciones Antropológicas*. Abya - Yala.

INEC. (2019). Retrieved from documentos/web-inec/POBREZA/2018/Diciembre-2018/201812_Pobreza.pdf

International Cooperative Alliance. (2019). *Datos y cifras*. Retrieved from https://www.ica.coop/es/cooperativas/datos-y-cifras

International Labour Organisation. (2019). *Work for a Brighter Future: global Comission on the future of work*. Genova: International Labour Office. Retrieved from https://www.ilo.org/wcmsp5/groups/public/---dgreports/---cabinet/documents/publication/wcms_662410.pdf

ISSE. (2019). *Rendición de Cuentas IEPS*. Retrieved from https://www.economiasolidaria.gob.ec/rendicion-de-cuentas-ieps/

Jácome, H. (2019). *Seminario Internacional Desafíos de la Economía Solidaria y Comunitaria: Acercamientos conceptuales desde las experiencias* (J. Ordóñez, Interviewer). Retrieved from https://grupoess2.wixsite.com/ecosolidariaycomuni

Jácome, V. (2019). *Seminario Internacional Desafíos de la Economía Solidaria y Comunitaria: Acercamientos conceptuales desde las experiencias* (J. Ordóñez, Interviewer). Retrieved from https://grupoess2.wixsite.com/ecosolidariaycomuni

Jiménez, J. (2016). *Avances y Desafíos de la Economía Popular y Solidaria en el Ecuador. Economía Popular y Solidaria: conceptos, prácticas y políticas públicas*. UPV-Hegoa.

Jokisch, B. (2001). Desde Nueva York a Madrid. *Ecuador Debate*, *54*, 59–79.

Korovkin, T. (2002). *Comunidades Indígenas, Economía del mercado y democracia en los Andes Ecuatorianos*. Abya - Yala.

Kowii, A. (2014). El Sumak Kawsay. In *Antología del Pensamiento Indigensita Ecuatoriano* (p. 168). CIM.

Krueger, R., & Casey, M. (2014). *Focus groups: A practical guide for applied research*. Sage publications.

Lanas, E. (2010). El trueque, una forma de economía solidaria en Pimampiro. *Sarence.*, *26*, 13–28.

Lanas, E. (2014). Políticas Públicas sobre Economía Solidaria en Ecuador. *Boletín Informativo Spondylu*, 1-24.

Laval, C., & Dardot, P. (2017). *La pesadilla que no acaba nunca*. Gedisa.

Luque, A. (2017). Promotion of transnational textile hyper-consumption: Fashion and excess as leitmotif. *Revista Chasqui*, *134*, 83–104.

Luque, A. (2018). Corruption in the transnational textile industry: An exception or the rule? *Empresa y Humanismo*, *21*(2), 123–184.

Luque, A. (2019). Gestión del conocimiento y su impacto en la economía mundial en el marco de una sociedad globalizada. *Revista Veritas and Research*, *1*(1), 54–63.

Luque, A., & Casado, F. (2020). Public Strategy and Eco-Social Engagement in Latin American States: An Analysis of Complex Networks Arising from Their Constitutions. *Journal Sustainability*, *12*(20), 1–29. doi:10.3390u12208558

Luque, A., & Herrero García, N. (2019). How corporate social (ir)responsibility in the textile sector is defined, and its impact on ethical sustainability: An analysis of 133 concepts. *Corporate Social Responsibility and Environmental Management*, *26*(6), 1–22. doi:10.1002/csr.1747

Luque, A., Ordóñez, J., & Ruales, V. (2017) La Responsabilidad Social en las Asociaciones de la Economía Popular y Solidaria. *II Congreso Internacional sobre Ciencia, Sociedad e Investigación Universitaria PUCE*. Retrieved from http://repositorio.pucesa.edu.ec/ handle/123456789/2223A

Luque, A., Ortega, T., & Carretero, P. A. (2019). La Justicia indígena en la comunidad de Tuntatacto (Ecuador): Moral o derecho'. *Revista Prisma Social*, *27*, 1–19.

Mason, P. (2016). *Poscapitalismo: Hacia un nuevo futuro*. Paidos.

Medina, G. (2019). *La Economía Popular y Solidaria en Ecuador: Políticas públicas y prácticas económicas no monetarias y sostenibles en los emprendimientos asociativos* (J. Ordóñez, Interviewer). Academic Press.

Ministry of Economic and Social Inclusion. (2013). Agenda de la revolución de la economía popular y solidaria 2011-2013. Quito, Ecuador: Author.

Miño, W. (2013). Historia del Cooperativismo en el Ecuador: Serie Historia de la Política Económica del Ecuador. Quito, Ecuador: Government of Ecuador, and Quito, Ecuador: Ministry Coordinator of Economic Policy.

Morgan, D. (1997). *The focus group guidebook* (Vol. 1). Sage.

Mossbrucker, H. (1990). *La Economía Campesina y el concepto "Comunidad" Un enfoque critico*. Instituto de Altos Estudios Peruanos.

Naranjo, C. (2016). *La economía Popular y solidaria en la legislación ecuatoriana. Serie Estudios sobre Economía Popular y Solidaria: Economía Solidaria Historias y prácticas de su fortalecimiento*. Publiasesores.

Obando, J. (2015). La Minga: Un instrumento vivo para el desarrollo comunitario. *Revista de Sociologia*, *5*(4), 82–100.

Oleas, J. (2016). *La economía Popular y solidaria en el Ecuador: una mirada institucional. Serie de Estudios sobre Economía Popular y Solidaria: Economía Solidaria Historias y prácticas de su fortalecimiento*. Publiasesores.

OLFSR (Organic Law of the Food Sovereignty Regime). (2009). Quito, Ecuador: Ecuador.

Oliván, F. (2019). *La Democracia Inencontrable. Una Arqueología de la Democracia*. Tirant lo Blanch.

OLSSE (Organic Law of Popular and Solidarity Economy). (2011). Corporación de Estudios y Publicaciones.

Oxfam. (2016). *Una Economía al servicio del 1%*. Recuperdo el 06 de 04 de 2019, de https://www-cdn.oxfam.org/s3fs-public/file_attachments/bp210-economy-one-percent-tax-havens-180116-es_0.pdf

Passet, R. (2013). *Las grandes representaciones del mundo y la economía a lo largo de la historia: del universo mágico al torbellino creador*. Madrid, Spain: Clave intelectual.

Patiño, O. (2012). *Memoria Oral del pueblo Saraguro*. Serie Estudios.

Pianovi, M. (2012). Análisis Comparado de Experiencias de Economía Popular y Solidaria en Tres Países del Mercosur: El caso de Argentina, Brasil y Paraguay. *La Saeta Universitaria*, *1*(1), 62–78.

Piketty, T. (2014). *La crisis del capital en el siglo XXI*. Anagrama.

Rabiee, F. (2004). Focus-group interview and data analysis. *The Proceedings of the Nutrition Society*, *63*(4), 655–660. doi:10.1079/PNS2004399 PMID:15831139

Richardson, C., & Rabiee, F. (2001). A question of access: An exploration of the factors that influence the health of young males aged 15 to 19 living in Corby and their use of health care services. *Health Education Journal*, *60*(1), 3–16. doi:10.1177/001789690106000102

Rodríguez, D., & Valldeoriola, J. (2007). *Metodología de la Investigación*. Universitat Oberta de Catalunya.

Saiz-Alvarez, J. M., Castillo-Nazareno, U. H., Matute de León, J. S., & Alcívar-Avilés, M. T. (2021). Post-COVID Indigenous Women Entrepreneurship: A Case of the Kichwa-Puruha in Ecuador. In N. Baporikar (Ed.), *Handbook of Research on Strategies and Interventions to Mitigate COVID-19 Impact on SMEs* (Vols. 1–2, pp. 225–234). IGI Global. doi:10.4018/978-1-7998-7436-2.ch021

Sánchez, F. (2012). La Cosmovisión Quichua en Ecuador: Una Perspectiva para la Economía Solidaria del Buen Vivir'. *Cuadernos Americanos*, *4*(142), 39–51.

Sánchez, J. (2016). *Institucionalidad y políticas para la economía popular y solidaria: balance de la experiencia ecuatoriana. Serie de Estudios sobre la Economía Popular y Solidaria Economía Solidaria. Historias y prácticas de su fortalecimiento*. Publiasesores.

Sassen, S. (2015). *Expulsiones: brutalidad y complejidad en la economía global*. Katz. doi:10.2307/j.ctvm7bdqr

SENPLADES. (2019). *Plan Toda una Vida*. Retrieved from http://www.planificacion.gob.ec/biblioteca/

SERCOP. (2019). *La compra pública en cifras: Boletín anual – 2018*. Retrieved from https://portal.compraspublicas.gob.ec/sercop/wp-content/uploads/downloads/2019/01/boletin_sercop_anual_2018-1.pdf

SSSE. (2019a). *Catastro sector no financiero y boletín financiero 2018*. Quito. Retrieved from http://www.seps.gob.ec/estadistica?boletin-financiero-sf-y-snf

SSSE. (2019b). Retrieved from https://servicios.seps.gob.ec/gosnf-internet/paginas/organizacion.jsf

Valle, M. (2019). *La Economía Popular y Solidaria en Ecuador: Políticas públicas y prácticas económicas no monetarias y sostenibles en los emprendimientos asociativos* (J. Ordóñez, Interviewer). Academic Press.

Velecela, P. (2017). Finanzas personales: La influencia de la edad en la toma de decisiones financieras. *Killkana Social.*, *1*(3), 81–88. doi:10.26871/killkana_social.v1i3.66

VIllalba, U. (2019). *Seminario Internacional Desafíos de la Economía Solidaria y Comunitaria: Acercamientos conceptuales desde las experiencias* (J. Ordóñez, Interviewer). Quito, Ecuador: Universidad Central del Ecuador. Retrieved from https://grupoess2.wixsite.com/ecosolidariaycomuni

Yépez, P. (2015). Tradiciones Indígenas en el mundo moderno y su incidencia en la educación intercultural. *Sophia, 18*(1), 231–251.

Zurita, R. (2019). *La Economía Popular y Solidaria en Ecuador: Políticas públicas y prácticas económicas no monetarias y sostenibles en los emprendimientos asociativos* (J. Ordóñez, Interviewer). Academic Press.

KEY TERMS AND DEFINITIONS

Anthropocene: Over the last several centuries, much of humanity has had such a negative impact on the environment, as well as other unpredictable consequences, that some scientists have described this period as a new geological age: the era of human impact on the Earth, or Anthropocene.

Consumerism: This is an economic, social, and political phenomenon. Postmodernity and the development of various models of production and consumption idealize the tendency to accumulate unnecessary goods and services, transforming the need for the acquisition of goods into excessive and indiscriminate consumption. This fact leads to the depletion of natural resources and an ecological imbalance resulting from increased waste and other adverse environmental impacts.

Economic Globalization: This is a phenomenon in an expansion that causes profound changes on the world stage. It revolves around trade, the flow of investment, financial capital, division of labor, and specialization. The concept is not limited only to economic variables since its effects extend to individuals, society, to the state. Developing countries are experiencing stagnation in the face of their inability to cope with globalization, which is compounded by poor management of their financial markets, leading to an increase in the income inequality gap. Economic globalization brings with it the mobilization of goods and capital, reduces the distance between borders, and energizes international trade with some alterations to sovereignty.

Public Policy: This refers to decisions and actions that a government takes when addressing public or collective issues.

Redistribution of Wealth: The transfer of wealth from one individual to another through a social mechanism such as taxation, charity, or public services. It aims to bridge the inequality gap between members of a society.

Resilience: Transformations within a complex system related to the capacity for self-organization while maintaining internal structure, together with the ability to create adaptive responses, generate knowledge, experience, and learning. Resilience and sustainability are directly related to changes within societies, economies, and the entire human system. The transformation of systems is inevitable since it allows systems to strengthen and maintain sustainability over time. The potential for change facilitates renewal and organization.

Rurality: This relates to the degree of industrialization and general development of a region. It is concerned with more sparsely populated areas containing spaces to develop primary activities, being a source of natural resources. It involves complex socio-economic cultural models interrelated through the exchange of goods as a basis for economic activities. It also concerns the move from the traditional to the modern as a vector of progress.

Social and Solidarity Economy: This places human beings as the first and last consideration in economic activities and is an alternative approach to the market economy. It relates to organizations, co-operatives, associations, or companies that aim to produce goods, services, and knowledge for economic purposes while simultaneously focusing on social implications and fostering solidarity.

Traditional Practices: Actions and knowledge produced by local communities over many generations through which their behavior and autochthonous environment may be better understood.

ENDNOTES

[1] "*Sumak* means perfection, beauty, goodness, fulfillment; and *Kawsay* is life, referring to a decent life, in harmony and balance with the universe and the human being. In short, *Sumak Kawsay* means Good Living" Kowii, (2014, p.168).

[2] See First Supplement No. 819 Tuesday, 16 August 2016 https://www.registroficial.gob.ec/index.php/registro-oficial-web/publicaciones/suplementos/item/8253-suplemento-al-registro-oficial-no-819

[3] The landowners controlled the land, having taken possession of the *hacienda* complexes left by the Jesuits on their expulsion in 1767. Furthermore, they took control of 49.3% of the indigenous serfs who lived on the *haciendas* as *huasipungueros*, while the other 50.6% lived as freemen in the villages, although sometimes they too provided their services as farmhands on the *haciendas* (Báez, Ospina, & Ramón, 2004).

[4] The *ayllus* are groups of similar kinship consisting of one or more families (Mossbrucker, 1990).

[5] Articles 1 and 4 of the Organic Law on Social and Solidarity Economy.

[6] An explanation is given to the effect that several Association members with the surname of Medina participated in the focus group. Medina is a common surname in the area analyzed.

[7] The celebration hosts.

[8] The people responsible for the church flower arrangements.

Chapter 13
Business Model Creation for Cost Saving in the New World Economic Order

Beatriz Olalla-Caballero
https://orcid.org/0000-0002-1042-2675
Pontifical University of Salamanca, Spain

Montserrat Mata
Deusto University, Spain

ABSTRACT

Globalization and economy features in this new world economic order due to SARS-CoV-2 pandemic crisis involve taking into account new ideas and proposals to keep the market share and to fight against competition. It is very important to consider and evaluate the business model of a company to drive all the objectives and the strategy towards the aimed position in the market to assure the market share in the future. Evaluation and analysis of a business model, together with new proposals regarding it may help a company to achieve all the objectives and to increase its competitiveness in the market.

INTRODUCTION

SARS-CoV-2 pandemic has made it challenging to address with standard macroeconomic tools, as Baldwin and Di Mauro (2020) explain, and there could be a world Gross Domestic Product (GDP) growth decrease of between 0.5 and 1.5%, being most of the impact attributed to lower demand. However, uncertainty should also be considered in that scenario. These moderate to principal contractions in demand may also be responsible for boosting unemployment and moderating price rises, according to Maital and Barzani (2020). This fact is the cause of an urgent need for enterprises to reinvent themselves while a creative economy is developed worldwide to decrease the pandemic's impact (Nobre, 2020). This fact may have involved a double market and economic evolution, which has led any company to change and benefit from the transformation. This fact has the goal of leading a healthy company and generating profits continu-

DOI: 10.4018/978-1-7998-7689-2.ch013

ously over time. Therefore, it is essential to consider themes such as co-creation, open innovation, and social responsibility. The concept of circular economy surrounds; in fact, this is a reality that companies have more or less strictly adopted. Based on the experience and the analysis of more than 15 companies, it has been seen that no one wants to lose this opportunity, and they have quickly incorporated some changes to be competitive. With the mindset of being a market leader, it is indispensable to think about promoting Environmental, Social, and Governance (ESG) criteria to be at the forefront of the market and because it is a factor analyzed by investors looking for good options for investment (Chen, 2019). The ability of these companies to attract them will enhance their value and image.

To become a benchmark reference in the market and offer a rising value, any leader, CEO (Chief Executive Officer), or CFO (Chief Financial Officer) needs to consider that they need a good business model and believe in the power of innovation. Nowadays, it cannot be forgotten that continuous changes have forced any company to adapt and adopt new techniques, which has to be inspired by this leader. There is a close link between innovation and business models (Palma-Ruiz, Saiz-Alvarez, & Herrero-Crespo, 2020). Carried out by the changing economic market, it has appeared several trends can be seen as a change of paradigm. Among those innovations can be mentioned the eco-innovation, a way to increase benefits and the company's public image, attracting investors and consequently improving its economic position in the global market (Garrido et al., 2014).

One remarkable point when talking about innovation is creativity, and thus, the main difference between companies is creativity. It is essential to consider that Canvas is the best-chosen option to build a creative and resilient business model, whose methodology is analyzed in this chapter. According to Naggar (2015), a good business model approach includes a deep understanding of the activities and resources to know how to finance them. Whatever the business model applied, a deep study and detailed analysis are required to clarify what will create value for the company and the customers. Conclusion: there have to be several changes to focus on a customer-centric mindset to develop and deliver suitable customer solutions. A new way of organization leads to innovation and ultimately a difference in the company's strategy (Kates & Galbraith, 2010). The company's final goal is to have the best economic profitability, and this logical goal implies a risk, which will be proportional to the desired or objective profitability.

For all these reasons, the Canvas model has been proposed as a good option; working on it and defining it with a clear idea will lead the company to better results, decreasing risks and placing it at the forefront of innovation. This chapter explains why this model can help any company ensure its profitability and, therefore, its permanence in the global market by supporting the strategy of innovation of products, processes, or services (Boons & Lüdeke-Freund, 2013).

This chapter aims to analyze all the issues to be taken into account when talking about business models and the benefits they can offer to a company regarding obtaining benefits and increasing the market share. All these facts are analyzed and prioritized. A business model proposal is detailed based on the business model defined for some Information Technologies (IT) services offered in an IT European firm. The authors of this chapter described and implemented this business model proposal in all these services to obtain value, gathering all the critical issues and critical success factors from the business model literature. Finally, a post-implementation review is developed to analyze the results and lessons from this experience to identify the Critical Success Factors (CSF) when defining and implementing business models.

SHORT TERM ECONOMY

In recent years, enterprises are fighting against a continuous transformation of the economy and markets, taking different strategies into account for this constant change. Economic rules and focus have constantly changed with globalization, creating an uncertain atmosphere where a corporation must make the correct path to success. Every few years, some technologies bring changes in the economy of almost all countries (Kwilinski, 2019). This success depends on many factors and issues, and obviously, on the enterprise's strategy and how agile a company is to constantly drive into the correct way. The quick and accurate movement is the most considerable success for the company. In this scenario, where to invest, policies to follow, Information and Communication Technology (ICT) development are examples of essential issues to be considered. Pradhan et al. (2019) studied how economic growth and ICT infrastructure development affect all stages of venture capital investment after analyzing 25 European countries between 1989 and 2016.

According to Fjeldstad and Snow (2018), the global economy is becoming digital, networked, and knowledge-based. Those features make firms constantly reconsider their business models and sometimes modify them if necessary, to adapt to new and changing conditions. There is another concept to be considered nowadays, and that is Circular Economy (CE). This new economy focuses on the circulation of materials in closed-loop production systems to reduce resource depletion and eliminate waste. In addition, this fact involves changing a company's business model (Henry et al., 2020), besides a difference in an enterprise's projects and risk management (Olalla-Caballero & Mata-Fernández, 2020).

Innovation capacity and competitiveness are crucial to afford that way to success and to maintain a company firmly in the market through the years. Companies search for innovations to attain new customers or maintain their market share (García-Sánchez et al., 2019). Business Model Innovation (BMI) consists of a systemic change that affects the companies' values proposition and how this value is generated (García-Muiña et al., 2020).

Human capital is also a critical success factor that might help a company fight in the market, consolidating itself in a vital position. For example, Prado-Prado et al. (2020) identify critical aspects for successfully implementing business participation programs. The networking perspective has also to be considered because networking rules are essential in current companies. In this line, social capital may also impact competitiveness and innovation, according to Capiello et al. (2020). They documented the effects of an innovation network established by a regional government institution in Italy on the performance of the participating firms. Innovation may make an enterprise more advanced, efficient, and, therefore, more productive, according to García-Sánchez et al. (2019). According to research developed in 28 European Union countries by Rusu and Dornean (2019), there is a positive relationship between entrepreneurial activity measured by innovation and job creation and economic competitiveness. Ghezzi and Cavallo (2020) explain how to face BMI through agile methods.

This competitiveness is also associated with businesses addressing the demands of clients and their ability to create a value anticipated by consumers (Vasilienė-Vasiliauskienė et al., 2019). This study details a competitiveness improvement strategy and shows that the deployment of the Business Canvas Model may accurately identify a realistic business photograph and its weaknesses. Competitiveness is also significant for a company when adapting to the information economy (Kwilinski, 2019). A mechanism for assessing competitiveness is suggested to be considered in a company in compliance with innovative approaches. Competitiveness may be viewed as a strategy to improve the macroeconomy in a country (Staehr & Vermeulen, 2019). Thus, it could be regarded as an essential factor to accelerate market share increase in a company. Competitiveness is also a combination of institutions, policies, and elements, which determine the productivity level of territory, according to Zeibote et al. (2019).

Kwilinski (2019) proposes a model, which involves three components: comparative evaluation of the competitiveness, the capacity of an enterprise to introduce new technologies, and integrated quantitative assessment of competitiveness. Farinha and Bagchi-Sen (2019) highlight the role of innovation in the competitiveness of Small and Medium-Sized Enterprises (SMEs) and innovation and entrepreneurship networks in enhancing the functions of a high-technology Portuguese industrial cluster. According to Amit and Zott (2012), business model innovation might also help companies stay ahead in product innovation and represent a source of future value. A business model that may create a new market or allow a company to develop and exploit new opportunities in existing markets (Amit & Zott, 2012) can significantly benefit the innovator. However, competitiveness and sustainability, designing and implementing Sustainable Business Models (SBMs) (Evans et al., 2017). They explain the concept of sustainable value as an important issue when considering business models. It is essential to believe that the pressure for businesses to respond to sustainability concerns is increasing (Joyce & Paquin, 2016). Sustainable business models may offer a competitive advantage, a growing brand reputation, and cost reduction (Nosratabadi et al., 2020). Besides those advantages, BMC is proven positive and significantly improves learning achievement (Hutasuhut et al., 2020).

Short-term strategies are focused on having a benefit in a period between three and six months, trying to cover necessities in this short term. These strategies are common when promoting new services or products, without forgetting that life cycles are getting shorter and customer needs change continuously (Teece, 2010). On the contrary, long-term strategies want to profit in four or five years, putting special attention on the general objectives and staying on the market as long as possible. Some of the advantages of short term strategies are the following ones:

- They are usually easier to implement.
- They try to use the talent already in the company avoiding the costly process of hiring new people.
- It reduces the time dedicated to preparing everything to launch a new product or service to demand less time for everybody.
- The feeling of the staff and even the clients is that of agility. This fact leads to the idea of a company with a brief adaptation period.
  On the contrary, some of the disadvantages are detailed below:
- It seems to be a quick solution without a solid base; it is seen as a company that does not want to miss the opportunity but without the capacity to adopt changes adequately in the short term.
- The communication plan has not been prepared well, so the message can be distorted or incomplete, creating confusion mainly between staff.
- It can be forgotten essential issues due to the urgency to start. Consequently, the investment made may not generate the expected benefits.

It is critical to surviving in the market to understand the investment behavior and customers' preferences for extended benefits. Traditional finance theories held that investment behavior is rational. Anyway, in the study carried out in this chapter. After studying the behavior of 15 companies from sectors as disparate as finance insurance or telco, it can be seen that investors do not act so rationally, primarily when they are influenced by emotional and rational elements, added to other sociological factors (Mak & Ip, 2017).

The environment where companies have to compete nowadays has changed radically. The market is now hypercompetitive, interdependent, and networked, so new ideas have to be used and applied to survive and grow. It has changed mainly due to globalization, which has carried on unique technological advantages, a shorter duration for competitive advantage, and the broadening of participation in every field, but especially in the development of companies (Von Hippel et al., 2011). So, firms must study how to improve benefits and set business strategies to make a profit in the long term when offering a product or a service. Firms need to think about some ideas: risks, but not in a traditional way but widening them to concepts as bankruptcy risk or credit risk, high transaction costs, or explanations of the behavior of investors under-reaction. The most critical points for any company to have long-term survival with healthy finances and constant profits improvement are detailed below.

Co-creation will be an essential point to be introduced in the company strategy because the benefits of the collaboration between customers and companies have been seen. Now is more important than before because the focus is on the client and their preferences. The final goal is to meet the demands of clients in the most efficient way. The importance of co-creation is primary for its links with technological platforms, facilitators of the emergence of new ideas and therefore of innovation, the customer participation, and to sum up, crucial to give better customer services. Everyone can benefit from widespread access to information, improving communication between all involved (Daxboeck, 2013). Co-creation will also help companies offer better customer satisfaction and innovation results and understand the customer, considering them as part of their value processes (Gummesson et al., 2014).

Another aspect of having in mind is that companies are no longer local. The global market and the complex and interconnected environment make it necessary to have a new business model, an innovation model based on the integration of external and internal ideas and the collaboration to create and shared value, a value that will allow it to survive more time and with better results. This issue has been called co-innovation, this has been considered a mega-trend, and it will require companies to cover several factors to be included in the co-innovation firms that lead the market (Lee et al., 2012). The use of technology and social networks has made it possible to share knowledge and ideas, where the main point is the innovation, which has turned into a platform based on collaborative arrangement, the sharing of ideas, convergent expertise, and co-creation with stakeholders and customers (Co-innovation)(Von Hippel et al., 2011). It is an excellent factor that facilitates creating value for the company and stakeholders.

It must cover all these points to have an agile leader because the company will have to change its strategic vision to have an innovative culture, becoming more and more common to have international strategic alliances. New leaders have to nurture cultural empathy as part of the key to success, and they need to be able to execute effective behavior. The old idea of a leader with broad knowledge is not enough in this new context. They have to prove that they have applied all that knowledge. They have to be competent from the point of view of an excellent performance tied to knowing (Gutierrez et al., 2008). More than ever, their ability to put failure into perspective, have a high level of resilience, and develop strategic and innovative thinking to push the company to change direction is essential (Pech, 2013). According to García-Muiña et al. (2020), BMI allows these practices to be considered operational and in the company's value creation strategy.

BUSINESS MODELS AND CANVAS ANALYSIS

It is crucial to understand and know the term Business Model (BM) and its origins. In 1994, Peter Druker introduced this concept in an HBR (Harvard Business Review) paper, talking about the company's set of assumptions. His vision was close to the definition of strategy given by Michael Porter, who thought it was necessary to understand the market and competitors to establish the way to do business (Porter, 2008), and several authors refer to Drucker's idea when talking about BM (Ovans, 2015). According to Osterwalder et al. (2005), it is a tool to understand how a company does business; it will have a set of objects, concepts, and relationships to express its business logic. It has two great functions: create value by defining a set of activities, and capture a portion of this value by creating a value, from the point of view of an activity that allows the company to have a competitive advantage (Chesbrough, 2006). It was used for the first time in processes and data modeling, but the idea extended and in the '90s was applied by practitioners working in emerging and disruptive new technologies. Anyway, after that, it was used in other spheres, and it is a term widely referenced nowadays by many authors, being appropriated for unpredictable, changing, and uncertain environments.

Due to its importance, it is necessary today to have a good business model for leading a successful company. A good BM has to focus on the source of the benefits: the customers, because they will choose this company or another, so it is essential to know who they are and what they want. This fact has to be combined with the company's strategy. According to Magretta (2002), strategy and business model are not the same. When the company has to deal with its competitors, the plan has to be applied. The business model can be excellent and innovative, but the rivals could use the same business model, but probably with another strategy, succeeding and becoming the leader. The development of a business model is part of the strategic planning of any company, and it implies changes at an individual and organizational level. Conceiving, creating, and executing a new and different strategy makes the company different from competitors. Nowadays, adopting a new model is necessary and provides the company with a halo of avant-garde, transparency, and quick response to changes in the global market. This fact will have two direct consequences: it will attract customers and investors, giving the company a better economic result, and if its answer to changes continues being quick, this status will be maintained in the future. Four new ideas appeared in the business model, and that deserves to be considered (McGrath, 2010):

- It is oriented more to an outside-in focus than to an inside-out. As a consequence of the changing global market, the idea is to analyze and see what the customers need, so flexibility has to be high.
- BM cannot be static. They need to change, experiment and learn to develop the best BM for the company.
- The market is dynamic, so it has to be the BM because what one day can be seen as the best sustainable model can turn into unsustainable in a short period. The CEO has to be aware of what is happening outside and adapt to have good benefits and continue to grow.
- Adopting a business model needs the development of a strategy based more on discovery than on planning.

The development of a BM is closely related to the strategy and the financial aspects. The capacity to renew the model is a key for the company's growth (Gamez-Gutierrez, & Saiz-Alvarez, 2021). The environment is changing, and practical financial management is fundamental to its growth and maintenance in an advantageous position than the competition, so it is the chosen BM. A BM may be defined as a system of resources and activities that might create value for the customer and, thus, benefit the company. Li (2020) explains different trends and variants of business models that may be considered in companies. Other business models may be developed and implemented, even agile (Ghezzi & Cavallo, 2020), but the most commonly recognized is the Business Model Canvas (BMC).

According to Amanullah et al. (2015), to create a good BMC, it is necessary to apply what has been called creativity. This creative process will generate ideas about business models, helping choose among the best ones for the company. The main idea is to forget the past, start from scratch, and try to ignore competitors to focus on the necessities of the customers, those unsatisfied, new ones, or candidates to be in the future. Canvas is a model created and designed by Alexander Osterwalder and Yves Pigneur and is a helpful tool to analyze and create new business models simply and comprehensively. His contribution is mainly because his model could answer how to create, capture and deliver value in a global and complex market (McFarlane, 2017). This model is integrated into the lean-startup methodology, based on finding and promoting new ways of creating, giving, and capturing value.

Among the benefits, the following ones can be mentioned (Gavrilova et al., 2014):

- Enhances the comprehension due to its image and its capacity to synthesize.
- Widen the focus points, being centered on the strategic and relevant topics for the company.
- Improve the strategic analysis.
- Integrate multiple perspectives, helping a better understanding and coordination between everyone.
- Creates engagement and involvement among people, being a focus of inspiration and so on improving creative thinking.
- It is focused on quality more than on quantity. Its construction is simple and carries on an agile mentality of planning that has to be reviewed, tested, and revamped frequently (Amanullah et al., 2015).

This model is based on nine building blocks covering four main business areas: customers, offer, infrastructure, and financial viability. Those nine blocks are the following ones (Osterwalder & Pigneur, 2010):

1. Customer Segment. It can be considered the heart of the BMC. The segments can be grouped by common behaviors, needs, or other attributes.
2. Value Propositions. This block solves a customer's need or problem, and it is related to the product or service offered to have a good economic return.
3. Channels can be owned, which will give a high margin or partner, with a lower margin. Among the first ones, it can also be distinguished between direct or indirect.
4. Customer Relationships are driven by customer retention, customer acquisition, or boosting sales (upselling). It has several categories that can co-exist with a specific customer segment: Personal assistance, Dedicated personal assistance, Self-service, Automated services, and Communities.
5. Revenue Streams. There are two different types: transaction revenues or recurring revenues. In addition, the way to generate them can be by asset sale, usage fee, subscription fees, and advertising, licensing, lending, brokerage fees.
6. Key Resources. They allow you to create and offer a value proposition.
7. Key Activities. These are actions that the company has to do to operate successfully. Moreover, they are categorized on production, platform, and problem-solving.

8. Key Partnerships. Some highlighted options include joint ventures, coopetition, the buyer-supplier relationship, or strategic alliances. In addition, the motivation for doing it goes from optimizing an economy of scale to reducing risk.
9. Cost Structure. It can be cost-driven or value-driven.

Watson (2005) evaluates business models through several components, such as competitors, customers, economy, management, products, and suppliers. Johnson et al. (2008) identify four elements in business models to be considered: Customer Value Proposition (CVP), profit formula, key resources, and critical processes. Some companies look for some challenges when creating and implementing a business model, such as (Evans et al., 2017):

- Keep and increase company benefits (profits, social or environmental).
- Company culture redefinition is defined with procedures, rules, or norms that may conflict with implementing a business model).
- Resources reallocation done to cover new business model implementation.
- Integration between technology and BMI. Regarding this issue, it is essential to consider that digital technologies are used to transform business models, according to Li (2020).
- Maintain and reinforce external relationships and the interest of stakeholders.
- Get the most considerable value from business model modeling methods and tools.

Shafer et al. (2005) explain how business models can serve a positive and decisive role in corporate management, although they must not be considered as a strategy in a company. Chesbrough (2010) explains how companies may obtain benefits by developing the capability to innovate their business models, detailing BMI barriers. Baden-Fuller and Morgan (2010) describe how business models classify businesses in a taxonomy or a typology.

Austin (2020) defines the BMC as strategic management and lean startup business model template and compares this model with Business Survival Growth Model (BSGM). There are several components to be taken into account in business models (customer, revenues, competitors, strategy, suppliers, information, resources, cost) and may be classified into four primary categories: strategic choices, the value network, creating value, and capturing value (Shafer et al., 2005). Osterwalder and Pigneur (2010) consider nine factors in a business model Canvas: customer segment, value proposition, channel, customer relationship, revenue stream, key resources, key activities, key partnership, and cost structure.

Other authors propose a Triple Layer Business Model Canvas (TLBMC) that considers new features added to the original BMC: environmental and social impact layers. It is extended by drawing connections across the three layers to support an integrated triple bottom line perspective of organizational impact (Joyce & Paquin, 2016). It allows a company to achieve a more sustainable perspective in the business model through a horizontal and vertical coherence among the three layers.

The SBM is centered on the company's collaboration to deliver sustainability, and it considers the interest of stakeholders but paying particular attention to the environment and social responsibility. It is closely related to concepts such as eco-innovation and eco-efficiency. This model will probably need to change what was defined as the firm's purpose and what was considered a value that will have to be rethought (Bocken et al., 2014).

A PROPOSAL TO CREATE VALUE IN A LONG TERM

BM may create value-gaining effectiveness in business model innovation, focusing on the three phases of collaboration with customers: value proposition definition, value provision design, and value-in-use delivery (Sjödin et al., 2020). Success aligns specific value creation and capture activities in each phase, and additional values may be generated.

When trying to identify how to create value in the long term implementing a business model, the following ones are considered in the services analyzed:

- **Customer loyalty and satisfaction**. It is vital to assure the market share and continue offering IT services in the mid and long-terms.
- **Competitiveness in the market**. It is essential to maintain the competitiveness in the market against other competitors to fight in this market to assure the market share in the long term.
- **A solid corporate image in markets and employees**. It is a fundamental issue to improve the corporate image to become a reference firm in the market because employment rotation reduces. After all, employees could find an excellent opportunity to work, avoiding taking all the knowledge with them leaving the company.
- **Benefits obtained maintaining or even increasing service quality**. Offering IT high-quality services is vital to be competitive in the market and to provide a differential value to customers among competitors.
- **Environmental adaptation capacity**. Flexibility and adaptability are two significant features to adapt and survive in a changing environment.

Several activities may be developed to identify value creation opportunities, agree on value distribution, design the value offering, decide on the profit formula, and refine value creation processes, according to Sjödin et al. (2020).

Considering all the information analyzed and the experience obtained from the business models implemented to offer IT services, a new way to work with Canvas based on the original one is proposed below:

1. **Customer Segment**. New techniques based on big data are needed to be applied to have a better result and to integrate customer behavior. Traditionally big data has been seen from the point of view of the four V's that specify its challenge: high velocity, large volume, wide variety, and uncertain veracity, but there is another V to be added and is the added value that big data can give to process or other activities like the analysis of the best segment to offer a new product or service (Kaufmann, 2019). The Chief Information Officer (CIO) will have to create a team to analyze and study the large and complex data storage. This team will be formed by consultants and people with knowledge in neuromarketing. The benefit of the collected data with the team's work will select the best customers for the product or service offered.
2. **Value Propositions**. Nowadays, it is more important than ever to know what the client is expecting to receive. As a result, firms have to be leaders in offering something that meets the required quality standards and is attractive enough to capture the client's interest in oversaturated markets endowed with offers and news. New services such as blockchain or powerful advertising campaigns can be issued before the service or product launch to reach this goal.

3. **Channels**. All the companies know different and multiple channels to communicate with clients; the difference is how to combine and use them. We must eliminate the idea that a channel is only for a particular sector, forget some channels' possible prejudices, and use them as a vehicle to transmit the new service or product that the company wants to offer.
4. **Customer Relationships**. It is more difficult to increase customer loyalty, so originality is necessary to establish a close link between the company and the customer. To do this, the work of the marketing department is more important than before. It has been proven that relationship marketing and customer loyalty is determinant in successful business operations (Ngoma & Ntale, 2019). The main point is to listen to the customer and to let him know he has been understood, so the concept of feedback is now mandatory. The company must have an eclectic group to analyze customers' opinions to provide the best answer and detect unfounded or false views.
5. **Revenue Streams**. It would be advisable to have a good service catalog to choose the best way to obtain better revenues. This catalog must be aligned with client necessities to be transparent and based on customer requirements and employees' contributions. The result has to be good enough to allow everyone to choose the best revenue stream.
6. **Key Resources**. The power of things like gamification and cooperative social media in a company has been proven. Employees are probably the most critical company asset, so it is determinant to let them cooperate. They will share not only documentation but also knowledge and, what is more important, ideas. The company will be transformed into a think tank.
7. **Key Activities**. As long as the key activities are identified, it will be possible to measure them and improve their quality. To get a more accurate calculation, the balanced scorecard can be used. The combination of optimum quality management and a good balance scorecard will allow the company to achieve the business purpose because it will be easier to focus on the most critical activities.
8. **Key Partnerships**. New alliances will be necessary. Nowadays, any company has to be updated, analyze and study new startups to create a win-win situation. Companies will also have to be alert about crowdfunding initiatives.
9. **Cost Structure.** To have a sound vision of the number of costs, the focus has to be on the company's cost model. In this case, it can be used and applied both in value-driven and cost-driven. Some company people have to downsize costs, giving a detailed level to optimize some of the costs and, therefore, obtain a profit.
10. **Competitors**. People's behavior regarding business has changed in the last years, and this has a clear reflection on how they react in their organizations. This fact will include not only aspects like individual or group behavior but also environmental and organizational behavior. It is crucial now to study the change through an analysis as PESTLE that explores the Political, Economic, Social, Technological, Legal, and Ecological issues that affect both employees and the organization (Buchanan & Huczynski, 2019).
11. **Strategy**. A leader's role has to be considered what they do, what kind of situations they lead, and what the market expects (Smircich & Morgan, 1982). They need to focus on what could happen in a changing environment. It is also essential to adapt ideas or ways of working from other models as lean.
12. **Stakeholders**. The possibilities of communication in the past were more limited than now. Social networks, especially virtual ones, have made it possible to interact with people and organizations with different and even contradictory points of view. These networks are known as Online Social

Networks (OSNs). Now it is possible to share information and have a quick feedback to allow the organization time to react to achieve the desired goal (Franchi et al., 2013).

There is a summary in Table 1 that gathers all these items and technological enablers and model sources:

Table 2 is based on the application of our model in the IT services industry. The relationship between CSFs and the technological enablers listed for every area or component in the business model is summarized. Also, we show on a 3-level scale how they collaborate to obtain every aspect of the long-term value created in the firm. A high contribution is assigned a "3", a medium contribution is given a "2," and a low contribution is set a "1."

Table 1. Areas and components in the business model proposal

Business model component/ area	Technological enablers and CSFs	Model source
Customer Segment	● Big Data (Needham, 2013) ● Neuromarketing (Renvoisé & Morin, 2006)	Business Model Canvas/ Business Survival Growth Model
Value Propositions	● Blockchain (Vigna & Casey, 2019) ● Services Catalogue (Rudolph, & Krcmar, 2009) ● Test advertisement campaign ● Standardization and normalization	Business Model Canvas
Channels	● The strategic combination of channels ● Targeted surveys (Vannette & Krosnick, 2017)	Business Model Canvas
Customer and Relationships	● Information flow, customers, and marketing synergies (Kotler, 2012). ● Complaints Management (Stauss & Seidel, 2019) ● Satisfaction surveys	Business Model Canvas/ Business Survival Growth Model
Revenue Streams	● Services Catalogue (Rudolph & Krcmar, 2009)	Business Model Canvas/ Business Survival Growth Model
Key Resources	● Social Media among employees (Connolly, 2020) ● Human Capital Management (Sripada, 2020; Olalla et al., 2012) ● Grants and development aids availability	Business Model Canvas/ Business Survival Growth Model
Key Activities	● Quality management and optimization activities (Saiz-Alvarez & Olalla-Caballero, 2021; Lakhal, Pasin & Limam, 2006; Taguchi & Phadke, 1989) ● Balanced Scorecard (Kaplan & Norton, 2005)	Business Model Canvas
Key Partnerships	● Startups (Thiel & Masters, 2014) ● Crowdfunding (Steinberg & DeMaria, 2012)	Business Model Canvas
Cost Structure	● Costs Model (Altmann & Kashef, 2014)	Business Model Canvas/ Business Survival Growth Model
Competitors	● Organizational behavioral analysis tools (Buchanan & Huczynski, 2019)	Business Survival Growth Model
Strategy	● Lean Management (Plenert, 2011) ● Leadership with clear vision (Smircich & Morgan, 1982)	Business Survival Growth Model
Stakeholders	● Virtual and physical networking (Franchi et al., 2013) ● Storytelling (Rodriguez, 2020)	Sustainable Business Model

Source. Authors

Table 2. Contribution of enablers and CSFs to long term value creation

VALUE CREATION / Technical enablers and CSFs	Customer loyalty and satisfaction	Competitiveness in the market	Corporate image and strong reference in the market and for employees	Benefits obtained maintaining or even increasing service quality	Changing environment adaptation capacity
Big Data	1	1	1	3	1
Neuromarketing	3	1	1	2	1
Blockchain	2	3	2	2	2
Services Catalogue	1	3	1	1	2
Test advertising campaign	3	2	3	1	1
Standardization and normalization	2	2	2	3	2
Strategic combination of channels	2	2	1	2	1
Targeted surveys	1	1	1	3	2
Information flow and synergies between customer and marketing department	3	2	3	1	1
Complaints Management	3	1	2	2	1
Satisfaction Surveys	3	1	3	2	1
Social Media among employees	1	1	3	2	2
Human Capital Management	1	2	2	2	2
Grants and development aids availability	1	1	2	2	1
Quality Management and Optimization Activities	1	2	3	3	1
Balanced Scorecard	1	2	1	2	1
Startups	1	2	1	1	3
Crowdfunding	1	3	2	1	2
Costs Model	1	2	1	2	1
Organizational Behavioral analysis tools	1	3	2	1	2
Lean Management	2	1	1	2	1
Leadership with clear vision	1	2	3	1	3
Virtual and physical networking	1	1	3	1	2
Storytelling	2	1	2	1	1

Source: Authors.

Regarding business models implementation, there are eight characteristics to be considered, according to the platform defined by Sorri et al. (2019): value, monetizing, producers, users, filtering, governance, resilience, and network effect. There are some problems related to business models that may be considered, according to Shafer et al. (2005): flawed assumptions underlying the core logic, limitations in the strategic choices considered, misunderstandings related to the value creation and value capture, and beliefs about the value network. Chesbrough (2010) explains the importance of the change of organizational processes regarding business models implementation. It is a critical issue to be considered, together with identifying internal leaders for business model change, because of the importance of managing the results of these processes and delivering a new business model for the company. Amit and Zott (2012) identify several questions to think about before launching a new business model in a company.

When considering a business model to be developed, several issues have to be considered: the company's activities and external environment (Vasilienė-Vasiliauskienė et al., 2019). In addition, when defining and implementing these areas or components in the business model, we recommended considering a social and an environmental layer for each element in the business model. When analyzing each aspect in the business model from both additional perspectives, there could be a complete view of all the issues that should be considered in every area of that business model (Joyce & Paquin, 2016). This fact could also allow the company to adopt circular economy practices (Olalla-Caballero & Mata-Fernández, 2020).

Considering factors and issues that may generate sustainability in a company, it is vital to take into account the following list, according to Nosratabadi et al. (2020): technology, target customers, partner networks, resources, customer interface, core competency, business processes, financial aspects, and value proposition. In addition, resilience is a factor that has been proven critical nowadays because new technologies can be a significant threat to business continuity, so it is necessary to evaluate the resilience of the chosen business model against the latest threats to ensure business continuity (Niemimaa et al., 2019).

CONCLUSION

Due to the terrible recession caused by SARS-CoV-2 (Nobre, 2020), firms should reconsider their business models trying to fit new rules in new economic scenarios and markets by considering that companies should be prepared for a changing world (Maital & Barzani, 2020). Companies should also learn from this new world economic order that they must be ready for the present and the future and the next crisis. The business model must be analyzed and fit for these new requirements, trying to get as much value as possible to achieve a more significant market share and stay in the market as a competitive enterprise.

Some perspectives and features of a business model have been analyzed and discussed in this research, highlighting their relevance. A new way to work with the Canvas business model based on the original one is proposed. The relationship among some technological enablers and CSFs and the value they may generate related to the proposed business model has also been highlighted to understand their synergies, considering that they surely help create value for the company. This value created is a vital issue in a changing market and guarantees that a company can afford this crisis and those new ones that may affect our economy in the future. It can be deduced that this proposal for working with the Canvas business model is a good option considering that the consequences of the pandemic may last for some years. This proposal can be adapted as far as the global economy changes and depending on leading a company. The company will have to study the area it is required to focus on: customer, offer, infrastructure, or financial viability.

It will also be a chance to consider modularizing this model, making it more flexible and adaptable to the new circumstances that may appear in the future. The power of this new way of working with Canvas will be more significant when firms and leaders work on each of its nine blocks to emphasize its weaker blocks, or due to the pandemic, it is necessary to reinforce.

Further research may be developed to analyze other features related to business models and their importance in value creation for a company, trying to identify and propose new business models that gather all the features and synergies. These models will be strong enough to afford new challenges in this new economic order, always considering technological enablers in this new digital economy.

REFERENCES

Altmann, J., & Kashef, M. M. (2014). Cost model-based service placement in federated hybrid clouds. *Future Generation Computer Systems*, *41*, 79–90. doi:10.1016/j.future.2014.08.014

Amanullah, A. N. A. A., Aziz, N. F. A., Hadi, F. N., & Ibrahim, J. (2015). Comparison of the business model canvas (BMC) among the three consulting companies. *International Journal of Computer Science and Information Technology Research*, *3*(2), 462–471.

Amit, R., & Zott, C. (2012). *Creating value through business model innovation*. Academic Press.

Austin, E. C. (2020). Business Survival Growth Model (BSGM) Canvas vs. Business Model Canvas (BMC). *European Journal of Business and Innovation Research*, *8*(1), 52–68. doi:10.37745/ejbir/vol8.no1.pp52-68.2020

Baden-Fuller, C., & Morgan, M. S. (2010). Business models as models. *Long Range Planning*, *43*(2-3), 156–171. doi:10.1016/j.lrp.2010.02.005

Baldwin, R., & Di Mauro, B. W. (2020). *Economics in the time of COVID-19: A new eBook*. VOX CEPR Policy Portal.

Bocken, N. M., Short, S. W., Rana, P., & Evans, S. (2014). A literature and practice review to develop sustainable business model archetypes. *Journal of Cleaner Production*, *65*, 42–56. doi:10.1016/j.jclepro.2013.11.039

Boons, F., & Lüdeke-Freund, F. (2013). Business models for sustainable innovation: State-of-the-art and steps towards a research agenda. *Journal of Cleaner Production*, *45*, 9–19. doi:10.1016/j.jclepro.2012.07.007

Buchanan, D. A., & Huczynski, A. A. (2019). Organizational Behaviour. Academic Press.

Cappiello, G., Giordani, F., & Visentin, M. (2020). Social capital and its effect on networked firm innovation and competitiveness. *Industrial Marketing Management. Quality Management & Business Excellence*, *31*(3-4), 297-311.

Chen, J. (2019). Environmental, Social and Governance (ESG) Criteria. *Investopedia Hentet*, *27*, 2019.

Chesbrough, H. (2006). *Open business models: How to thrive in the new innovation landscape*. Harvard Business Press.

Chesbrough, H. (2010). Business model innovation: Opportunities and barriers. *Long Range Planning*, *43*(2-3), 354–363. doi:10.1016/j.lrp.2009.07.010

Connolly, B. (2020). *Digital Trust: Social Media Strategies to Increase Trust and Engage Customers*. Bloomsbury Publishing.

Daxboeck, B. (2013). Value co-creation as a precondition for the development of a service business model canvas. *Studia Universitatis Babes Bolyai-Negotia*, *58*(4), 23–51.

Evans, S., Vladimirova, D., Holgado, M., Van Fossen, K., Yang, M., Silva, E. A., & Barlow, C. Y. (2017). Business model innovation for sustainability: Towards a unified perspective for creation of sustainable business models. *Business Strategy and the Environment*, *26*(5), 597–608. doi:10.1002/bse.1939

Farinha, L., & Bagchi-Sen, S. (2019). Following the Footprints of SME Competitiveness in a High-Technology Sector. In *Knowledge, Innovation and Sustainable Development in Organizations* (pp. 77–95). Springer. doi:10.1007/978-3-319-74881-8_6

Fjeldstad, Ø. D., & Snow, C. C. (2018). Business models and organization design. *Long Range Planning*, *51*(1), 32–39. doi:10.1016/j.lrp.2017.07.008

Franchi, E., Poggi, A., & Tomaiuolo, M. (2013). Open social networking for online collaboration. *International Journal of e-Collaboration*, *9*(3), 50-68.

Gamez-Gutierrez, J., & Saiz-Alvarez, J. M. (Eds.). (2021). Entrepreneurial Innovation for Securing Long-Term Growth in a Short-Term Economy. IGI Global.

García-Muiña, F. E., Medina-Salgado, M. S., Ferrari, A. M., & Cucchi, M. (2020). Sustainability Transition in Industry 4.0 and Smart Manufacturing with the Triple-Layered Business Model Canvas. *Sustainability*, *12*(6), 2364. doi:10.3390u12062364

García-Sánchez, A., Siles, D., & Vázquez-Méndez, M. D. M. (2019). Competitiveness and innovation: Effects on prosperity. *Anatolia*, *30*(2), 200–213. doi:10.1080/13032917.2018.1519179

Garrido, S., Brandenburg, M., Carvalho, H., & Cruz Machado, V. (2014). Eco-innovation and the development of business models. Lessons from experience and new frontiers in theory and practice. *Greening of Industry Networks Studies*, *2*.

Gavrilova, T., Alsufyev, A., & Yanson, A. S. (2014). Transforming canvas model: Map versus table. *International Journal of Knowledge. Innovation and Entrepreneurship*, *2*(2), 51–65.

Ghezzi, A., & Cavallo, A. (2020). Agile business model innovation in digital entrepreneurship: Lean startup approaches. *Journal of Business Research*, *110*, 519–537. doi:10.1016/j.jbusres.2018.06.013

Gummesson, E., Mele, C., Polese, F., Galvagno, M., & Dalli, D. (2014). Theory of value co-creation: A systematic literature review. *Managing Service Quality*, *24*(6), 643–683. doi:10.1108/MSQ-09-2013-0187

Gutierrez, B., Spencer, S., & Zhu, G. (2008, August). Thinking globally, leading locally: Chinese, Indian, and Western Leadership. Academy of Management Proceedings, 2008(1), 1-6.

Henry, M., Bauwens, T., Hekkert, M., & Kirchherr, J. (2020). A typology of circular startups: An Analysis of 128 circular business models. *Journal of Cleaner Production*, *245*, 118528. doi:10.1016/j.jclepro.2019.118528

Hutasuhut, S., Irwansyah, I., Rahmadsyah, A., & Aditia, R. (2020). Impact of Business Models Canvas Learning on improving learning achievement and entrepreneurial intention. *Jurnal Cakrawala Pendidikan*, *39*(1), 168–182. doi:10.21831/cp.v39i1.28308

Johnson, M. W., Christensen, C. M., & Kagermann, H. (2008). Reinventing your business model. *Harvard Business Review*, *86*(12), 57–68.

Joyce, A., & Paquin, R. L. (2016). The triple layered business model canvas: A tool to design more sustainable business models. *Journal of Cleaner Production*, *135*, 1474–1486. doi:10.1016/j.jclepro.2016.06.067

Kaplan, R. S., & Norton, D. P. (2005). The balanced scorecard: Measures that drive performance. *Harvard Business Review*, *83*(7), 172. PMID:10119714

Kates, A., & Galbraith, J. R. (2010). *Designing your organization: Using the STAR model to solve 5 critical design challenges*. John Wiley & Sons.

Kaufmann, M. (2019). Big data management canvas: A reference model for value creation from data. *Big Data and Cognitive Computing*, *3*(1), 19. doi:10.3390/bdcc3010019

Kotler, P. (2012). *Kotler on Marketing*. Simon and Schuster.

Kwilinski, A. (2019). A mechanism for assessing the competitiveness of an industrial enterprise in the information economy. *Research Papers in Economics and Finance*, *3*(1), 7–16. doi:10.18559/ref.2018.1.1

Lakhal, L., Pasin, F., & Limam, M. (2006). Quality management practices and their impact on performance. *International Journal of Quality & Reliability Management*, *23*(6), 625–646. doi:10.1108/02656710610672461

Lee, S. M., Olson, D. L., & Trimi, S. (2012). Co-innovation: Convergenomics, collaboration, and co-creation for organizational values. *Management Decision*, *50*(5), 817–831. doi:10.1108/00251741211227528

Li, F. (2020). The digital transformation of business models in the creative industries: A holistic framework and emerging trends. *Technovation*, *92*, 102012. doi:10.1016/j.technovation.2017.12.004

Magretta, J. (2002). Why business models matter. *Harvard Business Review*. PMID:12024761

Maital, S., & Barzani, E. (2020). The global economic impact of COVID-19: A summary of research. Samuel Neaman Institute for National Policy Research.

Mak, M. K., & Ip, W. H. (2017). An exploratory study of investment behaviour of investors. *International Journal of Engineering Business Management*, *9*. doi:10.1177/1847979017711520

McFarlane, D. A. (2017). Osterwalder's business model canvas: Its genesis, features, comparison, benefits. *Westcliff International Journal of Applied Research*, *1*(2), 24–28. doi:10.47670/wuwijar201712DAMC

McGrath, R. G. (2010). Business models: A discovery-driven approach. *Long Range Planning*, *43*(2-3), 247–261. doi:10.1016/j.lrp.2009.07.005

Naggar, R. (2015). The creativity canvas: A business model for knowledge and idea management. *Technology Innovation Management Review*, *5*(7), 50–58. doi:10.22215/timreview/914

Needham, J. (2013). *Disruptive Possibilities: How big data changes everything*. O'Reilly Media, Inc.

Ngoma, M., & Ntale, P. D. (2019). Word of mouth communication: A mediator of relationship marketing and customer loyalty. *Cogent Business & Management*, *6*(1), 1580123. doi:10.1080/23311975.2019.1580123

Niemimaa, M., Järveläinen, J., Heikkilä, M., & Heikkilä, J. (2019). Business continuity of business models: Evaluating the resilience of business models for contingencies. *International Journal of Information Management*, *49*, 208–216. doi:10.1016/j.ijinfomgt.2019.04.010

Nobre, G. F. (2020). *Creative Economy and Covid-19: Technology, automation and the new economy*. Academic Press.

Nosratabadi, S., Pinter, G., Mosavi, A., & Semperger, S. (2020). Sustainable banking; Evaluation of the European business models. *Sustainability*, *12*(6), 2314. doi:10.3390u12062314

Olalla, B., San José, C., & Mata, M. (2012). Factor humano: un elemento clave en la búsqueda de la eficiencia de los proyectos. In *VII Congreso Nacional VISION12*. Madrid: itSMF Spain.

Olalla-Caballero, B., & Mata-Fernández, M. (2020). Circular Economy and Risk Management Synergies in Disruptive Environments. In N. Baporikar (Ed.), *Handbook of Research on Entrepreneurship Development and Opportunities in Circular Economy*. IGI Global. doi:10.4018/978-1-7998-5116-5.ch005

Osterwalder, A., & Pigneur, Y. (2010). *Business model generation: a handbook for visionaries, game changers, and challengers*. John Wiley & Sons, Inc.

Osterwalder, A., Pigneur, Y., & Tucci, C. L. (2005). Clarifying business models: Origins, present, and future of the concept. *Communications of the Association for Information Systems*, *16*(1), 1. doi:10.17705/1CAIS.01601

Ovans, A. (2015). What is a business model? *Harvard Business Review*, *23*, 1–7.

Palma-Ruiz, J. M., Saiz-Alvarez, J. M., & Herrero-Crespo, A. (Eds.). (2020). *Handbook of Research on Smart Territories and Entrepreneurial Ecosystems for Social Innovation and Sustainable Growth*. IGI Global.

Pech, M. A. (2013). *The Financial Times Guide to Leadership: How to lead effectively and get results*. Pearson UK.

Plenert, G. J. (2011). *Lean management principles for information technology*. CRC Press. doi:10.1201/b11549

Porter, M. E. (2008). The five competitive forces that shape strategy. *Harvard Business Review*, *86*(1), 25–40. PMID:18271320

Pradhan, R. P., Arvin, M. B., Nair, M., Bennett, S. E., & Bahmani, S. (2019). Short-term and long-term dynamics of venture capital and economic growth in a digital economy: A study of European countries. *Technology in Society*, *57*, 125–134. doi:10.1016/j.techsoc.2018.11.002

Prado-Prado, J. C., García-Arca, J., & Fernández-González, A. J. (2020). People as the key factor in competitiveness: A framework for success in supply chain management. *Total Quality Management & Business Excellence*, *31*(3-4), 297–311. doi:10.1080/14783363.2018.1427499

Renvoisé, P., & Morin, C. (2006). *Neuromarketing: el nervio de la venta*. Editorial UOC.

Rodriguez, M. (2020). *Brand Storytelling: Put Customers at the Heart of Your Brand Story*. Kogan Page Publishers.

Rudolph, S., & Krcmar, H. (2009). Maturity model for IT service catalogues an approach to assess the quality of IT service documentation. *AMCIS 2009 Proceedings*, 750.

Rusu, V. D., & Dornean, A. (2019). The quality of entrepreneurial activity and economic competitiveness in European Union countries: A panel data approach. *Administrative Sciences*, *9*(2), 35. doi:10.3390/admsci9020035

Saiz-Álvarez, J. M., & Olalla-Caballero, B. (Eds.). (2021). Quality Management for Competitive Advantage in Global Markets. IGI Global.

Shafer, S. M., Smith, H. J., & Linder, J. C. (2005). The power of business models. *Business Horizons*, *48*(3), 199–207. doi:10.1016/j.bushor.2004.10.014

Sjödin, D., Parida, V., Jovanovic, M., & Visnjic, I. (2020). Value creation and value capture alignment in business model innovation: A process view on outcome-based business models. *Journal of Product Innovation Management*, *37*(2), 158–183. doi:10.1111/jpim.12516

Smircich, L., & Morgan, G. (1982). Leadership: The management of meaning. *The Journal of Applied Behavioral Science*, *18*(3), 257–273. doi:10.1177/002188638201800303 PMID:10260212

Sorri, K., Seppänen, M., Still, K., & Valkokari, K. (2019). Business Model Innovation with Platform Canvas. *Journal of Business Models*, *7*(2), 1–13.

Sripada, C. (Ed.). (2020). *Leading Human Capital in the 2020s: Emerging Perspectives*. SAGE Publishing India.

Staehr, K., & Vermeulen, R. (2019). Heterogeneous effects of competitiveness shocks on macroeconomic performance across euro area countries. *World Economy*, *42*(1), 68–86. doi:10.1111/twec.12675

Stauss, B., & Seidel, W. (2019). *Effective Complaint Management: The Business Case for Customer Satisfaction*. Springer. doi:10.1007/978-3-319-98705-7

Steinberg, S., & DeMaria, R. (2012). *The Crowdfunding Bible: How to raise money for any startup, video game or project*. Read.

Taguchi, G., & Phadke, M. S. (1989). Quality engineering through design optimization. In *Quality Control, Robust Design, and the Taguchi Method* (pp. 77–96). Springer. doi:10.1007/978-1-4684-1472-1_5

Teece, D. J. (2010). Business models, business strategy and innovation. *Long Range Planning*, *43*(2-3), 172–194. doi:10.1016/j.lrp.2009.07.003

Thiel, P. A., & Masters, B. (2014). *Zero to One: Notes on Startups or how to build the future*. Crown Business.

Vannette, D. L., & Krosnick, J. A. (Eds.). (2017). *The Palgrave handbook of survey research*. Springer.

Vasilienė-Vasiliauskienė, V., Vasiliauskas, A. V., Donculaitė, M., & Meidutė-Kavaliauskienė, I. (2019, May). Applying the Business Model Canvas to Increase Enterprise Competitiveness: A Case Study of Transport Company. In *Proceedings of the International Conference Transbaltica* (pp. 158-170). Springer.

Vigna, P., & Casey, M. J. (2019). *The truth machine: the blockchain and the future of everything*. HarperCollins.

Von Hippel, E. A., Ogawa, S., & de Jong, P. J. (2011). The age of the consumer-innovator. *MIT Sloan Management Review*, *23*, 1–10.

Watson, D. (2005). *Business Models*. Harriman House Ltd.

Zeibote, Z., Volkova, T., & Todorov, K. (2019). The impact of globalization on regional development and competitiveness: Cases of selected regions. Insights into Regional Development. *Entrepreneurship and Sustainability Center*, *1*(1), 33–47.

KEY TERMS AND DEFINITIONS

Adaptation Capacity: It is the readiness of a company to respond quickly to a changing environment, the capacity to be flexible enough to afford new challenges in a changing climate.

Business Model: It is the set of pieces that have to be used and put in a specific order to make the company run in the best way.

Eco-Innovation: This is the way to benefit by developing products or services, improving environmental sustainability, and using commercial strategies.

Ideation: It is the joining of the stages of an innovation cycle with the creative process steps. This concept can be conducted in a unique way or by an organization.

Open Innovation: This is how to improve and accelerate innovation through inputs and outputs to achieve a global expansion.

Sustainability: This is how a company can work, focusing not only on profitability but also on caring for environmental, cultural, and social aspects.

Value Creation: It refers to creating value for a company, increasing the benefits, or offering new or improved services or products to increase its competitiveness.

Section 2
Education

Chapter 14
Trends for Business Education Post COVID-19

Neeta Baporikar

https://orcid.org/0000-0003-0676-9913

Namibia University of Science and Technology, Namibia & University of Pune, India

ABSTRACT

COVID-19 has brought about tremendous changes in all occupations. Education in general and business education, in particular, is no exception. In the normal course, business education entailed students being on the campus as the courses are full-time residential with physical attendance to enable interaction and discussion. With COVID-19 lockdown and restrictions, the usual way of doing business is disrupted. Hence, by adopting systematic literature with grounded approach, the aim of this chapter is to understand the disruptions, faculty, and student difficulties and sketch out the future trends in business education post COVID-19.

INTRODUCTION

It is a truism to say that business schools and business education are big business (Pfeffer & Fong, 2004). According to Wilson and Wilson (2012), the phenomenal expansion of business schools worldwide, is a characteristic or feature which has made business schools a business. In the first generation of business schools in the late nineteenth to the early twentieth century, legitimacy could be traced to the creation of management employed by the state, industrialists, and entrepreneurs. Also, this generation saw the introduction of institutionalized management systems (such as accounting practices). Further, the second more academically rigorous generation in the seventy's garners legitimacy from national governments, which support business schools, and from universities, which recognized the growth and financial potential schools could bring. The third generation 1980s to present see issues of image and reputation as legitimacy providers and these include research rankings, citations, global performance rankings, and international accreditation bodies (Cooke & Alcadipani, 2015; Cummings, Bridgman, Hassard & Rowlinson, 2017).

DOI: 10.4018/978-1-7998-7689-2.ch014

Business schools present themselves as academic institutions mimicking the more established disciplines in universities. At the same time, they are expected to demonstrate their abilities to manage themselves as businesses and conduct research and teaching, which is considered "relevant" to practitioners and funding bodies (Wilson & Thomas, 2012). Our work in business schools and universities as academic scholars, in these times, leads us to consider these as research questions:

1. What are the disruptions in business education due to pandemics?
2. What are the faculty, and student difficulties in these pandemic times?
3. What are the future trends in business education post-pandemic?
4. What will the business school profile look like in the future?
5. What of research in the business school?

There is continuous questioning about the effectiveness and relevance of business education in general and MBA programs in recent years (Colby, Ehrlich, Sullivan, & Dolle, 2011; Martin, 2007; Mintzberg, 2004; Pfeffer & Fong, 2004). There are serious doubts about the business schools' ability to provide students with the skills required to function effectively in modern organizations and to prepare them for the professional demands and challenges of globalized business in a pluralistic world and most of the business schools seems have lost their way in the current scenario (Bennis & O'Toole, 2005). The questioning of business education effectiveness and relevance is all the more significant especially now due to the global health crisis which humanity is facing and enduring due to Covid 19. Hence, by adopting systematic literature and a grounded approach this chapter aims to understand the disruptions, faculty, and student difficulties and sketch out the future trends in business education post-Covid.

LITERATURE REVIEW

Characteristics of Business Education

Business education has been in much demand due to its ability to provide better employment opportunities and earning capacities. Some of the salient characteristics of business education include:

1. Focus on functional knowledge with the dominance of the business functions to enhance employable skills.
2. Focus on disciplinary knowledge acquisition with holistic teaching methods evolved to include case studies, thus moving to simulate the complexity of real-life business situations.
3. Focus on developing rational thinking and decision-making skills to be more productive and enable them to take a highly rational view of implementation and action.
4. Focus on analytical skills to enhance logical thinking and become knowledgeable about the business.
5. Focus on large corporate and powerful big companies that provide huge employment potential and are built on criteria of efficiency and profitability thereby favoring the education of technically rational managers.
6. Dominating the logic of the market that is the basis of the analytical framework to discuss all business issues. Firms are seen as groups of self-interested actors, which are conceived primarily as vehicles for maximizing return to shareholders.

7. Depicts managers as "agents" of shareholders, dedicating their careers to the sole purpose of creating private wealth, for themselves and shareholders as their "principals".
8. Attention to professional knowledge acquisition and training to ensure good professional judgment and practical reasoning.
9. Focus on motivation to improve and learn through "edutainment" from learning providers, who identify what skills are most relevant for them and entertainingly present them.
10. Focus on training through subject experts to ensure that there is a higher degree of knowledge acquisition through case method that encourages strategic scenario thinking or role-plays to understand complexities.

Criticism of Business Education

Business education reached its height in mid-1980 globally but soon after that, the cracks started appearing in the glamour of business education. There were various reasons among them were the scandals and inability of the business education to reinvent and meet society's expectations quickly. The issue of business educations creating more mercenaries rather than workforce worked for the common good and the huge backlash on the exploitation of natural resources making the world unsustainable especially for the underprivileged and developing economies (Dyllick, 2015). In the past two decades, business education has come under criticism on many fronts. Salient criticism against business education includes:

1. Business education has a focus on narrow functional knowledge instead of a broad issue-centered approach embracing business and society as embedded in a plurality of contexts: the dominance of the business functions comes at the expense of an integrated management perspective, embracing the external context, in a particular culture, society, nature, and history. There is little training in integrative thinking (Martin, 2009).
2. Business education focus is always on disciplinary knowledge acquisition instead of the development of an interdisciplinary and integrated perspective (Baporikar, 2010). Although teaching methods have evolved to include case studies, thus moving to simulate the complexity of real-life business situations, business education remains fundamentally disciplinary based and rests in silos, with little opportunity to deal with problems of the real world, which are mostly "messy" problems that cross boundaries (Khurana, 2007, p. 305).
3. Business education misses focus on critical thinking: effective leaders should have the capability to ask critical questions and they should be able to use multiple perspectives in understanding difficult situations. Business graduates often are surprisingly naïve about organizations and their management. They learn to take a highly rational view of implementation and action while failing to recognize that organizations are fundamentally complex and political organizations. They fail to understand why rational plans most of the time fail in implementation, why logical arguments are not accepted and why people say "yes" and then do not follow through (Datar, Garvin, Cullen, & Cullen, 2010, p. 92).
4. Business education always focuses strongly on analytical skills instead of soft skills, in particular social skills and personal skills (Kieser, 2011). Thus, management seems to be reduced to analysis and even further to technique, whereby integration, synthesis, and in particular soft skills are ignored and even got lost. More so in these critical and trying times, soft skills are exactly what managers need most to succeed in their day-to-day tasks and carry along with their people. In other words,

students learn analysis and thinking, but no action and reflection. They become knowledgeable about business but remain uneducated in the art and craft of management (Mintzberg, 2004).

5. Business education always has had a very selective focus. The focus of business school education favors the few, especially powerful big companies and corporations over the large majority of small and medium enterprises and companies. It favors western perspectives over the perspectives of the large majority of the global population. The focus is more on efficiency instead of the challenges of being effective. Moreover, business schools have shown to be very weak in supporting innovation and creativity, thereby favoring the education of technically rational managers over entrepreneurs (Baporikar, 2019a).

6. Business education prefers a dominating logic of the market meaning that it has a narrow view of the world. Idealized markets have become the analytical framework to discuss all business issues, but also business and society issues. The view is that firms are groups of self-interested actors conceived primarily as vehicles for maximizing return to shareholders. Hence the question remains as to how students will learn about the plurality of values and logic in the worlds of science, public policy, the arts, and other spheres of society (Colby et al., 2011; Hühn, 2014).

7. Business education in general has a missing and distorted focus on the importance of values and ethics. There is the dominance of amoral theories taught to students, depicting managers as "agents" of shareholders, dedicating their careers to the sole purpose of creating private wealth, for themselves and shareholders as their "principals," in effect stripping managers of any professional identity, self-respect and personal responsibility (Ghoshal, 2005; Khurana, 2007). This leaves business graduates unprepared for understanding and coping with the current challenges to the roles, responsibilities, and purpose of business in society and the importance of diplomacy and leadership (Gond, Igalens, & Bieger, 2011).

8. Business education does lack attention for self-knowledge and the reflective exploration of meaning (Riel & Martin, 2017). After all good professional judgment and practical reasoning is the result of critical reflections on one's perceptions and values as a prospective or actual manager and leader. Rarely does business education offer reflective spaces and purposely used to develop a dialogue with oneself about how one intends to act as a manager and leader and whom one wishes to become. Merely, addressing values and ethics by way of courses or modules is not sufficient. The challenges of values and ethics need to have a link and connection and provide students the opportunities for students' to make their efforts to explore the meaning for themselves (Baporikar, 2017a).

9. Business education, in general, lacks attention to learning to learn: in particular, self-redirected learning and self-determined learning have continuously decreased, partly due to the movement of business schools to become ever more student-oriented and making learning "fun." While motivation is important to successful learning, it should not come from entertainment, rather from the enjoyment of the learning process overall and the understanding of how useful the acquired knowledge and skills will be (Tubulingane & Baporikar, 2020). Business education and schools have relied heavily upon and focused on making education more about entertainment generally referred to as "edutainment". This approach and does not prepare students for being lifelong learners. Even they fail to identify personal development areas and pursue specific development activities, for overcoming their weakness. Business education creates dependent learners and they prefer learning providers, who identify what skills are most relevant for them and present them in an entertaining way (Kieser, 2011). If this were so then the very purpose of education fails from a societal point of

view. After all, education must propel an individual to be path seeking and experimental in pursuit of achieving for self and larger good of humankind rather than mere followers to achieve specific goals, and for that to happen there is a need to shift the perspectives on management education and innovate with the process of teaching, learning, curriculum and even student recruitment (Baporikar, 2017b).

10. Business education has always professed a learner-centered approach its emphasis is always on teaching more value-added courses. Thereby there is neglect or lack of attention to learning: how do faculty assure learning has happened? They are typically subject experts with little to no pedagogical training for assuring and measuring learning impact (Kieser, 2011). Hence, what is mostly assessed is to what degree knowledge has been acquired. The case method encourages strategic scenario thinking but creates the illusion that students can effectively handle the situation they have encountered in their case studies (Baporikar, 2016; 2008). However, there is very little to make sure and assess reflective learning takes place Hence there is a dire need to revisit the case method in its entirety to ensure relevance in the future of this widely used pedagogy in management education and more so in business schools (Bridgman, Cummings, & McLaughlin, 2016).

FUTURE BUSINESS EDUCATION ESSENTIALS

The obvious challenge, arising out of all the characteristics and criticism listed above, is to illustrate what kind of business school might be more appropriate (and robust) for the future especially post Covid. Indeed Henry Mintzberg (2004), the most consistent and insightful critic of management programs argues that management is an art, not a science and that the managerial task is all about practice. Hence, there is a critical need to place greater emphasis on managerial skill and capabilities and the virtues of critical and synthetic thinking offered by the study of the humanities and social sciences as well as conventional analytic thinking. We argue that schools will have to make substantial changes in what they research and teach. This means broadening the traditional focus of research and teaching in business schools to look more broadly at wider society, to embrace multi-disciplinary perspectives, and to turn its theoretical perspectives and research focus towards "big" questions. In turn, this means engaging largely in public and private policy debates – reclaiming the terrain of work, employment, and society.

So how does business education do this? Few strategies suggested including:

1. Develop a strong norm of learning and not primarily viewing management qualifications and degrees as increasing individual salaries (Baporikar, 2009).
2. Maintaining/developing research and teaching in the "mother" disciplines of management – for example, sociology, philosophy, psychology, economics, law, and mathematics.
3. Prioritize learning over "added value" or "value added courses and modules" in business education.
4. Place far greater emphasis on the ethical and moral questions endemic in modern capitalism.
5. Examine critically the role of business in wider society. Focus on the role of businesses and managers in society by going significantly beyond the current debates over corporate social responsibility, which arguably act as a convenient moral "cloak" for deeper questions over the accountability of managers for their actions and decisions.
6. Ensure that business education engages in research and teach "big questions" which impact organizations and society (Baporikar, 2015b). Examples include a wide range of topics ranging from, an

examination of why there is simultaneous obesity and poverty and starvation, the impact of social and economic policy. Understanding the impact and the risks of exogenous events such as climate change, disasters, and the impact of a newly emerging global economic order, changing geopolitical structures or political leadership dynamics, and key players in the world economy. The current problem based and industry solutions approach to research has diminished the value of research and made even the research undertaken in many business schools irrelevant (Koskela, 2017).

7. Global perspectives as managers operate increasingly globally, business schools themselves will have to become less insular and nationally oriented. There is a need to develop a global and integrated perspective to solve the problems and ensure effective decision-making that is holistic and inclusive rather than narrow and linear (Muff, 2013). For this there is a need to emphasize understanding of language, comparative social cultures and the impact of religion on global economic activity would seem essential parts of the teaching and research curriculum of business school soon (Baporikar, 2017a; 2017b).

If business education and schools do not undertake these changes, we argue that they are likely to become irrelevant and unnecessary institutions operating on the sidelines of key social, economic, and political issues. Hence, business schools and academic leaders must have the courage to build curricula, which develop simultaneously so-called T-shaped individuals, i.e. those who have significant disciplinary depth achieved through a liberal education involving critical, synthetic, and analytic thinking and appropriate training in the important functions and languages of management education. Unfortunately, the similarity in many business school curricula arises sadly from the mimetic and isomorphic tendencies.

FUTURE TRENDS IN BUSINESS EDUCATION

The trends in education are predicted in advance. But due to the changes in the current environment, trends are coming up faster than ever. Due to this global crisis of Covid 19, various changes will dominate the specialized business education space in the years to come. Figure 1 gives the trends in business education post-Covid to watch out followed by a brief discussion of each trend.

Artificial Intelligence: Artificial intelligence (AI) in a classroom has been a big topic whenever one discusses or thinks about technology integration in education. In the future, it's expected to be a priority for forward-thinking academic institutes. The way business schools make use of AI will vary. For instance, many institutes are using technology to automate administrative activities such as the admission process, some are using it for student enrolment and recruitment of domestic and international students by creating algorithms. Moreover, with the help of this AI and tech tools, faculty will get more free time as AI tools take care of mundane tasks such as grading, creating tests, etc.

Digital Content and eBooks: As technology gets more involved in our lives, traditional textbooks have started adding digital ad-on. To bring the costs down and enhance access and availability, business schools are predicted to buy digital content to promote the self-serve model, especially for specific subjects like accounting, finance, and quantitative methods. The idea is to allow students to avail themselves of an entire skill-based course from a reputable source while providing a tutor just for support.

Faculty Professional Development: Earlier the faculty and teaching community was seen as the never-ending source of knowledge. Their role was to be thorough at every little thing they taught their students. While this is true even today, faculty responsibility more than being comprehensive but also adapting themselves to newer and better ways of imparting knowledge and teaching in the class.

Figure 1. Business education trends post-Covid
Source: Author

Just as students are expected to adopt new learning methods and subjects as a result of the rise of technology, similarly, teachers will have to step up their game by embracing new roles and responsibilities. As it is, due to pandemic this change is seen right now. Instead of going from typical classrooms to conducting lectures in Zoom/ Microsoft Teams, faculty is bracing for online learning and teaching.

Genius Hour: To promote innovation, ingenuity, Google encourages its employees to devote 20 percent time to side projects. This is because the company believes that enabling people to work on something that interests them will eventually lead to better productivity and innovation. Similarly, business schools will be expected to have the "Genius Hour", where students are free to learn what makes them curious. This hour will look more open-ended and less organized. This hour's purpose is to take a break from a rigid, test-driven, and 'achievement-focused' learning environment. With this extra time, students will have the chance to explore their ideas and follow their instincts—without being assessed or monitored.

Immersive Education: With the help of extended reality, which is a mix of virtual, augmented, and mixed reality, faculty can provide immersive learning to students, no matter where they are. For example, with the help of a headset, a lesson about ancient industrialization in the early 1900 can come alive, as the student walks around the digital version of that time zone. Not only does this make learning fun, but it also encourages them to immerse themselves in the lesson.

Personalized Learning: Business schools will and no more can afford to have strict and standard structures or delivery mechanisms. The time has come to reckon that it is the generation of personalization, right from the recommendations for what to eat and what to see, to where and how they consume data. Platforms like Netflix and Amazon, along with Zomato, promote personalized convenience by removing restrictions related to location, device, and timing. Hence, education, too, is not far behind from delivering personalized education, especially since the speculations and debates around the traditional lecture process that does not work for every student. This is primarily because every individual has their unique strengths and weaknesses, and grasps concepts at their own pace. In a traditional classroom setting, going at each student's pace is impossible. Hence, the demand for personalized learning will increase with the realization that technology can aid and facilitate this process. With technology, students can get access to study material online, including documents and videos, allowing them to learn about concepts at their speed, anytime, anywhere.

Project-based Learning: As we enter the third decade, business schools are finally moving on to active learning. Gone will be the days when students sat passively at desks while professors lectured endlessly, expecting the class to soak up all the knowledge. The trend in the educational sector and more so in business schools will and is project-based learning wherein students will collaborate, think critically, and work in a group to develop innovative projects and come up with answers to complex questions. Business schools will need to bring in companies that offer students industry-relevant projects. This also will help and ensure students get to adapt to a new way of learning and also be in-sync with what the real world looks for.

STEAM Replaces STEM: For a long time business schools have focused on analytical skills development and hence, focused on recruiting students with strong Science, Technology, Engineering, Math (STEM) or inspiring pursuit of it. But now Science, Technology, Engineering, Art, and Math (STEAM) will replace STEM. The last few years have increased the popularity of the STEAM approach to learning. This is because various industries want professionals who are disciplined in the areas of creativity and art as well. Arts, includes humanities, language arts, dance, drama, music, visual arts, design, and new media. Today, global businesses and the world want to recruit candidates who do not just have technical knowledge but also can think creatively, come up with innovative solutions to solve problems, blend in with different cultures. It is here that business schools will have to shift their gears and propel towards adopting the STEAM approach and it is this approach that helps better than mere STEM to not only meet this requirement but develop holistic and grounded individuals.

So, if business education has to be more relevant and useful to the changing order in the global society and take headlong with the above future trends in business education, business schools will need to focus on:

1. Meaningful relationships with professors and peers. Develop an intimate setting, cultivating meaningful relationships between students and their professors, and students and their peers (Baporikar, 2015c).
2. Open doors, flexible office hours, and inviting professors who create an environment where students can question without fear due to relationships that hold meaning beyond the classroom.
3. Students get space and opportunity to create their learning community, involving leadership opportunities, field trips, and occasions for celebrating their successes. Provide more interaction among

fresher and entrants with more opportunities to network and work together in groups, facilitate class team projects, and so on.
4. Develop group identity early on with more meet and greets with professors, social interaction with school staff, more informal opportunities to get to know each other, and ensure leadership opportunities in all aspects of the student experience in the school and faculty.
5. Building upon the excellent history of entrepreneurship, the apprentice project, and experiential out of classroom learning enhances strong leadership skills (Baporikar, 2019a).
6. Programs of mentoring younger students help strengthen the experience of the business education program as a whole and give the mentoring students the responsibility and real-world context of coaching, leading, and develops integrity and conduct (Baporikar, 2019b).
7. Strong connections and an annual leadership summit with alumni who have leveraged their experience at alma mater into a leadership role in their career will provide current students with an idea of what they can achieve and keep the development of leadership skills as a central aim of the business education programs.
8. Provide students the opportunity to learn in a dynamic and engaging environment via experiential learning (Baporikar, 2017b). Offer variety in course design, the courses can allow for workshops, cases, presentations, event planning, and field trips that enable the students to learn about and encompass real-world issues and organizations as this allows students to experience and develop the skills necessary to prepare for the future. Students could likely utilize these skills through some form of co-op or internship program. Such a program would allow students summer employment in their preferred area of study, and expand their experiential learning experience through the real-world application (Baporikar, 2018b).
9. Provide more variety in experiential learning opportunities, different types of organizations (arts, non-profit, public systems such as health) Bring real-world issues into the classroom (e.g., climate change; disasters occurrence to contextualize learning to ensure finer engagement and quality student learning (Baporikar, 2020). Offer more interdisciplinary perspectives such as current political issues (e.g., management-political science-focused course) and also optional courses in basic workplace skills (e.g., PowerPoint, Excel, presentation skills, software applications that are used in the workplace).
10. Creativity and flexibility in program design (workshops/guest lecturers/case competitions/unique experiences), ensure creativity in curriculum design, by encouraging professors to include practical experience and cross-course collaboration to maximize learning potential. Professors should be given the flexibility to supplement class material with opportunities to hear guest lectures, attend case competitions and other unique experiences and students must be provided an opportunity to complete a program evaluation and a course evaluation that addresses creativity within their program (Baporikar, 2015a).

IMPLICATIONS

Transforming business education is complex and intertwined with research and faculty apart from closely connected issues that lead to a final question concerning the role and purpose of business education as a whole in the future: for whom do business schools create value? Although the business education and business school has been the major success story in the university in the last quarter of the century, if measured in terms of growth in demand and by looking at the MBA as the only truly global degree (Mintzberg, 2004), it has come under attack about its fundamental nature and value. Business education programs especially MBA are criticized for having become too customer-focused and too business-focused, at the expense of a truly professional orientation focused on the common good. Khurana (2007) concludes in his history of management education that leading business schools moved from a "tyranny of the faculty" to a "tyranny of the markets." While this shift may have gone furthest for the leading business schools, most of them live under both tyrannies.

Neither of them is healthy as tyranny or dominance of faculty means that education is seen through the lens of teaching, not learning. Students are taught, examined, and graded and they are not seen as partners or co-producers in a two-way learning process. If students have learned, what they were taught, they pass the exams and receive good grades. Faculty has a defining role in designing the courses, the programs, and the pedagogy (Baporikar & Parker, 2019). Research is seen as the prerogative of the individual faculty, not as a social obligation. It is an expression of their freedom of research and teaching.

All aspects of research, areas, and topics, theoretical or practical focus, national or international orientation, as well as the forms and channels of publications are objects of their free decisions. They are free to define them according to their scholarly preferences and experiences, their reputation building strategies, their economic interests, or their political convictions. Even if the school may have research priorities and programs of their own, which they try to get accepted by their faculty, but there are clear limits to the success of their "carrots and sticks." The higher the scholarly reputation of the faculty, the more likely it is, that they will use their status and their attractiveness to other schools to extract extra benefits and freedom from the demands of the school (Hühn, 2014). Engagement for institutional self-management and development (program management, leadership roles in committees and faculties, etc. will then become the domain of the less reputed faculty.

If they are under the tyranny of the market that is market dominance, it shows in different ways as well. Business schools build and strengthen their brand name through institutional strategies. Financial well-being and success, revenues, costs, and surplus, play an important role. They use marketing and communications to position the school and its particular strengths in an increasingly transparent and competitive landscape. Accreditations and rankings measure and demonstrate their comparative success and make it widely known to different stakeholders and the public. Dedicated faculty and administrators, who will make their demands known internally, thereby, are managing accreditations and rankings challenging faculty dominance (Baporikar, 2018a, 2018c; 2017a). They attract high-profile faculty and develop carefully their international networks of business school and corporate partners, who should reflect favorably on the school's reputation. Further, collaborative dynamics between business schools, but also between faculty and students, give way to competitive dynamics. The logic of secretiveness and holding back overtakes openness and sharing as student's selection is from the pool of applicants. The bigger this pool is and the lower the rate of acceptance, the higher is the school's reputation. Besides, the higher the reputation, the more increase in the made. Students are viewed as customers, who buy a service and whose demands have to be fulfilled. Success is measured by "customer satisfaction" surveys and that is a danger as the very educational purpose is likely to get lost in the process apart from quality being questionable (Baporikar, & Sony, 2020).

Faculty dominance and market dominance both are present in varying degrees in today's business education and business schools. They force different orientations on administration and leadership, be it the research interests of faculty or the market focus of the institution. Both have clear limitations and problems. What gets lost is the genuine educational mission that cannot be measured in terms of student satisfaction or starting salaries. What gets lost also is the professional contribution to the common good (Starkey, Tempest, & Cinque, 2019; Podolny, 2009).

If business education wants to attract and inspire talented students, if they want to secure political support, and if they want to keep the public trust, they have to start looking beyond their interests, those of their faculties and those of their direct "customers." They have to start thinking about their contributions to society. Do they educate the kind of managers and leaders society needs? Do they provide their graduates with social awareness and social competencies they will need to manage controversial issues in business and society? Will they be able to engage in solving the big economic and social issues we are collectively facing? Moreover, do they produce research that is accessible and useful for understanding and acting toward solving these issues?

The reforms based on the results of the Ford and Carnegie Foundation reports (Pierson, 1959; Gordon & Howell, 1959) have been very successful in embedding business administration in a research-based body of knowledge, thereby elevating its academic status. These reforms, however, did nothing toward making business administration more socially trustworthy. On the contrary, by basing their theories on a particular interpretation of neoclassical assumptions about the efficacy of markets, scholars came to rationalize individual selfishness as socially advantageous, which was enthusiastically embraced by the top management in many parts of the business world, in particular in the financial services. The defenders of personal responsibility and social trustworthiness were relegated to the back seats. As Augier and March (2011, p. 275) conclude in their critical analysis of the development of business schools in the USA, discussions of the role of management as a profession in creating a better world thereby have been made largely irrelevant, as discusses the role of the business school in improving society. Developing a constructive role for business schools in contributing to the pressing global challenges will need major changes in the dominant business school model, a model that has been developed in the USA, but that has become the dominant model for business schools in many other places as well.

SOLUTIONS AND RECOMMENDATIONS

Reforming business education means more than simply adding courses in the humanities. The entire business education curriculum must be infused with multidisciplinary, practical, and ethical questions and analyses reflecting the tangled challenges business leaders face. In revising the curricula, we emphatically do not advocate that business schools abandon science. Rather, they should encourage and reward science that illuminates the mysteries and ambiguities of today's business practices. Oddly, for all the emphasis business schools put on science, they do little in the one area of contemporary science that probably holds the greatest promise for business education cognitive science, and neuroscience. There, pioneering scientists are using functional magnetic resonance imaging technology to study how the brain behaves while making economic decisions, including gender differences and the role of trust.

The problem is not that business schools have embraced scientific rigor but that they have forsaken other ways of knowing. It is not a case of either/or. Manifestly, there are business professors who do research contributing to both science and practice (Dostaler & Tomberlin, 2013; Lee & Cassell, 2011). Besides, not every professor needs are such a skilled switch hitter. In practice, business schools need a variety of professors with different skills and interests, which, collectively, cover territory as broad and as deep as the challenges business managers face. As the late, Sumantra Goshal wrote, citing Clegg and

Ross-Smith, in a probing analysis of the problems with management education today "the task is not one of delegitimizing existing research approaches, but one of relegitimizing pluralism."

Rebalancing runs against the perceived self-interest of many faculties, not to mention the seemingly unstoppable trend in academia toward specialization (Kieser, 2011). We believe the most effective levers for overcoming this resistance are personnel policies related to recruitment, promotion, tenure, and other academic rewards (Baporikar, 2015a; Finch, Deephouse, O'Reilly, Massie, & Hillenbrand, 2016). Instead of blindly following the paths forged by trade schools or traditional academic departments, business schools must create their unique standards of excellence. However, many business school leaders now say their universities are forcing them to adopt the same standards for hiring and promotion used by graduate departments in the hard sciences. In our view, this is often an excuse for maintaining a dysfunctional (but comfortable) system. Law schools and schools of music, dentistry, pharmacy, and fine arts have all carved out standards that are appropriate for their various professions, and now business schools must have the courage to do the same (Lee & Cassell, 2011).

FUTURE RESEARCH DIRECTIONS

Some of the interesting research areas in business education would be to undertake studies and investigate the impacts and environmental influences on business education including issues of globalization, global sustainability, and advances in digital and social media. Another line of research would be to delve and explore the challenges and criticisms of business education covering issues of legitimacy, business model sustainability, and the need for change in business models. For us, we intend to further explore and take up studies on the ways and approaches to the re-invention of business schools and the creation of alternative models of management education and approaches for effective implementation and delivery of those models. A wider discussion of academic leadership and leadership in business schools is essential. In conclusion, these debates and criticisms of business schools need to be continued and addressed through empirical research that may also be contextual to the location of the business education. How to establish standards for business education that are benchmarked for quality but not so standardized that they do not meet the requirements of individual economies is also another interesting path to investigate.

After all healthy debates through research need to be undertaken so that ideas and innovation in business education are not only presented openly and constructively but also widely disseminated for the larger benefit of the education of global society.

CONCLUSION

As has been argued in this chapter, the future of business education has to be, responsible management education for a sustainable world. It will need fundamental changes in business and management education, management research, and managing faculty. This means the time has arrived to redefine the role of business education and business schools as social institutions with a clear public responsibility in a more technology integrated world. Business education world over is devoted overwhelmingly to technical training. This is ironic because even before Enron, studies showed that executives that fail--financially as well as morally--rarely do so from a lack of expertise. Rather, they fail because they lack interpersonal skills and practical wisdom; which Aristotle called prudence. Aristotle taught that genuine leadership consisted of the ability to identify and serve the common good. To do so requires more than technical training. It requires an education in moral reasoning, which must include history, philosophy, literature, theology, logic, and above all curriculum, methods, and metrics that ensure the development of foresight, conviction, and moral compass.

REFERENCES

Augier, M., & March, J. (2011). *The roots, rituals, and rhetorics of change: North American business schools after the Second World War*. Stanford University Press.

Baporikar, N. (2008). *Case Method: Cases in Management* (2nd ed.). Himalaya Publishing House.

Baporikar, N. (2009). Management Education- Challenges Ahead. Himalaya Publishing House.

Baporikar, N. (2010). Doctorate Education: A Practical Guide. Viva Books Private Limited.

Baporikar, N. (2015a). Understanding Professional Development for Educators. *International Journal of Sustainable Economies Management*, 4(4), 18–30. doi:10.4018/IJSEM.2015100102

Baporikar, N. (2015b). Strategies for Promoting Research Culture to Support Knowledge Society. *International Journal of Information Communication Technologies and Human Development*, 7(4), 58–72. doi:10.4018/IJICTHD.2015100104

Baporikar, N. (2015c). Collegiality as a strategy for excellence in academia. *International Journal of Strategic Change Management*, 6(1), 59–72. doi:10.1504/IJSCM.2015.069522

Baporikar, N. (2016). Contemporary Cases in Management. Himalaya Publishing House.

Baporikar, N. (2017a). *Management Education for Global Leadership*. IGI Global., doi:10.4018/978-1-5225-1013-0

Baporikar, N. (2017b). *Innovation and Shifting Perspectives in Management Education*. IGI Global. doi:10.4018/978-1-5225-1019-2

Baporikar, N. (2018a). Educational Leadership: A Global Perspective. In N. P. Ololube (Ed.), *Encyclopaedia of institutional leadership, policy, and management* (pp. 28–51). Pearl Publications.

Baporikar, N. (2018b). Improving Communication by Linking Student Centred Pedagogy and Management Curriculum Development. In N. P. Ololube (Ed.), *Encyclopaedia of institutional leadership, policy, and management* (pp. 369–386). Pearl Publications.

Baporikar, N. (2018c). Rankings and Academia in India. In B. Dutta & S. D. Reddy (Eds.), *University 5.0* (pp. 181–196). MTC Global.

Baporikar, N. (2019a). Significance and Role of Entrepreneurial University in Emerging Economies. *International Journal of Applied Management Sciences and Engineering*, 6(1), 46–61. doi:10.4018/IJAMSE.2019010104

Baporikar, N. (2019b). Preventing Academic Misconduct: Student-Centered Teaching Strategies. In D. Velliaris (Ed.), *Prevention and Detection of Academic Misconduct in Higher Education* (pp. 98–115). IGI Global. doi:10.4018/978-1-5225-7531-3.ch005

Baporikar, N. (2020). Finer Student Engagement via Quality and Lifelong Learning for Sustainable Education. *International Journal of Political Activism and Engagement*, 7(4), 38–55. doi:10.4018/IJPAE.2020100104

Baporikar, N., & Parker, S. (2019). Higher Education Quality and BRICS Network University Pact: Academic Leadership as a Booster. *International Journal of Political Activism and Engagement*, 6(4), 29–41. doi:10.4018/IJPAE.2019100103

Baporikar, N., & Sony, M. (2020). *Quality Management Principles and Policies in Higher Education*. IGI Global. doi:10.4018/978-1-7998-1017-9

Bieger, T. (2011). Business schools–from career training centers towards enablers of CSR: a new vision for teaching at business schools. *Business Schools and Their Contribution to Society*, 104-113.

Bridgman, T., Cummings, S., & McLaughlin, C. (2016). Restating the case: How revisiting the development of the case method can help us think differently about the future of the business school. *Academy of Management Learning & Education*, 15(4), 724–741. doi:10.5465/amle.2015.0291

Colby, A., Ehrlich, T., Sullivan, W. M., & Dolle, J. R. (2011). *Rethinking undergraduate business education: Liberal learning for the profession* (Vol. 20). John Wiley & Sons.

Cooke, B., & Alcadipani, R. (2015). Toward a global history of management education: The case of the Ford Foundation and the São Paulo School of Business Administration, Brazil. *Academy of Management Learning & Education*, 14(4), 482–499. doi:10.5465/amle.2013.0147

Cummings, S., Bridgman, T., Hassard, J., & Rowlinson, M. (2017). *A new history of management*. Cambridge University Press. doi:10.1017/9781316481202

Datar, S. M., Garvin, D. A., Cullen, P. G., & Cullen, P. (2010). *Rethinking the MBA: Business education at a crossroads*. Harvard Business Press.

Dostaler, I., & Tomberlin, J. (2013). The great divide between business schools research and business practice. *Canadian Journal of Higher Education*, 43(1), 115–128. doi:10.47678/cjhe.v43i1.1895

Dyllick, T. (2015). Responsible management education for a sustainable world: The challenges for business schools. *Journal of Management Development*, 34(1), 16–33. doi:10.1108/JMD-02-2013-0022

Finch, D., Deephouse, D. L., O'Reilly, N., Massie, T., & Hillenbrand, C. (2016). Follow the leaders? An analysis of convergence and innovation of faculty recruiting practices in US business schools. *Higher Education*, 71(5), 699–717. doi:10.100710734-015-9931-5

Ghoshal, S. (2005). Bad management theories are destroying good management practices. *Academy of Management Learning & Education*, 4(1), 75–91. doi:10.5465/amle.2005.16132558

Gond, J. P., Igalens, J., Swaen, V., & El Akremi, A. (2011). The human resources contribution to responsible leadership: An exploration of the CSR–HR interface. In *Responsible leadership* (pp. 115–132). Springer. doi:10.1007/978-94-007-3995-6_10

Gordon, R. A., & Howell, J. E. (1959). Higher education for business. *The Journal of Business Education*, *35*(3), 115–117. doi:10.1080/08832323.1959.10116245

Hühn, M. P. (2014). You reap what you sow: How MBA programs undermine ethics. *Journal of Business Ethics*, *121*(4), 527–541. doi:10.100710551-013-1733-z

Khurana, R. (2007). *From Higher Aims to Hired Hands*. Princeton University Press. doi:10.1515/9781400830862

Kieser, A. (2011). Between rigour and relevance: Co-existing institutional logics in the field of management science. *Society and Economy*, *33*(2), 237–247. doi:10.1556/SocEc.33.2011.2.1

Koskela, L. (2017). Why is management research irrelevant? *Construction Management and Economics*, *35*(1-2), 4–23. doi:10.1080/01446193.2016.1272759

Lee, B., & Cassell, C. (Eds.). (2011). *Challenges and controversies in management research* (Vol. 45). Routledge. doi:10.4324/9780203834114

Martin, R. (2007). How successful leaders think. *Harvard Business Review*, *85*(6), 60. PMID:17580648

Martin, R. L. (2009). *The opposable mind: How successful leaders win through integrative thinking*. Harvard Business Press.

Mintzberg, H. (2004). *Managers, not MBAs: A hard look at the soft practice of managing and management development*. Berrett-Koehler Publishers.

Muff, K. (2013). Developing globally responsible leaders in business schools: A vision and transformational practice for the journey ahead. *Journal of Management Development*, *32*(5), 487–507. doi:10.1108/02621711311328273

Pfeffer, J., & Fong, C. T. (2004). The business school 'business': Some lessons from the US experience. *Journal of Management Studies*, *41*(8), 1501–1520. doi:10.1111/j.1467-6486.2004.00484.x

Pierson, F. C. (1959). The education of American businessmen. *The Journal of Business Education*, *35*(3), 114–117. doi:10.1080/08832323.1959.10116244

Podolny, J. M. (2009). The buck stops (and starts) at business school. *Harvard Business Review*, *87*(6), 62–67.

Riel, J., & Martin, R. L. (2017). *Creating great choices: A leader's guide to integrative thinking*. Harvard Business Press.

Starkey, K., Tempest, S., & Cinque, S. (2019). Management education and the theatre of the absurd. *Management Learning*, *50*(5), 591–606. doi:10.1177/1350507619875894

Tubulingane, B. S., & Baporikar, N. (2020). Student Satisfaction Approach for Enhancing University Competitiveness. *International Journal of Technology-Enabled Student Support Services*, *10*(2), 31–54. doi:10.4018/IJTESSS.2020070103

Wilson, D. C., & Thomas, H. (2012). The Legitimacy of the Business of Business Schools: What's the Future? *Journal of Management Development*, *31*(4), 368–376. doi:10.1108/02621711211219040

KEY TERMS AND DEFINITIONS

Business: Pertains broadly to commercial, financial, and industrial activities.

Challenges: Something that by its nature or character serves as a call to make a special effort, a demand to explain, justify, or difficulty in an undertaking that is stimulating to one engaged in it.

Competence: Refers to the capacity of individuals/ employees to act in a wide variety of situations. It is their education, skills, experience, energy, and attitudes.

Development: Means 'steady progress' and stresses effective assisting in hastening a process or bringing about the desired end, a significant consequence or event, the act or process of growing, progressing, or developing.

E-Learning: Electronic learning (or e-Learning or eLearning) is a type of education where the medium of instruction in computer technology. In some instances, no in-person interaction takes place. It can be defined as a planned teaching/learning experience that uses a wide spectrum of technologies, mainly internet or computer-based, to reach learners.

Education: The process of formal knowledge giving process. The actions in process of imparting for acquiring general knowledge, developing the powers of reasoning and judgment, especially at schools, generally for preparing oneself or others for mature life.

Faculty: The entire teaching and administrative force of a university, college, or school.

Higher Education: The act or process of imparting and acquiring knowledge, developing the powers of reasoning and judgment, the act and practice of imparting knowledge, especially at college, or university, the theory of teaching and learning generally of preparing oneself or others intellectually for mature life.

Impact: To affect, the effect of coming into contact with a thing or person; the force exerted by a new idea, concept, technology, or ideology, the impression made by an idea, cultural movement, social group, it is to drive or press (an object) firmly into (another object, thing, etc.) to have an impact or strong effect (on).

Knowledge Development: The development of knowledge includes not only processes of external knowledge procurement (i.e., through cooperative efforts, consultants, new contacts, etc.) or the creation of specific knowledge resources like research and development departments. The formation of personal and technical knowledge networks is also part of the development of knowledge.

Learning: The knowledge acquired by systematic study in any field of scholarly application and includes the act or process of acquiring knowledge or skill, which generally lead to the modification of behavior through practice, training, or experience, practice, or exercise, and includes associative processes.

Management Education: The act or process of imparting or acquiring knowledge to develop the members of the executive or administration of an organization or business, managers, or employers collectively, or train in the techniques, practice, or science of managing, controlling, or dealing, in the skillful or resourceful use of materials, time, etc.

Student: Pupil, a person formally engaged in learning, especially one enrolled in a school or college; any person who studies, investigates, or examines thoughtfully.

Sustainability: Sustainability is the ability or capacity of something to maintain or to sustain itself.

Tacit: Expressed or understood without being directly stated or in words, to involve or indicate by inference, association, or necessary consequence, to contain potential sense.

Chapter 15
Developments and Global Trends in the Education and Business Sectors in the Post-COVID-19 Period:
The Mexican Case

Enriqueta Márquez
Universidad Anáhuac, Mexico

ABSTRACT

In this chapter, the author focuses on the reality of living through a pandemic that made people worldwide prioritize their matters of importance. Since the beginning of the pandemic, the educational sector was one of the most privileged ones thanks to the previous implementation of proper technologies and internet tools. The author will analyze the challenges faced by teachers, students, and parents, who had to adapt workplaces and focus their efforts to continuously innovate and capture the attention of students. On the business arena, the pandemic was a digital accelerator. Many businesses had to improve their digital platforms and different types of consumers emerged. The author will highlight the global consumer trends that emerged during the pandemic which will remain throughout the post-COVID-19 period and the challenges to capitalize on all the new trends that emerged to transform persons into better human beings and to contribute building a better world.

INTRODUCTION

Because of the Pandemic, the world economy changed. Purchasing habits, lifestyles, entertainment, amusement, study, and work itself have evolved. According to the Interactive Advertising Bureau (IAB, 2020), health contingencies caused 6 out of 10 Internet users to isolate themselves rigorously. As a result, more online purchases were made, 2 out of 3 people faced a change in household income, so they became more careful with managing income and savings, and 44% of Internet users increased their

DOI: 10.4018/978-1-7998-7689-2.ch015

Developments and Global Trends in the Education and Business Sectors in the Post-COVID-19 Period

family spending during the last quarter of 2020. Concerning the first quarter of 2021, caused by price increases in almost all product categories and purchases of new products such as vitamins and antigen tests to travel, continue with their daily activities, and ensure they remain healthy.

According to Salvatto (2021), the technological revolution we are experiencing is changing our reality like never before, bringing endless opportunities and threats that need to be considered. The post-Covid world is a mixture of speed and uncertainty, making people and companies learn to be flexible, adapting in weeks or hours to new business schemes, and using new technologies to solve customer and even family problems in a matter of minutes.

An example of this is how different communication media have reached 100 million users worldwide. Created in 1878, phones took 75 years to get 100 million users. Cell phones, launched in 1979, took 16 years. The Internet, started in 1990, seven years. Facebook, developed in 2004, four years and six months. WhatsApp, created in 2009, three years and four months, and Instagram, set in 2010, only required two years and four months. These figures explain the speed of new technologies and forms of communication that have become important communication and business platforms.

This chapter provides the elements to understand how the reality of living through a pandemic made people worldwide and in México prioritize their matters of importance to be adequately informed. In principle, people wanted to take care of their family health by getting the best benefits from the health system (70%). They also wanted to know about addressing and improving poverty issues caused by Covid19 to help their communities' needy (62%). Also, people were interested in managing mechanisms to strengthen educational systems (62%) and being aware of other issues, such as climate change (61%). (Edelman Trust Barometer, 2021).

Furthermore, trust all information sources such as search engines, traditional, social, and owned media were at record lows in trustfulness. Table 1 presents trust percentages in each source.

Table 1. Trust percentages in each source

Year	Search Engines	Traditional Media	Owned Media	Social Media
2020	62	61	46	40
2021	56	53	41	35

Source: Adapted from the Edelman Trust Barometer 2021.

According to Luque et al. (2020), Twitter has become more than just a social platform, as it helped spread positive and alarming pictures of the Covid19 situation by the primary domestic and global media to show the reality that turned out to be more severe than officially deemed and that was exposed by unofficial global media in different countries. Although some of these images were fake or not true, it made the media's credibility worldwide decrease.

The goal is to analyze the challenges faced in the educational sector and the business arena, describing the new types of consumers and global consumer trends that emerged during the pandemic, which will remain throughout the post-Covid19 period thanks to technological advances.

DEVELOPMENTS IN THE POST-COVID 19 PERIOD

For the first time in the world of the mass media, people felt uninformed, full of contradictory fake news or false information (60%). In contrast, the social and political aspects were left on the back burner. (Edelman Trust Barometer, 2021). Making simple decisions such as using a mask, understanding the right sanitation conditions in workplaces, or knowing the time and place to get the Covid19 vaccine became complex and even stressful situations for people.

For this reason, we went from Transmedia Storytelling to the new phenomenon of Transmedia Omnichannel. In Transmedia Storytelling, any media, whether traditional media, digital media, a business website, or a personal comment, could generate news, either through a formal statement or from a tweet. But with the Transmedia Omnichannel, people are more careful when they receive a message. They search for information in different media, basing their decisions on the data found in traditional and digital media sources. Also, they validate data integrity with friends or family members using WhatsApp or Facebook, as this strategy generates more confidence than viewing a YouTube video or posting on social networks, as social networks can contain fake news. As a result of the pandemic, consumers were eager to have information from various sources. They became selective of the final data they considered accurate or more convincing based on their decision-making process in simple matters like staying healthy.

From a medium- to long-term perspective, the current push for digitization needs must be backed by investments focused on economic recovery and the necessary complementary (business and public) intangible capital. If the funds are used in such a manner, a post-Covid19 scenario will likely lead to a pronounced increase in labor productivity growth (Roth, 2021).

The Coronavirus crisis has placed us quickly and intensely in a scenario of high volatility, uncertainty, complexity, and ambiguity where digitization is an essential element. This digital evolvement implies that companies generate new processes and rethink how they want to work with the new ways of doing things, seeking to become more efficient with their resources. Table 2 presents how companies perceive that digital transformation has created value in their organizations. The factors evaluated and perceived to have made the most value due to this digital transformation were Customer Experience/ Engagement, Mobile Technologies, and Digital Asset Management. (Jeffrey Group, 2020)

Table 2. Percent of digital transformation value to organizations

Customer Experience – Engagement	13.7	Data Mining - Analytics	10.6
Mobile Technologies	13.5	E-commerce	10.6
Digital Asset Management	13.0	Product Information Management	9.4
Cloud Computing Services	12.8	Internet of Things	6.5

Source: Adapted from Jeffrey Group (2020).

It is essential to mention the growth in the use of apps and digital platforms. Although they were already in a growing trend from previous years, their use intensified due to confinement. This fact is because while being at home and returning to a new post-Covid19 reality, people use this form of communication to continue working, studying, and contacting family and friends. Also, to make online purchases without leaving home, obtain information on current topics of interest, or simply as a means of entertainment. (IAB Mexico, 2020).

Table 3. Growth of the most popular apps during the pandemic

Netflix	Microsoft Teams	Zoom	Skype	Facetime
9,550%	1,100%	875%	550%	548%

Source: Adapted from Jeffrey Group (2020).

About health, the imposition of lockdowns during the different waves of the Covid19 outbreak was driven by the alarming projected spread of the disease, aiming to reduce the health impact of the epidemic but not to stop transmission completely, to suppression (Ferguson et al., 2020; Lacobucci, 2020). These lockdown restrictions and the resulting impact on social life and the economy are linked to at least two significant adverse public health consequences: reduction in physical exercise and mental health deterioration. A growing body of international studies show that lockdown policies harm mobility and outdoor recreational activity (Askitas et al., 2020); the adverse impact of Covid19 and lockdown restrictions on mental health has also recently been documented (Banks & Xu, 2020; Davillas & Jones, 2021).

When people could no longer do any physical conditioning indoors, due to the closure of gyms, and outdoors, due to mobility restrictions, coaches and trainers began to offer the same classes through electronic platforms such as Zoom and Google meet. This way, people could continue with their exercise routines, and this particular segment could continue operating. As soon as it was clear that Covid19 could be controlled with safe distancing and masks, many exterior activities such as Soccer and even the traditional 2021 Superbowl in the United States came back to normal.

Concerning physical, spiritual, and psychological well-being, people unable to leave their homes, regardless of the weather, saw the opportunity to continue exercising at home. Thus, increasing the sale of electronic exercising devices significantly, such as treadmills, elliptical trainers, fixed biceps, and rowing machines. Same for the video game industry in which they could dance, play sports, or do any kind of physical conditioning as well. Another effect was churches offering their traditional Sunday masses through YouTube and Zoom with the opportunity to interact and participate in Spiritual retirements, where participants received the talks and meditations via WhatsApp. Also, Psychologists and Nutritionists continued their therapies by Facetime or Zoom. They returned to their offices with face masks and the necessary social distance measures as soon as possible.

Weather conditions did not exacerbate the mental health costs of the pandemic. Promotion of the existing guidelines from public health authorities on regular indoor exercises should be further intensified during winter lockdowns since weather conditions affected people's outdoor physical activity. (Burdett, Davillas, Etheridge, 2021)

While countries finished with their vaccination campaigns, people had the opportunity to return to their sport and spiritual activities as they did before the pandemic. Still, others preferred to continue maintaining their exercise routines, therapies, and religious services through Zoom or Facebook because of the safety and practicality of not having to leave their home. This fact is an evolution that is here to stay even after the pandemic, and that these types of service providers will have to continue offering to their users.

Faced with uncertainty, people began to worry about keeping their jobs and how they could help in their communities without leaving home. Also, people worried about public support focused on the unemployed or companies that, due to their activity, were necessary to continue operating or bankrupted, mainly department stores, pubs, and restaurants.

Priorities changed overnight. Environmental problems were significant, but it was even more important to know how people would continue teaching or working from home; how their children will continue with their classes without having an estimated date to return to face-to-face courses. The challenge was solving how they would balance work, personal, and home school activities. Activities made in a limited space and without having the distractions of attending social gatherings or walking or going on vacations safely; having families to wait from health and work-related aspects and personal projects. After families had to postpone health, work-related and personal matters, significant changes emerged in their consumer behavioral patterns, study methods, and lifestyle habits.

One of the consumption trends that had already been observed and increased with the crisis was online shopping. It is foreseeable that some patterns and practices of the digital economy adopted out of necessity will remain part of new normality even after the pandemic problem is solved. On the one hand, to support the digital transformation process, the Government had the task of increasing the availability, accessibility, and affordability of the connectivity and broadband infrastructure to extend the benefits of digitization to the most significant number of business dimensions, regardless of their economic activity, geographic region, degree of urbanization, etc. On the other hand, it had the task of promoting the digital transformation of companies through training and financing to get the full benefits of digitization. Finally, proper competitive conditions were procured so that companies, particularly SMEs, had similar access conditions to markets, allowing them to enter digital markets successfully. (Navarro, 2021)

Prioritization was a constant in all people's lives, and it will continue to be so after the pandemic. To prioritize activities to carry out a daily task without the same number of employees. Prioritize economic resources to guarantee their existence in the event of employment scarcity or the case that the segment in which they operate did not reopen soon. Prioritize the patients who had to be seen first when hospitals were saturated; In the case of governments, prioritize the aspects that would help them quickly overcome the aftermath of Covid19. Prioritize which products to buy online and on which platforms, depending on delivery times. Prioritize who to meet with for a video call or focus on essential home activities after combining Home Office and Home School activities simultaneously. In having to leave home, prioritize the most critical actions during those hours they were away while staying healthy.

GLOBAL TRENDS IN THE EDUCATIONAL AND BUSINESS SECTORS

The pandemic caused a sharp contraction in economic activity since the primary measure adopted to control the spread of the virus was a substantial restriction of productive activities. This fact reduced the Gross Domestic Product (GDP) of most countries. For example, due to Mexico's economic activities limits, GDP was reduced by 8.5% in 2020 compared to 2019 (INEGI, 2020). Likewise, the use of digital platforms increased significantly in the educational and financial sectors. Businesses from transnational companies to Small and Medium Enterprises (SMEs) and even recreational and tourism services evolved. The result is that online sessions replaced face-to-face sessions. Additionally, payment forms and services offered through the companies' internet pages or apps increased significantly.

In Mexico, six out of ten SMEs sell online, and two ventured into this kind of app distribution channel derived from the pandemic (Asociación Mexicana de Ventas Online, 2020). This fact is an example that supports the expectation that this accelerated growth trend in the digitization of the economy and electronic commerce will continue in the future. Some of the digital economy practices adopted out of necessity today will remain as part of new normality. SMEs increasingly recognize the importance of electronic commerce as a high-growth distribution media that allowed them to diversify compared to traditional channels (Asociación Mexicana de Internet, 2020).

Table 4 shows the percent of internet penetration in different countries to show that countries with greater internet access were more likely to carry out more electronic commerce operations. Although this phenomenon also occurred in developing countries, where lower socioeconomic levels had internet access through their mobile phones.

Table 4. Internet penetration

Country	In %	Country	In %
Canada	98	Chile	58
United States	81	China	45
Argentina	63	Brazil	43
Mexico	61	Turkey	41

Source: Adapted from Navarro (2021).

The pandemic showed that 70% of jobs could be done remotely. However, only 2 out of 10 companies had the necessary working and digital culture to efficiently implement this new working modality (Coronado; Llanos, 2020). It has been one of the most remarkable changes and challenges of this period to adapt in a matter of days. Traditionally everything done had to be done remotely using digital platforms or taking those services offered directly to consumers' homes.

During and after the pandemic, people's priorities changed. Many people became more sensitive to being affected by this virus or losing a loved one to this disease. The world has changed, and two sectors in which these changes have been more tangible, which will be analyzed in-depth in the following sections of this chapter, is precisely the Education and Business sectors.

Challenges and New Trends in the Education Sector

Since the pandemic's beginning, the educational sector was one of the most privileged due to the previous implementation of proper technologies and Internet tools. Therefore, in just a few days in Mexico, preschool to Ph.D. studies classes migrated from the schools and universities classrooms to students' homes. In this way, the educational environment entered into a new Home School modality. Furthermore, thanks to their uninterrupted activities, the educational sector was one of the few capable of maintaining its revenue level.

As most jobs were kept, teens and adults continued with their studies, and some online programs even increased their tuition prices, given the higher demand. Many people wanted to study for years but did not enroll due to the lack of time. This new online modality avoids commuting times, and people

Developments and Global Trends in the Education and Business Sectors in the Post-COVID-19 Period

are at home attending to their families while studying, which contributed to the growth of this online consumption segment. Table 5 presents significant purchasing preferences when compared to the 2020s.

Table 5. Major purchasing preferences

Courier Services	Education	Payment of Services	Bank Services	Mobile Phone
52%	52%	75%	78%	78%

Source: Adapted from AMVO (*Asociación Mexicana de Venta Online*) (2021).

The challenges faced by teachers, students, and parents, while adapting workplaces and study materials to a digital format, they had to innovate continuously and implement teaching techniques to capture students' attention through a screen. The educational institutions had to offer immediate training to teachers to maintain a high academic standard to achieve the school objectives of the different cycles.

Figure 1. Typical Rules for a Home School Session
Source: Author

As for the **teachers**, they faced the following challenges:

1. To change from traditional teaching materials to remote session formats via digital platforms such as television, Zoom, Microsoft Teams, or Google Meet. When taught in person, teachers can interact and talk with students so that less material is required to be covered. In contrast, if students do not have the same level of participation in online classes, many different topics would have to be prepared in advance to be covered appropriately.
2. Establish rules for remote session interactions where students are requested to connect on time, keeping their computer or mobile device cameras always connected and their microphones muted until their participation is asked for with a respectful behavior towards teachers and student´s comments. Figure 1 shows some typical rules for a Home School Session by zoom or videoconference platforms.
3. Comply with the training requirements that educational institutions at all levels offered to teachers to give them tools such as Kahoot, Socrative, Classroom, or Reading. Platforms to be used during their sessions to make them more attractive for students and help keep their attention.
4. Design individual and team participation dynamics that could be carried out remotely and accordingly to the study program's objectives.
5. Establish evaluation and feedback procedures that promoted real student learning, with realistic and achievable metrics within a limited time frame.
6. In television sessions or where it was impossible to have live conversations between teachers and students, establish forms of communication and deliver the materials requested during the school year by using WhatsApp, text messages, or email.
7. In countries with face-to-face classes, it was a great challenge to establish security protocols such as masks at all times by teachers, administrators, and students. Also, it was challenging to achieve proper accommodation in classrooms to promote healthy distance between students. Another challenge was developing a health control of those attending the classes, such as taking the temperature at different times of the day or keeping an entire group under observation without attending college or university in the event of infected students.
8. To adapt to more extensive than usual courses or with the presence of international students since some courses, especially postgraduate ones, increased their online enrollment by offering the opportunity to people from different countries and cities to enroll. Such has been the success that many seminars, even after the pandemic, will continue with the online modality.

According to Núñez et al. (2020), our knowledge society requires more institutions and teachers that ease knowledge generation to create an excellent educational system that guarantees equality and improves quality to influence productivity growth positively and improve the quality of life of its citizens. To surmount the crisis caused by Covid19, the so-called digital natives need as much, or even a more complete and complex training than their predecessors, if they want to master the information to access skills and knowledge to solve all kinds of problems. As a result, they can develop an enriching life to create social wealth and well-being. This goal requires organizational changes, alignment of objectives, simplification of the current bureaucratization, and, most importantly, improvements to make the teaching and research profession attractive to new talent and motivate students in their training. It also requires establishing a solid and relevant information system that Artificial Intelligence and other Big Data analysis tools allow to provide the system with the necessary analytical capability to identify problems and propose innovative and flexible solutions.

Delving further into parents' perspective, the interaction of school closures and parents in economic distress will have long-term effects on children and teenagers. Fathers' earnings dropped to zero were about 7.5 percentage points less likely to have received additional paid learning resources (such as tutoring or learning apps) than fathers who did not experience a drop in earnings during the early months of the pandemic. Fathers whose earnings dropped to zero appear to have substituted reduced paid learning resources with time. Their children received about 30 more minutes of help with schoolwork per day. Mothers with earnings reductions to zero or reduced earnings more generally experienced mental health deterioration by 18% and 11%, respectively. The quality of parent-child interactions has also been affected, but only for fathers.

On the one hand, fathers whose earnings dropped to zero were less likely to talk regularly about matters with their children. On the other hand, they were also less likely to quarrel often with their children. For mothers, labor market shocks did not significantly affect their interactions with their children regarding fighting or talking about things that matter. Results suggest that these sources might be further aggravated when parents experiencing economic distress are obliged simultaneously to care for their children when proper care is shut down. (Hupkau, Isphording, Machin, & Ruiz-Valenzuela, 2021)

The previous study sustains that the main challenges faced by **parents** were:

1. Achieve a balanced schedule to support and supervise their children in school activities while at the same time carrying out their professional and home activities.
2. Establish study spaces at home that favor the concentration and learning of their children.
3. In the case of families with sufficient resources, looking for remote or in-person support would complement the missing gaps in their children's learning process.
4. Establish and differentiate school allotted time from healthy leisure time to achieve healthy coexistence with their children and avoid wear and tiredness from school duties that affect their family relationships.
5. Adapt patiently to all school and teacher requirements, trusting that all actions implemented by governments and educational institutions were for their children's well-being and proper learning.

Regarding students, school closures and other lockdown policies seem to have reduced the mortality associated with Covid19 in most countries (Dehning et al., 2020; Flaxman et al., 2020).

However, some differences were shown in the impact between individuals with low- and high-educated parents. First, parents with higher levels of education are more capable of substituting for the learning loss suffered by their children. Second, internet coverage for highly educated families is higher in most countries. Hence, they can benefit from the online resources while low-educated families cannot or can do it to a more limited extent. Third, while many children of low-educated families that experience educational mobility upward attain at most a secondary degree, most children of high-educated parents continue their academic career (Neidhoefer, Lustig, & Tommasi, 2021)

The reality was that students' age and educational level made the process either easier or more difficult. In the case of Junior high school, High School, University, and Postgraduate levels, it was the student`s responsibility to attend and pay attention to the teaching sessions regardless of whether they were face-to-face or online. While addressing preschool-age students was a more complicated process since they needed their parents' support and supervision during the online sessions to stay focused and comply with the expected learning objectives. At this level, greater cooperation among students, teachers, and parents was needed.

The challenges and new trends found in **students** were:

1. The need to meet the learning objectives regardless of whether the sessions were online or face-to-face.
2. Learn to use new technological tools such as Kahoot or Classroom as part of their school activities since they would continue to be used in the post-Covid period.
3. Focus and honesty about what they were learning since they did not have a teacher in front of them, and making sure they had all the needed materials at hand. Their responsibility was to focus and learn and not just copy the information from previous note sessions.
4. Maintain friendship relationships through digital platforms, as many countries continued with the online class modality, and there was no personal conviviality with their friends. The growth in digital platforms such as Messenger Kids, Playdates by Zoom, or playing video games online with their friends is a trend that increased during the pandemic. That will continue to be used even when all students return to classes in person.
5. Value the fact that attending College or University is to acquire knowledge, interact with other people, and create networking experiences. Figure 2 shows students during their Home School Sessions.

Figure 2. Students during their Home School Sessions
Source: Author.

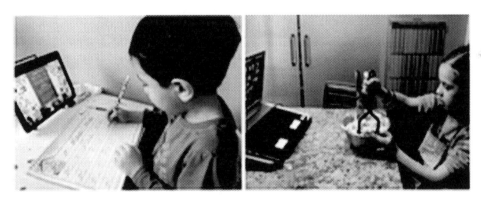

In short, it is critical to highlight the importance of keeping personal and institutional incentives in place so that both systems persevere on the path of change and improvement. Among these areas of action, and as a priority, changes should focus on the following:

1) Management of educational and research centers,
2) Selection, training, and promotion of teachers and researchers
3) Control of results, considering that any increase in education and science expenditure, which should be considered as an investment, must become a compelling incentive to launch, consolidate and achieve the expected educational objectives (De la Fuente, 2015).

Finally, the evolution of the institutions had to evolve to maintain the educational standards and achieve a safe return to the classrooms. It is necessary to capitalize on the new opportunities found in the online classes, such as those that involve the expansion of many local programs, both nationally and internationally.

DEVELOPMENTS AND NEW TRENDS IN THE BUSINESS ARENA

In the business arena, the pandemic was a digital accelerator. Many businesses had to improve their digital platforms, such as department stores and supermarkets, home delivery restaurants, digital banks offering more online transactions options to protect people by refraining them from visiting the branches. Digital platforms must improve to support work meetings and conferences by Zoom or Google Meet, promote workout sessions, provide medical consultations, experiment virtual tours in amusement parks, and foster the need for continuous innovation and new products sold through digital platforms like Netflix or video games. As a result, consumers are entertained. It is a fact that the pandemic increased the time spent on these platforms significantly. Figure 3 shows digitalization amid Covid19.

According to Sheth (2020), consumption habits are altered by changes in the context. Highlighting the following:

1) Social context: These are events in the consumer's life such as getting married, having children, relocating to another area or country, or even changing jobs.
2) Technological context: the use of the Internet, the emergence of smartphones, tablets, computer change, and online shopping.
3) Context of rules and regulations related to public and shared spaces: Maintaining clean public areas, respecting parking places with particular indications, or complying with the requirements requested for the use of common areas, whether public or private.
4) Context of natural disasters, as well as regional, national or global conflicts: These are less predictable events such as earthquakes, hurricanes, war, or the Covid19 pandemic itself where those affected and the people around them change their behavior, either to receive help or to be able to collaborate in the best of their abilities.

It is interesting to note how within the pandemic, digital, and natural disasters context, three other different types of consumers emerged, given the nature of the virus, the beliefs generated around it, and the medical indications to take care of ourselves and remain healthy, these new consumers are the following:

1) People who prefer to remain indoors: People who, despite having been vaccinated, continued to carry out their activities at home in lockdown, and after a year of not going out, are used to ordering groceries and accessories online to be delivered to their homes. During the morning, they do home office work while their children take online classes and organize meetings with their friends through zoom, which they enjoy widely. They even have services taken to their homes, such as a haircut or a bank messenger bringing a signature document. Although they could go out, these people saw the convenience of doing their daily activities at home and felt more secure by opting not to go out.

2) Mixed consumers: They are people who have applied a dual purchase scheme, either by making purchases and activities online when necessary or in person, in the absence of other options. These consumers have learned to take advantage of all the technological advances in business, and whenever possible, to enjoy going out for a walk, visit a shopping mall or even enjoy eating at a restaurant with a terrace.

Figure 3. Digitalization amid Covid19
Source: Adapted from Kotler, Kartajaya, and Setawan (2021).

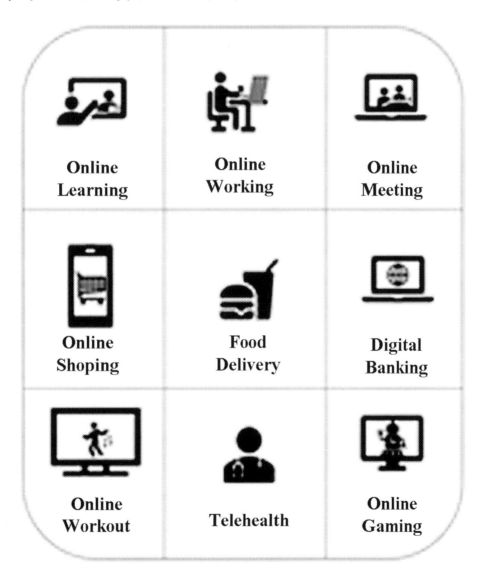

3) People who have never stayed at home and continued carrying out their normal activities because they need to work or just for pleasure. Primarily, people from the health, media, self-service, and pharmacy sectors always kept working, and it was thanks to these people, who never left home,

others were able to satisfy their basic needs. These consumers taught us that it was possible to go out without getting sick with the proper precautions. Although some of these groups continued traveling and following their routines, as if the pandemic did not exist, they suffer from the virus (AMVO, 2020)

Additionally, and according to their income level, two types of consumers were observed:

1) Consumers with savings and earnings: They can face the pandemic and its effects in a relaxed manner. These consumers took advantage of the available time at home to complete unfinished tasks and reorganize their activities without the burden of financial needs while maintaining a higher level of physical and mental health.

It is often forgotten to highlight those businesses that had significant growth due to the nature of the pandemic. Such was the case of companies like 3M, Clorox, Amazon, Mercado Libre, zoom, google meet, antibacterial gel manufacturers, companies that provide home repair and painting products, food and drink industries, and funeral homes, among many others. Not to mention pharmaceutical companies able to develop successful Covid19 vaccines. Many have double-digit growth and are publicly traded, with significant impact and value increase at stock markets. Table 6 presents Internet-bought products with higher growth rates.

Table 6. Internet bought product with higher growth rates

Food Delivery	66%	Pharmacy	41%
Clothes	57%	Supermarket	40%
Beauty and Personal Care	52%	Office	37%
Electronics	46%	Sports	33%
Videogames	41%		

Source: Adapted from AMVO (*Asociación Mexicana de Venta Online*)(2021).

2) Consumers lacking savings to overcome the crisis: They found themselves in severe economic difficulties when they lost their jobs or saw their income severely reduced. People who struggled with this and had stressful moments, and on occasions, suffered from health and mental related issues, set their goals to be financially prepared and avoid this from happening again. Some looked to relocate to countries that provide better support or seeked support from family members or friends. We also find groups of people whose businesses had to be shut down, such as bars and gymnasiums. They had to seek alternative income options in segments of great demand, such as Covid Testing services and the sale of face masks, among others. These are resilient people who did not let their guard down and learned the lesson to be better prepared and become less affected by future similar situations.

It is said that during the post-Covid19 period, things will come back to normal. However, after this pandemic, everything will change. So, all that was learned and experienced needs to be capitalized to become more humane and supportive.

Globally and in Mexico, confidence in companies was the least volatile during the pandemic period, maintaining a positive confidence level of 71%. In Mexico, companies were the only institutions to earn points since the last edition of the report (+ 1pt.) because they maintain employment and stakeholders' security in nonsecure environments defined by official changing guidelines related to Covid19's evolution and vaccination.

On the other hand, institutions such as NGOs fell to second place in trustiness with 67%, and the media obtained 53%, classified as neutral institutions. In comparison, the Mexican Government is the only institution in mistrust (44%), with 12 points less since the last measurement in May 2020. Companies are the only institutions considered competent and ethical in Mexico; companies are the only institutions respondents consider skilled in the country, with 40 points above the Government. (Edelman Trust Barometer, 2021). Table 7 shows us the levels of trust globally and in Mexico in companies, NGOs, Government, and the Media, where companies are the institutions most trusted.

Table 7. Trusted institutions

	Business	**NGOs**	**Government**	**Media**
World (mean)	61%	57%	53%	51%
Mexico	71%	67%	44%	53%

Source: Adapted from Edelman Trust Barometer (2021).

The reality is that in the face of a new virus, vaccines became the only hope to return to the previous lifestyle before the pandemic. An efficacious vaccine is essential to prevent further morbidity and mortality. Although some countries might deploy Covid19 vaccines on the strength of safety and immunogenicity data alone, vaccine development aims to gain direct evidence of vaccine efficacy in protecting humans' infection, and Covid19 to manufacture efficacious vaccines can be selectively upscaled. However, the most crucial efficacy endpoint, protection against severe disease and death, is difficult to assess in phase 3 clinical trials. (Hodgson S. et al., 2020).

According to Sassen (2014), the growth of inequality in the world in the last 30 years has been relentless. They were making it clear that the income gap between rich and emerging nations is large and growing. This aspect is evident in the development and distribution of Covid19 vaccines, where developed countries made negotiations with pharmaceutical companies, even before the production of vaccines began to secure the first batches for their citizens. While less resourceful countries were put on a waiting list and could start their vaccination schedules up to 3 months after the developed countries did. Even for the last Quarter of 2021, they still have not received the requested vaccines to complete their vaccination programs.

By August 2021, while the world had administered more than 4,586 million vaccines, in the United States, more than 353 million vaccines had been applied, while in Mexico, only about 73 million vaccines had been administered (Our World in data, 2021). This fact causes the United States and other countries to complete their vaccination programs within their entire population to reactivate their economies. In contrast, developing countries like Mexico continue with incremental Covid19 cases that generate spending on the health sector. Many people continue to be in confinement and using online school schemes. While Covid19 is already being controlled in some developed countries, Mexico is still lagging in its vaccinating programs and cannot reactivate its economy fully.

According to the National Survey of Occupation and Employment (ENOE) of June 2021, the economically active population amounted to 57 million 386 thousand people, of which 55.1 million (96%) were employed, while 2 million 309 thousand (4%) were unemployed. According to Luque et al. (2020), hence the need for changes in international regulations capable of encompassing all the complexity of the significant economic conglomerates, with criteria that transcend the state framework and break the apparent separation between a parent company and subsidiaries (Zubizarreta, 2019).

According to Euromonitor (2021), the global consumer trends that emerged during the Covid19 pandemic, which will remain throughout the post-Covid period, will be analyzed. These trends will be grouped into those directly related to people's lifestyles and those about society and the world.

People's lifestyle

1. Safety Obsessed: Demand contactless services, exceptional sanitation standards, and products that enhance hygiene and immunity. Taking care of health and remain healthy has become one of the most important aspects for individuals and families.
2. Prioritize to avoid being Shaken and Stirred: Reassess priorities and identities to pursue a more fulfilled life and improved mental resilience. Depression and mental health had a moderate or severe impact on 73% of global consumers´ everyday lives last year.
3. Thoughtful Thriftier: Budget cautiously and purchase value-added and affordable products and services. By experiencing or witnessing how many products and services sectors were left without receiving any income due to lockdowns, people became more aware of taking care of their income, savings and focusing spending habits on what created value for them.
4. Workplaces in New Spaces: Find a new work-life balance, as remote collaboration redefined the traditional office environment. More than half of the global consumers previously had a strict boundary between work or school and personal life.

Although it was sometimes complicated, people valued working without leaving their homes.

5. Playing with Time: Gain newfound flexibility, scheduling activities in a non-conventional order to suit individual time demands. Working from home and order products delivered at their doors promoted a balance between their life and work, which people want to continue having.
6. Outdoor Oasis: Reconnect with nature and turn to open-air venues for leisure and to safely socialize. It is an opportunity to get together with family and friends. Besides the impressive evolvement of products and services offered by companies so that their consumers can now experience their products outdoors.
7. Phygital Reality: Use digital tools to stay connected at home and facilitate safer procedures in brick-and-mortar outlets. This is another opportunity due to technology, where you can attend a meeting, a class, or even play a video game with friends from your cell phone or Ipad anytime, anywhere.

8. Craving Convenience: Desire the ease of on-the-go, impulse, and unanticipated occasions and simplicities of pre-pandemic life. They are valuing the ability to meet with co-workers, family, and friends continuously and safely.

Concerning society and the world

9. Restless and Rebellious: Distrust media and governments, defying misinformation and putting their needs first. In 2020, 29% of global consumers were actively involved in political and social issues. Every time there is a more outstanding analysis of the information received from different media sources, people now have a greater awareness of being protected from the virus. Concerns have shifted not only to think about yourself but also to watch over others while contributing in whatever way possible to safety.
10. Build Back Better: Expect purpose-driven initiatives that support the triple bottom line—people, planet, and profits. Nearly 70% of professionals expect consumers to be more concerned about sustainability than before COVID19. Consumers also expect specific actions from the Government and companies as it is everyone`s responsibility to help make a better place to live.

Cooperation among countries and companies to achieve faster solutions to problems in the world is an example of the trends mentioned above focused on the control of this pandemic and the prevention of other variants of the virus. The return to a family and friend's coexistence increase quality time, either in person or through the new technologies allowing many people from different countries to meet simultaneously. Outdoor activities will continue to be enjoyed, which during the pandemic in many countries was the only option of coexistence. Even more, some religious services will continue to be broadcasted through YouTube or Facebook. Also, there is a big possibility that physical-digital reality will be maintained due to the development and effectiveness of these new digital platforms. There will be occasions in which people will prefer to continue using e-commerce platforms. There will be a significant concern regarding security and health issues. Companies will most likely offer new working schemes, and people will manage their economy by keeping savings for any kind to overcome unexpected future events (Nielsen, 2020; Euromonitor, 2021).

FUTURE RESEARCH

Future research will analyze if there are changes in students' social interactions at different ages after returning to the face-to-face sessions, especially in those countries where schools and universities operated remotely for almost two years and where interactions were possible only through a screen. Also, it will be essential to analyze the enrollment trends for remote programs, such as specialized courses and postgraduate degrees maintained after the pandemic, and the preference of face-to-face classes for online classes.

It is also essential to analyze which technologies were more effective since their implementation at the beginning of the pandemic to improve teaching methods and accelerate learning creatively.

From a family point of view, it will be essential to analyze the effect on family members who no longer have a 24-hour interaction in the same place to work, study, and play while performing parenthood, executive, and professor roles simultaneously.

On the corporate side, it will be necessary to analyze the critical success factors in those countries that could achieve a rapid post-covid economic recovery.

Within omnichannel consumer behavior, it will be necessary to delve further into the preferred purchasing channels after the pandemic and how the communication messages impact the purchasing decision of consumers.

It will be essential to analyze the efficiency of new benefits packages offered by enterprises and their impact on achieving greater productivity and having a more balanced life. It will also be critical to detecting if media communications are more objective in transmitting facts and news with integrity.

Finally, it is crucial to analyze the success and efficiency of the programs implemented by the different stakeholders towards preventing another Pandemic and improving the environment to benefit the most vulnerable sectors of society.

CONCLUSION

Seven thousand, seven hundred and thirty million (7,730,000,000) people worldwide found themselves struggling with a Pandemic in just a few days, living many situations in different ways and incorporating new living, studying, and working habits in such a short time. Technology played a relevant role in how Covid19 was faced. The challenge now will be to capitalize on all the new trends that emerged throughout these months to transform persons into better human beings and build a better world in all aspects (INEGI, 2020).

To conclude, the main aspects generated by the pandemic during the post-Covid 19 period are linked to the opportunities that can be capitalized, taking advantage of everything that has been experienced by people, families, schools, companies, the health sector, and governments. The world economy changed as purchasing habits, lifestyle, entertainment, amusement, study, and work have evolved. 2 out of 3 people faced a change in household income.

In a world of information, people feel disinformed. They do not trust all information sources, such as search engines, traditional, social, and owned media, as they show low records of trustfulness (see Table 1). Transmedia storytelling has developed during the pandemic, as any media (traditional, digital, or private) generates news through a formal statement or a tweet.

Challenges faced by teachers, professors, students, and parents have been substantial while adapting workplaces and study materials to a digital format. They had to innovate continuously and implement teaching techniques to capture the attention of students through a screen. Educational institutions had to offer immediate training to teachers and professors to main a high academic standard to achieve the schools' goals at the different educational levels.

As shown in Table 7, there is increased confidence in firms' performance and a decreased confidence in the Government. Also, there is exponential growth in apps and digital platforms in socializing, doing business, and studying (see Tables 2 and 3).

Concerning physical, spiritual, and psychological well-being, people who were unable to leave their homes, regardless of weather conditions, saw the opportunity to continue exercising at home. As a result, electronic exercising devices sales increased significantly. The same situation happened in the video game

Developments and Global Trends in the Education and Business Sectors in the Post-COVID-19 Period

industry. Another effect was the case of churches that began offering their traditionally Sunday masses through YouTube and Zoom. Online shopping, remote work, and a new perception and acceptance of vaccine vaccination processes are other remarkable effects during this pandemic.

Both the world and people have changed. During the forced confinement periods, people realized the unnecessary activism, fast pace, consumerism, and unnecessary processes or activities they were involved in daily. People value having physical, mental, and spiritual health. They realized that world changes have modified lifestyles to prioritize products purchases required. They realized products and services could be purchased online, but others preferred to be consumed individually. Both online and face-to-face consumption trends will continue.

People were surprised to find out that they could work, study, and support their children during school days and have recreational activities to optimize their leisure time, an aspect that will also be maintained. Educational institutions incorporated new educational digital platforms, and the benefits of online courses will be kept as well.

Likewise, performing simple outdoor activities such as walking in a park or looking at the stars was highly valued to enjoy shared moments with family and friends that people could not have seen in months given the requested social distancing measures. Although stressful in the beginning, people who carried out many activities in the same space and at the same time later achieved a balance to perform them. This fact is a new trend that companies will have to consider in their new working schemes to allow flexibility.

Finally, people have learned to prioritize time for themselves and their families. In contrast, those who had the opportunity to be vaccinated enjoyed some peace of mind knowing that consequences would be less risky if they were to get the virus.

Analyzing media information will require greater veracity to provide facts that support the validity of the data transmitted and from what is expected from companies and governments in their environment and social support efforts. By leveraging all the technological advances, collaboration among the different stakeholders, and awareness for an integral well-being initiative for themselves and society, we will have a more complete and balanced life on a better planet.

Finally, the post-Covid19 world will

a) Be a mixture of speed and uncertainty that has made people and companies learn to be flexible, adapt almost instantly to new business schemes, and use new technologies to solve customers' needs and even family problems in a matter of minutes.
b) Create advice councils with experts on trending topics or those where the confusion is detected to generate a worldwide unification of information, such as avoiding contracting Covid19 even after being vaccinated or performing safe transactions on different purchasing websites.
c) Maximize the Omnichannel Storytelling, where people care when they are influenced by a message or an influencer. In this case, they look for information in different traditional and digital media sources to validate its integrity with friends and social networks.
d) Evolve, while maintaining all the new technologies and teaching apps, to an online and a hybrid system with online and in-person students in the same class. So, teaching and learning processes are more effective, as students can choose face-to-face, hybrid, and online.
e) Joint efforts between governments and corporations to complete the vaccination programs at their earliest convenience focused on economic recovery.
f) Maintain the already implemented technological advances while pushing for digitization needs backed with investments inserted into digital-related recovery packages close with the necessary

complementary (private and public) intangible capital. A post-Covid19 scenario will likely lead to a pronounced increase in labor productivity growth if funds are used correctly.

g) Maintain activities dealt with people's physical and mental health to be prepared to face future pandemic waves. Psychologists and nutritionists continued with their therapies using Facetime or Zoom. They will return to their offices with face masks and the necessary social distance measures as soon as possible. Gymnasiums and Spiritual services will continue offering their online and face-to-face services.

h) Continue sale channels, and more employees will provide services through these channels.

i) Evolve to offer benefits and cost savings approaches—working schemes where employees can work some days in the office and others at home.

j) Learn to live with Covid19 by maintaining the recommended safety measures being attentive to the application of vaccine reinforcements.

REFERENCES

Angus, A. (2021). *Euromonitor's "Top 10 Global Consumer Trends 2021"*. Euromonitor.

Askitas, N., Tatsiramos, K., & Verheyden, B. (2020). *Lockdown strategies, mobility patterns, and COVID19*. IZA Discussion Paper, 13293, University of Bonn, Germany.

Asociación de Internet, M. X. (2019). Estudio sobre Comercio Electrónico en México 2019. Asociación de Internet MX.

Asociación Mexicana de Ventas Online. (2020). *Estudio sobre Venta Online en PyMEs 2020*. Asociación Mexicana de Ventas Online.

Banks, J., & Xu, X. (2020). The mental health effects of the first two months of lockdown during the COVID19 pandemic in the UK. *Fiscal Studies*, *41*(3), 685–708. doi:10.1111/1475-5890.12239

Burdett, A., Davillas, A., & Etheridge, B. (2021). *Weather, psychological well-being and mobility during the first wave of the Covid19 pandemic*. ISER Working Paper Series, 2021-02, Institute for Social and Economic Research.

Coronado Contreras, L., & Llanos Reynoso, L. F. (Coords.). (2020). Home office. La nueva revolución industrial. Wolters Kluwer.

Davillas, A., & Jones, A. M. (2021). *The First Wave of the COVID19 Pandemic and Its Impact on Socioeconomic Inequality in Psychological Distress in the UK*. Discussion Paper, 14057. IZA.

De la Fuente, A., & Doménech, R. (2018). El nivel educativo de la población en España y sus regiones: Actualización hasta 2016. *Documento de Trabajo BBVA Research*, *18*(04), 1–25.

Dehning, J., Zierenberg, J., Spitzner, F. P., Wibral, M., Neto, J. P., Wilczek, M., & Priesemann, V. (2020). Inferring change points in the spread of COVID19 reveals the effectiveness of interventions. *Science*, *369*(6500), eabb9789. doi:10.1126cience.abb9789 PMID:32414780

Edelman, R. (2021). *Edelman Trust Barometer 2021*. https://www.edelman.com

Ferguson, N. (2020). Report 9: Impact of non-pharmaceutical interventions (NPIs) to reduce COVID19 mortality and healthcare demand. *Imperial College London*, *10*(77482), 491–497.

Flaxman, S., Mishra, S., Gandy, A., Unwin, H. J. T., Mellan, T. A., Coupland, H., Whittaker, C., Zhu, H., Berah, T., Eaton, J. W., Monod, M., Perez-Guzman, P. N., Schmit, N., Cilloni, L., Ainslie, K. E. C., Baguelin, M., Boonyasiri, A., Boyd, O., Cattarino, L., ... Bhatt, S. (2020). Estimating the effects of non-pharmaceutical interventions on COVID19 in Europe. *Nature*, *584*(7820), 257–261. doi:10.103841586-020-2405-7 PMID:32512579

Hodgson, S., Mansatta, K., Mallett, G., Harris, V., Emary, K. R. W., & Pollard, A. J. (2020). What defines an efficacious COVID19 vaccine? A review of the challenges assessing the clinical efficacy of vaccines against SARS-CoV-2. *The Lancet. Infectious Diseases*, *21*(2), e26–e35. doi:10.1016/S1473-3099(20)30773-8 PMID:33125914

Hupkau, C. (2021). In brief... Losses in lockdown: jobs, income, education and mental health. *CentrePiece - The Magazine for Economic Performance, 598*.

INEGI. (2020). *Resultados de la Encuesta Nacional sobre disponibilidad y uso de tecnologías de la Información de los Hogares 2019.* Press Release, 103/20, INEGI.

INEGI. (2021). *Encuesta Nacional de Ocupación y Empleo.* INEGI.

Instituto Federal de Telecomunicaciones. (2019). *Acuerdo mediante el cual la Procuraduría Federal del Consumidor y el Instituto Federal de Telecomunicaciones, determinan los derechos mínimos que deben incluirse en la carta a que hace referencia el artículo 191 de la Ley Federal de Telecomunicaciones y Radiodifusión.* Instituto Federal de Telecomunicaciones. http://www.ift.org.mx

Jeffrey Group. (2020). *El camino digital después del Covid19.* Jeffrey Group.

Kotler, P., Kartajaya, H., & Setiawan, I. (2021). *Marketing 5.0: Technology for Humanity.* Wiley.

Luque, A., Maniglio, F., Casado, F., & García-Guerrero, J. (2020). Transmedia Context and Twitter as Conditioning the Ecuadorian Government's Action. The Case of the Guayaquil Emergency, during the COVID19 Pandemic. *Tripodos*, *2*(47), 47–68. doi:10.51698/tripodos.2020.47p47-68

México, I. A. B. (2020). *Estudio de consumo de medios y dispositivos entre internautas mexicanos. El internauta frente al Covid 19.* IAB Mexico.

Navarro, I. (2021). *Las instituciones de competencia en México ante el COVID-19 y la recuperación económica. Documentos de Proyectos, 46662.* UN-CEPAL.

Neidhoefer, G., Lustig, N., & Tommasi, M. (2021). *Intergenerational transmission of lockdown consequences: Prognosis of the longer-run persistence of COVID19 in Latin America.* Working Papers, 571, ECINEQ (Society for the Study of Economic Inequality).

Núñez, C. (2020). *Sistema educativo, formación de capital humano, ciencia e investigación tras la COVID19. Policy Papers, 2020-15.* FEDEA.

Our World in data. (2021). *El Avance de la Vacunación.* Oxford University.

Roth, F. (2021). *The Productivity Puzzle – A Critical Assessment and an Outlook on the COVID19 Crisis. Hamburg Discussion Papers in International Economics, 8, Chair of International Economics.* University of Hamburg.

Salvatto, M., & Salvatto, A. (2021). *La batalla del futuro: algo en qué creer*. Ediciones Lea.

Sassen, S. (2014). *Expulsions: Brutality and Complexity in the Global Economy*. The President and Fellows of Harvard College.

Sheth, J. (2020). Impact of Covid19 on consumer behavior: Will the old habits return or die? *Journal of Business Research*, *117*, 280–283. doi:10.1016/j.jbusres.2020.05.059 PMID:32536735

Zubizarreta, J., Gonzalez, E., & Ramiro, P. (2019). Transnational corporations and the legal Architecture of impunity: Corporate Social Responsibility, *lex mercatoria* and human rights. *Revista de Economia (Curitiba)*, *28*, 41–54.

ADDITIONAL READING

Dijuluis, J. R. (2015). *The customer service revolution: overthrow conventional business, inspire employees, and change the world*. Greenleaf Book Group Press.

Eijlers, M. A., Boksem, M. A. S., & Smidts, A. (2020). Measuring Neural Arousal for Advertisements and Its Relationship with Advertising Success. *Frontiers in Neuroscience*, *14*, 736. Advance online publication. doi:10.3389/fnins.2020.00736 PMID:32765214

Fernández, J. D. (2014). *Mecanismos estratégicos en publicidad: de la USP a las lovemarks*. Advook.

Hopson, B., & Scally, M. (2015). *12 pasos para el éxito brindando servicio*. Macchi.

Kotler, P., & Fox, K. (1995). *Strategic Marketing for Educational Institutions*. Prentice-Hall.

Kotler, P., Kartajaya, H., & Setiawan, I. (2010). *Marketing 3.0*. Acción empresarial.

Kotler, P., Kartajaya, H., & Setiawan, I. (2019). *Marketing 4.0*. Wiley.

Kotler, P., & Kotler, M. (2015). *8 maneras de crecer, Estrategias de marketing para desarrollar tu negocio*. LID Editorial Empresarial.

Kotler, P., & Lane, K. (2012). *Dirección de marketing*. Pearson.

KEY TERMS AND DEFINITIONS

Digital Accelerator: It refers to the use of digital technology to transform as soon as possible an organization, its business model, its strategy, its customer experience, and other areas of the business.

Digital Natives: A person born or brought up during the age of digital technology and therefore familiar with computers and the Internet from an early age.

Fake News: False reports of events, written and read on websites. Many of us seem unable to distinguish fake news from the verified sort. Fake news creates significant public confusion about current events.

Home Office: A room in someone's home that is used for work. Today, technology allows employees or even entire offices to work remotely.

Home School: The education of students at home by their parents.

Omnichannel: It is a type of retail that integrates the different shopping methods available to consumers, such as online, in a physical store, or by telephone.

On Line: With or through a computer or mobile device, especially over a network.

Phygital Reality: Use digital tools to stay connected at home and facilitate safer procedures in brick-and-mortar outlets.

Transmedia: The technique of telling a single story across multiple platforms and formats using current digital technologies.

Transmedia Omnichannel: It searches or transmits information across multiple media such as social media, traditional media, or the internet.

Chapter 16
Initial Exploration of Cross-Generational Attitudes Towards Piracy of Chinese Online Literature

Rob Kim Marjerison
https://orcid.org/0000-0003-1181-8695
Wenzhou-Kean University, China

Sijia Jiang
Wenzhou-Kean University, China

ABSTRACT

This chapter seeks to provide initial evidence and provide a baseline for further exploration of Chinese cross-generational audiences' attitude differences towards online literature and digital piracy. Globalization has complicated the many disparate cultural, generational, and national perspectives on intellectual property (IP) protection. IP and IP protection continue to grow in importance in global commerce and international relations. How attitudes towards IP and online content, in particular, evolve generationally is an area of relative under exploration. Data was gathered through an online survey and indicates a trend towards increased awareness and acceptance of IP value and protection. This study provides insight into cross-generational audiences in the important market of China. It may be helpful to those interested in commerce in the areas of online publishing or related industries to help make business decisions in targeting and marketing, to those interested in global commerce and international relations, or those who are researchers in the areas of IP and IP protection.

DOI: 10.4018/978-1-7998-7689-2.ch016

Initial Exploration of Cross-Generational Attitudes Towards Piracy of Chinese Online Literature

INTRODUCTION

The relevance of this study is rooted in the more macro view of Intellectual Property (IP) in general and the legal concepts that attempt to protect the ownership of that often intangible property that is a creation of the mind, Intellectual Property Protection (IPP).

In the case of this study, intellectual property is focused on literature, a creation of the mind. However, the implications go far beyond writing poetry, stories, songs, and movie scripts (Hughes, 1988; Reichman & Samuelson, 1997). Intellectual property is the very essence of innovation (Granstrand, 2006; Maskus, 2000). In today's world, innovation is primarily, but not wholly, based on technological developments (Fagerberg, 2018; Maskus, 2000). Most technological development is built on the foundation of previous technology (Millar et al., 2018). The country with the most advanced technology is, therefore, best positioned to develop the next generation of technology (Galvão et al., 2017). Assuming that their technology is not copied, "stolen," or used by other countries without compensation, which would reduce or eliminate the competitive advantage of the owner, or creator, of the latest technology (Akhmetshin et al., 2018; Granstrand, 1999; Maskus, 2000). And therein, lies the core conceptual value of IP and IPP.

This study is focused on a small part of the global macro view of IP and IPP, but, even as a small brick on the wall, the attitudes towards IP and IPP of the citizenry of the largest, or second-largest national economy in the world, China, Yuki et al. (2018) is relevant. And will play a part in the development of the new world order in the not too distant future (Lake, 2018; Tarasova & Ashurkova, 2020; Yueh, 2020).

Therefore, the focus of this study is both relevant and timely. It is hoped that the findings of this study will contribute to future work in the area of IP and IPP as well as the related fields of IPP in the creative arts, which, as we have come to learn, play a societal role far more significant than simple entertainment (Delaney, 1997; Nouri, 2018).

Intellectual property includes a fairly broad spectrum of materials including; books of fiction, songs and music, art both two and three dimensional which includes architecture and even holographic light, videos and movies, performing arts and dance including recordings of same, literature including poems, stories and even legends both modern and old (Hughes, 1988; May & Sell, 2006). And finally the most obvious of all, technology. Technological innovation is often the result of considerable investment of resources, financial, intellectual and of the intangibles, time, effort and talent (Peng et al., 2020; Tao, 2018).

With these considerations in mind, it is possible for one to see how the micro view of how Chinese perceive one small piece of the overall IP picture as having relevance to the larger picture of IP and IPP protection in China and how it could play a role in the new world order that is emerging. Therefore, this chapter aims to contribute to this the much larger body of research on the perception, role, relevance, and ultimately, the importance of how Chinese view IP and IPP with specific consideration of one small part of IP, the popular and seemingly of little commercial importance, Chinese online literature.

Chinese online literature (COL) is also called Chinese internet literature (CIL). COL contains a variety of types of e-books and other materials (Lugg, 2011a). The most popular type is fiction Tse et al. (2012a), but there are others, including magazines, newspapers, and journal articles (Lovell, 2012a). With the rise of COL commercialization, both individual and commercial "pirate" behavior has occurred. "Pirate" in the case of Intellectual Property (IP) refers to the unauthorized use of IP and has substantial financial implications worldwide (Kwong et al., 2003a; Tunca & Wu, 2013a; Wan et al., 2009). The commonly pirated IP includes software, music CDs, films, movies, television content, and games. In China, pirated COL has increased in recent years and is very common (Brander et al., 2017; Mertha, 2018). There is a considerable research literature on the development of COL, the business opportunities that COL brings, the financial impact of pirated IP, and even the attitude towards IP piracy by gender (Amodu et al., 2020; SHADE, 2014). However, there appears to be a gap in the literature regarding the cross-generational audiences' attitude differences, particularly in China. This study aims to explore the attitudes of different generations of Chinese towards the piracy of IP.

Cross-generational research in the US consistently identifies generations by the terms Baby Boomer, Generation X, Generation Y, and Generation Z, Millenial (Ardueser & Garza, 2021; Lissitsa & Laor, 2021). However, except for the term "millennials," these terms are not widely used in China, or cross-generational demographic research in China (Chen & Naughton, 2017). Often, Chinese of different ages are referred to as part of a generation based on what period of recent Chinese history they lived in (Chen & Naughton, 2017). Considering the changes that have influenced China in the last few decades and the emergence and popularization of COL, the generation cohorts compared in this study are divided into post-70s, post-80s, and post-90s. Each generation has its unique characteristics and experiences which have contributed to different values, perceptions, and attitudes. For example, the post-90s generation grew up with digital products such as mobile phones and computers, so they are more closely linked to e-commerce and more knowledgeable about information technology. Due to rapid economic development, the post-90s live in an age of prosperity and have more discretionary purchasing power. Unlike the experiences of the post-80s and post-70s, the millennial generation has been exposed to e-books, smartphones, online video content, e-commerce, and e-payments since they were young. Many online content writers have targeted the post-90s and have become popular (Lovell, 2012a; Lugg, 2011a).

Previous generations had no access to any online content and, at times, limited access to printed content. As a result of their very different experiences, and vastly different economic circumstances, there is a possibility that the generations may have different views toward piracy of online IP. To explore this topic, information from all three generation cohorts was gathered and compared. Data was collected via an online survey designed to assess the public's attitudes towards pirated online content.

LITERATURE REVIEW - BACKGROUND

There appears to be a substantial body of literature based on research on topics related to Chinese online/internet literature, which boomed in the late 20th and early 21st century(Lovell, 2012a). Chinese online literature gained attention during that period from both writers and readers (Lugg, 2011b). Many writers, including Han Han and Guo Jingming, have high-school and college students as their target audiences they account for the most significant percentage of online readers (Lovell, 2012a). Online communities are more than simply platforms for distributing literature; they play an essential role in Chinese online literature commercialization (Tse & Gong, 2012b). Websites have emerged that make pirated online literature available, and their popularity has increased in line with the growth in the formal online literature industry (Ren & Montgomery, 2012a). Due to the extremely low risk of being detected and sued by the legal publisher, a large number of Chinese consumers support the commercial pirates, resulting in a large profit for the piracy industry (Ren & Montgomery, 2012a; Tunca & Wu, 2013b). Research related to Chinese software piracy shows that the users' perceived moral intensity has some influence on their attitudes to piracy (Chan et al., 2013a). It is also reported that consumers can rationalize their patronage of pirate content distributors in several ways, including an anti-big-business attitude combined with the perceived social benefit of low-cost access to literature (Kwong et al., 2003a). More recently, it has been found that gender is a factor in attitude to digital piracy, with males having a more positive attitude towards digital piracy than females (Tjiptono et al., 2016).

Chinese Online Literature

Chinese online literature is mainly free or low-fee (Lugg, 2011), especially in the case of amateur fiction, written by amateur writing enthusiasts (Lugg, 2011b; Ren & Montgomery, 2012a). In the past few decades, the writing of fiction and ease of access to publishing has increased. Content is filtered by end-user online communities rather than by established publishers like magazines or other traditional publishers (Lovell, 2012b; Ren & Montgomery, 2012a).

Online Paid Reading

As online reading has become more popular, driven by the business opportunity it presents, the Chinese online literature market has proliferated, and the Chinese online literature commercialization has taken off (Tse & Gong, 2012b). Online publishers typically sign a contract with the writer to obtain licensed access to the literature, which is then offered free of charge for a limited tie or limited amount of content. The readers are charged after finishing the "freemium" part of the literature. Typically, the "freemium" approach is when the first chapter or two of a publication or the first episode or two of a series is offered to readers free of charge. Subsequent chapters or installments must be purchased. When combined with the micropayment system, this type of offer is a successful business model that first emerged in 2003 and was created by the Qidian company. The audience or readers can have a trial reading of several chapters of the fiction free of change, while the content companies will realize the fiction's business value through the number of readers. However, after this, if audiences want to continue reading, they must pay for the upcoming chapters (Ren & Montgomery, 2012b; L. Zhao, 2021). Usually, pirated websites have unlicensed access and, while not charging for the content, will monetize the content by selling advertising shown on the reading page (Ren & Montgomery, 2012a).

Digital Piracy

Like software, film, and music content providers, many industries experience a significant negative financial impact due to digital piracy (Tjiptono et al., 2016). There are two types of digital goods piracy, individual piracy, and commercial piracy. Individual piracy refers to the illegal copy and sharing of digital goods by consumers. In contrast, commercial piracy is the unlawful copying and sale to consumers by a third party done for profit (Tunca & Wu, 2013b). According to Purwanto (2012), blocking illegal download sites cannot stop individual piracy. In terms of internet literature, commercial digital piracy outlets that offer illegally copied content allow consumers to purchase all kinds of content, including books, novels, magazines, and journal articles (Tjiptono et al., 2016).

Attention Economy

The attention economy is the approach to social media usage that seeks to monetize the attention or engagement of users by essentially selling the exposure of advertising or promotional content on social media platforms (Myllylahti, 2018; Zulli, 2018). It seeks to attract readers' attention to gain economic profit or material compensation (Hendricks & Vestergaard, 2019; Ryan et al., 2020). The Attention economy evolved due to the difficulties associated with controlling access to content (Tassi, 2018). As user satisfaction and enjoyment of free, often pirated, content has increased and preventing piracy of the content has proven to be nearly impossible to control, access to the users themselves has been commercialized into a profitable product (Ryan et al., 2020; Skågeby, 2009). Hence, the readers become both "the consumers and the products" (Ren & Montgomery, 2012a). By exploiting the Attention economy with pirated content, or access to pirated content, many pirate websites provide illegal access to genuine websites' VIP content and generate revenue through offering that content (Crogan & Kinsley, 2012; Ren & Montgomery, 2012b).

Motivation

Many Chinese piracy websites offer access to the legally available literature only on the formal online literature website (Ren & Montgomery, 2012a). Consumers tend to decide where they purchase online literature mainly based on price Yoon (2011), and more specifically, by considering the cost and benefit of each available option (Chan et al., 2013b). In other words, readers of online content can choose to purchase literature from a legal publisher or commercially pirated content, or individuals who are "technologically savvy" can download content themselves (Xia & Muppala, 2010). They decide which option to exercise based on the value rather than on what is considered to be ethical grounds (Wan et al., 2009). The legal authorities' possibility of detection and prosecution is extremely low for both individual piracy and commercial piracy (Tunca & Wu, 2013b).

Generation Cohorts

In a homogenous society, people in the same generation cohort tend to have similar values and attitudes, which are significantly influenced by the historical events they experienced during their formative years (Ng et al., 2016a). The generation cohorts model commonly used in America is divided into Baby Boomer, Generation X, Generation Y, and Generation Z (Grenčíková & Vojtovič, 2017; Ng et al., 2016a). However, as the target of this study is Chinese consumers, the model should be adapted to the situation. After a thorough analysis of significant Chinese historical events, Ng et al. (2016a) put forward a Chinese generation cohorts model which divided consumers into three broad groups, the era with limited choice, the great Gatsby generation, and the dreamers' generation. Ng's model is primarily based on changes in the political and economic situation, such as leadership and economic policy changes. With minor adaptation, the cohort periods used by Ng (2016b) is suitable for this research; hence, the generation cohorts in China are divided by every ten years into post-70s (1970-1979), post-80s (1980-1989), post-90s (1990-1999) and post-00s (2000-2009).

In adolescence, the post-1970s cohort received orthodox socialist values and traditional Chinese culture education (X. Zhao, 2019). After 1985, they began to receive the overall impact from the introduction of western culture, which resulted in a profound conflict of values (X. Zhao, 2019). The post-80s and post-90s youth are the generations growing up after the reformation and in the stage of deep modernization (Bao, 2019). They experienced a very different education due to the social and economic environment changes during their adolescent years compared to the post-70s. The post-80s generation is the first generation in China to come into contact with the Internet (Zhang, 2019). The Internet is a very influential aspect of the development of that group. The post-90s were born in a period of rapid economic development in China and have experienced mass adoption and access to the Internet, including the popularization driven by social media and e-commerce. The result is a more national view of public life in China (Golley & Kong, 2013; X. Zhao, 2019). If the "post-90s" are the "Internet" indigenous generation, then the "Post-00" is the "mobile Internet" indigenous generation (Cheng & Dai, 1995).

STATEMENT OF HYPOTHESIS

With different ages, consumers have different interests, demands, and attitudes (Herrando et al., 2019; San-Martín et al., 2015). Age has a significant relationship with people's attitude towards innovation and also towards original products vs. pirated products (Kwong et al., 2003b). The younger generation is more likely to readily accept innovation and change, such as mobile shopping (San-Martín et al., 2015). Research related to information technology issues suggests that the older the people are, the more opposition they have towards immoral or unethical matters related to IT and Internet-related activities (Peslak, 2008).

Based on the existing idea and research results reported above, the following hypotheses are formulated.

Research Question (RQ): What are the attitude differences between cross-generation Chinese audiences to online paid literature and piracy?

H1: Regarding online paid literature.
1a – Generation "Post-70s" has the most negative attitude to online paid reading.
1b – Generation "Post-90s" has the most positive attitude to online paid reading.
H2: Regarding digital literature piracy.
2a – Gen post-90s are more likely than Gen post-80s to support piracy.
2b – Gen post-90s are more likely than Gen post-70s to support piracy.

METHODOLOGY

Pilot Study

Interviews with three generations were conducted in pilot studies to determine the most useful and frequent responses to possible survey questions. Through phone calls, WeChat, and in-person interviews, every generation cohort had three participants (total 9) who participated in the pilot study. A pilot study can help researchers to test and refine methodology (Schachtebeck et al., 2018). In this chapter, the pilot study was used to test the clarity of questions and the sufficiency of answers in the survey.

Online Survey

A survey was designed in accordance with pilot study findings and previous related research design (Chan et al., 2013a). The survey was made available online via the popular social media platform WeChat. Because this research aims to explore people's attitudes, the online survey was determined to be the appropriate methodology. A common tool to assess public opinions, online surveys are an appropriate method (Lee et al., 2012). Compared with the traditional offline surveys, online surveys have the

advantage of anonymity, timeliness, respondent convenience, low cost, forced answering of questions, and so on (Roster et al., 2007). The assurance of anonymity and confidentiality was included at the beginning of the survey. The first question is age or year of birth to distribute the respondents into the designated age groups (post-70s, post-80s, and post-90s). The total number of surveys collected was 238, which included 86 males and 152 females. The number of "post-70s" and "post-80s" participants is 44 and 49, while the number of post 90s participants is 122. The rest are out-of-range participants consisting of 16 from "post-00" and "7 from post-60s". All respondents answered all the following questions about their opinion. From the Pilot Study, the survey question was, *Motivation to Purchase Online Paid Reading Material.*
Six options were identified as possible responses for the question:

- Quality
- Copyright
- Advertisement Interference
- Idols
- Variety of books
- No access to pirated content

All responses above are the most frequent response from the pilot study. The frequencies are 8 out of 9, 6 out of 9, 6 out of 9, 4 out of 9, 9 out of 9, and 4 out of 9.

1. Survey Questions on Online Literature Piracy

Seven considerations were provided to find out people's attitudes to piracy:

- Congregational psychology
- Personal benefit / Price
- Quality
- Variety access to pirate
- Anti-big business attitude
- The emergence of mobile network
- Ethical issues/copyright

In the combination of pilot study and literature review, there are six factors that most influence consumers' attitudes towards piracy. The benefits and costs of commercial piracy and individual piracy are different. Every component above leads to different thoughts and attitudes to the pros and cons of piracy (Kwong et al., 2003b). These options all come from literature review and have a relatively high frequency of appearance in the Pilot Study.

2. Survey Question on the Approach to Gain the Literature

Based on the frequency of repeated responses in the Pilot Study, five methods are indicated below to access pirated literature in China. Because these five are the most frequent answers to be chosen or added by the 9 participants, they are included. The frequencies are 6 out of 9, 5 out of 9, 5 out of 9, 5 out of 9, and 4 out of 9, respectively.

- Browser Search
- Search in a specific website
- Software Search
- Sharing through friends (Baidu Cloud network)
- Taobao

With the rapid development of the Internet and the pervasive connectivity available through either WiFi or 4G, the adoption of e-commerce in China has exploded. As a creative industry and business model, paid online literature faces stiff competition from pirated outlets. Commercial piracy has resulted in substantial revenue losses to the official online outlets of e-literature and threatens the viability of the business model. The five methods of acquiring literature online that are included within the scope of this study may not include all possibilities due to the limitations of the pilot study and the diversity of online reading approaches.

ANALYSIS / RESULTS

A total of 238 online survey questionnaire responses were collected.

Table 1. Age distribution

	0–19	20–29	30–39	40–49	+50	Total
Male	4	48	13	18	3	86
Female	12	74	36	26	4	152
Total	16	122	49	44	7	238

Source: Authors

Table 1 shows the gender and age group data. The groups of ages 0-19, 20-29, 30-39, 40-49 refer to the post-00s, post-90s, post-80s, and post-70s, respectively, while the 50+ represents were born before 1970. Due to the limitations of the data, the age group of 0-19 and 50+ are out of scope for this study.

Table 2 shows the percentage of the respondents' first choice in acquiring online literature by the different age groups. The most preferred way to access online resources is free genuine reading, with the highest score in all three generation cohorts (63.93%, 83.67%, 81.82%). However, the post-90s group has a relatively high percentage (21.31%) of acquiring free pirated resources as their first approach to online literature, which would explain why the post-90s have the lowest rate on free genuine resources when compared to the post-80s and the post-70s age groups.

Table 2. Distribution of the first approach to online literature with age comparison

	20–29	%	30–39	%	40–49	%	Total
First Approach to OL							
Genuine resource (paid)	15	12.30	5	10.2	4	9.09	24
Genuine resource (free)	78	63.93	41	83.67	36	81.82	155
Pirate resource (paid)	3	2.46	2	4.08	1	4.08	6
Pirate resource (free)	26	21.31	1	2.04	3	2.04	30
Total	122	100	49	100	44	100	215

Source: Authors

Table 3. Distribution of the second approach to online literature with age comparison

	20–29	%	30–39	%	40–49	%	Total
Second Approach to OL							
Genuine resource (paid)	32	26.23	22	44.90	18	40.91	72
Genuine resource (free)	36	29.51	14	28.57	15	34.09	65
Pirate resource (paid)	6	4.92	0	0.00	1	2.27	7
Pirate resource (free)	48	39.34	3	26.53	10	22.73	71
Total	122	100	49	100	44	100	215

Source: Authors

Similarly, Table 3 shows the percentage of respondents' second choice for the acquisition of online literature by different age groups. Whether respondents are likely to be willing to pay for genuine resources instead of pirated resources depends partly on which generation cohort to which they belong. The second approach question results show that the post-80s and post-70s are more likely to pay for the genuine resource than to access the free pirated resources. However, the post-90s are more likely to access free pirated resources, accounting for the largest part of the second approach for that age cohort.

Table 4 shows that the most popular way to find and access pirated content is by browser search (61.40%), while the second most used method is sharing with friends online (60.00%). The post-90s group has the largest percentage of users using the browser search and the sharing through friends (73.77% and 62.30%, respectively). The post-90s are more likely to have more ways to access pirated content.

Without consideration of the order of approach choice, Table 5, using the average and the mode, indicates the degree of different factors that influence the pirated online reading by age group. The mode indicates that quality (5 = strongly agree) is the most likely factor that leads people to access genuine online literature and has the most significant influence on the post-70s age group. Furthermore, the data shows a substantial likelihood of supporting the result that the post-90s have the highest pirated percentage (23.77% & 44.26%, respectively) as indicated in Tables 2 and 3. The averages shown imply that whether they can get free access to resources will have the biggest influence on their acquisition behaviors, while not knowing how to pirate or gain access to pirated content has the lowest influence on the post-90s cohort compared with the post-80s and post-70s groups.

Table 4. Ways and number of ways to pirate by age group

Ways	20 – 29	%	30 – 39	%	40 – 49	%	All ages
Browser Search	90	73.77	16	32.65	26	59.09	61.40
Search in a specific website	48	39.34	14	28.57	5	11.36	31.16
Software Search	38	31.15	9	18.37	10	22.73	26.51
Sharing through friends	76	62.30	28	57.14	25	56.82	60.00
Taobao	44	36.07	17	34.69	16	36.36	35.81
Number of ways	20 – 29	%	30 – 39	%	40 – 49	%	
1	37	30.33	28	57.14	20	45.45	
2	36	29.51	11	22.45	12	27.27	
3	21	17.21	7	14.29	10	22.73	
4	16	13.11	2	4.08	2	4.55	
5	12	9.84	1	2.04	0	0.00	
Total	122	100	49	100	44	100	

Source: Authors

Table 5. Degree of factor influences with age comparison (genuine)

	Average			Mode		
	20–29	30–39	40–49	20–29	30–39	40–49
Factors lead to Pirated OL						
Copyright	3.885	3.694	3.841	4	4	4
Quality	3.869	3.878	4.386	5	5	5
Idols	3.221	2.918	3.205	3	4	3
No free resource	3.721	3.490	3.386	3&4	3&4	3
Advertisement	3.566	3.653	3.682	4	4	4
No idea to pirate	3.041	3.347	3.500	3	3	3

Source: Authors

Similar to Table 5, Table 6 shows the degree of influence of the different factors on the reading of pirated online content by age group. According to the mode and mean of the degree of influence, the factors most influential in leading people to read pirated online literature are the cheaper/free price and the emergence of cloud storage, especially for the post-90s group. Moreover, copyright considerations and the disturbance of advertisements do not positively relate to how respondents prefer to gain access to pirated online literature.

Table 6. Degree of factor influences with age comparison (pirated)

	Average			Mode		
	20–29	30–39	40–49	20–29	30–39	40–49
Factors lead to Pirated OL						
It is cheaper/free	3.885	3.612	3.432	4	4	3
There are lots of pirated resources	3.598	3.122	3.273	3	3	3
I do not care about copyright	2.869	2.816	2.932	3	3	3
The emergence of mobile network disk (e.g., Baidu Cloud)	3.631	3.265	3.591	4	4	3
I do not mind the advertisement on pirated website	2.705	2.551	2.568	3	3	3&4
I have anti-bug business attitude	2.246	2.592	2.909	2	3	3
Many people use pirated resources (Group psychology)	3.090	3.122	3.432	3	3	3

Source: Authors

FINDINGS

The results of the first approach to online reading indicate that both H1a and H1b are preliminarily supported. The Generation "Post-90s" has the most positive attitude to online paid reading, while the Generation "Post-70s" has the most negative attitude (the 90s: 12.30%, 80s: 10.20%, 70s: 9.09%). However, the result of using a second approach to online reading conflicts with that, primarily because the post-80s and post-70s groups lack familiarity with the technology used to gain access to pirated resources. Further, the data tends to offer preliminary support of both H2a and H2b. For example, the percentage of the post-90s age group choosing pirated resources as their first/second approach to acquiring content is the highest of the three generations. The data shows that the Generation "Post-90s" is more favorable than either Generation "Post-80s" or Generation "Post-70s" in their willingness to support piracy of online content. The implications of these findings may imply a generalized view within a generational cohort towards pirated IP of all types, not just online literature. If so, the possible economic impact could extend far beyond the borders of China if, for example, the spillover effect extends into commercial, technological IP at a high level where cutting edge technology can give a company or a nation a substantial competitive advantage commercially, and even militarily because, as was pointed out early, technological innovation is built on previous innovations in the same field. On the other hand, should a society, in general, take a more supportive view of IPP, then there is more incentive for private section investment in R&D, which in turn can result in increased innovation and the subsequent economic development morphing into soft power on the global stage for China. Insight into these possibilities are the topics of necessary further research into how IPP is perceived and treated

CONCLUSION

In conclusion, the preliminary findings support both hypotheses, with different age groups having different attitudes to online paid reading and literature piracy. The Generation "Post-90s" has the most positive attitudes toward online paid reading and online literature piracy. The "Post-80s" and "Post-70s" are less open to paying for online reading and less knowledgeable in how to gain access to pirated content. Hence, the support of the "Post-80s" and "Post-70s" generations to online paid reading and piracy is less than the "Post-90s". This study establishes a baseline and identifies an empirically verifiable opportunity for further study of this topic and provides a better understanding of the Chinese online literature market. The value of this paper lies not in the findings alone, although there are significant commercial aspects to the online literature business model in China and the application of possible ways to monetize it. As well, it is possible that the findings could be generalized over different populations, especially when it comes to the use of the Attention Economy as a consequence of more online content being more easily copied or made available without charge. However, a more macro view of the findings of this study could be to see this study as a tiny part of the examination of the Chinese consumer, and by extension, the society's perception of IP and IPP of other kinds of IP, which, as discussed earlier may have a more far-reaching impact on the larger economy of China as well as the global economy. This could include future creations of IP as well as past IP. There is ample room for research in this area and much to be gained from examining the perceptions and attitudes of the consumer and society of China.

LIMITATIONS AND FUTURE RESEARCH

There are limitations to this study, specifically in the sample size and breakdown of age diversity. Additionally, this study did not consider other demographic factors of the respondents, such as the diversity of educational level, occupation, social-economic level. The independent variable of this research is the generation; hence, this paper only identifies trends in Chinese audiences' attitude differences across generations. A rigorous analysis of a larger sample size is the logical next step for further research and could include either together, or separately, more of these factors.

REFERENCES

Akhmetshin, E., Dzhavatov, D. K., Sverdlikova, E. A., Sokolov, M. S., Avdeeva, O. A., & Yavkin, G. P. (2018). The influence of innovation on social and economic development of the Russian Regions. *European Research Studies Journal*, *21*, 767–776.

Amodu, L., Isiguzoro, C., Omojola, O., Adeyeye, B., & Ajakaiye, L. (2020). Assessing audience's willingness to curb digital piracy: A gender perspective. *Cogent Social Sciences*, *6*(1), 1823602. doi:10.1080/23311886.2020.1823602

Ardueser, C., & Garza, D. (2021). Exploring Cross-Generational Traits and Management Across Generations in the Workforce: A Theoretical Literature Review. In *RAIS Conference Proceedings 2021* (No. 0011; RAIS Conference Proceedings 2021). Research Association for Interdisciplinary Studies. https://ideas.repec.org/p/smo/lpaper/0011.html

Bao, L. (2019). Deep Modernization: The Value Conflict and Identity of the Post-80s and Post-90s. 中国青年研究, *8*, 47–55.

Brander, J. A., Cui, V., & Vertinsky, I. (2017). China and intellectual property rights: A challenge to the rule of law. *Journal of International Business Studies*, *48*(7), 908–921. doi:10.105741267-017-0087-7

Chan, R. K., Ma, K. Y., & Wong, Y. H. (2013). The Software Piracy Decision-Making Process of Chinese Computer Users. *The Information Society*, *29*(4), 203–218. doi:10.1080/01972243.2013.792302

Chen, L., & Naughton, B. (2017). A Dynamic China Model: The Co-Evolution of Economics and Politics in China. *Journal of Contemporary China*, *26*(103), 18–34. doi:10.1080/10670564.2016.1206278

Cheng, Y., & Dai, J. (1995). Intergenerational mobility in modern China. *European Sociological Review*, *11*(1), 17–35. doi:10.1093/oxfordjournals.esr.a036347

Crogan, P., & Kinsley, S. (2012). Paying attention: Towards a critique of the attention economy. *Culture Machine*, 13.

Delaney, P. (1997). Pop Culture, "Gangsta Rap" and the "New Vaudeville." In *The Media in Black and White*. Routledge.

Fagerberg, J. (2018). *Innovation, Economic Development and Policy: Selected Essays*. Edward Elgar Publishing. doi:10.4337/9781788110266

Galvão, A., Mascarenhas, C., Gouveia Rodrigues, R., Marques, C. S., & Leal, C. T. (2017). A quadruple helix model of entrepreneurship, innovation and stages of economic development. *Review of International Business and Strategy*, *27*(2), 261–282. doi:10.1108/RIBS-01-2017-0003

Golley, J., & Kong, S. T. (2013). Inequality in intergenerational mobility of education in China. *China & World Economy*, *21*(2), 15–37. doi:10.1111/j.1749-124X.2013.12013.x

Granstrand, O. (1999). The Economics and Management of Intellectual Property. In *Books*. Edward Elgar Publishing. https://ideas.repec.org/b/elg/eebook/1651.html

Granstrand, O. (2006, January 19). Innovation and Intellectual Property Rights. *The Oxford Handbook of Innovation*. doi:10.1093/oxfordhb/9780199286805.003.0010

Grenčíková, A., & Vojtovič, S. (2017). Relationship of generations X, Y, Z with new communication technologies. *Problems and Perspectives in Management; Sumy*, *15*(2), 557–563.

Hasenhütl, G. (2018). The World Beyond Your Head: On Becoming an Individual in an Age of Distraction. *The Journal of Modern Craft*, *11*(3), 287–291. doi:10.1080/17496772.2018.1538631

Hendricks, V. F., & Vestergaard, M. (2019). The Attention Economy. In V. F. Hendricks & M. Vestergaard (Eds.), *Reality Lost: Markets of Attention, Misinformation and Manipulation* (pp. 1–17). Springer International Publishing. doi:10.1007/978-3-030-00813-0_1

Herrando, C., Jimenez-Martinez, J., & Hoyos, M. J. M.-D. (2019). Tell me your age and I tell you what you trust: The moderating effect of generations. *Internet Research*, *29*(4), 799–817. doi:10.1108/IntR-03-2017-0135

Hughes, J. (1988). The Philosophy of Intellectual Property. *The Georgetown Law Journal*, *77*(2), 287–366. https://heinonline.org/HOL/P?h=hein.journals/glj77&i=309

Kwong, K. K., Yau, O. H. M., Lee, J. S. Y., Sin, L. Y. M., & Tse, A. C. B. (2003a). The Effects of Attitudinal and Demographic Factors on Intention to Buy Pirated CDs: The Case of Chinese Consumers. *Journal of Business Ethics*, *47*(3), 223–235. doi:10.1023/A:1026269003472

Lake, D. A. (2018). Economic Openness and Great Power Competition: Lessons for China and the United States. *The Chinese Journal of International Politics*, *11*(3), 237–270. doi:10.1093/cjip/poy010

Lee, G., Benoit-Bryan, J., & Johnson, T. P. (2012). Survey Research in Public Administration: Assessing Mainstream Journals with a Total Survey Error Framework. Public Administration Review, 72(1).

Lissitsa, S., & Laor, T. (2021). Baby Boomers, Generation X and Generation Y: Identifying generational differences in effects of personality traits in on-demand radio use. *Technology in Society*, *64*, 101526. doi:10.1016/j.techsoc.2021.101526

Lovell, J. (2012a). Finding a Place: Mainland Chinese Fiction in the 2000s. *The Journal of Asian Studies*, *71*(1), 7–32. https://search.proquest.com/abicomplete/docview/921635142/abstract/A090375A55904F-E6PQ/1

Lovell, J. (2012b). Finding a Place: Mainland Chinese Fiction in the 2000s. *The Journal of Asian Studies, 71*(1), 7–32.

Lugg, A. (2011a). Chinese online fiction: Taste publics, entertainment, and Candle in the Tomb. *Chinese Journal of Communication*, *4*(2), 121–136. doi:10.1080/17544750.2011.565673

Lugg, A. (2011b). Chinese online fiction: Taste publics, entertainment, and Candle in the Tomb. *Chinese Journal of Communication*, *4*(2), 121–136. doi:10.1080/17544750.2011.565673

Maskus, K. E. (2000). *Intellectual Property Rights in the Global Economy*. Peterson Institute.

May, C., & Sell, S. K. (2006). *Intellectual property rights: A critical history*. Lynne Rienner Publishers Boulder.

Mertha, A. C. (2018). The Politics of Piracy. In *The Politics of Piracy*. Cornell University Press. https://www.degruyter.com/document/doi/10.7591/9781501728808/html

Millar, C., Lockett, M., & Ladd, T. (2018). Disruption: Technology, innovation and society. *Technological Forecasting and Social Change*, *129*, 254–260. doi:10.1016/j.techfore.2017.10.020

Myllylahti, M. (2018). An attention economy trap? An empirical investigation into four news companies' Facebook traffic and social media revenue. *Journal of Media Business Studies*, *15*(4), 237–253. doi:10.1080/16522354.2018.1527521

Ng, J. C. Y., Helminger, C. M., & Wu, Q. (2016a). A Generational Cohort Model for Consumers in China: The Rise and Fall of the Great Gatsby? *Indian Journal of Commerce and Management Studies. Nasik*, *7*(1), 53–66.

Ng, J. C. Y., Helminger, C. M., & Wu, Q. (2016b). A Generational Cohort Model for Consumers in China: The Rise and Fall of the Great Gatsby? *Indian Journal of Commerce and Management Studies; Nasik, 7*(1), 53–66. https://search.proquest.com/abicomplete/docview/1830724446/abstract/97CDFA8255094E01PQ/1

Nouri, M. (2018). The Power of Influence: Traditional Celebrity vs Social Media Influencer. *Pop Culture Intersections*. https://scholarcommons.scu.edu/engl_176/32

Peng, H., Tan, H., & Zhang, Y. (2020). Human capital, financial constraints, and innovation investment persistence. *Asian Journal of Technology Innovation*, *28*(3), 453–475. doi:10.1080/19761597.2020.17 70616

Peslak, A. R. (2008). Current Information Technology Issues and Moral Intensity Influences. *The Journal of Computer Information Systems*, *48*(4), 77–86.

Purwanto, D. (2012). *Kominfo Blokir 20 Situs "Download"*. Musik Ilegal.

Reichman, J. H., & Samuelson, P. (1997). Intellectual Property Rights in Data. *Vanderbilt Law Review*, *50*(1), 49–166. https://heinonline.org/HOL/P?h=hein.journals/vanlr50&i=91

Ren, X., & Montgomery, L. (2012). Chinese online literature: Creative consumers and evolving business models. *Arts Marketing*, *2*(2), 118–130.

Roster, C. A., Rogers, R. A., Hozier, G. C., Baker, K. G., & Albaum, G. (2007). Management of Marketing Research Projects: Does Delivery Method Matter Anymore in Survey Research? *Journal of Marketing Theory and Practice; Abingdon*, *15*(2), 127–144.

Ryan, C. D., Schaul, A. J., Butner, R., & Swarthout, J. T. (2020). Monetizing disinformation in the attention economy: The case of genetically modified organisms (GMOs). *European Management Journal*, *38*(1), 7–18. doi:10.1016/j.emj.2019.11.002

San-Martín, S., Prodanova, J., & Jiménez, N. (2015). The impact of age in the generation of satisfaction and WOM in mobile shopping. *Journal of Retailing and Consumer Services*, *23*, 1–8. doi:10.1016/j.jretconser.2014.11.001

Schachtebeck, C., Groenewald, D., & Nieuwenhuizen, C. (2018). Pilot Studies: Use and Misuse In South African SME Research. Acta Universitatis Danubius. Oeconomica, 14(1).

SHADE. L. R. (2014). Gender and digital policy: From global information infrastructure to internet governance. In The Routledge Companion to Media & Gender. Routledge.

Skågeby, J. (2009). Exploring qualitative sharing practices of social metadata: Expanding the attention economy. *The Information Society*, *25*(1), 60–72. doi:10.1080/01972240802587588

Tao, S. (2018). Evaluation of technology innovation in Hubei province. *Engineering Heritage Journal*, *2*(2), 9–10. doi:10.26480/gwk.02.2018.09.10

Tarasova, M. V., & Ashurkova, K. S. (2020). Trade Wars as a Reflection of the Global Economic Situation. *Вестник Тульского Филиала Финуниверситета, 1*. https://elibrary.ru/item.asp?id=43140164

Tassi, P. (2018). Media: From the Contact Economy to the Attention Economy. *International Journal of Arts Management*, *20*(3), 49–59. https://www.proquest.com/docview/2092791898/abstract/68C6DFA7518F402APQ/1

Tjiptono, F., Arli, D., & Viviea. (2016). Gender and digital privacy: Examining determinants of attitude toward digital piracy among youths in an emerging market. *International Journal of Consumer Studies*, *40*(2), 168–178. doi:10.1111/ijcs.12240

Tse, M. C., & Gong, M. (2012a). Online Communities and Commercialization of Chinese Internet Literature. *Journal of Internet Commerce*, *11*(2), 100–116. doi:10.1080/15332861.2012.689563

Tse, M. C., & Gong, M. (2012b). Online Communities and Commercialization of Chinese Internet Literature. *Journal of Internet Commerce*, *11*(2), 100–116. doi:10.1080/15332861.2012.689563

Tunca, T. I., & Wu, Q. (2013a). Fighting Fire with Fire: Commercial Piracy and the Role of File Sharing on Copyright Protection Policy for Digital Goods. *Information Systems Research; Linthicum*, *24*(2), 436-453, 495-496. http://search.proquest.com/abicomplete/docview/1399039152/E0DB27710BEF4738PQ/1center

Tunca, T. I., & Wu, Q. (2013b). Fighting Fire with Fire: Commercial Piracy and the Role of File Sharing on Copyright Protection Policy for Digital Goods. *Information Systems Research; Linthicum*, *24*(2), 436-453, 495-496.

Wan, W. W., Luk, C.-L., Yau, O. H., Alan, C., Sin, L. Y., Kwong, K. K., & Chow, R. P. (2009). Do traditional Chinese cultural values nourish a market for pirated CDs? *Journal of Business Ethics*, *88*(1), 185–196. doi:10.100710551-008-9821-1

Xia, R. L., & Muppala, J. K. (2010). A survey of bittorrent performance. *IEEE Communications Surveys and Tutorials*, *12*(2), 140–158. doi:10.1109/SURV.2010.021110.00036

Yoon, C. (2011). Theory of planned behavior and ethics theory in digital piracy: An integrated model. *Journal of Business Ethics*, *100*(3), 405–417. doi:10.100710551-010-0687-7

Yueh, L. Y. (2020, August). *Economic diplomacy in the 21st century: Principles and challenges* (Monograph August 2020). LSE IDEAS, London School of Economics and Political Science. https://www.lse.ac.uk/ideas/publications/updates/economic-diplomacy-in-the-21st-century-principles-and-challenges

Yuki, K., & Cen, Z. (2018). Effects of the Size of a Country on Its Economic Performance. In M. Tadokoro, S. Egashira, & K. Yamamoto (Eds.), *Emerging Risks in a World of Heterogeneity: Interactions Among Countries with Different Sizes, Polities and Societies* (pp. 19–44). Springer. doi:10.1007/978-981-10-7968-9_2

Zhang, X. (2019). "80后""90后""00后"文化属性的代演和代内演. 文教料, *14*, 52–53.

Zhao, L. (2021). The English Translation and Cultural Dissemination of Chinese Web Novels. *Communication across Borders: Translation & Interpreting*, *1*(1).

Zhao, X. (2019). Intergenerational Differences in Participation in Online Public Relations among the Post-1970s, Post-1980s and Post-1990s Generations. *Fujian University Journal - Humanities and Social Sciences Edition*, *4*, 151–160.

Zulli, D. (2018). Capitalizing on the look: Insights into the glance, attention economy, and Instagram. *Critical Studies in Media Communication*, *35*(2), 137–150. doi:10.1080/15295036.2017.1394582

KEY TERMS AND DEFINITIONS

Attention Economy: Attention economics is an approach to the management of information that treats human attention as a scarce commodity and applies economic theory to solve various information management problems (Hasenhütl, 2018). The attention economy is the collective human capacity to engage with the many elements in our environments that demand mental focus. The term reflects an acknowledgment that the human capacity for attention is limited and that the content and events vying for that attention far exceed that capacity (Whatis.com, 2021).

Millennial Generation (China and Other Countries): Definitions vary, but generally, Millennials are the generation that was born between 1981 and 1994/6.

Online Literature: Printed content available for download or viewing, online and generally, but not always, not available in print form. Maybe fiction, educational, informative, or news, and current events.

Chapter 17
How COVID-19 Has Stimulated Innovation in the Chinese Education Sector

Poshan Yu
https://orcid.org/0000-0003-1069-3675
Soochow University, China

Samuel Kwok
Xi'an Jiaotong-Liverpool University, China

Zhongyue Jiang
Independent Researcher, China

ABSTRACT

This chapter aims to investigate the impacts of COVID-19 in China's education sector. It will capture the dynamics of the interlinked changing relationships between the availability and use of education technology (EdTech) and the demand for online learning among various stakeholders in the Chinese education market. In addition, this chapter examines whether and how these relationships enhance operational efficiency via transforming the current business models in the sector, in particular due to the COVID-19 pandemic. By analyzing the current practices of the sector, this chapter will critically discuss the challenges and opportunities for technology in education and how these changes in turn drive stakeholders (including students, educators, and regulators) to respond and engage with each other, and how these stakeholder engagements impact the sustainable development of delivery modes, such as digital education and remote learning by using EdTech strategies in the sector.

DOI: 10.4018/978-1-7998-7689-2.ch017

INTRODUCTION

China's Education Under the New Normal

Education is a critical factor in any strategy to encourage economic development (Pana & Mosora, 2013). There are some circumstances when learners are pushed to the online option, such as being in a war (Rajab, 2018), being a worker, and not having time to attend regular classrooms (Bourne et al., 2005). Due to the COVID-19 pandemic, restrictions on mass gatherings and social distancing requirements have limited in-class teaching, which has resulted in a massive quick shift to online teaching methods (Ratten, 2020). Hence, the ever-growing demand for online instruction, along with the call to include technology in education, has led to the increased use of e-learning to promote positive student learning outcomes (Kowitlawakul et al., 2017). In this connection, e-learning content can be repeated as many times as needed creating a safe learning environment (Paquet & Marchionni, 2015). This chapter aims to investigate the impacts of COVID-19 in China's education sector. It will capture the dynamics of the interlinked changing relationships between the availability and use of education technology (EdTech) and the demand for online learning among various stakeholders in the Chinese education market.

Under COVID-19, China launched the "no class suspension" policy and operated a large-scale online education, which successfully dealt with the crisis of class suspension caused by the epidemic. This strategy formed a new model of online education in practice, which has far-reaching significance for the future development of China's education. In recent years, the potential market size of China's education and training is vast and maintains a rapid development trend. The main body of education in the training market is also expanded from the initial schools to social forces, training companies, or individuals. However, due to the continuous exploitation of the offline market, there is a surplus of offline traditional education and training institutions, so the industry pattern and structure are undergoing a new round of shuffling. Because of the development of EdTech, China can adjust the online education mode in time during the epidemic period. EdTech is used as an innovation of educational methods, and it contains digital education, remote learning, and online education. EdTech market is prominent in China, and its services have transformed the traditional education model in many countries, for the number of stakeholders is vast. For instance, reports show that Chinese parents give priority to children's education. They hope their children can graduate from famous universities and get stable and well-paid jobs.

Moreover, technology is promoting the development and adoption of education in China from a practitioner's perspective. In other words, the application and expectation of Internet technology and online learning technology in the field of educational technology in China are very high. In this connection, the Chinese government has issued several policies to promote the healthy development and fairness of digital and online education and develop "Internet + education," and encourage the development of online education among all eligible subjects. So far, online education in China has covered early childhood education, K12, higher degree education, and occupational education.

The Development of Online Education in the COVID-19 Era

Why is online education so popular? What is fueling the growth of e-learning in China? Compared to the traditional offline education model, online education has outstanding advantages. E-learning is flexible, convenient, and rich in resources; combining with artificial intelligence (AI), virtual reality (VR), augmented reality (AR), and other technologies, it can better meet users' personalized needs (Jun, 2020).

The epidemic has promoted the reflection and innovation of the whole world on education, enriched the content of education, broadened the horizon of education, from individuals to groups, from schools to society, from China to the world, and brought about the refreshment of education technology and means.

Distance learning has long roots in higher education, dating back to the correspondence courses of the 19th century. As communication technology advanced through the 20th century, connectivity became a source of competitive advantage and differentiation. E-learning represents an opportunity for students to have more personalized learning experiences and choose the subjects they wish to study (Joshua, 2020). With the continuous improvement of the platform business and the stricter teacher standards, China's online education has gradually penetrated various market segments, and the market size is expected to expand further. Compared with the highly competitive first-tier and second-tier cities, the third-tier and fourth-tier cities show more significant development potential. As the online education market in first-tier and second-tier cities tends to be saturated, the user groups of education and training platforms also start to shift to the third-tier and fourth-tier cities. While user transfer brings massive traffic, it also brings some challenges to the industry. For example, it requires online education products to be novel and straightforward enough, with clear and easy-to-learn content, high-cost performance, and excellent teachers and resources.

According to the current situation of China's education, online education is not perfect, and it still has some drawbacks. Therefore, the most suitable mode for China's education is the combination of online and offline, namely the "Internet + education" mode. The application of the Internet is shaping its unique education culture. Stakeholders (including students, parents, educators, and regulators) should fully explore the value of future-oriented education: resource sharing, personalized teaching, and social learning. These concepts should move education from online to offline, creating an interactive, hybrid future learning model. Based on the progress of the Internet and EdTech, teaching technology should be widely used in online education. In addition, the problem of the difference in the level of technological development among regions needs to be solved. Currently, in China, educational resources gather in first-tier cities. Teachers and students from rural areas find it hard to access high-quality materials. To this end, technologies including AI and big data are ideal ways of promoting more resources equally to students from China (Cheng, 2018).

Challenges & Opportunities of Education Under COVID-19

Under the tremendous pressure of coronavirus infectious disease, education is facing challenges around the globe. People need to avoid social activities since the virus can be spread by respiratory droplets, contact, aerosols, and the digestive tract. This has meant an increase in courses taught through digital communication methods (Krishnamurthy, 2020). Ministry of Education of China required schools at various levels to delay the spring semester and encouraged schools and social educational institutions to educate online. So, most schools and other educational institutions cannot have face-to-face classes. The epidemic has transformed China's education model and its business model. Moreover, COVID-19 poses a significant challenge to management education, especially for international students and courses with an experiential nature (Brammer & Clark, 2020). Many schools have to adopt online education for international students.

The restriction of offline education gives opportunities for EdTech and digital education to develop. In the educational realm, network goals as they currently exist can be broadly defined as regarding school improvement, broadening opportunities (including networking with non-school agencies, such as social services or businesses), and resource sharing (Muijs, West, & Mel, 2010). Digital devices are being increasingly adopted for learning and education purposes (Zawacki-Richter & Latchem, 2018). COVID-19 stimulates the reform and development of China's education. Digital education, distance education, online education, and educational technology are gradually applied to daily teaching. People also find the advantages and disadvantages of offline education and online education. Therefore, the business model of online education has further changed. The traditional business model cannot meet development needs, which gave birth to a new business model. At present, the OMO (Online-Merge-Offline) model is gradually accepted by people, and this mode combines online education and offline education organically and gives full play to their advantages.

Online Education-Related Business Models and Stakeholders in China

Different related business models have been formed in the Chinese market in the long-term development process of online education, digital education, and distance education. These business models also cater to the needs of various stakeholders in the market, and even benefit output has been formed between these models, which provides a reference for future education models.

There are three major stakeholders in online learning: administrators (or school management), teachers, and students. Because online learning provides a particular challenge to stakeholders, while they express their acceptance, there are some contradictions. Some innovational stakeholders, like new educational institutions, are willing to exercise, some conventional stakeholders, like traditional schools, think it is difficult to change the current education mode flexibly. So, these stakeholders affect the quality of online education, such as students' participation and learning quality, and greatly influence the development of the online learning industry to a large extent.

The school management hopes that online learning can attract a large number of students and develop the industry. Therefore, a huge investment has been made in technology, and there is a lack of attention to traditional curriculum management issues (such as learning styles, individual differences among students, appropriate curriculum activities, and material selection). Lack of proper training for online teachers and students is common. (Bass & Ritting, nd; Bates & Poole, 2003; Conrad & Donaldson, 2004) Regarding these issues, Palloff and Pratt (2003) indicated that online courses designed around learners often provide higher quality, thereby increasing learner satisfaction.

ANALYSIS AND MODELS

Analysis of Development of Online Education in China: How This Development Helps Enhance Operational Efficiency

In the early stages, due to the immature Internet technology, users' acceptance of online education was not high, and the economy was not good, so few people received online education. At that time, online education was achieved only by recording courses, and users could only watch videos. So, the market for online education is small. By 2011, many Internet companies had started to invest in online education and were pouring money into technical support. When live streaming appeared in China, online education had a more effective model. After that, the education platform emerged, and the government issued a number of policies to support information education (Figure 1).

Figure 1.

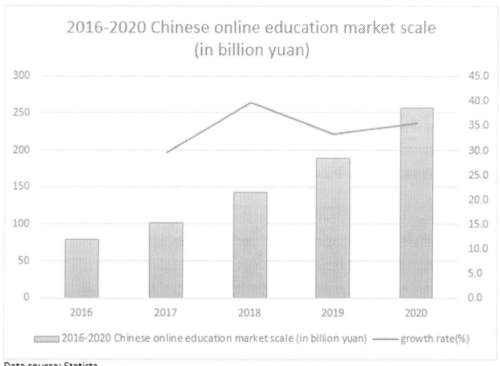

Data source: Statista

In 2020, the scale of China's online education market reached 257.3 billion yuan. Since 2016, the growth rate of the online education market scale has increased year by year. It is expected that the trend will not change in recent years. However, due to the epidemic situation in 2019 and 2020, the growth rate of the online education industry may slow down in recent years. Disruption to operations (including supply chains) as a result of natural and man-made disasters is an unavoidable risk that confronts firms (Ivanov & Dolgui, 2019; Chowdhury et al., 2019), with efficacy to threaten the survival of firms (Haraguchi & Lall, 2015). Evidence shows that disruption to operations has direct and immediate adverse consequences on operations systems and efficiency (Haraguchi & Lall, 2015). Though COVID-19 does not entirely disrupt the education operation, it has negative consequences on traditional education functions. Research indicates that resilient firms have mechanisms for dealing with disruptions, enabling such firms to reap superior performance outcomes (Yu et al., 2019). Therefore, it is necessary for industry practitioners in education to actively prepare for the transformation, in particular, under the epidemic situation.

For the future of education in China, the most likely scenario is a combination of online and offline. On the one hand, the development of online education products is based on integrating offline education course content. Only when the quality of course content is guaranteed, online technical support and platform interaction are meaningful. Offline education also needs to break through the platform's limitations, technology, space-time, and other aspects to reach more users. On the other hand, online education focuses on training and cannot wholly replace face-to-face education, especially personality and social skills education. Based upon Tencent's new smart education experience, the primary goal of implementing EdTech is to provide learners with timely process feedback and personalized learning solutions, which will help improve their performance. The second is to help teachers reduce repetitive labor and improve efficiency. The third is to help management reduce costs and increase efficiency (Ouyang, 2019).

In China, levels of technological development among areas are different, so the operational efficiency is different in different areas. How does online education achieve high operating efficiency? Senior management should focus on the overall situation, background operations, and methods that can be streamlined and deployed to areas that can add value to the student experience (Figure 2).

Figure 2.

In this cycle, the management may first analyze the environment to implement online education better, formulate solutions according to the different requirements, and allocate the corresponding resources to each target. Finally, various services can be delivered according to the conditions of other objectives. Each learning activity or teaching task should be evaluated according to its expected results. If the expected goal is not achieved, management needs to adjust its solution accordingly.

For example, the Chinese online education market adopts different solutions for early childhood and quality-oriented education, K12 education, higher education, vocational education, and other types of education (Figure 3).

Figure 3.

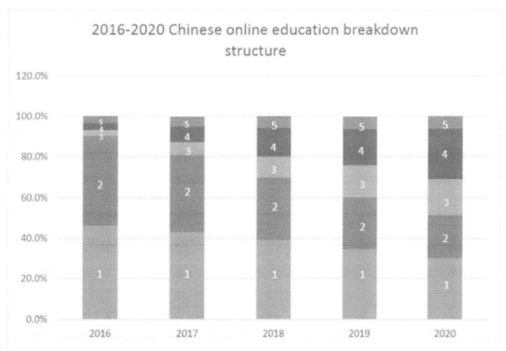

EdTech & Digital Education for Early Childhood and Quality-oriented Education

EdTech for early education is mainly associated with the implementation of intelligent robots. Since China has implemented a universal two-child policy, the number of children aged 0 to 6 has increased. Therefore, the number of early education institutions is growing, and the early education market is expanding. However, there are some problems in the development of early education in China, such as the single content of teaching materials, the shortage of teachers and management talents, etc. In general, China's early education industry still needs standardization and is expected to have huge development potential.

Digital Education for K12

As for K12 online education, China has issued relevant policies to support it as early as 2015. In July 2015, The State Council advocated encouraging Internet enterprises and social educational institutions to develop educational resources and provide online education services according to market demands in the Guidance on Actively Promoting the "Internet +" Action. In January 2017, the Ministry of Education put forward the 13th Five-Year Plan for National Education, which aims to develop modern distance education and online education. In April 2018, the Ministry of Education issued Education Informatization

2.0 Action Plan to accelerate the modernization of education and promote the economic development of education in the new era (Figure 4).

In China, the K12 group is relatively large, so online education significantly impacts the K12 group. From 2015 to 2020, the proportion of K12 online education users in the K12 group increases year by year. K12 online education is expected to overgrow. K12 online education focuses on subject education and quality-oriented education. Among them, online subject education is more, it mainly aims at test-taking ability, and the subject content is synchronized with the school, such as Chinese, English, and Mathematics. The goal of quality-oriented education is to develop physical and mental health, including art, sports, science and innovation, quality of life, and research and learning.

Figure 4.

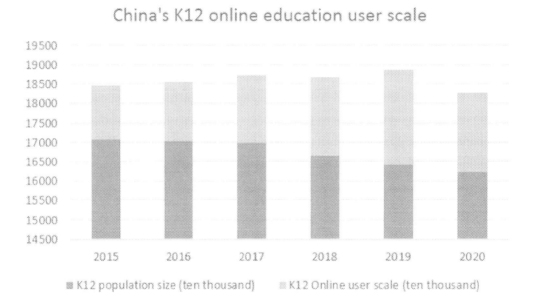

Data source: www.reportrc.com

Digital Education for Higher Degree Education

In higher education, the academic atmosphere is more liberal than K12, as students are more inclined to independent learning, learning to establish a thinking mode. After class, students have more time to choose personalized online education. In addition, in September 2014, the Ministry of Education promulgated the regulations on the Management of The Recruitment of Postgraduate students for 2015, which clearly indicates that the state recognizes the degree of undergraduate students who can graduate through online education. This provides educational opportunities for those with educational needs and is more widespread.

By taking Massive Open Online Courses (MOOC) in Chinese universities as an example, universities provide course resources at first around the MOOC platform. Then, different users choose courses, participate in teaching, complete homework and discussions, and finally, teachers answer questions to improve the course. In general, users have more flexibility and freedom to choose courses.

Remote Learning for Occupational Training and Adult Language

In May 2019, The State Council issued the Implementation Plan for the National Vocational Education Reform, which details efforts to ensure the success of vocational education in the New Era into concrete actions to promote the major reform and development of vocational education. Online vocational education mainly applies to skills training and certification test. Because vocational education involves many skilled industries, and some digital and information technology are widely used, digital technology and remote education are particularly commonly used in vocational education. For example, in the field of digital technology application, the curriculum focuses on the vocational education of big data, AI, 5G, AR / VR, and other technical applications and cultivates technical application-oriented talents. Also, video e-commerce focuses on Vocational Education in online audio-visual, online live broadcast, content creation, and community marketing to nurture creative talents and digital marketing talents. "Smart supply chain" focuses on the vocational education of smart logistics to develop logistics technical talents and supply chain financiers who master information technology.

Other Types of EdTech Education

Online education also applies to enterprise training. These enterprises often use the B2B business model for online education. Through online training, enterprises reduce the cost of training and have a formulated training system, significantly improving work efficiency.

The study model is the foundation of education reform. In the last ten years of development, the study model has involved a lot. Take K12 online education as an example, "one-to-one" model provides a different platform for teachers and students, its process is efficient, but the cost is high. In the real-time model, a teacher can face many students through real-time streaming. This model can give students and teachers have a sense of participation and interaction. The recording mode means that the course is recorded in advance, and students can play it repeatedly. Another common model is the question bank model, in which the supplier summarizes the topics of different subjects and provides students with many test questions. Some software also allows students to learn through their mistakes and enhance their learning achievement.

Due to the diversity of study models, some intelligent technologies are applied, such as AI. In November 2016, the 13th Five-Year Plan for the Development of National Strategic Emerging Industries pointed out that AI should be developed, the industrial ecology of AI should be cultivated, the technology of AI should be comprehensively integrated and penetrated all industries, and the intelligent upgrading should be gradually realized. In the notice "Action plan for AI innovation in colleges and universities" issued by the Ministry of Education in 2018, colleges and universities are required to "improve AI talents cultivation system" and "enhance the collaborative innovation and strategic research for AI" (Kong & Feng, 2017). With the increase of household consumption level and their education level, the role of AI in the education system has been accepted. Along with the support of the government and hardware, the AI industry is on the rise.

Take study English as an example. Some websites can correct the tense according to the context of words and sentences. The function could help students know their grammatical mistakes and assist teachers in correcting homework. Automatic Speech Recognition is also widespread in online education. It could test spoken English and correct pronunciation.

Moreover, a software called "Homework Help" uses image recognition technology, lets students take pictures, and then upload the topic. The system will give the analysis. Similar software is available in the United States–Volley. This software guide students to improve their ability to study by themselves. This could help them accumulate experience for future study. Some software allows teachers to design and teach their own subjects, and some educational platforms for K8 students combine learning with some games to increase students' interest. The software provides personalized learning for different students through big data analysis, optimizing the teaching methods and contents, therefore improving scientific and effective teaching.

Online Education-related Industries and Business Models in China: How these Models Impact the Stakeholder's Engagement

Based on the development of online education and the emphasis on K12 and higher education, the size of China's online education market has been growing steadily in the past five years (Figure 5).

Figure 5.

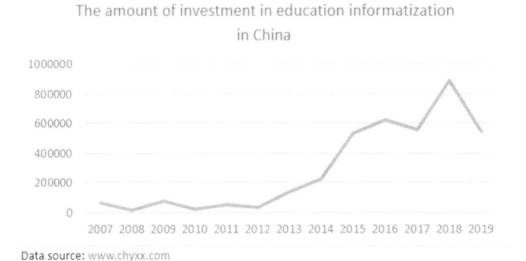

According to the data, the rate of investment in education informatization in China is increasing fast. The industrial structure of online education is also gradually optimized and upgraded. As a result, the online education industry has boomed in recent years, and the shares of listed companies that dabbled in the business have seen several rallies. For example, TCL is the largest online academic education service operator in China, taking a leading position in the online academic education service and Chinese Proficiency Test (HSK) service and actively developing Internet education and vocational education.

Nowadays, the online education market is seriously polarized, with high profit and high financing in the head market. In 2020, the education industry accumulated 103.4 billion yuan of financing, and the five companies with the largest amount of financing have accumulated 82.7 billion yuan, accounting for 80%. However, the customer acquisition cost of the whole industry continues to rise, and the industry generally suffers losses, which makes it difficult for small and medium-sized enterprises in the sector to survive.

The online education industry chain consists of three kinds of stakeholders:

1. upstream: resource supply, including hardware supply (like Polaris AI-assisted teaching system) and content resource supply (like college course contents).
2. midstream: service providers (like MOOC, Zuoyebang, i.e., Homework Help)
3. downstream: schools, teachers, and students.

The value proposition of service providers is to provide platforms and online courses to users, and the target customer segments are K12 and higher education students and teachers. Their distribution channels are software and cooperation with schools. During the engagement, the time spent creates a strong bond between institutions and their outside partners (Morrell et al., 2015). Adekalu et al. (2018) and Gorski (2016) suggested that the institutional administrators must create time and offer necessary support to enhance faculty and students' engagement.

In the online education market, the business models are multiple, so the stakeholder engagements react variously.

1. Business to Customer (B2C), a business model in which a merchant sells products and services directly to the user. At present, most online education enterprises in the market belong to the B2C model, such as VIPKID and 51Talk (both are online youth English platforms). B2C teaching scenarios are also constantly changing, from recorded courses to on-site recording courses, from classrooms to one-on-one and hybrid classes, to grasp consumers' psychology and meet the market's needs. However, this business model can easily cause copyright issues, such as video copying and secondary distribution.
2. Customer to Customer (C2C) is a business model in which users put things on the platform to trade. Like Taobao and Amazon, both educational institutions and individual lecturers can enter the platform to provide educational services to users in the online education market. The platform is just a medium for two sides. But there is an obvious flaw that product quality and other marginal factors are difficult to control.
3. Online to Offline (O2O), like Uber, some offline educational institutions have begun to offer online courses in the Internet era, combining online and offline teaching. For example, institutions start online teaching businesses in the initial offline training or add an offline business to the initial online settings. Some tuition software is positioned as offline tutoring, matching nearby teachers and students for one-on-one tuition. This business model makes full use of offline resources. However, this model may falsify data and make it challenging to ensure the quality of teaching.
4. Business to Business (B2B), a model for establishing business relationships between a company and other companies. For example, companies that provide online education services and technologies for companies, governments, schools, and groups are all B2B, such as the company's online

internal training and customer training. However, this model requires both parties to spend a lot of time polishing and cooperating, and it is difficult to succeed.

5. Business to Business to Customer (B2B2C) is a business model in which an enterprise cooperates with an offline education institution and allows individual teachers to enter into the platform and then provide curriculum resources to learners. Although both B2C and B2B2C are online, B2C has only dabbled in a single area, B2B2C online education platform serves as more of an educational carrier, learners can achieve knowledge of the different regions. For example, CCTalk (i.e., "Content, Community & Talk" real-time interactive education platform) is a comprehensive online knowledge learning platform that covers different topics such as knowledge, interests, social connection, and practical skills. With the "platform + tool + operation" trinity of advantages, CCtalk's territory is rapidly expanding.

Considering that each business model has disadvantages, there will also be a profit model between different business models (Figure 6).

Figure 6.

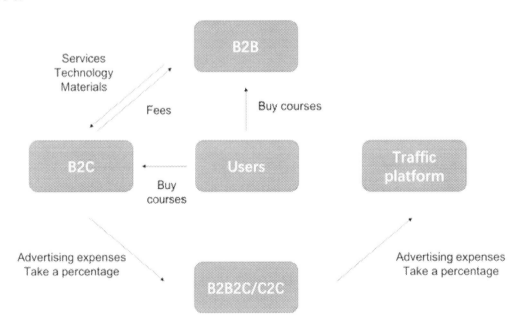

Comparing the Impacts of EdTech on Different Regions from the Perspective of Operational Efficiency and Stakeholder Engagement

Due to the unexpected outbreak of the epidemic, the construction of online education was rapid during the epidemic. The government immediately promoted the education platform and other supporting facilities.

In the early stage, the mainstream online teaching platforms in the market mainly were carried out in recorded broadcasts or live broadcasts of courses. They lacked perfect online interaction functions and limited communication between students and teachers. However, the problem was resolved after the network equipment was updated and the network traffic speed increased (Figure 7).

Figure 7.

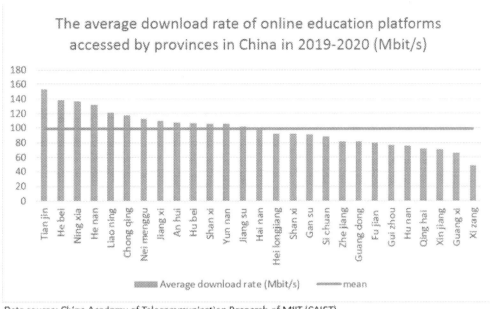

The graph above shows the average download rate of online education platforms accessed in different provinces during COVID-19. With the help of the Ministry of Education and other administrative agencies, the penetration rate and conversion rate of online education in remote areas have been significantly increased in a short time, the level of informatization in developed regions is developing rapidly.

The download rate is different in various regions. This is because the economic development of different provinces in China is not the same. Generally speaking, the economic development of southern China is better than that of northern China. Therefore, the infrastructure construction in southern China is more comprehensive, the intelligent system is better, and the operational efficiency and stakeholder engagement are higher (Figure 8).

The graph shows the different online education platforms and the average download rate in China. Different platforms reflect that online education in China is not single, as the online teaching methods are multiple. And their average download rates are generally high, which means online education is developed fast in China.

During this period, changes in education models have also led some companies to change their business models. Due to the pressure of the COVID-19 pandemic, offline education faces the following problems: delays in school start times, tight budgets, student refunds, and staff shortages. Although the world is working hard to control COVID-19, China has managed to control the pandemic quickly and effectively. To avoid the risk of breaking the capital chain, many offline education institutions have urgently deployed online education courses. However, the cost of online education is relatively low, and some enterprises seize the market with online education deployed in the early stage. Because of their advantages, are similar to "southern China"; they have high operational efficiency and stakeholder engagement.

Figure 8.

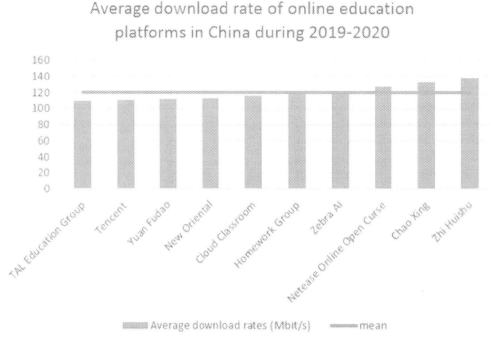

How Do the Authorities Regulate the Online Education in China?

In 2020, China's online education industry had a good market prospect, and sound policies will further promote the development of the industry.

Up to now, there is only one policy document that clearly uses the concept of "online education" in China, namely "Guidance on promoting the healthy development of online education" issued by the Ministry of Education on September 30, 2019, which comprehensively encourages the development of online education industry from the aspects of development goals and means, policy support system and management system. This guiding opinion points out that "online education is a new way of teaching and learning interaction by using modern information technologies such as the Internet and AI, and it is an important part of education services."

The understanding of the online education industry is not only to simply focus on the documents named "online education," but also to comprehensively focus on all regulatory requirements in the field of "network" and "education," and to comply with all regulatory requirements related to network behavior, such as network security, Internet information management, and specific network information service (such as blog, forum, post, live broadcast) form management requirements. In terms of personal information protection, a series of policy documents and regulations in the field of education management must also be complied with. Therefore, the government has gradually tightened supervision over the online education market. In August 2018, the Ministry of Justice issued the Regulations on the Implementation of the Law of the People's Republic of China on The Promotion of Private Education, stressing that private schools using Internet technology to implement online education should obtain a school permit and an Internet business license for the same level and type of education, and file with the government education department and the Ministry of Human Resources and Social Security. In November 2019, the Ministry of Education issued the "Notice on Improving the Special Governance and Rectification Mechanism of Off-campus Training Institutions," which aims to strengthen the online training mechanism. The education administrative department should train institutions in accordance with offline management policies and regulate online education and training mechanisms. In December 2019, the Ministry of Education also issued a notice forbidding harmful mobile applications (apps) from entering primary and secondary schools, stressing that apps containing content that violates teaching rules should be thoroughly checked and stopped immediately.

How Would These Rules Impact the Stakeholder's Behaviors in China?

These rules break the current school model and recognize the legitimacy of online education.

The Chinese education system is based on the industrial revolution. The system advocates large-scale education, emphasizes efficiency and advocates knowledge dissemination. Teachers, teaching materials, and classrooms become the "iron triangle" of education in this system.

There is a growing discussion about how regulations affect China's future education. Stakeholders are concerned about when and how the education system would be impacted. For example, should the Chinese education system, like the Stanford online high school, turn the focus of knowledge into the focus of students' knowledge, break the time and space constraints of education, and allow students to obtain knowledge and necessary credit recognition through online learning?

This is where the "one size fits all" argument is stranded. Why should people with different learning bases, interests, and habits be arranged in the same classroom? In the future, most of the problems can be solved by learning at home and in the library. Each person has a schedule, which can be adjusted at any time. No matter which school you are in, whether in the city or the countryside, you do not have to study every course step by step. It is autonomous learning based on personal interests and problem-solving needs, which is a large-scale network collaborative learning. Students may no longer need teachers to provide them with a complete knowledge structure. After completing their initial knowledge structure, they can construct their own personalized structure to meet their own learning through autonomous learning.

In the future, credits, educational levels, and schools are not significant. What matters is what you learn, what you share, what you build, and what you create.

The Change of Business Model of Digital Education and Remote Learning Before and After COVID-19

Before and after the epidemic, the most significant data are the online education user scale and Internet penetration rate (Figure 9).

In this connection, the data difference between 2019 and 2020 is the most significant in recent years.

Based upon our findings, COVID-19 is just a force accelerating transitional changes in teaching in schools and education departments. It has been recognized that schools and education should undergo extensive digital transformation to meet the needs of the younger generation and their digital future in China. Schools play a pivotal role in this regard: they should educate the younger generation to meet the needs of the future. However, the school strives to keep up with the latest developments in digital technology. In the following section, this chapter will examine how a private education company, i.e., New Oriental, responds to the COVID-19 by adjusting its business model.

Figure 9.

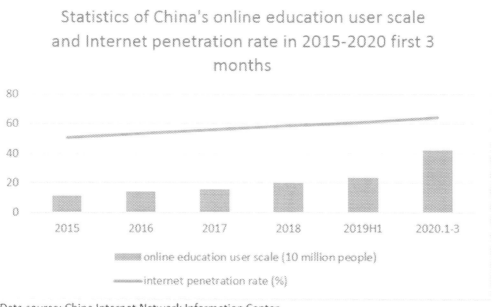

Data source: China Internet Network Information Center

Case Study: New Oriental

New Oriental was established in 1993. At the initial stage, its industrial chain and operation mode were relatively single, and its customers were all applicants who took English exams to study abroad. At this stage, New Oriental's course prices were lower than market prices, and "free" teaching materials were provided, attracting a large number of students. Since then, due to the ever-increasing demand for English proficiency in China's market, the increasing demand for studying abroad, and the rapid development of the English test and training market, the scope of the New Oriental market has expanded rapidly. It provides training for students studying abroad, some fundamental English training for K12 students, and services for early education, higher education, and skills training, but this training is basically offline courses.

The outbreak of the COVID-19 epidemic has brought great challenges to the education field, but it has also brought major innovations. New Oriental is no exception. It faces the following issues:

1. All students have switched to online remote courses, and the degree of acceptance between the students and their parents is unclear;
2. Before the outbreak of the epidemic, most teachers in New Oriental taught offline and had almost no online teaching experience. During the epidemic, they should receive relevant online teaching training, and the company needs to be equipped with necessary online teaching settings in a short time;

3. New Oriental's own online education platform cannot support a large number of students and interactive courses. It needs to expand and upgrade the platform in a short time.

However, after the upgrade, New Oriental became one of the most successful organizations in the education field by changing its business model to deal with the uncertainty caused by COVID-19. Teachers and students quickly became familiar with the new online education arrangements.

Based on New Oriental's experience, this study found that under the impetus of COVID-19, the profound impact on the education field is emerging in some ways:

1. The penetration and transformation of technology to education will be normal. With the integration of technology and education, to a certain extent, students used to take classroom lessons as the core, and now this model has gradually transformed into a dual-core model of classroom and online.
2. The transformation of education methods is gradually taking shape. Before it became popular, people talked about pure offline education or online education. The lock-down caused by COVID-19 will bring more opportunities to use OMO (Online-Merge-Offline) mode, which organically integrates offline and online education.
3. More cooperation between educational institutions and IT companies is gradually developing. The capital sector will further increase investment in education, which will promote a closer integration of education and science and technology.

Currently, discussions on China's (online) education reform are still brewing. Although students, teachers, and other stakeholders across the country have experienced online education, this does not mean that the future of education will always be online. Offline education and online education are not substitutes but cooperative and complementary relationships.

Many things in offline education cannot be directly replaced by online education, so the OMO mode will inevitably appear. In addition, our research has the following findings:

1. Fragmentation

The fragmentation of knowledge itself does not bring advantages. The advantage lies in the value that the effective use of fragmentation brings to users. This value becomes the fragmentation demand of users, and this fragmentation demand changes through contextual changes. For instance, some psychological reports show that when facing the screen instead of the real scene, people's maximum attention is only 25 minutes. Therefore, fragmentation can enable students to improve efficiency to a certain extent.

2. Auxiliary online learning has become the norm

For example, more and more auxiliary online learning platforms are designed to help users learn efficiently.

However, due to the rapid growth of online education in 2020, competition in the online education market will be more brutal in 2021, so it is particularly important to look for new market opportunities, e.g., other than the first- and second-tier cities, that is, the third- and fourth-tier cities in China (Figure 10).

Figure 10.

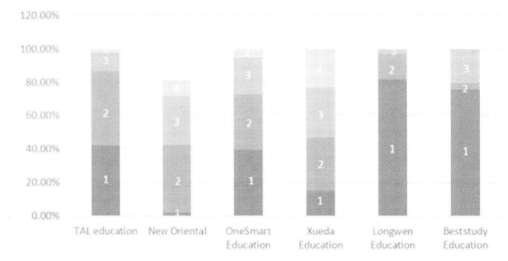

1 — first-tier cities
2 — new first tier cities
3 — second-tier cities
4 — third tier and below cities

Data source: Statista

By the end of this year, the online education market in the first and second-tier cities has become saturated. Take K12 education as an example, the proportion of major educational institutions in the first and second-tier cities has exceeded 90%, and it is not easy to have space for growth. The changes brought by the COVID-19 epidemic are: on the one hand, users' tolerance is improved under the background of limited choice, and users in low-tier cities also only choose online education mode during the COVID-19 epidemic period; On the other hand, how to open up online education market opportunities in schools is the key.

Although the government has promoted education informatization in the past, the application of EdTech in lower-tier cities is not widespread. Currently, there are many products available on the market. Schools in third- and fourth-tier cities will have more opportunities to receive support from online educational resources. Besides, the relatively mature application of online education technology and products, at least in terms of cognition, expects to increase the popularity of online education in lower-tier cities.

Sustainable Development of Digital Education

Education and learning are systematic projects, and the sustainable development of online education and remote education has become the key to China's education market. To make online education sustainable:

1. The market needs standardized development. Adhering to standardized management is the trend of future growth.
2. Continuously improve the display form of educational technology. The advantage of the Internet is that students can obtain transparent information and solve remote interaction problems. However, to transform the freshness brought by educational technology into a lasting attraction and enhance user trust, it is not enough to rely on online education platforms alone. AI and other applications can give education a broader space for development, and they can help solve many standardized and personalized teaching problems.
3. Adhere to the content as the main body. Digital education and online education are the extension of traditional education, the core of which is still education. Respecting the rules of knowledge teaching, insisting on content as the main body, and making products meet customers' needs are the rules that should be followed in the field of education.

CONCLUSION

The report of the 19th National Congress of the Communist Party of China points out that the main social contradictions in China have been transformed into the contradiction between the people's growing needs for a better life and unbalanced and inadequate development. This imbalance is pronounced in the field of education. Although China's information construction and digital economy development are at the forefront of the world, the Internet application in culture and education still needs to be deepened. The "Internet plus education" undoubtedly expands the coverage of high-quality educational resources, conducive to narrowing the gap between education and promoting the optimal allocation of educational resources. The application of digital education, online learning, and remote learning immensely helped develop and innovate education in China.

In China, the rapid demand growth for online education benefits from the rapid development of the Internet industry in recent years. The COVID-19 epidemic's outbreak once again stimulates the new momentum of relevant sectors. It brings a rare opportunity for educational innovation. Although at the beginning of the outbreak, both teachers and students had to use the Internet for online education. However, after the epidemic situation was controlled in China, many courses were carried out online. Nowadays, online education accounts for a more significant proportion of all education modes. Moreover, in the post-COVID-19 era, the education industry has a more prominent trend; that is, the combination of online and offline education will further become the driving needs of education development. According to the cases of some enterprises, OMO mode is a new and effective education mode at present, which can help the sustainable development of education.

Based on the above discussion, this chapter proposes the following suggestions to improve the business efficiency of online education:

1. Solve technical problems. Hardware requirements are the basis for promoting online education. All subsequent facilities are built on hardware. Therefore, the issue of insufficient technology must be solved, especially in some remote low-tier cities.
2. The nature of the subject may limit the integration with online education. For example, the way Chinese students learn English relies on memory, while the subject of chemistry is an experiment. In terms of chemistry courses, online education has no obvious advantages over traditional educa-

tion. Therefore, online education institutions need to take special measures for specialized classes, such as establishing public offline laboratories.
3. The learning efficiency of students varies. In offline learning, students' learning scenarios are relatively random, and there will inevitably be many cases of low learning efficiency. This requires online education to conduct an individualized classification of students and use personalized teaching methods. Of course, students' self-discipline is also crucial.
4. Given the different management systems of online education platforms, strengthening supervision has become an essential measure for online education. The government should improve the supervision and management mechanism and solve the registration and qualification problems of online education institutions and platforms from the source.

Faced with opportunities and challenges, education enterprises should first have sufficient input energy, including technology, teaching, and research. Only by providing sufficiently high-quality educational products and services can their reputation, brand, and capital become the energy accumulation for sustainable development. In such a circular market, online education enterprises need to be user-oriented and find a breakthrough in their development.

This chapter has critically discussed the development of online education and the challenges in COVID-19, and it also analyses the "Internet + education" mode in China. More research could be done on how AI-based online teaching and offline teaching can be integrated and innovated and how this transformation will affect business decisions (especially in higher education).

REFERENCES

Adekalu, S. O., Krauss, S. E., Ismail, I. A., & Suandi, T. (2018). Teaching Professors' Challenges about Community Engagement Outreach and Intervention in Nigerian Universities. *International Journal of Academic Research in Business & Social Sciences*, *8*(8), 191–204. doi:10.6007/IJARBSS/v8-i8/4458

Bass, L., & Ritting, L. (n.d.). *Technology in education.* https://www.uri.edu/personal/lbas2219/

Bates, A. W., & Poole, G. (Eds.). (2003). Effective teaching with technology in higher education: Foundations for success. Jossey Bass Publishers.

Bourne, J., Harris, D., & Mayadas, F. (2005). *Online Engineering Education: Learning Anywhere*. Academic Press.

Brammer, S., & Clark, T. (2020). COVID-19 and management education: Reflections on challenges, opportunities, and potential futures. *British Journal of Management*, *31*(1), 453–456.

Yu, C. (2018, November 29). 17Edtech banks on AI to bridge education gap. *China Daily.* http://www.chinadaily.com.cn/cndy/2018-11/29/content_37329506.htm

Chowdhury, M. M. H., Quaddus, M., & Agarwal, R. (2019). Supply chain resilience for performance: Role of relational practices and network complexities. *Supply Chain Management*, *24*(5), 659–676. doi:10.1108/SCM-09-2018-0332

Conrad, R. M., & Donaldson, J. A. (Eds.). (2004). Engaging the online learner: Activities and resources for creative instruction. Jossey Bass Publishers.

Gorski, I. (2016). Engaging faculty across the community engagement continuum. *Journal of Public Scholarship in Higher Education*, *6*(1), 108–123.

Haraguchi, M., & Lall, U. (2015). Flood risks and impacts: A case study of Thailand's floods in 2011 and research questions for supply chain decision making. *International Journal of Disaster Risk Reduction*, *14*, 256–272. doi:10.1016/j.ijdrr.2014.09.005

Ivanov, D., & Dolgui, A. (2019). Low-certainty-need (LCN) supply chains: A new perspective in managing disruption risks and resilience. *International Journal of Production Research*, *57*(15–16), 5119–5136. doi:10.1080/00207543.2018.1521025

Kobb, J. (2020, March 3). Living beyond the moment. *China Daily*. https://www.chinadaily.com.cn/a/202003/18/WS5e716450a31012821727fe1e.html

Jun, J. (2020, October 25). Hottest Online Education Startups in China. *Pandaily*. https://pandaily.com/7-hottest-online-education-startups-in-china/

Kong, L. Q., & Feng, Y. (2017). Development Difficulties and Transformation of Paths of Entrepreneurship Education for College and University Students in the Period of New Normal. *Education and Vocation*, *15*, 66–71.

Kowitlawakul, Y., Chan, M. F., Tan, S. S. L., Soong, A. S. K., & Chan, S. W. C. (2017). Development of an e-learning research module using multimedia instruction approach. *CIN: Computers, Informatics. Nursing*, *35*(3), 158–166. PMID:27811511

Krishnamurthy, S. (2020). The future of business education: A commentary in the shadow of the COVID-19 pandemic. *Journal of Business Research*, *117*(1), 1–54. doi:10.1016/j.jbusres.2020.05.034 PMID:32501309

Morrell, E., Sorensen, J., & Howarth, J. (2015). The Charlotte Action Research Project: A Model for Direct and Mutually Beneficial Community–University Engagement. *Journal of Higher Education Outreach & Engagement*, *19*(1), 105.

Muijs, D., West, M., & Mel, A. (2010). Why network? Theoretical perspectives on networking. *School Effectiveness and School Improvement*, *21*(1), 5–26. doi:10.1080/09243450903569692

Ouyang, S. (2019, December 4). Tencent launches new smart education solution. *China Daily*. https://www.chinadaily.com.cn/a/201912/04/WS5de77c66a310cf3e3557bfef.html

Palloff, R. M., & Pratt, K. (Eds.). (2003). The virtual student: A profile and guide to working with online learners. Jossey Bass.

Pana, M. C., & Mosora, C. (2013). From quantity to quality in addressing the relationship between education and economic development. *Procedia: Social and Behavioral Sciences*, *93*, 911–915. doi:10.1016/j.sbspro.2013.09.302

Paquet, F., & Marchionni, C. (2015). E-learning and IV therapy: Can learning be fun? *Vascular Access*, 9(3), 11–22.

Rajab, K. D. (2018). The Effectiveness and Potential of e-Learning in War Zones: An Empirical Comparison of Face-to-Face and Online Education in Saudi Arabia. *IEEE Access: Practical Innovations, Open Solutions*, 6, 6783–6794. doi:10.1109/ACCESS.2018.2800164

Ratten, V. (2020). Coronavirus disease (COVID-19) and sports entrepreneurship. *International Journal of Entrepreneurial Behaviour & Research*, 26(6), 1379–1388. doi:10.1108/IJEBR-06-2020-0387

Yu, W., Jacobs, M. A., Chavez, R., & Yang, J. (2019). Dynamism, disruption orientation, and resilience in the supply chain and the impacts on financial performance: A dynamic capabilities perspective. *International Journal of Production Economics*, 218, 352–362. doi:10.1016/j.ijpe.2019.07.013

Zawacki-Richter, O., & Latchem, C. (2018). Exploring four decades of research in computers & education. *Computers & Education*, 122, 136–152. doi:10.1016/j.compedu.2018.04.001

KEY TERMS AND DEFINITIONS

AI: The acronym "artificial intelligence" is a new technical science for simulating, extending, and expanding the theory, method, technology, and application system of human intelligence.

AR: The acronym "augmented reality" is computer-generated text, images, 3D models, music, video, and other virtual information simulated and applied to the real world. The two kinds of information complement each other to "augment" the real world.

Digital Education: It refers to the teaching activities in which teachers and learners follow modern educational theories and use digital teaching resources and modes to train the interdisciplinary talents with innovative consciousness and innovative ability to meet the needs of the new century.

EdTech: A combination of "education" and "technology" refers to software designed to enhance teacher-led learning in classrooms and improve students' education outcomes.

K12: (Kindergarten through twelfth grade). It is the abbreviation of pre-school education to high school education.

Operational Efficiency: It is primarily a metric that measures the efficiency of profit earned as a function of operating costs. The greater the operational efficiency, the more profitable a firm or investment is.

Remote Learning: It refers to the use of media such as television and the Internet; it breaks the boundaries of time and space and is different from the traditional school accommodation teaching model.

Stakeholder Engagement: It is the process used by an organization to engage relevant stakeholders for a purpose to achieve accepted outcomes.

VR: The acronym "virtual reality" occurs when the computer simulates the virtual environment to give people a sense of environmental immersion.

Chapter 18
Decision-Making Styles of the Next Generation of Chinese Business Leaders

Rob Kim Marjerison
https://orcid.org/0000-0003-1181-8695
Wenzhou-Kean University, China

Jing Pan
University of Warwick, UK

ABSTRACT

This study seeks to explore the relationships between decision-making styles, academic performance, and gender of educated Chinese millennials. As the millennial generation of college graduates in China comes of age, they will move into leadership roles in public and commercial organizations. They will have influence over considerable financial assets as well as economic and public policy which translates into global impact. There is a gap in the existing literature on the topic. This study utilized online self-report questionnaires to gather data, and the general decision-making style test to assess respondents' decision-making models culminating in correlation analysis and t-test. Based on the findings of related research, the authors hypothesized that there would be a difference in the decision-making styles based on gender and that there would be a significant difference in academic performance based on the decision-making styles. The findings may be of interest to a variety of those interested in decision-making styles, Chinese millennials, and future leaders of China.

INTRODUCTION

As China continues to grow economically and assert its position on the world stage, an understanding of the goals, strategies and tactics of those making decisions regarding economic policy both today and in the future is important to various parties worldwide. The generation of leaders that opened up China and have overseen the economic development is rapidly approaching retirement age, and the subsequent

DOI: 10.4018/978-1-7998-7689-2.ch018

generations who will eventually become decision-makers have a very different frame of reference and have had a very different set of experiences than their parents' and grandparents' generations (Peng et al., 2019). Existing research on the decision-making styles of Chinese decision-makers is not abundant, and much is of limited relevance given the relatively rapid and significant shift in circumstances since the opening up of China to international commerce began in the 1970s. Additionally, findings in the existing body of research regarding decision-making styles indicate a considerable variance from generation to generation (Ding et al., 2020; Lakshika & Ahzan, 2021; Rašković et al., 2020).

Recruiting, hiring and promotion of employees is often largely based on the academic performance of the candidates (Baert et al., 2018; Soon et al., 2020). Particularly in China, academic performance is given considerable weight in the selection process for hiring by both private companies and government agencies (Mok & Jiang, 2017; Teng et al., 2019). Decision-making styles have been demonstrated to be related to academic performance (Bista, 2019; MacCann et al., 2020; Saya, 2015). For these reasons, when considering the decision-making styles of the next generation of decision-makers, it is helpful to examine the relationship between academic performance and decision-making styles.

There has been a shift since the opening up of China in the societal norms and values with regards to women in leadership roles in both political and commercial organizations (Leung, 2003; McKeen, 2005). China has grown in influence and importance on the global stage, becoming one of the few superpowers (Cernat, 2020; Myles, 2018). As the trend seems likely to continue Sun (2017), it is relevant to consider how the increasing influence of women may affect the future decisions made in China that impact the interaction between China other superpowers as well as smaller players on the global stage. Therefore, this study investigates how the decision-making of Chinese millennials is influenced by their gender.

Decision-making has been identified as one of the ways that managers and leaders effectively manage change in a business environment (Erven, 2001). It plays a key role in a firm's success. People tend to classify bad decisions as unconscious and unavoidable consequences of the human decision-making process; however, the existing literature points to another view that decision-making skills can be acquired. Not only should leaders be able to adapt their behavior in changing situations but adapting their decision-making models may be beneficial (Bradley & Price, 2021; Hubbard, 2017). For those that match the respondent demographic of this study, once aware of their preferences and the strengths and weaknesses of their approaches, they can make good use of strengths and develop weaknesses (Sadler & Spicer, 2005). Business leaders may find that awareness of decision-making styles and subsequent implementation of adaptive behaviors may provide business benefits (Jewell et al., 2020; Levin & Liu, 2021). Researchers across a variety of disciplines may find that the results of this research are helpful and make a contribution to their respective fields of inquiry. However, good decision-making could be critical to a company's success (Alharahsheh & Pius, 2021; Subrahmanyam, 2018).

Decision-making has long been a topic of interest, and the body of research-based knowledge on the subject is considerable, especially on related topics, including the relationship between decision-making and team effectiveness, leadership, team and decision speed and relationship between demographics and leadership, but there has been little consideration of the impact of gender, decision-making styles and academic other performance specifically in China.

Companies can use the findings of this study in conjunction with the results of related research to predict good decision-making ability and to support the recruitment of potential managers as employees successfully Baroda et al. (2019), of whom most are college graduates, so it is necessary to investigate the millennial generation's decision-making models and understand the factors that affect those decision-making styles. It is hoped that the findings of this study will help decision-makers and future decision-makers to improve their decision-making skills.

This topic might be of interest to policymakers, business leaders, Human Resources professionals, and those whose research interests include; decision-making, variables affecting academic performance, and gender studies.

This paper is an attempt to lessen that gap in the existing research, specifically by seeking to identify and quantify the presence and level of the relationships between gender, decision-making style and academic performance.

BACKGROUND

Review of Related Literature

All organizations' systems are imperfect, and wrong decisions are made from time to time (Katz & Kahn, 1978). As a result, addressing questions of how decision-making could become more effective is relevant. In the ten years preceding this study, interest and activity in research in the area of decision-making has increased with considerable focus on how people make managerial decisions and specifically why cognitive distortions occur (Dong et al., 2018; Schildkamp, 2019). Much of the research is focused on attempting to identify how bias is related to heuristics and may influence business decisions either in *peius* or *in melius* (Artinger et al., 2015; Azar, 2014). Some scholars also believe that cognitive biases have a negative effect on business choices (Abatecola, 2017).

To reduce biases during the process of decision-making, scholars have tried to develop techniques and methods through research like using the promising de-biasing techniques like the cross-disciplinary checklist or using MBTI® testing to track decision makers' personality types to identify and track the biases (Furnham, 2020; Mendes et al., 2019). Further, it has been demonstrated that the use of checklists and MBTI® testing can help reduce bias in complex organizations (Mendes et al., 2019). Individuals with frequent quality control mechanisms and more complex and diverse personalities are more likely to make decisions than individuals with no control, fewer participants, and individuals with slight differences in personality (Cristofaro, 2017).

Scholars have also studied the factors that affect the decision-making process. Some results show that "agreement-seeking behavior, group trust, and cognitive diversity can have positive effects on decision outcomes" (Parayitam & Papenhausen, 2016). Research conducted by Dooley et al. (1999) noted that perceived trustworthiness plays an important role and that cognition-based trust can increase the benefits of cognitive conflict and that affect-based trust can reduce problems associated with cognitive conflict.

Among the existing research on decision-making skills, there is relatively little dissension on how best to define and measure DMS (Rowland, 2004; Wood & Bandura, 1989). And few exceptions to the broad methodology used to measure DMS across borders (Rowland, 2004). As stated above, there is a gap in the literature on the specific topic of this study; however, the existing research does indicate that gender can be a factor in some cases (Bakewell & Mitchell, 2006; Powell & Ansic, 1997; Radecki & Jaccard, 1996).

Age has also been identified as a factor in decision-making styles McMorris (1999); and Chavda et al. (2015) with skills generally improving from elementary age Karnes (1993) through adolescence Nelson (1984) at least through college age (Rocha, 2012). Again, there exists a gap in the research in the specific topic of this study which is explored with the aim not of whether age is a factor, but rather how age is a factor in the specific demographic identified in this study.

In recent studies, scholars have studied the elements which affect managers' decision-making results (Mendes et al., 2019). Some research has been conducted to investigate the relationship between demographics and leadership or decision-making style, and have shown that there is not a significant difference in the decision-making models and leadership styles of those used among non-profit organizational leaders Uzonwanne (2007) but that decisions making styles may vary within the same non-profit organizations as a function of the age of the decision-makers (Uzonwanne, 2016). Decision-making styles in for-profit organizations has also been explored and has revealed a consensus in the predominance of Rational decision-making skills, which have been used by older, possibly more experienced and senior executives (Alkhawlani et al., 2021; Fatima et al., 2020; Gurkov, 2015).

For these studies, most of the early researchers focused on cognitive biases and the relationships between demographics and manager's decision-making styles. Using psychological instruments may be one of the useful ways to help decision-makers better understand themselves and control decision outcomes (Lysonski & Durvasula, 2013; Phillips et al., 1984). Predicting the performance through external factors like decision-making styles can also be an excellent way to make this distinction (Bărbuță-Mișu et al., 2019; Rus et al., 2019).

Becoming aware of people's own preferred decision-making styles can be an important step to help individuals reduce biases and overcome weaknesses in decision-making processes and in developing effective decision-making skills (Rowland, 2004; Spicer & Sadler-Smith, 2006). Completion and understanding of the results of the GDMS test would enable individuals to improve their decision-making capabilities (Betsch & Iannello, 2009; Loo, 2000b; Tadriss-Hasani & Rahmansersht, 2020). Once aware of their preferences and the strengths and weaknesses of their approaches, individuals can then seek to develop those areas where they are weaker or work with others who exhibit styles that complement their own (Sadler & Spicer, 2005).

Employment, both within the private and public sectors in China, has historically been heavily influenced by academic performance, and while the educational system has morphed over the recent decades, academic performance remains a major determining factor in employment (Alon, 2009; Teng et al., 2019).

The literature related to decision-making styles in China is limited and further limited by the questionable relevance of the findings reported prior to the present era of political and commercial leadership due to the rapid and significant changes in China (Warner & Zhu, 2018; Xue & Wang, 2012). The majority of the recent existing literature on decision-making styles in China is focused tightly on consumer behavior; thus, almost no current research on the decision-making styles of non-commercial leadership in China has been conducted Jiang and Luo (2021); however, due to the interwoven relationship between government and corporate enterprises in present-day China Yu (2018) and Xue et al. (2018), within the context of this study, it is appropriate to assume some similarity to those in political leadership roles, and those in commercial leadership roles (Lau et al., 2020; Si et al., 2017).

Most of these studies have studied the factors which influence managers' decision-making styles and processes. However, there has been less consideration of the influence of gender differences on decision-making styles, and in particular, within the context of China. In a review of the existing literature on decision-making and gender in China on which to build a foundation for this study, care was taken to consider the context and period during which the findings were reported.

It should also be noted that while some aspects of Chinese society and culture have remained largely unchanged for centuries, other elements have changed considerably since the opening up of China for international commerce less than two generations ago (Peng & Luo, 2021; Perry, 2018; Xiao et al., 2017). While changes in cultural and societal norms and the roles of women in China is well outside the scope of this study, it should be noted that there have been changes since the opening up less than two generations ago; specifically, there have been significant changes in the number and context of leadership roles that women play socially, politically and commercially in China in the last 1-2 generations (Huang et al., 2018; Mattison et al., 2021; Riley, 1997; Xiong et al., 2018)

As college-educated Millennials are the most likely source for potential new hires for organizations in China and are the most likely to emerge as the next generation of leaders, it is important to understand their decision-making behavior. As a result, after we understand the psychological reasons behind their decision-making process, it is relevant to investigate the relationship between genders, college students (educated or soon to be educated Millennials), decision-making styles, and academic performance. Thus, the research question is, what factors actually affect the decision-making styles of this demographic?

HYPOTHESIS

Based on the literature review mentioned above, the following hypotheses are put forth:

H1. There will be a significant difference in the decision-making styles (Rational, Intuitive, Dependent, Spontaneous, and Avoidant) used among college students based on gender.
H2. There will be no significant difference in the decision-making styles (Rational, Intuitive, Dependent, Spontaneous, and Avoidant) used among college students based on gender.
H3. There will be a significant difference in the academic performance (GPA) used among college students based on the decision-making styles (Rational, Intuitive, Dependent, Spontaneous, and Avoidant).
H4. There will be no significant difference in the academic performance (GPA) used among college students based on the decision-making styles (Rational, Intuitive, Dependent, Spontaneous, and Avoidant).

METHODOLOGY – DESIGN OF THE STUDY

The research aims to investigate the relationships between gender, decision-making styles, and academic performance for Chinese millennials and identify what strategic plans organizations could implement to improve their effectiveness by inferring their decision-making styles.

Since there is little data about Chinese millennials' decision-making styles, and a relatively large amount of primary data needs to be collected, a quantitative methodology would be most appropriate in this study to investigate the demographic factors and decision-making styles. An online survey is well suited to meet these conditions.

The review of existing literature revealed the existence of valid and relevant instrument that had been successfully developed, tested, and deployed on a closely related topic under different circumstances. The survey instrument was previously used by Scott and Bruce (1995).

Questions were used to identify gender, age, academic performance, and five general decision-making styles: Rational, Intuitive, Dependent, Avoidant, and Spontaneous. To test the constructs desired, the survey instrument was organized to reflect the following: Questions 7-9 represented the Rational model;

10-12 represented the Intuitive model; Questions 13-15 represented the Dependent model; Questions 16-18 represented the Avoidant model, while Questions 19-21 represented the Spontaneous model.

The respondents were self-selected and were primarily enrolled in one of several Chinese universities. To attempt to determine if there is a connection between these factors and students' decision-making styles, an online survey containing 21 questions was well suited for this purpose and topic. The survey was completed by 321 people through social media Wechat, with the data collected and stored on the WeChat survey platform. The survey results were filtered, and the data of respondents who did not complete the survey completely was discarded. The data was then analyzed.

ANALYSIS

As mentioned, the data of decision-making models was collected using the GDMS scale in five dimensions: Rational, Intuitive, Dependent, Avoidant, and Spontaneous models. The first step in examining the data was to identify the respondents by gender and to confirm that they were part of the desired demographic by age. Of 321 respondents, 162 were male, and 159 were female, which is a highly satisfactory distribution given that gender is on the test variables in this study. Of the respondents, 83% were university undergraduate students, which fits the profile of educated or likely to become college-educated millennials. These results are indicated in Figure 1.

Figure 1. The respondents' gender and educational level
Source: Authors

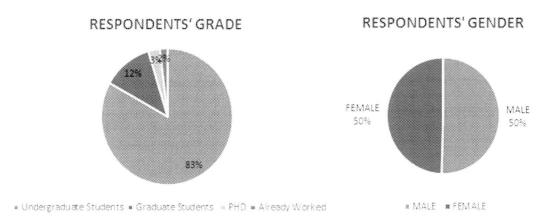

H1 studied the decision-making models used among Chinese millennials (Rational, Intuitive, Dependent, Spontaneous, and Avoidant) based on the difference in gender. This hypothesis was tested by a t-test through SPSS. Spontaneous (p = 0.093), Avoidant (p = 0.080), and Dependent decision-making model (p = 0.532) reported no statistically significant difference in gender. However, with Intuitive and Rational decision-making models, results found a significant difference in gender. The p-value reported $p < 0.05$ on Intuitive (p = 0.019) and Rational (p = 0.039) decision-making models. Through specific contrast, the data indicates that for Intuitive decision-making models (t=2.39, P=0.02), the average value of female (9.74) was significantly higher than the average value of Male (8.42). In contrast, the average value of female (11.65) of Rational decision-making models (t=-2.09,P=0.04) was significantly lower than the average value of Male (12.62).

Therefore, H1 was partially supported in the case of Intuitive and Rational decision-making and not supported in the case of Spontaneous, Avoidant, and Dependent decision-making.

Likewise, H2 was partially supported in the case of Avoidant, Dependents, and Spontaneous decision-making and not supported in the cases of Intuitive and Rational decision-making styles. The findings from this analysis are provided in Table 1.

Table 1. The significant differences on college students' decision-making models by gender

	Female (N=162)	Male (N=159)	t	p
Spontaneous	9.69 ± 2.97	8.72 ± 2.94	1.693	0.093
Avoidant	10.26 ± 3.38	9.19 ± 2.86	1.766	0.08
Dependent	11.30 ± 2.82	10.98 ± 2.36	0.627	0.532
Intuitive	9.74 ± 2.84	8.42 ± 2.90	2.391	0.019*
Rational	11.65 ± 2.78	12.62 ± 1.98	-2.093	0.039*
*p<0.05 ** p<0.01				

Source: Authors.

H3 and H4 required the analysis of the academic performance based on the different decision-making models (Rational, Intuitive, Dependent, Avoidant, and Spontaneous). Correlation analysis was used to study the correlation between GPA and decision-making models and used the Pearson correlation coefficient to indicate the strength of correlation.

Table 2. The Pearson correlation coefficient between GPA and five decision-making models

	GPA	Grades & Efforts
Spontaneous	-0.196**	-0.006
Avoidant	-0.218**	-0.244**
Dependent	0.066	-0.101
Intuitive	0.143	-0.13
Rational	0.132	0.511**
*p<0.05 ** p<0.01		

Source: Authors.

The results, presented in Table II show that the correlation coefficient between GPA and Rational, Intuitive and Dependent models was close to 0, thus indicating that there is no correlation between GPA and Rational, Intuitive and Dependent models. However, the correlation coefficient between GPA and Spontaneous is -0.196, while Avoidant was reported as -0.218, which indicated a significant negative correlation between GPA and Spontaneous and Avoidant models. Therefore, H3 was also partially supported in the cases of Spontaneous and Avoidant but not supported in the cases of Rational, Intuitive, and Dependent in this situation. Likewise, the H4, which stated the there was no difference between the decision-making styles of the respondents based on academic performance, was partially supported in the cases of Rational, Intuitive, and Dependent decision-making styles, but not supported in the cases of Spontaneous and Avoidant decision-making styles. The findings from this analysis are provided in Table 2.

FINDINGS AND DISCUSSION

The decision-making models as used by Chinese millennials are discussed. The results of the data analysis are somewhat complicated by the number of factors included in the GDM, which resulted in the mixed results of partially supporting, and not supporting, all of the four hypotheses, with some constraints.

It was also determined that more respondents used the Rational decision-making model than any other model.

In the case of H1, which states that there will be significant differences in the decision-making styles, (Rational, Intuitive, Dependent, Spontaneous and Avoidant) used among respondents based on gender. It was found that in the case of Intuitive and Rational decision-making, H1 was supported, and in the case of Spontaneous, Avoidant and Dependent decision-making styles, H1 was not supported.

In the case of H2, which states that there will be no significant difference in the decision-making styles (Rational, Intuitive, Dependent, Spontaneous and Avoidant) used among respondents based on gender, the results reveal that H2 was partially supported, in the case of Avoidant, Dependent and Spontaneous decision-making, and not supported in the cases of Intuitive and Rational decision-making styles. The results of the data analysis showed that Intuitive and Rational decision-making models reported a significant difference in gender, with females being more likely to engage in Intuitive DMSs. Therefore, H2 was not wholly accepted. By comparing the average value, the researcher found that more women used the Intuitive decision-making model than men while more men used the Rational decision-making model than women.

While these findings may be interpreted as supporting H1 and not supporting H2 at the macro level, a further examination of the data, with consideration of all the five decision-making styles, shows meaningful results, well worthy of exploration, examination, and discussion. The relationship between gender and Intuitive and Rational decision-making indicates that males are more likely to engage in Rational decision-making, that is decision-making that as defined by Scott and Bruce (1995) as more likely to be based on logic and structured approaches while simultaneously women are more likely to use Intuitive decision-making which is more likely to be based on hunches, feelings, and impressions. This apparent contrast in findings is worthy of further exploration, which is outside the scope of the present study but which is addressed by an abundance of literature focused on gender and DMSs of populations that differ from the focus of this study (Delaney et al., 2015; Páez Gallego et al., 2020; Uzonwanne, 2015).

Examination of the findings are a more granular level, reveal that the styles are Spontaneous and Avoidant do not correlate to gender, as reported by the respondents in this study which can be interpreted to mean that males and females do not differ in their behavior when avoiding decision-making, nor when it comes to makes a rash or impulsive decision on short notice. This lack of difference, where previous research had often indicated different behaviors could possibly be attributed to the cultural differences between the previous research respondents and those in this study as other findings in the existing research on the topic of cultural behaviors, while only peripherally related to this study, consistently indicate that variations in behavior may be related to cultural differences. A determination on this matter is outside the scope of this study but well worth further exploration and subsequent research.

H3 states that there will be a significant difference in the academic performance (GPA) used among college students based on the decision-making styles (Rational, Intuitive, Dependent, Spontaneous and Avoidant). The correlation coefficient between GPA and Spontaneous and Avoidant is -0.196 and -0.218, respectively, which indicated a significant negative correlation between GPA and Spontaneous and Avoidant models while the other three styles, Rational, Intuitive, and Dependent, the results show there is no connection. In this case, H3 was also partially accepted.

In the case of H4, which states that there will be no difference in the decision-making styles (Rational, Intuitive, Dependent, Spontaneous and Avoidant) of the target demographic based on academic performance, again the results are divided with the correlation coefficient between GPA and Spontaneous and Avoidant at -0.196 and -0.218, respectively, which indicates a significant negative correlation between GPA and Spontaneous and Avoidant models. In these two factors, H4 was not accepted, while in the other three factors of Rational, Intuitive and Dependent, there appears to be no significant correlation, therefore, supporting H4.

While these findings may be technically interpreted as supporting H3 and not supporting H4 at the macro level, the number, five, of decision-makings styles are worthy of individual attention and a further examination of the data at a more granular level, with consideration of all the five decision-making styles shows meaningful results, well worthy of exploration, study and discussion.

The lack of a relationship between GPA and Rational, Intuitive and Dependent decision-making styles indicates that these three styles are not of critical relevance to academic performance, which in itself may indicate a potential to provide insight into the decision-makings styles of the target demographic, for example, the Dependent style, which is not related to GPA according to the results, could indicate that the higher performers in this demographic are not easily influenced by others, which is as expected, but also suggests that those with lower academic performance are likewise not influenced by others. This finding is potentially interesting for a number of reasons and may be of interest for further research by those whose interests lie closer to leadership, leadership development, and related topics, which are outside the scope of this study.

The negative relationships observed between GPA and Spontaneous and Avoidant potentially indicate that consistent Avoidant decision-making, or Spontaneous and Impulsive decision-making, is highly likely to create difficulties in studies resulting in poorer academic performance. This relationship also agrees with the findings of previous other researchers whose views are that Rational decision-makers would typically rather deal with, rather than avoid the problems or decisions they face (Abubakar et al., 2019; Phillips et al., 1984).

It suggests that if we can encourage and maintain using a Rational approach to handle problems, it could potentially help with solving avoidance-related issues, and improve performance.

CONCLUSION

This study explored the relationship between gender and the decision-making models (Rational, Intuitive, Dependent, Spontaneous, and Avoidant) gender and academic performance (GPA) of Chinese millennials. This topic is relevant.

Gender does have some influence on decision-making styles, as discussed above, when it comes to Intuitive and Rational decision-making styles, with females significantly more likely to use Intuitive DMS and males more likely to use Rational DMSs. Although care should be taken in the generalization of this finding due to vast differences in culture and educational systems, this finding is consistent with previously reported findings in other countries (Aliman et al., 2017; Delaney et al., 2015; Lin et al., 2019; Mehta, 2020; Pavlić & Vukić, 2019).

Likewise, academic performance is related to decision-making styles, as discussed above, where Avoidant and Spontaneous decision-making styles are likely to result in poorer academic performance.

The Rational decision-making approach is the most frequently used approach and is suggested as a focus for those who seek to improve decision-making skills which may result in better academic performance. This is suggested because of the positive relationship with academic performance. The Rational decision-makers' choices will maximize the academic outcomes, and they will choose the alternative that rates the highest, resulting in the situation where they will get the maximum benefits (Abubakar et al., 2019; Doukianou et al., 2019). Rational decision-making, using logical and structured approaches, are more useful than postponing or avoiding making decisions. Thus, millennials, especially those who are pursuing higher education, should focus on developing their Rational decision-making approaches. This finding is consistent with the existing literature, and like to be generalizable across broader sections of society to include anyone who is interested in improving their decision-making performance (Abubakar et al., 2019; Eells, 2016; Power et al., 2019).

Further, assuming the premise of this study, that those with better academic performance are more likely to attain employment in both the private and public sections organizations, and are more likely to advance once on those organizations, it seems likely that the future leaders in China are less likely to use Avoidance and Spontaneous DMS. Likewise, it seems likely that women, as given their increasing numbers in leadership positions in both the public Xiajuan et al. (2017) and commercial organizations (Cooke, 2016; Wang & Shirmohammadi, 2016) over time, and potentially to influence DMSs most often exhibited within those same organizations, will drive an increased reliance on Intuitive and Rational decision-making styles.

LIMITATIONS AND FURTHER INVESTIGATION

The limitations of this study should also be noted. Firstly, since it uses self-report questionnaires to collect data, accurate judgments made by respondents about themselves are required, and the potential for bias and distortion may interfere with the results (Brenner & DeLamater, 2016; Louie & Ward, 2010; Spicer & Sadler-Smith, 2005). For instance, respondents tend to claim traits that make them feel good and deny those that do not; thus, social desirability bias may appear (Marquis et al., 1986; McCullagh & Rosemberg, 2015). Secondly, the findings of Loo (2000) provides evidence that the GDMS is unlikely to show social desirability bias. It should also be recognized that the data was collected within a relatively short period of time, four weeks, which is a short period for collecting data and which may result in a lack of characteristic diversity. Further testing over more extended periods of time would be suggested. In addition, the age and personality of the respondents also could be the critical factors that influence the decision-making models and, in doing so, would increase the contribution of the study by including not only future decision-makers, but also the present generation of decision-makers. On this topic, it should be considered that the generally accepted age of leaders in China is quite mature (Smith, 2019; Zhu &

Mukhin, 2021). With that in mind, there actually exists a two-generation gap between millennials and the present senior leadership of most public and government organizations in China, so further research on different generations would be worthwhile.

Most importantly, this study makes apparent the need for further research in the level of granularity of exploration within the five decision-making styles identified by Scot and Bruce (1995) and upon which the foundation of this study rests. Each of the five styles is worthy of individual consideration and validation and should be explored independently. Such research would necessitate a more comprehensive instrument and different analytical approach, but would provide a more clear picture of the relationships between the variables in this study and, in doing so, greater add to the contribution of this study.

REFERENCES

Abatecola, G., Caputo, A., & Cristofaro, M. (2017). Reviewing cognitive distortions in managerial decision-making | Toward an integrative co-evolutionary framework |. *Journal of Management Development*, *37*(5), 409–424. doi:10.1108/JMD-08-2017-0263

Abatecola, G., Caputo, A., & Cristofaro, M. (2018). Reviewing cognitive distortions in managerial decision-making: Toward an integrative co-evolutionary framework. *Journal of Management Development*, *37*(5), 409–424. doi:10.1108/JMD-08-2017-0263

Abubakar, A. M., Elrehail, H., Alatailat, M. A., & Elçi, A. (2019). Knowledge management, decision-making style and organizational performance. *Journal of Innovation & Knowledge*, *4*(2), 104–114. doi:10.1016/j.jik.2017.07.003

Alharahsheh, H. H., & Pius, A. (2021). Exploration of Employability Skills in Business Management Studies Within Higher Education Levels: Systematic Literature Review. *Research Anthology on Business and Technical Education in the Information Era*, 1147–1164.

Aliman, N. K., Ariffin, Z. Z., & Hashim, S. M. (2017). Generation Y Muslim Female and Male Decision-making Styles in Malaysia: Are They Different? *Journal of Research in Marketing*, *7*(2), 534–543. doi:10.17722/jorm.v7i2.184

Alkhawlani, M. A. S., Bohari, A. M., & Shamsuddin, J. (2021). The moderating effect of crisis experience on the relationship between transformational leadership, decision-making styles and crisis management in Yemen organizations. *International Journal of Business Continuity and Risk Management*, *11*(2–3), 156–171. doi:10.1504/IJBCRM.2021.116277

Alon, S. (2009). The Evolution of Class Inequality in Higher Education: Competition, Exclusion, and Adaptation. *American Sociological Review*, *74*(5), 731–755. doi:10.1177/000312240907400503

Artinger, F., Petersen, M., Gigerenzer, G., & Weibler, J. (2015). Heuristics as adaptive decision strategies in management. *Journal of Organizational Behavior*, *36*(S1), S33–S52. doi:10.1002/job.1950

Azar, O. H. (2014). The default heuristic in strategic decision-making: When is it optimal to choose the default without investing in information search? *Journal of Business Research*, *67*(8), 1744–1748. doi:10.1016/j.jbusres.2014.02.021

Baert, S., Marx, I., Neyt, B., Van Belle, E., & Van Casteren, J. (2018). Student employment and academic performance: An empirical exploration of the primary orientation theory. *Applied Economics Letters*, *25*(8), 547–552. doi:10.1080/13504851.2017.1343443

Bakewell, C., & Mitchell, V.-W. (2006). Male versus female consumer decision-making styles. *Journal of Business Research*, *59*(12), 1297–1300. doi:10.1016/j.jbusres.2006.09.008

Bărbuţă-Mişu, N., Madaleno, M., & Ilie, V. (2019). Analysis of risk factors affecting firms' financial performance—Support for managerial decision-making. *Sustainability*, *11*(18), 4838. doi:10.3390u11184838

Baroda, S., & Dhankar, N. (2019). Analysis of Managerial Decision-making Skills of Prospective Managers. Haryana School of Business, 127.

Betsch, C., & Iannello, P. (2009). 14 Measuring individual differences in intuitive and deliberate decision-making styles. *Foundations for Tracing Intuition: Challenges and Methods*, 251.

Bradley, S., & Price, N. (2021). *Critical Thinking: Proven Strategies To Improve Decision-making Skills, Increase Intuition And Think Smarter*. Createspace Independent Pub.

Brenner, P. S., & DeLamater, J. (2016). Lies, damned lies, and survey self-reports? Identity as a cause of measurement bias. *Social Psychology Quarterly*, *79*(4), 333–354. doi:10.1177/0190272516628298 PMID:29038609

Cernat, R. (2020). *The Dispute Revival for the Superpower Status*. Academic Press.

Chavda, M. D., & Trivedi, B. S. (2015). Impact of Age on Skills Development in Different Groups of Students. *International Journal of Information and Education Technology (IJIET)*, *5*(1), 55–59. doi:10.7763/IJIET.2015.V5.476

Cooke, F. L. (2016). Women in management in China. In *Women in Management Worldwide* (pp. 213–228). Gower.

Delaney, R., Strough, J., Parker, A. M., & de Bruin, W. B. (2015). Variations in decision-making profiles by age and gender: A cluster-analytic approach. *Personality and Individual Differences*, *85*, 19–24. doi:10.1016/j.paid.2015.04.034 PMID:26005238

Dimock, M. (2019). Defining generations: Where Millennials end and Generation Z begins. *Pew Research Center*, *17*(1), 1–7.

Ding, N., Xu, X., Yang, H., Li, Y., & van Heughten, P. (2020). Decision-making styles of Chinese business students. *Journal of Education for Business*, *95*(6), 351–358. doi:10.1080/08832323.2019.1654968

Dong, Y., Zha, Q., Zhang, H., Kou, G., Fujita, H., Chiclana, F., & Herrera-Viedma, E. (2018). Consensus reaching in social network group decision-making: Research paradigms and challenges. *Knowledge-Based Systems*, *162*, 3–13. doi:10.1016/j.knosys.2018.06.036

Dooley, R. S., & Fryxell, G. E. (1999). Attaining decision quality and commitment from dissent: The moderating effects of loyalty and competence in strategic decision-making teams. *Academy of Management Journal*, *42*(4), 389–402.

Doukianou, S., Doukianou, S., Daylamani-Zad, D., Zad, D. D., Lameras, P., & Dunwell, I. (2019). *Reinforcing Rational Decision-making in a Risk Elicitation task through Visual Reasoning*. Academic Press.

Eells, E. (2016). *Rational decision and causality*. Cambridge University Press.

Erven, B. L. (2001). *Becoming an Effective Leader Through Situational Leadership*. Department of Agricultural, Environment, and Development Economics, Ohio State University Extension.

Fatima, S., Khan, M., Rosselli, M., & Ardila, A. (2020). Age, executive functioning, and decision-making styles in adults: A moderated mediation model. *Neuropsychology, Development, and Cognition. Section B, Aging, Neuropsychology and Cognition*, *27*(3), 338–350. doi:10.1080/13825585.2019.1614142 PMID:31084251

Furnham, A. (2020). Myers-Briggs type indicator (MBTI). Encyclopedia of Personality and Individual Differences, 3059–3062.

Gurkov, I. (2015). Corporate parenting styles of the multinational corporation: A subsidiary view. In *The Future of Global Organizing*. Emerald Group Publishing Limited. doi:10.1108/S1745-886220150000010003

Huang, J., Kumar, S., & Hu, C. (2018). Gender differences in motivations for identity reconstruction on social network sites. *International Journal of Human-Computer Interaction*, *34*(7), 591–602. doi:10.1080/10447318.2017.1383061

Hubbard, E. (2017). 7.9 Improving Decision-making. *Career Skills for Surgeons*, 136.

Jewell, P., Reading, J., Clarke, M., & Kippist, L. (2020). Information skills for business acumen and employability: A competitive advantage for graduates in Western Sydney. *Journal of Education for Business*, *95*(2), 88–105. doi:10.1080/08832323.2019.1610346

Jiang, J., & Luo, Z. (2021). Leadership Styles and Political Survival of Chinese Communist Party Elites. *The Journal of Politics*, *83*(2), 777–782. doi:10.1086/710144

Karnes, F. A., Deason, D. M., & D'Ilio, V. (1993). Leadership Skills and Self-Actualization of School-Age Children1. *Psychological Reports*, *73*(3_part_1), 861–862. doi:10.1177/00332941930733pt122

Katz, D., & Kahn, R. L. (1978). *The social psychology of organizations* (Vol. 2). Wiley New York.

Lakshika, V., & Ahzan, M. (2021). Decision-making Styles of Sri Lankan Millennial: Are They Different? *Sri Lanka Journal of Marketing*, *7*(1), 46. doi:10.4038ljmuok.v7i1.56

Lau, W. K., Li, Z., & Okpara, J. (2020). An examination of three-way interactions of paternalistic leadership in China. *Asia Pacific Business Review*, *26*(1), 32–49. doi:10.1080/13602381.2019.1674031

Leung, A. S. (2003). Feminism in transition: Chinese culture, ideology and the development of the women's movement in China. *Asia Pacific Journal of Management*, *20*(3), 359–374. doi:10.1023/A:1024049516797

Levin, M., & Liu, Y. (2021). Teaching RA theory to develop future business practitioners' decision-making skills. *Journal of Marketing Theory and Practice*, 1–13. doi:10.1080/10696679.2021.1901593

Lin, X., Featherman, M., Brooks, S. L., & Hajli, N. (2019). Exploring Gender Differences in Online Consumer Purchase Decision-making: An Online Product Presentation Perspective. *Information Systems Frontiers*, *21*(5), 1187–1201. doi:10.100710796-018-9831-1

Loo, R. (2000a). A psychometric evaluation of the general decision-making style inventory. *Personality and Individual Differences*, *29*(1), 895–905. doi:10.1016/S0191-8869(99)00241-X

Loo, R. (2000b). A psychometric evaluation of the general decision-making style inventory. *Personality and Individual Differences*, *29*(5), 895–905. doi:10.1016/S0191-8869(99)00241-X

Louie, G. H., & Ward, M. M. (2010). Sex disparities in self-reported physical functioning: True differences, reporting bias, or incomplete adjustment for confounding? *Journal of the American Geriatrics Society*, *58*(6), 1117–1122. doi:10.1111/j.1532-5415.2010.02858.x PMID:20487076

Lysonski, S., & Durvasula, S. (2013). Consumer decision-making styles in retailing: Evolution of mindsets and psychological impacts. *Journal of Consumer Marketing*, *30*(1), 75–87. doi:10.1108/07363761311290858

MacCann, C., Jiang, Y., Brown, L. E. R., Double, K. S., Bucich, M., & Minbashian, A. (2020). Emotional intelligence predicts academic performance: A meta-analysis. *Psychological Bulletin*, *146*(2), 150–186. doi:10.1037/bul0000219 PMID:31829667

Marquis, K. H., Marquis, M. S., & Polich, J. M. (1986). Response bias and reliability in sensitive topic surveys. *Journal of the American Statistical Association*, *81*(394), 381–389. doi:10.1080/01621459.1986.10478282

Mattison, S. M., MacLaren, N. G., Liu, R., Reynolds, A. Z., Baca, G. D., Mattison, P. M., Zhang, M., Sum, C.-Y., Shenk, M. K., Blumenfield, T., von Rueden, C., & Wander, K. (2021). Gender Differences in Social Networks Based on Prevailing Kinship Norms in the Mosuo of China. *Social Sciences*, *10*(7), 253. doi:10.3390ocsci10070253

McCullagh, M. C., & Rosemberg, M.-A. (2015). Social desirability bias in self-reporting of hearing protector use among farm operators. *The Annals of Occupational Hygiene*, *59*(9), 1200–1207. doi:10.1093/annhyg/mev046 PMID:26209595

McKeen, C. A. (2005). Gender roles: An examination of the hopes and expectations of the next generation of managers in Canada and China. *Sex Roles*, *52*(7), 533–546. doi:10.100711199-005-3719-5

Mcmorris, T. (1999). Cognitive development and the acquisition of decision-making skills. *International Journal of Sport Psychology*.

Mehta, R. (2020). Gender-based differences in consumer decision-making styles: Implications for marketers. *Decision (Washington, D.C.)*, *47*(3), 319–329.

Mendes, F. F., Mendes, E., & Salleh, N. (2019). The relationship between personality and decision-making: A Systematic literature review. *Information and Software Technology*, *111*, 50–71. doi:10.1016/j.infsof.2019.03.010

Mok, K. H., & Jiang, J. (2017). Massification of higher education: Challenges for admissions and graduate employment in China. In *Managing international connectivity, diversity of learning and changing labour markets* (pp. 219–243). Springer. doi:10.1007/978-981-10-1736-0_13

Myles, A. (2018). The world's newest economic superpower? *Company Director*, *34*(4), 46–47.

Nelson, G. D. (1984). *Assessment of Health Decision-making Skills of Adolescents.* Academic Press.

Páez Gallego, J., De-Juanas Oliva, Á., García-Castilla, F. J., & Muelas, Á. (2020). Relationship Between Basic Human Values and Decision-Making Styles in Adolescents. *International Journal of Environmental Research and Public Health*, *17*(22), 8315. doi:10.3390/ijerph17228315 PMID:33182771

Parayitam, S., & Papenhausen, C. (2016). Agreement-seeking behavior, trust, and cognitive diversity in strategic decision-making teams: Process conflict as a moderator. *Journal of Advances in Management Research*, *13*(3), 292–315. doi:10.1108/JAMR-10-2015-0072

Pavlić, I., & Vukić, M. (2019). Decision-making styles of Generation Z consumers in Croatia. *Ekonomska Misao i Praksa*, *1*, 79–95. https://hrcak.srce.hr/index.php?show=clanak&id_clanak_jezik=322669

Peng, J., Feng, T., Zhang, J., Zhao, L., Zhang, Y., Chang, Y., Zhang, Y., & Xiao, W. (2019). Measuring decision-making competence in Chinese adults. *Journal of Behavioral Decision Making*, *32*(3), 266–279.

Peng, L., & Luo, S. (2021). Impact of social economic development on personality traits among Chinese college students: A cross-temporal meta-analysis, 2001–2016. *Personality and Individual Differences*, *171*, 110461. doi:10.1016/j.paid.2020.110461

Perry, E. J. (2018). Introduction: Chinese political culture revisited. In Popular Protest and Political Culture in Modern China (pp. 1–14). Routledge.

Phillips, S. D., Pazienza, N. J., & Ferrin, H. H. (1984). Decision-making styles and problem-solving appraisal. *Journal of Counseling Psychology*, *31*(4), 497–502. doi:10.1037/0022-0167.31.4.497

Powell, M., & Ansic, D. (1997). Gender differences in risk behaviour in financial decision-making: An experimental analysis. *Journal of Economic Psychology*, *18*(6), 605–628. doi:10.1016/S0167-4870(97)00026-3

Power, D. J., Cyphert, D., & Roth, R. M. (2019). Analytics, bias, and evidence: The quest for rational decision-making. *Journal of Decision Systems*, *28*(2), 120–137. doi:10.1080/12460125.2019.1623534

Radecki, C. M., & Jaccard, J. (1996). Gender-Role Differences in Decision-Making Orientations and Decision-Making Skills1. *Journal of Applied Social Psychology*, *26*(1), 76–94. doi:10.1111/j.1559-1816.1996.tb01839.x

Rašković, M., Ding, Z., Hirose, M., Žabkar, V., & Fam, K.-S. (2020). Segmenting young-adult consumers in East Asia and Central and Eastern Europe–The role of consumer ethnocentrism and decision-making styles. *Journal of Business Research*, *108*, 496–507. doi:10.1016/j.jbusres.2019.04.013

Riley, N. E. (1997). Gender Equality in China: Two Steps Forward, One Step Back. In *China Briefing*. Routledge.

Rocha, M. (2012). Transferable skills representations in a Portuguese college sample: Gender, age, adaptability and vocational development. *European Journal of Psychology of Education, 27*(1), 77–90. doi:10.100710212-011-0067-4

Rowland, K. D. (2004). Career decision-making skills of high school students in the Bahamas. *Journal of Career Development, 31*(1), 1–13. doi:10.1177/089484530403100101

Rus, M., Tasente, T., & Sandu, M. L. (2019). Study regarding the perception on the personality traits in managerial decision-making. *Journal of Danubian Studies and Research, 9*(2).

Sadler, E., & Spicer, D. P. (2005). An examination of the general decision-making style questionnaire in two UK samples. *Journal of Managerial Psychology, 20*(2), 137–149. doi:10.1108/02683940510579777

Saya, G. (2015). *The relationship of academic procrastination and decision-making styles among university students*. Academic Press.

Schildkamp, K. (2019). Data-based decision-making for school improvement: Research insights and gaps. *Educational Research, 61*(3), 257–273. doi:10.1080/00131881.2019.1625716

Scott, S., & Bruce, R. (1995). Decision-making style: The development and assessment of a new measure. *Educational and Psychological Measurement, 55*(5), 818–831. doi:10.1177/0013164495055005017

Si, W., Farh, J.-L., Qu, Q., Fu, P. P., & Kang, F. (2017). Paternalistic Leadership in China: A Latent Profile Analysis of its Antecedents and Outcomes. *Academy of Management Proceedings, 2017*(1), 15057. doi:10.5465/AMBPP.2017.15057abstract

Smith, C. J. (2019). *China: In the Post-Utopian Age*. Routledge. doi:10.4324/9780429039324

Soon, J.-J., Lee, A. S.-H., Lim, H.-E., Idris, I., & Eng, W. Y.-K. (2020). Cubicles or corner offices? Effects of academic performance on university graduates' employment likelihood and salary. *Studies in Higher Education, 45*(6), 1233–1248. doi:10.1080/03075079.2019.1590689

Spicer, D. P., & Sadler-Smith, E. (2005). An examination of the general decision-making style questionnaire in two UK samples. *Journal of Managerial Psychology, 20*(2), 137–149. doi:10.1108/02683940510579777

Spicer, D. P., & Sadler-Smith, E. (2006). Organizational learning in smaller manufacturing firms. *International Small Business Journal, 24*(2), 133–158. doi:10.1177/0266242606061836

Subrahmanyam, S. (2018). Corporate leadership: A study of the decision-making skills in growing in the corporate world. *International Journal of Research, 5*(1), 2348–6848.

Sun, J. Y., & Li, J. (2017). Women in leadership in China: Past, present, and future. *Current Perspectives on Asian Women in Leadership*, 19–35.

Tadriss-Hasani, M., & Rahmansersht, H. (2020). Provide a mathematical model for determining decision-making styles and improving its effectiveness in the face of data uncertainty. *Modern Research in Decision-making, 5*(2), 1–20.

Teng, W., Ma, C., Pahlevansharif, S., & Turner, J. J. (2019). Graduate readiness for the employment market of the 4th industrial revolution: The development of soft employability skills. *Education + Training, 61*(5), 590–604. doi:10.1108/ET-07-2018-0154

Uzonwanne, F. (2015). Leadership styles and decision-making models among corporate leaders in non-profit organizations in North America. *Journal of Public Affairs*, *15*(3), 287–299. doi:10.1002/pa.1530

Uzonwanne, F. C. (2007). *Leadership style and decision-making models among corporate leaders in non-profit organizations*. Academic Press.

Uzonwanne, F. C. (2016). Influence of age and gender on decision-making models and leadership styles of non-profit executives in Texas, USA. *The International Journal of Organizational Analysis*, *24*(2), 186–203. doi:10.1108/IJOA-05-2013-0667

Wang, J., & Shirmohammadi, M. (2016). Women leaders in China: Looking back and moving forward. *Advances in Developing Human Resources*, *18*(2), 137–151. doi:10.1177/1523422316641399

Warner, M., & Zhu, Y. (2018). The challenges of managing 'new generation' employees in contemporary China: Setting the scene. *Asia Pacific Business Review*, *24*(4), 429–436. doi:10.1080/13602381.2018.1451130

Wood, R., & Bandura, A. (1989). Impact of conceptions of ability on self-regulatory mechanisms and complex decision-making. *Journal of Personality and Social Psychology*, *56*(3), 407–415. doi:10.1037/0022-3514.56.3.407 PMID:2926637

Xiajuan, G., & Lijun, Y. (2017). Women's political participation in China. In *Changing State-Society Relations in Contemporary China* (pp. 249–265). World Scientific.

Xiao, F., Zhang, J., & Long, B. (2017). The Predicament, Revitalization, and Future of Traditional Chinese Festivals. *Western Folklore*, 181–196.

Xiong, H., Deng, J., & Yuan, J. (2018). From Exclusion to Inclusion: Changes in Women's Roles in Folk Sports and Indigenous Physical Culture in China. *The International Journal of the History of Sport*, *35*(15–16), 1603–1621. doi:10.1080/09523367.2018.1493456

Xue, H. B., & Wang, X. X. (2012). Face consciousness and decision-making styles: An empirical study of young-adult Chinese consumers. *International Journal of China Marketing*, *2*(2), 60–73.

Xue-ling, L., Li, C., Yu-jie, L., Jia, S., & Ling, Z. (2018). Influence of institutional environment on the construction of corporate relations: An empirical research based on China's transition. *Nankai Business Review*, *21*(5), 41–50.

Yu, J. (2018). The belt and road initiative: Domestic interests, bureaucratic politics and the EU-China relations. *Asia Europe Journal*, *16*(3), 223–236. doi:10.100710308-018-0510-0

Zhu, J., & Mukhin, N. (2021). The Modern Regency: Leadership Transition and Authoritarian Resilience of the Former Soviet Union and China. *Communist and Post-Communist Studies*, *54*(1–2), 24–44. doi:10.1525/j.postcomstud.2021.54.1-2.24

KEY TERMS AND DEFINITIONS

Cognitive Distortions: A pattern of thoughts that are fundamentally inaccurate and often negatively based (Abatecola et al., 2018).

Decision-Making Styles: Decision-making is the selection of a procedure to weigh alternatives and find a solution to a problem. It is the action or process of making decisions, especially important ones (Bavolar & Bacikova-Sleskova, 2020).

GDMS: The general decision-making style test attributed to Scott and Bruce (1995) which defined 5 decision-making styles: (a) Rational: logical and structured approaches to decision-making; (b) Intuitive: reliance upon hunches, feelings and impressions; (c) Dependent: reliance upon the direction and support of others; (d) Avoidant: postponing or avoiding making decisions; (e) Spontaneous: impulsive and prone to making "snap" or "spur of the moment" decisions.

MBTI® Testing: Myers-Briggs' theory is an adaptation of the theory of psychological types produced by Carl Gustav Jung. It is based on 16 personality types (Jung, 1921).

Millennial Generation: There are various definitions of generational groupings based on age, but most are similar. One well known and accepted definition is "Those born between 1982 and 2000" (Dimock, 2019).

APPENDIX A

Questionnaire

Gender & Decision-making Style & Academic Performance

1. What's your gender?
   - Female 女
   - Male 男
2. What's your grade?
   - Freshman 大一
   - Sophomore 大二
   - Junior 大三
   - Senior 大四
   - Master's degree 研究生
   - PHD 博士
   - Already Working 已工作
3. What's your GPA ranking?
   - TOP5%
   - TOP15%
   - TOP30%
   - TOP50%
   - TOP70%
   - After 70%
4. What's your GPA?
   - 3.8-4.0
   - 3.8-4.0
   - 3.6-3.8
   - 3.3-3.6
   - 3.0-3.3
   - Under 3.0
5. When do you go to sleep?
   - 10pm-11pm
   - 11pm-12pm
   - 12pm-1am
   - 1am-2am
   - After 2am.
   - Before 10 pm
6. I got good grades when I made an effort.
   - Strongly disagree 非常不同意
   - 2
   - 3
   - 4
   - Strongly Agree 非常同意

7. I double-check my information sources to be sure I have the correct facts before making decisions.
   - ○ Strongly disagree 非常不同意
   - ○ 2
   - ○ 3
   - ○ 4
   - ○ Strongly Agree 非常同意
8. I make decisions logically and systematically.
   - ○ Strongly disagree 非常不同意
   - ○ 2
   - ○ 3
   - ○ 4
   - ○ Strongly Agree 非常同意
9. My decision-making requires careful thought and consideration of various options in terms of a specific goal.
   - ○ Strongly disagree 非常不同意
   - ○ 2
   - ○ 3
   - ○ 4
   - ○ Strongly Agree 非常同意
10. When making decisions, I rely upon my instincts/ intuition.
    - ○ Strongly disagree 非常不同意
    - ○ 2
    - ○ 3
    - ○ 4
    - ○ Strongly Agree 非常同意
11. When I make a decision, it is more important for me to feel the decision is right than to have a Rational reason for it.
    - ○ Strongly disagree 非常不同意
    - ○ 2
    - ○ 3
    - ○ 4
    - ○ Strongly Agree 非常同意
12. When I make a decision, I trust my inner feelings and reactions.
    - ○ Strongly disagree 非常不同意
    - ○ 2
    - ○ 3
    - ○ 4
    - ○ Strongly Agree 非常同意
13. I often need the assistance of other people when making important decisions.
    - ○ Strongly disagree 非常不同意
    - ○ 2
    - ○ 3
    - ○ 4
    - ○ Strongly Agree 非常同意

14. I rarely make important decisions without consulting other people.
    ○ Strongly disagree 非常不同意
    ○ 2
    ○ 3
    ○ 4
    ○ Strongly Agree 非常同意
15. I use the advice of other people in making my important decisions.
    ○ Strongly disagree 非常不同意
    ○ 2
    ○ 3
    ○ 4
    ○ Strongly Agree 非常同意
16. I avoid making important decisions until the pressure is on.
    ○ Strongly disagree 非常不同意
    ○ 2
    ○ 3
    ○ 4
    ○ Strongly Agree 非常同意
17. I postpone decision-making whenever possible.
    ○ Strongly disagree 非常不同意
    ○ 2
    ○ 3
    ○ 4
    ○ Strongly Agree 非常同意
18. I put off making decisions because thinking about them makes me uneasy.
    ○ Strongly disagree 非常不同意
    ○ 2
    ○ 3
    ○ 4
    ○ Strongly Agree 非常同意
19. I generally make snap decisions.
    ○ Strongly disagree 非常不同意
    ○ 2
    ○ 3
    ○ 4
    ○ Strongly Agree 非常同意
20. I often make quick decisions.
    ○ Strongly disagree 非常不同意
    ○ 2
    ○ 3
    ○ 4
    ○ Strongly Agree 非常同意

21. I often make impulsive decisions.
    - Strongly disagree 非常不同意
    - 2
    - 3
    - 4
    - Strongly Agree 非常同意
22. What kind of university are you from?
    - 国内传统大学
    - 中外合办大学
    - 国外大学
    - 其他
23. Are you the leader in school organizations/clubs?
    - 是
    - 未曾担任

Compilation of References

Aaker, D. A. (1991). *Managing Brand Equity: Capitalizing on the Value of a Brand Name*. Free Press.

Aaker, D. A. (1996). *Building Strong Brands*. Free Press.

Aaker, D. A. (2004). *Brand Portfolio Strategy*. Free Press.

Aaker, D. A., & Jacobson, R. (1994). The Financial Information Content of Perceived Quality. *JMR, Journal of Marketing Research*, *31*(2), 191–201. doi:10.1177/002224379403100204

Aaker, D. A., & Jacobson, R. (2001). The Value Relevance of Brand Attitude in High – Technology Markets. *JMR, Journal of Marketing Research*, *38*(4), 485–493. doi:10.1509/jmkr.38.4.485.18905

Aaker, D. A., & Joachimsthaler, E. (2000). *Brand Leadership*. The Free Press.

Abatecola, G., Caputo, A., & Cristofaro, M. (2017). Reviewing cognitive distortions in managerial decision-making I Toward an integrative co-evolutionary framework I. *Journal of Management Development*, *37*(5), 409–424. doi:10.1108/JMD-08-2017-0263

Abubakar, A. M., Elrehail, H., Alatailat, M. A., & Elçi, A. (2019). Knowledge management, decision-making style and organizational performance. *Journal of Innovation & Knowledge*, *4*(2), 104–114. doi:10.1016/j.jik.2017.07.003

Acosta, A. (2013). *El Buen Vivir. In Sumak kawsay una oportunidad para imaginar otro mundo*. Icaria.

Acosta, A. (2017). Los buenos convivires: Filosofías sin filósofos, Prácticas sin teorías. *Estudios Críticos del Desarrollo V*, *7*(12), 153–192. doi:10.35533/ecd.0712.aa

Adekalu, S. O., Krauss, S. E., Ismail, I. A., & Suandi, T. (2018). Teaching Professors' Challenges about Community Engagement Outreach and Intervention in Nigerian Universities. *International Journal of Academic Research in Business & Social Sciences*, *8*(8), 191–204. doi:10.6007/IJARBSS/v8-i8/4458

Adhiarna, N., Hwang, Y. M., Park, M. J., & Rho, J. (2013). An integrated framework for RFID adoption and diffusion with a stage-scale-scope cubicle model: A case of Indonesia. *International Journal of Information Management*, *33*(2), 378–389. doi:10.1016/j.ijinfomgt.2012.10.001

Ahmad, A., Alshurideh, M. T., Al Kurdi, B. H., & Salloum, S. A. (2021). Factors Impacts Organization Digital Transformation and Organization Decision Making During Covid19 Pandemic. *Studies in Systems. Decision and Control*, *334*, 95–106.

Aikman, S. N., Min, K. E., & Graham, D. (2006). Food attitudes, eating behavior, and the information underlying food attitudes. *Appetite*, *47*(1), 111–114. doi:10.1016/j.appet.2006.02.004 PMID:16621134

Ailawadi, K. L., Lehmann, D. R., & Neslin, S. A. (2003). Revenue Premium as an Outcome Measure of Brand Equity. *Journal of Marketing*, *67*(4), 1–17. doi:10.1509/jmkg.67.4.1.18688

Ajzen, I. (1991). The theory of planned behavior. *Organizational Behavior and Human Decision Processes*, *50*(2), 179–211. doi:10.1016/0749-5978(91)90020-T

Ajzen, I. (2020). The theory of planned behavior: Frequently asked questions. *Human Behavior and Emerging Technologies*, *2*(4), 314–324. doi:10.1002/hbe2.195

Ajzen, I., & Manstead, A. S. (2007). Changing health-related behaviors: An approach based on the theory of planned behavior. In M. Hewstone, J. B. F. de Wit, K. van den Bos, H. Schut, & M. Stroebe (Eds.), *The Scope of Social Psychology: Theory and Applications* (pp. 43–63). Psychology Press.

Akhmetshin, E., Dzhavatov, D. K., Sverdlikova, E. A., Sokolov, M. S., Avdeeva, O. A., & Yavkin, G. P. (2018). The influence of innovation on social and economic development of the Russian Regions. *European Research Studies Journal*, *21*, 767–776.

Al Khasawneh, M., Abuhashesh, M., Ahmad, A., Masa'deh, R., & Alshurideh, M. T. (2021). Customers' Online Engagement with Social Media Influencers' Content Related to COVID 19. *Studies in Systems. Decision and Control*, *334*, 385–404.

Alba, L., Coll, C., Sáez, S., Alonso, L., Pérez, H., Palma, S., Vallés, V., & Ortiz, S. (2021). New-onset psychosis: A case report of brief psychosis related to COVID-19 infection. *Psychiatry Research*, *301*, 113975. doi:10.1016/j.psychres.2021.113975 PMID:33990069

Alexander, B., & Blazquez Cano, M. (2020). Store of the future: Towards a (re)invention and (re)imagination of physical store space in an omnichannel context. *Journal of Retailing and Consumer Services*, *55*(August), 101913. doi:10.1016/j.jretconser.2019.101913

Alharahsheh, H. H., & Pius, A. (2021). Exploration of Employability Skills in Business Management Studies Within Higher Education Levels: Systematic Literature Review. *Research Anthology on Business and Technical Education in the Information Era*, 1147–1164.

Aliaga-Ortega, L., Adasme-Berríos, C., Méndez, C., Soto, C., & Schnettler, B. (2019). Processed food choice based on the theory of planned behavior in the context of nutritional warning labels. *British Food Journal*, *121*(12), 3266–3280. doi:10.1108/BFJ-10-2018-0695

Alicke, K.; Rexhausen, D., & Seyfert, A. (2017). *Supply Chain 4.0 in consumer goods*. McKinsey & Company.

Aliman, N. K., Ariffin, Z. Z., & Hashim, S. M. (2017). Generation Y Muslim Female and Male Decision-making Styles in Malaysia: Are They Different? *Journal of Research in Marketing*, *7*(2), 534–543. doi:10.17722/jorm.v7i2.184

Alkhawlani, M. A. S., Bohari, A. M., & Shamsuddin, J. (2021). The moderating effect of crisis experience on the relationship between transformational leadership, decision-making styles and crisis management in Yemen organizations. *International Journal of Business Continuity and Risk Management*, *11*(2–3), 156–171. doi:10.1504/IJBCRM.2021.116277

Allaire, Y., & Firsirotu, M. (1984). Theories of organizational culture. *Organization Studies*, *5*(3), 193–226. doi:10.1177/017084068400500301

Alon, S. (2009). The Evolution of Class Inequality in Higher Education: Competition, Exclusion, and Adaptation. *American Sociological Review*, *74*(5), 731–755. doi:10.1177/000312240907400503

Al-Qatawneh, M. I. (2014). The Impact of Organizational Structure on Organizational Commitment: A Comparison between Public and Private Sector Firms in Jordan. *European Journal of Business and Management*, *6*(12), 23–32.

Compilation of References

Alsmadi, S. (2007). Green marketing and the concern over the environment: Measuring environmental consciousness of Jordanian consumers. *Journal of Promotion Management*, *13*(3–4), 339–361. doi:10.1080/10496490802306905

Al-Swidi, A., Mohammed Rafiul Huque, S., Haroon Hafeez, M., & Noor Mohd Shariff, M. (2014). The role of subjective norms in theory of planned behavior in the context of organic food consumption. *British Food Journal*, *116*(10), 1561–1580. doi:10.1108/BFJ-05-2013-0105

Alter, S. K. (2006). SE models and their mission and money relationships. *Social Entrepreneurship: New Models of Sustainable Social Change*.

Altmann, J., & Kashef, M. M. (2014). Cost model-based service placement in federated hybrid clouds. *Future Generation Computer Systems*, *41*, 79–90. doi:10.1016/j.future.2014.08.014

Amanullah, A. N. A. A., Aziz, N. F. A., Hadi, F. N., & Ibrahim, J. (2015). Comparison of the business model canvas (BMC) among the three consulting companies. *International Journal of Computer Science and Information Technology Research*, *3*(2), 462–471.

Ambrose, S. C., Anaza, N. A., & Rutherord, B. N. (2017). The role of prior sales experience of buyers and duration in buyer-seller relationships. *The Marketing Management Journal*, *27*(1), 16–30.

Amit, R., & Zott, C. (2012). *Creating value through business model innovation*. Academic Press.

Amodu, L., Isiguzoro, C., Omojola, O., Adeyeye, B., & Ajakaiye, L. (2020). Assessing audience's willingness to curb digital piracy: A gender perspective. *Cogent Social Sciences*, *6*(1), 1823602. doi:10.1080/23311886.2020.1823602

Anderlini, L., & Sabourian, H. (1998). Algunas notas sobre la economía del trueque, dinero y crédito. In *Trueque, intercambio y valor: Aproximaciones Antropológicas*. Abya - Yala.

Andino, V. (2013). *Políticas Públicas para la Economía Popular y Solidaria Caso de Estudio de Ecuador*. RELIESS.

Andino, V. (2014). Continuidades y rupturas entre los enfoques de economía solidaria y desarrollo local. In Y. Jubeto, L. Guridi, & V. Fernández (Eds.), *Diálogos sobre Economía Popular y Solidaria en Ecuador* (p. 121). UPV-Hegoa.

Andrade, C., Cáceres, M., & Vásquez, A. (2014). Cosmovisión andina, Sumak Ally Kawsay y economía comunitaria. In Y. Jubeto, L. Guridi, & V. Fernández (Eds.), *Diálogos sobre Economía Popular y Solidaria en Ecuador* (pp. 174–178). UPV-Hegoa.

Angus, A. (2020). *How Is COVID19 Affecting The Top 10 Global Consumer Trends 2020?* Euromonitor International.

Angus, A. (2021). *Euromonitor's "Top 10 Global Consumer Trends 2021"*. Euromonitor.

Ansoff, I. H. (1997). *La dirección estratégica en la práctica empresarial* (2nd ed.). Pearson.

Ansoff, I. H., & Mcdonell, E. (1990). *Implanting Strategic Management* (2nd ed.). Prentice-Hall.

Arbeláez-Campillo, D. F., Dudareva, A., & Marianna, M. J. (2019). Las pandemias como factor perturbador del orden geopolítico en el mundo globalizado. *Cuestiones Políticas*, *36*(63), 134–150.

Arbeláez-Campillo, D. F., & Villasmil, J. J. (2020). Escenarios prospectivos de un nuevo orden internacional que se vislumbra luego de la pandemia COVID-19. *Telos. Revista de Estudios Interdisciplinarios en Ciencias Sociales*, *22*(3), 494–508. doi:10.36390/telos223.02

Arconada Muñoz, D. (2016). La Experiencia de Cliente y la Omnicanalidad. *Contact Center*, (83), 18–21.

Ardebili, A. T., & Rickertsen, K. (2020). Personality traits, knowledge, and consumer acceptance of genetically modified plant and animal products. *Food Quality and Preference*, *80*, 103825. doi:10.1016/j.foodqual.2019.103825

Ardueser, C., & Garza, D. (2021). Exploring Cross-Generational Traits and Management Across Generations in the Workforce: A Theoretical Literature Review. In *RAIS Conference Proceedings 2021* (No. 0011; RAIS Conference Proceedings 2021). Research Association for Interdisciplinary Studies. https://ideas.repec.org/p/smo/lpaper/0011.html

Arévalo Pardo, N. J., Perez-Uribe, R., & Ocampo-Guzmán, D. (2015). *MIIGO (Modelo de intervención e innovación de la gestión organizacional): Intervención e innovación de la estructura organizacional*. Universidad EAN.

Arias, A. D., Hernández, A., & Pérez-Uribe, R. I. (2018). Model of Modernization for Organizational Management Component Evaluation. In R. Perez-Uribe, C. Salcedo-Perez, & D. David Ocampo-Guzman (Eds.), *Handbook of Research on Intrapreneurship and Organizational Sustainability in SMEs* (pp. 217–249). IGI Global. doi:10.4018/978-1-5225-3543-0.ch011

Arnaud, N., Mills, C. E., Legrand, C., & Maton, E. (2016). Materializing Strategy in Mundane Tools: ¿the Key to Coupling Global Strategy and Local Strategy Practice? *British Journal of Management*, 27(1), 38–57. doi:10.1111/1467-8551.12144

Aronsson, H., Abrahamsson, M., & Spens, K. (2011). Developing lean and agile health care supply chains. *Supply Chain Management*, 16(3), 176–183. doi:10.1108/13598541111127164

Arora, R., Arora, P. K., Kumar, H., & Pant, M. (2020). Additive Manufacturing Enabled Supply Chain in Combating COVID-19. *Journal of Industrial Integration and Management*, 05(04), 495–505. doi:10.1142/S2424862220500244

Artinger, F., Petersen, M., Gigerenzer, G., & Weibler, J. (2015). Heuristics as adaptive decision strategies in management. *Journal of Organizational Behavior*, 36(S1), S33–S52. doi:10.1002/job.1950

Arzubiaga, U., Castillo-Apraiz, J., & Palma-Ruiz, J. M. (2020). Organisational learning as a mediator in the host-home country similarity–international firm performance link: The role of exploration and exploitation. *European Business Review*, 33(3), 409–426. doi:10.1108/EBR-09-2019-0238

Askitas, N., Tatsiramos, K., & Verheyden, B. (2020). *Lockdown strategies, mobility patterns, and COVID19*. IZA Discussion Paper, 13293, University of Bonn, Germany.

Aslam, F., Mohti, W., & Ferreira, P. (2020). Evidence of Intraday Multifractality in European Stock Markets during the recent Coronavirus (COVID-19) Outbreak. *International Journal of Financial Studies*, 8(2), 31. doi:10.3390/ijfs8020031

Asociación de Internet, M. X. (2019). Estudio sobre Comercio Electrónico en México 2019. Asociación de Internet MX.

Asociación Mexicana de Ventas Online. (2020). *Estudio sobre Venta Online en PyMEs 2020*. Asociación Mexicana de Ventas Online.

Assembly, C. (2008). *Acta 055, Sumario 30 of May 2008*. Quito, Ecuador: Gobierno de Ecuador. Retrieved from https://montecristivive.com/wp-content/uploads/2014/05/acta-055-30-05-2008.pdf

Asti, W. P., Handayani, P. W., & Azzahro, F. (2021). Influence of Trust, Perceived Value, and Attitude on Customers' Repurchase Intention for E-Grocery. *Journal of Food Products Marketing*, 27(3), 157–171. doi:10.1080/10454446.2021.1922325

Augier, M., & March, J. (2011). *The roots, rituals, and rhetorics of change: North American business schools after the Second World War*. Stanford University Press.

Austin, E. C. (2020). Business Survival Growth Model (BSGM) Canvas vs. Business Model Canvas (BMC). *European Journal of Business and Innovation Research*, 8(1), 52–68. doi:10.37745/ejbir/vol8.no1.pp52-68.2020

Azar, O. H. (2014). The default heuristic in strategic decision-making: When is it optimal to choose the default without investing in information search? *Journal of Business Research*, 67(8), 1744–1748. doi:10.1016/j.jbusres.2014.02.021

Compilation of References

Bacq, S., & Lumpkin, G. (2020). Social Entrepreneurship and COVID-19. *Journal of Management Studies*.

Baden-Fuller, C., & Morgan, M. S. (2010). Business models as models. *Long Range Planning*, *43*(2-3), 156–171. doi:10.1016/j.lrp.2010.02.005

Badenhop, A., & Frasquet, M. (2021). Online Grocery Shopping at Multichannel Supermarkets: The Impact of Retailer Brand Equity. *Journal of Food Products Marketing*, *27*(2), 89–104. doi:10.1080/10454446.2021.1894296

Baert, S., Marx, I., Neyt, B., Van Belle, E., & Van Casteren, J. (2018). Student employment and academic performance: An empirical exploration of the primary orientation theory. *Applied Economics Letters*, *25*(8), 547–552. doi:10.1080/13504851.2017.1343443

Báez, R., Ospina, P., & Ramón, G. (2004). *Desarrollo Local con énfasis en la gestión de los recursos naturales: Una breve Historial del espacio ecuatoriano*. Camaren.

Baker, R. K., & White, K. M. (2010). Predicting adolescents' use of social networking sites from an extended theory of planned behaviour perspective. *Computers in Human Behavior*, *26*(6), 1591–1597. doi:10.1016/j.chb.2010.06.006

Bakewell, C., & Mitchell, V.-W. (2006). Male versus female consumer decision-making styles. *Journal of Business Research*, *59*(12), 1297–1300. doi:10.1016/j.jbusres.2006.09.008

Baldwin, R., & Di Mauro, B. W. (2020). *Economics in the time of COVID-19: A new eBook*. VOX CEPR Policy Portal.

Bandura, A. (2004). Health promotion by social cognitive means. *Health Education & Behavior*, *31*(2), 143–164. doi:10.1177/1090198104263660 PMID:15090118

Banerjee, A. (2019). *Portafolio: El mito de bajar los impuestos a las empresas para subir la inversión*. Retrieved from https://www.portafolio.co/internacional/el-falso-mito-de-bajar-los-impuestos-para-impulsar-la-inversion-534814

Banks, J., & Xu, X. (2020). The mental health effects of the first two months of lockdown during the COVID19 pandemic in the UK. *Fiscal Studies*, *41*(3), 685–708. doi:10.1111/1475-5890.12239

Baños González, M., & de Aguilera Moyano, J. (2017). Las comunicaciones en el nuevo paradigma de marketing. Experiencias, relevancia, engagement y personalización. Presentación. *Revista ICONO14 Revista Científica de Comunicación y Tecnologías Emergentes*, *15*(2), 1–15. doi:10.7195/ri14.v15i2.1098

Bao, L. (2019). Deep Modernization: The Value Conflict and Identity of the Post-80s and Post-90s.中国青年研究, *8*, 47–55.

Baporikar, N. (2009). Management Education- Challenges Ahead. Himalaya Publishing House.

Baporikar, N. (2010). Doctorate Education: A Practical Guide. Viva Books Private Limited.

Baporikar, N. (2016). Contemporary Cases in Management. Himalaya Publishing House.

Baporikar, N. (2008). *Case Method: Cases in Management* (2nd ed.). Himalaya Publishing House.

Baporikar, N. (2015a). Understanding Professional Development for Educators. *International Journal of Sustainable Economies Management*, *4*(4), 18–30. doi:10.4018/IJSEM.2015100102

Baporikar, N. (2015b). Strategies for Promoting Research Culture to Support Knowledge Society. *International Journal of Information Communication Technologies and Human Development*, *7*(4), 58–72. doi:10.4018/IJICTHD.2015100104

Baporikar, N. (2015c). Collegiality as a strategy for excellence in academia. *International Journal of Strategic Change Management*, *6*(1), 59–72. doi:10.1504/IJSCM.2015.069522

Baporikar, N. (2017a). *Management Education for Global Leadership*. IGI Global., doi:10.4018/978-1-5225-1013-0

Baporikar, N. (2017b). *Innovation and Shifting Perspectives in Management Education*. IGI Global. doi:10.4018/978-1-5225-1019-2

Baporikar, N. (2018a). Educational Leadership: A Global Perspective. In N. P. Ololube (Ed.), *Encyclopaedia of institutional leadership, policy, and management* (pp. 28–51). Pearl Publications.

Baporikar, N. (2018b). Improving Communication by Linking Student Centred Pedagogy and Management Curriculum Development. In N. P. Ololube (Ed.), *Encyclopaedia of institutional leadership, policy, and management* (pp. 369–386). Pearl Publications.

Baporikar, N. (2018c). Rankings and Academia in India. In B. Dutta & S. D. Reddy (Eds.), *University 5.0* (pp. 181–196). MTC Global.

Baporikar, N. (2019a). Significance and Role of Entrepreneurial University in Emerging Economies. *International Journal of Applied Management Sciences and Engineering*, 6(1), 46–61. doi:10.4018/IJAMSE.2019010104

Baporikar, N. (2019b). Preventing Academic Misconduct: Student-Centered Teaching Strategies. In D. Velliaris (Ed.), *Prevention and Detection of Academic Misconduct in Higher Education* (pp. 98–115). IGI Global. doi:10.4018/978-1-5225-7531-3.ch005

Baporikar, N. (2020). Finer Student Engagement via Quality and Lifelong Learning for Sustainable Education. *International Journal of Political Activism and Engagement*, 7(4), 38–55. doi:10.4018/IJPAE.2020100104

Baporikar, N., & Parker, S. (2019). Higher Education Quality and BRICS Network University Pact: Academic Leadership as a Booster. *International Journal of Political Activism and Engagement*, 6(4), 29–41. doi:10.4018/IJPAE.2019100103

Baporikar, N., & Sony, M. (2020). *Quality Management Principles and Policies in Higher Education*. IGI Global. doi:10.4018/978-1-7998-1017-9

Barberá de la Torre, R. (2012). Globalización. In J. Malfeito (Ed.), *Introducción a la economía mundial* (pp. 467–489). Delta Publicaciones.

Bărbuță-Mișu, N., Madaleno, M., & Ilie, V. (2019). Analysis of risk factors affecting firms' financial performance—Support for managerial decision-making. *Sustainability*, 11(18), 4838. doi:10.3390u11184838

Baroda, S., & Dhankar, N. (2019). Analysis of Managerial Decision-making Skills of Prospective Managers. Haryana School of Business, 127.

Barreto, L., Amaral, A., & Pereria, T. (2017) Industry 4.0 implications in logistics: an overview. *Proceedings of the Manufacturing Engineering Society International Conference MESIC 2017*. 10.1016/j.promfg.2017.09.045

Barría, C. (2020, March 30) Coronavirus: "Estamos frente a una crisis generalizada del capitalismo democrático mundial y del no democrático, como el de China". *BBC News / Mundo*. https://www.bbc.com/mundo/noticias-52055657

Barrios, S., Görg, H., & Strobl, E. (2003). Foreign Direct Investment, Competition and Industrial Development in the Host Country. *European Economic Review*, 49(7), 1761–1784. doi:10.1016/j.euroecorev.2004.05.005

Barros, I., Palma-Ruiz, J. M., Cantarero-Prieto, D., & González-Moreno, S. E. (2017). Las empresas familiares en el desarrollo regional: un llamado al reenfoque de la investigación en México. In Los Retos del Cambio Económico Actual: Revisión y Aplicaciones para el Caso Mexicano (pp. 128–152). Ediciones de Laurel / Universidad Autónoma de Chihuahua.

Bask, A., Rajahonka, M., Laari, S., Solakivi, T., Töyli, J., & Ojala, L. (2018). Environmental sustainability in shipper-LSP relationships. *Journal of Cleaner Production*, 172, 2986–2998. doi:10.1016/j.jclepro.2017.11.112

Compilation of References

Bass, L., & Ritting, L. (n.d.). *Technology in education.* https://www.uri.edu/personal/lbas2219/

Bates, A. W., & Poole, G. (Eds.). (2003). Effective teaching with technology in higher education: Foundations for success. Jossey Bass Publishers.

Baum, W. M. (2002, May). The Harvard pigeon lab under Herrnstein. *Journal of the Experimental Analysis of Behavior*, *77*(3), 347–355. doi:10.1901/jeab.2002.77-347 PMID:12083686

BBC. (2020). *Mundo-Noticias: BBC News.* Obtenido de BBC: https://www.bbc.com/mundo/noticias-52748371

Beldad, A., & Hegner, S. (2018). Determinants of Fair-Trade Product Purchase Intention of Dutch Consumers According to the Extended Theory of Planned Behaviour, The Moderating Role of Gender. *Journal of Consumer Policy*, *41*(3), 191–210. doi:10.100710603-018-9384-1

Belhadi, A., Kamble, S., Jabbour, C. J. C., Gunasekaran, A., Ndubisi, N. O., & Venkatesh, M. (2021). Manufacturing and service supply chain resilience to the COVID-19 outbreak: Lessons learned from the automobile and airline industries. *Technological Forecasting and Social Change*, *163*, 120447. doi:10.1016/j.techfore.2020.120447 PMID:33518818

Bello, P. W. (2005). *Deglobalization: Ideas for a New World Economy.* Zed Books.

Bello, P. W. (2013). *Capitalism's Last Stand? Deglobalization in the Age of Austerity.* Zed Books. doi:10.5040/9781350218895

Bendle, N. T., Farris, P. W., Pfeifer, P. E., & Reibstein, D. J. (2016). *Marketing Metrics: The Manager's Guide to Measuring Marketing Performance* (3rd ed.). Pearson Education, Inc.

Bensel, P., Gunther, O., Tribowski, C., & Vogeler, S. (2008). Cost-benefit sharing in cross-company RFID applications: a case study approach, ICIS 2008 Proceedings, 129.

Berger, P. D., & Nasr, N. I. (1998). Customer Lifetime Value: Marketing Models and Applications. *Journal of Interactive Marketing*, *12*(1), 17–30. doi:10.1002/(SICI)1520-6653(199824)12:1<17::AID-DIR3>3.0.CO;2-K

Bergsten, C. F. (2000). The Backlash against Globalization. *Tokyo 2000: The Annual Meeting of the Trilateral Commission.*

Betsch, C., & Iannello, P. (2009). 14 Measuring individual differences in intuitive and deliberate decision-making styles. *Foundations for Tracing Intuition: Challenges and Methods*, 251.

Bhagwati, J. (2004). *In Defence of Globalization.* Oxford University Press.

Bhattacharya, M., Chu, C. H., Hayya, J., & Mullen, T. (2010). An exploratory study of RFID adoption in the retail sector. *Operations Management Research*, *3*(1-2), 80–89. doi:10.100712063-010-0029-z

Bhushan, V., & Rai, S. (2021). Knowledge, attitude, and practices regarding COVID19 outbreak among the personnel providing emergency services in India. *International Journal of Academic Medicine*, *7*(2), 107–112. doi:10.4103/IJAM.IJAM_2_21

Bieger, T. (2011). Business schools–from career training centers towards enablers of CSR: a new vision for teaching at business schools. *Business Schools and Their Contribution to Society*, 104-113.

Bill of the Organic Law on Social and Solidarity Economy. (2017). Quito, Ecuador: Gobierno de Ecuador. Retrieved from http://2013-2017. observatoriolegislativo.ec/media/archivos_leyes/Objeci%C3%B3n_Total_ Presidente_de_la_Rep%C3%BAblica_Tr._275224.pdf

Blattberg, R. C., Byung-Do, K., & Neslin, S. A. (2008). Database Marketing: Analyzing and Managing Customers. New York, NY: Springer-Verlag. doi:10.1007/978-0-387-72579-6

Blattberg, R. C., Malthouse, E. C., & Neslin, S. A. (2009, May). Customer Lifetime Value: Empirical Generalizations and Some Conceptual Questions. *Journal of Interactive Marketing*, *23*(2), 157–168. doi:10.1016/j.intmar.2009.02.005

Blauw, J. N., & During, W. E. (1990). Adoption of an organizational innovation: Total quality control in industrial firms. *International Journal of Production Research*, *28*(10), 1831–1846. doi:10.1080/00207549008942837

Bocken, N. M., Short, S. W., Rana, P., & Evans, S. (2014). A literature and practice review to develop sustainable business model archetypes. *Journal of Cleaner Production*, *65*, 42–56. doi:10.1016/j.jclepro.2013.11.039

Boolkin, J. (2017). *Good reads: Best books for social entrepreneurs and changemakers*. Academic Press.

Boons, F., & Lüdeke-Freund, F. (2013). Business models for sustainable innovation: State-of-the-art and steps towards a research agenda. *Journal of Cleaner Production*, *45*, 9–19. doi:10.1016/j.jclepro.2012.07.007

Borda, J. (2016). *La Fábrica del Futuro: Humana, inteligente, tecnológica y digital*. Sisteplant.

Bordo, M. (2017). *The Second Era of Globalization is Not Yet Over: An Historical Perspective*. NBER Working Papers.

Bornstein, D. (2007). *How to change the world: Social entrepreneurs and the power of new ideas*. Oxford University Press.

Borsellino, V., Kaliji, S. A., & Schimment, E. (2020). COVID-19 Drives Consumer Behaviour and Agro-Food Markets towards Healthier and More Sustainable Patterns. *Sustainability*, *12*(20), 8366. doi:10.3390u12208366

Botero, A. J. L. (2011). *Modelo de direccionamiento estratégico para PYMES*. Universidad EAN.

Bourne, J., Harris, D., & Mayadas, F. (2005). *Online Engineering Education: Learning Anywhere*. Academic Press.

Bown, C. P. (2019). The 2018 US-China trade conflict after forty years of special protection. *China Economic Journal*, *12*(2), 109–136. doi:10.1080/17538963.2019.1608047

Bradley, S., & Price, N. (2021). *Critical Thinking: Proven Strategies To Improve Decision-making Skills, Increase Intuition And Think Smarter*. Createspace Independent Pub.

Bramanti, A., & Ratti, R. (1997). The multi-faceted dimensions of local development. In R. Ratti, A. Bramanti, & R. Gordon (Eds.), *The Dynamics of Innovative Regions: The GREMI Approach* (pp. 3–44). Ashgate.

Brammer, S., & Clark, T. (2020). COVID-19 and management education: Reflections on challenges, opportunities, and potential futures. *British Journal of Management*, *31*(1), 453–456.

Brander, J. A., Cui, V., & Vertinsky, I. (2017). China and intellectual property rights: A challenge to the rule of law. *Journal of International Business Studies*, *48*(7), 908–921. doi:10.105741267-017-0087-7

Breier, M., Kallmuenzer, A., Clauss, T., Gast, J., Kraus, S., & Tiberius, V. (2021). The role of business model innovation in the hospitality industry during the COVID-19 crisis. *International Journal of Hospitality Management*, *92*, 102723. doi:10.1016/j.ijhm.2020.102723

Brenner, P. S., & DeLamater, J. (2016). Lies, damned lies, and survey self-reports? Identity as a cause of measurement bias. *Social Psychology Quarterly*, *79*(4), 333–354. doi:10.1177/0190272516628298 PMID:29038609

Bridgman, T., Cummings, S., & McLaughlin, C. (2016). Restating the case: How revisiting the development of the case method can help us think differently about the future of the business school. *Academy of Management Learning & Education*, *15*(4), 724–741. doi:10.5465/amle.2015.0291

Brounen, D., Kok, N., & Quigley, J. (2014). Energy literacy and capitalization. *Energy Economics*, *38*(7), 42–50.

Compilation of References

Brown, I., & Russell, J. (2007). Radio frequency identification technology: An exploratory study on adoption in the South African retail sector. *International Journal of Information Management, 27*(4), 50–265. doi:10.1016/j.ijinfomgt.2007.02.007

Browning, G., & Kilmister, A. (2006). *Critical and Post-Critical Political Economy*. Palgrave Macmillan. doi:10.1057/9780230501522

Brown, M., Young, S. G., & Sacco, D. F. (2021). Competing motives in a pandemic: Interplays between fundamental social motives and technology use in predicting (Non)Compliance with social distancing guidelines. *Computers in Human Behavior, 123*, 106892. doi:10.1016/j.chb.2021.106892

Buchanan, D. A., & Huczynski, A. A. (2019). Organizational Behaviour. Academic Press.

Buchanan, B., Cao, C. X., & Chen, C. (2018). Corporate social responsibility, firm value, and influential institutional ownership. *Journal of Corporate Finance, 52*, 73–95. doi:10.1016/j.jcorpfin.2018.07.004

Bui, T. L. H. (2010). The Vietnamese consumer perception on corporate social responsibility. *Journal of International Business Research, 9*(1), 75–87.

Bunduchi, R., Weisshaar, C., & Smart, A. U. (2011). Mapping the benefits and costs associated with process innovation: The case of RFID adoption. *Technovation, 31*(9), 505–521. doi:10.1016/j.technovation.2011.04.001

Burbano, A., Saka, B., Rardin, R., & Rossetti, M. (2009). Technology assessment for an inventory management process in a hospital unit. In *Proceedings of the 2009 industrial engineering research conference* (pp. 791–796). Academic Press.

Burdett, A., Davillas, A., & Etheridge, B. (2021). *Weather, psychological well-being and mobility during the first wave of the Covid19 pandemic*. ISER Working Paper Series, 2021-02, Institute for Social and Economic Research.

Caiado, R. G., Filho, W. L., Quelhas, O. L. G., de Mattos, D. L., & Avila, L. V. (2018). A literature-based review on potentials and constraints in the implementation of the sustainable development goals. *Journal of Cleaner Production, 198*, 1276–1288. doi:10.1016/j.jclepro.2018.07.102

Čaić, M., Mahr, D., & Oderkerken-Schröder, G. (2019). Value of social robots in services: Social cognition perspective. *Journal of Services Marketing, 29*(2), 178–205.

Calderón-Hernández, G. (2017). *La generación de conocimiento en estrategia organizacional en Colombia*. Universidad Sergio Arboleda and Ascolfa.

Cali, M. (2018). The impact of the US-China trade war on East Asia. *VoxEU. Org, 16*.

Caligiuri, P., De Cieri, H., Minbaeva, D., Verbeke, A., & Zimmermann, A. (2020). International HRM insights for navigating the COVID-19 pandemic: Implications for future research and practice. *Journal of International Business Studies, 51*(5), 697–713. doi:10.105741267-020-00335-9 PMID:32836500

Camacho, M. (2002). Direccionamiento estratégico: Análisis de una herramienta poderosa. *Revista VíaSalud, 21*, 6–12.

Cango, C. (2019). *La Economía Popular y Solidaria en Ecuador: Políticas públicas y prácticas económicas no monetarias y sostenibles en los emprendimientos asociativos* (J. Ordoñez, Interviewer). Academic Press.

Cao, Q., Baker, J., Wetherbe, J., & Gu, V. (2012). Organizational adoption of innovation: Identifying factors that influence RFID adoption in the healthcare industry. *Proceedings of the European Conference on Information Systems*, 94.

Cappiello, G., Giordani, F., & Visentin, M. (2020). Social capital and its effect on networked firm innovation and competitiveness. *Industrial Marketing Management. Quality Management & Business Excellence, 31*(3-4), 297-311.

Carr, A. S., Zhang, M., Klopping, I., & Min, H. (2010). RFID technology: Implications for healthcare organizations. *American Journal of Business*, *25*(2), 25–40. doi:10.1108/19355181201000008

Carroll, A. B. (1991). The pyramid of corporate social responsibility: Toward the moral management of organizational stakeholders. *Business Horizons*, *34*(4), 39–48. doi:10.1016/0007-6813(91)90005-G

Carter, C. R., & Rogers, D. S. (2008). A framework of sustainable chain management: Moving toward new theory. *International Journal of Physical Distribution & Logistics Management*, *38*(5), 360–387. doi:10.1108/09600030810882816

Castro, J. (2019, June 11). *Qué es la cadena de suministro Supply Chain 4.0 y qué puede hacer por tu negocio*. Blog Corponet. https://blog.corponet.com.mx/que-es-la-cadena-de-suministro-o-supply-chain-4-0-y-que-puede-hacer-por-tu-negocio

Castro, A. A. (2010). *Direccionamiento estratégico y crecimiento empresarial: algunas reflexiones en torno a su relación*. Universidad del Norte.

Catania, A. C. (2013). Learning (5th ed.). Cornwall on Hudson, NY: Sloan Publishing.

CEPAL. (2020). *Estudio Económico de América Latina y el Caribe 2020: Principales condicionantes de las políticas fiscal y monetaria en la era pospandemia de COVID-19* (LC/PUB.20). Comisión Económica para América Latina y el Caribe (CEPAL).

Cernat, R. (2020). *The Dispute Revival for the Superpower Status*. Academic Press.

Certo, S. (2001). *Administración moderna: diversidad, calidad, ética y el entorno global* (8th ed.). Pearson Education.

CETDIR. (2007). Dirección estratégica integrada. *Ingeniería Industrial*, *28*(1), 14–23.

Chan, K.-M., Yuen, Y., & Wong, H. (2013). *Realities of social service purchasing in China: A political transaction cost perspective*. Academic Press.

Chandra, Y., Lee, E. K. M., & Tjiptono, F. (2021). Public versus private interest in social entrepreneurship: Can one serve two masters? *Journal of Cleaner Production*, *280*, 124499. doi:10.1016/j.jclepro.2020.124499

Chang, S., Klabjan, D., & Vossen, T. (2010). Optimal radio frequency identification deployment in a supply chain network. *International Journal of Production Economics*, *125*(1), 71–83. doi:10.1016/j.ijpe.2010.01.004

Chan, R. K., Ma, K. Y., & Wong, Y. H. (2013). The Software Piracy Decision-Making Process of Chinese Computer Users. *The Information Society*, *29*(4), 203–218. doi:10.1080/01972243.2013.792302

Chan, R. Y. K. (2001). Determinants of Chinese consumers' green purchase behavior. *Psychology and Marketing*, *18*(4), 389–413. doi:10.1002/mar.1013

Chan, R. Y., & Lau, L. B. (2002). Explaining green purchasing behavior: A cross-cultural study on American and Chinese consumers. *Journal of International Consumer Marketing*, *14*(2–3), 9–40. doi:10.1300/J046v14n02_02

Chapin, C., & Roy, S. S. (2021). A Spatial Web Application to Explore the Interactions between Human Mobility. Government Policies. and COVID19 Cases. *Journal of Geovisualization and Spatial Analysis*, *5*(1), 12. doi:10.100741651-021-00081-y

Chau, P. Y., & Tam, K. Y. (1997). Factors affecting the adoption of open systems: An exploratory study. *Management Information Systems Quarterly*, *21*(1), 1–24. doi:10.2307/249740

Chavda, M. D., & Trivedi, B. S. (2015). Impact of Age on Skills Development in Different Groups of Students. *International Journal of Information and Education Technology (IJIET)*, *5*(1), 55–59. doi:10.7763/IJIET.2015.V5.476

Compilation of References

Chen, B., Wan, J., Shu, L., Li, P., Mukherjee, M., & Yin, B. (2018). Smart Factory of Industry 4.0: Key Technologies, Application Case, and Challenges. *IEEE Access: Practical Innovations, Open Solutions*, *6*, 6505–6519. doi:10.1109/ACCESS.2017.2783682

Cheng, Y., & Dai, J. (1995). Intergenerational mobility in modern China. *European Sociological Review*, *11*(1), 17–35. doi:10.1093/oxfordjournals.esr.a036347

Chen, J. (2019). Environmental, Social and Governance (ESG) Criteria. *Investopedia Hentet*, *27*, 2019.

Chen, L., & Naughton, B. (2017). A Dynamic China Model: The Co-Evolution of Economics and Politics in China. *Journal of Contemporary China*, *26*(103), 18–34. doi:10.1080/10670564.2016.1206278

Chen, X., & Kelly, T. F. (2015). B-Corps—A Growing Form of SE: Tracing Their Progress and Assessing Their Performance. *Journal of Leadership & Organizational Studies*, *22*(1), 102–114. doi:10.1177/1548051814532529

Chen, Y., Han, Z., Cao, K., Zheng, X., & Xu, X. (2020). Manufacturing upgrading in industry 4.0 era. *Systems Research and Behavioral Science*, *37*(4), 766–771. doi:10.1002res.2717

Cherrafi, A., Garza-Reyes, J. A., Kumar, V., Mishra, N., Ghobadian, A., & El-Fezazi, S. (2018). Lean, green practices and process innovation: A model for green supply chain performance. *International Journal of Production Economics*, *206*, 79–92. doi:10.1016/j.ijpe.2018.09.031

Chesbrough, H. (2006). *Open business models: How to thrive in the new innovation landscape*. Harvard Business Press.

Chesbrough, H. (2010). Business model innovation: Opportunities and barriers. *Long Range Planning*, *43*(2-3), 354–363. doi:10.1016/j.lrp.2009.07.010

Choi, D., & Johnson, K. K. P. (2019). Influences of environmental and hedonic motivations on intention to purchase green products: An extension of the theory of planned behavior. *Sustainable Production and Consumption*, *18*, 145–155. doi:10.1016/j.spc.2019.02.001

Chowdhury, B., & Khosla, R. (2007). RFID-based hospital real-time patient management system. In *6th IEEE/ACIS international conference on computer and information science (ICIS 2007)* (pp. 363-368). IEEE. 10.1109/ICIS.2007.159

Chowdhury, M. M. H., Quaddus, M., & Agarwal, R. (2019). Supply chain resilience for performance: Role of relational practices and network complexities. *Supply Chain Management*, *24*(5), 659–676. doi:10.1108/SCM-09-2018-0332

Christopher, M. (2000). The Agile Supply Chain Competing in Volatile Markets. *Industrial Marketing Management*, *29*(1), 37–44. doi:10.1016/S0019-8501(99)00110-8

Cicopa. (2014). *Cooperativas y empleo: un informe mundial*. Bruselas: CICOPA & Grupo Desjardins. Retrieved from http://www.cicopa.coop/cicopa_old/IMG/pdf/ cooperativas_y_empleo_cicopa_es__web_1_pagina.pdf

Clauss, T., Kraus, S., Kallinger, F. L., Bican, P. M., Brem, A., & Kailer, N. (2020). Organizational ambidexterity and competitive advantage: The role of strategic agility in the exploration-exploitation paradox. *Journal of Innovation & KNOWLEDGE*. doi:10.1016/j.jik.2020.07.003

Código Orgánico de Organización Territorial. (2010). *Autonomía y Descentralización*. Lexis.

Coe, D. T., Helpman, E., & Hoffmaister, A. W. (1997). International R&D spillovers and institutions. *European Economic Review*, *53*(7), 723–741. doi:10.1016/j.euroecorev.2009.02.005

Colby, A., Ehrlich, T., Sullivan, W. M., & Dolle, J. R. (2011). *Rethinking undergraduate business education: Liberal learning for the profession* (Vol. 20). John Wiley & Sons.

Colmenares, E. A. M. (2012). Investigación-acción participativa: Una metodología integradora del conocimiento y la acción. Voces y Silencios. *Revista Latinoamericana de Educación, 3*(1), 102–115.

Colombatto, E. (2020, Nov 27). *Opinion: The WTO drifts toward irrelevance.* Geopolitical Intelligence Services GIS. https://www.gisreportsonline.com/opinion-the-wto-drifts-toward-irrelevance,economy,3373.html

Comín, F. (2011). *Historia económica mundial.* Alianza Editorial.

Comisión Económica para América Latina y El Caribe (CEPAL). (2002). *Globalización y desarrollo.* Santiago de Chile.

Comisión Económica para América Latina y El Caribe (CEPAL). (2017). *La inversión extranjera directa en América Latina y El Caribe.* Santiago de Chile.

Comisión Económica para América Latina y El Caribe. (2020). *Repositorio: CEPAL.* Obtained from CEPAL:https://repositorio.cepal.org/bitstream/handle/11362/45734/S2000438_es.pdf?sequence=4&isAllowed=y

Connolly, B. (2020). *Digital Trust: Social Media Strategies to Increase Trust and Engage Customers.* Bloomsbury Publishing.

Conrad, R. M., & Donaldson, J. A. (Eds.). (2004). Engaging the online learner: Activities and resources for creative instruction. Jossey Bass Publishers.

Constitution of the Republic of Ecuador CRE. (2008). Government of Ecuador.

Cooil, B., Keiningham, T. L., Aksoy, L., & Hsu, M. (2007). A Longitudinal Analysis of Customer Satisfaction and Share of Wallet: Investigating the Moderating Effect of Customer Characteristics. *Journal of Marketing, 71*(1), 67–83. doi:10.1509/jmkg.71.1.067

Cooke, B., & Alcadipani, R. (2015). Toward a global history of management education: The case of the Ford Foundation and the São Paulo School of Business Administration, Brazil. *Academy of Management Learning & Education, 14*(4), 482–499. doi:10.5465/amle.2013.0147

Cooke, F. L. (2016). Women in management in China. In *Women in Management Worldwide* (pp. 213–228). Gower.

Coppelli Ortiz, G. (2018). La globalización económica del siglo XXI. Entre la mundialización y la desglobalización. *Estudios Internacionales (Santiago), 50*(191), 57–80. doi:10.5354/0719-3769.2018.52048

Coraggio, J. (2014). *La presencia de la Economía Popular y Solidaria y su institucionalización en América Latina, 16.* Ginebra. Retrieved from https://www.coraggioeconomia.org/ jlc/archivos%20para%20descargar/A%20Ponencia%20ES%20estados%20generales%20junio%202011.pdf

Coronado Contreras, L., & Llanos Reynoso, L. F. (Coords.). (2020). Home office. La nueva revolución industrial. Wolters Kluwer.

Coronado, D., Acosta, M., & Fernández, A. (2008). Attitudes to innovation in peripheral economic regions. *Research Policy, 37*(6-7), 1009–1021. doi:10.1016/j.respol.2008.03.009

Costanzo, L. A., Vurro, C., Foster, D., Servato, F., & Perrini, F. (2014). Dual-Mission Management in Social Entrepreneurship: Qualitative Evidence from Social Firms in the United Kingdom. *Journal of Small Business Management, 52*(4), 655–677. doi:10.1111/jsbm.12128

Crogan, P., & Kinsley, S. (2012). Paying attention: Towards a critique of the attention economy. *Culture Machine, 13.*

Cruz, R. W. L. (2016). *La estructura organizacional y el análisis de la capacidad institucional: un referente en la Universidad de los Llanos.* Universidad Nacional de Colombia.

Compilation of References

Cummings, S., Bridgman, T., Hassard, J., & Rowlinson, M. (2017). *A new history of management*. Cambridge University Press. doi:10.1017/9781316481202

Curry, B., Foxall, G. R., & Sigurdsson, V. (2010, May). On the tautology of the matching law in consumer behavior analysis. *Behavioural Processes*, *84*(1), 390–399. doi:10.1016/j.beproc.2010.02.009 PMID:20178838

Dabic, M., González-Loureiro, M., & Furrer, O. (2014). Research on the strategy of multinational enterprises: Key approaches and new avenues. *BRQ Business Research Quarterly*, *17*(2), 129–148. doi:10.1016/j.brq.2013.09.001

Dagnoli, J. (1991). Consciously green. *Advertising Age*, *62*(38), 14–14.

Danley, S. (2020 December 6). Eight in ten consumers changed their eating habits due to COVID-19. *Food Business News*. Available at: https://www.foodbusinessnews.net/articles/16226-eight-in-ten-consumers-changed-their-eating-habits-due-to-covid-19

Daros, G. (2007). Economía Solidaria: Aspectos teóricos y experiencias. *Unircoop*, *5*(1), 9–19.

Daros, G., & Flores, R. (2006). Realidad y perspectivas de la Economía Popular en Ecuador. In J. Pérez & M. Rodrigán (Eds.), *La Economía Popular en Iberoamérica*. Fundibes.

Das, B. C., & Mukherjee, B. N. (2000). *Integral Calculus* (50th ed.). U. N. Dhur & Sons Private Limited.

Datar, S. M., Garvin, D. A., Cullen, P. G., & Cullen, P. (2010). *Rethinking the MBA: Business education at a crossroads*. Harvard Business Press.

Davies, I. A., Haugh, H., & Chambers, L. (2019). Barriers to SE Growth. *Journal of Small Business Management*, *57*(4), 1616–1636. doi:10.1111/jsbm.12429

Davillas, A., & Jones, A. M. (2021). *The First Wave of the COVID19 Pandemic and Its Impact on Socioeconomic Inequality in Psychological Distress in the UK*. Discussion Paper, 14057. IZA.

Davison, M., & McCarthy, D. (1988). *The matching law: A research review*. Lawrence Erlbaum Associates, Inc.

Davis-Sramek, B., Ishfaq, R., Gibson, B. J., & Defee, C. (2020). Examining retail business model transformation: A longitudinal study of the transition to omnichannel order fulfillment. *International Journal of Physical Distribution & Logistics Management*, *50*(5), 557–576. doi:10.1108/IJPDLM-02-2019-0055

Daxboeck, B. (2013). Value co-creation as a precondition for the development of a service business model canvas. *Studia Universitatis Babes Bolyai-Negotia*, *58*(4), 23–51.

de Chernatony, L., & McDonald, M. H. B. (2003). *Creating Powerful Brands in Consumer, Service and Industrial Markets* (3rd ed.). Elsevier / Butterworth – Heinemann.

De la Fuente, A., & Doménech, R. (2018). El nivel educativo de la población en España y sus regiones: Actualización hasta 2016. *Documento de Trabajo BBVA Research*, *18*(04), 1–25.

de la Republica de Colombia, C. (2004). *Ley 905 de 2004*. Retrieved from http://web.presidencia.gov.co/leyes/2004/agosto/Ley%20No.%20905.pdf

De La Torre, L., & Sandoval, C. (2004). *La Reciprocidad en el Mundo Andino*. Abya Yala.

De Marco, A., Cagliano, A. C., Nervo, M. L., & Rafele, C. (2012). Using System Dynamics to assess the impact of RFID technology on retail operations. *International Journal of Production Economics*, *135*(1), 333–344. doi:10.1016/j.ijpe.2011.08.009

DeAngelis, S. (2021 May 24). *The Changing Face of Retail*. Available at: https://enterrasolutions.com/blog/the-changing-face-of-retail/

Dees, J. G. (2007). Taking social entrepreneurship seriously. *Society*, *44*(3), 24–31. doi:10.1007/BF02819936

Defourny, J., & Nyssens, M. (2006). Defining SE. *SE: At the Crossroads of Market. Public Policies and Civil Society*, *7*, 3–27.

Dehning, J., Zierenberg, J., Spitzner, F. P., Wibral, M., Neto, J. P., Wilczek, M., & Priesemann, V. (2020). Inferring change points in the spread of COVID19 reveals the effectiveness of interventions. *Science*, *369*(6500), eabb9789. doi:10.1126cience.abb9789 PMID:32414780

Delaney, P. (1997). Pop Culture, "Gangsta Rap" and the "New Vaudeville." In *The Media in Black and White*. Routledge.

Delaney, R., Strough, J., Parker, A. M., & de Bruin, W. B. (2015). Variations in decision-making profiles by age and gender: A cluster-analytic approach. *Personality and Individual Differences*, *85*, 19–24. doi:10.1016/j.paid.2015.04.034 PMID:26005238

Demarest, A. A. (2020 June 10). New Survey Reveals Covid-19's Impact on American Food Habits. *Forbes*. Available at: https://www.forbes.com/sites/abigailabesamis/2020/06/10/new-survey-reveals-covid-19s-impact-on-american-food-habits/?sh=18697fdf6a77

Deng, J., Zhou, F., Hou, W., Silver, Z., Wong, C. Y., Chang, O., Drakos, A., Zuo, Q. K., & Huang, E. (2021). The prevalence of depressive symptoms, anxiety symptoms and sleep disturbance in higher education students during the COVID-19 pandemic: A systematic review and meta-analysis. *Psychiatry Research*, *301*, 113863. doi:10.1016/j.psychres.2021.113863 PMID:33984824

Denison, D., & Neale, W.S. (1996). *Denison organizational culture survey: facilitator guide*. Aviat.

Denison, R., & Mishra, A. (1995). Toward a theory of organizational culture and effectiveness. *Organization Science*, *6*(2), 204–223. doi:10.1287/orsc.6.2.204

Deshpande, S., Basil, M. D., & Basil, D. Z. (2009). Factors Influencing Healthy Eating Habits among College Students: An Application of the Health Belief Model. *Health Marketing Quarterly*, *26*(2), 145–164. doi:10.1080/07359680802619834 PMID:19408181

Dess, G. G., & Lumpkin, G. T. (2003). *Dirección estratégica: Creando ventajas competitivas*. McGraw-Hill Interamericana.

Deutscher, F., Zapkau, F. B., Schwens, C., Baum, M., & Kabst, R. (2016). Strategic orientations and performance: A configurational perspective. *Journal of Business Research*, *69*(2), 849–861. doi:10.1016/j.jbusres.2015.07.005

Dimock, M. (2019). Defining generations: Where Millennials end and Generation Z begins. *Pew Research Center*, *17*(1), 1–7.

Ding, N., Xu, X., Yang, H., Li, Y., & van Heughten, P. (2020). Decision-making styles of Chinese business students. *Journal of Education for Business*, *95*(6), 351–358. doi:10.1080/08832323.2019.1654968

Dixit, A. K., & Nalebuff, B. J. (1991). *Pensar estratégicamente: un arma decisiva en los negocios, la política y la vida diaria*. Antoni Bosch.

Dong, E., Du, H., & Gardner, L. (2020). An interactive web-based dashboard to track COVID-19 in real time. *The Lancet. Infectious Diseases*, *20*(5), 533–534. doi:10.1016/S1473-3099(20)30120-1 PMID:32087114

Compilation of References

Dong, Y., Zha, Q., Zhang, H., Kou, G., Fujita, H., Chiclana, F., & Herrera-Viedma, E. (2018). Consensus reaching in social network group decision-making: Research paradigms and challenges. *Knowledge-Based Systems*, *162*, 3–13. doi:10.1016/j.knosys.2018.06.036

Donoso, E. (2014). *Lecciones de las prácticas económicas de las comunidades indígenas Andino-Amazonicas para ser aplicadas en las PYMES*. Retrieved from http://repositorio.flacsoandes.edu.ec:8080/handle/10469/7518

Dooley, R. S., & Fryxell, G. E. (1999). Attaining decision quality and commitment from dissent: The moderating effects of loyalty and competence in strategic decision-making teams. *Academy of Management Journal*, *42*(4), 389–402.

Dosi, G., Nelson, R. R., & Winter, S. G. (2000). *The nature and dynamics of organizational capabilities* (G. Dosi, R. R. Nelson, & S. G. Winter, Eds.). Oxford University Press.

Dostaler, I., & Tomberlin, J. (2013). The great divide between business schools research and business practice. *Canadian Journal of Higher Education*, *43*(1), 115–128. doi:10.47678/cjhe.v43i1.1895

Doukianou, S., Doukianou, S., Daylamani-Zad, D., Zad, D. D., Lameras, P., & Dunwell, I. (2019). *Reinforcing Rational Decision-making in a Risk Elicitation task through Visual Reasoning*. Academic Press.

Draper, A. (2004). The principles and application of qualitative research. *The Proceedings of the Nutrition Society*, *63*(4), 641–646. doi:10.1079/PNS2004397 PMID:15831137

Driedonks, C., Gregor, S., Wassenaar, A., & Wassenaar, A. (2005). Economic and social analysis of the adoption of B2B electronic marketplaces: A case study in the Australian beef industry. *International Journal of Electronic Commerce*, *9*(3), 49–72. doi:10.1080/10864415.2005.11044337

Dubé, J. P., Smith, M. M., Sherry, S. B., Hewitt, P. L., & Stewart, S. H. (2021). Suicide behaviors during the COVID-19 pandemic: A meta-analysis of 54 studies. *Psychiatry Research*, *301*, 113998. doi:10.1016/j.psychres.2021.113998 PMID:34022657

Duprey, R. (2020). *Uber eats gains Grubhub lags during Coronavirus pandemic*. Motley Fool. https://www.fool.com/investing/2020/04/09/uber-eats-gains-grubhub-lags-during-coronavirus-pa.aspx

Dwyer, F. R. (1989). Customer Lifetime Valuation to Support Marketing Decision Making. *Journal of Direct Marketing*, *3*(4), 8–15. doi:10.1002/dir.4000030404

Dyllick, T. (2015). Responsible management education for a sustainable world: The challenges for business schools. *Journal of Management Development*, *34*(1), 16–33. doi:10.1108/JMD-02-2013-0022

ECLAC & ILO. (2020). Employment trends in an unprecedented crisis: policy challenges. In *Employment Situation in Latin America and the Caribbean* (Issue 23 (LC/TS.2020/128)). United Nations. https://repositorio.cepal.org/bitstream/handle/11362/46309/4/S2000600_en.pdf

Edelman, R. (2021). *Edelman Trust Barometer 2021*. https://www.edelman.com

Eells, E. (2016). *Rational decision and causality*. Cambridge University Press.

Efstathiou, V., Michopoulos, I., Yotsidi, V., Smyrnis, N., Zompola, C., Papadopoulou, A., Pomini, V., Papadopoulou, M., Tsigkaropoulou, E., Tsivgoulis, G., Douzenis, A., & Gournellis, R. (2021). Does suicidal ideation increase during the second COVID-19 lockdown? *Psychiatry Research*, *301*, 113990. doi:10.1016/j.psychres.2021.113990 PMID:34020218

Eftimov, T., Popovski, G., Petković, M., Seljak, B. K., & Dragi Kocev, D. (2020). COVID-19 pandemic changes the food consumption patterns. *Trends in Food Science & Technology*, *104*, 268–272. doi:10.1016/j.tifs.2020.08.017 PMID:32905099

Eggers, F. (2020). Masters of disasters? Challenges and opportunities for SMEs in times of crisis. *Journal of Business Research*, *116*, 199–208. doi:10.1016/j.jbusres.2020.05.025 PMID:32501306

Eng, T.-Y., & Spickett-Jones, J. G. (2009a). An investigation of marketing capabilities and upgrading performance of manufacturers in mainland China and Hong Kong. *Journal of World Business*, *44*(4), 463–475. doi:10.1016/j.jwb.2009.01.002

Eroglu, C., Kurt, A. C., & Elwakil, O. S. (2016). Stock Market Reaction to Quality, Safety, and Sustainability Awards in Logistics. *Journal of Business Logistics*, *37*(4), 329–345. doi:10.1111/jbl.12145

Erven, B. L. (2001). *Becoming an Effective Leader Through Situational Leadership*. Department of Agricultural, Environment, and Development Economics, Ohio State University Extension.

Esch, F. R. (2007). *Strategie und Technik der Markenführung* (4th ed.). Vahlen.

Esch, F. R. (2008). Brand identity: the guiding star for successful brands. In B. H. Schmitt & D. L. Rogers (Eds.), *Handbook on Brand and Experience Management* (pp. 58–73). Edward Elgar Publishing. doi:10.4337/9781848446151.00010

Esch, F. R., Langner, T., & Rempel, J. E. (2005). Ansätze zur Erfassung und Entwicklung der Markenidentität. In F. R. Esch (Ed.), *Moderne Markenführung, Grundlagen – Innovative Ansätze – Praktische Umsetzungen* (4th ed., pp. 103–129). Springer Gabler Verlag., doi:10.1007/978-3-8349-4541-9_4

Esquivel, G. (2020). The Economic Impacts of the Pandemic in Mexico. *Economía UNAM*, *17*(51). Advance online publication. doi:10.22201/fe.24488143e.2020.51.543

Evans, S., Vladimirova, D., Holgado, M., Van Fossen, K., Yang, M., Silva, E. A., & Barlow, C. Y. (2017). Business model innovation for sustainability: Towards a unified perspective for creation of sustainable business models. *Business Strategy and the Environment*, *26*(5), 597–608. doi:10.1002/bse.1939

Evers, A. (2005). Mixed Welfare Systems and Hybrid Organizations: Changes in the Governance and Provision of Social Services. *International Journal of Public Administration*, *28*(9–10), 737–748. doi:10.1081/PAD-200067318

Evtodieva, T. E., Chernova, D. V., Ivanova, N. V., & Kisteneva, N. S. (2019). Logistics 4.0. In S. Ashmarina & M. Vochozka (Eds.), *Sustainable Growth and Development of Economic Systems* (pp. 207–219). Springer. doi:10.1007/978-3-030-11754-2_16

Evtodieva, T. E., Chernova, D. V., Voitkevich, N. I., Khramtsova, E. R., & Gorgodze, T. E. (2017). Transformation of logistics organizations forms under the conditions of a modern economy. In E. G. Popkova (Ed.), *Russia and the European Union* (pp. 177–182). Springer. doi:10.1007/978-3-319-55257-6_24

Fade, S. (2004). Using interpretative phenomenological analysis for public health nutrition and dietetic research: A practical guide. *The Proceedings of the Nutrition Society*, *63*(4), 647–653. doi:10.1079/PNS2004398 PMID:15831138

Fagerberg, J. (2018). *Innovation, Economic Development and Policy: Selected Essays*. Edward Elgar Publishing. doi:10.4337/9781788110266

Fagerstrøm, A., & Sigurdsson, V. (2016). Experimental analyses of consumer choices. In G. R. Foxall (Ed.), *The Routledge Companion to Consumer Behavior Analysis* (pp. 25–39). Routledge.

Faizah, S. I., & Husaeni, U. A. (2019). Economic Empowerment for Poor Women Using Grameen Bank Model in Indonesia. *KnE Social Sciences*, 880–913.

Fana, M., Tolan, S., Torrejón Pérez, S., Urzi Brancati, M. C., & Fernández-Macías, E. (2020). The COVID confinement measures and EU labour markets. In *JCR Technical Reports*. Publications Office of the European Union. doi:10.2760/079230

Compilation of References

Farinha, L., & Bagchi-Sen, S. (2019). Following the Footprints of SME Competitiveness in a High-Technology Sector. In *Knowledge, Innovation and Sustainable Development in Organizations* (pp. 77–95). Springer. doi:10.1007/978-3-319-74881-8_6

Fatima, S., Khan, M., Rosselli, M., & Ardila, A. (2020). Age, executive functioning, and decision-making styles in adults: A moderated mediation model. *Neuropsychology, Development, and Cognition. Section B, Aging, Neuropsychology and Cognition, 27*(3), 338–350. doi:10.1080/13825585.2019.1614142 PMID:31084251

Feldstein, M. (2000). *Aspects of Global Economic Integration: Outlook for the Future.* NBER Working Papers 7899.

Feng, C.-M., & Chern, C.-H. (2008). Key Factors Used by Manufacturers to Analyze Supply-Chain Operational Models: An Empirical Study among Notebook Computer Firms. *International Journal of Management; Poole, 25*(4), 740-755,779.

Ferguson, N. (2020). Report 9: Impact of non-pharmaceutical interventions (NPIs) to reduce COVID19 mortality and healthcare demand. *Imperial College London, 10*(77482), 491–497.

Fernández G.R. (2001). *Manual para el desarrollo y crecimiento empresarial.* 3R Editores.

Fernández, J. C. (2010). *Sistema de Derecho Económico Internacional.* Aranzadi.

Fernández-Villacañas, M.A. (2018) Las plataformas logísticas 4.0 y la mejora del comercio global: Creando ventaja competitiva logística y desarrollo sostenible. *VI Simposio Internacional Online de Logística y Competitividad, High Logistics Simposios.*

Fernández-Villacañas, M. A. (2019) Desarrollo e Implementación de Plataformas Logísticas de Carga 4.0. *Proceedings of Primer Congreso Internacional de Tecnología e Innovación en Logística 4.0.*

Fernández-Villacañas, M. A. (2020). The New Concept of Logistics Platforms 4.0: Creating Competitiveness Within the Paradigm of Global Sustainable Logistics. In U. Akkucuk (Ed.), *Handbook of Research on Sustainable Supply Chain Management for the Global Economy* (pp. 36–62). IGI Global. doi:10.4018/978-1-7998-4601-7.ch003

Ferraro, E. (2004). *Reciprocidad, don y deuda Formas de relaciones de intercambios en los Andes de Ecuador: la comunidad de Pesillo.* Abya - Yala.

Ferrer, A. (1998). América Latina y la globalización. *Revista CEPAL, 10*, 155–168.

Ferrer, G., Dew, N., & Apte, U. (2010). When is RFID right for your service? *International Journal of Production Economics, 124*(2), 414–425. doi:10.1016/j.ijpe.2009.12.004

Finch, D., Deephouse, D. L., O'Reilly, N., Massie, T., & Hillenbrand, C. (2016). Follow the leaders? An analysis of convergence and innovation of faculty recruiting practices in US business schools. *Higher Education, 71*(5), 699–717. doi:10.100710734-015-9931-5

Fishbein, M., & Ajzen, I. (1975). *Belief, Attitude, Intention, and Behavior: An Introduction to Theory and Research.* Addison-Wesley.

Fisher, J. A., & Monahan, T. (2008). Tracking the social dimensions of RFID systems in hospitals. *International Journal of Medical Informatics, 77*(3), 176–183. doi:10.1016/j.ijmedinf.2007.04.010 PMID:17544841

Fjeldstad, Ø. D., & Snow, C. C. (2018). Business models and organization design. *Long Range Planning, 51*(1), 32–39. doi:10.1016/j.lrp.2017.07.008

Flaxman, S., Mishra, S., Gandy, A., Unwin, H. J. T., Mellan, T. A., Coupland, H., Whittaker, C., Zhu, H., Berah, T., Eaton, J. W., Monod, M., Perez-Guzman, P. N., Schmit, N., Cilloni, L., Ainslie, K. E. C., Baguelin, M., Boonyasiri, A., Boyd, O., Cattarino, L., ... Bhatt, S. (2020). Estimating the effects of non-pharmaceutical interventions on COVID19 in Europe. *Nature*, *584*(7820), 257–261. doi:10.103841586-020-2405-7 PMID:32512579

Fonseca, C. (1974). Modalidades de la Minka. In Reciprocidad e intercambio en los Andes peruanos (p. 88). Lima, Peru: Industrial.

Food Insight. (2020 April 14). Consumer Survey: COVID-19's Impact on Food Purchasing, Eating Behaviors and Perceptions of Food Safety. *Food Insight*. Available at: https://foodinsight.org/consumer-survey-covid-19s-impact-on-food-purchasing/

FoodMatters. (2020 June 4). COVID-19 is changing consumer behaviour. *FoodMatters*. Available at: https://www.foodmatters.co.uk/industry-insight/covid-19-is-changing-consumer-behaviour/

Forker, L. B., & Mendez, D. (2001). An analytical method for benchmarking best peer suppliers. *International Journal of Operations & Production Management*, *21*(1–2), 195–209. doi:10.1108/01443570110358530

Fosso Wamba, S., Anand, A., & Carter, L. (2013). A Literature Review of RFID enabled Healthcare Applications and Issues. *International Journal of Information Management*, *33*(5), 875–891. doi:10.1016/j.ijinfomgt.2013.07.005

Fosso Wamba, S., Gunasekaran, A., Bhattacharya, M., & Dubey, R. (2016). Determinants of RFID adoption intention by SMEs: An empirical investigation. *Production Planning and Control*, *27*(12), 979–990. doi:10.1080/09537287.2016.1167981

Fosso Wamba, S., & Ngai, E. W. (2015). Importance of Issues Related to RFID enabled Healthcare Transformation Projects: Results from a Delphi Study. *Production Planning and Control*, *26*(1), 19–33. doi:10.1080/09537287.2013.840015

Fournier, S. (1998, March). Consumers and Their Brands: Developing Relationship Theory in Consumer Research. *The Journal of Consumer Research*, *24*(4), 343–373. doi:10.1086/209515

Fournier, S., Solomon, M. R., & Englis, B. G. (2008). When brands resonate. In B. H. Schmitt & D. L. Rogers (Eds.), *Handbook on Brand and Experience Management* (pp. 35–57). Edward Elgar Publishing. doi:10.4337/9781848446151.00009

Foxall, G. R. (2005). *Understanding Consumer Choice*. Palgrave Macmillan. doi:10.1057/9780230510029

Foxall, G. R. (2007). *Explaining Consumer Choice*. Palgrave Macmillan. doi:10.1057/9780230599796

Foxall, G. R. (2010). *Interpreting Consumer Choice: The Behavioral Perspective Model*. Routledge.

Foxall, G. R. (2016). Consumer behavior analysis comes of an age. In G. R. Foxall (Ed.), *The Routledge Companion to Consumer Behavior Analysis* (pp. 3–21). Routledge.

Franchi, E., Poggi, A., & Tomaiuolo, M. (2013). Open social networking for online collaboration. *International Journal of e-Collaboration*, *9*(3), 50-68.

Francisco, P., & Bergoglio, J. (2015). *Carta Encíclica Laudato Si: sobre el cuidado de la casa común. Vaticano*. Retrieved from http://w2.vatican.va/content/dam/ francesco/pdf/encyclicals/documents/papa-francesco_20150524_enciclica-laudato-si_sp.pdf

Frazzon, E., Rodriguez, C. M., Pereira, M., Pires, M., & Uhlmann, I. (2019). Towards Supply Chain Management 4.0. *Brazilian Journal of Operations & Production Management*, *16*(2), 180–191. doi:10.14488/BJOPM.2019.v16.n2.a2

Frederick, W. C. (2006). *Corporation, be good!: The story of corporate social responsibility*. Dog Ear Publishing.

Compilation of References

Fuentelsaz, L., Polo, Y., & Maicas, J. P. (2003). Economía digital y estrategia empresarial: Un análisis desde la dirección estratégica. *Revista de Empresa, 5*, 57–63.

Fumero, A., Marrero, R. J., Voltes, D., & Penate, W. (2018). Personal and social factors involved in internet addiction among adolescents: A meta-analysis. *Computers in Human Behavior, 86*, 387–400. doi:10.1016/j.chb.2018.05.005

Furnham, A. (2020). Myers-Briggs type indicator (MBTI). Encyclopedia of Personality and Individual Differences, 3059–3062.

Gadenne, D., Sharma, B., Kerr, D., & Smith, T. (2011). The influence of consumers' environmental beliefs and attitudes on energy-saving behaviours. *Energy Policy, 39*(12), 7684–7694. doi:10.1016/j.enpol.2011.09.002

Galent, M., & Soborski, R. (2020). Introduction to the special issue: globalization thirty years on: promises, realities and morals for the future. *The International Journal of Interdisciplinary Global Studies, 15*(4), 23–35. doi:10.18848/2324-755X/CGP/v15i04/0-0

Galvão, A., Mascarenhas, C., Gouveia Rodrigues, R., Marques, C. S., & Leal, C. T. (2017). A quadruple helix model of entrepreneurship, innovation and stages of economic development. *Review of International Business and Strategy, 27*(2), 261–282. doi:10.1108/RIBS-01-2017-0003

Gálvez, A. E. J., Cuéllar, L. K., Restrepo, R. C., Berna, C. A., & Cortés, J. A. (2014). *Análisis estratégico para el desarrollo de las MiPymes en Colombia*. Programa Editorial Universidad del Valle. doi:10.25100/peu.35

Gamez-Gutierrez, J., & Saiz-Alvarez, J. M. (Eds.). (2021). Entrepreneurial Innovation for Securing Long-Term Growth in a Short-Term Economy. IGI Global.

García de la Cruz, J. M. (2008). La globalización económica. In *Sistema económico mundial* (pp. 53–74). Thomson Editores.

García-Muiña, F. E., Medina-Salgado, M. S., Ferrari, A. M., & Cucchi, M. (2020). Sustainability Transition in Industry 4.0 and Smart Manufacturing with the Triple-Layered Business Model Canvas. *Sustainability, 12*(6), 2364. doi:10.3390u12062364

García-Muñoz Aparicio, C., Pérez Sánchez, B., & Navarrete Torres, M. del C. (2020). Las Empresas ante el COVID-19. *Revista de Investigación En Gestion Industrial, Ambiental, Seguridad y Salud En El Trabajo- GISST, 2*(2), 85–143. doi:10.34893/gisst.v2i2.83

García-Sánchez, A., Siles, D., & Vázquez-Méndez, M. D. M. (2019). Competitiveness and innovation: Effects on prosperity. *Anatolia, 30*(2), 200–213. doi:10.1080/13032917.2018.1519179

Garrido, S., Brandenburg, M., Carvalho, H., & Cruz Machado, V. (2014). Eco-innovation and the development of business models. Lessons from experience and new frontiers in theory and practice. *Greening of Industry Networks Studies, 2*.

Gavetti, G. (2005). Cognition and Hierarchy: Rethinking the Microfoundations of Capabilities' Development. *Organization Science, 16*(6), 599–617. doi:10.1287/orsc.1050.0140

Gavrilova, T., Alsufyev, A., & Yanson, A. S. (2014). Transforming canvas model: Map versus table. *International Journal of Knowledge. Innovation and Entrepreneurship, 2*(2), 51–65.

Gereffi, G., & Frederick, S. S. (2010). *The Global Apparel Value Chain, Trade and the Crisis: Challenges and Opportunities for Developing Countries*. doi:10.1596/1813-9450-5281

Ghadge, A., Dani, S., Ojha, R., & Caldwell, N. (2017). Using risk sharing contracts for supply chain risk mitigation: A buyer-supplier power and dependence perspective. *Computers & Industrial Engineering*, *103*, 262–270. doi:10.1016/j.cie.2016.11.034

Ghezzi, A., & Cavallo, A. (2020). Agile business model innovation in digital entrepreneurship: Lean startup approaches. *Journal of Business Research*, *110*, 519–537. doi:10.1016/j.jbusres.2018.06.013

Ghosh, I. (2020). *How China Overtook the U.S. as the World's Major Trading Partner.* Visual Capitalist. https://www.visualcapitalist.com/china-u-s-worlds-trading-partner/

Ghoshal, S. (2005). Bad management theories are destroying good management practices. *Academy of Management Learning & Education*, *4*(1), 75–91. doi:10.5465/amle.2005.16132558

Gil Robles, M. A. (2020). Organizational Transformation During COVID-19. *IEEE Engineering Management Review*, *48*(3), 31–36. doi:10.1109/EMR.2020.3014280

Gilpin, R. (2001). *Global Political Economy: Understanding the International Economic Order.* Princeton University Press. doi:10.1515/9781400831272

Goldin, I., & Reinert, K. (2007). *Globalización para el desarrollo.* The World Bank.

Golley, J., & Kong, S. T. (2013). Inequality in intergenerational mobility of education in China. *China & World Economy*, *21*(2), 15–37. doi:10.1111/j.1749-124X.2013.12013.x

Gond, J. P., Igalens, J., Swaen, V., & El Akremi, A. (2011). The human resources contribution to responsible leadership: An exploration of the CSR–HR interface. In *Responsible leadership* (pp. 115–132). Springer. doi:10.1007/978-94-007-3995-6_10

González, A. F., Curtis, C., Washburn, I. J., & Shirsat, A. R. (2019). Factors in tourists' food decision processes: A US-based case study. *Journal of Tourism Analysis: Revista de Análisis Turístico*, *27*(1), 2–19. doi:10.1108/JTA-01-2019-0002

Gordon, R. A., & Howell, J. E. (1959). Higher education for business. *The Journal of Business Education*, *35*(3), 115–117. doi:10.1080/08832323.1959.10116245

Gorski, I. (2016). Engaging faculty across the community engagement continuum. *Journal of Public Scholarship in Higher Education*, *6*(1), 108–123.

Granger, C. W. J., & Newbold, P. (1974). Spurious regressions in econometrics. *Journal of Econometrics*, *2*(2), 111–120. doi:10.1016/0304-4076(74)90034-7

Granstrand, O. (2006, January 19). Innovation and Intellectual Property Rights. *The Oxford Handbook of Innovation.* doi:10.1093/oxfordhb/9780199286805.003.0010

Granstrand, O. (1999). The Economics and Management of Intellectual Property. In *Books.* Edward Elgar Publishing. https://ideas.repec.org/b/elg/eebook/1651.html

Gratz, K. L., Mann, A. J. D., & Tull, M. T. (2021). Suicidal ideation among university students during the COVID19 pandemic: Identifying at-risk subgroups. *Psychiatry Research*, *302*, 114034. doi:10.1016/j.psychres.2021.114034 PMID:34098158

Green, P. E., & Rao, V. R. (1971, August). Conjoint measurement for quantifying judgmental data. *JMR, Journal of Marketing Research*, *8*(3), 355–363. doi:10.2307/3149575

Grenčíková, A., & Vojtovič, S. (2017). Relationship of generations X, Y, Z with new communication technologies. *Problems and Perspectives in Management; Sumy*, *15*(2), 557–563.

Compilation of References

Griffin, A. (2008). *New strategies for reputation management: Gaining control of issues, crises & corporate social responsibility*. Kogan Page Publishers.

Grönroos, C. (1994). *Marketing y gestión de servicios*. Ediciones Díaz de Santos S.A.

Grunert, S. C. (n.d.). *Everybody seems concerned about the environment: But is this concern reflected in (Danish) consumers' food choice?* Academic Press.

Guagnano, G. A., Stern, P. C., & Dietz, T. (1995). Influences on Attitude-Behavior Relationships: A Natural Experiment with Curbside Recycling. *Environment and Behavior*, *27*(5), 699–718. doi:10.1177/0013916595275005

Guamán, J. (2017). *La perspectiva indígena de la equidad, la reciprocidad y la solidaridad como aporte a la construcción de un Nuevo Orden Económico Internacional*. Retrieved from https://es.scribd.com/document/130539491/La-perspectiva-indigena-de-la-equidad-la-reciprocidad-y-la-solidaridad

Gudiel, K. C., Marjerison, R. K., & Zhao, Y. (2021). Scope for Sustainability in the Fashion Industry Supply Chain: Technology and Its Impact. In Entrepreneurial Innovation for Securing Long-Term Growth in a Short-Term Economy (pp. 71–89). IGI Global.

Guerrero-Lorente, J., Gabor, A. F., & Ponce-Cueto, E. (2020). Omnichannel logistics network design with integrated customer preference for deliveries and returns. *Computers & Industrial Engineering*, *144*(March), 106433. doi:10.1016/j.cie.2020.106433

Guevara, D. (1957). *Las Mingas en el Ecuador: orígenes, tránsito, supervivencia*. Universitaria.

Gujarati, D. N. (2003). *Basic Econometrics* (4th ed.). McGraw – Hill, Inc.

Gummesson, E., Mele, C., Polese, F., Galvagno, M., & Dalli, D. (2014). Theory of value co-creation: A systematic literature review. *Managing Service Quality*, *24*(6), 643–683. doi:10.1108/MSQ-09-2013-0187

Gunay, G. N., & Baker, M. J. (2011). The factors influencing consumers' behaviour on wine consumption in the Turkish wine market. *EuroMed Journal of Business*, *6*(3), 324–334. doi:10.1108/14502191111170150

Gupta, S., & Lehmann, D. R. (2005). *Managing Customers as Investments*. Wharton Business School Publishing.

Gupta, S., Lehmann, D. R., & Stuart, J. A. (2004). Valuing Customers. *JMR, Journal of Marketing Research*, *41*(1), 7–18. doi:10.1509/jmkr.41.1.7.25084

Gurkov, I. (2015). Corporate parenting styles of the multinational corporation: A subsidiary view. In *The Future of Global Organizing*. Emerald Group Publishing Limited. doi:10.1108/S1745-886220150000010003

Gutierrez, B., Spencer, S., & Zhu, G. (2008, August). Thinking globally, leading locally: Chinese, Indian, and Western Leadership. Academy of Management Proceedings, 2008(1), 1-6.

Haarhaus, T., & Liening, A. (2020). Building dynamic capabilities to cope with environmental uncertainty: The role of strategic foresight. *Technological Forecasting and Social Change*, *155*(3), 120033. doi:10.1016/j.techfore.2020.120033

Haass, R. N. (2008). The age of non-polarity: What will follow U. S. dominance? *Foreign Affairs*, *87*(3), 44–56.

Hakala, H. (2011). Strategic Orientations in Management Literature: Three Approaches to Understanding the Interaction between Market, Technology, Entrepreneurial and Learning Orientations. *International Journal of Management Reviews*, *13*(2), 199–217. doi:10.1111/j.1468-2370.2010.00292.x

Halbritter, G., & Dorfleitner, G. (2015). The wages of social responsibility - where are they? A critical review of ESG investing. *Review of Financial Economics*, *26*, 25–35. doi:10.1016/j.rfe.2015.03.004

Haraguchi, M., & Lall, U. (2015). Flood risks and impacts: A case study of Thailand's floods in 2011 and research questions for supply chain decision making. *International Journal of Disaster Risk Reduction*, *14*, 256–272. doi:10.1016/j.ijdrr.2014.09.005

Hardt, M., & Negri, A. (2002). *Empire*. Harvard University Press.

Harland, C. M., Caldwell, N. D., Powell, P., & Zheng, J. (2007). Barriers to supply chain information integration: SMEs adrift of eLands. *Journal of Operations Management*, *25*(6), 1234–1254. doi:10.1016/j.jom.2007.01.004

Harrison, R. (1972). Understanding your organization's charter. *Harvard Business Review*, (May-June), 119–128.

Harvey, D. (2007). *Breve historia del neoliberalismo*. Akal.

Hasenhütl, G. (2018). The World Beyond Your Head: On Becoming an Individual in an Age of Distraction. *The Journal of Modern Craft*, *11*(3), 287–291. doi:10.1080/17496772.2018.1538631

Hassinen, M., & Marttila-Kontio, M. (2008). EMS coordination in large scale emergencies using automated patient monitoring. In *2008 Second International Conference on Pervasive Computing Technologies for Healthcare* (pp. 86-87). IEEE. 10.1109/PCTHEALTH.2008.4571035

Helfat, C. E., & Peteraf, M. A. (2003). The dynamic resource-based view: Capability lifecycles. *Strategic Management Journal*, *24*(10), 997–1010. doi:10.1002mj.332

Henderson, J. M., & Quandt, R. E. (1980). Microeconomic Theory: A Mathematical Approach (3rd ed.). McGraw-Hill Book Company.

Hendricks, V. F., & Vestergaard, M. (2019). The Attention Economy. In V. F. Hendricks & M. Vestergaard (Eds.), *Reality Lost: Markets of Attention, Misinformation and Manipulation* (pp. 1–17). Springer International Publishing. doi:10.1007/978-3-030-00813-0_1

Henry, M., Bauwens, T., Hekkert, M., & Kirchherr, J. (2020). A typology of circular startups: An Analysis of 128 circular business models. *Journal of Cleaner Production*, *245*, 118528. doi:10.1016/j.jclepro.2019.118528

Hernández Zubizarreta, J., & Ramiro, P. (2016). *Contra la Lex Mercatoria*. Icaria.

Herrando, C., Jimenez-Martinez, J., & Hoyos, M. J. M.-D. (2019). Tell me your age and I tell you what you trust: The moderating effect of generations. *Internet Research*, *29*(4), 799–817. doi:10.1108/IntR-03-2017-0135

Herrnstein, R. J. (1961, July). Relative and absolute strength of response as a function of frequency of reinforcement. *Journal of the Experimental Analysis of Behavior*, *4*(3), 267–272. doi:10.1901/jeab.1961.4-267 PMID:13713775

Herrnstein, R. J. (1970, March). On the law of effect. *Journal of the Experimental Analysis of Behavior*, *13*(2), 243–266. doi:10.1901/jeab.1970.13-243 PMID:16811440

Herrnstein, R. J. (1997). The matching law: Papers in psychology and economics. In H. Rachlin & D. Laibson (Eds.). Russel Sage Foundation.

Higgs, S., & Thomas, J. (2016). Social influences on eating. *Current Opinion in Behavioral Sciences*, *9*, 1–6. doi:10.1016/j.cobeha.2015.10.005

Hill, W. L., & Jones, G. R. (1996). *Administración estratégica: un enfoque integrado* (3rd ed.). McGrawHill.

Hinterhuber, H. H. (1994). The European way to lean management. *The International Executive*, *36*(3), 275–290. doi:10.1002/tie.5060360303

Compilation of References

Hitt, M. A., Ireland, R. D., Camp, S. M., & Sexton, D. L. (2001). Strategic entrepreneurship: Entrepreneurial strategies for wealth creation. *Strategic Management Journal*, *22*(6–7), 479–491. doi:10.1002mj.196

Hoang, L. T. P., & Pham, H. T. T. (2016). An Analysis of Vietnamese Footwear Manufacturers' Participation in the Global Value Chain Where They Are and Where They Should Proceed? *VNU Journal of Science: Economics and Business, 32*(5E). https://js.vnu.edu.vn/EAB/article/view/4063

Hockerts, K. (2017). Determinants of social entrepreneurial intentions. *Entrepreneurship Theory and Practice*, *41*(1), 105–130. doi:10.1111/etap.12171

Hodgson, S., Mansatta, K., Mallett, G., Harris, V., Emary, K. R. W., & Pollard, A. J. (2020). What defines an efficacious COVID19 vaccine? A review of the challenges assessing the clinical efficacy of vaccines against SARS-CoV-2. *The Lancet. Infectious Diseases*, *21*(2), e26–e35. doi:10.1016/S1473-3099(20)30773-8 PMID:33125914

Hoffman, K. D., & Bateson, J. E. G. (2008). Services Marketing. In Acta Theologica (4e ed.). doi:10.4314/actat.v27i2.52312

Holmqvist, M., & Stefansson, G. (2006). 'Smart goods' and mobile RFID a case with innovation from Volvo. *Journal of Business Logistics*, *27*(2), 251–272. doi:10.1002/j.2158-1592.2006.tb00225.x

Hossain, M. (1988). *Credit for alleviation of rural poverty: The Grameen Bank in Bangladesh* (Vol. 65). Intl Food Policy Res Inst.

Hossain, M. M., & Prybutok, V. R. (2008). Consumer acceptance of RFID technology: An exploratory study. *IEEE Transactions on Engineering Management*, *55*(2), 316–328. doi:10.1109/TEM.2008.919728

Howell, J. (2007). Civil Society In China: Chipping away at the edges. *Development*, *50*(3), 17–23. doi:10.1057/palgrave.development.1100416

Hristov, J. (2020). Pro-capitalist violence and globalization Lessons from Latin America. In The Routledge Handbook of Transformative Global Studies. Routledge.

Hsiao, Y.-C. (2021). (in press). Impacts of course type and student gender on distance learning performance: A case study in Taiwan. *Education and Information Technologies*. Advance online publication. doi:10.100710639-021-10538-8 PMID:33867809

Huanacuni, F. (2010). *Vivir Bien / Buen Vivir: Filosofía, políticas, estrategias y experiencias regionales*. Instituto Internacional de Integración. Retrieved from https://www.escr-net.org/sites/default/files/Libro%20Buen%20Vivir%20y%20Vivir%20Bien_0.pdf

Huang, J., Kumar, S., & Hu, C. (2018). Gender differences in motivations for identity reconstruction on social network sites. *International Journal of Human-Computer Interaction*, *34*(7), 591–602. doi:10.1080/10447318.2017.1383061

Hubbard, E. (2017). 7.9 Improving Decision-making. *Career Skills for Surgeons*, 136.

Hughes, J. (1988). The Philosophy of Intellectual Property. *The Georgetown Law Journal*, *77*(2), 287–366. https://heinonline.org/HOL/P?h=hein.journals/glj77&i=309

Hühn, M. P. (2014). You reap what you sow: How MBA programs undermine ethics. *Journal of Business Ethics*, *121*(4), 527–541. doi:10.100710551-013-1733-z

Humpbrey, C., & Hugb Jones, S. (1998). *Trueque intercambio y valor: Aproximaciones Antropológicas*. Abya - Yala.

Humphrey, J., & Schmitz, H. (2002). How does insertion in global value chains affect upgrading in industrial clusters? *Regional Studies*, *36*(9), 1017–1027. doi:10.1080/0034340022000022198

Hupkau, C. (2021). In brief... Losses in lockdown: jobs, income, education and mental health. *CentrePiece - The Magazine for Economic Performance, 598.*

Hutasuhut, S., Irwansyah, I., Rahmadsyah, A., & Aditia, R. (2020). Impact of Business Models Canvas Learning on improving learning achievement and entrepreneurial intention. *Jurnal Cakrawala Pendidikan, 39*(1), 168–182. doi:10.21831/cp.v39i1.28308

Iacovou, C. L., Benbasat, I., & Dexter, A. S. (1995). Electronic data interchange and small organizations: Adoption and impact of technology. *Management Information Systems Quarterly, 19*(4), 465–485. doi:10.2307/249629

Ibarra-Nava, I., Cardenas-de la Garza, J. A., Ruiz-Lozano, R. E., & Salazar-Montalvo, R. G. (2020). Mexico and the COVID-19 Response. *Disaster Medicine and Public Health Preparedness, 1–2*(4), e17–e18. Advance online publication. doi:10.1017/dmp.2020.260 PMID:32713412

ILO. (2021). *COVID-19 and the World of Work.* https://www.ilo.org/global/topics/coronavirus/lang--en/index.htm

INEC. (2019). Retrieved from documentos/web-inec/POBREZA/2018/Diciembre-2018/201812_Pobreza.pdf

INEGI. (2020). *Encuesta sobre el Impacto Económico Generado por COVID-19 en las Empresas 2020 (ECOVID-IE): Síntesis metodológica.* Instituto Nacional de Estadística y Geografía.

INEGI. (2020). *Resultados de la Encuesta Nacional sobre disponibilidad y uso de tecnologías de la Información de los Hogares 2019.* Press Release, 103/20, INEGI.

INEGI. (2021). *Encuesta Nacional de Ocupación y Empleo.* INEGI.

INEGI. (2021). *Gross Domestic Product per Economic Activity.* https://www.inegi.org.mx/temas/pib/

Instituto Federal de Telecomunicaciones. (2019). *Acuerdo mediante el cual la Procuraduría Federal del Consumidor y el Instituto Federal de Telecomunicaciones, determinan los derechos mínimos que deben incluirse en la carta a que hace referencia el artículo 191 de la Ley Federal de Telecomunicaciones y Radiodifusión.* Instituto Federal de Telecomunicaciones. http://www.ift.org.mx

International Cooperative Alliance. (2019). *Datos y cifras.* Retrieved from https://www.ica.coop/es/cooperativas/datos-y-cifras

International Labour Organisation. (2019). *Work for a Brighter Future: global Comission on the future of work.* Genova: International Labour Office. Retrieved from https://www.ilo.org/wcmsp5/groups/public/---dgreports/---cabinet/documents/publication/wcms_662410.pdf

Irwin, D. (2005). *Free Trade under Fire.* Princeton University Press.

ISSE. (2019). *Rendición de Cuentas IEPS.* Retrieved from https://www.economiasolidaria.gob.ec/rendicion-de-cuentas-ieps/

Itakura, K. (2020). Evaluating the impact of the US–China trade war. *Asian Economic Policy Review, 15*(1), 77–93. doi:10.1111/aepr.12286

Ivanov, D., & Dolgui, A. (2019). Low-certainty-need (LCN) supply chains: A new perspective in managing disruption risks and resilience. *International Journal of Production Research, 57*(15–16), 5119–5136. doi:10.1080/00207543.2018.1521025

Jackson, T. (1993). *Clean Production Strategies Developing Preventive Environmental Management in the Industrial Economy.* CRC Press.

Compilation of References

Jácome, H. (2019). *Seminario Internacional Desafíos de la Economía Solidaria y Comunitaria: Acercamientos conceptuales desde las experiencias* (J. Ordóñez, Interviewer). Retrieved from https://grupoess2.wixsite.com/ecosolidariaycomuni

Jácome, V. (2019). *Seminario Internacional Desafíos de la Economía Solidaria y Comunitaria: Acercamientos conceptuales desde las experiencias* (J. Ordóñez, Interviewer). Retrieved from https://grupoess2.wixsite.com/ecosolidariaycomuni

Jarillo, C. (1992). *Dirección Estratégica*. McGraw-Hill.

Jayadi, A., & Aziz, H. A. (2017). Comparative advantage analysis and products mapping of Indonesia, Malaysia, Philippines, Singapore, Thailand and Vietnam export products. *Journal of Development Economics*, *2*(1), 12–27.

Je˙zewska-Zychowicz, M., Plichta, M., & Królak, M. (2020). Consumers' Fears Regarding Food Availability and Purchasing Behaviors during the COVID-19 Pandemic: The Importance of Trust and Perceived Stress. *Nutrients*, *12*(9), 2852. doi:10.3390/nu12092852 PMID:32957585

Jeffrey Group. (2020). *El camino digital después del Covid19*. Jeffrey Group.

Jenkins, R. (2004). Globalization, production, employment, and poverty: Debates and evidence. *Journal of International Development*, *16*(1), 1–12. doi:10.1002/jid.1059

Jennings, M., Munuera, L., & Tong, D. (2011). *An Assessment of China's 2020 Carbon Intensity Target*. Grantham Institute for Climate Change Report GR1.

Jewell, P., Reading, J., Clarke, M., & Kippist, L. (2020). Information skills for business acumen and employability: A competitive advantage for graduates in Western Sydney. *Journal of Education for Business*, *95*(2), 88–105. doi:10.1080/08832323.2019.1610346

Jeyaraj, A., Rottman, J. W., & Lacity, M. C. (2006). A review of the predictors, linkages, and biases in IT innovation adoption research. *Journal of Information Technology*, *21*(1), 1–23. doi:10.1057/palgrave.jit.2000056

Jiang, J., & Luo, Z. (2021). Leadership Styles and Political Survival of Chinese Communist Party Elites. *The Journal of Politics*, *83*(2), 777–782. doi:10.1086/710144

Jiménez, J. (2016). *Avances y Desafíos de la Economía Popular y Solidaria en el Ecuador. Economía Popular y Solidaria: conceptos, prácticas y políticas públicas*. UPV-Hegoa.

Jiménez, J. C. (2009). Etapas del desarrollo de la economía mundial. In *Lecciones sobre Economía Mundial* (pp. 47–67). Aranzadi.

Jin, H., Lin, Z., & McLeay, F. (2020). Negative emotions, positive actions: Food safety and consumer intentions to purchase ethical food in China. *Food Quality and Preference*, *85*, 103981. doi:10.1016/j.foodqual.2020.103981

Jo, W., Kim, J., & Choi, J. (2018). *Who are the multichannel shoppers, and how can retailers use them? Evidence from the French apparel industry*. Emerald Insight.

Johnson, G., & Scholes, K. (1997). *Dirección Estratégica: Análisis de la estrategia de las organizaciones*. Prentice Hall.

Johnson, M. W., Christensen, C. M., & Kagermann, H. (2008). Reinventing your business model. *Harvard Business Review*, *86*(12), 57–68.

Jokisch, B. (2001). Desde Nueva York a Madrid. *Ecuador Debate*, *54*, 59–79.

Joyce, A., & Paquin, R. L. (2016). The triple layered business model canvas: A tool to design more sustainable business models. *Journal of Cleaner Production*, *135*, 1474–1486. doi:10.1016/j.jclepro.2016.06.067

Jun, J. (2020, October 25). Hottest Online Education Startups in China. *Pandaily*. https://pandaily.com/7-hottest-online-education-startups-in-china/

Jun, M., & Cal, S. (2003). Key Obstacles to EDI Success: From the US Small Manufacturing Companies' Perspective. *Industrial Management & Data Systems*, *103*(3), 192–203. doi:10.1108/02635570310465670

Kabir, A., Miah, S., & Islam, A. (2018). Factors influencing eating behavior and dietary intake among resident students in a public university in Bangladesh: A qualitative study. *PLoS One*, *13*(6), e0198801. Advance online publication. doi:10.1371/journal.pone.0198801 PMID:29920535

Kalantaridis, C. (2006). A study into the localization of rural businesses in five European countries. *European Planning Studies*, *14*(1), 61–78. doi:10.1080/09654310500339133

Kapferer, J. N. (2004). *The New Strategic Brand Management: Creating and Sustaining Brand Equity Long Term* (3rd ed.). Kogan Page.

Kaplan, R. S., & Norton, D. P. (2005). The balanced scorecard: Measures that drive performance. *Harvard Business Review*, *83*(7), 172. PMID:10119714

Kaplinsky, R. (2000). Globalization and unequalisation: What can be learned from value chain analysis? *The Journal of Development Studies*, *37*(2), 117–146. doi:10.1080/713600071

Karnes, F. A., Deason, D. M., & D'Ilio, V. (1993). Leadership Skills and Self-Actualization of School-Age Children1. *Psychological Reports*, *73*(3_part_1), 861–862. doi:10.1177/00332941930733pt122

Kasper, W. (2015). *Libertad Económica y Desarrollo*. Universidad Francisco Marroquin.

Katare, B., Marshall, M. I., & Valdivia, C. B. (2021). Bend or break? Small business survival and strategies during the COVID-19 shock. *International Journal of Disaster Risk Reduction*, *61*, 102332. doi:10.1016/j.ijdrr.2021.102332

Kates, A., & Galbraith, J. R. (2010). *Designing your organization: Using the STAR model to solve 5 critical design challenges*. John Wiley & Sons.

Katz, D., & Kahn, R. L. (1978). *The social psychology of organizations* (Vol. 2). Wiley New York.

Kaufmann, M. (2019). Big data management canvas: A reference model for value creation from data. *Big Data and Cognitive Computing*, *3*(1), 19. doi:10.3390/bdcc3010019

Keller, K. L. (1993). Conceptualizing, Measuring, Managing Customer-Based Brand Equity. *Journal of Marketing*, *57*(1), 1–22. doi:10.1177/002224299305700101

Keller, K. L., & Lehmann, D. R. (2006). Brands and Branding: Research Findings and Future Priorities. *Marketing Science*, *25*(6), 740–759. doi:10.1287/mksc.1050.0153

Kerin, R. A., & Sethuraman, R. (1998). Exploring the Brand Value – Shareholder Value Nexus for Customer Goods Companies. *Journal of the Academy of Marketing Science*, *26*(14), 260–273. doi:10.1177/0092070398264001

Ketchen, D. J. Jr, & Craighead, C. W. (2020). Research at the Intersection of Entrepreneurship, Supply Chain Management, and Strategic Management: Opportunities Highlighted by COVID-19. *Journal of Management*, *46*(8), 1330–1341. doi:10.1177/0149206320945028

Khalek, A. A. (2014). Young consumers' attitude towards halal food outlets and JAKIM's halal certification in Malaysia. *Procedia: Social and Behavioral Sciences*, *121*, 26–34. doi:10.1016/j.sbspro.2014.01.1105

Khurana, R. (2007). *From Higher Aims to Hired Hands*. Princeton University Press. doi:10.1515/9781400830862

Compilation of References

Kieser, A. (2011). Between rigour and relevance: Co-existing institutional logics in the field of management science. *Society and Economy, 33*(2), 237–247. doi:10.1556/SocEc.33.2011.2.1

Kim, D., & Lim, U. (2017). SE as a Catalyst for Sustainable Local and Regional Development. *Sustainability, 9*(8), 1427. doi:10.3390u9081427

Kim, S., & Garrison, G. (2010). Understanding users' behaviors regarding supply chain technology: Determinants impacting the adoption and implementation of RFID technology in South Korea. *International Journal of Information Management, 30*(5), 388–398. doi:10.1016/j.ijinfomgt.2010.02.008

Kim, Y., & Han, H. (2010). Intention to pay conventional-hotel prices at a green hotel – a modification of the theory of planned behavior. *Journal of Sustainable Tourism, 18*(8), 1014–1037. doi:10.1080/09669582.2010.490300

Kitchell, S. (1997). CEO characteristics and technological innovativeness: A Canadian perspective. *Canadian Journal of Administrative Sciences/Revue Canadienne des Sciences de l'Administration, 14*(2), 111–121, DOI: doi:10.1111/j.1936-4490.1997.tb00123

Klein, M. (2015). *Foreign Direct Investment and Intellectual Property Protection in Developing Countries*. Center for Applied Economics and Policy Research (CAEPR) Working Paper, 018.

Kobb, J. (2020, March 3). Living beyond the moment. *China Daily.* https://www.chinadaily.com.cn/a/202003/18/WS5e716450a31012821727fe1e.html

Komolov, O. (2020). Deglobalization and the "Great Stagnation". *International Critical Thought, 10*(3), 424–439. doi:10.1080/21598282.2020.1846582

Komulainen, H., & Saraniemi, S. (2019). Customer centricity in mobile banking: A customer experience perspective. *International Journal of Bank Marketing, 37*(5), 1082–1102. doi:10.1108/IJBM-11-2017-0245

Kong, L. Q., & Feng, Y. (2017). Development Difficulties and Transformation of Paths of Entrepreneurship Education for College and University Students in the Period of New Normal. *Education and Vocation, 15*, 66–71.

Korovkin, T. (2002). *Comunidades Indígenas, Economía del mercado y democracia en los Andes Ecuatorianos*. Abya-Yala.

Koskela, L. (2017). Why is management research irrelevant? *Construction Management and Economics, 35*(1-2), 4–23. doi:10.1080/01446193.2016.1272759

Kotler, P. (2012). *Kotler on Marketing*. Simon and Schuster.

Kotler, P., Kartajaya, H., & Setiawan, I. (2021). *Marketing 5.0: Technology for Humanity*. Wiley.

Kowii, A. (2014). El Sumak Kawsay. In *Antología del Pensamiento Indigensita Ecuatoriano* (p. 168). CIM.

Kowitlawakul, Y., Chan, M. F., Tan, S. S. L., Soong, A. S. K., & Chan, S. W. C. (2017). Development of an e-learning research module using multimedia instruction approach. *CIN: Computers, Informatics. Nursing, 35*(3), 158–166. PMID:27811511

Koziej, S. (2020, May 5). *The U.S. and China: The rivalry escalates irrelevance*. Geopolitical Intelligence Services GIS. https://www.gisreportsonline.com/the-us-and-china-the-rivalry-escalates,defense,3155,report.html

Krasnova, H., Weser, L., & Ivantysynova, L. (2008). Drivers of RFID adoption in the automotive industry. AMCIS 2008 Proceedings, 287.

Krishnamurthy, S. (2020). The future of business education: A commentary in the shadow of the COVID-19 pandemic. *Journal of Business Research, 117*(1), 1–54. doi:10.1016/j.jbusres.2020.05.034 PMID:32501309

Krueger, R., & Casey, M. (2014). *Focus groups: A practical guide for applied research*. Sage publications.

Kuo, S., Ou, H.-T., & Wang, C. J. (2021). Managing medication supply chains: Lessons learned from Taiwan during the COVID-19 pandemic and preparedness planning for the future. *Journal of the American Pharmacists Association*, *61*(1), e12–e15. doi:10.1016/j.japh.2020.08.029 PMID:32919923

Kuratko, D. F., & Audretsch, D. B. (2009). Strategic Entrepreneurship: Exploring Different Perspectives of an Emerging Concept. *Entrepreneurship Theory and Practice*, *33*(1), 1–17. doi:10.1111/j.1540-6520.2008.00278.x

Kuznar, L. A. (2021). A tale of two pandemics: Evolutionary psychology, urbanism, and the biology of disease spread deepen sociopolitical divides in the U.S. *Humanities and Social Sciences Communications*, *8*(1), 42. doi:10.105741599-021-00719-8

Kwilinski, A. (2019). A mechanism for assessing the competitiveness of an industrial enterprise in the information economy. *Research Papers in Economics and Finance*, *3*(1), 7–16. doi:10.18559/ref.2018.1.1

Kwong, K. K., Yau, O. H. M., Lee, J. S. Y., Sin, L. Y. M., & Tse, A. C. B. (2003a). The Effects of Attitudinal and Demographic Factors on Intention to Buy Pirated CDs: The Case of Chinese Consumers. *Journal of Business Ethics*, *47*(3), 223–235. doi:10.1023/A:1026269003472

Lake, D. A. (2018). Economic Openness and Great Power Competition: Lessons for China and the United States. *The Chinese Journal of International Politics*, *11*(3), 237–270. doi:10.1093/cjip/poy010

Lakhal, L., Pasin, F., & Limam, M. (2006). Quality management practices and their impact on performance. *International Journal of Quality & Reliability Management*, *23*(6), 625–646. doi:10.1108/02656710610672461

Lakshika, V., & Ahzan, M. (2021). Decision-making Styles of Sri Lankan Millennial: Are They Different? *Sri Lanka Journal of Marketing*, *7*(1), 46. doi:10.4038ljmuok.v7i1.56

Lam, A. (2006). Organizational innovation. In J. Fagerberg, D. C. Mowery, & R. R. Nelson (Eds.), *The Oxford Handbook of Innovation* (pp. 115–147). Oxford University Press.

Lanas, E. (2014). Políticas Públicas sobre Economía Solidaria en Ecuador. *Boletín Informativo Spondylu*, 1-24.

Lanas, E. (2010). El trueque, una forma de economía solidaria en Pimampiro. *Sarence.*, *26*, 13–28.

Lascurain, M. (2017). Challenges of economic globalization. *Revista de Relaciones Internacionales y de Estrategia de Seguridad*, *12*(1), 23–50.

Lascurain, M., & Villafuerte, L. F. (2016). Primera globalización económica y las raíces de la inequidad social en México. *Ensayos de Economía*, *26*(48), 67–90. doi:10.15446/ede.v26n48.59858

Lau, W. K., Li, Z., & Okpara, J. (2020). An examination of three-way interactions of paternalistic leadership in China. *Asia Pacific Business Review*, *26*(1), 32–49. doi:10.1080/13602381.2019.1674031

Laval, C., & Dardot, P. (2017). *La pesadilla que no acaba nunca*. Gedisa.

Lee, G., Benoit-Bryan, J., & Johnson, T. P. (2012). Survey Research in Public Administration: Assessing Mainstream Journals with a Total Survey Error Framework. Public Administration Review, 72(1).

Lee, K., Song, J., & Kwak, J. (2015). An Exploratory Study on the Transition from OEM to OBM: Case Studies of SMEs in Korea. *Industry and Innovation*. https://www.tandfonline.com/doi/pdf/10.1080/13662716.2015.1064257?needAccess=true

Lee, B., & Cassell, C. (Eds.). (2011). *Challenges and controversies in management research* (Vol. 45). Routledge. doi:10.4324/9780203834114

Lee, L. S., Fiedler, K. D., & Smith, J. S. (2008). Radio frequency identification (RFID) implementation in the service sector: A customer-facing diffusion model. *International Journal of Production Economics*, *112*(2), 587–600. doi:10.1016/j.ijpe.2007.05.008

Lee, R. (2009). The Emergence of SEs in China. *The Quest for Space and Legitimacy.*, *2*, 21.

Lee, S. M., Olson, D. L., & Trimi, S. (2012). Co-innovation: Convergenomics, collaboration, and co-creation for organizational values. *Management Decision*, *50*(5), 817–831. doi:10.1108/00251741211227528

Le, F., Olivier, B., & Mognol, J. H. (2013). Sustainable manufacturing: Evaluation and modeling of environmental impacts in additive manufacturing. *International Journal of Advanced Manufacturing Technology*, *69*(9-12), 1927–1939. doi:10.100700170-013-5151-2

Leggett, A. (2020). Bringing green food to the Chinese table: How civil society actors are changing consumer culture in China. *Journal of Consumer Culture*, *20*(1), 83–101. doi:10.1177/1469540517729009

Lemes, A., & Machado, T. (2007). *SMEs and Their Space in the Latin American Economy*. https://www.eumed.net/eve/resum/07-enero/alb.htm

Leone, R. P., Rao, V. R., Keller, K. L., Luo, A. M., McAlister, L., & Srivastava, R. (2006). Linking Brand Equity to Customer Equity. *Journal of Service Research*, *9*(2), 125–138. doi:10.1177/1094670506293563

Leonidou, C. N., & Leonidou, L. C. (2011). Research into environmental marketing/management: A bibliographic analysis. *European Journal of Marketing*, *45*(1-2), 68–103. doi:10.1108/03090561111095603

Lesser, R., & Reeves, M. (2020). *5 Priorities for Leaders in the New Reality of COVID-19*. World Economic Forum. https://www.weforum.org/agenda/2020/05/5-things-leaders-succeed-new-reality- coronavirus/

Leung, A. S. (2003). Feminism in transition: Chinese culture, ideology and the development of the women's movement in China. *Asia Pacific Journal of Management*, *20*(3), 359–374. doi:10.1023/A:1024049516797

Leung, Z. C., Ho, A. P., Tjia, L. Y., Tam, R. K., Chan, K., & Lai, M. K. (2019). Social Impacts of Work Integration SE in Hong Kong–Workfare and Beyond. *Journal of Social Entrepreneurship*, *10*(2), 159–176. doi:10.1080/19420676.2018.1541007

Levin, M., & Liu, Y. (2021). Teaching RA theory to develop future business practitioners' decision-making skills. *Journal of Marketing Theory and Practice*, 1–13. doi:10.1080/10696679.2021.1901593

Li, C. (2011). *A customized lean model for a Chinese aerospace OEM (Original Equipment Manufacturer)*. https://dspace.lib.cranfield.ac.uk/handle/1826/5716

Li, F. (2020). The digital transformation of business models in the creative industries: A holistic framework and emerging trends. *Technovation*, *92*, 102012. doi:10.1016/j.technovation.2017.12.004

Li, J., Zhang, D., & Su, B. (2019). The Impact of Social Awareness and Lifestyles on Household Carbon Emissions in China. *Ecological Economics*, *160*, 145–155. doi:10.1016/j.ecolecon.2019.02.020

Li, L. (2018). China's manufacturing locus in 2025: With a comparison of "Made-in-China 2025" and "Industry 4.0.". *Technological Forecasting and Social Change*, *135*, 66–74. doi:10.1016/j.techfore.2017.05.028

Li, L., & Benton, W. C. (2006). Hospital technology and nurse staffing management decisions. *Journal of Operations Management*, *24*(5), 676–691. doi:10.1016/j.jom.2005.06.001

Lilien, G. L., Kotler, P., & Sridhar Moorthy, K. (1992). Marketing Models. Englewood Cliffs, NJ: Prentice-Hall, Inc.

Lim, H.-R., & An, S. (2021). Intention to purchase wellbeing food among Korean consumers: An application of the Theory of Planned Behavior. *Food Quality and Preference*, *88*, 104101. doi:10.1016/j.foodqual.2020.104101 PMID:33071469

Lin, B.-W. (2004). Original equipment manufacturers (OEM) manufacturing strategy for network innovation agility: The case of Taiwanese manufacturing networks. *International Journal of Production Research*, *42*(5), 943–957. doi:10.1080/00207540310001622449

Lindblom, A., & Lindblom, T. (2018). Applying the Extended Theory of Planned Behavior to Predict Collaborative Consumption Intentions. In A. Smedlund, A. Lindblom, & L. Mitronen (Eds.), *Collaborative Value Co-creation in the Platform Economy. Translational Systems Sciences, 11*. Springer. doi:10.1007/978-981-10-8956-5_9

Lin, S., Cai, S., Sun, J., Wang, S., & Zhao, D. (2019). Influencing mechanism and achievement of manufacturing transformation and upgrading. *Journal of Manufacturing Technology Management*, *30*(1), 213–232. doi:10.1108/JMTM-05-2018-0126

Lin, X., Featherman, M., Brooks, S. L., & Hajli, N. (2019). Exploring Gender Differences in Online Consumer Purchase Decision-making: An Online Product Presentation Perspective. *Information Systems Frontiers*, *21*(5), 1187–1201. doi:10.100710796-018-9831-1

Li, R. (2020). Reinvent Retail Supply Chain: Ship-from-Store-to-Store. *Production and Operations Management*, *29*(8), 1825–1836. doi:10.1111/poms.13195

Lissardy, G. (2020). *Coronavirus: los 2 grandes escenarios mundiales que plantean algunos expertos para después de la pandemia*. BBC News/Mundo. https://www.bbc.com/mundo/noticias-internacional-52526090

Lissitsa, S., & Laor, T. (2021). Baby Boomers, Generation X and Generation Y: Identifying generational differences in effects of personality traits in on-demand radio use. *Technology in Society*, *64*, 101526. doi:10.1016/j.techsoc.2021.101526

Liu, A.-J., Li, J., & Gómez, M. I. (2020). Factors Influencing Consumption of Edible Insects for Chinese Consumers. *Insects*, *11*(1), 10. doi:10.3390/insects11010010 PMID:31861955

Logue, A. W. (2002, May). The living legacy of the Harvard Pigeon Lab: Quantitative analysis in the wide world. *Journal of the Experimental Analysis of Behavior*, *77*(3), 357–366. doi:10.1901/jeab.2002.77-357 PMID:12083687

Loo, R. (2000a). A psychometric evaluation of the general decision-making style inventory. *Personality and Individual Differences*, *29*(1), 895–905. doi:10.1016/S0191-8869(99)00241-X

López-Hernández, A. M., & López, M. (2019). Estudio omnicanal de las empresas minorista del sector cosmético en España. *Red Marka - Revista de Marketing Aplicado*, *23*(2), 19–41.

López, I. I. A., Ocampo, G. D., & Pérez–Uribe, R. (2013). *Model of Modernization for organizational Management (MMOM)*. Ediciones EAN., doi:10.13140/2.1.3437.4727

Lorenzo-Romero, C., Andrés-Martínez, M. E., & Mondéjar-Jiménez, J. A. (2020). Omnichannel in the fashion industry: A qualitative analysis from a supply-side perspective. *Heliyon*, *6*(6), e04198. Advance online publication. doi:10.1016/j.heliyon.2020.e04198 PMID:32577571

Louie, G. H., & Ward, M. M. (2010). Sex disparities in self-reported physical functioning: True differences, reporting bias, or incomplete adjustment for confounding? *Journal of the American Geriatrics Society*, *58*(6), 1117–1122. doi:10.1111/j.1532-5415.2010.02858.x PMID:20487076

Compilation of References

Louviere, J. J., Hensher, D. A., & Swait, J. D. (2000). *Stated Choice Methods: Analysis and Applications.* Cambridge University Press. doi:10.1017/CBO9780511753831

Lovell, J. (2012a). Finding a Place: Mainland Chinese Fiction in the 2000s. *The Journal of Asian Studies, 71*(1), 7–32. https://search.proquest.com/abicomplete/docview/921635142/abstract/A090375A55904FE6PQ/1

Lovell, J. (2012b). Finding a Place: Mainland Chinese Fiction in the 2000s. *The Journal of Asian Studies, 71*(1), 7–32.

Lozano, L. J., Perez-Uribe, R., & Ocampo-Guzmán, D. (2015). *MIIGO (Modelo de intervención e innovación de la gestión organizacional): Intervención e innovación de la cultura organizacional.* Universidad EAN.

Luce, R. D., & Tukey, J. W. (1964, January). Simultaneous conjoint measurement: A new type of fundamental measurement. *Journal of Mathematical Psychology, 1*(1), 1–27. doi:10.1016/0022-2496(64)90015-X

Luger, J., Raisch, S., & Schimmer, M. (2018). Dynamic balancing of exploration and exploitation: The contingent benefits of ambidexterity. *Organization Science, 29*(3), 449–470. doi:10.1287/orsc.2017.1189

Lugg, A. (2011a). Chinese online fiction: Taste publics, entertainment, and Candle in the Tomb. *Chinese Journal of Communication, 4*(2), 121–136. doi:10.1080/17544750.2011.565673

Luque, A., Ordóñez, J., & Ruales, V. (2017) La Responsabilidad Social en las Asociaciones de la Economía Popular y Solidaria. *II Congreso Internacional sobre Ciencia, Sociedad e Investigación Universitaria PUCE.* Retrieved from http://repositorio.pucesa.edu.ec/ handle/123456789/2223A

Luque, A. (2017). Promotion of transnational textile hyper-consumption: Fashion and excess as leitmotif. *Revista Chasqui, 134,* 83–104.

Luque, A. (2018). Corruption in the transnational textile industry: An exception or the rule? *Empresa y Humanismo, 21*(2), 123–184.

Luque, A. (2019). Gestión del conocimiento y su impacto en la economía mundial en el marco de una sociedad globalizada. *Revista Veritas and Research, 1*(1), 54–63.

Luque, A., & Casado, F. (2020). Public Strategy and Eco-Social Engagement in Latin American States: An Analysis of Complex Networks Arising from Their Constitutions. *Journal Sustainability, 12*(20), 1–29. doi:10.3390u12208558

Luque, A., & Herrero García, N. (2019). How corporate social (ir)responsibility in the textile sector is defined, and its impact on ethical sustainability: An analysis of 133 concepts. *Corporate Social Responsibility and Environmental Management, 26*(6), 1–22. doi:10.1002/csr.1747

Luque, A., Maniglio, F., Casado, F., & García-Guerrero, J. (2020). Transmedia Context and Twitter as Conditioning the Ecuadorian Government's Action. The Case of the Guayaquil Emergency, during the COVID19 Pandemic. *Tripodos, 2*(47), 47–68. doi:10.51698/tripodos.2020.47p47-68

Luque, A., Ortega, T., & Carretero, P. A. (2019). La Justicia indígena en la comunidad de Tuntatacto (Ecuador): Moral o derecho'. *Revista Prisma Social, 27,* 1–19.

Lynch, S., & Barnes, L. (2020). Omnichannel fashion retailing: Examining the customer decision-making journey. *Journal of Fashion Marketing and Management, 24*(3), 471–493. doi:10.1108/JFMM-09-2019-0192

Lysonski, S., & Durvasula, S. (2013). Consumer decision-making styles in retailing: Evolution of mindsets and psychological impacts. *Journal of Consumer Marketing, 30*(1), 75–87. doi:10.1108/07363761311290858

MacCann, C., Jiang, Y., Brown, L. E. R., Double, K. S., Bucich, M., & Minbashian, A. (2020). Emotional intelligence predicts academic performance: A meta-analysis. *Psychological Bulletin*, *146*(2), 150–186. doi:10.1037/bul0000219 PMID:31829667

Madden, T. J., Fehle, F., & Fournier, S. (2006). Brands Matter: An Empirical Demonstration of the Creation of Shareholder Value Through Branding. *Journal of the Academy of Marketing Science*, *34*(2), 224–235. doi:10.1177/0092070305283356

Madero Gómez, S., Ortiz Mendoza, O. E., Ramírez, J., & Olivas-Luján, M. R. (2020). Stress and myths related to the COVID-19 pandemic's effects on remote work. *Management Research: Journal of the Iberoamerican Academy of Management*. doi:10.1108/MRJIAM-06-2020-1065

Madlberger, M. (2009). A model of antecedents of RFID adoption intention in the supply chain. In *Proceedings of the 42nd Hawaii International Conference on System Sciences*-2009 (pp. 1-10). IEEE.

Madrid, F., & Diaz-Rebolledo, J. (2020). *México: Red de Universidades Anáhuac*. Obtained from Red de Universidades Anáhuac: https://www.anahuac.mx/mexico/cicotur/sites/default/files/2020-03/Doc06_Coronavirus_Turismo_CICOTUR.pdf

Madsen, J. (2001). Trade barriers and the collapse of world trade during the Great Depression. *Southern Economic Journal*, *67*(4), 848–868. doi:10.2307/1061574

Madueny, S., Oluremi, A., Fadeyi, O., & Akintunde, M. (2015). Impact of organization structure on organization performance. *International Conference on African Development Issues (CU-ICADI)*. Retrieved from https://www.researchgate.net/publication/291336611

Magretta, J. (2002). Why business models matter. *Harvard Business Review*. PMID:12024761

Mainardes, E. W., Rosa, C. A. de M., & Nossa, S. N. (2020). Omnichannel strategy and customer loyalty in banking. *International Journal of Bank Marketing*, *38*(4), 799–822. doi:10.1108/IJBM-07-2019-0272

Maital, S., & Barzani, E. (2020). The global economic impact of COVID-19: A summary of research. Samuel Neaman Institute for National Policy Research.

Mak, A. H. N., Lumbers, M., Eves, A., & Chang, R. C. Y. (2012). Factors influencing tourist food consumption. *International Journal of Hospitality Management*, *31*(3), 928–936. doi:10.1016/j.ijhm.2011.10.012

Mak, M. K., & Ip, W. H. (2017). An exploratory study of investment behaviour of investors. *International Journal of Engineering Business Management*, *9*. doi:10.1177/1847979017711520

Man, C. K., & Terence, Y. Y. K. (2011). An overview of SE development in China and Hong Kong. *Journal of Ritsumeikan Social Sciences*, *5*, 165–178.

Manso, C. F. J. (1991). *Curso de dirección estratégica comercial*. ESIC Editorial.

Mao, H., Liu, S., & Zhang, J. (2015). How the effects of IT and knowledge capability on organizational agility are contingent on environmental uncertainty and information intensity. *Information Development*, *31*(4), 358–382. doi:10.1177/0266666913518059

Ma, Q. (2005). *Non-governmental organizations in contemporary China: Paving the way to civil society?* Routledge. doi:10.4324/9780203029367

Marcati, A., Guido, G., & Peluso, A. M. (2008). The role of SME entrepreneurs' innovativeness and personality in the adoption of innovations. *Research Policy*, *37*(9), 1579–1590. doi:10.1016/j.respol.2008.06.004

Compilation of References

Marín-Idárraga, D. A. (2012). Estructura organizacional y sus parámetros de diseño: Análisis descriptivo en pymes industriales de Bogotá. *Estudios Gerenciales*, *28*(123), 43–63. doi:10.1016/S0123-5923(12)70204-8

Marín-Idárraga, D. A., Hurtado González, J. M., & Cabello Medina, C. (2016). The Antecedents of Exploitation-Exploration and Their Relationship with Innovation: A Study of Managers' Cognitive Maps. *Creativity and Innovation Management*, *25*(1), 18–37. doi:10.1111/caim.12139

Marinova, D., & Phillimore, J. (2003). Models of Innovation. In L. V. Shavinina (Ed.), *The International Handbook on Innovation* (pp. 44–53). Elsevier Science Ltd. doi:10.1016/B978-008044198-6/50005-X

Maroo, P. (2016). Need for Deployment of RFID Technology in Indian Hospitals. In *Proceedings - International Conference on Industrial Engineering and Operations Management* (pp. 3427-3431). Academic Press.

Marquis, K. H., Marquis, M. S., & Polich, J. M. (1986). Response bias and reliability in sensitive topic surveys. *Journal of the American Statistical Association*, *81*(394), 381–389. doi:10.1080/01621459.1986.10478282

Marshall, D., McCarthy, L., McGrath, P., & Claudy, M. (2015). Going above and beyond: How sustainability culture and entrepreneurial orientation drive social sustainability supply chain practice adoption. *Supply Chain Management*, *20*(4), 434–454. doi:10.1108/SCM-08-2014-0267

Mart, C. J. (2020). Walmart China. *Evolución de los formatos comerciales hasta la omnicanalidad, 3*, 110–120.

Martínez, A., Romero, L., & Jimenez, M. (2017). La ominicanalidad como medio de homogeneización de la experiencia de compra. In XXIX Congreso de Marketing Aemark 2017 (pp. 1597-1599). Sevilla: ESIC.

Martínez-Ruiz, M. P., & Gómez-Cantó, C. M. (2016). Key External Influences Affecting Consumers' Decisions Regarding Food. *Frontiers in Psychology*, *7*. Advance online publication. doi:10.3389/fpsyg.2016.01618 PMID:27803686

Martin, R. (2007). How successful leaders think. *Harvard Business Review*, *85*(6), 60. PMID:17580648

Martin, R. L. (2009). *The opposable mind: How successful leaders win through integrative thinking*. Harvard Business Press.

Maskus, K. E. (2000). *Intellectual Property Rights in the Global Economy*. Peterson Institute.

Mason, P. (2016). *Poscapitalismo: Hacia un nuevo futuro*. Paidos.

Masters, J. M., Allenby, G. M., LaLonde, B. J., & Maltz, A. (1992). On the adoption of DRP. *Journal of Business Logistics*, *13*(1), 47. doi:10.1108/09574099410805117

Mattison, S. M., MacLaren, N. G., Liu, R., Reynolds, A. Z., Baca, G. D., Mattison, P. M., Zhang, M., Sum, C.-Y., Shenk, M. K., Blumenfield, T., von Rueden, C., & Wander, K. (2021). Gender Differences in Social Networks Based on Prevailing Kinship Norms in the Mosuo of China. *Social Sciences*, *10*(7), 253. doi:10.3390ocsci10070253

May, C., & Sell, S. K. (2006). *Intellectual property rights: A critical history*. Lynne Rienner Publishers Boulder.

McCullagh, M. C., & Rosemberg, M.-A. (2015). Social desirability bias in self-reporting of hearing protector use among farm operators. *The Annals of Occupational Hygiene*, *59*(9), 1200–1207. doi:10.1093/annhyg/mev046 PMID:26209595

McFarlane, D. A. (2017). Osterwalder's business model canvas: Its genesis, features, comparison, benefits. *Westcliff International Journal of Applied Research*, *1*(2), 24–28. doi:10.47670/wuwijar201712DAMC

McGrath, R. G. (2010). Business models: A discovery-driven approach. *Long Range Planning*, *43*(2-3), 247–261. doi:10.1016/j.lrp.2009.07.005

McKeen, C. A. (2005). Gender roles: An examination of the hopes and expectations of the next generation of managers in Canada and China. *Sex Roles*, *52*(7), 533–546. doi:10.100711199-005-3719-5

McMichael, A. J. (2020). *Climate change and human health. Risks and responses*. World Health Organization.

Mcmorris, T. (1999). Cognitive development and the acquisition of decision-making skills. *International Journal of Sport Psychology*.

McMullen, J. S., & Shepherd, D. A. (2006). Entrepreneurial Action and The Role of Uncertainty in The Theory of The Entrepreneur. *Academy of Management Review*, *31*(1), 132–152. doi:10.5465/amr.2006.19379628

Medina, G. (2019). *La Economía Popular y Solidaria en Ecuador: Políticas públicas y prácticas económicas no monetarias y sostenibles en los emprendimientos asociativos* (J. Ordóñez, Interviewer). Academic Press.

Mehta, R. (2020). Gender-based differences in consumer decision-making styles: Implications for marketers. *Decision (Washington, D.C.)*, *47*(3), 319–329.

Mehta, R., Singh, H., Banerjee, A., Bozhuk, S., & Kozlova, N. (2020). Comparative analysis of the consequences of purchasing models transformation within the global digitalization of the economy. *IOP Conference Series. Materials Science and Engineering*, *940*(1), 012071. Advance online publication. doi:10.1088/1757-899X/940/1/012071

Mehta, S., Saxena, T., & Purohit, N. (2020). The New Consumer Behaviour Paradigm amid COVID-19: Permanent or Transient? *Journal of Health Management*, *22*(2), 291–301. doi:10.1177/0972063420940834

Menachemi, N., & Brooks, R. G. (2006). EHR and other IT adoption among physicians: Results of a large-scale state wide analysis. *Journal of Healthcare Information Management*, *20*(3), 79–87. PMID:16903665

Mendes, F. F., Mendes, E., & Salleh, N. (2019). The relationship between personality and decision-making: A Systematic literature review. *Information and Software Technology*, *111*, 50–71. doi:10.1016/j.infsof.2019.03.010

Mertha, A. C. (2018). The Politics of Piracy. In *The Politics of Piracy*. Cornell University Press. https://www.degruyter.com/document/doi/10.7591/9781501728808/html

México, I. A. B. (2020). *Estudio de consumo de medios y dispositivos entre internautas mexicanos. El internauta frente al Covid 19*. IAB Mexico.

Meyer, K. E., Ding, Y., Li, J., & Zhang, H. (2018). Overcoming distrust: How state-owned enterprises adapt their foreign entries to institutional pressures abroad. In *State-Owned Multinationals* (pp. 211–251). Springer. doi:10.1007/978-3-319-51715-5_9

Millar, C., Lockett, M., & Ladd, T. (2018). Disruption: Technology, innovation and society. *Technological Forecasting and Social Change*, *129*, 254–260. doi:10.1016/j.techfore.2017.10.020

Minbashrazgah, M. M., Maleki, F., & Torabi, M. (2017). Green chicken purchase behavior: The moderating role of price transparency. *Management of Environmental Quality*, *28*(6), 902–916. doi:10.1108/MEQ-12-2016-0093

Ministry of Economic and Social Inclusion. (2013). Agenda de la revolución de la economía popular y solidaria 2011-2013. Quito, Ecuador: Author.

Miño, W. (2013). Historia del Cooperativismo en el Ecuador: Serie Historia de la Política Económica del Ecuador. Quito, Ecuador: Government of Ecuador, and Quito, Ecuador: Ministry Coordinator of Economic Policy.

Mintzberg, H. (2004). *Managers, not MBAs: A hard look at the soft practice of managing and management development*. Berrett-Koehler Publishers.

Mintzberg, H., Quinn, J. B., & Ghoshal, S. (1999). *El proceso estratégico*. Prentice Hall.

Mizik, N., & Jacobson, R. (2008). The Financial Value Impact of Perceptual Brand Attributes. *JMR, Journal of Marketing Research*, *45*(1), 15–32. doi:10.1509/jmkr.45.1.15

Mogre, R., Gadh, R., & Chattopadhyay, A. (2009). Using survey data to design a RFID centric service system for hospitals. *Service Science*, *1*(3), 189–206. doi:10.1287erv.1.3.189

Mok, K. H., & Jiang, J. (2017). Massification of higher education: Challenges for admissions and graduate employment in China. In *Managing international connectivity, diversity of learning and changing labour markets* (pp. 219–243). Springer. doi:10.1007/978-981-10-1736-0_13

Montreuil, B. (2011). Toward a Physical Internet: Meeting the global logistics sustainability grand challenge. *Logistics Research*, *3*(2-3), 1–29. doi:10.100712159-011-0045-x

Montreuil, B., Meller, R. D., & Ballot, E. (2010). Towards a Physical Internet: the impact on logistics facilities and material handling systems design and innovation. In K. Gue (Ed.), *Progress in Material Handling Research* (pp. 1–23). Material Handling Industry of America.

Morales, Y. R., Villasmil, J. J., & Martínez, R. D. (2019). Democracia a la palestra: ¿Gobierno del pueblo o degeneración del poder? *Revista de Ciencias Sociales*, *25*, 236–252.

Morgan, D. (1997). *The focus group guidebook* (Vol. 1). Sage.

Morrell, E., Sorensen, J., & Howarth, J. (2015). The Charlotte Action Research Project: A Model for Direct and Mutually Beneficial Community–University Engagement. *Journal of Higher Education Outreach & Engagement*, *19*(1), 105.

Mossbrucker, H. (1990). *La Economía Campesina y el concepto "Comunidad" Un enfoque critico*. Instituto de Altos Estudios Peruanos.

Muff, K. (2013). Developing globally responsible leaders in business schools: A vision and transformational practice for the journey ahead. *Journal of Management Development*, *32*(5), 487–507. doi:10.1108/02621711311328273

Muijs, D., West, M., & Mel, A. (2010). Why network? Theoretical perspectives on networking. *School Effectiveness and School Improvement*, *21*(1), 5–26. doi:10.1080/09243450903569692

Munerah, S., Koay, K. Y., & Thambiah, S. (2021). Factors influencing non-green consumers' purchase intention: A partial least squares structural equation modelling (PLS-SEM) approach. *Journal of Cleaner Production*, *280*, 124192. doi:10.1016/j.jclepro.2020.124192

Murphy, B., Benson, T., McCloat, A., Mooney, E., Elliott, C., Dean, M., & Lavelle, F. (2021). Changes in Consumers' Food Practices during the COVID-19 Lockdown, Implications for Diet Quality and the Food System: A Cross-Continental Comparison. *Nutrients*, *13*(1), 20. doi:10.3390/nu13010020 PMID:33374619

Musaiger, A. O. (1993). Socio-Cultural and Economic Factors Affecting Food Consumption Patterns in the Arab Countries. *Journal of the Royal Society of Health*, *113*(2), 68–74. doi:10.1177/146642409311300205 PMID:8478894

Muttakin, M. B., & Khan, A. (2014). Determinants of corporate social disclosure: Empirical evidence from Bangladesh. *Advances in Accounting*, *30*(1), 168–175. doi:10.1016/j.adiac.2014.03.005

Myles, A. (2018). The world's newest economic superpower? *Company Director*, *34*(4), 46–47.

Myllylahti, M. (2018). An attention economy trap? An empirical investigation into four news companies' Facebook traffic and social media revenue. *Journal of Media Business Studies*, *15*(4), 237–253. doi:10.1080/16522354.2018.1527521

Naggar, R. (2015). The creativity canvas: A business model for knowledge and idea management. *Technology Innovation Management Review*, 5(7), 50–58. doi:10.22215/timreview/914

Nair, S. R., & Maram, H. K. (2014). Consumer Behavior in Choice of Food and Branding. *The Future of Entrepreneurship*, 7th Annual Conference of the EuroMed Academy of Business.

Nair, S.R., & Shams, R.S.M. (2020). Impact of store-attributes on food and grocery shopping behavior: insights from an emerging market context. *EuroMed Journal of Business, 16*(3), 324-343. doi:10.1108/EMJB-10-2019-0128 doi:10.1108/EMJB-10-2019-0128

Nair, S. R. (2018a). Analyzing the relationship between store attributes, satisfaction, patronage-intention and lifestyle in food and grocery store choice behavior. *International Journal of Retail & Distribution Management, 46*(1), 70–89. doi:10.1108/IJRDM-06-2016-0102

Nair, S. R. (2018b). Consumption dynamics and demographics effect on food and grocery shopping behaviour. *IIMS Journal of Management Science, 9*(2), 137–154. doi:10.5958/0976-173X.2018.00013.1

Najera, P., Lopez, J., & Roman, R. (2011). Real-time location and inpatient care systems based on passive RFID. *Journal of Network and Computer Applications, 34*(3), 980–989. doi:10.1016/j.jnca.2010.04.011 PMID:34170999

Namkung, Y., & Jang, S. (2007). Does Food Quality Really Matter in Restaurants? Its Impact on Customer Satisfaction and Behavioral Intentions. *Journal of Hospitality & Tourism Research (Washington, D.C.), 31*(3), 387–409. doi:10.1177/1096348007299924

Naranjo, C. (2016). *La economía Popular y solidaria en la legislación ecuatoriana. Serie Estudios sobre Economía Popular y Solidaria: Economía Solidaria Historias y prácticas de su fortalecimiento*. Publiasesores.

Navarro, M. & Sabalza, X. (2016) Reflexiones sobre la Industria 4.0 desde el caso vasco. *Ekonomiaz. Revista vasca de Economía, 89*, 142-173.

Navarro, I. (2021). *Las instituciones de competencia en México ante el COVID-19 y la recuperación económica. Documentos de Proyectos, 46662*. UN-CEPAL.

Needham, J. (2013). *Disruptive Possibilities: How big data changes everything*. O'Reilly Media, Inc.

Neidhoefer, G., Lustig, N., & Tommasi, M. (2021). *Intergenerational transmission of lockdown consequences: Prognosis of the longer-run persistence of COVID19 in Latin America*. Working Papers, 571, ECINEQ (Society for the Study of Economic Inequality).

Neilson, D. (2020). Epistemic violence in the time of coronavirus: From the legacy of the western limits of Spivak's 'can the subaltern speak' to an alternative to the 'neoliberal model of development'. *Educational Philosophy and Theory, 53*(8), 760–765. doi:10.1080/00131857.2020.1750092

Nelson, G. D. (1984). *Assessment of Health Decision-making Skills of Adolescents*. Academic Press.

Ng, J. C. Y., Helminger, C. M., & Wu, Q. (2016b). A Generational Cohort Model for Consumers in China: The Rise and Fall of the Great Gatsby? *Indian Journal of Commerce and Management Studies; Nasik, 7*(1), 53–66. https://search.proquest.com/abicomplete/docview/1830724446/abstract/97CDFA8255094E01PQ/1

Ngai, E. W. T., Cheng, T. C. E., Lai, K. H., Chai, P. Y. F., Choi, Y. S., & Sin, R. K. Y. (2007). Development of an RFID-based traceability system: Experiences and lessons learned from an aircraft engineering company. *Production and Operations Management, 16*(5), 554–568. doi:10.1111/j.1937-5956.2007.tb00280.x

Ng, J. C. Y., Helminger, C. M., & Wu, Q. (2016a). A Generational Cohort Model for Consumers in China: The Rise and Fall of the Great Gatsby? *Indian Journal of Commerce and Management Studies. Nasik, 7*(1), 53–66.

Ngoma, M., & Ntale, P. D. (2019). Word of mouth communication: A mediator of relationship marketing and customer loyalty. *Cogent Business & Management, 6*(1), 1580123. doi:10.1080/23311975.2019.1580123

Nguyen, N. T. T. (n.d.). *The reform of Vietnamese Economic institutions under the impact of Free Trade Agreements A case study of the EU and Vietnam Free Trade Agreement*. Academic Press.

Niederman, F., Mathieu, R. G., Morley, R., & Kwon, I.-W. (2007). Examining RFID applications in supply chain management. *Communications of the ACM, 50*(7), 92–101. doi:10.1145/1272516.1272520

Niemimaa, M., Järveläinen, J., Heikkilä, M., & Heikkilä, J. (2019). Business continuity of business models: Evaluating the resilience of business models for contingencies. *International Journal of Information Management, 49*, 208–216. doi:10.1016/j.ijinfomgt.2019.04.010

Nobre, G. F. (2020). *Creative Economy and Covid-19: Technology, automation and the new economy*. Academic Press.

Nordhagen, S., Igbeka, U., Rowlands, H., Heneghan, E., & Tench, J. (2021). COVID19 and small enterprises in the food supply chain: Early impacts and implications for longer-term food system resilience in low- and middle-income countries. *World Development, 141,* 105405.

Nosratabadi, S., Pinter, G., Mosavi, A., & Semperger, S. (2020). Sustainable banking; Evaluation of the European business models. *Sustainability, 12*(6), 2314. doi:10.3390u12062314

Nouri, M. (2018). The Power of Influence: Traditional Celebrity vs Social Media Influencer. *Pop Culture Intersections*. https://scholarcommons.scu.edu/engl_176/32

Núñez, C. (2020). *Sistema educativo, formación de capital humano, ciencia e investigación tras la COVID19. Policy Papers, 2020-15*. FEDEA.

Nystrand, B. T., & Olsen, S. O. (2020). Consumers' attitudes and intentions toward consuming functional foods in Norway. *Food Quality and Preference, 80*, 103827. doi:10.1016/j.foodqual.2019.103827

Obando, J. (2015). La Minga: Un instrumento vivo para el desarrollo comunitario. *Revista de Sociologia, 5*(4), 82–100.

Obi, J., Ibidunni, A. S., Tolulope, A., Olokundun, M. A., Amaihian, A. B., Borishade, T. T., & Fred, P. (2018). Contribution of small and medium enterprises to economic development: Evidence from a transiting economy. *Data in Brief, 18*, 835–839. doi:10.1016/j.dib.2018.03.126 PMID:29900247

OCDE. (2020a). *Covid-19 en América Latina y el Caribe: Panorama de las respuestas de los gobiernos a la crisis.* https://www.oecd.org/coronavirus/policy-responses/covid-19-en-america-latina-y-el-caribe-panorama-de-las-respuestas-de-los-gobiernos-a-la-crisis-7d9f7a2b/

OCDE. (2020b). *Generar confianza ante una recuperación incierta*. https://www.oecd.org/perspectivas-economicas

Olabuenga, R. J. I. (1995). *Sociología de las organizaciones*. Universidad de Deusto.

Olalla, B., San José, C., & Mata, M. (2012). Factor humano: un elemento clave en la búsqueda de la eficiencia de los proyectos. In *VII Congreso Nacional VISION12*. Madrid: itSMF Spain.

Olalla-Caballero, B., & Mata-Fernández, M. (2020). Circular Economy and Risk Management Synergies in Disruptive Environments. In N. Baporikar (Ed.), *Handbook of Research on Entrepreneurship Development and Opportunities in Circular Economy*. IGI Global. doi:10.4018/978-1-7998-5116-5.ch005

Oleas, J. (2016). *La economía Popular y solidaria en el Ecuador: una mirada institucional. Serie de Estudios sobre Economía Popular y Solidaria: Economía Solidaria Historias y prácticas de su fortalecimiento*. Publiasesores.

OLFSR (Organic Law of the Food Sovereignty Regime). (2009). Quito, Ecuador: Ecuador.

Oliván, F. (2019). *La Democracia Inencontrable. Una Arqueología de la Democracia*. Tirant lo Blanch.

Oliveira, T., & Martins, M. F. (2010). Firms' patterns of e-business adoption: Evidence for the European Union-27. *Electronic Journal of Information Systems Evaluation, 13*(1), 47–56.

Oliveira, T., & Martins, M. F. (2011). Literature review of information technology adoption models at firm level. *Electronic Journal of Information Systems Evaluation, 14*(1), 110–121.

OLSSE (Organic Law of Popular and Solidarity Economy). (2011). Corporación de Estudios y Publicaciones.

OMS. (2020). *Orientaciones para el Público: OMS*. Obtained from Organización Mundial de la Salud: https://www.who.int/es/emergencies/diseases/novel-coronavirus-2019/advice-for-public/q-a-coronaviruses

Oomen, D., Nijhof, A. D., & Wiersema, J. R. (2021). The psychological impact of the COVID19 pandemic on adults with autism: A survey study across three countries. *Molecular Autism, 12*(1), 21. doi:10.118613229-021-00424-y PMID:33658046

Ortega-Vivanco, M. (2020). Efectos del Covid19 en el comportamiento del consumidor: Caso Ecuador. *RETOS. Revista de Ciencias de la Administración y Economía, 10*(20), 233–247.

Osterwalder, A., & Pigneur, Y. (2010). *Business model generation: a handbook for visionaries, game changers, and challengers*. John Wiley & Sons, Inc.

Osterwalder, A., Pigneur, Y., & Tucci, C. L. (2005). Clarifying business models: Origins, present, and future of the concept. *Communications of the Association for Information Systems, 16*(1), 1. doi:10.17705/1CAIS.01601

Our World in data. (2021). *El Avance de la Vacunación*. Oxford University.

Ouyang, S. (2019, December 4). Tencent launches new smart education solution. *China Daily*. https://www.chinadaily.com.cn/a/201912/04/WS5de77c66a310cf3e3557bfef.html

Ovans, A. (2015). What is a business model? *Harvard Business Review, 23*, 1–7.

Oxfam. (2016). *Una Economía al servicio del 1%*. Recuperdo el 06 de 04 de 2019, de https://www-cdn.oxfam.org/s3fs-public/file_attachments/bp210-economy-one-percent-tax-havens-180116-es_0.pdf

Oyserman, D., Coon, H. M., & Kemmelmeier, M. (2002). Rethinking Individualism and Collectivism: Evaluation of Theoretical Assumptions and Meta-Analyses. *Psychological Bulletin, 128*(1), 3–72. doi:10.1037/0033-2909.128.1.3 PMID:11843547

Pache, A.-C., & Santos, F. (2012). Inside the Hybrid Organization: Selective Coupling as a Response to Competing Institutional Logics. *Academy of Management Journal, 56*(4), 972–1001. doi:10.5465/amj.2011.0405

Pacho, F. (2020). What influences consumers to purchase organic food in developing countries? *British Food Journal, 122*(12), 3695–3709. doi:10.1108/BFJ-01-2020-0075

Páez Gallego, J., De-Juanas Oliva, Á., García-Castilla, F. J., & Muelas, Á. (2020). Relationship Between Basic Human Values and Decision-Making Styles in Adolescents. *International Journal of Environmental Research and Public Health, 17*(22), 8315. doi:10.3390/ijerph17228315 PMID:33182771

Compilation of References

Palloff, R. M., & Pratt, K. (Eds.). (2003). *The virtual student: A profile and guide to working with online learners.* Jossey Bass.

Palma-Ruiz, J. M., Barros-Contreras, I., & Gnan, L. (Eds.). (2020). Handbook of Research on the Strategic Management of Family Businesses. IGI Global. doi:10.4018/978-1-7998-2269-1

Palma-Ruiz, J. M., Saiz-Alvarez, J. M., & Herrero-Crespo, A. (Eds.). (2020). Handbook of Research on Smart Territories and Entrepreneurial Ecosystems for Social Innovation and Sustainable Growth. IGI Global.

Palma-Ruiz, J. M., Castillo-Apraiz, J., & Gómez-Martínez, R. (2020). Socially Responsible Investing as a Competitive Strategy for Trading Companies in Times of Upheaval Amid COVID-19: Evidence from Spain. *International Journal of Financial Studies, 8*(3), 41. doi:10.3390/ijfs8030041

Palomares, G. (2006). *Relaciones internacionales en el siglo XXI*. Tecnos.

Pana, M. C., & Mosora, C. (2013). From quantity to quality in addressing the relationship between education and economic development. *Procedia: Social and Behavioral Sciences, 93*, 911–915. doi:10.1016/j.sbspro.2013.09.302

Paquet, F., & Marchionni, C. (2015). E-learning and IV therapy: Can learning be fun? *Vascular Access, 9*(3), 11–22.

Parayitam, S., & Papenhausen, C. (2016). Agreement-seeking behavior, trust, and cognitive diversity in strategic decision-making teams: Process conflict as a moderator. *Journal of Advances in Management Research, 13*(3), 292–315. doi:10.1108/JAMR-10-2015-0072

Park, C. W., MacInnis, D. J., & Priester, J. (2008). Brand attachment and a strategic brand exemplar. In B. H. Schmitt & D. L. Rogers (Eds.), *Handbook on Brand and Experience Management* (pp. 3–17). Edward Elgar Publishing. doi:10.4337/9781848446151.00007

Parra, R. (2020). Una perspectiva del mundo que se nos avecina. *Revista de la Universidad del Zulia, 11*(29), 3–5. doi:10.46925/rdluz.29.01

Passet, R. (2013). *Las grandes representaciones del mundo y la economía a lo largo de la historia: del universo mágico al torbellino creador*. Madrid, Spain: Clave intelectual.

Patiño, O. (2012). *Memoria Oral del pueblo Saraguro*. Serie Estudios.

Paul, J., & Rana, J. (2012). Consumer behavior and purchase intention for organic food. *Journal of Consumer Marketing, 29*(6), 412–422. doi:10.1108/07363761211259223

Pavlić, I., & Vukić, M. (2019). Decision-making styles of Generation Z consumers in Croatia. *Ekonomska Misao i Praksa, 1*, 79–95. https://hrcak.srce.hr/index.php?show=clanak&id_clanak_jezik=322669

Paz, M. D. R., & Delgado, F. J. (2020). Consumer Experience and Omnichannel Behavior in Various Sales Atmospheres. *Frontiers in Psychology, 11*(August), 1–11. doi:10.3389/fpsyg.2020.01972 PMID:32849155

Pech, M. A. (2013). *The Financial Times Guide to Leadership: How to lead effectively and get results*. Pearson UK.

Peel, Q. (2009, May 4) El primer paso de un nuevo orden geopolítico. *Cronista, Impresa General*. https://www.cronista.com/impresa-general/el-primer-paso-de-un-nuevo-orden-geopolitico-20090504-0035.html

Peng, H., Tan, H., & Zhang, Y. (2020). Human capital, financial constraints, and innovation investment persistence. *Asian Journal of Technology Innovation, 28*(3), 453–475. doi:10.1080/19761597.2020.1770616

Peng, J., Feng, T., Zhang, J., Zhao, L., Zhang, Y., Chang, Y., Zhang, Y., & Xiao, W. (2019). Measuring decision-making competence in Chinese adults. *Journal of Behavioral Decision Making, 32*(3), 266–279.

Peng, L., & Luo, S. (2021). Impact of social economic development on personality traits among Chinese college students: A cross-temporal meta-analysis, 2001–2016. *Personality and Individual Differences*, *171*, 110461. doi:10.1016/j.paid.2020.110461

Peng, M. W., & Chen, H. (2011). Strategic Responses to Domestic and Foreign Institutional Pressures. *International Studies of Management & Organization*, *41*(2), 88–105. doi:10.2753/IMO0020-8825410204

Peng, Y., Li, J., Xia, H., Qi, S., & Li, J. (2015). The effects of food safety issues released by we media on consumers' awareness and purchasing behavior: A case study in China. *Food Policy*, *51*, 44–52. doi:10.1016/j.foodpol.2014.12.010

Peppers, D., & Rogers, M. (2004). *Managing Customer Relationships*. John Wiley & Sons.

Pérez–Uribe, R. (2012). *El ambiente laboral y su incidencia en el desempeño de las organizaciones: estudio de las mejores empresas para trabajar en Colombia* (PhD Dissertation). Universidad Antonio de Nebrija.

Pérez–Uribe, R. (2007). Estructura y Cultura organizacional en la PYME Colombiana: Análisis en empresas Bogotanas. *Cuadernos Americanos*, *38*, 73–85.

Pérez–Uribe, R. (2011). *Compromiso de la alta gerencia como eje en el desarrollo de una cultura organizacional de excelencia y su efecto en el desempeño de la firma: Un estudio en medianas empresas del sector de maquinaria y equipo en la ciudad de Bogotá*. Editorial Académica Española.

Pérez–Uribe, R. (2018). *Gerencia Estratégica Corporativa*. Ediciones Ecoe.

Pérez-Uribe, R., Ocampo-Guzmán, D., Ospina-Bermeo, J., Cifuentes-Valenzuela, J., & Cubillos-Leal, C. A. (2016). *MIIGO - Modelo de Intervención e Innovación para el direccionamiento estratégico*. Ediciones EAN. doi:10.21158/9789587564143

Perez-Uribe, R., Ocampo-Guzmán, D., Salcedo-Perez, C., Piñeiro-Cortes, L., & Ramírez-Salazar, M. P. (2020). Preface. In R. Perez-Uribe, D. Ocampo-Guzmán, C. Salcedo-Perez, L. Piñeiro-Cortes, & M. P. Ramírez-Salazar (Eds.), *Handbook of Research on Increasing the Competitiveness of SMEs*. IGI Global. doi:10.4018/978-1-5225-9425-3

Pérez-Uribe, R., & Ramírez-Salazar, M. P. (2018). Organizational Components that Explain the Management of Innovation and Knowledge in Colombian SMEs. In R. Perez-Uribe, C. Salcedo-Perez, & D. David Ocampo-Guzman (Eds.), *Handbook of Research on Intrapreneurship and Organizational Sustainability in SMEs* (pp. 1–27). doi:10.4018/978-1-5225-3543-0.ch001

Perry, E. J. (2018). Introduction: Chinese political culture revisited. In Popular Protest and Political Culture in Modern China (pp. 1–14). Routledge.

Pertuz, R. A. (2013). Estudio de los tipos de estructura organizacional de los institutos universitarios venezolanos. *Revista Electrónica de Investigación Educativa*, *15*(3), 53–67.

Peslak, A. R. (2008). Current Information Technology Issues and Moral Intensity Influences. *The Journal of Computer Information Systems*, *48*(4), 77–86.

Petrovici, D. A., Ritson, C., & Ness, M. (2004). The Theory of Reasoned Action and Food Choice. *Journal of International Food & Agribusiness Marketing*, *16*(1), 59–87. doi:10.1300/J047v16n01_05

Pfeffer, J., & Fong, C. T. (2004). The business school 'business': Some lessons from the US experience. *Journal of Management Studies*, *41*(8), 1501–1520. doi:10.1111/j.1467-6486.2004.00484.x

Phillips, S. D., Pazienza, N. J., & Ferrin, H. H. (1984). Decision-making styles and problem-solving appraisal. *Journal of Counseling Psychology*, *31*(4), 497–502. doi:10.1037/0022-0167.31.4.497

Pianovi, M. (2012). Análisis Comparado de Experiencias de Economía Popular y Solidaria en Tres Países del Mercosur: El caso de Argentina, Brasil y Paraguay. *La Saeta Universitaria, 1*(1), 62–78.

Pierson, F. C. (1959). The education of American businessmen. *The Journal of Business Education, 35*(3), 114–117. doi:10.1080/08832323.1959.10116244

Pigni, F., & Ugazio, E. (2009). Measuring RFID benefits in supply chains. *AMCIS 2009 Proceedings*, 635.

Piketty, T. (2014). *La crisis del capital en el siglo XXI*. Anagrama.

Piketty, T., & Goldhammer, A. (2014). *Capital in the twenty-first century*. The Belknap Press of Harvard University Press. doi:10.4159/9780674369542

Pisedtasalasai, A. (2021). Hedging stocks in crises and market downturns with gold and bonds: Industry analysis. *Asian Economic and Financial Review, 11*(1), 1–16. doi:10.18488/journal.aefr.2021.111.1.16

Plenert, G. J. (2011). *Lean management principles for information technology*. CRC Press. doi:10.1201/b11549

Podolny, J. M. (2009). The buck stops (and starts) at business school. *Harvard Business Review, 87*(6), 62–67.

Pop, R.-A., Săplăcan, Z., & Alt, M.-A. (2020). Social Media Goes Green—The Impact of Social Media on Green Cosmetics Purchase Motivation and Intention. *Information (Basel), 11*(9), 447. doi:10.3390/info11090447

Porter, M. E. (1990). The competitive advantage of nations. *Competitive Intelligence Review, 1*(1), 14–14. doi:10.1002/cir.3880010112

Porter, M. E. (2008). The five competitive forces that shape strategy. *Harvard Business Review, 86*(1), 25–40. PMID:18271320

Povey, R., Conner, M., Sparks, P., Rhiannon, J., & Shepherd, R. (2000). The theory of planned behaviour and healthy eating: Examining additive and moderating effects of social influence variables. *Psychology & Health, 14*(6), 991–1006. doi:10.1080/08870440008407363 PMID:22175258

Powell, M., & Ansic, D. (1997). Gender differences in risk behaviour in financial decision-making: An experimental analysis. *Journal of Economic Psychology, 18*(6), 605–628. doi:10.1016/S0167-4870(97)00026-3

Power, D. J., Cyphert, D., & Roth, R. M. (2019). Analytics, bias, and evidence: The quest for rational decision-making. *Journal of Decision Systems, 28*(2), 120–137. doi:10.1080/12460125.2019.1623534

Pradhan, R. P., Arvin, M. B., Nair, M., Bennett, S. E., & Bahmani, S. (2019). Short-term and long-term dynamics of venture capital and economic growth in a digital economy: A study of European countries. *Technology in Society, 57*, 125–134. doi:10.1016/j.techsoc.2018.11.002

Prado-Prado, J. C., García-Arca, J., & Fernández-González, A. J. (2020). People as the key factor in competitiveness: A framework for success in supply chain management. *Total Quality Management & Business Excellence, 31*(3-4), 297–311. doi:10.1080/14783363.2018.1427499

Prahalad, C. K., & Bettis, R. A. (1986). The dominant logic: A new linkage between diversity and performance. *Strategic Management Journal, 7*(6), 485–501. doi:10.1002mj.4250070602

Prasad, E., & ... . (2003). *Effects of Financial Globalization on Developing Countries: Some Empirical Evidence*. International Monetary Fund.

Premkumar, G., & Roberts, M. (1999). Adoption of new information technologies in rural small businesses. *Omega, 27*(4), 467–484. doi:10.1016/S0305-0483(98)00071-1

Purwanto, D. (2012). *Kominfo Blokir 20 Situs "Download"*. Musik Ilegal.

Puttaiah, M. H., Raverkar, A. K., & Avramakis, E. (2020 December 10). *All change: how COVID-19 is transforming consumer behaviour*. Available at: https://www.swissre.com/institute/research/topics-and-risk-dialogues/health-and-longevity/covid-19-and-consumer-behaviour.html

PWC-Chile. (2020). *Nuestros Servicios: PWC*. Obtained from PWC: https://www.pwc.com/cl/es/Nuestros-Servicios/COVID19-como-puede-responder-tu-empresa-ante-la-crisis.html

Pyle, J. L. (1999). Third World Women and Global Restructuring. In J. Chafetz (Ed.), *Handbook of the Sociology of Gender* (pp. 81–104). Kluwer.

Pyle, J. L. (2001). *International Encyclopedia of the Social & Behavioral Sciences*. Elsevier.

Qi, X., & Ploeger, A. (2019). Explaining consumers' intentions towards purchasing green food in Qingdao, China: The amendment and extension of the theory of planned behavior. *Appetite*, *133*, 414–422. doi:10.1016/j.appet.2018.12.004 PMID:30537527

Quach, S., Barari, M., Vit Moudry, D., & Quach, K. (2020). Service integration in omnichannel retailing and its impact on customer experience. *Journal of Retailing and Consumer Services*, 102267. doi:10.1016/j.jretconser.2020.102267

Rabiee, F. (2004). Focus-group interview and data analysis. *The Proceedings of the Nutrition Society*, *63*(4), 655–660. doi:10.1079/PNS2004399 PMID:15831139

Radecki, C. M., & Jaccard, J. (1996). Gender-Role Differences in Decision-Making Orientations and Decision-Making Skills1. *Journal of Applied Social Psychology*, *26*(1), 76–94. doi:10.1111/j.1559-1816.1996.tb01839.x

Radojevi'c, V., Tomaš Simin, M., Glavaš Trbi'c, D., & Mili'c, D. (2021). A Profile of Organic Food Consumers—Serbia Case-Study. *Sustainability*, *13*(1), 131. doi:10.3390u13010131

Rai, A., & Patnayakuni, R. (1996). A structural model for CASE adoption behavior. *Journal of Management Information Systems*, *13*(2), 205–234. doi:10.1080/07421222.1996.11518129

Rajab, K. D. (2018). The Effectiveness and Potential of e-Learning in War Zones: An Empirical Comparison of Face-to-Face and Online Education in Saudi Arabia. *IEEE Access: Practical Innovations, Open Solutions*, *6*, 6783–6794. doi:10.1109/ACCESS.2018.2800164

Ramanathan, A. (2020 September 30). Elevating consumer experience in a phygital world. *Retail News*. Available at: https://retail.economictimes.indiatimes.com/news/industry/elevating-consumer-experience-in-a-phygital-world/78406271

Ramírez-Garzón, M. T., Perez-Uribe, R., & Espinoza-Mosqueda, R. (2020). Organizational components that explain profitability as a key factor of competitiveness. Colombian SMEs Case. In R. Perez-Uribe, D. Ocampo-Guzmán, C. Salcedo-Perez, L. Piñeiro-Cortes, & M. P. Ramírez-Salazar (Eds.), *Handbook of Research on Increasing the Competitiveness of SMEs* (pp. 26–53). IGI Global. doi:10.4018/978-1-5225-9425-3.ch002

Ramírez-Salazar, M. P. (2016). *Modelo de Innovación Abierta Colaborativa para la Banca de Fomento, Caso Bancóldex* (PhD Dissertation). Universidad Antonio de Nebrija & Universidad EAN. DOI: doi:10.13140/RG.2.2.12496.92166

Ramírez-Salazar, M. P., Perez-Uribe, R., & Salcedo-Perez, C. (2018). A Triple Helix Model Based on Open Collaborative Innovation in Colombia: A Proposal for Higher Education Institutions. In N. Suja & J. M. Saiz-Alvarez (Eds.), *Handbook of Research on Ethics, Entrepreneurship, and Governance in Higher Education* (pp. 238–261). IGI Global. doi:10.4018/978-1-5225-5837-8.ch011

Rašković, M., Ding, Z., Hirose, M., Žabkar, V., & Fam, K.-S. (2020). Segmenting young-adult consumers in East Asia and Central and Eastern Europe–The role of consumer ethnocentrism and decision-making styles. *Journal of Business Research*, *108*, 496–507. doi:10.1016/j.jbusres.2019.04.013

Ratten, V. (2020). Coronavirus disease (COVID-19) and sports entrepreneurship. *International Journal of Entrepreneurial Behaviour & Research*, *26*(6), 1379–1388. doi:10.1108/IJEBR-06-2020-0387

Rauch, A., Wiklund, J., Lumpkin, G. T., & Frese, M. (2009). Entrepreneurial Orientation and Business Performance: An Assessment of Past Research and Suggestions for the Future. *Entrepreneurship Theory and Practice*, *33*(3), 761–787. doi:10.1111/j.1540-6520.2009.00308.x

Razumovskaia, E., Yuzvovich, L., Kniazeva, E., Klimenko, M., & Shelyakin, V. (2020). The Effectiveness of Russian Government Policy to Support SMEs in the COVID-19 Pandemic. *Journal of Open Innovation*, *6*(4), 160. doi:10.3390/joitmc6040160

Reaidy, P. J., Gunasekaran, A., & Spalanzani, A. (2015). Bottom-up approach based on Internet of Things for order fulfillment in a collaborative warehousing environment. *International Journal of Production Economics*, *159*, 29–40. doi:10.1016/j.ijpe.2014.02.017

Reichman, J. H., & Samuelson, P. (1997). Intellectual Property Rights in Data. *Vanderbilt Law Review*, *50*(1), 49–166. https://heinonline.org/HOL/P?h=hein.journals/vanlr50&i=91

Rempel, P., Mader, P., & Kuschke, T. (2013). An empirical study on project-specific traceability strategies. *2013 21st IEEE International Requirements Engineering Conference (RE)*, 195–204. 10.1109/RE.2013.6636719

Ren, X., & Montgomery, L. (2012). Chinese online literature: Creative consumers and evolving business models. *Arts Marketing*, *2*(2), 118–130.

Renvoisé, P., & Morin, C. (2006). *Neuromarketing: el nervio de la venta*. Editorial UOC.

Repko, M., & Thomas, L. (2020 September 29). 6 ways the coronavirus pandemic has forever altered the retail landscape. *CNBC*. Available at: https://www.cnbc.com/2020/09/29/how-coronavirus-pandemic-forever-altered-retail.html

Requeijo, J. (2012). *Economía Mundial*. McGraw Hill.

Reyes-Martínez, L., Barboza-Carrasco, M., & Vicuña-Tapia, H. (2017). Diagnóstico Cultura Organizacional de la Empresa Grupo Fadomo Reproser, S.A. de C.V. *Revista de Desarrollo Económico.*, *4*(12), 67–78.

Reyes, P. M., Li, S., & Visich, J. K. (2012). Accessing Antecedents and Outcomes of RFID Implementation in Health Care. *International Journal of Production Economics*, *136*(1), 137–150. doi:10.1016/j.ijpe.2011.09.024

Reyes, P. M., Li, S., & Visich, J. K. (2016). Determinants of RFID adoption stage and perceived benefits. *European Journal of Operational Research*, *254*(3), 801–812. doi:10.1016/j.ejor.2016.03.051

Richardson, C., & Rabiee, F. (2001). A question of access: An exploration of the factors that influence the health of young males aged 15 to 19 living in Corby and their use of health care services. *Health Education Journal*, *60*(1), 3–16. doi:10.1177/001789690106000102

Riel, J., & Martin, R. L. (2017). *Creating great choices: A leader's guide to integrative thinking*. Harvard Business Press.

Riley, N. E. (1997). Gender Equality in China: Two Steps Forward, One Step Back. In *China Briefing*. Routledge.

Rocha, M. (2012). Transferable skills representations in a Portuguese college sample: Gender, age, adaptability and vocational development. *European Journal of Psychology of Education*, *27*(1), 77–90. doi:10.100710212-011-0067-4

Rodríguez, D., & Valldeoriola, J. (2007). *Metodología de la Investigación*. Universitat Oberta de Catalunya.

Rodriguez, M. (2020). *Brand Storytelling: Put Customers at the Heart of Your Brand Story*. Kogan Page Publishers.

Rodríguez-Torrico, P., San-Martín, S., & San José Cabezudo, R. (2020). The role of omnichannel tendency in digital information processing. *Online Information Review*, *44*(7), 1347–1367. doi:10.1108/OIR-08-2019-0272

Rodríguez, V. J. (2005). *Cómo aplicar la administración estratégica a la pequeña y mediana empresa* (5th ed.). Thompson.

Rogers, E. M. (1995). *Diffusion of Innovations* (4th ed.). Free Press. doi:10.2307/30036530 10.1146/annurev.soc.28.110601.141051

Rosati, F., & Diniz, L. G. (2019). Addressing the Sustainable Development Goals in sustainability reports: The relationship with institutional factors. *Journal of Cleaner Production*, *215*, 1312–1326. doi:10.1016/j.jclepro.2018.12.107

Roster, C. A., Rogers, R. A., Hozier, G. C., Baker, K. G., & Albaum, G. (2007). Management of Marketing Research Projects: Does Delivery Method Matter Anymore in Survey Research? *Journal of Marketing Theory and Practice; Abingdon*, *15*(2), 127–144.

Roth, F. (2021). *The Productivity Puzzle – A Critical Assessment and an Outlook on the COVID19 Crisis. Hamburg Discussion Papers in International Economics, 8, Chair of International Economics*. University of Hamburg.

Rowland, K. D. (2004). Career decision-making skills of high school students in the Bahamas. *Journal of Career Development*, *31*(1), 1–13. doi:10.1177/089484530403100101

Roy, D. (2019). Managerial grid in macroeconomic perspective: An empirical study (2008–2017). *Journal of Transnational Management*, *24*(3), 165–184. doi:10.1080/15475778.2019.1632636

Rudolph, S., & Krcmar, H. (2009). Maturity model for IT service catalogues an approach to assess the quality of IT service documentation. *AMCIS 2009 Proceedings*, 750.

Ruggie, J. (1982). International regimes, transactions, and change: Embedded Liberalism in the post-war economic order. *International Organization*, *36*(2), 379–415. doi:10.1017/S0020818300018993

Rus, M., Tasente, T., & Sandu, M. L. (2019). Study regarding the perception on the personality traits in managerial decision-making. *Journal of Danubian Studies and Research*, *9*(2).

Rust, R. T., Lemon, K. N., & Zeithaml, V. A. (2004). Return on Marketing: Using Customer Equity to Focus Marketing Strategy. *Journal of Marketing*, *68*(1), 109–127. doi:10.1509/jmkg.68.1.109.24030

Rusu, V. D., & Dornean, A. (2019). The quality of entrepreneurial activity and economic competitiveness in European Union countries: A panel data approach. *Administrative Sciences*, *9*(2), 35. doi:10.3390/admsci9020035

Ru, X., Wang, S., Chen, Q., & Yan, S. (2018). Exploring the interaction effects of norms and attitudes on green travel intention: An empirical study in eastern China. *Journal of Cleaner Production*, *197*(Part 1), 1317–1327. doi:10.1016/j.jclepro.2018.06.293

Ryan, C. D., Schaul, A. J., Butner, R., & Swarthout, J. T. (2020). Monetizing disinformation in the attention economy: The case of genetically modified organisms (GMOs). *European Management Journal*, *38*(1), 7–18. doi:10.1016/j.emj.2019.11.002

Sachs, J. (2008). *Common Wealth: Economics for a Crowded Planet*. Penguin Group.

Sadler, E., & Spicer, D. P. (2005). An examination of the general decision-making style questionnaire in two UK samples. *Journal of Managerial Psychology*, *20*(2), 137–149. doi:10.1108/02683940510579777

Saiz-Álvarez, J. M., & Olalla-Caballero, B. (Eds.). (2021). Quality Management for Competitive Advantage in Global Markets. IGI Global.

Saiz-Álvarez, J. M., Leitao, J., & Palma-Ruiz, J. M. (Eds.). (2019). Entrepreneurship and Family Business Vitality: Surviving and Flourishing in the Long Term. Springer International Publishing AG. doi:10.1007/978-3-030-15526-1

Saiz-Álvarez, J. M. (2018a). An Entrepreneurship-based Model to Foster Organizational Wellbeing. In P. Ochoa, M. T. Lepeley, & P. Essens (Eds.), *Wellbeing for Sustainability in the Global Workplace* (pp. 159–178). Routledge. doi:10.4324/9780429470523-8

Saiz-Álvarez, J. M. (2018b). Managing Social Innovation through CSR 2.0 and the Quadruple Helix. A Socially Inclusive Business Strategy for the Industry 4.0. In A. Guerra (Ed.), *Organizational Transformation and Managing Innovation in the Fourth Industrial Revolution* (pp. 228–244). IGI Global.

Saiz-Álvarez, J. M. (2022). *Emerging Business Models and the New World Economic Order* (1st ed.). IGI Global. https://www.igi-global.com/submission/book-project-chapters/?projectid=1032c361-0b19-48a4-8f0d-6ae9b2dc9dce

Saiz-Alvarez, J. M., Castillo-Nazareno, U. H., Matute de León, J. S., & Alcívar-Avilés, M. T. (2021). Post-COVID Indigenous Women Entrepreneurship: A Case of the Kichwa-Puruha in Ecuador. In N. Baporikar (Ed.), *Handbook of Research on Strategies and Interventions to Mitigate COVID-19 Impact on SMEs* (Vols. 1–2, pp. 225–234). IGI Global. doi:10.4018/978-1-7998-7436-2.ch021

Saiz-Alvarez, J. M., Vega-Muñoz, A., Acevedo-Duque, A., & Castillo, D. (2020). B Corps: A Socioeconomic Approach for the COVID-19 Post-crisis. *Frontiers in Psychology*, *11*, 1867. doi:10.3389/fpsyg.2020.01867 PMID:32849095

Saloner, G., Shepard, A., & Podolny, J. (2005). *Administración estratégica*. LimusaWiley.

Salvatto, M., & Salvatto, A. (2021). *La batalla del futuro: algo en qué creer*. Ediciones Lea.

Sambamurthy, V., Bharadwaj, A., & Grover, V. (2003). Shaping Agility Through Digital Options: Reconceptualizing the Role of Information Technology in Contemporary Firms. *Management Information Systems Quarterly*, *27*(2), 237–263. doi:10.2307/30036530

Sánchez, F. (2012). La Cosmovisión Quichua en Ecuador: Una Perspectiva para la Economía Solidaria del Buen Vivir'. *Cuadernos Americanos*, *4*(142), 39–51.

Sánchez, J. (2016). *Institucionalidad y políticas para la economía popular y solidaria: balance de la experiencia ecuatoriana. Serie de Estudios sobre la Economía Popular y Solidaria Economía Solidaria. Historias y prácticas de su fortalecimiento*. Publiasesores.

San-Martín, S., Prodanova, J., & Jiménez, N. (2015). The impact of age in the generation of satisfaction and WOM in mobile shopping. *Journal of Retailing and Consumer Services*, *23*, 1–8. doi:10.1016/j.jretconser.2014.11.001

Sanna-Randaccio, M., & Veurgeles, R. (2003). Global Innovation strategies of MNE's: implications for host economies. In J. Cantwell & J. Molero (Eds.), *Multinational Enterprises, Innovative Strategies and Systems of Innovation, New Horizons in International Business*. Edward Elgar Publishing.

Santabárbara, J., Lasheras, I., Lipnicki, D. M., Bueno-Notivol, J., Pérez-Moreno, M., López-Antón, R., De la Cámara, C., Lobo, A., & Gracia-García, P. (2021). Prevalence of anxiety in the COVID-19 pandemic: An updated meta-analysis of community-based studies. *Progress in Neuro-Psychopharmacology & Biological Psychiatry*, *109*, 110207. doi:10.1016/j.pnpbp.2020.110207 PMID:33338558

Santana Juárez, M. V., Santana Castañeda, G., Sánchez Carillo, C., Sánchez Carrillo, R., & Ortega Alcántara, R. (2020). COVID-19 en México: Asociación espacial de cara a la fase tres. *Hygeia; Revista Brasileira de Geografia Médica e da Saúde*, 36–48. doi:10.14393/Hygeia0054317

Saran, C. (2005). Costs Set to Rise as RFID and Barcodes Battle. *Computer Weekly*, 2-8. doi:10.1108/01443571011029994

Sassen, S. (2014). *Expulsions: Brutality and Complexity in the Global Economy*. The President and Fellows of Harvard College.

Sassen, S. (2015). *Expulsiones: brutalidad y complejidad en la economía global*. Katz. doi:10.2307/j.ctvm7bdqr

Saya, G. (2015). *The relationship of academic procrastination and decision-making styles among university students*. Academic Press.

Schachtebeck, C., Groenewald, D., & Nieuwenhuizen, C. (2018). Pilot Studies: Use and Misuse In South African SME Research. Acta Universitatis Danubius. Oeconomica, 14(1).

Scherrer-Rathje, M., Boyle, T. A., & Deflorin, P. (2009). Lean, take two! Reflections from the second attempt at lean implementation. *Business Horizons*, *52*(1), 79–88. doi:10.1016/j.bushor.2008.08.004

Schildkamp, K. (2019). Data-based decision-making for school improvement: Research insights and gaps. *Educational Research*, *61*(3), 257–273. doi:10.1080/00131881.2019.1625716

Schon, D. (1967). *Technology and social change*. Delacorte. doi:10.1016/j.techfore.2020.120054

Schwab, K., & Malleret, T. (2020). *COVID-19: The Great Reset*. World Economic Forum, Forum Publishing.

Scott, S., & Bruce, R. (1995). Decision-making style: The development and assessment of a new measure. *Educational and Psychological Measurement*, *55*(5), 818–831. doi:10.1177/0013164495055005017

SENPLADES. (2019). *Plan Toda una Vida*. Retrieved from http://www.planificacion.gob.ec/biblioteca/

SERCOP. (2019). *La compra pública en cifras: Boletín anual – 2018*. Retrieved from https://portal.compraspublicas.gob.ec/sercop/wp-content/uploads/downloads/2019/01/boletin_sercop_anual_2018-1.pdf

Serrano-Bedia, A. M., Palma-Ruiz, J. M., & Flores-Rivera, C. (2019). Innovation and Family Firms: Past and Future Research Perspectives. In Handbook of Research on Entrepreneurial Leadership and Competitive Strategy in Family Business (pp. 371–398). IGI Global. doi:10.4018/978-1-5225-8012-6.ch018

SHADE. L. R. (2014). Gender and digital policy: From global information infrastructure to internet governance. In The Routledge Companion to Media & Gender. Routledge.

Shafer, S. M., Smith, H. J., & Linder, J. C. (2005). The power of business models. *Business Horizons*, *48*(3), 199–207. doi:10.1016/j.bushor.2004.10.014

Shams, R., Vrontis, D., Belyaeva, Z., Ferraris, A., & Czinkota, M. R. (2020). Strategic agility in international business: A conceptual framework for "agile" multinationals. *Journal of International Management*, *100737*. doi:10.1016/j.intman.2020.100737

Shankar, V. (2009). The Evolution of Markets: Innovation Adoption, Diffusion, Market Growth, New Product Entry, and Competitor Responses. In S. Shane (Ed.), *The Handbook of Technology and Innovation Management* (pp. 57–112). John Wiley & Sons Ltd.

Sharma, A., & Citurs, A. (2005). Radio frequency identification (RFID) adoption drivers: A radical innovation adoption perspective. AMCIS 2005 Proceedings, 211.

Compilation of References

Sharma, A., Citurs, A., & Konsynski, B. (2007). Strategic and institutional perspectives in the adoption and early integration of radio frequency identification (RFID). In *2007 40th Annual Hawaii International Conference on System Sciences (HICSS'07)*. IEEE.

Sharma, A., Dominic, T., & Benn, K. (2008). Strategic and institutional perspectives in the evaluation, adoption and early integration of radio frequency identification (RFID): an empirical investigation of current and potential adopters. In *Proceedings of the 41st Annual Hawaii International Conference on System Sciences (HICSS 2008)* (pp. 407-407). IEEE. 10.1109/HICSS.2008.412

Sharma, P., & Chrisman, J. J. (1999). Toward a Reconciliation of the Definitional Issues in the Field of Corporate Entrepreneurship. *Entrepreneurship Theory and Practice*, *23*(3), 11–28. doi:10.1177/104225879902300302

Shen, H., Fu, M., Pan, H., Yu, Z., & Chen, Y. (2020). The impact of the COVID-19 pandemic on firm performance. *Emerging Markets Finance & Trade*, *56*(10), 2213–2230. doi:10.1080/1540496X.2020.1785863

Sherer, S. (2010). Information systems and healthcare: An institutional theory perspective on physician adoption of electronic health records. *Communications of the Association for Information Systems*, *27*(7), 127–140. doi:10.17705/1CAIS.02607

Sheth, J. (2020). Impact of Covid-19 on consumer behavior: Will the old habits return or die? *Journal of Business Research*, *117*, 280–283. doi:10.1016/j.jbusres.2020.05.059 PMID:32536735

Shieh, M.-D., Chen, C.-N., & Lin, M.-C. (2018). Discussion of Correlations between Green Advertising Design and Purchase Intention based on Consumers' Environmental Attitude. *Ekoloji*, *27*(106), 1153–1159.

Shin, Y. H., Im, J., Jung, S. E., & Severt, K. (2018). The theory of planned behavior and the norm activation model approach to consumer behavior regarding organic menus. *International Journal of Hospitality Management*, *69*, 21–29. doi:10.1016/j.ijhm.2017.10.011

Shin, Y. H., Jung, S. E., Im, J., & Severt, K. (2020). Applying an extended theory of planned behavior to examine state-branded food product purchase behavior: The moderating effect of gender. *Journal of Foodservice Business Research*, *23*(4), 358–375. doi:10.1080/15378020.2020.1770043

Short, J. C., Ketchen, D. J. Jr, Shook, C. L., & Ireland, R. D. (2010). The Concept of "Opportunity" in Entrepreneurship Research: Past Accomplishments and Future Challenges. *Journal of Management*, *36*(1), 40–65. doi:10.1177/0149206309342746

Sidaoui, K., Jaakkola, M., & Burton, J. (2020). AI feel you: Customer experience assessment via chatbot interviews. *Journal of Service Management*, *31*(4), 745–766. doi:10.1108/JOSM-11-2019-0341

Sigurdsson, V., & Foxall, G. R. (2016). Experimental analyses of choice and matching: from the animal laboratory to the marketplace. In G. R. Foxall (Ed.), *The Routledge Companion to Consumer Behavior Analysis* (pp. 78–95). Routledge.

Silva, C. (2009). Globalización: Dimensiones y políticas públicas. *Holográmatica*, *10*, 3–25.

Sirmon, D. G., Hitt, M. A., & Ireland, R. D. (2007). Managing firm resources in dynamic environments to create value: Looking inside the black box. *Academy of Management Review*, *32*(1), 273–292. doi:10.5465/amr.2007.23466005

Si, W., Farh, J.-L., Qu, Q., Fu, P. P., & Kang, F. (2017). Paternalistic Leadership in China: A Latent Profile Analysis of its Antecedents and Outcomes. *Academy of Management Proceedings*, *2017*(1), 15057. doi:10.5465/AMBPP.2017.15057abstract

Sjödin, D., Parida, V., Jovanovic, M., & Visnjic, I. (2020). Value creation and value capture alignment in business model innovation: A process view on outcome-based business models. *Journal of Product Innovation Management*, *37*(2), 158–183. doi:10.1111/jpim.12516

Skågeby, J. (2009). Exploring qualitative sharing practices of social metadata: Expanding the attention economy. *The Information Society*, *25*(1), 60–72. doi:10.1080/01972240802587588

Skrentny, J. D. (1993). Concern for the environment: A cross-national perspective. *International Journal of Public Opinion Research*, *5*(4), 335–352. doi:10.1093/ijpor/5.4.335

Smircich, L., & Morgan, G. (1982). Leadership: The management of meaning. *The Journal of Applied Behavioral Science*, *18*(3), 257–273. doi:10.1177/002188638201800303 PMID:10260212

Smith, C. J. (2019). *China: In the Post-Utopian Age*. Routledge. doi:10.4324/9780429039324

Sodhi, M. S., & Tang, C. S. (2011). SEs as supply-chain enablers for the poor. *Socio-Economic Planning Sciences*, *45*(4), 146–153. doi:10.1016/j.seps.2011.04.001

Soon, J.-J., Lee, A. S.-H., Lim, H.-E., Idris, I., & Eng, W. Y.-K. (2020). Cubicles or corner offices? Effects of academic performance on university graduates' employment likelihood and salary. *Studies in Higher Education*, *45*(6), 1233–1248. doi:10.1080/03075079.2019.1590689

Sorri, K., Seppänen, M., Still, K., & Valkokari, K. (2019). Business Model Innovation with Platform Canvas. *Journal of Business Models*, *7*(2), 1–13.

Spekman, R. E., & Sweeney, P. J. II. (2006). RFID: From concept to implementation. *International Journal of Physical Distribution & Logistics Management*, *36*(10), 736–754. doi:10.1108/09600030610714571

Spicer, D. P., & Sadler-Smith, E. (2006). Organizational learning in smaller manufacturing firms. *International Small Business Journal*, *24*(2), 133–158. doi:10.1177/0266242606061836

Srinivasan, V., Park, C. S., & Chang, D. R. (2005). An Approach to the Measurement Analysis and Prediction of Brand Equity and Its Sources. *Management Science*, *51*(9), 1433–1448. doi:10.1287/mnsc.1050.0405

Sripada, C. (Ed.). (2020). *Leading Human Capital in the 2020s: Emerging Perspectives*. SAGE Publishing India.

SSSE. (2019a). *Catastro sector no financiero y boletín financiero 2018*. Quito. Retrieved from http://www.seps.gob.ec/estadistica?boletin-financiero-sf-y-snf

SSSE. (2019b). Retrieved from https://servicios.seps.gob.ec/gosnf-internet/paginas/organizacion.jsf

Staehr, K., & Vermeulen, R. (2019). Heterogeneous effects of competitiveness shocks on macroeconomic performance across euro area countries. *World Economy*, *42*(1), 68–86. doi:10.1111/twec.12675

Stahl, F., Heitmann, M., Lehmann, D. R., & Neslin, S. A. (2012). The Impact of Brand Equity on Customer Acquisition, Retention, and Profit Margin. *Journal of Marketing*, *76*(4), 44–63. doi:10.1509/jm.10.0522

Starkey, K., Tempest, S., & Cinque, S. (2019). Management education and the theatre of the absurd. *Management Learning*, *50*(5), 591–606. doi:10.1177/1350507619875894

Stauss, B., & Seidel, W. (2019). *Effective Complaint Management: The Business Case for Customer Satisfaction*. Springer. doi:10.1007/978-3-319-98705-7

Steenkamp, J.-B. E. M. (1993). Food Consumption Behavior. In E-European Advances in Consumer Research, 1. Provo, UT: Association for Consumer Research.

Steinberg, S., & DeMaria, R. (2012). *The Crowdfunding Bible: How to raise money for any startup, video game or project*. Read.

Compilation of References

Strandhagen, J. O., Vallandingham, L. R., Fragapane, G., Strandhagen, J. W., Stangeland, A. B. H., & Sharma, N. (2019). Logistics 4.0 and emerging sustainable business models. *Advanced Manufacturing*, *5*(4), 23–32.

Suárez, V., Suarez Quezada, M., Oros Ruiz, S., & Ronquillo De Jesús, E. (2020). Epidemiología de COVID-19 en México: Del 27 de febrero al 30 de abril de 2020. *Revista Clínica Española*, *220*(8), 463–471. doi:10.1016/j.rceng.2020.05.008

Subrahmanyam, S. (2018). Corporate leadership: A study of the decision-making skills in growing in the corporate world. *International Journal of Research*, *5*(1), 2348–6848.

Suki, N. M. (2016). Green product purchase intention: Impact of green brands, attitude, and knowledge. *British Food Journal*.

Suki, N. M. (Ed.). (2017). *The Handbook of Research on Leveraging Consumer Psychology for Effective Customer Engagement*. IGI Global. doi:10.4018/978-1-5225-0746-8

Sullivan Mort, G., Weerawardena, J., & Carnegie, K. (2003). Social entrepreneurship: Towards conceptualisation. *International Journal of Nonprofit and Voluntary Sector Marketing*, *8*(1), 76–88. doi:10.1002/nvsm.202

Sun, J. Y., & Li, J. (2017). Women in leadership in China: Past, present, and future. *Current Perspectives on Asian Women in Leadership*, 19–35.

Sun, Y., Luo, B., Wang, S., & Fang, W. (2020). What you see is meaningful: Does green advertising change the intentions of consumers to purchase eco-labeled products? *Business Strategy and the Environment*.

Sun, Y., Yang, C., Shen, X. L., & Wang, N. (2020). When digitalized customers meet digitalized services: A digitalized social cognitive perspective of omnichannel service usage. *International Journal of Information Management*, *54*(July), 102200. doi:10.1016/j.ijinfomgt.2020.102200

Swafford, P. M., Ghosh, S., & Murthy, N. (2006). The antecedents of supply chain agility of a firm: Scale development and model testing. *Journal of Operations Management*, *24*(2), 170–188. doi:10.1016/j.jom.2005.05.002

Sykes, T. A., Venkatesh, V., & Rai, A. (2011). Explaining physicians' use of EMR systems and performance in the shakedown phase. *Journal of the American Medical Informatics Association: JAMIA*, *18*(2), 125–130. doi:10.1136/jamia.2010.009316 PMID:21292704

Szymańska, O., Adamczak, M., & Cyplik, P. (2017). Logistics 4.0 - a new paradigm or set of known solutions? *Research in Logistics and Production*, *7*(4), 299–310. doi:10.21008/j.2083-4950.2017.7.4.2

Tadriss-Hasani, M., & Rahmansersht, H. (2020). Provide a mathematical model for determining decision-making styles and improving its effectiveness in the face of data uncertainty. *Modern Research in Decision-making*, *5*(2), 1–20.

Taguchi, G., & Phadke, M. S. (1989). Quality engineering through design optimization. In *Quality Control, Robust Design, and the Taguchi Method* (pp. 77–96). Springer. doi:10.1007/978-1-4684-1472-1_5

Tam, J. L. M. (2011). The moderating effects of purchase importance in customer satisfaction process: An empirical investigation. *Journal of Consumer Behaviour*, *10*(4), 205–215. doi:10.1002/cb.330

Tang, C. S., & Veelenturf, L. P. (2019). The Strategic Role of Logistics in the Industry 4.0 Era. *Transportation Research Part E, Logistics and Transportation Review*, *129*, 1–11. doi:10.1016/j.tre.2019.06.004

Tao, S. (2018). Evaluation of technology innovation in Hubei province. *Engineering Heritage Journal*, *2*(2), 9–10. doi:10.26480/gwk.02.2018.09.10

Tarasova, M. V., & Ashurkova, K. S. (2020). Trade Wars as a Reflection of the Global Economic Situation. *Вестник Тульского Филиала Финуниверситета*, *1*. https://elibrary.ru/item.asp?id=43140164

Tassi, P. (2018). Media: From the Contact Economy to the Attention Economy. *International Journal of Arts Management*, *20*(3), 49–59. https://www.proquest.com/docview/2092791898/abstract/68C6DFA7518F402APQ/1

Teece, D. J. (2010). Business models, business strategy and innovation. *Long Range Planning*, *43*(2-3), 172–194. doi:10.1016/j.lrp.2009.07.003

Teng, W., Ma, C., Pahlevansharif, S., & Turner, J. J. (2019). Graduate readiness for the employment market of the 4th industrial revolution: The development of soft employability skills. *Education + Training*, *61*(5), 590–604. doi:10.1108/ET-07-2018-0154

Teo, H. H., Wei, K. K., & Benbasat, I. (2003). Predicting intention to adopt interorganizational linkages: An institutional perspective. *Management Information Systems Quarterly*, *27*(1), 19–49. doi:10.2307/30036518

Tewari, A., & Gupta, B. B. (2020). An Analysis of Provable Security Frameworks for RFID Security. In *Handbook of Computer Networks and Cyber Security* (pp. 635–651). Springer., doi:10.1007/978-3-030-22277-2_25

Theodoridou, G., Tsakiridou, E., Kalogeras, N., & Mattas, K. (2017). Food Consumption Patterns in Times of Economic Recession. *International Journal of Food and Beverage Manufacturing and Business Models*, *2*(1), 56–69. doi:10.4018/IJFBMBM.2017010105

Thiel, P. A., & Masters, B. (2014). *Zero to One: Notes on Startups or how to build the future*. Crown Business.

Thoben, K. D., Wiesner, S., & Wuestet, T. (2017). "Industrie 4.0" and Smart Manufacturing – A Review of Research Issues and Application Examples. *International Journal of Automotive Technology*, *11*, 4–19.

Thompson, A., & Strickland, A. J. (2004). *Administración estratégica: textos y casos* (13th ed.). McGraw-Hill.

Thuemmler, C., Buchanan, W., & Kumar, V. (2007). Setting safety standards by designing a low-budget and compatible patient identification system based on passive RFID technology. *International Journal of Healthcare Technology and Management*, *8*(5), 571–583. doi:10.1504/IJHTM.2007.013524

Tian, R., Chui, C. H.-K., & Hu, X. (2018). Emergent models and strategies of SEs in China. *Asia Pacific Journal of Social Work and Development*, *28*(2), 111–127. doi:10.1080/02185385.2018.1453372

Tiwari, P., Bhat, A. K., & Tikoria, J. (2017). An empirical analysis of the factors affecting social entrepreneurial intentions. *Journal of Global Entrepreneurship Research*, *7*(1), 1–25. doi:10.118640497-017-0067-1

Tjiptono, F., Arli, D., & Viviea. (2016). Gender and digital privacy: Examining determinants of attitude toward digital piracy among youths in an emerging market. *International Journal of Consumer Studies*, *40*(2), 168–178. doi:10.1111/ijcs.12240

Tokatli, N. (2013). Toward a better understanding of the apparel industry. *Journal of Economic Geography*, *13*(6), 993–1101. doi:10.1093/jeg/lbs043

Tokatli, N., & Kizilgün, Ö. (2004). Upgrading in the Global Clothing Industry: Mavi Jeans and the Transformation of a Turkish Firm from Full-Package to Brand-Name Manufacturing and Retailing. *Economic Geography*, *80*(3), 221–240. doi:10.1111/j.1944-8287.2004.tb00233.x

Tombe, T., & Zhu, X. (2019). Trade, migration, and productivity: A quantitative analysis of china. *The American Economic Review*, *109*(5), 1843–1872. doi:10.1257/aer.20150811

Tornatzky, L. G., Fleischer, M., & Chakrabarti, A. K. (1990). *The processes of technological innovation*. Lexington Books. doi:10.1007/BF02371446

Compilation of References

Tornatzky, L. G., & Klein, K. J. (1982). Innovation characteristics and innovation adoption-implementation: A meta-analysis of findings. *IEEE Transactions on Engineering Management*, 29(1), 28–45. doi:10.1109/TEM.1982.6447463

Torres-Toukoumidis, A., González-Moreno, S. E., Pesántez-Avilés, F., Cárdenas-Tapia, J., & Valles-Baca, H. G. (2021). Políticas públicas educativas durante la pandemia: Estudio comparativo México y Ecuador. *Education Policy Analysis Archives*, 29, 88. doi:10.14507/epaa.29.6362

Torri, L., Tuccillo, F., Bonelli, S., Piraino, S., & Leoned, A. (2020). The attitudes of Italian consumers towards jellyfish as novel food. *Food Quality and Preference*, 79, 103782. doi:10.1016/j.foodqual.2019.103782

Toubia, O. (2018). Conjoint Analysis. In N. Mizik & D. M. Hanssens (Eds.), *Handbook of Marketing Analytics* (pp. 52–75). Edward Elgar Publishing. doi:10.4337/9781784716752.00011

Tse, M. C., & Gong, M. (2012a). Online Communities and Commercialization of Chinese Internet Literature. *Journal of Internet Commerce*, 11(2), 100–116. doi:10.1080/15332861.2012.689563

Tubulingane, B. S., & Baporikar, N. (2020). Student Satisfaction Approach for Enhancing University Competitiveness. *International Journal of Technology-Enabled Student Support Services*, 10(2), 31–54. doi:10.4018/IJTESSS.2020070103

Tunca, T. I., & Wu, Q. (2013a). Fighting Fire with Fire: Commercial Piracy and the Role of File Sharing on Copyright Protection Policy for Digital Goods. *Information Systems Research; Linthicum*, 24(2), 436-453, 495-496. http://search.proquest.com/abicomplete/docview/1399039152/E0DB27710BEF4738PQ/1center

Tunca, T. I., & Wu, Q. (2013b). Fighting Fire with Fire: Commercial Piracy and the Role of File Sharing on Copyright Protection Policy for Digital Goods. *Information Systems Research; Linthicum*, 24(2), 436-453, 495-496.

Türkel, S., Uzunoğlu, E., Kaplan, M. D., & Vural, B. A. (2016). A Strategic Approach to CSR Communication: Examining the Impact of Brand Familiarity on Consumer Responses. *Corporate Social Responsibility and Environmental Management*, 23(4), 228–242. doi:10.1002/csr.1373

Tu, Y. J., Zhou, W., & Piramuthu, S. (2009). Identifying RFID-embedded objects in pervasive healthcare applications. *Decision Support Systems*, 46(2), 586–593. doi:10.1016/j.dss.2008.10.001

Tversky, A. (1972). Elimination by aspects: A theory of choice. *Psychological Review*, 79(4), 281-299. https://psycnet.apa.org/doi/10.1037/h0032955

Tyrväinen, O., Karjaluoto, H., & Saarijärvi, H. (2020). Personalization and hedonic motivation in creating customer experiences and loyalty in omnichannel retail. *Journal of Retailing and Consumer Services*, 57.

Tzeng, C. T., Chiang, Y. C., Chiang, C. M., & Lai, C. M. (2008). Combination of radio frequency identification (RFID) and field verification tests of interior decorating materials. *Automation in Construction*, 18(1), 16–23. doi:10.1016/j.autcon.2008.04.003

UNCAD. (2020 October). *COVID-19 and E-commerce, Findings from a survey of online consumers in 9 countries.* Available at https://unctad.org/system/files/official-document/dtlstictinf2020d1_en.pdf

UNDP. (2009). *Human Development Report 2009: Overcoming Barriers–Human Mobility and Development*, NY.

Universidad Autónoma de México. (2018). El Comercio Electrónico y principios económico-comerciales. *Biblioteca Juridica Virtual del Instituto de Investigaciones Jurídicas de la UNAM*, 1.

Universidad de Catalunya. (2018). La logística como fuente de valor añadido al eCommerce. *Oikonomics*, 28-30.

Uzonwanne, F. C. (2007). *Leadership style and decision-making models among corporate leaders in non-profit organizations.* Academic Press.

Uzonwanne, F. (2015). Leadership styles and decision-making models among corporate leaders in non-profit organizations in North America. *Journal of Public Affairs*, *15*(3), 287–299. doi:10.1002/pa.1530

Uzonwanne, F. C. (2016). Influence of age and gender on decision-making models and leadership styles of non-profit executives in Texas, USA. *The International Journal of Organizational Analysis*, *24*(2), 186–203. doi:10.1108/IJOA-05-2013-0667

Valencia-Maldonado, G., & Erazo, M. A. (2016). El reto de la planificación estratégica en las Pymes. *Revista Publicando*, *3*(8), 335–344.

Valentini, S., Neslin, S. A., & Montaguti, E. (2020). Identifying omnichannel deal-prone segments, their antecedents, and their consequences. *Journal of Retailing*, *96*(3), 310–327. doi:10.1016/j.jretai.2020.01.003

Valle, M. (2019). *La Economía Popular y Solidaria en Ecuador: Políticas públicas y prácticas económicas no monetarias y sostenibles en los emprendimientos asociativos* (J. Ordóñez, Interviewer). Academic Press.

Van der Togt, R., Bakker, P. J., & Jaspers, M. W. (2011). A framework for performance and data quality assessment of Radio Frequency Identification (RFID) systems in health care settings. *Journal of Biomedical Informatics*, *44*(2), 372–383. doi:10.1016/j.jbi.2010.12.004 PMID:21168526

Van Doorn, J., Mende, M., Noble, S. M., Hulland, J., Ostrom, A. L., Grewal, D., & Petersen, J. A. (2017). Domo arigato Mr. Roboto: Emergence of automated social presence in organizational frontlines and customers' service experiences. *Journal of Service Research*, *20*(1), 43–58. doi:10.1177/1094670516679272

Vannette, D. L., & Krosnick, J. A. (Eds.). (2017). *The Palgrave handbook of survey research*. Springer.

Varma, P., Junge, M., Meaklim, H., & Jackson, M. L. (2021). Younger people are more vulnerable to stress, anxiety, and depression during COVID-19 pandemic: A global cross-sectional survey. *Progress in Neuro-Psychopharmacology & Biological Psychiatry*, *109*, 110236. doi:10.1016/j.pnpbp.2020.110236 PMID:33373680

Vasilienė-Vasiliauskienė, V., Vasiliauskas, A. V., Donculaitė, M., & Meidutė-Kavaliauskienė, I. (2019, May). Applying the Business Model Canvas to Increase Enterprise Competitiveness: A Case Study of Transport Company. In *Proceedings of the International Conference Transbaltica* (pp. 158-170). Springer.

Vazquez-Bustelo, D., & Avella, L. (2006). Agile manufacturing: Industrial case studies in Spain. *Technovation*, *26*(10), 1147–1161. doi:10.1016/j.technovation.2005.11.006

Velecela, P. (2017). Finanzas personales: La influencia de la edad en la toma de decisiones financieras. *Killkana Social.*, *1*(3), 81–88. doi:10.26871/killkana_social.v1i3.66

Venkatesh, V., Sykes, T. A., & Venkatraman, S. (2014). Understanding e-Government portal use in rural India: Role of demographic and personality characteristics. *Information Systems Journal*, *24*(3), 249–269. doi:10.1111/isj.12008

Verdict Medical Devices. (2017). *Radio-frequency identification technology in healthcare*. https://www.medicaldevice-network.com/comment/commentradio-frequency-identification-technology-in-healthcare-5848545/

Verma, V. K., & Chandra, B. (2018). An application of theory of planned behavior to predict young Indian consumers' green hotel visit intention. *Journal of Cleaner Production*, *172*, 1152–1162. doi:10.1016/j.jclepro.2017.10.047

Verstraeten, R., Van Royen, K., Ochoa-Avilés, A., Penafiel, D., Holdsworth, M., Donoso, S., Maes, L., & Kolsteren, P. (2014). A Conceptual Framework for Healthy Eating Behavior in Ecuadorian Adolescents: A Qualitative Study. *PLoS One*, *9*(1), e87183. doi:10.1371/journal.pone.0087183 PMID:24489865

Vickers, I. (2010). *SE and the environment: A review of the literature*. Third Sector Research Centre Working Paper, 22.

Compilation of References

Vidal, A. E. (2004). *Diagnóstico organizacional: evaluación sistémica del desempeño empresarial en la era digital*. Ecoe.

Vigna, P., & Casey, M. J. (2019). *The truth machine: the blockchain and the future of everything*. HarperCollins.

VIllalba, U. (2019). *Seminario Internacional Desafíos de la Economía Solidaria y Comunitaria: Acercamientos conceptuales desde las experiencias* (J. Ordóñez, Interviewer). Quito, Ecuador: Universidad Central del Ecuador. Retrieved from https://grupoess2.wixsite.com/ecosolidariaycomuni

Von Borgstede, C., Andersson, M., & Johnsson, F. (2013). Public attitudes to climate change and carbon mitigation—Implications for energy-associated behaviours. *Energy Policy*, *57*, 182–193. doi:10.1016/j.enpol.2013.01.051

Von Hippel, E. A., Ogawa, S., & de Jong, P. J. (2011). The age of the consumer-innovator. *MIT Sloan Management Review*, *23*, 1–10.

Walińska, E., & Dobroszek, J. (2021). The functional controller for sustainable and value chain management: Fashion or need? A sample of job advertisements in the COVID19 period. [Switzerland]. *Sustainability*, *13*(13), 7139. doi:10.3390u13137139

Wang, H., Alon, I., & Kimble, C. (2015). Dialogue in the dark: Shedding light on the development of SEs in China. *Global Business and Organizational Excellence*, *34*(4), 60–69. doi:10.1002/joe.21615

Wang, J., Bao, J., Wang, C., & Wu, L. (2017). The impact of different emotional appeals on the purchase intention for green products: The moderating effects of green involvement and Confucian cultures. *Sustainable Cities and Society*, *34*, 32–42. doi:10.1016/j.scs.2017.06.001

Wang, J., & Shirmohammadi, M. (2016). Women leaders in China: Looking back and moving forward. *Advances in Developing Human Resources*, *18*(2), 137–151. doi:10.1177/1523422316641399

Wang, K. S. (2016) Logistics 4.0 Solution: New Challenges and Opportunities. *6th International Workshop of Advanced Manufacturing and Automation*. 10.2991/iwama-16.2016.13

Wang, Y. M., Wang, Y. S., & Yang, Y. F. (2010). Understanding the determinants of RFID adoption in the manufacturing industry. *Technological Forecasting and Social Change*, *77*(5), 803–815. doi:10.1016/j.techfore.2010.03.006

Wan, L. C., Chan, E. K., & Luo, X. (2021). ROBOTS COME to RESCUE: How to reduce perceived risk of infectious disease in Covid19-stricken consumers? *Annals of Tourism Research*, *88*, 103069. doi:10.1016/j.annals.2020.103069 PMID:33071394

Wan, W. W., Luk, C.-L., Yau, O. H., Alan, C., Sin, L. Y., Kwong, K. K., & Chow, R. P. (2009). Do traditional Chinese cultural values nourish a market for pirated CDs? *Journal of Business Ethics*, *88*(1), 185–196. doi:10.100710551-008-9821-1

Warner, M., & Zhu, Y. (2018). The challenges of managing 'new generation'employees in contemporary China: Setting the scene. *Asia Pacific Business Review*, *24*(4), 429–436. doi:10.1080/13602381.2018.1451130

Watanabe, E. A. M., Alfinito, S., Curvelo, I. C. G., & Hamza, K. M. (2020). Perceived value, trust and purchase intention of organic food: A study with Brazilian consumers. *British Food Journal*, *122*(4), 1070–1184. doi:10.1108/BFJ-05-2019-0363

Watanabe, E. H., Da Silva, R. M., Blos, M. F., Junqueira, F., Filho, D. J., & Miyagi, P. E. (2018). Framework to evaluate the performance and sustainability of a dispersed productive system. *Journal of the Brazilian Society of Mechanical Sciences and Engineering*, *40*(6), 277–286. doi:10.100740430-018-1032-9

Watson, D. (2005). *Business Models*. Harriman House Ltd.

Weismeier-Sammer, D. (2011). Entrepreneurial behavior in family firms: A replication study. *Journal of Family Business Strategy*, *2*(3), 128–138. doi:10.1016/j.jfbs.2011.07.003

White, C. L., Nielsen, A. E., & Valentini, C. (2017). CSR research in the apparel industry: A quantitative and qualitative review of existing literature. *Corporate Social Responsibility and Environmental Management*, *24*(5), 382–394. doi:10.1002/csr.1413

White, K., Habib, R., David, J., & Hardisty, D. J. (2019). How to SHIFT Consumer Behaviors to be More Sustainable: A Literature Review and Guiding Framework. *Journal of Marketing*, *83*(3), 22–49. doi:10.1177/0022242919825649

White, T. L., Thomas-Danguin, T., Olofsson, J. K., Zucco, G. M., & Prescott, J. (2020). Thought for food: Cognitive influences on chemosensory perceptions and preferences. *Food Quality and Preference*, *79*, 103776. doi:10.1016/j.foodqual.2019.103776

WHO. (2020). *WHO Timeline - COVID-19*. Newsroom. https://www.who.int/news-room/detail/27-04-2020-who-timeline---covid-19

Wicks, A. M., Visich, J. K., & Li, S. (2006). Radio frequency identification applications in healthcare. *International Journal of Healthcare Technology and Management*, *7*(6), 522–540. doi:10.1504/IJHTM.2006.010414

Wieland, H., Koskela-Huotari, K., & Vargo, S. L. (2016). Extending actor participation in value creation: An institutional view. *Journal of Strategic Marketing*, *24*(3–4), 210–226. doi:10.1080/0965254X.2015.1095225

Wilson, D. C., & Thomas, H. (2012). The Legitimacy of the Business of Business Schools: What's the Future? *Journal of Management Development*, *31*(4), 368–376. doi:10.1108/02621711211219040

Winkelhaus, S., & Grosse, E. (2019). Logistics 4.0: A systematic review towards a new logistics system. *International Journal of Production Research*, *1*, 18–43.

Winter, S. G. (2003). Understanding dynamic capabilities. *Strategic Management Journal*, *24*(10), 991–995. doi:10.1002mj.318

Wong, W. K., Leung, S. Y. S., Guo, Z. X., Zeng, X. H., & Mok, P. Y. (2012). Intelligent product cross-selling system with radio frequency identification technology for retailing. *International Journal of Production Economics*, *135*(1), 308–319. doi:10.1016/j.ijpe.2011.08.005

Wood, R., & Bandura, A. (1989). Impact of conceptions of ability on self-regulatory mechanisms and complex decision-making. *Journal of Personality and Social Psychology*, *56*(3), 407–415. doi:10.1037/0022-3514.56.3.407 PMID:2926637

Woo, E., & Kim, Y. G. (2019). Consumer attitudes and buying behavior for green food products: From the aspect of green perceived value (GPV). *British Food Journal*, *121*(2), 320–332. doi:10.1108/BFJ-01-2018-0027

World Economic Forum. (2020) *The Global Risks Report 2020*. Author.

Xia, D., Zhang, M., Yu, Q., & Tu, Y. (2019). Developing a framework to identify barriers of Green technology adoption for enterprises. *Resources, Conservation and Recycling*, *143*, 99–110. doi:10.1016/j.resconrec.2018.12.022

Xiajuan, G., & Lijun, Y. (2017). Women's political participation in China. In *Changing State-Society Relations in Contemporary China* (pp. 249–265). World Scientific.

Xiao, F., Zhang, J., & Long, B. (2017). The Predicament, Revitalization, and Future of Traditional Chinese Festivals. *Western Folklore*, 181–196.

Xia, R. L., & Muppala, J. K. (2010). A survey of bittorrent performance. *IEEE Communications Surveys and Tutorials*, *12*(2), 140–158. doi:10.1109/SURV.2010.021110.00036

Compilation of References

Xiong, H., Deng, J., & Yuan, J. (2018). From Exclusion to Inclusion: Changes in Women's Roles in Folk Sports and Indigenous Physical Culture in China. *The International Journal of the History of Sport*, *35*(15–16), 1603–1621. doi:10.1080/09523367.2018.1493456

Xue, H. B., & Wang, X. X. (2012). Face consciousness and decision-making styles: An empirical study of young-adult Chinese consumers. *International Journal of China Marketing*, *2*(2), 60–73.

Xue-ling, L., Li, C., Yu-jie, L., Jia, S., & Ling, Z. (2018). Influence of institutional environment on the construction of corporate relations: An empirical research based on China's transition. *Nankai Business Review*, *21*(5), 41–50.

Yakasai, A. B. M., & Jusoh, W. J. W. (2015). Testing the Theory of Planned Behavior in Determining Intention to Use Digital Coupon among University Students. *Procedia Economics and Finance*, *31*, 186–193. doi:10.1016/S2212-5671(15)01145-4

Yang, X., Dong, X., Jiang, Q., & Liu, G. (2019). Factors influencing public concern about environmental protection: An analysis from China. *Discrete Dynamics in Nature and Society*, *2019*, 2019. doi:10.1155/2019/5983160

Yan, H.-D. (2012). Entrepreneurship, Competitive Strategies, and Transforming Firms from OEM to OBM in Taiwan. *Journal of Asia-Pacific Business*, *13*(1), 16–36. doi:10.1080/10599231.2012.629877

Yao, W., Chu, C. H., & Li, Z. (2012). The adoption and implementation of RFID technologies in healthcare: A literature review. *Journal of Medical Systems*, *36*(6), 3507–3525. doi:10.100710916-011-9789-8 PMID:22009254

Yazici, H. J. (2014). An Exploratory Analysis of Hospital Perspectives on Real Time Information Requirements and Perceived Benefits of RFID Technology for Future Adoption. *International Journal of Information Management*, *34*(5), 603–621. doi:10.1016/j.ijinfomgt.2014.04.010

Yépez, P. (2015). Tradiciones Indígenas en el mundo moderno y su incidencia en la educación intercultural. *Sophia*, *18*(1), 231–251.

Yi, H., Li, G., Li, L., Loyalka, P., Zhang, L., Xu, J., Kardanova, E., Shi, H., & Chu, J. (2018). Assessing the quality of upper-secondary vocational education and training: Evidence from China. *Comparative Education Review*, *62*(2), 199–230. doi:10.1086/696920

Yong, J. N. C., Ziaei, S. M., & Szulczyk, K. R. (2021). The impact of COVID19 pandemic on stock market return volatility: Evidence from Malaysia and Singapore. *Asian Economic and Financial Review*, *11*(3), 191–204. doi:10.18488/journal.aefr.2021.113.191.204

Yoon, C. (2011). Theory of planned behavior and ethics theory in digital piracy: An integrated model. *Journal of Business Ethics*, *100*(3), 405–417. doi:10.100710551-010-0687-7

Young, D. R. (2001). Organizational Identity in Nonprofit Organizations: Strategic and Structural Implications. *Nonprofit Management & Leadership*, *12*(2), 139–157. doi:10.1002/nml.12202

Yu, C. (2018, November 29). 17Edtech banks on AI to bridge education gap. *China Daily*. http://www.chinadaily.com.cn/cndy/2018-11/29/content_37329506.htm

Yu, X. (2016). Social Entrepreneurship in China's Nonprofit Sector. The Case of Innovative Participation of Civil Society in Post-disaster Reconstruction. *China Perspectives*, *2016*(3), 53–61. doi:10.4000/chinaperspectives.7051

Yueh, L. Y. (2020, August). *Economic diplomacy in the 21st century: Principles and challenges* (Monograph August 2020). LSE IDEAS, London School of Economics and Political Science. https://www.lse.ac.uk/ideas/publications/updates/economic-diplomacy-in-the-21st-century-principles-and-challenges

Yu, J. (2018). The belt and road initiative: Domestic interests, bureaucratic politics and the EU-China relations. *Asia Europe Journal*, *16*(3), 223–236. doi:10.100710308-018-0510-0

Yuki, K., & Cen, Z. (2018). Effects of the Size of a Country on Its Economic Performance. In M. Tadokoro, S. Egashira, & K. Yamamoto (Eds.), *Emerging Risks in a World of Heterogeneity: Interactions Among Countries with Different Sizes, Polities and Societies* (pp. 19–44). Springer. doi:10.1007/978-981-10-7968-9_2

Yu, L. (2020). The emergence of social entrepreneurs in China. *Journal of the International Council for Small Business*, *1*(1), 32–35. doi:10.1080/26437015.2020.1714359

Yun, G., Yalcin, M. G., Hales, D. N., & Kwon, H. Y. (2019). Interactions in sustainable supply chain management: A framework review. *International Journal of Logistics Management*, *30*(1), 140–173. doi:10.1108/IJLM-05-2017-0112

Yu, W., Jacobs, M. A., Chavez, R., & Yang, J. (2019). Dynamism, disruption orientation, and resilience in the supply chain and the impacts on financial performance: A dynamic capabilities perspective. *International Journal of Production Economics*, *218*, 352–362. doi:10.1016/j.ijpe.2019.07.013

Yu, X. (2013). *The governance of SEs in China*. SE Journal.

Zawacki-Richter, O., & Latchem, C. (2018). Exploring four decades of research in computers & education. *Computers & Education*, *122*, 136–152. doi:10.1016/j.compedu.2018.04.001

Zeibote, Z., Volkova, T., & Todorov, K. (2019). The impact of globalization on regional development and competitiveness: Cases of selected regions. Insights into Regional Development. *Entrepreneurship and Sustainability Center*, *1*(1), 33–47.

Zhang, X. (2019). "80后""90后""00后"亚文化属性的代际演变和代内演进. 文教资料, *14*, 52–53.

Zhao, L. (2021). The English Translation and Cultural Dissemination of Chinese Web Novels. *Communication across Borders: Translation & Interpreting*, *1*(1).

Zhao, M. (2020, September 13). *The SE Emerges in China (SSIR)*. https://ssir.org/articles/entry/the_social_enterprise_emerges_in_china

Zhao, X. (2019). Intergenerational Differences in Participation in Online Public Relations among the Post-1970s, Post-1980s and Post-1990s Generations. *Fujian University Journal - Humanities and Social Sciences Edition*, *4*, 151–160.

Zhao, E. Y., & Wry, T. (2016). Not All Inequality Is Equal: Deconstructing the Societal Logic of Patriarchy to Understand Microfinance Lending to Women. *Academy of Management Journal*, *59*(6), 1994–2020. doi:10.5465/amj.2015.0476

Zhongqun, S. (2011). *Road of Strategic Transformation for Chinese OEM Enterprises: Issues and Countermeasures*. Academic Press.

Zhu, J., & Mukhin, N. (2021). The Modern Regency: Leadership Transition and Authoritarian Resilience of the Former Soviet Union and China. *Communist and Post-Communist Studies*, *54*(1–2), 24–44. doi:10.1525/j.postcomstud.2021.54.1-2.24

Zhu, Q., & Sarkis, J. (2016). Green marketing and consumerism as social change in China: Analyzing the literature. *International Journal of Production Economics*, *181*, 289–302. doi:10.1016/j.ijpe.2016.06.006

Zhu, S., & He, C. (2018). Upgrading in China's apparel industry: International trade, local clusters and institutional contexts. *Post-Communist Economies*, *30*(2), 193–215. doi:10.1080/14631377.2017.1362099

Zhu, S., & Pickles, J. (2014). Bring In, Go Up, Go West, Go Out: Upgrading, Regionalization and Delocalisation in China's Apparel Production Networks. *Journal of Contemporary Asia*, *44*(1), 36–63. doi:10.1080/00472336.2013.801166

Compilation of References

Zhu, X., Mukhopadhyay, S. K., & Kurata, H. (2012). A review of RFID technology and its managerial applications in different industries. *Journal of Engineering and Technology Management*, *29*(1), 152–167. doi:10.1016/j.jengtecman.2011.09.011

Zmud, R. W. (1984). An examination of push-pull theory applied to process innovation in knowledge work. *Management Science*, *30*(6), 727–738. doi:10.1287/mnsc.30.6.727

Zubizarreta, J., Gonzalez, E., & Ramiro, P. (2019). Transnational corporations and the legal Architecture of impunity: Corporate Social Responsibility, *lex mercatoria* and human rights. *Revista de Economia (Curitiba)*, *28*, 41–54.

Zulli, D. (2018). Capitalizing on the look: Insights into the glance, attention economy, and Instagram. *Critical Studies in Media Communication*, *35*(2), 137–150. doi:10.1080/15295036.2017.1394582

Zurita, R. (2019). *La Economía Popular y Solidaria en Ecuador: Políticas públicas y prácticas económicas no monetarias y sostenibles en los emprendimientos asociativos* (J. Ordóñez, Interviewer). Academic Press.

About the Contributors

José Manuel Saiz-Alvarez has a Ph.D. in Economic and Business Sciences, Universidad Autónoma de Madrid, Spain. Ph.D. in Political Sciences and Sociology, Universidad Pontificia de Salamanca, Spain. Prof. Saiz-Alvarez is a research professor, Catholic University of Avila, Spain, and a Visiting professor, Universidad Católica de Santiago de Guayaquil, Ecuador, and Universidad Autónoma de Manizales, Colombia. International researcher, CEIEF-Universidad de Santiago de Chile. Officially accredited in Spain by ANECA. Regular member, Mexican Academy of Sciences and Accademia Tiberina già Pontificia, Italy. GEM Jalisco member and Business Controller accredited by the College of Economists of Madrid, Spain. He was a research professor, Tecnológico de Monterrey, Mexico, and member of the National System of Researchers of Mexico. Director for BA Doctoral Studies, Universidad Nebrija, Spain. Professor, Universidad Pontificia de Salamanca, Spain, and Universidad Alfonso X El Sabio, Spain. Academic leader, Tecnológico de Monterrey, Mexico. Diploma of Recognition, The House of Representatives from the Capitol of Puerto Rico. Honor Diploma, Universitatea Valahia din Targoviste, Romania. Honorary Professor, Universidad Autónoma de Madrid, Spain. Who's Who in the World since 2011.

* * *

Neeta Baporikar is currently Professor (Management) at Harold Pupkewitz Graduate School of Business (HP-GSB), Namibia University of Science and Technology, Namibia. Prior to this, she was Head-Scientific Research, with the Ministry of Higher Education CAS-Salalah, Sultanate of Oman, Professor (Strategic Management and Entrepreneurship) at IIIT Pune and BITS India. With more than a decade of experience in the industry, consultancy, and training, she made a lateral switch to research and academics in 1995. Prof Baporikar holds D.Sc. (Management Studies) USA, Ph.D. in Management, the University of Pune INDIA with MBA (Distinction) and Law (Hons.) degrees. Apart from this, she is an external reviewer, Oman Academic Accreditation Authority, Accredited Management Teacher, Qualified Trainer, FDP from EDII, Doctoral Guide, and Board Member of Academic and Advisory Committee in accredited B-Schools. She has to her credit many conferred doctorates, is a member of the international and editorial advisory board, reviewer for Emerald, IGI, Inderscience, etc., published numerous refereed papers, and authored books in the area of entrepreneurship, strategy, management, and higher education.

Danny Barbery has a PhD in Business Administration (Universidad de Nebrija, Madrid), Master's Degree in Business Management and Companies Creation (Universidad de Nebrija, Madrid), Master's Degree in Management and Strategic Marketing (Escuela de Organización Industrial, Madrid), Master's Degree in Business Administration (ESPAE, Guayaquil). Dean of the Faculty of Communication Sciences

About the Contributors

and the Faculty of Tourism and Hospitality, Universidad Espíritu Santo. He has contributed to scientific publications related to consumer behavior, entrepreneurship, family businesses and brand management in high impact indexed journals and editorials such as IGI Global and Springer.

Aitor Bengoetxea Alkorta, Added Professor of Labour and Social Security Law at the Faculty of Law and Director of GEZKI (Institute of Cooperative Law and Social Economy) at the University of the Basque Country. Donostia / San Sebastián. (Basque Country).

Fa-Hsiang Chang specializes in dynamic regional development, the pattern of industry structure and urban formation in both theoretical model and empirical studies. He is currently working on the effect of dynamic agglomeration externalities on regional economic efficiency under the urban system perspective, with the support of some external funding.

Mingyi Chen is pursuing a graduate degree in the field of Management period. His research interests include social cause awareness, social enterprises, and social entrepreneurship.

Rongjuan Chen is an Assistant Professor at the College of Business and Public Management of Wenzhou-Kean University. She teaches in the management information systems, management science, and business analytics areas. Her research interests include collective psychology and behavior in social media, individual's information processing, and decision making and judgment in management and marketing-related areas.

Alicia Coduras has a Ph.D. in Political Sciences and Sociology, Pompeu Fabra University, Spain. B.Sc. in Economics and Business Administration, University of Barcelone. She has been a Professor at the University of Barcelone and Pompeu Fabra University, and Technical Director of GEM (Global Entrepreneurship Monitor) Spain and Saudi Arabia, and GEM Global Staff. She is now GEM/GERA (Global Entrepreneurship Research Association) staff and Specialized Statistician in Opinometre Institute, Spain. She has published in prestigious and peer-reviewed journals such as Journal of Business Research, Journal of Small Business Strategy, Journal of Small Business and Enterprise Development, Industrial Marketing Management, International Advances in Economic Research, Investigaciones Regionales, Management Decision, Regional Studies, and Strategic Change.

Dennisse Coronel-Arellano has a PhD (c) in Marketing Sciences (University de València, Valencia); Master degree in Management in emerging markets (Institute of Business Studies, Moscow); Master degree in Business Administration (Universitat de València, Valencia). Account Director in Lucky Ecuador.

Jiawei Feng is pursuing a graduate degree in the field of Management period. Her research interests include social cause awareness, social enterprises, and social entrepreneurship.

Carmen Romelia Flores-Morales is a full professor at the School of Accounting and Administration (FCA) at the Autonomous University of Chihuahua in Mexico. She holds a Ph.D. in Business Administration from FCA. She is a member of the National System of Researchers (CONACYT) and holds the Recognition of Desirable Profile by the Secretariat of Public Education (SEP-PROMEP). Currently, she serves as Secretary of Planning and Institutional Development at FCA. She has published in scientific journals, books and participated in national and international scientific workshops and conferences.

Sijia Jiang is a graduate of the Global Studies Program at Wenzhou-Kean University. Her academic and research interest is in the confluence of applied and theoretical Intellectual Property Rights and Protections in post Globalization Sino-US Trade.

Shampy Kamboj is an Assistant Professor in Department of Management Studies (DoMS) at National Institute of Technology (NIT) Hamirpur, Himachal Pradesh (HP), India. She earned her Ph.D. from Indian Institute of Technology (IIT) Roorkee, Uttarakhand (UK), India. Prior to join NIT Hamirpur, she has worked as an Assistant Professor and Programme leader in Amity School of Business at Amity University, Noida campus (Delhi-NCR). Her research interests are in the area of Information Systems (IS) and Marketing Management including Social Media Marketing, Sustainability, Customer Co-Creation, Service Innovation, Customer Engagement, M-commerce research. Dr. Kamboj has to her credit research papers as well as chapters in ABDC, SSCI, ESCI and Scopus indexed journals/edited books. She has received 5th & 6th ADMAA (Amity Directorate of Management & Allied Areas) "Best Researcher Award" in 18th International Business Conference INBUSH ERA World Summit 2017-2018 at Amity University, Noida (DelhiNCR). Besides, being on the reviewer panel of reputed journals of Science direct (Elsevier), Emerald, Springer, Taylor and Francis, IGI Global, Inderscience and Wiley, she has also reviewed research papers submitted in several International conferences in USA, UK, Italy, Spain and many more. She has visited countries like Bangkok, Thailand and United Kingdom for presentation of her research work in International conference and workshop.

Samuel Kwok is a transdisciplinary (TD) professional practitioner - namely an international accountant, an entrepreneur, and a professional doctorate on Work-Based Learning. He is a member of the Chartered Accountants Worldwide, a Fellow of ICAEW, ACCA, HKICPA, and an Academic Fellow of the Association of International Accoutants-UK. Samuel is an international certified chartered eCommerce specialist (ICEC-USA) and is appointed as an Industry Expert by the Bureau of Science & Technology of Suzhou Municipal People's Government. With background in KPMG, Deloitte, member of senior management team in two public listed companies, and running his own consultancy firm before joining IBSS in 2016, Dr. Kwok engaged in various cross-border finance & business strategy development projects such as: - the lead consultant of the Chinese Gold and Silver Exchange Society of Hong Kong assisted on the fouding of 'Shenzhen-Hong Kong Gold Connect'. - the chief consultant of the Sino-Swiss Eco-Industrial Park, Zhenjiang and organized a Press Conference for the Ministry of Commerce of China Government in 2014 at Basel, Switzerland. He focuses on Practice-led research. Book, chapter, articles and Conference presentation are published on the topics of Industry Analysis, Corporate Auditing practice, and e-luxury branding management practice. Instead of perfecting the know, he is opening up a new research direction on Culture management in Narrative Policy Framework research. He won the Best Paper award from the Shanghai Gold Exchange, and won a Teaching Excellence Award from an UK Accountancy body. He has been interviewed by XinHua News Agency, AB Magazine(ACCA), & 21st Century Business Herald. Dr. Kwok is the Academic Director of the Executive Education, IBSS. He is always a watch connoisseur and aficionados of fine horology.

About the Contributors

Arturo Luque is a full professor at the Technical University of Manabí, Ecuador, and a member of the Euro-Mediterranean Observatory on Public Policies and Democratic Quality at the University King Juan Carlos (Spain). He holds a Ph.D. in Social Sciences and Law and a Master of two years in Labor Relations. He supervises several doctoral theses (Ph.D.) in Córdoba (Spain) and the Basque Country (GEZKI Institute) like a director and co-director. It has 45 indexed articles, and his latest publications include topics about corporate social (Ir)responsibility (How corporate social (ir)responsibility in the textile sector is defined, and its impact on ethical sustainability: An analysis of 133 concepts), transnational companies (The transnational textile companies relationship with the environment: a Delphi analysis approach) and their relations with ethics (Corruption in the transnational textile industry: an exception or the rule?), social economy and a cooperative system like economic alternative (Socially responsible public management: case spinning development in Ecuador), media analysis and social conflicts (Analysis of the indigenous uprising of Ecuador, 2019).

Rob Kim Marjerison is Asst Professor of Global Business at Wenzhou-Kean University in Wenzhou, China. His previous affiliations include teaching internationally at Universities in Bhutan, Mexico, India and Korea. Dr. Marjerison has a PhD in International Business from the International School of Management in Paris France, a Master of Science in Information Systems from Louisiana State University, and a Masters in Public Administration from California State University. His research interests include Sino-US Trade, Sustainable Economic Development, Organizational and New venture Assessment and Social Entrepreneurship.

Enriqueta Márquez is PhD in Business Sciences specialized in International Business Management from the Antonio Nebrija University in Spain. She has a Master's Degree in Marketing and Advertising from the Anahuac University, and graduated with honors from the Bachelor's Degree in Marketing from the Monterrey Technological Institute. Her work experience began at SONY Electronics, where she later specialized in consumer companies such as Conagra Foods, Herdez and Nestlé. Since 2008, while working at Nestlé, she began her teaching career as a Professor at the Anahuac University, teaching classes in the Marketing Master program, Media Planning Masters, the PhD in Communication and Strategic Marketing and the Doctorate in Leadership and Management of Higher Education Institutions. Currently she continues with her lecture and is Founder and General Director of Transcendence, a company focused on providing Marketing courses and consultancies to national and international companies. She has more than 21 years of experience in Marketing and 12 years teaching classes at Master degree and PhD level.

Montserrat Mata Fernández has a B.Sc. in Computer Science with a Master in Business Management and several certifications as PMP Certification and ITIL v3 Foundation, among others. Collaborator in articles and papers. Wide experience as Project Manager, dealing with national and international projects.

Suja R. Nair is a holder of Ph.D, MBA and BA(Hons.) degrees with over 25 years of work experience that includes Corporate, Academics and Research. She is an Independent Researcher and Author since 1999, and has been handling Strategic Marketing as a Co-entrepreneur at Educe Micro Research, Bangalore, India, since 2002. As a prolific writer she has written many text-books in the areas of Marketing Research, Consumer Behavior, Retail Management and Organizational Behavior, which are widely read and recommended by leading universities/institutes in India. Her papers/chapters have been published in referred Indian Journals and top International publications such as Inderscience Publishers, Elsevier,

Emerald Group Publishing, IGI Global & Palgrave Macmillan. She has 43 publications to her credit. She is the Editor of 'Handbook of Research on Ethics, Entrepreneurship and Governance in Higher Education', Editor of 'International Journal of Big Data Management' and an Editorial Board Member of 'IAFOR Journal of Education'. Her fields of research interest include Cause-related marketing, Consumer Behavior, Ethics in Higher Education, Education Management, Retail Food Shopping Behavior and Women-entrepreneurship.

Beatriz Olalla-Caballero has a PhD in Computer Science, Information Technologies and Knowledge Society, Pontifical University of Salamanca, Spain. MSc in Quality Engineer, American Society for Quality. BSc in Telecommunication Engineer, University of Valladolid (Spain). Project Management Professional and ITIL Expert. Several years working in Information Technologies services and Quality and Projects Management. Author of papers and articles about quality, projects and Information Technologies.

Jaime Leonidas Ordóñez Salcedo is a PhD student at the University of the Basque Country - Master in Administration of the Organizations of the Social and Solidarity Economy at the Indoamérica Technological University - Dynamizer in the Movement of Social and Solidarity Economy in the city of Loja – Ecuador.

Jesús Manuel Palma-Ruiz is a full professor in the School of Accounting and Administration at the Autonomous University of Chihuahua (UACH) in Mexico, teaching in graduate and undergraduate programs. He is a member of the National System of Researchers (SNI-CONACYT) in Mexico. He has published in indexed journals, recently including the Sustainability European Business Review, International Journal of Financial Studies, Academia Revista Latinoamericana de Administración, and co-edited books with IGI Global and Springer. His research interests include international and strategic management and entrepreneurship.

Jing Pan received the B.S.degree in Global Business from Wenzhou-Kean University, China, and the M.S. degree in Business with Accounting & Finance in University of Warwick, UK. Her areas of research include sustainable business models, trade, and economy.

Rafael Pérez-Uribe has a Ph.D. in Business Sciences, Nebrija University, Spain. Diploma of Advanced Studies in Applied Economics, Nebrija University, Spain. Master's Degree in Organizational Management, EAN University, Colombia. Maître es Sciences, University of Quebec to Chicoutimi, Canada. Specialist in Evaluation and Construction of Management Indicators for Higher Education, School of Business Administration. Postgraduate Studies as Kenkyusei (Associate Researcher) in Total Quality Control and Quality Circles, Fukushima University, Japan. Business Administrator, Universidad Jorge Tadeo Lozano, Colombia. Director of the G3pymes Research Group and Associate Professor to the Management of Research, EAN University, Colombia.

Neeraj Kumar Phookan is currently pursuing his Doctoral studies in the Centre for Management Studies (CMS), North Eastern Regional Institute of Science and Technology (Under MHRD), Nirjuli, Arunachal Pradesh. He has completed his Post Graduate Degree in Master of Business Administration from Atal Bihari Vajpayee- Indian Institute of Information Technology and Management (ABV-IIIT), Gwalior, Madhya Pradesh with specialization in Marketing and Operations domain. He has more than

About the Contributors

four years of combined industry and academic experience. He has attended and presented in many international/national conferences and workshops, and published in a few journals. His research interests are in the field of brand experience, consumer behaviour, green marketing, environmental sustainability.

Maria Ramirez has a Ph.D. in Management at Universidad EAN. Ph.D. in Entrepreneurial Sciences at Universidad Nebrija, Spain. Master's in Business Management at Université du Quebec, Canada, and Universidad EAN, Colombia. Graduate degree in Management Indicators to Evaluate Higher Education Institutions, Universidad EAN, Colombia. B.A. in Business Administration, Universidad EAN, Colombia. B.A. in Education, Universidad Pedagógica Nacional, Colombia.

Muhammad Roomi is Vice Dean – Executive Education & Professor of Entrepreneurship, Prince Mohammad Bin Salman College (MSBC), Saudi Arabia. Prior to joining MBSC, he served as the Director of the Executive MBA program and MSc Management and Entrepreneurship program at the Cranfield School of Management, UK. He also held a principal lectureship at the University of Bedfordshire, where he played a major role in developing the business school's graduate programs portfolio. He was also instrumental in setting up the research agenda for the Centre for Women's Enterprise, with a focus on the growth and development of women-owned enterprises in the UK and other Asian and Islamic countries. He has acted as a consultant to national governments including the UK, Qatar, Oman, Bangladesh, Malaysia, Pakistan, Vietnam, and Honduras; multi-lateral agencies such as the World Bank, Asian Development Bank, European Union Higher Education Social Fund, ILO, and UN-APCTT; and private organizations including CIPE Int., LEAD Int., and InfoTech Ltd. Besides working with entrepreneurs, Dr Roomi works with charities and corporates on how to encourage and implement intrapreneurship, and has received several teaching and research awards, Muhammad Roomi is a fellow of the Higher Education Academy - UK (HEA), National Council for Entrepreneurship Education - UK (NCEE), Leadership for Environment and Development (LEAD), and European Entrepreneurship Educators Program (3ep). Professor Roomi has been an invited member of the judging panel for UK Corporate Entrepreneurship Awards, the Asian Entrepreneur Awards, and The Case Centre's case method competitions. He has also served as the chair of Marsh Farm Community Development Trust, UK (2009 – 2015) and the Vice Chair of the Institute of Small Business and Entrepreneurship, UK (2008-2010).

Debasish Roy is currently a Ph.D. Research Scholar in Marketing Management at Sikkim University, Gangtok, India with backgrounds in Postgraduate Diploma in Transportation and Logistics Management from Indian Institute of Social Welfare and Business Management (IISWBM) - India's one of the premier Business Schools, and Bachelor of Science (Honors) in Economics from the University of Calcutta.

Carlos Salcedo has a Bachelor of Science in Business Administration. Master of Science in Economic Development. Ph.D. in Business Science. University professor and researcher.

Luis Raúl Sánchez-Acosta currently serves as the director of the School of Accounting and Administration (FCA) at the Autonomous University of Chihuahua in Mexico and teaches in the postgraduate programs at FCA. He has held several leadership positions within the university. He has published in indexed journals and participated in national and international conferences. His research interests are accounting, finance, and corporate strategy.

Bijoylaxmi Sarmah has received her Doctoral research (Ph.D) at the Department of Management Studies, IIT Roorkee, Uttarakhand (India) and M.B.A degree from North-Eastern Regional Institute of Management under Dibrugarh University. She is currently serving as Assistant Professor and Head of the Centre at North-Eastern Regional Institute of Science & Technology, Arunachal Pradesh (India). She has published in various reputed journals such as International Journal of Information Management, Internet Research, Online Information Review, International Journal of Innovation Science and in International Journal of Contemporary Hospitality Management. Her research interests are Shared value, Service innovation and value co-creation.

Ariana Soria Loor has a marketing degree and media certification (Universidad Santa María, Guayaquil). Creative in Norlop JWT.

Herik Germán Valles-Baca is currently the Provost for Academic Affairs at the Autonomous University of Chihuahua in Mexico. He served as the director of the School of International Economics during 2010-2016 and has held several leadership positions within the university. He has published in national and international indexed journals and co-authored books. He has performed as a guest speaker at several regional conferences and events. His research interests include economics, international business, and topics in higher education.

José Vargas-Hernández has a Ph.D. in Public Administration and a Ph.D. in Organizational Economics. He is a member of the National System of Researchers of Mexico and a research professor at the University Center for Economic and Managerial Sciences, University of Guadalajara, Mexico. He has undertaken studies in Organizational Behavior and has a Master's of Business Administration. He has published four books and more than 200 papers in international journals and reviews (some translated to English, French, German, Portuguese, Farsi, Chinese, etc.) and more than 300 essays in national journals and reviews. He has obtained several international awards and recognitions.

Poshan (Sam) Yu is a Lecturer in Accounting and Finance in the International Cooperative Education Program of Soochow University (China). He is also an External Professor of FinTech and Finance at SKEMA Business School (China), a Visiting Professor at Krirk University (Thailand) and a Visiting Researcher at the Australian Studies Center of Shanghai University (China). Sam leads FasterCapital (Dubai, UAE) as a Regional Partner (China) and serves as a Startup Mentor for AIC RAISE (Coimbatore, India). His research interests include financial technology, regulatory technology, public-private partnerships, mergers and acquisitions, private equity, venture capital, start-ups, intellectual property, art finance, and China's "One Belt One Road" policy.

Index

A

academic performance 365-369, 371-374, 383
Accessibility 183, 222, 308
Actions 20, 30, 39-40, 43-44, 46-47, 53, 61, 82, 87, 91-92, 136, 140, 190-191, 193, 220, 246, 251-252, 256, 258-259, 265-266, 302, 308, 351
Adaptation Capacity 285
Agile 86, 101, 110, 115-119, 124, 179, 201, 269, 271, 273
Agility 43, 59, 116
AI 292, 344-345, 351, 356, 364
American Customer Satisfaction Index (ACSI)® 128, 130, 144, 151, 153, 158
Ancestral Practices 242-244
ANOVA 97
Antecedents 60, 63, 65-66, 68-72, 79, 198-200, 202, 204-205, 207
Anthropocene 265
Anthropocentrism 243
AR 344, 351, 364
Association of Southeast Asian Nations (ASEAN) 182
Attention Economy 329-330, 337, 342
attitude 20, 65-70, 79, 111, 140, 164, 201, 326, 328-329, 331, 336-337

B

B Corporations 222, 241
Behavior Intentions 60, 63, 69-70
Beijing Social Enterprise Initiatives 219, 241
Benchmarking 200, 213
brand development 163-164, 171-172, 178-179
Business management 42, 108, 110
Business Model 40, 184, 216, 218, 267-275, 277, 279, 285, 298, 324, 329, 333, 337, 345-346, 351, 354, 357-359

C

Capitalism 1-14, 17, 102-103, 259
CETDIR 82, 98
Change Management 114
Chinese online literature 326-329, 337
Circular Economy 101, 268-269, 279
Co-creation 268, 271
Cognitive Distortions 367, 382
Competence 206, 302
Competitiveness 22, 53, 109, 124, 165-166, 172, 267, 269-270, 285
Consumer Centrality 196
Consumer Induction Factor (CIF) 125-126, 128-130, 144, 151, 153, 158
Consumer-Centered Strategy 196
Consumerism 243, 265, 321
Consumers 32, 60-72, 88, 101, 110, 114, 123-124, 127, 133, 135, 137, 139-142, 158, 164, 178, 183-188, 190-193, 215, 217, 246, 269, 304-306, 309, 314, 316, 320, 325, 328-332
Contingency 39-41, 44, 49, 59, 135
Contingency Perspective 49, 59
Cost Savings 21
Cost Structure 274
Country Brand Value (CBV) 125, 128-130, 144, 151, 158
COVID-19 18, 39-53, 60-65, 67-68, 70-72, 79, 99-100, 103-105, 116, 118, 197, 204, 206-207, 214-215, 222-223, 225-235, 287, 343-347, 355, 357-362
Crisis 1-3, 7-10, 12-14, 17-18, 34, 39-41, 43, 49, 53, 61-62, 99-101, 103-104, 116, 118-119, 184, 245, 267, 279, 288, 292, 306, 308, 311, 344
Cronbach's Alpha 22, 38
cross-generation 331
Customer Centricity 64, 71-72, 79
Customer experience 128, 185, 306, 324

Customer Journey 71, 183, 191-192, 196
Customer Satisfaction 71, 79, 128, 130, 144, 151, 153, 158, 199, 271, 296

D

Decision-making models 365-366, 368, 370-374
Decision-Making Styles 365-375, 382
Deglobalization 1, 3, 7, 10-14, 17
Digital Accelerator 304, 314, 324
Digital Economy 5, 113, 117, 119, 123, 280, 308-309, 361
Digital Education 343-346, 349-350, 357, 360-361, 364
Digital Natives 311, 324
Disruptive Environment 101, 117-118, 123
Disruptive Technology 123
DOI 203, 213

E

Early-Stage 25, 38
Early-Stage Companies 25, 38
ECLAC 3, 41-42, 59
Eco-Innovation 268, 274, 285
Economic activity 39, 42, 44, 81, 249, 308
Economic Crisis 17-18, 34, 184, 245
Economic Globalization 2-6, 8-11, 13-14, 17, 265
EdTech 343-345, 347, 349, 351, 354, 360, 364
E-Learning 302, 344-345
Embedded Social Enterprise 241
Employment 20, 38, 41-42, 65, 81, 129, 144, 151, 154, 165, 176, 244-246, 249, 288, 291, 308, 317-318, 368, 374
Enterprises 6, 20, 40-44, 47, 49, 53, 81-82, 88, 164, 171-172, 176, 178-179, 182, 198, 214-215, 220-221, 241, 244, 246, 267, 269-270, 308, 320, 349, 351, 353, 355, 361-362, 368
Entrepreneurship 17, 25, 38, 40, 42, 214-216, 270
ESG Criteria 109, 123
European Union (EU) 20, 102, 104, 182, 269
Extension of Theory of Planned Behavior (TPB) 79

F

Factors influencing food consumption 60
Faculty 287-288, 292-293, 295-296, 298, 302, 353
Fake News 306, 325
Financial Crisis 1-2, 7-8, 13, 17, 100, 245
Food behavior 60, 63, 65, 68-71, 79
Food Consumption Behavior 62-65, 67-68, 70-72, 79
Fragile States Index (FSI)® 132, 144, 151, 158

G

GDMS 368, 370, 374, 382
GEM 19, 21-22, 27, 30, 38
Global Entrepreneurship Monitor 38
Global Innovation Index (GII)® 128, 130, 144, 151, 153, 158
Global Logistics 108, 114, 117-119, 124

H

Health Care Industry 198-199, 207
Healthy Food Consumption 60-61, 66, 72, 79
Higher Education 12, 19, 302, 345, 348, 350, 352-353, 358, 362, 374
Home Office 46, 308, 325
Home School 308-310, 313, 325
Hybrid Environments 196

I

Ideation 285
INEGI 39, 42, 44-46, 48-52, 59, 308, 320
Information and Communications Technology 59
Inseparability Is the Service 196
Institutional support 53
intellectual property 130, 182, 326-327
intellectual property protection 327
Investment 6, 8, 12-13, 19, 30, 34-35, 109, 129, 165, 168-169, 175-176, 178-179, 202, 220, 243, 246, 249, 265, 268-270, 327, 336, 346, 352, 364
Isoattribute Curve 125-126, 132, 141-143, 147-148, 158
Isopartworth Line 125-126, 142, 158

J

Job Quality Index (JQI) 144, 151, 158

K

K12 344, 348-353, 358, 360, 364
Knowledge Development 302

L

Lean Production System (LPS) 166, 182
Logistics 4.0 99, 102, 110, 113-114, 116-119, 124

M

Management Education 292, 296, 298, 302, 345

Index

manufacturing transformation 166
MBTI® Testing 367, 382
Millennial Generation 328, 342, 365-366, 382
MMOM 80-81, 83-84, 94, 98
MSMEs 20, 81, 98
Multichannel 64, 72, 185-186, 196

N

Neoliberalism 8, 10-11, 13, 17, 100, 153
NES Questionnaire 22, 38
New Logistics 101-102, 110-111, 113-114, 118, 124
New Public Management 216, 241
New World Economic Order 80-84, 87, 89-91, 100, 102, 110, 118, 124, 267, 279
North-South Gap 18, 35, 38

O

OEM manufacturing 163
Omnichannel 71, 114, 183-188, 190-191, 193, 306, 320, 325
Online Literature 326-330, 332-337, 342
Open Innovation 268, 285
Operational Efficiency 206, 343, 346, 348, 354-355, 364
Organizational Components 80-81, 83-85, 98
Organizational strategy 42, 53
Original Design Manufacturer (ODM) 167, 182
Original Equipment Manufacturer (OEM) 165, 167, 182

P

Pandemic 8, 13-14, 18-22, 24-25, 29-30, 32, 34-35, 40-43, 46, 49, 53, 60-65, 67-68, 70-72, 79, 99-101, 103-105, 116, 118, 153, 183-184, 188-191, 193, 197, 206-207, 214-215, 222, 267, 279-280, 293, 304-309, 312, 314, 316-321, 343-344, 355
Patient Monitoring 197-198
Phygital 64, 70-72, 79, 190, 196, 325
Phygital Experience 72, 79
Phygital Reality 71, 190, 325
piracy 326, 328-333, 336-337
Post-New World Economic Order 99, 101-103, 105, 109, 116, 118-119, 124
Principal Components 21-22, 24, 38
Principal Components Method 38
Prioritize 40, 167, 218, 304-305, 308, 321
Profitability 8, 11, 80, 88, 98, 109, 140, 268, 285
Public Policy 219, 247, 249, 265, 365

Purchase intention 63, 65-66, 164, 214
P-Value 98, 370

R

Redistribution 243, 252, 265
Remote Learning 343-344, 351, 357, 361, 364
Resilience 30, 265, 271, 279
RFID Adoption Intention 197-203, 206-207
RFID Technology 197-199, 201-203, 206-207, 213
Rurality 265

S

Satisfaction 68, 70-71, 79, 128, 130, 144, 151, 153, 158, 199, 203, 205, 271, 297, 330, 346
Service Inseparability 196
Small and Medium-Sized Enterprises (SME) 40-41, 43-44, 164, 182, 270, 353
Social and Solidarity Economy 244-249, 266
Social Enterprise 214-215, 219, 241
Social enterprise awareness 214
Social Welfare Corporations 217, 241
Societal Shifts and Changes 79
Solidarity 5, 8, 242-249, 251-255, 258-259, 266
SOP 213
South-South Gap 38
Stakeholder Engagement 218, 354-355, 364
Stakeholders 20, 138, 217-220, 241, 271, 274, 296, 317, 320-321, 343-346, 353, 357, 359, 364
State of Emergency 41, 59
Statgraphics Centurión XVI 98
Stimulus, Organism, Reply (SOR) 196
Strategic Direction 42-43, 80-82, 84-88, 90-92, 98
Supply Chain Management 4.0 99, 115-116, 124
Sustainable Consumption 79
Sustainable Development 19, 80, 108, 173, 175, 217, 221, 343, 360-362
Sustainable Logistics 99, 101-102, 108-109, 118, 124

T

Tacit 303
Technical Shutdown 47-48, 59
Theory of Planned Behavior 60, 63, 66-67, 69, 79
TOE Framework 203, 213
Total Quality Control 200, 213
Traditional Practices 258, 266
Transmedia 306, 320, 325

Transmedia Omnichannel 306, 325
Trust 53, 63, 65-66, 186, 193, 297, 305-306, 317, 320, 367

V

Value Creation 167, 215, 271, 275, 279-280, 285
Vision 47, 82-83, 98, 114, 163, 185, 222, 245, 271-272
VR 344, 351, 364

W

Word-of-Mouth 192, 196

Y

Year of Civil Society 219, 241

Recommended Reference Books

IGI Global's reference books are available in three unique pricing formats:
Print Only, E-Book Only, or Print + E-Book.

Shipping fees may apply.

www.igi-global.com

ISBN: 978-1-7998-1048-3
EISBN: 978-1-7998-1049-0
© 2020; 605 pp.
List Price: US$ **285**

ISBN: 978-1-5225-8933-4
EISBN: 978-1-5225-8934-1
© 2020; 667 pp.
List Price: US$ **295**

ISBN: 978-1-7998-0357-7
EISBN: 978-1-7998-0359-1
© 2020; 451 pp.
List Price: US$ **235**

ISBN: 978-1-7998-0070-5
EISBN: 978-1-7998-0071-2
© 2020; 144 pp.
List Price: US$ **175**

ISBN: 978-1-5225-6980-0
EISBN: 978-1-5225-6981-7
© 2019; 339 pp.
List Price: US$ **235**

ISBN: 978-1-5225-5390-8
EISBN: 978-1-5225-5391-5
© 2018; 125 pp.
List Price: US$ **165**

Do you want to stay current on the latest research trends, product announcements, news, and special offers?
Join IGI Global's mailing list to receive customized recommendations, exclusive discounts, and more.
Sign up at: **www.igi-global.com/newsletters**.

Publisher of Peer-Reviewed, Timely, and Innovative Academic Research

www.igi-global.com   Sign up at www.igi-global.com/newsletters   facebook.com/igiglobal   twitter.com/igiglobal   linkedin.com/igiglobal

Ensure Quality Research is Introduced to the Academic Community

Become an Evaluator for IGI Global Authored Book Projects

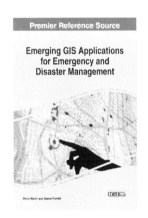 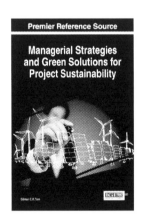  

The overall success of an authored book project is dependent on quality and timely manuscript evaluations.

Applications and Inquiries may be sent to:
development@igi-global.com

Applicants must have a doctorate (or equivalent degree) as well as publishing, research, and reviewing experience. Authored Book Evaluators are appointed for one-year terms and are expected to complete at least three evaluations per term. Upon successful completion of this term, evaluators can be considered for an additional term.

If you have a colleague that may be interested in this opportunity, we encourage you to share this information with them.

IGI Global Author Services

Providing a high-quality, affordable, and expeditious service, IGI Global's Author Services enable authors to streamline their publishing process, increase chance of acceptance, and adhere to IGI Global's publication standards.

Benefits of Author Services:

- **Professional Service:** All our editors, designers, and translators are experts in their field with years of experience and professional certifications.
- **Quality Guarantee & Certificate:** Each order is returned with a quality guarantee and certificate of professional completion.
- **Timeliness:** All editorial orders have a guaranteed return timeframe of 3-5 business days and translation orders are guaranteed in 7-10 business days.
- **Affordable Pricing:** IGI Global Author Services are competitively priced compared to other industry service providers.
- **APC Reimbursement:** IGI Global authors publishing Open Access (OA) will be able to deduct the cost of editing and other IGI Global author services from their OA APC publishing fee.

Author Services Offered:

English Language Copy Editing
Professional, native English language copy editors improve your manuscript's grammar, spelling, punctuation, terminology, semantics, consistency, flow, formatting, and more.

Scientific & Scholarly Editing
A Ph.D. level review for qualities such as originality and significance, interest to researchers, level of methodology and analysis, coverage of literature, organization, quality of writing, and strengths and weaknesses.

Figure, Table, Chart & Equation Conversions
Work with IGI Global's graphic designers before submission to enhance and design all figures and charts to IGI Global's specific standards for clarity.

Translation
Providing 70 language options, including Simplified and Traditional Chinese, Spanish, Arabic, German, French, and more.

Hear What the Experts Are Saying About IGI Global's Author Services

"Publishing with IGI Global has been **an amazing experience** for me for sharing my research. The **strong academic production** support ensures quality and timely completion." – **Prof. Margaret Niess, Oregon State University, USA**

"The service was **very fast, very thorough, and very helpful** in ensuring our chapter meets the criteria and requirements of the book's editors. I was **quite impressed and happy** with your service." – **Prof. Tom Brinthaupt, Middle Tennessee State University, USA**

Learn More or Get Started Here:

For Questions, Contact IGI Global's Customer Service Team at cust@igi-global.com or 717-533-8845

IGI Global
PUBLISHER of TIMELY KNOWLEDGE
www.igi-global.com

Celebrating Over 30 Years of Scholarly Knowledge Creation & Dissemination

www.igi-global.com

InfoSci®-Books

A Database of Nearly 6,000 Reference Books Containing Over 105,000+ Chapters Focusing on Emerging Research

GAIN ACCESS TO **THOUSANDS** OF REFERENCE BOOKS AT **A FRACTION** OF THEIR INDIVIDUAL LIST **PRICE**.

InfoSci®-Books Database

The **InfoSci®-Books** is a database of nearly 6,000 IGI Global single and multi-volume reference books, handbooks of research, and encyclopedias, encompassing groundbreaking research from prominent experts worldwide that spans over 350+ topics in 11 core subject areas including business, computer science, education, science and engineering, social sciences, and more.

Open Access Fee Waiver (Read & Publish) Initiative

For any library that invests in IGI Global's InfoSci-Books and/or InfoSci-Journals (175+ scholarly journals) databases, IGI Global will match the library's investment with a fund of equal value to go toward **subsidizing the OA article processing charges (APCs) for their students, faculty, and staff** at that institution when their work is submitted and accepted under OA into an IGI Global journal.*

INFOSCI® PLATFORM FEATURES

- Unlimited Simultaneous Access
- No DRM
- No Set-Up or Maintenance Fees
- A Guarantee of No More Than a 5% Annual Increase for Subscriptions
- Full-Text HTML and PDF Viewing Options
- Downloadable MARC Records
- COUNTER 5 Compliant Reports
- Formatted Citations With Ability to Export to RefWorks and EasyBib
- No Embargo of Content (Research is Available Months in Advance of the Print Release)

*The fund will be offered on an annual basis and expire at the end of the subscription period. The fund would renew as the subscription is renewed for each year thereafter. The open access fees will be waived after the student, faculty, or staff's paper has been vetted and accepted into an IGI Global journal and the fund can only be used toward publishing OA in an IGI Global journal. Libraries in developing countries will have the match on their investment doubled.

To Recommend or Request a Free Trial:
www.igi-global.com/infosci-books

eresources@igi-global.com • Toll Free: 1-866-342-6657 ext. 100 • Phone: 717-533-8845 x100

www.igi-global.com

Publisher of Peer-Reviewed, Timely, and Innovative Academic Research Since 1988

IGI Global's Transformative Open Access (OA) Model:
How to Turn Your University Library's Database Acquisitions Into a Source of OA Funding

Well in advance of Plan S, IGI Global unveiled their OA Fee Waiver (Read & Publish) Initiative. Under this initiative, librarians who invest in IGI Global's InfoSci-Books and/or InfoSci-Journals databases will be able to subsidize their patrons' OA article processing charges (APCs) when their work is submitted and accepted (after the peer review process) into an IGI Global journal.

How Does it Work?

Step 1: **Library Invests in the InfoSci-Databases:** A library perpetually purchases or subscribes to the InfoSci-Books, InfoSci-Journals, or discipline/subject databases.

Step 2: **IGI Global Matches the Library Investment with OA Subsidies Fund:** IGI Global provides a fund to go towards subsidizing the OA APCs for the library's patrons.

Step 3: **Patron of the Library is Accepted into IGI Global Journal (After Peer Review):** When a patron's paper is accepted into an IGI Global journal, they option to have their paper published under a traditional publishing model or as OA.

Step 4: **IGI Global Will Deduct APC Cost from OA Subsidies Fund:** If the author decides to publish under OA, the OA APC fee will be deducted from the OA subsidies fund.

Step 5: **Author's Work Becomes Freely Available:** The patron's work will be freely available under CC BY copyright license, enabling them to share it freely with the academic community.

Note: This fund will be offered on an annual basis and will renew as the subscription is renewed for each year thereafter. IGI Global will manage the fund and award the APC waivers unless the librarian has a preference as to how the funds should be managed.

Hear From the Experts on This Initiative:

"I'm very happy to have been able to make one of my recent research contributions *freely available* along with having access to the *valuable resources* found within IGI Global's InfoSci-Journals database."

– **Prof. Stuart Palmer**, Deakin University, Australia

"Receiving the support from IGI Global's OA Fee Waiver Initiative *encourages me to continue my research work without any hesitation.*"

– **Prof. Wenlong Liu**, College of Economics and Management at Nanjing University of Aeronautics & Astronautics, China

For More Information, Scan the QR Code or Contact: IGI Global's Digital Resources Team at eresources@igi-global.com.

Are You Ready to Publish Your Research?

IGI Global offers book authorship and editorship opportunities across 11 subject areas, including business, computer science, education, science and engineering, social sciences, and more!

Benefits of Publishing with IGI Global:

- Free one-on-one editorial and promotional support.
- Expedited publishing timelines that can take your book from start to finish in less than one (1) year.
- Choose from a variety of formats, including: Edited and Authored References, Handbooks of Research, Encyclopedias, and Research Insights.
- Utilize IGI Global's eEditorial Discovery® submission system in support of conducting the submission and double-blind peer review process.
- IGI Global maintains a strict adherence to ethical practices due in part to our full membership with the Committee on Publication Ethics (COPE).
- Indexing potential in prestigious indices such as Scopus®, Web of Science™, PsycINFO®, and ERIC – Education Resources Information Center.
- Ability to connect your ORCID iD to your IGI Global publications.
- Earn honorariums and royalties on your full book publications as well as complimentary copies and exclusive discounts.

Join Your Colleagues from Prestigious Institutions, Including:

Learn More at: www.igi-global.com/publish
or Contact IGI Global's Aquisitions Team at: acquisition@igi-global.com

Purchase Individual IGI Global InfoSci-OnDemand Book Chapters and Journal Articles

InfoSci®-OnDemand

Pay-Per-View Articles and Chapters from IGI Global

For More Information, Visit: www.igi-global.com/e-resources/infosci-ondemand

Browse through nearly 150,000+ articles/chapters to find specific research related to their current studies and projects that have been contributed by international researchers from prestigious institutions, including MIT, Harvard University, Columbia University, and many more.

Easily Identify, Acquire, and Utilize Published Peer-Reviewed Findings in Support of Your Current Research:

Accurate and Advanced Search: Utilize the advanced InfoSci-OnDemand search engine to identify research in your area of interest.

Affordably Acquire Research: Provide an affordable alternative to purchasing an entire reference book or scholarly journal.

Fast and Easy One-Click Shopping: Simply utilize the OnDemand "Buy Now" button on the webpage.

Instantly Download/Access Your Content: Receive an immediate link to download your InfoSci-OnDemand content to your personal computer and device.

Access Anywhere, Anytime, and on Any Device: Additionally, receive access to your OnDemand articles and chapters through a personal electronic library.

Benefit from the InfoSci Platform Features: Providing formatted citations, full-text PDF and HTML format, no embargo of content, no DRM, and more.

*"It really provides **an excellent entry into the research literature of the field**. It presents a manageable number of **highly relevant sources** on topics of interest to a wide range of researchers. The sources are **scholarly, but also accessible** to 'practitioners'."*

- Ms. Lisa Stimatz, MLS, University of North Carolina at Chapel Hill, USA

Interested in Additional Savings and Acquiring Multiple Articles and Chapters Through InfoSci-OnDemand?

Subscribe to InfoSci-OnDemand Plus

Learn More

Printed in the United States
by Baker & Taylor Publisher Services